California Real Estate Law

TEXT AND CASES

EIGHTH EDITION

California Real Estate Law

TEXT AND CASES

EIGHTH EDITION

by

Ted H. Gordon, M.B.A., J.D.

California Bar Association, Inactive Member

Golden Gate University, Adjunct Professor, Retired

California Real Estate Law, Eighth Edition
Ted H. Gordon

Vice President/Editorial Director: Dave Shaut

Acquisitions Editor: Sara Glassmeyer

Developmental Editor: Michelle Melfi

Senior Marketing and Sales Manager:
Mark Linton

Content Project Management: PrePressPMG

Senior Manufacturing Coordinator: Charlene
Taylor

Senior Art Director: Pamela Galbreath

Cover Designer: Jeff Bane, CMB Design
Partners

Cover Image: Mark Rasmussen, Tom
Schmucker, and Photo168/Dreamstime.com

Image Permissions Editor: Deanna Ettinger

Text Permissions Editor: Mardell Glinski Schultz

Figures 2.1, 2.2, 6.1 and 16.1 reprinted by
permission, Judicial Council of California.

Figures 5.1, 5.2, 5.3, 5.4, 5.5, 5.6, 6.2, 6.3, 6.4,
6.5, 6.6, 13.3 and 23.1 reprinted by permission,
California Association of REALTORS®.
Endorsement not implied.

Figures 22.1 reprinted by permission, Chicago
Title Insurance Company.

For product information and technology assistance, contact us
at **OnCourse Learning & Sales Support, 1-855-733-7239.**

For permission to use material from this text or product.

Library of Congress Control Number: 2010923184

ISBN-13: 978-0-538-73613-8

ISBN-10: 0-538-73613-5

OnCourse Learning
3100 Cumberland Blvd Suite 1450
Atlanta, GA 30339
USA

Printed in the United States of America
1 2 3 4 5 6 7 8   17 16 15

To Matt, Iris and Madison

Contents

Preface xx

Foreword xxv

Table of Legal Abbreviations xxvi

1 NATURE OF PROPERTY 2
PROPERTY RIGHTS IN A DEMOCRACY 2

Absolute Rights Abolished • All Rights Relative • Balancing Rights • Restrictions on Use

PROPERTY AS A CREATION OF LAW 7

What Is Property? • Bundle of Rights • Not Absolute but Abolishable

STUDY QUESTIONS (TRUE–FALSE) 10

2 JUDICIAL SYSTEM AND HISTORY 12
NATURE AND SOURCE OF LAW 12

Nature of Law • Two Legal Systems • Stare Decisis

IMPLEMENTATION: THE COURTS 15

State Trial Courts • California's Appellate Courts • Federal Courts

IMPLEMENTATION: ALTERNATIVE DISPUTE RESOLUTION 23

Importance of Alternative Dispute Resolution

LEGAL TERMS AND CONCEPTS 27

Jurisdiction • Venue • Statute of Limitations • Statute of Frauds • Parol Evidence Rule • Doctrine of "Reasonableness" • Dictum

HISTORY OF CALIFORNIA LAND 31

Early History • Ownership by Californians • Government Ownership

STUDY QUESTIONS (TRUE–FALSE) 32

3 ELEMENTS OF PROPERTY 34

COMPONENTS OF PROPERTY 34

Ownership • Types of Property • Importance of Distinction • Elements of Real Property

SPECIFIC ELEMENTS OF REAL PROPERTY 41

Land • Airspace • Minerals • Crops and Other Vegetation • Water • Fixtures

FIXTURES 46

Definition • Tests of a Fixture • Intent of the Owner • Method of Attachment • Adaptability of the Item • Relationship of the Parties • Agreement between the Parties • Priorities between Secured Parties • Exceptions When Fixtures Are Removable

STUDY QUESTIONS (TRUE–FALSE) 50

4 CONTRACTS AND DAMAGES 52

NATURE AND CLASSIFICATION OF CONTRACTS 52

Definition • Bilateral and Unilateral Contracts • Express and Implied Contracts • Executed and Executory Contracts • Validity and Enforceability • Illusory Contracts

ELEMENTS OF A CONTRACT 56

Mutual Assent • Offer • Acceptance • When Acts Become Effective • Consideration • Legal Object • Competent Parties • Writing under the Statute of Frauds

DISCHARGE AND UNENFORCEABILITY OF CONTRACTS 64

Modification • Rescission • Novation • Accord and Satisfaction • Cancellation • Statute of Frauds • Statute of Limitations • Bankruptcy

REMEDIES FOR BREACH 66

Definition of Breach • Damages • Specific Performance • Rescission • Other Remedies

LIQUIDATED DAMAGES FOR BREACH OF A REAL ESTATE CONTRACT 68

Liquidated Damages • Old Law • Current Law • Exceptions • Sale of Residential Property • Sales of Nonresidential Property • Installment Sales Contracts

GENERAL DAMAGES FOR BREACH OF A REAL ESTATE CONTRACT 72

Minimal Damages • General Damages • Special Damages

STUDY QUESTIONS (TRUE–FALSE) 75

5 DEPOSIT RECEIPTS 76

NATURE OF DEPOSIT RECEIPTS 76

Multipurpose Document • No Standard Form • Caution in Drafting

ANALYSIS OF CALIFORNIA ASSOCIATION OF REALTORS®, DEPOSIT RECEIPT 80

(1) Buyer's Identity • (2) Description • (3) Agency Confirmation • (4) Finance Terms—In General • (4) Finance—Initial Deposit • (5) Finance—Increased Deposit • (6) Finance—First Loan • (7) Finance—Additional Financing Terms • (8) Finance—Balance and Total Purchase Price • (9) Finance—Verification of Down Payment and Closing Costs • (10) Finance—Loan Applications • (11) Loan Contingency • (12) Loan Terms—Contingency Removal • (13) Loan Terms—No Loan Contingency • (14) Finance—Appraisal Contingency and Removal • (15) Finance—All Cash Offer • (16) Finance—Buyer Stated Financing • (17) Allocation of Costs—Introduction • (18) Wood Destroying Pest Inspection • (19) Other Inspections and Reports • (20) Government Requirements and Retrofits • (21) Escrow and Title • (22) Other Costs • (23) Closing—Possession • (24) Closing—Possession Transfer • (25) Statutory Disclosures and Cancellation Rights • (26) Condominium/Planned Unit Development Disclosures • (27) Items Included and Excluded • (28) Condition of Property • (29) Buyer's Investigation and Matters Affecting Property • (30) Disclosures, Addenda and Other Terms • (31) Title and Vesting • (32) Sale of Buyer's Property • (33) Time Periods and Contingencies • (34) Seller's Right to Cancel • (35) Effect of Buyer's Removal of Contingencies • (36) Effect of Cancellation on Deposits • (37) Repairs • (38) Final Walk Through (Verification) • (39) Prorations • (40) Selection of Service Providers • (41) Multiple Listing Service • (42) Equal Housing Opportunity • (43) Attorney Fees • (44) Definitions • (45) Broker Compensation • (46) Joint Escrow Instructions • (47) Liquidated Damages • (48) Mediation • (49) Arbitration • (50) Terms and Conditions of Offer • (51) Time of Essence: Entire Contract • (52) Offer and Expiration • (53) Buyer's Signature • (54) Acceptance of Offer • (55) Seller's Signature • (56) Confirmation of Acceptance • (57) Real Estate Broker • (58) Broker's Signature: Not Party • (59) Escrow Holder • (60) Presentation of Offer • (61) Rejection of Offer

DISCLOSURES TO BUYER 133

General Duty Disclosures • Residential Disclosure Statements • Natural Hazard Disclosure Statements • Other Statutory Disclosures

STUDY QUESTIONS (TRUE–FALSE) 140

6 LISTING AGREEMENTS 142

NATURE OF LISTING AGREEMENTS 142

Employment Contract • Agency and Contract • Requirements • Accepting Deposits • Uncashed Checks as Deposits • Appraisals for Listing Price

TYPES OF LISTINGS 145

Open Listing • Exclusive Agency • Exclusive Right to Sell

SPECIAL LISTING FORMS 145

Net Listing • Option Listing • Multiple Listing

BROKER'S RIGHT TO COMPENSATION 146

Amount by Agreement • Problems • Writing Mandatory • Procuring Cause • Ready, Willing, and Able Buyer • Safety Clause

SPECIAL COMMISSION SITUATIONS 149

Withdrawal Requires Commission • Default by Buyer • Probate Sales • After Expiration of Listing

ANALYSIS OF CALIFORNIA ASSOCIATION OF REALTORS®, LISTING AGREEMENT 154

(1) Name of Seller • (2) Name of Broker • (3) Commencement Date • (4) Termination Date • (5) Exclusive Right to Sell • (6) Irrevocable Right • (7) Description of Property • (8) Items Excluded and Included • (9) List Price • (10) Terms of Sale • (11) Notice: Commission Negotiable • (12) Commission: Amount • (13) Commission: Sale • (14) Commission: Safety Clause • (15) Commission: Withdrawal from Sale • (16) Commission: Buyer Default • (17) Additional Compensation • (18) MLS Fee Compensation • (19) Cooperate with Other Brokers • (20) Commission: Assignment • (21) Prior Broker's Claim • (22) Title • (23) Multiple Listing Service • (24) Seller's Warranties to Broker • (25) Broker's and Seller's Duties • (26) Acceptance of Deposit • (27) Agency Relationship • (28) Security and Insurance • (29) Lockbox • (30) For Sale Sign • (31) Equal Housing Opportunity • (32) Attorney Fees • (33) Additional Terms • (34) Management Approval • (35) Dispute Resolution • (36) Entire Agreement • (37) Sellers' Signatures • (38) Broker Signatures

OTHER DOCUMENTS REQUIRED 169

Residential Disclosure Statement • FIRPTA Withholding Statement • California's Onerous Withholding • Agency Disclosure Statement • Sales of Mobile Homes • Sale of Condominiums

STUDY QUESTIONS (TRUE–FALSE) 178

7 NONPOSSESSORY INTERESTS 180

NATURE OF EASEMENTS 180

Definition and Nature • Types of Easements • Purpose of Easement • Profit á Prendre

CREATION OF EASEMENTS 182

Grant and Reservation • Implied Easements • Easement by Prescription

USE, MAINTENANCE, AND REPAIR OF EASEMENTS 187

By the Terms of the Easement • Statutory Duty of Repair • Limited Rights of Improvement • Interference with Easement Use

TERMINATION OF EASEMENTS 188

Common Methods of Termination • Nonuse Generally Does Not Terminate • Termination by Estoppel • Destruction and Misuse

LICENSES 192

Definition • Written or Oral • Irrevocable License

DEDICATION OF PROPERTY 195

Nature and Definition • Common Law and Statutory Dedication • Special Rules for Implied Easements

STUDY QUESTIONS (TRUE–FALSE) 197

8 ESTATES IN LAND 198

CLASSIFICATION OF ESTATES 198

Characteristics of an Estate • Duration of an Estate • Quality of an Estate • Estate's Time of Enjoyment • Number of Owners

FREEHOLD ESTATES 200

Nature of Freehold Estates • Fee Simple Absolute Estates • Fee Simple Defeasible Estates • Life Estate • Rule against Perpetuities

NONFREEHOLD ESTATES 207

Nature of Tenancy • Eviction Procedure • Types of Tenancies • Estate for Years • Periodic Tenancy • Tenancy at Will • Tenancy at Sufferance • Advantages of a Written Lease

STUDY QUESTIONS (TRUE–FALSE) 212

9 VOLUNTARY TRANSFERS OF PROPERTY 214

NATURE AND TYPES OF DEEDS 214

Nature of Deeds • Grant Deeds • Quitclaim and Related Deeds • Warranty Deeds • Originally No Other Warranties • Warning to Brokers

REQUIREMENTS FOR A VALID DEED   221

Basic Requirements • Competent Grantor • Competent Grantee • Adequate Property Description • Words of Conveyance • Legal Delivery • Acceptance

WILLS AND INTESTACY   224

Types of Wills • Intestacy • Terminology Used with Wills • Escheat

LAND SALES CONTRACTS   226

Definition • Seller's Right and Duties • Buyer's Rights and Duties • Reasons for Demise • Trustee's Sale • Advantages and Disadvantages to Seller • Advantages and Disadvantages to Buyer

STUDY QUESTIONS (TRUE–FALSE)   230

10 INVOLUNTARY TRANSFERS OF PROPERTY   232

NATURE OF ADVERSE POSSESSION   232

Definition • Use of Adverse Possession • Comparison to Easement by Prescription

REQUIREMENTS OF ADVERSE POSSESSION   233

Basic Requirements • Notorious Occupation • Hostile (Adverse) Possession • Claim of Right or Color of Title • Five Years' Continuous Possession • Payment of Taxes

CONDEMNATION (EMINENT DOMAIN)   238

Nature and Definition • Inverse Condemnation • Dedication as Disguised Condemnation • Distinction from Police Power

CONDEMNATION GUIDELINES   244

Limitations on Condemnation • For the Public Good • Just Compensation

ADDITIONS AND SUBTRACTIONS BY WATER   245

Nature of the Problem • Gradual Gain of Land • Sudden Removal of Land

STUDY QUESTIONS (TRUE–FALSE)   246

11 JOINT OWNERSHIP   248

CO-OWNERSHIP   248

Types of Co-ownership • Nature of Co-ownership

JOINT TENANCY   249

Nature of Joint Tenancy • Survivorship • Severance • Four Unities

TENANCY IN COMMON 254

Nature of Tenancy • Creation • Rights of Tenants

COMMUNITY PROPERTY 257

Origin of Community Property • Nature • Domestic Part-
nerships • Management and Control • Separate Property •
Community Property • Division of Community Property •
Secretive Transfers

COMMUNITY PROPERTY WITH RIGHT OF
SURVIVORSHIP 266

OTHER FORMS OF JOINT OWNERSHIP 266

Many Forms • General Partnerships • Limited
Partnership • Joint Venture • Corporations • Limited
Liability Company • Syndications • Real Estate Investment
Trusts • Condominiums • Cooperatives • Common
Interest Developments

STUDY QUESTIONS (TRUE–FALSE) 271

CHAPTER SUPPLEMENT REAL ESTATE SYNDICATIONS 272

Nature of Syndications • Regulations for Syndicators •
Regulated by the Department of Corporations • Typical
Syndication Process

12 LANDOWNER'S LIABILITY FOR INJURIES 278

DUTY OWED TO PEOPLE ON THE OWNER'S
PROPERTY 278

General Liability • Law Before 1968 • Problems with
Old Law • New Rule • End Result

DUTY OWED TO PEOPLE OFF THE OWNER'S
PROPERTY 281

General Rule • Exceptions for Adjoining Property •
Exceptions for Sidewalks

LIABILITY OF LANDLORD FOR INJURIES 284

General Background • Four Major Areas of Exposure

NUISANCES 286

Definition • Classification • Public and Private Nuisances •
Remedies for a Nuisance • Balancing the Equities

TREES 290

General Problems • Ownership of Trees • Right to Cut
Neighbor's Overhanging Branches

FENCES 291

Obligation to Pay • Spite Fences

ENCROACHMENTS 292

Nature and Definition • Remedies

STORM DAMAGE   293

Creating Dangerous Conditions   •   Failure to Correct
Dangerous Conditions

LATERAL AND SUBJACENT SUPPORT   294

Nature and Development   •   Lateral Support   •   Subjacent
Support   •   Eminent Domain by State

STUDY QUESTIONS (TRUE–FALSE)   296

13   LEASES AND EVICTION   298

LIMITATIONS ON LANDLORD'S REMEDIES   298

Originally No Limitations   •   Modern Restrictions   •   Violation
Does Not Terminate Lease

EVICTION PROCESS   301

Regulated by Statute   •   Steps in Eviction   •   Termination of
Tenancy   •   Unlawful Detainer Action   •   Eviction by the
Sheriff   •   Writ of Immediate Possession   •   Defense Strategy
•   Special Tenancies

LANDLORD–TENANT RELATIONSHIP   309

Governed by Law   •   Governed by Contract   •   No Standard
Form Lease   •   CAR Lease Analyzed

ANALYSIS OF A LEASE   317

(1) Lease and Demise   •   (2) List of Occupants   •   (3) Term   •
(4) Rent Payment   •   (5) Advance Deposits   •   (6) Amounts of
Advance Deposits   •   (7) Refund of Advance Deposits   •
(8) Interest on Deposit   •   (9) Management of Advance
Deposits   •   (10) Late Charges   •   (11) Parking   •   (12) Storage   •   (13) Utilities   •   (14) Condition of Premises   •
(15) Maintenance and Fitness (Habitability)   •   (16) Retaliatory
Eviction   •   (17) Neighborhood Conditions   •   (18) Pets   •
(19) Rules and Regulations   •   (20) Condominium and Planned
Unit Development   •   (21) Alterations   •   (22) Keys and
Locks   •   (23) Covenant of Quiet Enjoyment   •   (24) Entry   •
(25) Right of Reentry   •   (26) Signs   •   (27) Assignment and
Sublease   •   (28) Right to Assign and Sublease   •   (29) Joint
and Individual Obligations   •   (30) Various Disclosure
Notices   •   (31) Possession   •   (32) Tenant's Obligations upon
Vacating Premises   •   (33) Pre-Move Out Inspection   •
(34) Breach of Contract and Early Termination   •   (35) Abandonment   •   (36) Disposing of Abandoned Personal Property   •
(37) Temporary Relocation   •   (38) Damages to Premises   •
(39) Insurance   •   (40) Waterbeds   •   (41) Antiwaiver   •
(42) Notices   •   (43) Manner of Service   •   (44) Notice
Period   •   (45) Tenant Estoppel Certificate   •   (46) Credit
Check   •   (47) Mediation   •   (48) Attorney Fees   •

(49) Other Terms–Exculpatory Clause • (50) Entire Contract and Modification • (51) Agency • (52) Interpreter and Translator   • (53) Broker's Disclaimers • (54) Tenant's Signature • (55) Discrimination • (56) Guarantee

STUDY QUESTIONS (TRUE–FALSE)   342

14   RECORDING SYSTEM 344

NATURE AND EFFECT OF RECORDING   344

Recording Optional • Effect of Recording • Constructive Notice • Recording Requirements • Bona Fide Purchaser • Priorities • Title Insurance

GENERAL PRIORITIES   350

Unrecorded Documents • Effect of Recording • Effect of Improper Recording • Effect of Notice • Chain of Title • Transferee of a Bona Fide Purchaser

SPECIAL PRIORITIES   354

Mechanic's Liens • Judgment Liens • Future Advances under Deed of Trust

LIS PENDENS   356

Nature • Purpose • Use by Some Attorneys

RECORDING LIMITS   360

Problem • Periods

STUDY QUESTIONS (TRUE–FALSE)   361

15   MORTGAGES AND DEEDS OF TRUST 362

SECURITY AND OBLIGATION   362

Nature of Security • Security Separate from Obligation • Nature of Obligation • Promissory Note • Classification of Notes

COMPARISON OF MORTGAGES AND DEEDS OF TRUST   367

Deed of Trust • Mortgage

CLAUSES COMMON IN PROMISSORY NOTES AND DEEDS OF TRUST   370

Acceleration Clauses • Assignment of Rents Clause • Late Charges Clause • Prepayment Clause • Prepayment Fees • Wraparound Deeds of Trust • Blanket Deed of Trust • Future Advances Clause • Partial Release Clause • Subordination Agreements

DISCLOSURE AND LIMITS ON FINANCE CHARGES   376

Usury • Federal Truth in Lending Law • Real Property Loan Law • Loan Applications • Real Property Securities Dealers • Predatory Lending Law • Subprime Loans

DEFICIENCY JUDGMENTS   384

Nature of Deficiency • Restrictions on Deficiency Judgments • Purchase Money Instruments • Purpose of Deficiency Statutes • Exemption for Fraudulent Loans

FORECLOSURE PROCESS AND PROCEDURE   390

Nature of Trustee's Foreclosure • Trustee's Foreclosure Process • Judicial Foreclosure • Sale of Residential Property in Foreclosure

EFFECTS OF FORECLOSURE ON OTHER EXISTING DEEDS OF TRUST   400

General Rule • Effect of Junior's Foreclosure • Effect of Senior's Foreclosure • Options for Junior Lienor

TRANSFER OF SECURED PROPERTY   403

Right to Transfer • Subject To • Assumption • Novation

STUDY QUESTIONS (TRUE–FALSE)   404

16 INVOLUNTARY LIENS   406

NATURE OF INVOLUNTARY LIENS   406

Creation • Effect of Lien

ATTACHMENT LIENS   406

Nature • Old Attachment Law • Current Statutes • Limitations on Use of Attachments • Procedure to Obtain Attachment • Attachment of Real Estate

JUDGMENT LIENS   409

Nature • Interest Rate • Recorded to Be a Lien • Property Attached • Duration of Lien • General Priority

EXECUTION LIENS   415

Nature of Writ of Execution • Creation of an Execution Lien • Enforcement of the Lien

MECHANIC'S LIEN   416

Definition and Nature of Lien • Definition of Mechanic • Procedures to Obtain a Lien • Various Remedies for a Mechanic • Protections for Owner • Notice of Nonresponsibility

STUDY QUESTIONS (TRUE–FALSE)   428

17 PROPERTY TAXES 430

NATURE OF TAXES AND TAXABLE PROPERTY 430

Nature and Types of Taxes • Effect of Nonpayment • Exempt Property • Exemptions

TAX COLLECTION PROCESS 432

Due Dates • Tax-Defaulted Property • Redemption • Subject to Power of Sale

TAXING PROCEDURE 436

Proposition 13 • Tax Limits • Value Roll-Back to 1975 • Inflation Factor Increase • Senior Citizen Legislation • Over 55 or Disabled Carryover Basis

CALCULATION OF TAXES 443

Taxes before July 1978 • Taxes since July 1978 • Sample Tax Calculations

PRIORITY OF TAX LIENS 444

Normal Priority Rules Inapplicable • Priority over Private Liens • Priority to Federal Tax Liens • Priority between Tax Deeds

STUDY QUESTIONS (TRUE–FALSE) 447

18 HOMESTEADS 448

NATURE AND AMOUNT 448

Nature • Amount • Equity Protection • Effect of Increase

PRIORITIES 453

Recording Priority • Dwelling House Exemption • Effect

CREATION AND TERMINATION 454

Creation Requirements • Termination of Homestead

STUDY QUESTIONS (TRUE–FALSE) 456

19 PRIVATE RESTRICTIONS ON LAND 458

NATURE OF PRIVATE RESTRICTION 458

Types of Restrictions • Effect of Restrictions • Creation of Restrictions

CONDITIONS AND COVENANTS 459

Conditions in Contracts • Conditions in Real Property Law • Covenant • Comparison of Covenants and Conditions • Construction of Ambiguous Language

CONDITIONS RUNNING WITH THE LAND 463

Nature • Requirements • Equitable Servitude

GENERAL PLAN RESTRICTIONS (SUBDIVISIONS) 464

Nature and Purpose • Equitable Servitude • Modification and Termination

TERMINATION AND UNENFORCEABILITY 466

Enforcement • Defenses to Enforcement • Natural Termination

STUDY QUESTIONS (TRUE–FALSE) 469

20 ZONING 470

NATURE OF ZONING 470

Definition and Use • Zoning History • Authority for Zoning • Limits on Zoning • Distinct from Eminent Domain

EXPANDED USES OF ZONING AND PLANNING 472

New Orientations • General Plan • Regional Planning • Broadened Use of Zoning • Growth Limitations and Character

RELIEF FROM ZONING 478

Sources of Relief • Legislative Relief • Judicial Relief • Administrative Relief

STUDY QUESTIONS (TRUE–FALSE) 483

21 ENVIRONMENTAL CONTROLS AND SUBDIVISION LAWS 484

NEED FOR CONTROLS 484

Spaceship Earth • Recent Power

FEDERAL ENVIRONMENTAL LAWS 485

National Environmental Policy Act • Other Legislation

CALIFORNIA ENVIRONMENTAL LAWS 486

Environmental Quality Act • Government Projects • Significant Effect • Timing and Procedure

HAZARDOUS WASTE LAWS 490

Legislation • Typical Hazardous Wastes • People Liable • Innocent Landowner Exception • New Owner Restoring Property Exception • Lender and Fiduciary Exemption • Purchaser Protections

CALIFORNIA SUBDIVISION LAWS 495

Two Separate Statutes

SUBDIVIDED LANDS ACT   495

Nature of Statute • Definition of Subdivision • Procedure for Compliance

SUBDIVISION MAP ACT   498

Nature of the Statute • Definition of Subdivision • Obtaining the Final Map • Dedication Requirements • Exceptions to Obtaining the Final Map • Condominium Conversions • Vested Rights

STUDY QUESTIONS (TRUE–FALSE)   502

22 TITLE INSURANCE AND ESCROW   504

NATURE OF TITLE INSURANCE   504

Purpose • Legally Optional • Nature of Policy and Company

TYPES OF TITLE POLICIES   507

Types of Policies • Elements of a Policy • Difference between Policies

NATURE OF ESCROW AND ESCROW COMPANIES   520

Use and Definition • Regulation of Escrow

ESCROW IS A DOUBLE AGENT   521

Dual Agency • Limited Agency • Elements of an Escrow • Delivery, Title, and Risk

REAL ESTATE SETTLEMENT PROCEDURES ACT   526

Nature of RESPA (Reg. X) • Good Faith Estimate Form • Limits On Good Faith Estimate Increase • Three Categories of GFE Charges • Example of Allowed Changes to GFE

STUDY QUESTIONS (TRUE–FALSE)   534

23 AGENCY AND BROKER'S RELATIONSHIP   536

NATURE AND CREATION OF AGENCY RELATIONSHIPS   536

Nature of Agency • Classification of Agencies • Comparison to Employee Relationship • Comparison to Independent Contractors • Creation of Express Agency • Creation of Implied Agency • Termination of Agency Relationship • Real Estate Activities on Internet

REAL ESTATE BROKERS   540

Definition of Broker • Salespersons • Status of Real Estate Broker • Whose Agent Is Broker?

REGULATION OF BROKERS   546

Basic Regulations • Handling of Deposits • Unlawful Acts of Brokers • Unlawful Acts as Individuals • Other Regulations • Real Estate Recovery Fund • No Special Liability When Acting as Principal

BROKER'S OBLIGATION TO CLIENTS   553

Nature of Duties • Duty of Good Faith • Duty of Full Disclosure • Duty of Loyalty: No Adverse Interest • Duty to Use Professional Standard of Care • Duty to Account

BROKER'S OBLIGATION TO THIRD PERSONS   555

General Duties • Fraud • Secret Profits • Negligence • Principal's Contracts • Disclosure of Property's Condition

STUDY QUESTIONS (TRUE–FALSE)   561

APPENDIX A: USEFUL WEB SITES   562

APPENDIX B: ANSWERS TO STUDY QUESTIONS   566

APPENDIX C: SAMPLE TEST #1   574

APPENDIX D: SAMPLE TEST #2   590

APPENDIX E: ANSWERS TO SAMPLE
                       TESTS #1 AND #2   608

Glossary of Real Estate and Legal Terms   626

Index of Cases   643

Index of Codes   646

Subject Index   652

Preface

In the time since the publication of the seventh edition of *California Real Estate Law*, changes have been made in California real estate property law. New laws include those covering subprime loans, predatory lending, good faith estimates, new requirements on advertising, and higher limits on homesteads. This edition provides expanded coverage laws that have taken on greater importance, such as the Americans with Disabilities Act, water law, use of the Internet in selling property, domestic partnerships, view easements, and real estate syndications. This revision has many more sample forms to supplement the readings. All the changes to this supplement are detailed later in this Preface.

FIVE GOALS OF THIS BOOK

This edition continues the five goals that have made previous editions of this book so popular. The goals are: balanced and concise statements of the law, expanded coverage on key areas of the law, testing materials, practical application, and digested case analysis.

The first goal of this book is to provide a well-organized, balanced, and concise statement of key areas of California property law. The basic principles are clearly and concisely stated. These doctrines are then supported by a discussion explaining the nature and purpose of the laws.

Second, some areas of the law are so commonly encountered that expanded and more detailed material is needed for a practical and useful understanding of the law. For example, deposit receipts, listing agreements, and leases are all broken down clause by clause. The legal effect of each provision is carefully explained so that the forms are fully understood in their legal context. In addition, the book offers detailed analysis of the common clauses in promissory notes and deeds of trust.

The eviction process, foreclosure of deeds of trust, and environmental law also receive expanded treatment beyond that ordinarily found in similar texts.

Third, it is important to evaluate just how well the reader understands the law. As a valuable learning tool, this edition contains two appendices that together contain 220 multiple-choice questions, with answers, and more importantly, an explanation of WHY a particular answer is correct.

Fourth, the emphasis of the book is on practical application. Abstract legal principles provide only a theoretical understanding of the law unless they are tied to practical applications. Where appropriate, practical tips are provided that come from the author's experience both as an attorney and as a real estate broker.

The last goal is to include the opportunity for case analysis. No more than two cases are in a chapter, so as not to overwhelm the reader. These cases are well digested and purposely omit references to deleted material, to make the cases more readable. These digested cases also provide practical examples of the legal principles as they arise in common situations and offer discussion and restatement of the applicable real estate laws.

Besides being a tool for learning the law, this book serves as a handy reference. Throughout the book, important legal points contain references to codes or cases, which allow additional research and supplemental investigation for a deeper understanding of a legal point. Besides the normal subject index, the book contains both an index by case names and a listing by code sections for quick reference.

NEW CHANGES TO THIS EDITION

- Chapter 2: The chapter now adds a copy of Judicial Council complaint to understand how a complaint looks, and adds a copy of the Judicial Council info for the small claims court plaintiff (discussing who can file, where to file, how to serve the defendant, counter-claims, trial, and more).
- Chapter 3: The chapter now includes information on acquiring a security interest in real and personal property, how to perfect that security interest, a sample UCC-1 form, and how to transfer those interests with a sample bill of sale and grant deed. Water has taken on added importance, and the chapter has expanded coverage of water law, including riparian rights and prior appropriation rights, and adds a table on the exact process to obtain a water permit.

- Chapter 4: The chapter more fully explains counteroffers and now gives sample forms for counteroffer and counter to the counteroffer. The chapter adds a sample form to cancel a contract. Finally, the chapter mentions specified high-priced condominium sales having special exemption to 3% limitation on liquidated damages.

- Chapter 5: The biggest change to this chapter is replacing the 2004 version of the CAR deposit receipt with the 4/28/10 version and analyzes that version clause by clause. The chapter adds many new forms: CAR receipt for increase deposit, CAR statewide buyer and seller advisory, CAR contingency for sale or purchase of other property, CAR contingency removal, CAR extension of time addendum, and CAR addendum. The chapter discusses the right to inspect the property and cancel the agreement as the buyer's "absolute and sole discretion" may make the contract unenforceable. There is expanded material on drafting of contingencies and the satisfaction or waiver of contingencies. Finally, the chapter adds information on the unresolved potential for arbitration under federal preemption under the Federal Arbitration Act if the arbitration clause does not meet California's statutory requirements for arbitration.

- Chapter 6: The chapter provides expanded information on probate sales by the independent administration of estates act, and includes a Judicial Council form for report of sale and order confirming sale of real property. The chapter adds a CAR notice of prospective buyer/transferee, and changed from CAR residential listing agreement to the CAR general listing agreement for all property before analyzing that listing agreement clause-by-clause.

- Chapter 7: The chapter adds material on view easements as well as adding a sample grant of easement form and a sample license agreement.

- Chapter 8: There is now a discussion on today's use of life estates and the fact they still have uses.

- Chapter 10: The chapter now discusses the limitations of condemnation as restricted by Proposition 99.

- Chapter 11: The chapter adds a section on domestic partnerships. The chapter also adds an appendix to the chapter providing extensive discussion on the nature and use of real estate syndications. Syndications are added as an appendix making its reading optional, despite its importance, as such material if often not included in this type of law textbook.

- Chapter 13: The chapter offers expanded coverage of eviction under Section 8 federally subsided housing and disposing of abandoned personal property. The chapter adds material on vacating a lease by a tenant who is the victim of domestic violence, and on the Americans With Disability Act, including prohibitions against discrimination against the disabled. Finally the chapter includes an updated CAR residential lease form before analyzing that form clause-by-clause.

- Chapter 14: The chapter expands discussion of the need for a preliminary change of ownership report, and updates the new language required in the acknowledgment form. The chapter also adds a new section on transfer tax stamps and includes a copy of transfer tax affidavit. The form is required to record documents where there will be potential transfer tax stamps.

- Chapter 15: The chapter provides expanded coverage on level payment promissory notes and of rescission rights under Regulation Z. It covers the new topics of constant reduction of principal loans, negative amortization, special requirements in the Real Property Loan Law for subprime loans, and a new section on Subprime loans and the new laws governing such loans. The book adds sample forms on full reconveyance of deed of trust, three-day rescission notice (Reg-Z), notice of default, request for special notice of default, and notice of trustee's sale. Additionally, the chapter adds a diagram of the difference between level payment and constant reduction of principal notes. It adds a table explaining the risks of purchase money deeds of trust to a holder, both non-tax and tax consideration involved, and how to minimize some of the risks of such loans.

- Chapter 16—*Involuntary Liens*: The chapter explains and expands method of an owner's process to obtain a waiver of potential mechanic's lien from the contractor and others by use of the waiver of mechanics lien. It supplements that discussion with sample forms waiver of mechanic's lien by general contractor, conditional waiver and release (of mechanic's lien) upon progress payment, unconditional waiver and release (of mechanic's lien) upon progress payment, and conditional waiver and release (of mechanic's lien) upon final payment. The book adds a sample preliminary 20-day notice form, and updates the abstract of judgment form.

- Chapter 17: This chapter updates the preliminary change of ownership report form to include coverage for domestic partners.

- Chapter 18: The chapter updates the homestead amounts to the new, higher amounts, and updates the figure providing examples of homestead calculation as well as the table of recent homestead increases.

- Chapter 19: There is new material on the scope of restrictions and how they can be used.
- Chapter 22: The new Homeowner's title insurance Policy is substituted for older CLTA title policy. The chapter adds a new section on RESPA including good faith estimates and how they are calculated and regulated. The chapter then adds a copy of HUD's Good Faith Estimate and their Settlement Statement forms.
- Chapter 23: The chapter adds a new section on real estate activities on the Internet and includes a copy of CAR's Independent Contractor Agreement form.

LIMITATIONS ON BOOK ON LAW

The book is not a substitute for an attorney. Facts of individual cases may affect the application of the law in subtle variation that only a lawyer can recognize. Additionally, interpretation of statutes and cases is a matter of opinion—not fact. The law is constantly changing, with new statutes added each year supplemented by hundreds of new case citations. You should seek the services of an attorney for any analysis of the law and for any legal problems, and you should not rely on any book, including this book, to analyze or decide the legal rights of any individual factual situation. Finally, the forms included in this book are for illustrative purposes only, and should not, nor are they designed to, be used in individual situations.

GENERAL INFORMATION

I have used the pronouns "he" or "she" in sentences with the sole intent of signifying the neuter gender, applicable to a man or a woman. Sentences read easier with the pronoun "he" or "she" instead of "he/she" or similar words. While I have tried to balance the appearances of two pronouns, the intent is to keep the gender neutral and inoffensive.

Any comments on the content of the book, its format, information about new laws, and suggestions on improvements are enthusiastically encouraged and very welcome. Such feedback resulted in revision of each previous edition and expansion in selected areas.

Ted H. Gordon
San Rafael, California

Foreword

(To the First Edition)

The study of law in the United States originally approximated the apprentice system: one "read" law in an attorney's office and assisted that attorney. The next stage in legal education was the establishment of law schools, where instructors lectured to students on the broad legal rules. Under this system, the student was totally removed from client contact. Then, roughly a hundred years ago, Harvard Professor of Law C. C. Langdell put his students to studying appellate cases, and the case system of legal study was born. It provided the student with concrete examples of how the broad legal rules were applied as between actual people, the plaintiff and the defendant, and gave the student some insight into the many variations in results that could, did, and still do stem from even slight variations in the factual situations to which broad legal rules are applied.

This casebook covers the standard topics discussed in a basic text or reference in real estate law, while incorporating the advantage of the case method. It has been designed for use as the text for collegiate real estate law classes, as a guide for real estate brokers and property owners, and as a quick reference for attorneys. In addition to covering the standard areas of concern, it gives expanded coverage of leases and deeds of trust, explains the nature and problems of damages for breach of a contract to sell real property, and offers an introduction to environmental law problems. The cases selected provide adequate coverage of real estate law. The tables, diagrams, and explanatory materials facilitate understanding of legal relationships and legal principles. The book is a very useful and valuable learning and operating tool.

Joe H. Munster, Jr., J.D., S.J.D.
Professor of Law, Past Associate Dean
University of California
Hastings College of the Law

Table of Legal Abbreviations

B.&P.C.	Business and Professions Code of California
C.	California Reports (the official decisions of the California Supreme Court from 1850 to 1934)
C.2d	California Reports, Second Series (decisions from 1934 to 1969)
C.3d	California Reports, Third Series (decisions from 1969 to 1991)
C.4th	California Reports, Fourth Series (decisions from 1991 to date)
C.A.	California Appellate Reports (the official decisions of the California Court of Appeal from 1905 to 1934)
C.A.2d	California Appellate Reports, Second Series (decisions from 1934 to 1969)
C.A.3d	California Appellate Reports, Third Series (decisions from 1969 to 1991)
C.A.4th	California Appellate Reports, Third Series (decisions from 1991 to date)
Cal. Code Reg.	Code of Regulations (replaced Administrative Code)
Cal. Const.	California Constitution
C.C.	Civil Code of California
C.C.P.	Code of Civil Procedure of California
Comm.C.	Commercial Code (California's adopted version of the Uniform Commercial Code)
Comm.Regs.	Regulations of the California Real Estate Commissioner
Corp.C.	Corporations Code of California
F.	Federal Reporter (official decisions of the Federal Court of Appeal from 1880 to 1924)

F.2d	Federal Reporter, Second Series (decisions from 1924 to date)
Fam.C.	Family Code of California
Fin.C.	Financial Code of California
F.Supp.	Federal Supplement (official decisions of the U.S. District Court from 1932 to date)
Gov.C.	Government Code of California
H.&S.C.	Health and Safety Code of California
Ins.C.	Insurance Code of California
I.R.C.	Internal Revenue Code (federal)
Lab.C.	Labor Code of California
Ops.Cal.Att.Gen.	Opinions of the Attorney General of California
P.	Pacific Reporter (decisions of the California Supreme Court and selected opinions of the Court of Appeal from 1883 to 1931)
P.2d	Pacific Reporter, Second Series (decisions from 1931 to date)
Penal.C.	Penal Code of California
Prob.C.	Probate Code of California
Pub.Res.C.	Public Resources Code of California
R.&T.C.	Revenue and Taxation Code of California
Rev.Rul.	Official interpretation by the Internal Revenue Service of the tax code
S.Ct.	Supreme Court Reporter (decisions of the U.S. Supreme Court from 1882 to date)
Sts.Hy.C.	Streets and Highway Code of California
U.C.C.	Uniform Commercial Code
Un.I.C.	Unemployment Insurance Code of California
U.S.	United States Reports (official decisions of the U.S. Supreme Court from 1754 to date)
U.S.C.	United States Code
Wat.C.	Water Code of California

PROPERTY RIGHTS IN A DEMOCRACY

Absolute Rights Abolished

Many people still think of property in terms of the ancient doctrine of feudal law, in which a man's home was his castle. Under this concept, the owner exercised absolute dominion over his land. Trespassers were shot, neighbors' rights disregarded, and the public welfare ignored. However, with increasing urbanization and the rise of the middle class, the landowner's rights became circumscribed by the rights of others. To protect the common welfare, laws were developed to cover waste, lateral and subjacent support, nuisance, zoning, land planning, building codes, and other police powers.

All Rights Relative

In a democracy, all property and personal rights are, by definition, relative to and circumscribed by the rights and privileges of others in that society. Consequently, each right or privilege must be balanced against similar, equivalent, and superior rights. Furthermore, each new variable or change in circumstances alters the factors that are balanced against each other.

Balancing Rights

The rights of *private property* have traditionally been protected by the democratic concept and constitutional safeguards. The Fourteenth Amendment to the U.S. Constitution prevents any *state* from depriving any person of property without due process of law. The California Constitution contains a similar restriction. The Fifth Amendment to the federal Constitution places similar limitations on

Nature of Property

the *federal* government. Thus, any taking of property rights requires due process and, under the Fifth Amendment, compensation for any taking. The Fourteenth Amendment also prohibits *states* from denying any person "equal protection of the laws." Similarly, for example, the rights of *free speech* have been protected. When these two constitutionally protected rights conflict, the more important right in the particular situation will prevail. The outcome in each situation depends on the particular circumstances that must be balanced against each other.

Examples of Balancing

Free speech is generally guaranteed on publicly owned property that is fully open to the public. *Jamison v. Texas (1942) 318 U.S. 413.* At the other extreme, the First Amendment right of free speech is generally prohibited on purely privately owned property, like a person's home, which is used exclusively for private purposes. *Bread v. Alexandria (1951) 341 U.S. 622.* Hence, employees may not picket their employer's private home. *Annenberg v. So. Cal. Dist. Council (1974) 38 C.A.3d 637.*

Further Examples

Between the extremes of totally public and totally private property, restrictions on the use of property change dramatically depending on numerous factors. The courts consider and balance the nature of the public or private uses involved, the number and type of persons using the property, and the character of the property itself. For example, peaceful demonstrations could not be restricted at a privately owned railroad station, unless the demonstrations interfered with station operations. *In re Hoffman (1967) 67 C.2d 845.* However, even peaceful, nondisruptive demonstrations were prohibited in front of a county jail, under the theory that such structures were designed for security purposes as opposed to public uses. *Adderly v. Florida (1966) 385 U.S. 39.*

Restrictions on Use

Numerous restrictions prohibit property owners from freely using their property as they wish. A few of the more common restrictions follow.

Constitutional Restrictions

The owner of a wholly owned company town, consisting entirely of private property, may not prohibit demonstrators from distributing anti-Soviet literature.

Nuisance

An owner may not use residential property for a garbage dump or a copper smelter.

Private Covenants, Conditions, and Restrictions

A real estate developer may place covenants, conditions, and restrictions on a subdivision, such as to prohibit any lot owner from building a home below a certain price or above a certain size.

Police Power

A local government may use zoning to prohibit an individual from constructing an apartment building in a purely single-family residential neighborhood. It may also use building codes to require all buildings to meet certain wiring and construction standards.

APPLY THE LAW

Robins v. Pruneyard Shopping Center
23 C.3d 899 (1979)

[Several demonstrators (the appellants) entered a large, privately owned regional shopping center and, in a peaceful, quiet, and orderly manner, sought to solicit support for their cause and to collect signatures for a petition to the president of the United States. The shopping center owners (the respondents), through their security guards, ordered the demonstrators off the premises. Faced with the possibility of being arrested for trespassing, the demonstrators left the shopping center and filed a lawsuit seeking free access to the premises for free speech rights.

To decide this case, the court has to balance the rights of Free Speech, which are guaranteed by the First Amendment of the Constitution, against the equally important rights of Private Property, which are guaranteed by the Fifth Amendment. When two equally important rights are in conflict, obviously only one can win. The court has reversed itself several times in its history of deciding which right is the most important.

Before 1946, private property rights always prevailed. Then, in 1946, the U.S. Supreme Court held that privately owned streets of a company town serve the same function as public streets. Because you could not prohibit free speech on public streets, the Court ruled you could not prohibit free speech on privately owned streets. As the Court stated: "the more an owner, for his own advantage, opens up his property for the use by the public in general, the more do his rights become circumscribed by the statutory and constitutional rights of owners who use it."

In 1968, the U.S. Supreme Court extended the doctrine, by holding that the common areas of a shopping center served the same function as public streets. Therefore, free speech rights prevailed over private property rights on shopping centers, and owners could not evict peaceful demonstrators.

However, in 1972, the conservative Berger Court reversed itself and overturned its previous holdings under the liberal Warren Court. The U.S. Supreme Court held that an owner could evict demonstrators from distributing pamphlets and information unrelated to the business purposes of the shopping center. Private property rights, under the Fifth Amendment, prevailed over free speech rights of the First Amendment.

In 1979, the issue is before the California Supreme Court, which must interpret California laws in light of federal rulings. The trial court found for the shopping center owners, and the demonstrators appealed.]

NEWMAN, JUSTICE. All private property is held subject to the power of the government to regulate its use for the public welfare.

Property rights must yield to the public interest served by zoning laws, to environmental needs, and to many other public concerns (see, e.g., the California Coastal Act, the California Water Quality Control Act, the Subdivision Map Act, and the Subdivision Lands Act).

We do not minimize the importance of the constitutional guarantee attaching to private ownership of property; but as long as 50 years ago it was already thoroughly established in this country that the rights preserved to the individual by these constitutional provisions are held in subordination to the rights of society. Although one owns property, he may not do with it as he pleases any more than he may act in accordance with his personal desires. As the interest of society justifies restraints upon individual conduct, so, also, does it justify restraints upon the use to which property may be devoted. It was not intended by these constitutional provisions to so far protect the individual in the use of his property as to enable him to use it to the detriment of society. By thus protecting individual rights, society did not part with the power to protect itself or to promote its general well-being. Where the interest of the individual conflicts with the interest of society, such individual interest is subordinated to the general welfare.

The power to regulate property is not static; rather, it is capable of expansion to meet new conditions of modern life. Property rights must be

APPLY THE LAW

continued

continued

redefined in response to a swelling demand that ownership be responsible and responsive to the needs of the social whole. Property rights cannot be used as a shibboleth to cloak conduct that adversely affects the health, the safety, the morals, or the welfare of others.

In assessing the significance of the growing importance of the shopping center, we stress also that to prohibit expressive activity in the centers would impinge on constitutional rights beyond speech rights. Courts have long protected the right to petition as an essential attribute of governing. To protect free speech and petitioning is a goal that surely matches the protecting of health and safety, the environment, aesthetics, property values, and other societal goals that have been held to justify reasonable restrictions on private property rights.

No California statute prescribes that shopping center owners provide public forums. But the State Constitution reads, "Every person may freely speak, write, and publish his or her sentiments on all subjects, being responsible for the abuse of this right. A law may not restrain or abridge liberty of speech or press." Though the framers could have adopted the words of the federal Bill of Rights, they chose not to do so. Special protections thus accorded speech are marked in this court's opinions. A protective provision more definitive and inclusive than the First Amendment is contained in our state constitutional guarantee of the right of free speech and press.

Past decisions on speech and private property testify to the strength of liberty of speech in this state. [The court case known as] *Diamond I* held that distributing leaflets and soliciting initiative signatures at a shopping center are constitutionally protected. Though the court relied partly on federal law, California precedents also were cited. The fact that those opinions cited federal law that subsequently took a divergent course does not diminish their usefulness as precedent. The duty of this court is to help determine what "liberty of speech" means in California. Federal principles are relevant but not conclusive so long as federal rights are protected.

In re Lane extended the assurance of protected speech to the privately owned sidewalk of a grocery store. "Certainly, this sidewalk is not private in the sense of not being open to the public. The public is openly invited to use it in gaining access to the store and in leaving the premises. Thus, in our view it is a public area in which members of the public may exercise First Amendment rights."

The issue arose too in *In re Hoffman*, where Vietnam War protesters had attempted to distribute leaflets in the Los Angeles Union Station, owned by three private companies. It housed a restaurant, snack bar, cocktail lounge, and magazine stand in addition to facilities directly related to transporting passengers. The public was free to use the whole station. Chief Justice Traynor's opinion made it clear that property owners as well as government may regulate speech as to time, place, and manner.

Nonetheless, a railway station is like a public street or park. Further, the test is not whether petitioners' use of the station was a railway use, but whether it interfered with that use.

APPLY THE LAW
continued

The opinion thus affirms that the public interest in peaceful speech outweighs the desire of property owners for control over their property. The shopping center may no more exclude individuals who wear long hair, who are black, who are members of the John Birch Society, or who belong to the American Civil Liberties Union, merely because of these characteristics or associations, than may the City of San Rafael. Justice Mosk described the extensive use of private shopping centers. His observations on the role of the centers in our society are even more forceful now than when he wrote. The California Constitution broadly proclaims speech and petition rights. Shopping centers to which the public is invited can provide an essential and invaluable forum for exercising those rights.

We conclude that the California Constitution protects speech and petitioning, reasonably exercised, in shopping centers even when the centers are privately owned.

By no means do we imply that those who wish to disseminate ideas have free rein. We noted above Chief Justice Traynor's endorsement of time, place, and manner rules. Further, as Justice Mosk stated: "It bears repeated emphasis that we do not have under consideration the property or privacy rights of an individual homeowner or the proprietor of a modest retail establishment." As a result of advertising and the lure of a congenial environment, 25,000 persons are induced to congregate daily to take advantage of the numerous amenities offered by the shopping center there. A handful of additional orderly persons soliciting signatures and distributing handbills in connection therewith, under reasonable regulations adopted by defendant to assure that these activities do not interfere with normal business operations, would not markedly dilute defendant's property rights.

The judgment rejecting appellants' request that Pruneyard be enjoined from denying access to circulate the petition is reversed. [The individuals may enter at reasonable times, in reasonable numbers, and demonstrate in a peaceful, nondisruptive manner.]

PROPERTY AS A CREATION OF LAW

What Is Property?

Two theories define the nature of property. The first is the *natural rights* doctrine, which holds that property exists independent of law. Under this doctrine, property cannot be taken away or substantially limited by the legislature. The second theory, and the one accepted today, is the *creation of law* doctrine. Under this doctrine, property is a creation of law and has no existence without the protection of law.

Bundle of Rights

Property in modern societies is nothing more than a basis of expectations—a *bundle of rights*—created by, existing under, and protected through laws. These expectations include the right to use and possess the property to the exclusion of others, the right to sell or will the property to others, and the right to grow crops and build on the land. These rights, protected by law, have value. Without that law there is no more property—only land. Thus, it is the protected rights of individuals to exclusive use of their property, and not the physical elements (land, building, and fixtures), that form the basis and the legal concept of property.

Not Absolute but Abolishable

The collective rights known as property are protected by law, but they are not absolute and guaranteed to the owner. Because the governments created property, they can also uncreate or remove many of these rights, thereby eliminating the benefits of ownership.

Example

Before January 1, 1977, property belonging to a decedent received a free **stepped-up basis** to date of death without subjection to capital gains tax computations. This significant tax advantage to property owners was then largely eliminated by the government. Thus, heirs and beneficiaries of the decedent received the decedent's property at the decedent's old tax basis. If the heirs and beneficiaries later sold the property, they were subject to capital gains, generally equal to the sales price less the decedent's original purchase price. Because decedents often purchased real estate many years before their death, the capital gains often became very costly, significantly reducing the effective net value of the property ownership. Several years later, Congress finally rescinded this legislation, restoring the tax break that originally existed. Thus, one of the values of property ownership—transference on death—was significantly reduced, then later reinstated.

Under the same type of power, the government could declare that all property owned at death would automatically revert to the state. *In re Estate of Larkin (1966) 65 C.2d 60.* The only difference between the tax adjustment and the right to pass property on death through inheritance is one of degree.

Some Limitations

However, the state's power to affect private property, like the private citizen's rights in a democracy, is not absolute. Among other requirements, any taking or regulation of private property by the government must meet the demands of **due process** and **equal protection** of the Fourteenth Amendment to the U.S. Constitution.

APPLY THE LAW

In re Estate of Larkin
65 C.2d 60 (1966)

[A California resident, having no heirs in this country, left his estate to a Russian living in the U.S.S.R. The State of California tried to claim the estate under the doctrine of escheat, alleging that the gift was invalid for want of a qualified heir by reason of the reciprocity required for aliens under Probate Code 259.]

TROBRINER, JUSTICE. That statute makes the validity of such gifts conditional upon the existence of reciprocal rights on the part of the United States citizens to share without discrimination in the estates governed by the law of the foreign beneficiary's own country. Section 259 uses the words "reciprocal rights" to mean merely that United States residents and citizens have the same rights as residents and citizens of the alien's country. It does not require equal rights be granted by the inheritance laws of the two countries. We may require no more than a demonstration that the law of the foreign country, as written and as consistently applied in practice, enables our citizens to inherit economically significant property interests on terms of full equality with the residents of that country.

The Attorney General introduced evidence tending to establish that Soviet legal theory does not recognize the concept of "natural rights." Even if we were to accept the hypothesis that a system of inheritance predicated upon "natural right" is, for that reason, more secure, we think it unlikely that the legislature intended to impose such a requirement. Few nations could meet it; our own certainly could not.

The right to succession [to inherit property] is not an inherent or natural right. It is only by virtue of the statute that an heir is given the right to receive any of his ancestor's estate.

Rights of succession to the property of a deceased, whether by will or by intestacy, are of statutory creation, and only by sufferance. Nothing in the Federal Constitution forbids the legislature of a state to limit, condition, or even abolish the power of testamentary disposition over property within its jurisdiction. So broad is the power of the state to determine the title to the property of a person dying and leaving property within its boundaries that it may take the property itself and deny any rights of anyone to succeed thereto, either by will or by succession.

APPLY THE LAW
continued

Unquestionably, the range of items that can be owned by Soviet citizens and, hence, inherited by their American heirs, is more limited than in our country. Soviet law permits no private ownership of "means of production" and prohibits "speculation" in securities and commodities. These restrictions do not, however, necessarily negate the existence of a meaningful regime of reciprocal inheritance rights unless the items that can be owned are so limited in number or value as to be economically negligible.

It is common knowledge that there is scarcely a government in Europe that has not embarked upon a program of socialization of industry in greater or lesser degree.

Reciprocity with the Soviet Union does not extend to realty because of the fact that title to all Soviet land vests in the state. This limitation, however, does not affect the ownership of buildings. A building owner enjoys the indefeasible right to the perpetual use of the land supporting and surrounding his building, and may assign this right on sale of the building.

The record clearly establishes that citizens of the United States enjoy a reciprocal right to inherit from Soviet estates on the same terms and conditions as Soviet citizens. Judgment reversed. [The Soviet citizen may inherit the estate.]

[By dicta, in a case involving a similar reciprocal inheritance statute of another state, the U.S. Supreme Court indicated it would probably invalidate California's statute if it ever came to Court. *389 U.S. 429 at 433.*]

STUDY QUESTIONS (TRUE–FALSE)

1. Owners of totally private property may find themselves legally unable to evict unwanted demonstrators and pickets from their property.

2. Private property, totally located within California, is only and exclusively regulated by California statutes and California legal decisions.

3. The First Amendment rights of free speech are superior to and always take priority over private property rights.

4. Private property rights generally give way to and are bound by public rights when the general welfare of the public is involved.

5. Even though aliens live in a foreign country and have never visited the United States, they may still inherit

property by will from a U.S. citizen living in California.

6. In America, ownership of property is a natural right guaranteed by the U.S. Constitution.

7. All countries of the world permit law-abiding citizens of that country to own real property if they are able to afford it.

8. California's control over property is so broad that it may legally abolish a citizen's right to will property on death.

9. Anytime that the state significantly limits a use of private property previously enjoyed by the owner, the state must pay just compensation to the owner.

10. Legally, the term property does not relate to the physical assets, but rather describes the legal concept of ownership of a bundle of rights over the physical asset.

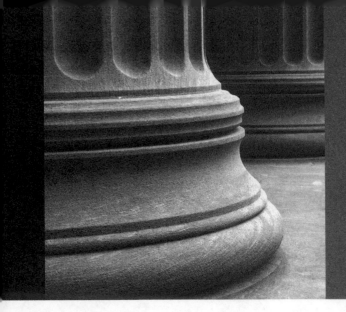

NATURE AND SOURCE OF LAW

Nature of Law

Law is a system of rules and enforcement methods by which society regulates and controls the conduct and affairs of its members. Laws replace the primitive concept of *might makes right* with a peaceful procedure that provides the individual with a nonviolent method of resolving personal disputes.

Two Legal Systems

The American legal system evolved from one or the other of two concepts. Either the system developed from the **civil law** concept of ancient Roman law, or it arose from the **common law** system of English law.

Civil Law

Civil law evolved in almost all of Europe except England. It operates on the concept of establishing numerous rules designated to cover and define the entire span of human conduct. In theory, for every given situation, one need only look to the detailed statutes to find society's (or the emperor's) regulation of that conduct.

Common Law

Common law originated almost exclusively in England and was the legal system brought to this country by our nation's founders. The law builds and expands, one small step at a time, through a case-by-case approach. Each judgment rendered by a court is a definition of a dispute or conduct. One need only look to a case involving a similar act or problem to know the law on that point.

Judicial System and History

Stare Decisis

The basis of the common law system is the principle of **stare decisis.** This concept is one of *predictability*, providing stability to the legal system: Once a judgment is rendered it becomes recorded. In a similar dispute in the future, the problem should be resolved in the same manner as the earlier case. Of course, it is rare that two cases ever arise on the exact same factual pattern. Consequently, most courts use similar cases as guidelines, trying to apply the law consistently, but nevertheless feeling free to interpret existing law in light of the factual pattern existing in the particular case before them.

Courts Bound

Only inferior, lower courts are *bound by* decisions of higher courts and must follow that higher court's earlier rulings. Courts of equal stature, although not required to follow one another's rulings, usually do so unless clearly convinced that the equal court's earlier decision is wrong. Finally, higher courts (which generally receive a case only by appeal) decide the rule of law on their own, unbound by the lower court's precedent.

Flexibility Insured

Having the law evolve one step at a time ensures flexibility so that laws can develop and adapt to a growing society with changing values. For example, the 1954 U.S. Supreme Court case of *Brown v. Board of Education* overruled the *separate but equal* doctrine of the 1896 U.S. Supreme Court. Also, courts may *distinguish* an earlier case based on the exact facts of that earlier case, thus limiting the earlier decision to the precise issue resolved.

Hart v. Burnett
15 C. 530 (1860)

[The court in rendering its decision was forced to review the doctrine of *stare decisis*, that is, to decide if it was bound by a prior decision.]

BALDWIN JUSTICE. The reason given for this rule of *stare decisis* is that rights vest by decisions, which affirm a title under a given state of facts, and therefore it would be unjust to deprive a party of property acquired under such circumstances.

A solemn decision upon a point of law, arising in any given case, becomes an authority in a like case, because it is the highest evidence that we can have of the law applicable to the subject. The judges are bound to follow that decision so long as it stands unreversed, unless it can be shown that the law was misunderstood or misapplied in that particular case. If a decision has been made upon solemn argument and mature deliberation, the presumption is in favor of its correctness. The community has a right to regard it as a just declaration of the law, and to regulate their actions and contracts by it.

It would, therefore, be extremely inconvenient to the public if precedents were not duly regarded and implicitly followed. It is by the notoriety and stability of such rules that the professional men can give safe advice to those who consult them; and people in general can venture with confidence to buy and trust, and to deal with each other. If judicial decisions were to be lightly disregarded, we should disturb and unsettle the great landmarks of property.

When a rule has been once deliberately adopted and declared, it ought not to be disturbed unless by a court of appeal or review, and never by the same court, except for very cogent reasons, and upon a clear manifestation of error; and if the practice were otherwise, it would be leaving us in a state of perplexing uncertainty as to the law.

The Supreme Court of the United States illustrates what it means by a settled course of adjudication. In a case now under consideration there have been two decisions in the highest courts of law in the State upon the identical question now in judgment, and which were in conformity to a settled course of adjudication for twenty years past.

We might admit the general doctrine, as contended for, that a single decision or two decisions on a question of property are decisive and conclusive. As a general rule, however flagrantly erroneous these decisions were, we yet hold that this principle, like all general rules, has and must have its exceptions. It would devolve upon us then to show that to this rule there were exceptions, and next that this case constitutes one of them.

Suppose this State Supreme Court had decided, on its first organization, that the public lands belonged to this State, and that, therefore, the patents of the General Government were void. The United States Courts, of course, hold a contrary doctrine. Suppose that this decision had been consistently

APPLY THE LAW
continued

maintained ever since the existence of the State until the present time, when the question came up for review again. Would we be bound, and would any Court be bound, its predecessors to the contrary notwithstanding, to hold to this doctrine as the permanent, unalterable law of this tribunal? If so, it must be held to be the true doctrine for all time. Then, it not being recognized by the Federal tribunals, we should have a perpetual conflict of opinions and jurisdictions, and practical revolution or civil war; or, at least, two irreconcilable systems of law and sets of rights prevailing in the State (and sometimes that does happen).

The High Court of Errors and Appeals of Mississippi overruled a former decision of the Court of that State. The decision was of long standing, being one of the earliest cases in that Court after its organization. We are fully sensible that the stability of jurisprudence requires an adherence to the decisions of our Courts. If solemn judgments once made are lightly departed from, it shakes the public confidence in the law and throws doubt and distrust on its administration. Yet even this reluctance to interfere with previous adjudications does not require us to shut our eyes upon all improvements in the science of the law, or requires us to be stationary while all around is in progression. Perhaps no general rule can be laid down on the subject. The circumstances of each particular case, the extent of influence upon contracts and interests that the decisions may have had; whether it may be only doubtful, or clearly against principle; whether sustained by some authority, or opposed to all; are all matters to be judged whenever the Court is called on to depart from a prior determination.

IMPLEMENTATION: THE COURTS

State Trial Courts

In June 1998, California voters passed Proposition 220, which allowed for the merger of **municipal** and **superior courts.** By the end of 2000, all counties in California had merged their superior and municipal courts. Before the consolidation, superior courts handled civil trials involving disputes over $25,000; probate, divorces, adoptions, and other family matters; criminal felonies; and appeals from municipal court trials. Municipal courts handled civil actions under $25,000, criminal misdemeanors, and infractions and appeals from small claims trials. California now has only two trial courts.

Superior Court

The new superior court has jurisdiction over all court matters previously handled by superior and municipal courts, and the municipal court will be abolished. However, the superior court will retain an appellate division to handle appeals from misdemeanors and infractions and from civil trials under $25,000 in damages.[1]

Civil cases are almost always commenced by filing a complaint, and California, in an attempt to streamline and make complaints easier to draft, requires the initial pages use the Judicial Council form. A sample of one such form is Figure 2.1.

Small Claims Court

The **small claims court** provides a simple, unstructured atmosphere for presentation of claims for damages not in excess of $7,500 for individuals ($5,000 for businesses). Additionally, the court is now authorized to issue equitable relief such as rescission, restitution, reformation, and specific performance. This relief may be in lieu of, or in addition to, money damages. *C.C.P. 116.220* and *116.221.*

However, there are certain waivers and special restrictions on the use of small claims courts. Although the jurisdictional limit is $7,500 for individuals ($5,000 for businesses), a person may not file more than two actions a year in excess of $2,500. Small claims courts no longer hear unlawful detainer actions. A collection agency or an assignee of any claim is denied access to small claims court. There are no rules of evidence or formal pleadings, and participants may not be represented by attorneys. Although the defendant may appeal an unfavorable decision, the plaintiff, by choosing this court, waives the right to appeal any decision of the court. Any appeal lies in the

---

1 The superior court still retains the concept of less-costly litigation procedures that existed for smaller cases under the economic litigation rules available in the old municipal courts. Cases that would have been filed in the old municipal courts are now called *limited civil cases.* To so qualify, the amount in controversy must be $25,000 or less (not including attorneys' fees, costs, and interest). Furthermore, cases must not be a type excluded by statute nor seek a type of equitable relief that the old municipal courts could not grant (such as permanent injunctions, divorces, etc.). *C.C.P. 85.* If the amount in controversy is less than $10,000, the rules are even more relaxed, and the filing fee is less as there is no court reporter's fee. *Gov.C. 72055.*

These limited civil cases are much less expensive litigation. The law severely limits the amount of discovery (such as only one deposition, and a limit of 35 interrogatory questions). At trials, live witnesses may not be needed. A party can introduce affidavits of any witness, including expert witnesses, provided the other side had 30 days of advance notice. *C.C.P. 98.* Additionally, the time to get to trial (the court docket) is generally much faster.

All cases that are not limited civil cases are called unlimited civil cases and follow the normal rules of litigation and discovery. To prevent someone from over-inflating the value of their case so as to qualify as an unlimited civil case, plaintiffs generally lose their right to court costs if at trial they do not win more than $25,000. *C.C.P. 1033.* Somewhat like in the old municipal courts, the plaintiff may not be awarded any amount in damages exceeding $25,000 (exclusive of costs, attorneys' fees, and interest). The distinctions between limited and unlimited civil cases are quite technical, and this footnote only highlights a few of the major differences.

FIGURE 2.1   Complaint.

PLD-PI-001

ATTORNEY OR PARTY WITHOUT ATTORNEY *(Name, State Bar number, and address):*	FOR COURT USE ONLY

TELEPHONE NO: FAX NO. *(Optional):*

E-MAIL ADDRESS *(Optional):*

ATTORNEY FOR *(Name):*

SUPERIOR COURT OF CALIFORNIA, COUNTY OF

STREET ADDRESS:

MAILING ADDRESS:

CITY AND ZIP CODE:

BRANCH NAME:

PLAINTIFF:

DEFENDANT:

☐ DOES 1 TO _____

COMPLAINT—Personal Injury, Property Damage, Wrongful Death

☐ **AMENDED** *(Number):*

Type *(check all that apply):*

☐ **MOTOR VEHICLE**   ☐ **OTHER** *(specify):*

☐ **Property Damage**   ☐ **Wrongful Death**

☐ **Personal Injury**   ☐ **Other Damages** *(specify):*

Jurisdiction *(check all that apply):*

☐ **ACTION IS A LIMITED CIVIL CASE**

Amount demanded ☐ **does not exceed $10,000**

☐ **exceeds $10,000, but does not exceed $25,000**

☐ **ACTION IS AN UNLIMITED CIVIL CASE (exceeds $25,000)**

☐ **ACTION IS RECLASSIFIED by this amended complaint**

☐ **from limited to unlimited**

☐ **from unlimited to limited**

CASE NUMBER:

1. **Plaintiff** *(name or names):*

   alleges causes of action against **defendant** *(name or names):*

2. This pleading, including attachments and exhibits, consists of the following number of pages:

3. Each plaintiff named above is a competent adult

   a. ☐ **except** plaintiff *(name):*

   (1) ☐ a corporation qualified to do business in California

   (2) ☐ an unincorporated entity *(describe):*

   (3) ☐ a public entity *(describe):*

   (4) ☐ a minor ☐ an adult

   (a) ☐ for whom a guardian or conservator of the estate or a guardian ad litem has been appointed

   (b) ☐ other *(specify):*

   (5) ☐ other *(specify):*

   b. ☐ **except** plaintiff *(name):*

   (1) ☐ a corporation qualified to do business in California

   (2) ☐ an unincorporated entity *(describe):*

   (3) ☐ a public entity *(describe):*

   (4) ☐ a minor ☐ an adult

   (a) ☐ for whom a guardian or conservator of the estate or a guardian ad litem has been appointed

   (b) ☐ other *(specify):*

   (5) ☐ other *(specify):*

   ☐ Information about additional plaintiffs who are not competent adults is shown in Attachment 3.

Page 1 of 3

Form Approved for Optional Use
Judicial Council of California
PLD-PI-001 [Rev. January 1, 2007]

COMPLAINT—Personal Injury, Property Damage, Wrongful Death

Code of Civil Procedure, § 425.12
www.courtinfo.ca.gov

American LegalNet, Inc.
www.FormsWorkflow.com

FIGURE 2.1 (*Continued*).

SHORT TITLE:	CASE NUMBER:

4. ☐ Plaintiff *(name):*

   is doing business under the fictitious name *(specify):*

   and has complied with the fictitious business name laws.

5. Each defendant named above is a natural person
   a. ☐ **except** defendant *(name):*
      (1) ☐ a business organization, form unknown
      (2) ☐ a corporation
      (3) ☐ an unincorporated entity *(describe):*

      (4) ☐ a public entity *(describe):*

      (5) ☐ other *(specify):*

   c. ☐ **except** defendant *(name):*
      (1) ☐ a business organization, form unknown
      (2) ☐ a corporation
      (3) ☐ an unincorporated entity *(describe):*

      (4) ☐ a public entity *(describe):*

      (5) ☐ other *(specify):*

   b. ☐ **except** defendant *(name):*
      (1) ☐ a business organization, form unknown
      (2) ☐ a corporation
      (3) ☐ an unincorporated entity *(describe):*

      (4) ☐ a public entity *(describe):*

      (5) ☐ other *(specify):*

   d. ☐ **except** defendant *(name):*
      (1) ☐ a business organization, form unknown
      (2) ☐ a corporation
      (3) ☐ an unincorporated entity *(describe):*

      (4) ☐ a public entity *(describe):*

      (5) ☐ other *(specify):*

   ☐ Information about additional defendants who are not natural persons is contained in Attachment 5.

6. The true names of defendants sued as Does are unknown to plaintiff.
   a. ☐ Doe defendants *(specify Doe numbers):* _____ were the agents or employees of other named defendants and acted within the scope of that agency or employment.
   b. ☐ Doe defendants *(specify Doe numbers):* _____ are persons whose capacities are unknown to plaintiff.

7. ☐ Defendants who are joined under Code of Civil Procedure section 382 are *(names):*

8. This court is the proper court because
   a. ☐ at least one defendant now resides in its jurisdictional area.
   b. ☐ the principal place of business of a defendant corporation or unincorporated association is in its jurisdictional area.
   c. ☐ injury to person or damage to personal property occurred in its jurisdictional area.
   d. ☐ other *(specify):*

9. ☐ Plaintiff is required to comply with a claims statute, **and**
   a. ☐ has complied with applicable claims statutes, **or**
   b. ☐ is excused from complying because *(specify):*

**COMPLAINT—Personal Injury, Property
Damage, Wrongful Death**

FIGURE 2.1 (*Continued*).

PLD-PI-001

SHORT TITLE:	CASE NUMBER:

10. The following causes of action are attached and the statements above apply to each *(each complaint must have one or more causes of action attached):*
    a. ☐ Motor Vehicle
    b. ☐ General Negligence
    c. ☐ Intentional Tort
    d. ☐ Products Liability
    e. ☐ Premises Liability
    f. ☐ Other *(specify):*

11. Plaintiff has suffered
    a. ☐ wage loss
    b. ☐ loss of use of property
    c. ☐ hospital and medical expenses
    d. ☐ general damage
    e. ☐ property damage
    f. ☐ loss of earning capacity
    g. ☐ other damage *(specify):*

12. ☐ The damages claimed for wrongful death and the relationships of plaintiff to the deceased are
    a. ☐ listed in Attachment 12.
    b. ☐ as follows:

13. The relief sought in this complaint is within the jurisdiction of this court.

14. **Plaintiff prays** for judgment for costs of suit; for such relief as is fair, just, and equitable; and for
    a. (1) ☐ compensatory damages
       (2) ☐ punitive damages
       The amount of damages is *(in cases for personal injury or wrongful death, you must check (1)):*
       (1) ☐ according to proof
       (2) ☐ in the amount of: $

15. ☐ The paragraphs of this complaint alleged on information and belief are as follows *(specify paragraph numbers):*

Date:

▶

_____   _____
(TYPE OR PRINT NAME)   (SIGNATURE OF PLAINTIFF OR ATTORNEY)

superior court, where the action shall be heard as if it were a new matter.

Small claims court can be a wonderful vehicle to resolve minor disputes, but it must be used with care. In one case, a tenant sued a former landlord for refund of her security deposit. Following a common practice, the landlord countersued the former tenant for costs of cleaning the carpet. The tenant won on her complaint, and the landlord lost on the counterclaim. The landlord appealed. There was a new trial in superior court, but only on the tenant's claim. The landlord was prevented from including his action because, as to that action, he lost in the small claims court. *Anderson v. Superior Court (1991) 226 C.A.3d 698.*

The California Judicial Council publishes a short, excellent summary of the information needed for filing, serving, trying, collecting, and obtaining additional help with small claims court cases. See Figure 2.2 for a copy of this form.

California's Appellate Courts

The state's appellate courts are the superior court, the courts of appeal, and the Supreme Court. The sole function of appellate courts is to correct a serious legal mistake made by a judge at a lower level. The appellate court accepts the trial court's finding of fact, unless that fact is totally unsupported by any reasonable evidence. Thus, if a jury or judge acting as a trier of fact erroneously believes a lying witness or draws an incorrect but possible inference from the facts, there is nothing to appeal. The only checks and balances (safeguards) built into the appeal system are for serious legal errors.

Superior Court

Besides being a trial court of general jurisdiction, the superior court is also an appellate court for decisions of the small claims courts and, to the extent that counties have not abolished their municipal courts, of municipal courts as well. As a general rule, a decision by the superior court is final and nonappealable as to small claims court cases. *C.C.P. 1180.1.*

District Court of Appeal

There are five district courts of appeal, which hear and decide cases appealed from the superior court.

California Supreme Court

Although the Supreme Court has original jurisdiction in a few specific areas, the court basically functions as the state's highest

FIGURE 2.2   Info for the small claims ct. plaintiff.

SC-150

INFORMATION FOR THE SMALL CLAIMS PLAINTIFF

This information sheet is written for the person who sues in the small claims court. It explains some of the rules of and some general information about the small claims court. It may also be helpful for the person who is sued.

WHAT IS SMALL CLAIMS COURT?

Small claims court is a special court where disputes are resolved quickly and inexpensively. The rules are simple and informal. The person who sues is the **plaintiff**. The person who is sued is the **defendant**. In small claims court, you may ask a lawyer for advice before you go to court, but you cannot have a lawyer in court. Your claim cannot be for more than $5,000 if you are a business or public entity or for more than $7,500 if you are a natural person (including a sole proprietor). (*See below for an exception.*) If you have a claim for more than this amount, you may sue in the civil division of the trial court or you may sue in the small claims court and give up your right to the amount over the limit. You cannot, however, file more than two cases in small claims court for more than $2,500 each during a calendar year.

WHO CAN FILE A CLAIM?

1. You must be at least *18 years old* to file a claim. If you are not yet 18, tell the clerk. You may ask the court to appoint a **guardian ad litem**. This is a person who will act for you in the case. The guardian ad litem is usually a parent, a relative, or an adult friend.
2. A person who sues in small claims court must first make a **demand**, if possible. This means that you have asked the defendant to pay, and the defendant has refused. If your claim is for possession of property, you must ask the defendant to give you the property.
3. Unless you fall within two technical exceptions, you must be the **original owner** of the claim. This means that if the claim is assigned, the buyer cannot sue in the small claims court.

You must also appear at the small claims hearing yourself unless you filed the claim for a corporation or other entity that is not a natural person.

4. If a corporation files a claim, an employee, an officer, or a director must act on its behalf. If the claim is filed on behalf of an association or another entity that is not a natural person, a regularly employed person of the entity must act on its behalf. A person who appears on behalf of a corporation or another entity must not be employed or associated solely for the purpose of representing the corporation or other entity in the small claims court. **You must file a declaration with the court to appear in any of these instances.** (See *Authorization to Appear on Behalf of Party*, form SC-109.)

WHERE CAN YOU FILE YOUR CLAIM?

You must sue in the right court and location. This rule is called **venue**. Check the court's local rules if there is more than one court location in the county handling small claims cases.

If you file your claim in the wrong court, the court will dismiss the claim unless all defendants personally appear at the hearing and agree that the claim may be heard.

The right location may be any of these:
1. Where the defendant lives or where the business involved is located;
2. Where the damage or accident happened;

3. Where the contract was signed or carried out;
4. If the defendant is a corporation, where the contract was broken;
5. For a retail installment account or sales contract or a motor vehicle finance sale:
   a. Where the buyer lives;
   b. Where the buyer lived when the contract was entered into;
   c. Where the buyer signed the contract; or
   d. Where the goods or vehicle are permanently kept.

SOME RULES ABOUT THE DEFENDANT (including government agencies)

1. You must sue using the defendant's *exact legal name*. If the defendant is a business or a corporation and you do not know the exact legal name, check with the state or local licensing agency, the county clerk's office, or the Office of the Secretary of State, Corporate Status Unit at *www.ss.ca.gov/business*. Ask the clerk for help if you do not know how to find this information. If you do not use the defendant's exact legal name, the court may be able to correct the name on your claim at the hearing or after the judgment.

2. If you want to sue a government agency, you must first file a claim with the agency before you can file a lawsuit in court. Strict time limits apply. If you are in a Department of Corrections or Youth Authority facility, you must prove that the agency denied your claim. Please attach a copy of the denial to your claim.

HOW DOES THE DEFENDANT FIND OUT ABOUT THE CLAIM?

You must make sure the defendant finds out about your lawsuit. This has to be done according to the rules or your case may be dismissed or delayed. The correct way of telling the defendant about the lawsuit is called **service of process**. This means giving the defendant a copy of the claim. **YOU CANNOT DO THIS YOURSELF.** Here are four ways to serve the defendant:
1. **Service by a law officer** — You may ask the marshal or sheriff to serve the defendant. A fee will be charged.
2. **Process server** — You may ask anyone who is *not a party* in your case and who is at least *18 years* to serve the defendant. The person is called a **process server** and must personally give a copy of your claim to the defendant. The person must also sign a proof of service form showing when

the defendant was served. Registered process servers will do this for you for a fee. You may also ask a friend or relative to do it.
3. **Certified mail** — You may ask the clerk of the court to serve the defendant by certified mail. The clerk will charge a fee. You should check back with the court prior to the hearing to see if the receipt for certified mail was returned to the court. **Service by certified mail must be done by the clerk's office except in motor vehicle accident cases involving out-of-state defendants.**
4. **Substituted service** — This method lets you serve another person instead of the defendant. You must follow the procedures carefully. You may also wish to use the marshal or sheriff or a registered process server.

*Except for an action against the Registrar of the Contractors State License Board, a $4,000 limit applies if a "defendant guarantor . . . is required to respond based upon the default, actions, or omissions of another" ($2,500 if the defendant guarantor does not charge a fee for the service).

Page 1 of 2

Form Adopted for Mandatory Use
Judicial Council of California
SC-150 [Rev. January 1, 2008]

INFORMATION FOR THE PLAINTIFF
(Small Claims)

Code of Civil Procedure,
§§ 116.110 et seq., 116.220(c), 116.340(g)
www.courtinfo.ca.gov

American LegalNet, Inc.
www.FormsWorkflow.com

FIGURE 2.2   (Continued).

4. **Substituted service** (continued)

A copy of your claim must be left
— at the defendant's business with the person in charge;
OR
— at the defendant's home with a competent person who is at least 18 years old. The person who receives the claim must be told about its contents. Another copy must be mailed, first class postage prepaid, to the defendant at the address where the paper was left. The service is not complete until 10 days after the copy is mailed.

No matter which method of service you choose, the defendant must be served by a certain date or the trial will be postponed. If the defendant lives in the county, service must be completed at least 15 days before the trial date. This period is at least 20 days if the defendant lives outside the county.

The person who serves the defendant must sign a court paper showing when the defendant was served. This paper is called a Proof of Service (form SC-104). It must be signed and returned to the court clerk as soon as the defendant has been served.

WHAT IF THE DEFENDANT ALSO HAS A CLAIM?

Sometimes the person who was sued (the **defendant**) will also have a claim against the person who filed the lawsuit (the **plaintiff**). This claim is called the Defendant's Claim. The defendant may file this claim in the same lawsuit. This helps to resolve all of the disagreements between the parties at the same time.

If the defendant decides to file the claim in the small claims court, the claim may not be for more than $5,000 or $7,500 if the defendant is a natural person (*see reverse). If the value of the claim is more than this amount, the defendant may either give up the amount over $5,000 or $7,500 and sue in the small claims court or file a motion to transfer the case to the appropriate court for the full value of the claim.

The defendant's claim must be served on the plaintiff at least 5 days before the trial. If the defendant received the plaintiff's claim 10 days or less before the trial, then the claim must be served at least 1 day before the trial. Both claims will be heard by the court at the same time.

WHAT HAPPENS AT THE TRIAL?

Be sure you are on time for the trial. The small claims trial is informal. You must bring with you all witnesses, books, receipts, and other papers or things to prove your case. You may ask the witnesses to come to court voluntarily. You may also ask the clerk of the court to issue a **subpoena**. A subpoena is a court order that requires the witness to go to trial. The witness has a right to charge a fee for going to the trial. If you do not have the records or papers to prove your case, you may also get a court order prior to the trial date requiring the papers to be brought to the trial. This order is called a Small Claims Subpoena and Declaration (form SC-107).

If you settle the case before the trial, you must file a **dismissal** form with the clerk.

The court's decision is usually mailed to you after the trial. It may also be hand delivered to you when the trial is over and after the judge has made a decision. The decision appears on a form called the Notice of Entry of Judgment (form SC-130).

WHAT HAPPENS AFTER JUDGMENT?

The court may have ordered one party to pay money to the other party. The party who wins the case and collects the money is called the **judgment creditor**. The party who loses the case and owes the money is called the **judgment debtor**. Enforcement of the judgment is **postponed** until the time for appeal ends or until the appeal is decided. This means that the judgment creditor cannot collect any money or take any action until this period is over. Generally both parties may be represented by lawyers after judgment. More information about your rights after judgment is available on the back of the Notice of Entry of Judgment form. The clerk may also have this information on a separate sheet.

HOW TO GET HELP WITH YOUR CASE

1. **Lawyers** — Both parties may ask a lawyer about the case, but a lawyer may not represent either party in court at the small claims trial. Generally, after judgment and on appeal, both parties may be represented by lawyers.

2. **Interpreters** — If you do not speak English well, bring an adult who is not a witness to interpret for you, or ask the court clerk for an interpreter at least five days before your court date. A court-provided interpreter may not be available or there may be a fee for using a court interpreter unless you qualify for a fee waiver. You may ask the court for a list of interpreters and also the Application for Waiver of Court Fees and Costs (form FW-001).

3. **Waiver of fees** — The court charges fees for some of its procedures. Fees are also charged for serving the defendant with the claim. The court may excuse you from paying these fees if you cannot afford them. Ask the clerk for the Information Sheet on Waiver of Court Fees and Costs (form FW-001-INFO) to find out if you meet the requirements so that you do not have to pay the fees.

4. **Night and Saturday court** — If you cannot go to court during working hours, ask the clerk if the court has trials at **night** or on **Saturdays**.

5. **Parties who are in jail** — If you are in jail, the court may excuse you from going to the trial. Instead, you may ask another person who is not an attorney to go to the trial for you. You may mail written declarations to the court to support your case.

6. **Accommodations** — If you have a disability and need assistance, immediately ask the court to help accommodate your needs. If you are hearing impaired and need assistance, notify the court immediately.

7. **Forms** — You can get small claims forms and more information at the California Courts Self-Help Center Web site (www.courtinfo.ca.gov), your county law library, or the courthouse nearest you.

8. **Small claims advisors** — The law requires each county to provide assistance in small claims cases free of charge. (Small claims advisor information):

SC- 150 [Rev. January 1, 2008]

INFORMATION FOR THE PLAINTIFF
(Small Claims)

Page 2 of 2

appeals court. The court has discretionary review. Generally, the court decides to accept a case for review (to grant **certiorari**) only if it deems the issue of significant magnitude and social importance. Thus, only a small ratio of the total cases appealed to the court is ever accepted as worthy of review by the six associate justices and the chief justice.

Federal Courts

The federal courts exist as a totally separate judicial system, hearing only cases involving violation of federal statutes and matters specifically authorized by congressional legislation. An appeal from the California Supreme Court, if a federal question was involved, would go directly to the U.S. Supreme Court, rather than beginning at the bottom at the district court level.

District Court

The **district court** is a trial court of limited jurisdiction, whose civil cases are limited almost exclusively to cases involving a federal question (such as bankruptcy or racial discrimination) or a claim of at least $75,000 between parties who are residents of different states. *28 U.S.C. 1332.*

Courts of Appeal

There are 11 courts of appeal, whose function is to hear appeals from the district courts, as well as certain orders from administrative agencies and decisions of the tax court.

U.S. Supreme Court

The Supreme Court acts as an appellate court for the federal courts of appeal and accepts cases from the state supreme courts if a federal question is involved. The Court has discretionary powers of review and accepts only those few cases that involve an issue of significant magnitude and social importance. The Court also possesses limited original jurisdiction to act as a trial court in limited circumstances.

IMPLEMENTATION: ALTERNATIVE DISPUTE RESOLUTION

Importance of Alternative Dispute Resolution

The high cost of litigation and the crowded court calendars have encouraged the use of **alternative dispute resolution (ADR)**. ADR is a method of settling disputes outside of court, most commonly through mediation or arbitration. The California Association of Realtors®' deposit receipts and listing agreements require mediation and offer a means of arbitration. These forms are commonly used in real estate (and in many other commercial settings). To help enforce mediation clauses, the courts have held that if the contract requires mediation before filing a lawsuit, then failing to enter mediation means the prevailing party in the lawsuit will not be entitled to attorneys' fees. *Leamon v. Krfajkiewcz (203) 106 C.A.4th 570.*

Mediation

Mediation is a process in which a neutral third party, called a mediator, tries to help the parties reach a compromise and resolution. The process is voluntary, and the parties can quit at any time. In many cases, the parties will meet without attorneys in an informal setting. The mediation process depends heavily on the style of the mediator and the authority given to the mediator. Most commonly, the mediator acts as a facilitator, seeking to help the clients reach an agreement without imposing his or her views into the process. The mediator has no authority to award his or her own decision. The resolution, if any, must come from mutual agreement by the parties.

Arbitration

Arbitration is the equivalent of an informal, abbreviated trial held outside the judicial system under the guidance of an arbitrator. The arbitrator seeks to hear the evidence and arrive at an appropriate award. In theory, the award should parallel what would happen at trial. The arbitrator seeks justice and is not concerned with compromise or agreement between the parties. The arbitration process can be *nonbinding*, meaning that the parties are free to litigate if they are unhappy with the results. Most real estate contracts using arbitration, including those by the California Association of REALTORS®, make the arbitration *binding*. This means that the courts will enforce the arbitrator's award and the parties (with a few minor exceptions) give up their rights to a court trial (see Table 2.1).

Arbitrators and Mediators

The parties are free to select anyone that they want to arbitrate or mediate and to use any procedure acceptable to both parties. Usually, whoever writes the contracts specifies the rules and the agency that will provide the arbitrators and mediators. Probably the two most commonly used groups in California, and the ones allowed in the standard California Association of REALTORS®' contracts, are the *American Arbitration Association* (AAA) and the *Judicial Arbitration and Mediation Services, Inc.* (JAMS). AAA is a nationwide, nonprofit organization of professional mediators, whereas JAMS is a privately held corporation using only retired judges. Both groups

TABLE 2.1 Comparison of arbitration and mediation.

	Arbitration	Mediation
Required	Mandatory if the parties elect arbitration when they fill out the contract forms. In real estate contracts, they initial the arbitration clause.	Voluntary and at the discretion of the parties. (Some real estate forms hold that the parties waive their right to attorneys' fees if they do not first go through mediation.)
Presence required	The parties are required to stay through the entire process.	At any time in the process, a party can leave and thus end the mediation process.
Role of leader	Arbitrator. Acts like a judge, hearing evidence and making a decision based on the facts. Theoretically, the results should be roughly similar to what a court might award.	Mediator. Acts as a facilitator to help the individual parties arrive at a resolution that is comfortable to them. Does not necessarily equal the result that would be rendered in court.
Attorneys' fees	Most contracts provide that the arbitrator can award attorneys' fees to the winning party.	Usually not awarded. Often, attorneys are not even involved in "basic" contract mediation cases.
Award	Most real estate contracts that use arbitration provide that the results shall be final. The courts will enforce the award.	Generally, in real estate contracts, the courts are not bound by any decision of the mediator.
Goal	One winner, one loser.	Two winners (a "win–win" situation).

have adopted standardized rules to guide and govern the mediation and arbitration process.

Comments on Alternative Dispute Resolution

The following comments reflect the personal opinions of the author, and although I think many other real estate attorneys share these views, they are still only one person's opinion.

In **deposit receipts**, the mediation clauses seem unwise because of the time, inflexibility of the parties, seriousness of the issues, and voluntary participation. Disputes often arise days before close of escrow, when loan commitments are of limited duration and other buyers may be waiting with contingent offers. In **listing agreements**, mediation may offer an expedient and inexpensive attempt at resolving seller–broker disputes. The author disfavors arbitration because of the limited rights to discovery and the fear that too often an award seems to split the difference (divide the baby in two).

Also on the negative side of arbitration is the fact that, except for very rare circumstances, an arbitrator's award is immune from court review. The California Supreme Court stated that "there is a risk that the arbitrator will make a mistake." However, the court went on to say that the parties have agreed "to bear that risk in return for a quick, inexpensive and conclusive resolution to their dispute." As the Supreme Court stated at the end of its opinion, "the existence of an error of law apparent on the face of the [arbitrator's] award that causes substantial injustice does not provide grounds for judicial review." *Moncharish v. Heily & Blasé et al. (1992) 3 C.4th 1.*

When drafting arbitration clauses, it is the author's opinion that the clause should require a lawyer with 10 years of real estate experience or a retired judge. The clause should further incorporate the provisions of *Evidence Code 1152.5*, which holds that everything discussed in mediation or arbitration is confidential and cannot be used in court. It is helpful to require the arbitrator to include the facts justifying the award so that you do not end up with a one-sentence award specifying just the amount of the decision. Finally, the clause should provide a simple, expedient method of selecting arbitrators and setting the matter for hearing.

Because this section involves only a personal opinion, the author feels compelled to inject a rather technical note. The U.S. Supreme Court holds that binding arbitration clauses are not reviewable by the courts, and the parties must accept the risk that the arbitrator might commit errors of law. *Hall Street Associates LLC v. Mattel Inc., 552 U.S. 576, 128 S.Ct. 1396 (2008).* However, California holds that if arbitrators are required to follow the law, then an arbitrator's errors of law can be reviewed by the courts if: (1) the arbitration clause specifically provides for such judicial review, (2) the contract is bound by California law, and (3) the clause is not governed by the Federal Arbitration Act. Cable *Connection v. Direct TV (2008) 44 C.4th 1334.* The author believes few, if any, standardized real estate contracts specifically provided for judicial review. Further drafting such a clause is highly technical, involves decisions if review should probably be under *C.C.P. 638*, and may be beyond what the law allows a real estate broker to do. In summary, arbitration clauses in real estate contracts are far more complex than apparent from a casual reading.

Also, the right to file a *lis pendens* applies only to court actions and not to arbitration proceedings. Thus, during arbitration a buyer loses the right to threaten the seller with filing a notice that litigation is pending thereby tying up the property. *Manhattan Loft, LLC v. Mercury Liquors, Inc. (2009) 173 C.A.4th 1040.*

LEGAL TERMS AND CONCEPTS

Jurisdiction

Jurisdiction is the power or authority of a court to hear and decide a case. For example, only superior courts are given the power to hear domestic cases (e.g., dissolution or adoption).

Venue

Venue is the proper court to hear a matter. It has no relation to jurisdiction. Jurisdiction refers to the authority of a court to hear a case, whereas venue describes which court, of those courts having jurisdiction, is the proper one to hear a case. Location determines which the proper court to hear a case is. For example, all superior courts have the jurisdiction to hear cases for foreclosure of a $25,000 mechanic's lien, but only the court in the county where the land is located has venue.

Statute of Limitations

The **statute of limitations** is actually a series of statutes providing that lawsuits must be filed within specific periods or else the rights become unenforceable. For example, personal injury action must be filed within two years of the injury; actions involving oral contracts have a two-year period; the period for suits alleging damages to real or personal property is three years; and actions involving written contracts have a four-year limitation. *C.C.P. 337, 340.*

Statute of Frauds

The **statute of frauds** is a series of laws designed to prevent fraud and perjury by requiring certain contracts to be in writing, or to have some form of written memorandum of the contractual terms signed by the party, before those contracts may be enforceable in a court of law. *C.C. 1624.* Real estate contracts that must be in writing to be enforceable include contracts for the sale of real property, leases for a term over one year, listing agreements, options, powers of attorney, and any other contract conveying an interest in land.

Thus, even if the seller orally agrees to sell a property for $100,000, and the buyer shakes hands and agrees to buy it for that price, neither party can go to court to enforce that agreement. If either the buyer or the seller refuses to perform under that agreement, the other party lacks a legal remedy. The agreement is not binding and enforceable because it is not in writing as required by the statute of frauds. Of course, the parties are free to complete the transaction voluntarily, if they so desire.

Parol Evidence Rule

The **parol evidence rule** holds that once there has been a written contract, oral (**parol**) testimony (*evidence*) may not be introduced in court to contradict the terms of the written agreement. However, oral terms may be admissible if the evidence is not inconsistent with the written terms of the contract. *C.C.P. 1856.* The parol evidence rule is one of the reasons why people drafting contracts must use extreme care and caution.

Doctrine of "Reasonableness"

The law frequently uses the concept of *reasonableness*. Courts frequently decide an issue based on what a "reasonable person" would do, or what constitutes "reasonable notice," or other such tests of reasonableness. Unfortunately, such terms lack explicit definitions, because they are factual questions to be decided by a jury. Is a person in a certain situation acting as a reasonable person would do? The jury hears the evidence and decides. Attorneys can frequently estimate how juries are most likely to act in a particular factual pattern based on their own experience and the reading of similar cases.

Dictum

Opinions or statements expressed by a judge in his opinion, even though not directly related to the precise legal point on which the case rests, are called **dicta**. Because these statements are not necessary to the decision, they are not binding as precedent, because otherwise the court would be *legislating* by deciding issues of law not before that court. However, dictum is often persuasive evidence of how a court might rule when faced with a case involving the issue discussed by the judge.

If a case involving a manslaughter conviction were before a judge, any statements by the judge about how he or she might rule on a real estate deposit receipt case would obviously be unrelated to that criminal action. Such statements would be dicta and nonbinding.

Of course, most dicta are closely related to the case and require a careful reading to determine which parts of the court decision are actually dicta and which part is the binding decision. For example, a court might say certain loans are assumable in a case involving residential property. A careful reading might then reveal that any statement by the court concerning application of loan assumability to commercial property would be dictum. The real importance to nonattorneys is to realize, when reading cases, that every pronouncement by the court is not law.

APPLY THE LAW

Ellis v. Klaff
96 C.A.2d 471 (1950)

[Defendants, the tenants, executed a written five-year lease for land that required them to construct a *building* or *buildings* as soon as possible in accordance with local building code requirements. When they failed to erect such a building, the plaintiff (landlord) sued for damages for breach of the lease. Defendants argued that the construction clause was unenforceable under the statute of frauds, since it was overly vague. Furthermore, defendants contended that parol evidence could not be introduced to supply the missing terms.]

SHINN, JUSTICE. Since the lease agreement was for a term of more than one year, its essential provisions were required by the statute of frauds to be in writing.

The evidentiary consequences of the statute of frauds are in many respects similar to those of the parol evidence rule. Both require exclusion of extrinsic evidence which would vary, contradict, or add to the terms of the written agreement under consideration. Both permit reception of such evidence to identify the subject matter of the contract from the written description; explain the meaning of ambiguous, abstruse, or technical expressions; and assist in interpreting the expressed intentions of the parties in the light of circumstances existing at the time of execution. It must be recognized, however, that there is a basic distinction between the two rules, which, in certain circumstances, becomes of controlling significance.

The parol evidence rule is a principle of law, premised upon the hypothesis that, when the parties have voluntarily expressed their agreement in written form, the writing represents a complete integration of their understanding. It is not calculated to, nor does it in practice, exert any compulsion upon the parties to put their entire understanding in writing. It does not, therefore, render inadmissible proof of contemporaneous oral agreements collateral to, and not inconsistent with, a written contract where the latter is either incomplete or silent on the subject, and the circumstances justify an inference that it was not intended to constitute a final inclusive statement of the transaction.

continued

The statute of frauds, on the other hand, is designed to prevent fraud and perjury by requiring certain contracts to be evidenced exclusively in writing. In order to effectuate that purpose, it demands that every material term of an agreement within its provisions be reduced to written form, whether the parties desire to do so or not. To be sufficient, the required writing must be one which states with reasonable certainty (a) each party to the contract, (b) the land, goods, or other subject-matter to which the contract relates, and (c) the terms and conditions of all the promises constituting the contract and by whom and to whom the promises are made: Unless the writing, considered alone, expresses the essential terms with sufficient certainty to constitute an enforceable contract, it fails to meet the demands of the statute.

Accordingly, where the statute of frauds, rather than the parol evidence rule, is invoked, it follows that recovery may not be predicated upon parol proof of material terms omitted from the written memorandum, even though the oral understanding is entirely consistent with, and in no way tends to vary or contradict, the written instrument. The whole object of the statute would be frustrated if any substantive portion of the agreement could be established by parol evidence.

The lease expressly provided that the lessee's obligation to build was one of the elements of consideration. It was clearly an essential term of the agreement and, as such, was required by the statute of frauds to be expressed in the writing with sufficient certainty to evidence an enforceable contract. The construction clause in the lease, as written, however, is too vague and uncertain to give rise to a contractual duty. Aside from the requirement that the "building or buildings" comply with the city building code, the lease is manifestly incomplete in failing to specify whether the lessee was to construct one or more buildings and is wholly silent as to the size, type, materials, location, cost, appearance, or any other details of construction.

The language of the construction clause thus shows that, at the time of the execution of the lease, the parties expected to supplement it by a future agreement with respect to the improvement of the property. Although the terms of a contract need not be stated in the minutest detail, it is requisite to enforceability that it must evidence a meeting of the minds upon the essential features of the agreement, and that the scope of the duty and limits of acceptable performance be at least sufficiently defined to provide a rational basis for the assessment of damages. Tested by these settled rules, the construction clause in the present lease upon its face is manifestly unenforceable.

Under these principles, the extrinsic evidence relied upon by plaintiffs to cure the deficiencies of the construction clause was inadmissible, since its purpose and effect were to add material terms to the lease as written, and thereby prove by parol that a contract existed which could be proven solely by a writing as required by the statute of frauds.

Plaintiffs seek to justify receipt of the parol evidence upon the ground that it was merely explanatory of an ambiguity in the writing. The provision in the lease for construction of a "building or buildings" clearly indicates that the number of structures required, whether one or more, was to be left to future arrangement. There is, of course, ambiguity and uncertainty in the writing in that respect, but it arises from the absence of any expressed agreement as to the very essence of the obligation to improve the property. The parol evidence was introduced to prove that a single building was to be erected, which was not expressed in the writing.

This was an attempt, not to resolve an ambiguity, but to supply essentials of a complete agreement which were lacking in the writing. It is clear that the receipt of parol evidence for the purpose of adding substantial terms to an otherwise unenforceable writing would be contrary to the requirements of the statute of frauds and destructive of its purpose.

[Therefore, there can be no default by the tenant, since there is no enforceable requirement to construct any buildings. The statute of frauds holds the construction to be invalid, null, and void.]

HISTORY OF CALIFORNIA LAND

Early History

When California was discovered in 1542 by the Spanish, title to all of its land was claimed by the king of Spain. Beginning in 1769, Spanish settlers began colonizing California land, ultimately establishing 21 *missions* (church settlements), four *presidios* (military forts), three *pueblos* (towns), and approximately 25 *ranches* (large private-land grants for farming and grazing). California became part of Mexico when Mexico won independence from Spain in 1821. From 1821 until 1848, when the United States annexed California, only an additional 480 ranches were granted. Thus, most of California's cities and the large private ownership of land did not develop until after annexation or statehood.

Mexican Influence Retained

The 1848 Treaty of Guadalupe Hidalgo provided that the United States would recognize the property rights of Mexican citizens in California. Thus, California adopted **community property,** a

Spanish concept, as part of its law. Finally, procedures were authorized for legitimization of Spanish and Mexican land grants by the authentication of these grants, and the issuance of U.S. *patents* (deeds) to that land.

Ownership by Californians

Private individuals acquired private-property rights in California from 1853 through the process of *preemption*, whereby persons could buy up to 160 acres of land from the federal government for $1.25 per acre. Settlers could also acquire up to 160 acres (later increased to 640 acres) almost free by cultivating the land continuously for five years (later reduced to three years). This often-used method of free acquisition existed from 1862 to 1935 under the Homestead Act. Certain other private grants were legitimized for existing mining claims, and approximately 11.5 million acres were granted to the railroads to aid in the building of the transcontinental railroad.

Government Ownership

Today, the federal government owns approximately 45 percent of the total land area of California. The state owns about 3 percent and the local governments approximately 2 percent of the total land. The balance, approximately 50 percent, is privately owned.

STUDY QUESTIONS (TRUE–FALSE)

1. English law evolved as a form of civil law whereby the courts follow case law of similar, prior decisions.

2. The rule of *stare decisis* holds that higher courts, as well as lower courts, should within reason be bound by the decision of trial courts.

3. Small claims court is an informal court where attorneys are not allowed and normal rules of evidence are not followed. If plaintiffs lose in this court, they waive their right to appeal the judge's decision.

4. In counties that still have municipal courts, such courts may hear any unlawful detainer action, provided the total amount of damages claimed is $25,000 or less.

5. Appellate courts do not correct erroneous findings of fact made by a jury.

6. Generally, there is no right to appeal to the California Supreme Court, and the court decides on its own what cases, if any, it will accept for review.

7. An appeal from the California Supreme Court goes to the federal district court.

8. Every court having proper venue has jurisdiction, although not every court that has proper jurisdiction has venue.

9. The statute of frauds applies to perjury committed during the course of a lawsuit.

10. The federal government owns only a small percentage of the total land in California.

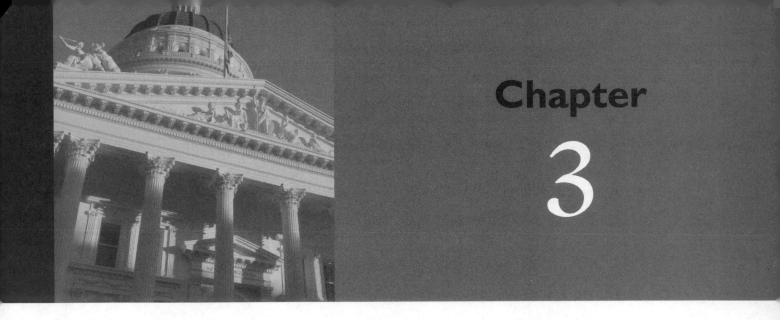

Chapter

3

COMPONENTS OF PROPERTY

Ownership

The Civil Code defines **ownership** as the right of someone to possess and use an item to the exclusion of everyone else. *C.C. 654.* Anything that may be owned is called **property**.

Types of Property

Property is divided into **real property**, which is considered immovable, and **personal property**, which is movable. No other categories of property exist. *C.C. 657.* Real property is fully defined by the Civil Code, including all its components. Personal property is defined in a negative manner, to include all property that is not real property. Real property is what most people think of as real estate. Thus, land and buildings are real property. However, the legal definition is broader and also includes fixtures attached to the real property, easements, and other appurtenances incidental to the property, as well as certain mineral rights belowground and air rights above the land.

Historical Evolution

The division between real and personal property evolved during the feudal period in England. The distinction depended largely on the authority that had the right to administer that property on the owner's death. The king's courts, preoccupied with preservation of the feudal structure and the control of wealth, dealt only with land. All other property, the personal property, was of little economic importance.

The serfs had little of value in those times, and their estates passed through church courts. With the development of capitalism and the

Elements of Property

decline of the feudal structure, personal property became as important as, if not more important than, real property. However, for historical reasons, because the two types evolved under separate legal systems, they have many different rules and legal concepts.

Importance of Distinction

The distinction between real and personal property is important because of the different laws involved.

Jurisdiction

Real estate is subject to the law of the state in which it is located. Thus, property located in California is subject to California's law regarding acquisition, transfer, and inheritance. Personal property, conversely, is normally regulated by the law of the owner's permanent residence, called **domicile**, regardless of where the property is actually located.

Assume that a California resident dies without a will (**intestate**) while visiting in New York. Further assume that this person owns land and personal property in both states. The personal property of both New York and California would pass by the laws of California, the domicile of the decedent. The California real estate would pass in accordance with California statutes, whereas the New York property would be inherited according to the laws governing New York property.

Taxes

The amount, type, and due date of taxes vary significantly between real property and personal property. In one case, the owner of the *Queen Mary* argued that the ship was personal property and therefore subject to only personal property taxes. The courts held that, although it floated on water, because the ship had been permanently attached to the land and could no longer function as a ship, it was real estate and therefore subject to the significantly higher real property taxes. *Specialty Restaurants Corp. v. Los Angeles (1977) 67 C.A.3d 924.*

Methods of Transfer

Real property can be transferred voluntarily only by an instrument in writing. Personal property passes by delivery, and written evidence of the transfer is not needed unless required by special statute. Generally, transfer of title to real property is evidenced by a deed, whereas title to personal property is certified by a bill of sale. Furthermore, most documents affecting title to real estate may be recorded, whereas, with few exceptions, instruments affecting personal property may not be recorded. See Figure 3.1 on methods of transferring real and personal property.

Acquiring a Security Interest

With real property the lender uses a deed of trust (mortgage in most other states), which is given its priority by recording in the county where the property is located. (See Figure 15.3.) Conversely, a security interest in personal property held by a California debtor is normally perfected and given priority by filing a UCC-1 statement with the California Secretary of State. (See Figure 3.2).

Enforcing a Security Interest

A deed of trust is normally foreclosed by filing a notice of default, waiting 90 days, and then publishing notice of sale once a week for three weeks (plus a few other notice requirements). After this approximately four-month period, the property is sold to the highest bidder at a sale held in the county where the property is located. *C.C. 2924.* Alternatively, the creditor could foreclose by a lawsuit filed in the county where the property lies. A security interest in personal property can be foreclosed by a lawsuit or if the collateral is represented by documents of title, seek to take possession of the documents or the goods that are covered. *U.C.C. 9601.* The time frame depends on the provisions of the security agreement, provided the method is commercially reasonable.

Judgment Liens and Involuntary Sales

Judgments are recorded in the county recorder's office and become a lien on all real estate owned by the debtor in that county for a period of 10 years from the date of the judgment. Generally, judgment liens do not attach to personal property. The one exception concerns

FIGURE 3.1   Transfer documents of personal vs. real property.

Bill of Sale
(For Personal Property)

I, Ted Gordon, of _____(Address)_____, the Seller, do hereby transfer, sell, and deliver to John Doe, _____(Address)_____, the Buyer, the following:

Used GE Model 1234 Refrigerator,
Used 8-foot red and blue used drapes, and

for the sum of five hundred dollars ($500), receipt of which is now acknowledged. I covenant and guarantee that I am the sole and lawful owner of the above items, that I have the right to sell those items, and that they are free and clear of any liens or encumbrances.

Date: _____   (Signed) *Ted Gordon*

When Recorded Mail To, And
Mail Tax Statements To:
Mr. & Mrs. John Buyer
123 Jones Street
San Rafael, CA 94903
Assessor's Parcel Number
123-44-5678

Grant Deed
(For Real Property)

Documentary Transfer Tax of $_____
    [ ] Computed on full value of property conveyed, or
    [ ] Computed on full value less value of liens remaining at time of sale
  The Above Declarations Are Made By The Undersigned Grantor(s)

For good and valuable consideration, the receipt of which is hereby acknowledged:

TED H. GORDON

Does hereby grant to:

JOHN BUYER and JOAN BUYER, Husband and Wife, as Community Property

The following described real property in the state of California, county of __*Marin*__, City Of __*San Rafael*__,

Lot #1 of Block A, as shown on that certain map entitled "Tract 12345," and filed for record on January 15, 1990, as Book 123 in Page 567, in the Official Records of the County of Marin, State of California.

Date:_____   _____ */s/ TED H. GORDON* _____

(Notary)

FIGURE 3.2   UCC-1 (financing statement).

UCC FINANCING STATEMENT
FOLLOW INSTRUCTIONS (front and back) CAREFULLY

A. NAME & PHONE OF CONTACT AT FILER {optional}

B. SEND ACKNOWLEDGEMENT TO: (Name and Address)

Mr. John Doe
12345 Able Street
San Francisco, CA 94123

THE ABOVE SPACE IS FOR FILING OFFICE USE ONLY

1. DEBTOR'S EXACT FULL LEGAL NAME – insert only <u>one</u> debtor name (1a or 1b) – do not abbreviate or combine names

1a. ORGANIZATION'S NAME			
1b. INDIVIDUAL'S LAST NAME McDebtor	FIRST NAME William	MIDDLE NAME Henry	SUFFIX Jr.

OR

1c. MAILING ADDRESS 800 Third Street	CITY Greenbrae	STATE CA	POSTAL CODE 94904	COUNTRY USA

	ADD'L INFO RE ORGANIZATION DEBTOR	1e. TYPE OF ORGANIZATION	1f. JURISDICTION OF ORGANIZATION	1g. ORGANIZATIONAL ID#, if any ☐ NONE

2. ADDITIONAL DEBTOR'S EXACT FULL LEGAL NAME – insert only <u>one</u> debtor name (2a or 2b) – do not abbreviate or combine names

2a. ORGANIZATION'S NAME			
2b. INDIVIDUAL'S LAST NAME McDebtor	FIRST NAME Mary	MIDDLE NAME Francis	SUFFIX

OR

2c. MAILING ADDRESS 800 Third Street	CITY Greenbrae	STATE CA	POSTAL CODE 94004	COUNTRY USA

	ADD'L INFO RE ORGANIZATION DEBTOR	2e. TYPE OF ORGANIZATION	2f. JURISDICTION OF ORGANIZATION	2g. ORGANIZATIONAL ID#, if any ☐ NONE

3. SECURED PARTY'S NAME (or NAME of TOTAL ASSIGNEE of ASSIGNOR S/P) – insert only <u>one</u> secured party name (3a or 3b)

3a. ORGANIZATION'S NAME			
3b. INDIVIDUAL'S LAST NAME	FIRST NAME	MIDDLE NAME	SUFFIX

OR

3c. MAILING ADDRESS	CITY	STATE	POSTAL CODE	COUNTRY

4. This FINANCING STATEMENT covers the following collateral:

Refrigerator (Sears Model 45678), living room drapes (made by XYZ Company, Fabric #4569, Red Color) and lawn chairs and table (made by ABC Company, Model 879-999).

5. ALTERNATIVE DESIGNATION (if applicable): ☐ LESSEE/LESSOR ☐ CONSIGNEE/CONSIGNOR ☐ BAILEE/BAILOR ☒ SELLER/BUYER ☐ AG.LIEN ☐ NON-UCC FILING

6. ☐ This FINANCING STATEMENT is to be filed [for record] [or recorded] in the REAL ESTATE RECORDS.   Attach Addendum   [if applicable] | 7. Check to REQUEST SEARCH REPORT(S) on Debtor(s) [ADDITIONAL FEE]   [optional]   ☐ All Debtors ☐ Debtor 1 ☐ Debtor 2

8. OPTIONAL FILER REFERENCE DATA

FILING OFFICE COPY – NATIONAL UCC FINANCING STATEMENT (FORM UCC1) – CALIFORNIA (REV. 01/01/08) business judgments, which may be filed with the California secretary of state. Once filed, these judgments become a lien on most business property owned by the debtor with the state of California for a period of five years from the date of the judgment. The procedures for pre-judgment attachments, levies, and execution sales are different for real and personal property.

Elements of Real Property

Real property is defined by the code to include three basic classes or elements.

Land

The first and most obvious element of real estate is the physical land itself. However, the code concept of land is broad, including minerals and earth underneath the land, as well as limited quantities of airspace above the land. *C.C. 659.*

Fixtures

Second, real estate consists of those items permanently attached to the land as **fixtures**. Included in the code definition of fixtures are things attached to the land by roots (such as trees, vines, or shrubs); embedded in the land (walls or fences); permanently resting on the land (buildings or swimming pools); or permanently attached to any of the preceding (the traditional concept of fixtures, like sink units and some furnishings). *C.C. 660.*

Appurtenances

Finally, real property includes those things and rights incidental or **appurtenant** to the land. Included in this category are easements, water rights, mineral rights, and other such items used with the land for its benefit. *C.C. 662.*

APPLY THE LAW

Geothermal Kinetics v. Union Oil Co. of California
75 C.A.3d 61 (1977)

[In 1951, the property called *The Geysers* in Sonoma County was divided between the surface landowner and a grant of minerals to the subsurface owners. At the time of this division, geothermal resources were relatively unknown and of no importance. In 1973, Geothermal Kinetics, the respondent, purchased rights to the subsurface minerals, spent $400,000 drilling a well, and produced a lucrative source of geothermal power. The appellants, owners of the surface land, claimed that they owned the geothermal resources.]

continued

SCOTT, JUSTICE. Appellants' primary contention is that geothermal energy is not a mineral; they argue that the resource is not steam, rocks, or the underground reservoir but the heat transported to the surface by means of steam. A mineral, appellants claim, must have physical substance and heat is merely a property of a physical substance. In support of this contention, appellants cite several definitions of "mineral" containing reference to "substance." Appellants then reason that, because they own everything in the property except for "mineral" substances, they own the geothermal resources.

Respondent contends that, since the parties did not specify particular minerals that were intended to be within the scope of the grant nor include any limitations on it, the grant conveyed the broadest possible estate. It urges that the grant is to be interpreted in favor of the grantee. Respondent urges that we not adopt a mechanistic approach based upon textbook definitions of the term "mineral"; instead we should adopt a "functional" approach which focuses upon the purposes and expectations generally attendant to mineral estates and surface estates. Since normally the owner of the mineral estate seeks to extract valuable resources from the earth, whereas the surface owner generally desires to utilize land and such resources as are necessary for his enjoyment of the land, the geothermal resources should follow the mineral estate. We agree with respondent's contention.

Geothermal energy is a naturally occurring phenomenon whose origin is the heat of the interior of the earth. The geothermal resources of *The Geysers* is apparently due to a layer of molten or semi-molten rock, called "magma," which has risen from the interior of the earth. This intrusion of hot magma expels gases and liquids which combine with ancient water trapped in the surrounding sediment to form a geothermal fluid. This fluid converts to steam which circulates in a sedimentary formation and transports minerals and heat from the magma toward the surface. At *The Geysers*, wells drilled bring geothermal steam to the surface. Respondent's well is approximately 7,200 feet deep. The extracted hot steam, which contains minerals, powers steam turbines to produce commercially valuable electric power.

In the construction of a grant or reservation of an interest in real property, a court seeks to determine the intent of the parties, giving effect to a particular intent over a general intent. In the present case, the 1951 grant of mineral rights makes no specific mention of geothermal resources; hence, the general intent of the parties must be ascertained.

Initially, we observe that as a general rule a grant or reservation of all minerals includes all minerals found on the premises whether or not known to exist. Thus, the fact that the presence of geothermal resources may not have been known to one or both parties to the 1951 conveyance is of no consequence.

APPLY THE LAW
continued

The court found that the production of energy from geothermal resources is analogous to the production of energy from such other mineral resources as coal, oil, and natural gas in that materials containing energy are extracted from the earth and transported to facilities where this energy is transformed into electrical energy. The fact that extracted coal, oil, and natural gas contain chemical energy while geothermal resources contain thermal energy is not significant; uranium ore is not denied the status of a mineral because it contains nuclear energy instead of chemical energy.

Several courts have held that the grant or reservation of a mineral estate does not include rights to surface or subsurface water. However, such cases concern water that is part of the normal groundwater system. As the trial court found, the water and steam components of geothermal resources are part of a separate water system cut off from these surface and subsurface waters by a thick mineral cap. Only insignificant amounts of groundwater enter the geothermal water system. Unlike the surface and subsurface waters, the origin of geothermal water is not rainfall, but water present at the time of the formation of the geologic structure. Because rainfall does not replenish geothermal water, it is a depletable deposit.

Judgment is affirmed [and the respondent owns all geothermal resources as part of the mineral rights].

SPECIFIC ELEMENTS OF REAL PROPERTY

Land

The physical element, the land, is obviously considered real property. This consists of whatever composition the land takes, such as soil, rock, or other substances.

Airspace

Airspace is an integral part of the realty. In modern times, the ability to sell one's airspace separate from one's surface land has given new importance to this element of real property. Condominiums include a sale of airspace. Furthermore, many buildings are constructed over land owned by another. For example in New York City the 54-story Pan American building rests above Grand Central Station.

Ownership Rights Historically Unlimited

Originally, a property owner could claim unlimited ownership in the airspace above his property. His rights were infinite, extending to the center of the heavens. However, with the advent of the airplane and modern air travel, not to mention the potential of space exploration, such ownership rights became impractical.

Current Limits on Ownership

To meet the needs of society, California now restricts an owner's rights in airspace to that which can *reasonably* and *beneficially be used*. This somewhat vague concept permits the owner to occupy the airspace on which he has built or may envision building, or which is necessary to prevent unreasonable interference with the use of the property. However, in all cases the determination of reasonableness of use is a factual question that must be decided case by case.

Rights of Aircraft

California permits aircraft to fly within the federally mandated airways. The minimum altitude is federally set at 1,000 feet over congested areas but not less than 500 feet over the nearest structure. California codes have incorporated by reference the federal standards, unless such altitudes pose a hazard to persons or property on the land. *Pub.Res.C. 21403*. However, most cases involving aircraft concern the annoyance caused by low-flying airplanes during takeoffs and landings.

Minerals

Real property also includes certain rights in minerals below the ground. Such rights are limited to minerals and excavation directly below one's land. Depending on the type of mineral, the landowner may or may not have an actual ownership interest in the mineral.

Solid Minerals

Solid minerals, such as coal, ores, and metals, are part of the land. The landowner has actual ownership over these minerals, and as part of the real estate they pass automatically with any deed, unless specifically excluded. They are called *minerals in place*. If their ownership is transferred separately from the surface land, the transfer also includes the right of surface entry to mine these minerals, unless the deed specifically excludes such entry.

Liquid Minerals

Liquid minerals include gas, oil, geothermal steam, and other transitory elements. There is no ownership interest in these minerals;

rather, the owner merely has the *right to drill* under his land. The right to drill, of course, includes the right of extraction. However, unlike solid minerals, these liquid elements lie in pools and channels under the land. On drilling, the change in pressure causes these minerals to flow toward the well. Because there is no ownership interest, the owner may extract all minerals under that land, even if this depletes pools lying under a neighbor's land.

Thus, if a pool of oil lies under an owner's land and extends under the land of hundreds of other neighbors, the owner still has the right to drill and extract all the oil, even though no neighbors would then have any oil. However, the owner has no right to drill beyond the property boundaries. Such slant drilling is illegal, and any oil obtained by drilling that extends beyond an owner's boundaries belongs to the person on whose land the drilled hole extends.

Crops and Other Vegetation

Real estate includes **fructus**, which are crops, trees, and shrubs attached to the land by roots. Trees, shrubs, vines, and grasses that grow naturally, called *fructus naturales*, pass automatically as part of the land, unless actually or constructively severed. A second category of plants includes crops that are specifically planted, cultivated, and harvested. These crops, known as *fructus industriales*, usually pass with the land. However, with agriculturally leased land, these crops remain the property of the tenant until the expiration of the lease, at which time the landlord is generally entitled to any unharvested crops. *C.C. 819.*

Severance Changes Status

Once the crops or plants are actually severed, they become personal property. They may also be constructively severed, by which the law fictionally imagines the plants as severed for legal purposes when, in fact, they are still growing and embedded in the soil. Plants sold under a contract of sale or bound by a chattel mortgage are considered constructively severed and bound by the laws of personal property. *Comm.C. 9105f, 9102.*

Water

Water law is a complex area and in depth coverage is far beyond the scope of this book. However, the water shortage in California makes water law an important topic. Water is *owned* by the State, and landowners can only acquire *rights to use* that water. California divides most water into surface water and underground water. *Surface water* is water that flows over the top of land without a fixed channel, or runs in a stream, or lies in a lake. Basically, it is all water lying on top of land that is not in a navigable river. *Underground waters* are streams and bodies of water lying under the surface of the land.

California uses two different sets of laws for surface water. It is easier to understand why the two surface systems of water law are so different by understanding where they developed. The first system is Riparian Rights, which originated at old English Common Law and in the Eastern United States, where water was plentiful. The second system is Prior Appropriation Rights, which evolved in the Western United States where water is scarce and is insufficient to meet the needs of the population.

Additionally, water can often be sold when considered in the public's best interest. *Water C. 109* and *1244.* The most famous California case involves the transfer of water from Owens Valley to Los Angles. Originally, Owners Valley was a fertile land awash with water. By 1930, Owens Valley was, by many accounts, rendered almost unfarmable because most of the water was shipped to Los Angeles through the specially constructed aqueducts.

Riparian Rights

Riparian Rights concern use of surface water adjacent to streams, ponds, or lakes. Owners of land adjacent to those surface waters have the right to use that water subject to the rights of any other owners who also abut those waters. By analogy, ownership is somewhat like tenants in common except that the landowners have a right to use the water, but no rights of ownership. One's use of the water is bound by and subject to the reasonable rights of all others having property fronting on that body of water. What is reasonable is a factual question to be decided on a case-by-case basis, although domestic needs have a higher priority than water for irrigation. *Water C. 106.*

Prior Appropriation Rights

The Prior Appropriation Rights apply to surface water not acquired under the Riparian Rights system. In other words, it applies to water used by landowners who do not front on a watercourse. Overly simplified, the concept holds that the first person to take surface water for a beneficial use has a right to continue taking the same reasonable amount of water each year as needed for his or her actual beneficial use. If other people later take that water for beneficial use, they do so in order of priority. The first person has prior right, then, to the extent water remains, it goes to the person who was second in taking that water, and so on. It is based on the concept of first in time is first in right. Currently, the only way to acquire Prior Appropriation Rights in California is through the permit process governed by the State Water Resources Control Board. *Water C. 1225* and *1250.* (See Table 3.1)

TABLE 3.1 Permit process to obtain water by appropriation.

SUMMARY OF PROCEDURE TO OBTAIN WATER PERMIT (APPROPRIATION RIGHTS)

Step	Board's Role	Applicant's Role
File An Application	The State Water Resources Control Board ("SWRCB") engineers are available to review and help prepare the application.	Prepare the application. The form is lengthy and requires supporting maps and other documents. File in the office of the SWRCB with appropriate fee.
Preliminary Acceptance	The SWRCB reviews the application to make sure it is complete and if so accepts the permit for processing. Priority arises from time of this Acceptance.	Provide any additionally requested information within 60 days or the application will be rejected.
Environmental Review	The engineers determine if an environmental impact report is required.	If the project could affect the environment you will have to pay for and submit an environmental impact report.
Public Notice	The SWRCB sends the applicant a notice of hearing on the application.	Applicant must post the notice and in some cases publish it in a local newspaper.
Protests	Anyone objecting to applicant's project can notify the SWRCB.	You must seek to resolve the protests of those who object so they will withdraw their objection.
Hearing	The SWRCB holds a public hearing on the application.	If applicant did not resolve the disputes with those who object, applicant presents all evidence for application at the hearing.
Permit Issued	If the SWRCB approves the application, it issues a permit for the water appropriation.	Applicant must pay whatever permit fees are required for the issuance of a permit.

Doctrine of Correlative Rights

Water is a precious commodity in California, and one's right to use the water is always relative to the rights of others entitled to similar use. *Wat. C. 100, 101.* When the water supply is insufficient, the doctrine of correlative rights allocates to each owner a reasonable share, according to a certain hierarchy of needs. Thus, one owner may not use water for agricultural needs until everyone's domestic needs are satisfied. *Wat. C. 106.*

Fixtures

Fixtures, also considered part of the real estate, automatically pass with a deed to the property.

FIXTURES

Definition

Fixtures are items of personal property that have become attached so permanently to the real estate as to be considered part of it. For example, bricks are items of personal property. However, when they are cemented together to form a building, their permanent attachment to the land changes their character to real property.

Tests of a Fixture

Difficulty arises when someone tries to classify a particular item as a fixture. Whether an item is a fixture depends on the particular circumstances between the parties, the nature of the item, and its relationship to the thing to which it is attached. The courts have devised five variables (tests) to analyze an item. Any potential fixture must be evaluated in light of the five tests. These criteria are best remembered by the mnemonic word *MARIA:* method of attachment, adaptability, relationship of the parties, intent, and agreement between the parties.

Intent of the Owner

The intent of the owner is the controlling and most significant of the five tests. However, the obvious difficulties, if not impossibilities, in determining the owner's true intentions have often led the courts to look to other criteria (such as method of attachment or adaptability) for circumstantial evidence and manifestations of that intent. If the courts conclude that the owner intended the item to be a fixture, then it is a part of the realty. Thus, if an owner claims to have never intended a mirror glued to the wall and secured by molly bolts to be a fixture, the court would easily conclude that at the time of attachment the owner really "intended" the item to be a fixture and part of the realty.

Method of Attachment

The method of attachment test is probably the most familiar. This objective test holds that if the item is permanently attached (as by means of cement, plaster, nails, bolts, or screws), such that removal of the item would cause damage to the premises, then the item is considered so annexed to the realty as to become a fixture. Thus, walnut paneling glued to the wall becomes part of the realty. Similarly, a bathroom mirror securely bolted into the wall is a fixture. Conversely, a mirror that is only hung on a nail like a picture frame is not considered attached to the realty.

Adaptability of the Item

The adaptability test assumes that an item custom made or specially fabricated for a particular location, and which is ordinary and essential to the use of that building, is a fixture. The court reasons that the item's essential and somewhat unique characteristic, which is not readily usable in other locations, evidences the party's intent that the item not be removed as personal property. Rather, the implication is that the party intended the item to be a permanent fixture.

A key is normally thought of as an item of personal property. However, the keys to the front door of a house are so uniquely adapted to that house as to be an integral part of the property. Therefore, the courts conclude that these keys are part of the real property and pass with the real estate.

Relationship of the Parties

The relationship of the parties usually becomes significant when all other tests are inconclusive. All other facts being equal, certain parties are favored by law, and the item's nature is resolved in that party's favor. The buyer prevails over a seller, on the assumption that the buyer should receive everything essential to the full use and enjoyment of the premises. By the same logic, the lender (beneficiary or mortgagee) is favored over the borrower. The tenants are liberally favored over the landlord on the conclusion that the tenants, recognizing that they have a limited tenancy, generally tend not to benefit the landlord with a windfall over and above rent.

Agreement between the Parties

Finally, the parties may agree between themselves that an item is and shall remain personal property; such an agreement will be binding. Thus, an agreement that buildings and other structures erected by a tenant will remain personal property will be enforced, even though they would otherwise obviously be real property. *Oroville-Wyandotte Irr. Dist. v. Ford (1941) 47 C.A.2d 531.* Generally, however, such an agreement is not binding on third parties without notice.

Priorities between Secured Parties

Just as it is possible to acquire a lien on real estate, so, too, can someone obtain a lien on personal property. In California, such liens, however created, are almost always evidenced by a document called a **financing statement**, also commonly known as a UCC-1 Statement. Typically, these liens arise when a buyer purchases an item of personal property (such as a water heater), and the vendor (seller) retains title under a conditional sales contract or claims a security interest in that item until the cost of the item is fully paid. When the item that the vendor retains a security interest in is subsequently attached to the real estate as a fixture, problems often arise. As part of the realty, conflict over ownership of the item arises between holders of deeds of trust who claim that the item is part of the realty and, therefore, security for their lien and the claim of the seller that the item is still personal property bound by lien.

As a general rule, a seller of personal property that becomes a fixture can obtain priority over any subsequently recorded interest against the real estate. To gain priority the seller must, within 20 days after the item is attached to the real estate, (1) file the financing statement with the secretary of state in Sacramento and (2) record the financing statement in the county where the real estate lies. If the fixture has priority, the seller can remove the item, repairing any damage caused by its removal. *Comm. C. 9313.*

Exceptions When Fixtures Are Removable

There are two exceptions to the general rule that fixtures are part of the real estate and hence unseverable from it.

Trade Fixtures

The first exception relates to **trade fixtures**. This doctrine only applies to landlord–tenant situations. Trade fixtures are to be removed by the tenant on termination of the lease if they were installed for *trade, manufacture, ornament,* or *domestic use,* and if their removal will not cause irreparable damage to the premises because of their integral association with the use of that property. *C.C. 1019.* Usually, the fixtures are not considered integral to the realty if the damage caused by their removal is slight or if the tenant will compensate the landlord for that damage. Thus, a tenant was allowed to remove sink bowls, dresserettes, and mirrors attached to the wall by means of lag bolts on payment of the damages caused by their removal. *Beebe v. Richards (1953) 115 C.A.2d 589.*

Good-Faith Improver

The second exception relates to an innocent trespasser who installs fixtures on another's land believing in good faith that the property was his. The *good-faith improver* may remove the fixtures only on payment of all expenses related to their removal, unless to do so would be inequitable or unjust under all the circumstances. The statutes provide relief to a *good-faith trespasser* who makes improvements, but offers no relief to a willful trespasser. *C.C. 871.1-871.7.*

APPLY THE LAW

M. P. Moller, Inc. v. Wilson
8 C.2d 31 (1936)

[Mr. Ferguson purchased a one-ton pipe organ for his home. The store owner (the plaintiff) sold the musical instrument under a conditional sales contract. Under the agreement, Ferguson took possession of the organ and installed it in his home, but the plaintiff retained title until the instrument was fully paid. Ferguson then defaulted on both the organ payments and his mortgage payments. Ferguson's home was foreclosed, and the defendant purchased the home at the foreclosure sale. The defendant, as the new owner, claimed he owned the organ, because it was a fixture and therefore part of the real estate. The plaintiff stated that the organ remained personal property and therefore, under the conditional sales contract, he retained title. The case arose before the new 1981 statutes covering such disputes.]

THE COURT. The only question, therefore, is whether the organ was real or personal property. If the former, in the absence of actual or constructive notice of the plaintiff's rights, it passed to the defendant upon the purchase of the residence. If, on the other hand, it retained its character as personal property, the owner of the realty could pass no greater title than he had and the plaintiff may successfully assert his rights in this action.

When a pipe organ has been installed in a church and an agreement executed that the seller should retain title until the full purchase price was paid, it has been held that as against a subsequent purchaser the organ became a part of the realty. The decisions in those cases rested upon the facts appearing that the structure, architectural design, and embellishments of the building comprehended the organ as an integral part thereof, as to furnish conclusive evidence of an intention that the annexation should be permanent. In cases involving a pipe organ installed in a theater as between lessor and lessee, the organ was held not to be a fixture, although in one case to remove the organ required removal and replacement of some parts of the wall.

APPLY THE LAW

continued

This divergence, however, is apparent merely and is the result of the application of what has come to be recognized as the tests of whether an article becomes a fixture when physical annexation fails as a sufficient and adequate test. This court has recognized the test of intention to make the article a permanent addition to the realty as manifested by the physical facts, and has accepted the character of the annexation and the use for which the article is designed as subsidiary elements employed for the purpose of testing the intention of permanency. Thus, whether an article is or was physically affixed to the building is one of the criteria in determining whether there was an intention to make it a permanent accession to the real property.

It must also appear from the nature of the chattel that if used for the purpose for which it was designed, it would naturally and necessarily be annexed to and become a permanent and integral part of some realty. In other words, it would become essential to the ordinary and convenient use of the property to which it was annexed. This is an obvious and necessary test derived from cases holding in some instances that articles affixed to the realty are nevertheless personalty [personal property] when they are not essential to the ordinary and convenient use of the property and can be detached therefrom without serious injury to the freehold.

Whether under the circumstances of each case the property has lost its character as personalty and has become a fixture is primarily a question of fact to be determined by the evidence. Tested by the foregoing criteria, the evidence supports the trial court's conclusion that the pipe organ as between the parties hereto retained its character as personal property. The judgment is affirmed. [The plaintiff–seller is the rightful owner.]

STUDY QUESTIONS (TRUE–FALSE)

1. The landowner owns the airspace up to a distance of one mile.

2. Although a deed does not mention minerals, all gold and silver under the land automatically pass with the deed when it is not specifically excluded.

3. Landowners *own* all the gas and oil located directly under their land.

4. Growing plants and trees embedded in the soil always remain part of the real estate.

5. The landowner has certain rights to use adjacent water, but no direct ownership rights in the water.

6. The method of attachment is the most important test for a fixture.

7. The relationship test holds that the tenant always prevails over the landlord.

8. The parties may agree between themselves that a building will be personal property and, as between them, the building will be so treated, although such an agreement is not binding on third parties.

9. A financing statement is a statement that a buyer executes to obtain a mortgage.

10. Even though an item qualifies as a fixture, it may remain personal property to a tenant who uses the item in a trade, business, or profession.

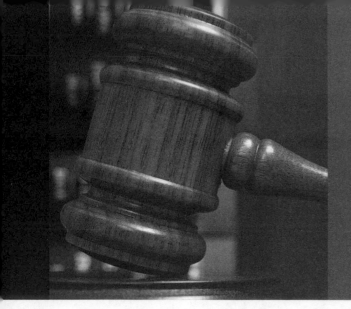

NATURE AND CLASSIFICATION OF CONTRACTS

Definition

A contract is an agreement between the parties to do or not to do something, which the law will enforce. This legally enforceable obligation and relationship arises from the consent of the parties.

Mere Agreement Insufficient

The mere exchange of promises or acts is by itself insufficient, especially when that exchange of promises or acts relates to simple social commitments. For example, even though an offer to come to dinner is accepted by the invitee, the agreement is unenforceable and not a contract. A contract requires an exchange of promises or acts, supported by consideration, and made by parties competent to contract. If one of the essential elements is missing, such as in an agreement to come to dinner where there is no consideration, then no contract is created.

Bilateral and Unilateral Contracts

Contracts can be classified as bilateral or unilateral. In a **bilateral contract**, each side exchanges a promise for the other side's promise. Most contracts, including real estate contracts, are bilateral. A deposit receipt is bilateral because the seller exchanges the promise to sell for the buyer's promise to buy, and vice versa. Once made, the contract may be enforced by either party, even though the individual obligations of the parties remain unperformed.

Contracts and Damages

In a **unilateral contract**, one side exchanges a promise for an act. A reward for finding a lost dog is an example: The dog owner promises to pay a reward for the return of the dog. Only the act (return of the dog) and not the promise (to find the dog) creates the contract. Option agreements are another type of unilateral contract.

Options

An **option** is an offer to sell property to another for a specified price and at set terms for a specific period. It is a unilateral contract, because the buyer has no obligation to complete the purchase. If the buyer elects to purchase the property, it must be within the set time and on the exact terms of the agreement. The option is supported by consideration; therefore, it cannot be revoked or withdrawn during the option period. If the option is not exercised during that period, the option expires and has no further validity.

Both parties need to ensure that the option is carefully drafted. When the option is exercised, it is transformed into a purchase and sales agreement. The agreement must contain all of the essential terms necessary for the sale. The most common problem with options arises from poorly defined terms and conditions. If certain terms are vague or left for future negotiation, the option can become unenforceable. In one case, the buyer exercised an option that held that the seller would subordinate to a deed of trust for a new construction loan. However, the terms of the construction loan were not defined, so the court held that the option was a mere agreement to agree. As such the option was unenforceable, and the property owner could sell his property to another buyer with a higher offer. *Roven v. Miller (1959) 168 C.A.2d 391.* If you are going to use an option, be sure it is tightly drawn, or the document may be unenforceable.

Express and Implied Contracts

Contracts can be either express or implied. Express contracts exist when the contract's terms are stated in words, either oral or written. Almost all real estate contracts are express, and because of the statute of frauds, most real estate agreements (except leases for periods of one year or less) must be in writing to be enforceable. Implied contracts arise solely from the acts of the parties, under the rationale that sometimes actions speak louder than words. The terms of those contracts are inferred from the parties' conduct, because no actual terms have been spoken.

Executed and Executory Contracts

Distinctions exist between executed and executory contracts. An executed contract is one that has been fully performed by both parties. Conversely, an executory contract is one in which something remains to be done; all the terms or duties have not yet been fulfilled. This distinction is often important in questions involving consideration, legality, the statute of frauds, and modification of written contracts by executed oral agreements.

Validity and Enforceability

Validity is another classification for contracts.

Valid Contract

A valid contract is a good, legally binding contract.

Void Contract

A void contract is a totally unenforceable agreement of no legal effect. It is a noncontract. For example, a contract to buy real estate that is executed by a minor is totally **void**. *C.C. 33.*

Voidable Contract

A voidable contract appears to be valid; however, it lacks one of the essential elements to become a contract. Thus, it may be avoided by one of the parties. Typical examples are contracts induced by fraud, duress, undue influence, coercion, or mistake. Generally, contracts made by minors (except those involving real estate or for necessities of life) are voidable by the minor during the minority or within a short time thereafter on return of the consideration. *C.C. 34–36.* Thus, a person forced into a contract by fraud can either withdraw from the contract, without liability, or accept the contract and enforce all its terms.

Conflicts will sometimes arise over wording in contracts giving rise to voidable contracts. Often these ambiguities are merely the result of sloppy drafting. For example, assume that a seller is going to remain on the property after close of escrow by paying rent equal to principal, interest, taxes, and insurance (PITI). In a San Jose case, a sloppy broker wrote "seller rentback equal to PITI." Was the rent equal to the seller's old PITI or the new buyer's PITI? Usually, the buyer's new loan payments and increased taxes exceed the seller's old payments. Another example might concern property containing commercial leases. Brokers tend to categorize leases as *gross leases* (where the landlord pays all the expenses and the tenant merely pays a specified rent) down to *net–net–net* (triple net) leases (where the tenant pays both rent and is responsible for maintenance, insurance, taxes, and repairs). However, terms such as *net*, *net–net*, and *net–net–net* leases are words commonly used, but not legally defined. They may have slightly, or even completely, different meaning to different people. The notation to the type of leases should be spelled out, not merely abbreviated. In short, care must be taken in drafting contracts or the contract might be voidable.

Unenforceable Contract

An **unenforceable contract** appears valid, but will not be enforced by the courts because of a legal defense available to one of the parties. Typical examples are contracts that violate the statute of frauds or the statute of limitations. Thus, if Barbara borrowed $100,000 on an unsecured promissory note and four years after the due date has not made any payments, then the lender cannot collect the loan. The four-year statute of limitations for written obligations would render this contractual obligation unenforceable.

Illusory Contracts

An **illusory contract** is an agreement that appears to be a contract but, because one party is not really bound by the agreement, fails to reach the level of a contract. It is a mere unenforceable agreement, which either party can ignore. Such agreements are often treated as contracts, either because both parties want to perform or because both parties are ignorant of their true noncontractual nature.

Illusory contracts arise when one party is given the freedom to withdraw at whim. These "contracts" are typically found in situations in which brokers and laypersons draft agreements providing for contingencies that are subject to one party's *subjective* desires. For example, an agreement was subject to a party's approval of a "satisfactory lease." The court held the contract illusory, because so many factors determine what makes a lease satisfactory, including taste, desires, and judgment, that an objective *reasonable person* standard could not be imposed. The courts interpose requirements of "good faith" and "reasonableness" on many "satisfaction" clauses, which has the effect of saving many contingency contracts. However, it is wise to avoid drafting any agreements contingent on satisfaction unless one is copying a clause from a book drafted by an attorney or taken from a form approved by the courts.

ELEMENTS OF A CONTRACT

Mutual Assent

Valid contracts require an offer and an acceptance, sometimes collectively called **mutual** assent. Furthermore, the agreement must be supported by *consideration*, involve a *legal object* or purpose, and be made by parties having the *capacity to contract*. Finally, certain contracts, such as most real estate contracts, must be in writing.

Offer

The **offer** signifies one party's present intent to be legally bound by a proposal. The offer must show a present contract intent, which is definite and certain in its terms and that is communicated to the other party. Offers that are obviously stated in anger or in jest are not intended as true offers and will not create a contract, even if accepted. Difficulty frequently arises in distinguishing preliminary negotiations from offers. Such cases are generally controlled by the objective test of whether a reasonable person would believe the proposal was an offer. Finally, if an offer is vague, uncertain, or leaves essential terms to be agreed on later, the offer cannot give rise to a contract. For example, a lease that gives the tenant the right to renew the lease "upon terms to be then agreed upon" was unenforceable. The court held that too many important terms and conditions were left to future agreement. No legal obligation was created between the parties; hence, no option agreement existed. *Ablett v. Clauson (1954) 43 C.2d 280.*

Generally Revocable

Generally, offers may be revoked at any time, even if the offer states that it is irrevocable. The typical real estate deposit form states that the offer is good for a certain period. Even so, the buyer may revoke the offer at any time before its acceptance.

Sometimes Irrevocable

If the offer is supported by consideration, then it may not be revoked. A typical example is an option wherein one party paid money or other consideration to ensure that the offer could be accepted at any time during the stated option period. Also, unilateral contracts are **irrevocable** once performance has begun, although the contract itself may be accepted only by full performance.

Termination of Offer

Offers terminate automatically upon the death or insanity of the offeror. They also terminate at the end of the period stated in the offer or, if no time limit is mentioned, on the passage of a *reasonable time*. Finally, an offer ends once it has been rejected. Thus, a seller who once rejects an offer in a deposit receipt may not later have a change of mind and accept that offer. If the seller later tries to accept the offer, after having once rejected it, the "acceptance" becomes a new offer. The buyer can accept or reject, but unless the offer is accepted, no contract is created.

Acceptance

An offer may be accepted only by an unqualified agreement to be bound by all the terms of the offer. The person accepting must know about and have the power to accept the offer and, furthermore, must normally communicate this **acceptance** to the offeror. Additionally, the offer must be accepted before it is revoked, extinguished by lapse of time, or otherwise terminated.

Thus, if a deposit receipt submitted to the seller states that the offer is open for 48 hours, the seller cannot accept on the forty-ninth hour. The offer dies by its own terms on the forty-eighth hour.

Complete Acceptance

Litigation frequently arises over acceptances that are not precise agreements to all the terms of the offer. An acceptance of less than all the terms, or an acceptance that incorporates new and additional terms, is not an acceptance. Rather, it is a rejection of the offer and a proposal for a new offer. *C.C. 1585*. Such new offers are often known as "counteroffers" and Figure 4.1 is an example of a counteroffer to purchase real estate. If that counteroffer is rejected, the counteroffer is often called a counter to the counteroffer. See Figure 4.2.

Example of Nonacceptance

An offer contained in a deposit receipt may provide for the seller to take back a purchase money deed of trust for $40,000, payable at $400 per month. If, before signing, the seller were to add the words "or more" after the amount so that it would read "payable at $400 or more per month," the contract could not then be accepted. Legally,

FIGURE 4.1   Counter Offer.

COUNTER OFFER

This counter offer (called "the Counter Offer" in this document) is made under the terms below and using the following definitions.

Definitions

A. *The Property.* The term "the Property" refers to that single-family residence at 12345 Maple Street, in San Francisco, California.

B. *Buyer.* The term "Buyer" refers to Richard and Martha Jones, husband and wife, jointly and severally, and the people who desire to purchase the Property.

C. *Seller.* The term "Seller" refers to Gary and Joyce Heffern, husband and wife, jointly and severally, and the owners of the Property.

D. *The Offer.* The term "the Offer" refers to that offer made by Buyer on May 23, 2010 to Seller to purchase the Property.

Terms of the Counter Offer

1. *The Offer Acceptable with Modifications.* The Seller is not willing to accept the Offer as submitted, but offers the following counter offer:

   A. *Price.* The purchase price shall be $780,000. The down payment shall be the same three percent, which shall be $23,400, and the 20% down payment would then be $156,000. The balance would be paid by new first loan on the terms and conditions specified in the Offer.

   B. *Refrigerator and Drapes Excluded.* The refrigerator and the custom made drapes are the personal property of the seller, which seller will take with them, and therefore will be excluded as items included in the purchase of the Property.

2. *All Other Terms the Same.* All other terms of the Offer remain the same.

3. *Seller May Accept Other Offers.* Until this Counter Offer is accepted, the Seller may continue keeping the property on the market and may accept any other offer or offers.

4. *Manner of Acceptance.* This Counter Offer shall only be accepted and become binding when signed by the Buyer and a signed copy is delivered to the Seller or to Seller's real estate broker.

5. *Expiration of Counter Offer.* This Counter Offer shall expire and be null and void unless accepted by Buyer on or before May 25, 2010 by 10:00 P.M.

Date: _____   Time: _____   Seller Gary Heffern: _____

Date: _____   Time: _____   Seller Joyce Heffern: _____

Acceptance of Counter Offer

We, the Buyer, accept the above Counter Offer, and acknowledge that we have a copy.

Date: _____   Time: _____   Buyer Richard Jones: _____

Date: _____   Time: _____   Buyer Martha Jones: _____

FIGURE 4.2   Counter-to-Counter Offer.

COUNTER TO THE COUNTER OFFER

This Counter to the Counter Offer (called "the Counter to the Counter Offer" in this document) is made under the terms below and using the following definitions.

Definitions

A. *The Property.* The term "the Property" refers to that single-family residence at 12345 Maple Street, in San Francisco, California.

B. *Buyer.* The term "Buyer" refers to Richard and Martha Jones, husband and wife, jointly and severally, and people who desire to purchase the Property.

C. *Seller.* The term "Seller" refers to Gary and Joyce Heffern, husband and wife, jointly and severally, and the owners of the Property.

D. *The Offer.* The term "the Offer" refers to that offer made by Buyer on May 23, 2010 to purchase the Property from Seller.

E. *Counter Offer.* The term "the Counter Offer" refers to that Counter Offer made by Seller dated May 25, 2010 offer to sell the Property to Buyer.

Terms of the Counter Offer

1. *The Counter Offer Acceptable with Modifications.* The Buyer is not willing to accept Seller's Counter Offer as submitted, but offers the following Counter to the Counter Offer:

   A. *Price.* The purchase price shall be $750,000. The down payment shall be the same three percent, which shall be $22,500, and the 20% down payment would then be $150,000. The balance would be paid by new first loan on the terms and conditions specified in the Offer.

2. *All Other Terms the Same.* All other terms of the Offer, except as modified by the Counter Offer, remain the same.

3. *Manner of Acceptance.* This Counter to the Counter Offer shall only be accepted and binding when signed by the Seller and a signed copy is delivered to the Seller or to Seller's real estate broker.

4. *Expiration of Counter Offer.* This Counter to the Counter Offer shall expire and be null and void unless accepted by Seller on or before May 29, 2010 by 8:00 P.M.

Date: _____   Time: _____   Buyer Richard Jones: _____

Date: _____   Time: _____   Buyer Martha Jones: _____

Acceptance of Counter to Counter Offer

We, the Seller, accept the above Counter to the Counter Offer, and acknowledge that we have a copy.

Date: _____   Time: _____   Seller Gary Heffern: _____

Date: _____   Time: _____   Seller Joyce Heffern: _____

such a change terminates the offer, leaving no contract at all. *Born v. Koop (1962) 200 C.A.2d 519.* As a practical matter, however, few parties realize the legal significance of such an act, proceeding instead as if they had a contract.

Communication of Acceptance

Once a party decides to accept an offer, this acceptance must be communicated in the appropriate manner. If the offer specifies the means of acceptance, no other method is acceptable. When the offer does not specify a particular mode of acceptance, any reasonable method qualifies. Thus, if the offer is delivered by mail, it may be accepted by mail, by telegram, or by personal delivery.

Generally, with certain exceptions, silence does not constitute acceptance. In unilateral contracts, completion of the requested act is acceptance.

When Acts Become Effective

Time elements and effectiveness of certain acts can significantly affect the formation of contracts. Certain acts become effective only when fully communicated, whereas other acts take effect on dispatch. (See Table 4.1.)

Example of Effectiveness

Acceptance and revocation of offers are effective when sent. Counteroffers and rejections of offers are effective upon receipt by the other party. Thus, for example, assume that on May 1 the seller receives an offer to buy that owner's property. Further assume that on May 2 the buyer revokes the offer; the revocation is not received by the seller until May 4. Ignorant of the revocation, on May 3 the seller accepts the buyer's offer. Under California law there is no contract, because the offer was withdrawn before it was accepted. *C.C. 1587.*

TABLE 4.1 When Acts Become Effective.

By	Act	When Effective
Offeror	Offer	Upon receipt
	Revocation	When sent
Offeree	Acceptance	When sent
	Rejection	Upon receipt
	Counteroffer	Upon receipt

Gibbs v. American Savings & Loan Assn.
217 C.A.3d 1372 (1990)

[The facts of this case are somewhat typical of the factual questions brokers sometimes face in presenting offers and counteroffers for the purchase of real estate. The issue involves when a contract is formed and how an offer may be revoked. In this case, American Savings and Loan Association (American) acquired a home through foreclosure that they then wished to sell. Mr. and Mrs. Gibbs (the Gibbses) submitted an offer that American lost and never acted on. Finally, the Gibbses resubmitted their $180,000 offer to American. At this point, the dates and time become critical.

1. On June 6, 1985, at 9:00 A.M., the Gibbses receive a counteroffer from American.
2. On June 6, 1985, at 9:39 A.M., the Gibbses sign the counteroffer accepting the new terms.
3. On June 6, 1985, at 10:00 A.M., they give the signed counteroffer to their private mail room employee for immediate mailing.
4. On June 6, 1985, at 11:00 A.M., by telephone, American notifies the Gibbses that by error the counteroffer neglected to state the purchase price should have been $189,000; therefore, the original counteroffer was revoked.
5. On June 6, 1985, in the morning, the Gibbses' clerk mails at the post office all the company mail, including the Gibbses' signed counteroffer.

The Gibbses sued American claiming that they had a signed contract for *$180,000*. American claimed there was no contract because they verbally revoked their counteroffer before the Gibbses' acceptance was valid. They claimed the acceptance had to be deposited in the U.S. mails to be valid. The trial court agreed, and the Gibbses appealed].

LUCAS, JUSTICE. Barbara Gibbs further testified that the clerk brought the mail to the Woodland Hills Post Office and returned with her receipt by 10:15 A.M. on June 6. However, the certified mail receipt was not produced at trial [meaning the court didn't believe this testimony], and the envelope in which the signed counteroffer was mailed to American Savings was postmarked June 7, not June 6. According to the Domestic Mail Manual of the United States Postal Service, the date shown in the meter postmark of any time of mail must be the actual date of deposit. The manual provides that metered mail bearing the wrong date of mailing shall be run through a canceling machine or otherwise postmarked to show the proper date. The postmarked envelope constitutes substantial evidence that the acceptance was mailed on June 7, not June 6.

continued

Civil Code section 1583 provides: "Consent is deemed to be fully communicated between the parties as soon as the party accepting a proposal has put his acceptance in the course of transmission to the proposer." This rule has long been interpreted to require that the acceptance be placed out of the control of the accepting party in order to be considered "in the course of transmission." Typically, this is found when the acceptance is delivered to the post office. California's "effective upon posting" rule holds that an acceptance of an offer is effective and deemed communicated upon its deposit in the mail.

The postmark on the counteroffer in the case before us shows such deposit occurred on June 7, not on June 6. The counteroffer was not placed in the course of transmission beyond the control of the offeree when Barbara Gibbs gave it to the mail clerk in her office with instructions to deliver it to the post office. It was placed in the course of transmission when it was deposited with the Postal Service on June 7, 1985.

It is basic contract law that an offer may be revoked any time prior to acceptance. On the morning of June 6 [American Savings telephoned Barbara Gibbs] and stated that American Savings was revoking the counteroffer. Inasmuch as the counteroffer was revoked on June 6, prior to the Gibbs' acceptance, no contract was formed.

A similar result was reached [when] the buyers delivered their signed acceptance to their attorney who was to mail to the seller. Before the attorney mailed the signed acceptance to the seller, the seller revoked the offer. The court held delivery to the buyer's attorney did not constitute posting. No contract was formed because the seller's revocation preceded the mailing of the acceptance.

We see no reason to depart from this well-reasoned law. The judgment is affirmed. [There is no contract.]

Consideration

Consideration is the essential element that makes offer and acceptance legally enforceable. Generally, every executory contract requires consideration to be valid; thus, even a witnessed gift promised in writing is unenforceable, if unexecuted, because it lacks consideration. Conversely, executed contracts are enforceable even if they lack consideration.

Nature of Consideration

Consideration requires either (1) a benefit given or agreed to be given to the promisor or someone designated or (2) a detriment suffered or agreed to be suffered by the promisee or another designated individual. The promisor must bargain for and receive something not previously legally entitled to, or the promisee does, or is obligated to do, or refrains from doing something previously legally entitled to do.

Types of Consideration

The consideration must have legal value, although it need not necessarily be economically valuable or even equivalent in value to the other party's benefit or detriment. For example, $1 could be consideration for an option to purchase a $100,000 parcel of real estate.

Illusory Contracts

In bilateral contracts, both sides must be bound by mutual promises or the contract is illusory and unenforceable. The promise can be conditional (e.g., subject to financing), provided the condition can be objectively measured or evaluated. Subjective conditions (such as "if I like it" or "as to how much I want to pay") are so nebulous as to be unmeasurable and therefore incapable of contract formation.

Legal Object

The requirement of a *legal object* means that the purpose of the contract must be lawful. An agreement to commit murder or a lease for a house of prostitution could not create a valid, enforceable contract.

Competent Parties

Finally, the parties must be legally competent to contract. Legal capacity generally means that the parties are over age 18, of sound mind, and not deprived of their civil liberties. Anyone else must contract through a duly appointed representative, such as a guardian or conservator.

Writing under the Statute of Frauds

The statute of frauds requires certain contracts, including most real estate contracts, to be in writing to be valid. The statute holds that certain contracts are unenforceable unless that contract, or some note or memorandum about that contract, is in writing and signed or executed by the party being sued. *C.C. 1624.* The purpose of this statute is to prevent fraud and perjury. The writing need not be a formal document. A summary of the terms written on several cocktail napkins and including the person's signed nickname or initials would be sufficient.

Real Estate Contracts

Real estate contracts that must be in writing include leases and other contracts that cannot be performed within one year from date of execution. Also included are contracts for the sale of real estate or of any interest in real estate. Additionally, under the *equal dignities rule*, the appointment of an agent to enter into any of the preceding contracts must be in writing. Deposit receipts, listing agreements, options, easements, and deeds of trust must all be in writing. *C.C. 1624.*

Because an agreement of sale, for example, must be in writing to be valid, then, under the equal dignities rule, so must an agreement appointing an agent to sell real estate also be in writing. Similarly, the equal dignities rule holds that any agreement modifying such a written contract must also be written.

Listing Agreements

Without a written employment or compensation agreement, the broker may not recover a commission, even if the seller intentionally misleads the broker into acting without such a written agreement. *Kroger v. Baur (1941) 46 C.A.2d 801.*

DISCHARGE AND UNENFORCEABILITY OF CONTRACTS

Modification

Frequently, the parties desire to modify or alter a contract. Written contracts can be amended only by three methods. *C.C. 1698.*

1. *Written contract.* A new written contract can modify an existing written contract. Thus, if a person has entered into a deposit receipt to purchase property and wishes to extend the escrow closing date or to modify other terms, a new contract must be executed.

2. *Executed oral agreement.* A fully executed oral agreement can modify or cancel a written contract. This rule is an exception to the equal dignities rule, which holds that contracts required to be in writing can be modified only by another written agreement. By using the term *written agreement* instead of *written contract*, that statute states that no consideration is required. Thus, in one case, a landlord rented premises to a tenant for $675 a month and later agreed orally to accept $300 a month. Several months later the landlord demanded $675 a month for all future and back months. As to the $300 rents already accepted, an executed oral agreement existed, and the landlord was barred from collecting more. However, the future rents remained at $675, because as to the future rents the agreement was not executed. *Stoltenberg v. Harveston (1934) 1 C.2d 264.*

3. *Oral contract allowed by law or contract.* If the agreement is not required by the statute of frauds or other law to be in writing,

then the written contract may be modified by an oral contract, supported by new consideration. The one exception is that if the written contract expressly prohibits modification by oral contracts, then an oral contract may not be used. However, because most real estate contracts must be written under the statute of frauds, this method is rarely used in real estate agreements.

Rescission

A **rescission** extinguishes a contract by *unmaking* it. All obligations are terminated retroactive to the time of the contract formation. Each party returns that which will restore the other person to the precontract position. Executory contracts can be mutually rescinded by a written or oral agreement. *C.C. 1689*. Thus, if a buyer and seller wish to abrogate a deposit receipt, they can rescind the agreement. The seller returns the deposit and anything else of the buyer's, and the buyer returns anything of the seller's. The net effect is as if the contract never existed. For the parties' mutual protection, there always should be a written rescission agreement. Should the seller wish to retain the deposit as damages, then cancellation is the appropriate remedy.

Additionally, one party can generally force a (unilateral) rescission on such grounds as fraud, duress, undue influence, mistake, or failure of consideration. *C.C. 1689*.

Novation

A **novation** is the acceptance of a new contract in substitution for the old agreement, with the intent that the new agreement will extinguish the original contract.

Accord and Satisfaction

An **accord and satisfaction** substitutes a new agreement for the old contract, with the provision that once the new contract is fully satisfied, the original obligation is fully extinguished. If the new contract is breached, the damaged party sues under the old contract. In a novation, however, the new contract immediately extinguishes the old agreement; hence, any suit for breach would be under the new contract.

Cancellation

Cancellation is a common method of terminating contracts, although it is frequently misunderstood. (*Termination* has subtle legal distinctions from *cancellation*, although it is used in this book in its common usage—as synonymous with cancellation.) When a contract is canceled or terminated, the parties are abolishing all unperformed (*executory*) terms of that contract. However, the parties retain any claims for breaches or performances already occurring *(executed)*. *C.C. 1699.*

Many brokers terminate a contract by having the parties execute a cancellation agreement. However, such an agreement still leaves the parties liable for any previous breaches or acts already done. Anyone canceling a contract should include within that document a release agreement covering all prior rights. *C.C. 1541.* A release is a discharge or abandonment of any legal obligation. In other words, it is a binding waiver of any claims or breaches available to a party. (See Figure 4.3 for cancellation agreement).

Statute of Frauds

As was discussed earlier in this chapter, the statute of frauds requires certain contracts to be in writing to be valid. If the statute is violated, there is a defense to the enforcement of that contract.

Statute of Limitations

Similarly, the statute of limitations provides that, unless the lawsuit is commenced within the prescribed time limit, the contract becomes unenforceable. The statute is discussed in more detail in Chapter 2.

Bankruptcy

A bankruptcy terminates contractual obligations, provided the obligation is properly scheduled in the bankruptcy petition.

REMEDIES FOR BREACH

Definition of Breach

A material breach (an unjustified failure to perform by one party) provides the injured party with the option of recovering under one or more remedies.

Damages

The injured party may sue to recover money damages to compensate for the harm reasonably and foreseeably arising from that breach. Special or unusual damages unknown or unlikely to have been known by the breaching party at the time of entering into the contract are not recoverable. *C.C. 3300.*

FIGURE 4.3 Cancellation of Contract.

CANCELLATION OF CONTRACT, RELEASE OF ALL CLAIMS, AND TERMINATION OF ESCROW

This Cancellation of Contract, Release of All Claims, and Termination of Escrow (called "the Agreement" in this document), are made under the terms below and using the following definitions.

Definitions

A. *The Property.* The term "the Property" refers to that single-family residence at 12345 Maple Street, in San Francisco, California.

B. *Buyer.* The term "Buyer" refers to Richard and Martha Jones, husband and wife, who are the people who executed the Purchase Agreement to purchase the Property.

C. *Seller.* The term "Seller" refers to Gary and Joyce Heffern, husband and wife, and who are the owners of the Property and the people who executed the Purchase Agreement to sell the Property.

D. *Purchase Agreement.* The term "Purchase Agreement" refers to that C.A.R. residential purchase agreement executed between Buyer and Seller on May 23, 2010 for the purchase of the Property.

E. *Escrow.* The term "Escrow" refers to that escrow the parties opened at XYZ title Company, whose address is 6789 Third Street, San Francisco, CA, being escrow number 1234-5.

Cancellation, Release, and Escrow

1. *Purchase Agreement Cancelled.* The Purchase Agreement is hereby cancelled and terminated, effective as of the date of this Agreement.

2. *Portion of Deposit Returned.* The purchase Agreement was accompanied by a deposit of $10,500, (the "Deposit"), which was less than 3% of the purchase prince for the Property, and the parties agree and acknowledge that Seller suffered damages only in the amount of $7,000. Seller shall retain $7,000 of the Deposit, and release and return $3,500 to Buyer, less all costs of escrow.

3. *Escrow Cancelled.* The Escrow is hereby cancelled, and XYZ title Company is now directed by both parties to: (a) terminate the Escrow, (b) release and issue a check to Seller for $7,000, (c) pay itself for all costs of Escrow incurred to date including the cancellation of Escrow, and (d) return and issue a check of any and all remaining funds in Escrow to Buyer.

4. *Release.* Each party forever remises, releases and discharges the other from any and all claims, loses and liabilities of any nature, in law or equity, known or unknown, that either party may have against the other party. Each party acknowledges that is a general release, and expressly waives Civil Code section 1542, which provides: "A general release does not extent to claims which the creditor does not know or suspect to exist in his favor at the time of executing the release, which if known by him must have materially effected his settlement with the debtor."

5. *Miscellaneous Provisions.* Time is of the essence. Each party agrees to promptly execute any and all documents necessary to carry out the terms and intent of this Agreement. Each party releases and indemnifies escrow holder from any claims arising out of that Escrow. Paragraph headings are for convenience only and not to be used in interrupting this Agreement.

Date: _____ Seller Gary Heffern: _____ Seller Joyce Heffern: _____

Date: _____ Buyer Richard Jones: _____ Buyer Martha Jones: _____

Specific Performance

Specific performance is a remedy in contract actions involving the sale of real property, the transfer of unique personal property, and other situations in which the legal remedy of damages is inadequate to compensate the injured party. *C.C. 3384–3387.* In specific performance cases, the court forces the parties to perform the contract (e.g., to transfer title on the contract for the sale of a house).

In practice, specific performance has many drawbacks. In real estate contracts, for example, the buyer requesting this remedy must be ready, willing, and able to perform (e.g., have the money) at all times, even though it might take years to get to court. The seller of real estate requesting this remedy must keep the property until trial and not sell it to others, even though the purpose of selling is to dispose of the property. Although specific performance is useful, it is not often the preferred remedy in real estate contracts.

Rescission

Rescission actions are brought by a party to annul or extinguish the contract, retroactive to its formation. (This concept was discussed more fully earlier in this chapter.)

Other Remedies

Infrequently, special circumstances may warrant an injunction to prevent one party from breaching a contract. Sometimes an action in declaratory relief is used to obtain a court determination of the rights and obligations of the parties to the contract. For example, suppose that property is bound by a condition in the deed, which restricts it to residential use. If Jim, through changed circumstances, can render the condition invalid, he can ignore it. If he is wrong, he will lose the property. Rather than risk title, Jim can ask the court to declare what rights he would have if he were to violate the condition.

Generally, a breach of contract allows only contract remedies and does not give rise to tort actions. However, in extremely rare cases, the mere breach of contract may also involve an action in tort for willful or negligent action.

LIQUIDATED DAMAGES FOR BREACH OF A REAL ESTATE CONTRACT

Liquidated Damages

Liquidated damages are an amount of money both parties agree to at the time that the contract is made that shall be paid in the event one party breaches the contract. In other words, the amount of damages is agreed on before a violation of the contract ever occurs. Generally, the parties do not have to prove the amount of actual damages suffered, because they have agreed beforehand as to the amount. In real estate contracts, the parties often agree that, in the event that the buyer breaches the contract and refuses to complete the purchase, the seller can retain the buyer's deposit as liquidated damages. The law of California has varied as to the enforceability of such provisions and the requirements needed to make valid liquidated damage provisions.

Old Law

Under the law before 1978, almost every attempt to draft a valid liquidated **damages clause** tied to the amount of the deposit for the purchase of real estate failed. *Greenbach Bros. Inc. v. Burns (1966) 245 C.A.2d 767.* Sellers were unable to prove that actual damages were impractical to calculate and that an honest, good-faith attempt had been made by the parties to estimate the anticipated damages.

Current Law

Recognizing the hardship to sellers, the legislature passed new statutes, reversing most of California's existing laws. Effective in 1978, most liquidated damages provisions are totally valid. These clauses will be fully enforced unless the party seeking to invalidate the clause can perform the difficult task of proving in court that the amount is unreasonable under the circumstances existing at the time the contract was made. *C.C. 1671b.*

Exceptions

Certain situations create special exceptions to the general validity of liquidated damages clauses.

Noncommercial Transactions

Liquidated damages provisions in contracts for the purchase or rental of personal property used for personal or household purposes and leases of dwelling units for the tenant or tenant's dependents are invalid and unenforceable unless they meet the strict requirements of the old law. Hence, these clauses are valid only if (1) the amount of damages is fixed by a reasonable attempt to estimate the actual damages and (2) the actual damages are impractical or extremely difficult to calculate. *C.C. 1671c,d.*

Real Estate

Liquidated damages provisions in contracts for the sale of real estate are valid only if certain conditions (discussed later) are met.

Sale of Residential Property

Residential property is defined as dwellings of not more than four residential units in which the buyer intends to live immediately after the sale. *C.C. 1675a.* Liquidated damages clauses in contracts for the sale of residential property are valid only if the following conditions are met.

Reasonableness

The amount actually paid (by cash or check) must be reasonable. If the amount is equal to or less than 3 percent of the purchase price, it will be presumed to be reasonable. Hence, the seller may retain the deposit as liquidated damages unless the buyer can prove in court that the amount is unreasonable. If the amount of the deposit is more than 3 percent of the purchase price, it will be presumed unreasonable unless the seller can justify the amount. However, in no event, regardless of the percentage specified, may the seller recover or retain more than actual damages. *C.C. 1675c,d.* In determining the reasonableness of liquidated damages, the court must consider circumstances existing when the contract was made, as well as, contracts or sales made within six months of the buyer's default. *C.C. 1675e.* [If the sale is for *certain* high-priced residential condominiums within a 20 or more unit building, there is a special exception beginning in 2010 that increases the liquidated damages amount from 3 percent of the contract price to 6 percent. *Civil Code 1675.*]

Deposit Actually Paid

If the deposit is all or a part of the liquidated damages, then such damages cannot exceed the amount of the deposit actually paid. The rationale is that buyers could expect to lose earnest money that they paid. Thus, if a clause calls for $10,000 liquidated damages and the buyer paid only a $5,000 deposit, damages can never be more than $5,000. (It could be less if the seller's actual damages are less.)

Typeface

The liquidated damages provision of any contract must be printed in at least 10-point boldface type or in red ink and at least 8-point type. *C.C. 1677b.* In typewritten contracts, the material is printed entirely in capital letters, which appears satisfactory.

Initialed

All liquidated damages provisions of any contract must be initialed or signed by all parties to that contract. *C.C. 1677a.* If a series of payments constitutes liquidated damages, a separate liquidated damages clause must be signed by the parties after each payment. *C.C. 1678.*

Suppose that a contract calls for an $8,000 deposit, $4,000 payable on execution of the agreement, $3,000 on satisfaction of all conditions, and the final $1,000 on close of escrow. When the $3,000 and $1,000 payments are made, the liquidated damages provision must again be reinitialed or such amounts will be excluded as liquidated damages. (See Table 4.2.)

TABLE 4.2 Liquidated Damages Provisions.

I. GENERAL APPLICATION

Limitations Liquidated damages provisions are favored and encouraged, except in (1) the sale or lease of personal property or services to consumer, and (2) the sale or lease of residential housing. In these two areas, sellers and landlords traditionally have substantially unequal bargaining power, so liquidated damages are disfavored.

Favored In all other contracts, liquidated damages clauses are enforceable unless the other party proves that the clause was unreasonable under the circumstances at the time the contract was made—a very difficult burden. *C.C.1671.*

II. REAL ESTATE APPLICATION

General rule All liquidated damages clauses are valid and enforceable if reasonable at the time that they were made. *C.C.1671.* The exceptions are set out in this table.

Residential purchase Liquidated damages provisions covering the buyer's default of a contract to purchase a one-to four-family dwelling where the buyer intends to reside are valid only if four conditions are met.

1. The provision was reasonable at the time the purchase contract was made.
2. The provision is in 10-point or other statutory-size type and initialed by each party to the contract.
3. If the down payment is all or part of the liquidated damages, the damages may not exceed the amount of the down payment actually paid. If the down payment is later increased (for example from $5,000 to $10,000 on release of all contingencies), the clause must be reinitialed at the time of the increase, or the increase is not included in these damages.
4. If the liquidated damages amount to over 3% of the purchase price, the party proves it was reasonable in amount. (If 3% or under, the amount is presumed reasonable, unless the buyer proves otherwise.)

Other purchases Liquidated damages provisions in all nonresidential purchase contracts are valid if (1) the approved clause is in 10-point type, (2) it is initialed by all the parties and (3) the provision was reasonable at the time it was made. *C.C.1671, 1677.*

Residential leases Liquidated damages provisions are only valid if it is extremely difficult or impractical to fix actual damages (the pre-1978 rule). *C.C. 1671(d).*

Sales of Nonresidential Property

Liquidated damages provisions in other real estate sales contracts are valid and enforceable if reasonable in amount, and if the liquidated damages clause is printed in at least 10-point type and initialed or signed by each party to the contract. *C.C. 1676, 1677.* The clause can only be invalidated if the other party can show that the liquidated damages provision was unreasonable at the time that the contract was made—a difficult task. *C.C. 1671.*

Installment Sales Contracts

Liquidated damages provisions are still invalid and unenforceable in installment sales contracts for real estate. *C.C. 1681.*

GENERAL DAMAGES FOR BREACH OF A REAL ESTATE CONTRACT

Minimal Damages

If the buyer defaults on a contract to purchase real property (deposit receipt) and the seller elects damages as a remedy (as opposed to specific performance or rescission), the amount of damages recoverable is usually small. Punitive damages are not available in a breach of contract action, *C.C. 3294,* and tort damages based on emotional distress are normally inapplicable. General damages are recoverable, but usually minimal or nonexistent, and special damages merely reimburse the seller for expenses actually incurred.

General Damages

The amount of general damages is the difference, if any, between the contract price and the market price at the time of the breach. *C.C. 3307.* Only if the market declines during this period—a rare occurrence in California over so short a time span—does the seller realize any general damages.

Increase in Value

If the market value increases, so that at the time of the breach the market price is greater than the contract price, the seller has actually profited from the breach. The property can now be sold to someone else at a higher price. Therefore, the seller is not injured by the breach and can recover no general damages. *Freedman v. Rector (1951) 37 C.2d 16.*

No Change in Value

Similarly, if there is no change in the market price, there will be no difference between market price and contract price, and, hence, no damages. *Fleischer v. Cosgrove (1956) 145 C.A.2d 14.*

Decrease in Value

If the market declines during this time, which is infrequent under present conditions, then damages will be recoverable. However, once the breach occurs, damages are fixed, and further decline in the market value will not affect the amount of damages. *Bouchard v. Orange (1953) 117 C.A.2d 521.*

Special Damages

Even though the seller may receive no general damages, compensation is made for actual expenses incurred because of the breach. Expenses of the first sale are generally disallowed on the theory that they would have been incurred had the contract been performed and, therefore, to permit them would place the seller in a better position than had there been no breach. The expenses of the second sale, the resale, are normally recoverable. Additionally, the courts have allowed recovery of the amount of mortgage interest, fire insurance, and taxes accruing during the period between the resale and the original breach. *Allen v. Enomoto (1964) 228 C.A.2d 805.*

APPLY THE LAW

Royer v. Carter
37 C.2d 544 (1951)

TRAYNOR, JUSTICE. Defendant has appealed from a judgment for damages for breach of a contract to purchase real property. On August 23, 1948, defendant agreed to buy plaintiff's house and lot for $24,000 and paid $1,000 down. Because she was unable to secure the additional funds necessary to complete the purchase, defendant defaulted on the contract, and the plaintiff put the property back on the market late in September. The following December plaintiff was able to resell the property for $18,500. The trial court awarded damages equal to the difference between the contract price and the price at which the property was resold [$5,500] plus the expenses incurred in connection with the first sale, but less the amount of the down payment.

The trial court awarded damages based on a finding that the value of the property to plaintiff under Civil Code Section 3307 was equal to the resale price of $18,500. The resale took place approximately three months after the date of defendant's breach, and it is undisputed that the value of the property was declining during that period. Various witnesses gave their opinions as to the value of the property at the time of the breach, the lowest estimate being $22,500. Although the resale price was evidence of the value of the property to plaintiff at the time of the resale, the trial court's failure to make an adjustment for the admitted decline in the market was erroneous, unless the damages are to be computed as of the date of the breach.

In cases involving sales of real property, however, it has generally been held that the value of the property to the seller is to be determined as of the date of the breach [$24,000 − $22,500 = $1,500 in damages].

APPLY THE LAW

continued

The defendant contends that the trial court also erred in allowing as additional damages $45 in escrow charges, $40 in title charges, and $420 in broker's fees paid in connection with the first sale. When, as under Section 3307, the measure of damages is designed to assure to the vendor the benefit of his bargain [his profit], additional damages should not be allowed for expenses that would have been incurred had the contract been performed. To do so would place the vendor in a better position than he would have been in had there been no breach.

In many cases, however, the vendee's breach may make it necessary for the vendor to incur additional expenses to realize the benefit of his bargain. Injustice could result if the vendor were not allowed to recover damages for additional expenses caused him by the vendee's breach. Thus, in a case where the property is sold at the market value and that value remains constant until after the breach, and the property is then resold at the same price, the vendor could recover no damages under Section 3307. He would be forced to pay, however, in addition to the expenses of the first sale, the expenses of the resale. When such additional expenses are the natural consequence of the breach, they may be recovered in addition to those provided for in Section 3307.

It does not follow that the actual expenses of the first sale will necessarily be equal to the additional expenses caused by the vendee's breach. If all of the contemplated expenses of the first sale are actually paid and the property does not change in value, ordinarily the additional expense of reselling made necessary by the breach will be equal to those incurred in the first sale.

In the present case, however, it appears that all the contemplated expenses of the first sale were not paid and that the cost of reselling at the market value at the time of the breach would have been less than the cost of selling at the contract price. Under the terms of her agreement with the broker, plaintiff was not obligated to pay the full commission on the first sale in case of defendant's default. She paid only $420, thus saving $780 of the anticipated expense of the first sale.

Because the cost of a sale under the usual brokerage contract [in 1942] is 5 percent of the purchase price, what the cost would have been at the time of the defendant's breach cannot be determined in the absence of a finding of the market value of the property at that time. On retrial, the trial court, in computing the additional damages caused by defendant's breach, should allow an amount equal to the difference between the cost of selling the property at its value at the time of the breach and $780, the amount the anticipated expenses of the first sale were reduced by defendant's default. The judgment is reversed. [Damages are to be determined at date of breach; they would be $1,500 plus certain limited damages of resale.]

STUDY QUESTIONS (TRUE–FALSE)

1. An unenforceable contract is an example of an executory contract.

2. A deposit receipt is an example of a unilateral contract.

3. A contract to buy real estate, executed by a minor, is void and of no force or effect.

4. If an offer states that it is irrevocable, then that offer cannot be revoked by the offeror.

5. If a buyer offers to purchase a seller's house for $300,000, and the seller rejects the offer, the offer may not be accepted later.

6. If the buyer offers to buy the seller's property for $300,000, and the seller accepts on the condition that the buyer pay all closing costs, there is no contract.

7. If an agreement lacks consideration, it is not an enforceable agreement.

8. If someone can absolutely and positively prove the existence of an oral contract to buy real estate, it will be enforced by the courts.

9. Under the law since 1978, liquidated damages clauses are not only enforceable, but also presumed to be the amount of the seller's damages if the amount is under 3 percent of the selling price.

10. Usually, the seller is unable to prove and recover any significant general damages on breach of a contract to buy real estate.

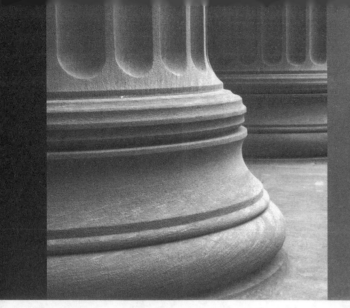

NATURE OF DEPOSIT RECEIPTS

Multipurpose Document

The deposit receipt is usually the first document executed in the process of purchasing property. It typically accomplishes four separate, independent functions.

Offer

The deposit receipt is an offer by the buyer to purchase the seller's property. As an offer, the document is governed by all the rules of offers in general. Thus, even though a period for acceptance is normally stated in the document, the offer may nevertheless be revoked at any time prior to its actual acceptance.

Contract

The deposit receipt becomes a binding bilateral contract if the seller accepts the offer without alteration or modification. However, as is common, if the seller adds new terms and then signs the document, the seller has rejected and extinguished the buyer's offer. The seller has created a counteroffer, which becomes a contract only if accepted without modification by the buyer. At some point in the process, a proper acceptance usually occurs, creating a binding contract.

Receipt for Deposit

The deposit receipt functions as a receipt for the buyer, acknowledging payment of the deposit toward the purchase of the property.

Commission Agreement

Most deposit receipts contain a separate contract between the seller and broker, covering the broker's right to a sales commission. The

Deposit Receipts

broker operating without a listing agreement must look exclusively to the deposit receipt clause for the commission. If the broker has a listing agreement, then the deposit receipt becomes a second contract covering the commission. If there are two contracts and the terms conflict, the later executed document (the deposit receipt) controls.

Under most listing agreements, if a buyer agrees to unconditionally purchase property under the exact terms of the listing, the broker then earns a commission. A later rescission or breach will not deprive the broker of fees. *Debble v. Stearns (1947) 82 C.A.2d 296.* The unfairness of this situation led the California Association of REALTORS® (CAR) to include a commission agreement that reduced the brokers' rights to fees. Commission is earned when the sale is consummated or prevented by the acts of the seller. Brokers also wanted a new commission form, because they rarely found buyers purchasing on the exact terms of the listing. Technically, then, brokers earned no commission (although once sellers accepted the new offer and sold the property, they would have agreed to the new terms). *Lathrop v. Gauger (1954) 127 C.A.2d 754.* However, to avoid any potential for dispute, sound practice requires a new commission agreement for offers different from the old listing. Thus, both sellers and brokers benefit from having a new commission agreement in the deposit receipt.

No Standard Form

Surprisingly, many brokers believe that deposit receipts follow a standard form. However, each real estate board may have its own form, which varies in certain key provisions from the forms used by other real estate boards. For example, the San Jose real estate board form had a printed provision that the seller would automatically pay for the title report. In small print on the back of the Marin County board form was the provision that once the termite report was available the seller and the buyer could negotiate whether the work was to be done and which party would pay for it, or the contract could be terminated.

Read Carefully

Many brokers have been involved in painful, embarrassing litigation because they assumed that the paragraphs of small print were all standard. A prudent broker carefully reads all the fine print of any form, because he or she is often charged with knowledge of the form's contents.

Caution in Drafting

In drafting a deposit receipt, the broker or other drafting party must exercise considerable caution. First, any ambiguities in the contract are interpreted against the drafting party. *Nakatsukasa v. Wade (1954) 128 C.A.2d 86.* Second, if the original contract requires considerable drafting or complex wording, the broker–drafter may be guilty of practicing law without a license. Finally, certain "boilerplate" clauses may be broader than intended or even inapplicable to the situation at hand.

Commissioner's Requirements

The California real estate commissioner has set numerous requirements affecting brokers. The two most important requirements, that are sometimes overlooked on deposit receipts, concern changes and blank spaces. All blank spaces in the deposit receipt must be filled in. *Comm. Regs. 2900.* Furthermore, any additions, deletions, or alterations on the form must be initialed and dated by all parties who have signed the contract. *Comm. Regs. 2901.*

APPLY THE LAW

Meyer v. Benko
55 C.A.3d 937 (1976)

[Plaintiffs, the buyers, executed a deposit receipt for the purchase of defendant's property. The deposit receipt provided for the buyers to obtain a new Federal Housing Administration (FHA) loan and for the seller to pay for any work required by the FHA. Defendant, the seller, signed the agreement. Buyers then obtained a loan commitment conditioned on a new roof being installed on the home in accordance with FHA standards. Seller refused to pay for the roof; hence, buyers were unable to obtain their loan and consummate the sale. Plaintiffs then sued for damages and specific performance. One of the principal issues at trial centered on whether the deposit receipt constituted a contract. The trial court ruled that it was not a contract, and plaintiffs appealed.]

APPLY THE LAW

continued

STEPHENS, JUSTICE. Every contract requires the mutual assent or consent of the parties. The existence of mutual consent is determined by objective rather than subjective criteria, the test being what the outward manifestations of consent would lead a reasonable person to believe.

Accordingly, the primary focus in determining the existence of mutual consent is upon the acts of the parties involved. In the case at bar, this focus is directed toward the Deposit Receipt and related documents, and the actions of the parties during the period of time encompassing the execution of these documents.

The utilization of the objective test of mutual consent demonstrates that the Deposit Receipt is in fact a contract. The fact that this document was signed by both parties indicates that the parties entered into an enforceable agreement. Ordinarily, one who accepts or signs an instrument, which on its face is a contract, is deemed to assent to all of its terms.

Although the parties introduced conflicting testimony as to whether or not the terms of the Deposit Receipt were explained to the defendants before they signed that document, this evidence was not sufficient to establish a lack of mutual consent. The general rule is that when a person with the capacity of reading and understanding an instrument signs it, he is, in the absence of fraud and imposition, bound by its contents, and he is estopped from saying that its explicit provisions are contrary to his intentions or understanding.

In addition, the material factors common to a contract for the sale of real property are contained within the terms of the Deposit Receipt. The Deposit Receipt named the sellers, named the buyers, identified the property being sold, and specified the price for which that property was being sold. Further, it detailed the method of financing the transaction, as well as providing an allocation of various incidental costs and duties. The presence of these material factors upon the face of the document raises two inferences, both of which indicate the existence of mutual consent. First, these factors indicate that the parties had proceeded beyond the stage of mere preliminary negotiations and into the stage of actual contract formation. Moreover, the presence of this material in the document gave notice to the subscribing parties, notably the defendants, that they were entering into a binding contract by subscribing their signatures upon that document. The evidence introduced by the defendants relating to their lack of knowledge about the implications of the terms contained in the Deposit Receipt fails to rebut these inferences.

In toto, the various facts discussed above lead to the inescapable conclusion that, based upon an objective test of contract formation, the parties mutually assented to the formation of a contract on the terms and conditions set forth in the Deposit Receipt. Accordingly, pursuant to the

continued

term obligating the seller to pay for FHA appraisal and to do any necessary work at his expense, the defendants were bound to pay for the new roof.

Defendants contend that a material mistake of fact—namely, the defendants' belief that they would not be obligated to install a new roof upon the residence—prevented contract formation. A unilateral mistake of fact may be the basis of relief. However, such a unilateral mistake may not invalidate a contract without a showing that the other party to the contract was aware of the mistaken belief and unfairly utilized that mistaken belief in a manner enabling him or her to take advantage of the other party. Defendants have failed to present any evidence in support of either requirement.

The judgment is reversed [and the deposit receipt is a valid, enforceable contract].

ANALYSIS OF CALIFORNIA ASSOCIATION OF REALTORS®, DEPOSIT RECEIPT

The numbers preceding the headings in this section correspond to the circled boldface numbers on the real estate purchase contract and receipt for deposit from the CAR (Figure 5.1).

New CAR Form

In 2000, CAR released two new, separate CAR deposit receipt forms. Buyers, sellers, and brokers must note which CAR form is being used and decide if its provisions are applicable to their situation. This supplement will just highlight one of the changes on the CAR form. As always, revised forms bring new wording and challenges, and each form should be thoroughly studied before use.

The New CAR Form Is "As Is"

In the year 2000, CAR revised its residential purchase agreement, Form RPA-11. Considerable changes were made to the form, probably none as significant as paragraph 7. This paragraph stated that the property "is sold in its present condition on the date of acceptance." As worded, the property is being sold "as is," although nowhere in the form does it actually use the words *as is*. In 2010 CAR revised its form, making many changes, including using the terminology "as is" in paragraph 9 to describe the condition of the property.

Other CAR Forms Available

CAR provides a number of forms for use in real estate transactions, and these are currently sold to both individuals and CAR members.

FIGURE 5.1   CAR deposit receipt.

CALIFORNIA ASSOCIATION OF REALTORS ®

CALIFORNIA
RESIDENTIAL PURCHASE AGREEMENT
AND JOINT ESCROW INSTRUCTIONS
For Use With Single Family Residential Property — Attached or Detached
(C.A.R. Form RPA-CA, Revised 4/10)

Date _____

1. **OFFER:**
   A. **THIS IS AN OFFER FROM** _____ ("Buyer").   ①
   B. **THE REAL PROPERTY TO BE ACQUIRED** is described as _____   ②
   _____, Assessor's Parcel No. _____, situated in
   _____, County of _____, California ("Property").
   C. **THE PURCHASE PRICE** offered is _____
   _____ (Dollars $ _____).
   D. **CLOSE OF ESCROW** shall occur on _____ (date) (or ☐ _____ **Days** After Acceptance).
2. **AGENCY:**
   A. **DISCLOSURE:** Buyer and Seller each acknowledge prior receipt of a "Disclosure Regarding Real Estate Agency Relationships" (C.A.R. Form AD).
   B. **POTENTIALLY COMPETING BUYERS AND SELLERS:** Buyer and Seller each acknowledge receipt of a disclosure of the possibility of multiple representation by the Broker representing that principal. This disclosure may be part of a listing agreement, buyer representation agreement or separate document (C.A.R. Form DA). Buyer understands that Broker representing Buyer may also represent other potential buyers, who may consider, make offers on or ultimately acquire the Property. Seller understands that Broker representing Seller may also represent other sellers with competing properties of interest to this Buyer.   ③
   C. **CONFIRMATION:** The following agency relationships are hereby confirmed for this transaction:
   Listing Agent _____ (Print Firm Name) is the agent of (check one):
   ☐ the Seller exclusively; or ☐ both the Buyer and Seller.
   Selling Agent _____ (Print Firm Name) (if not the same as the Listing
   Agent) is the agent of (check one): ☐ the Buyer exclusively; or ☐ the Seller exclusively; or ☐ both the Buyer and Seller. Real Estate Brokers are not parties to the Agreement between Buyer and Seller.
3. **FINANCE TERMS:** Buyer represents that funds will be good when deposited with Escrow Holder.
   A. **INITIAL DEPOSIT:** Deposit shall be in the amount of . . . .$ _____
   (1) Buyer shall deliver deposit directly to Escrow Holder by personal check, ☐ electronic funds transfer,
   ☐ Other _____ within 3 business days after acceptance   ④
   (or ☐ Other_____);
   OR (2) (If checked) ☐ Buyer has given the deposit by personal check (or ☐ _____)
   to the agent submitting the offer (or to ☐ _____), made payable to
   _____. The deposit shall be held uncashed until Acceptance and
   then deposited with Escrow Holder (or ☐ into Broker's trust account) within **3** business days after
   Acceptance (or ☐ Other_____).
   B. **INCREASED DEPOSIT:** Buyer shall deposit with Escrow Holder an increased deposit in the amount of . . . .$ _____
   within _____ **Days** After Acceptance, or ☐ _____.
   If a liquidated damages clause is incorporated into this Agreement, Buyer and Seller shall sign a   ⑤
   separate liquidated damages clause (C.A.R. Form RID) for any increased deposit at the time it is
   deposited.
   C. **LOAN(S):**
   (1) FIRST LOAN: in the amount of . . . .$ _____
   This loan will be conventional financing or, if checked, ☐ FHA, ☐ VA, ☐ Seller (C.A.R. Form SFA),
   ☐ assumed financing (C.A.R. Form PAA), ☐ Other _____. This loan shall be at a fixed   ⑥
   rate not to exceed _____% or, ☐ an adjustable rate loan with initial rate not to exceed _____%.
   Regardless of the type of loan, Buyer shall pay points not to exceed _____% of the loan amount.
   (2) ☐ **SECOND LOAN** in the amount of . . . .$ _____
   This loan will be conventional financing or, if checked, ☐ Seller (C.A.R. Form SFA), ☐ assumed
   financing (C.A.R. Form PAA), ☐ Other _____. This loan shall be at a fixed rate not to
   exceed _____% or, ☐ an adjustable rate loan with initial rate not to exceed _____%. Regardless
   of the type of loan, Buyer shall pay points not to exceed _____% of the loan amount.
   (3) FHA/VA: For any FHA or VA loan specified above, Buyer has **17 (or ☐ _____) Days** After
   Acceptance to Deliver to Seller written notice (C.A.R. Form FVA) of any lender-required repairs or
   costs that Buyer requests Seller to pay for or repair. Seller has no obligation to pay for repairs or
   satisfy lender requirements unless otherwise agreed in writing.
   ⑦ D. **ADDITIONAL FINANCING TERMS:** _____
   _____
   E. **BALANCE OF PURCHASE PRICE OR DOWN PAYMENT** in the amount of . . . .$ _____
   to be deposited with Escrow Holder within sufficient time to close escrow.
   ⑧ F. **PURCHASE PRICE (TOTAL):** . . . .$ _____

Buyer's Initials (_____)(_____)   Seller's Initials (_____)(_____)

RPA-CA REVISED 4/10 (PAGE 1 OF 8) Print Date BD Apr 10

Reviewed by _____ Date _____

CALIFORNIA RESIDENTIAL PURCHASE AGREEMENT (RPA-CA PAGE 1 OF 8)

Source: Reprinted with permission, *California Association of REALTORS®.* Endorsement not implied.

FIGURE 5.1 (Continued).

Property Address: _____   Date: _____

(9) **G. VERIFICATION OF DOWN PAYMENT AND CLOSING COSTS:** Buyer (or Buyer's lender or loan broker pursuant to 3H(1)) shall, within **7 (or _____) Days** After Acceptance, Deliver to Seller written verification of Buyer's down payment and closing costs. (If checked, ☐ verification attached.)

H. LOAN TERMS:

(10) **(1) LOAN APPLICATIONS:** Within **7 (or ☐ _____) Days** After Acceptance, Buyer shall Deliver to Seller a letter from lender or loan broker stating that, based on a review of Buyer's written application and credit report, Buyer is prequalified or preapproved for any NEW loan specified in 3C above. (If checked, ☐ letter attached.)

(11) **(2) LOAN CONTINGENCY:** Buyer shall act diligently and in good faith to obtain the designated loan(s). Obtaining the loan(s) specified above **is a contingency** of this Agreement unless otherwise agreed in writing. Buyer's contractual obligations to obtain and provide deposit, balance of down payment and closing costs **are not contingencies** of this Agreement.

(12) **(3) LOAN CONTINGENCY REMOVAL:**
(i) Within **17 (or ☐ _____) Days** After Acceptance, Buyer shall, as specified in paragraph 14, in writing remove the loan contingency or cancel this Agreement;
OR (ii) (If checked) ☐ the loan contingency shall remain in effect until the designated loans are funded.

(13) **(4) ☐ NO LOAN CONTINGENCY** (If checked): Obtaining any loan specified above is NOT a contingency of this Agreement. If Buyer does not obtain the loan and as a result Buyer does not purchase the Property, Seller may be entitled to Buyer's deposit or other legal remedies.

(14) **I. APPRAISAL CONTINGENCY AND REMOVAL:** This Agreement is (**or**, if checked, ☐ is NOT) contingent upon a written appraisal of the Property by a licensed or certified appraiser at no less than the specified purchase price. If there is a loan contingency, Buyer's removal of the loan contingency shall be deemed removal of this appraisal contingency (**or**, ☐ if checked, Buyer shall, as specified in paragraph 14B(3), in writing remove the appraisal contingency or cancel this Agreement within **17 (or ____) Days** After Acceptance). If there is no loan contingency, Buyer shall, as specified in paragraph 14B(3), in writing remove the appraisal contingency or cancel this Agreement within **17 (or ☐ ____) Days** After Acceptance.

(15) **J. ☐ ALL CASH OFFER** (If checked): Buyer shall, within **7 (or ☐ _____) Days** After Acceptance, Deliver to Seller written verification of sufficient funds to close this transaction. (If checked, ☐ verification attached.)

(16) **K. BUYER STATED FINANCING:** Seller has relied on Buyer's representation of the type of financing specified (including but not limited to, as applicable, amount of down payment, contingent or non contingent loan, or all cash). If Buyer seeks alternate financing, (i) Seller has no obligation to cooperate with Buyer's efforts to obtain such financing, and (ii) Buyer shall also pursue the financing method specified in this Agreement. Buyer's failure to secure alternate financing does not excuse Buyer from the obligation to purchase the Property and close escrow as specified in this Agreement.

4. ALLOCATION OF COSTS (If checked): Unless otherwise specified in writing, **this paragraph** only determines who is to pay for the inspection, test or service ("Report") mentioned; it **does not determine who is to pay for any work recommended or identified in the Report.**

A. INSPECTIONS AND REPORTS:

(17) **(1)** ☐ Buyer ☐ Seller shall pay for an inspection and report for wood destroying pests and organisms ("Wood Pest Report") prepared by _____ a registered structural pest control company.

(18) **(2)** ☐ Buyer ☐ Seller shall pay to have septic or private sewage disposal systems inspected _____.
(3) ☐ Buyer ☐ Seller shall pay to have domestic wells tested for water potability and productivity _____.

(19) **(4)** ☐ Buyer ☐ Seller shall pay for a natural hazard zone disclosure report prepared by _____.
(5) ☐ Buyer ☐ Seller shall pay for the following inspection or report _____.
(6) ☐ Buyer ☐ Seller shall pay for the following inspection or report _____.

B. GOVERNMENT REQUIREMENTS AND RETROFIT:

(20) **(1)** ☐ Buyer ☐ Seller shall pay for smoke detector installation and/or water heater bracing, if required by Law. Prior to Close Of Escrow, Seller shall provide Buyer written statement(s) of compliance in accordance with state and local Law, unless exempt.
(2) ☐ Buyer ☐ Seller shall pay the cost of compliance with any other minimum mandatory government retrofit standards, inspections and reports if required as a condition of closing escrow under any Law. _____.

C. ESCROW AND TITLE:

(21) **(1)** ☐ Buyer ☐ Seller shall pay escrow fee _____.
Escrow Holder shall be _____.
(2) ☐ Buyer ☐ Seller shall pay for **owner's** title insurance policy specified in paragraph 12E _____.
Owner's title policy to be issued by _____.
(Buyer shall pay for any title insurance policy insuring Buyer's **lender**, unless otherwise agreed in writing.)

D. OTHER COSTS:

(22) **(1)** ☐ Buyer ☐ Seller shall pay County transfer tax or fee _____.
(2) ☐ Buyer ☐ Seller shall pay City transfer tax or fee _____.
(3) ☐ Buyer ☐ Seller shall pay Homeowners' Association ("HOA") transfer fee _____.
(4) ☐ Buyer ☐ Seller shall pay HOA document preparation fees _____.
(5) ☐ Buyer ☐ Seller shall pay for any private transfer fee _____.
(6) ☐ Buyer ☐ Seller shall pay for the cost, not to exceed $ _____, of a one-year home warranty plan, issued by _____, with the following optional coverages:
☐ Air Conditioner ☐ Pool/Spa ☐ Code and Permit upgrade ☐ Other: _____.
Buyer is informed that home warranty plans have many optional coverages in addition to those listed above. Buyer is advised to investigate these coverages to determine those that may be suitable for Buyer.
(7) ☐ Buyer ☐ Seller shall pay for _____.
(8) ☐ Buyer ☐ Seller shall pay for _____.

Buyer's Initials (_____)(_____)   Seller's Initials (_____)(_____)

RPA-CA REVISED 4/10 (PAGE 2 OF 8)   Reviewed by _____ Date _____

FIGURE 5.1 *(Continued).*

Property Address: _____   Date: _____

5. **CLOSING AND POSSESSION:**
   A. Buyer intends (or ☐ does not intend) to occupy the Property as Buyer's primary residence.
   B. **Seller-occupied or vacant property:** Possession shall be delivered to Buyer at 5 PM or (☐ _____ ☐ AM/☐ PM), on the date
   of Close Of Escrow; ☐ on _____; or ☐ no later than _____ **Days** After Close Of Escrow.

(23)   If transfer of title and possession do not occur at the same time, Buyer and Seller are advised to: **(i)** enter into a written
   occupancy agreement (C.A.R. Form PAA, paragraph 2); and **(ii)** consult with their insurance and legal advisors.
   C. **Tenant-occupied property:**
         (i) **Property shall be vacant at least 5 (or** ☐ _____) **Days** Prior to Close Of Escrow, unless otherwise agreed in writing.
         Note to Seller: If you are unable to deliver Property vacant in accordance with rent control and other applicable
         Law, you may be in breach of this Agreement.

(24)   **OR (ii)** (if checked) ☐ **Tenant to remain in possession.** (C.A.R. Form PAA, paragraph 3)
   D. At Close Of Escrow, **(i)** Seller assigns to Buyer any assignable warranty rights for items included in the sale, and **(ii)** Seller shall
   Deliver to Buyer available Copies of warranties. Brokers cannot and will not determine the assignability of any warranties.
   E. At Close Of Escrow, unless otherwise agreed in writing, Seller shall provide keys and/or means to operate all locks, mailboxes,
   security systems, alarms and garage door openers. If Property is a condominium or located in a common interest subdivision,
   Buyer may be required to pay a deposit to the Homeowners' Association ("HOA") to obtain keys to accessible HOA facilities.
6. **STATUTORY DISCLOSURES (INCLUDING LEAD-BASED PAINT HAZARD DISCLOSURES) AND CANCELLATION RIGHTS:**
   A. **(1)** Seller shall, within the time specified in paragraph 14A, Deliver to Buyer, if required by Law: **(i)** Federal Lead-Based Paint
   Disclosures (C.A.R. Form FLD) and pamphlet ("Lead Disclosures"); and **(ii)** disclosures or notices required by sections 1102
   et. seq. and 1103 et. seq. of the Civil Code ("Statutory Disclosures"). Statutory Disclosures include, but are not limited to, a
   Real Estate Transfer Disclosure Statement ("TDS"), Natural Hazard Disclosure Statement ("NHD"), notice or actual
   knowledge of release of illegal controlled substance, notice of special tax and/or assessments (or, if allowed, substantially
   equivalent notice regarding the Mello-Roos Community Facilities Act and Improvement Bond Act of 1915) and, if Seller has
   actual knowledge, of industrial use and military ordnance location (C.A.R. Form SPQ or SSD).
   (2) Buyer shall, within the time specified in paragraph 14B(1), return Signed Copies of the Statutory and Lead Disclosures to Seller.
   (3) In the event Seller, prior to Close Of Escrow, becomes aware of adverse conditions materially affecting the Property, or any
   material inaccuracy in disclosures, information or representations previously provided to Buyer, Seller shall promptly
   provide a subsequent or amended disclosure or notice, in writing, covering those items. **However, a subsequent or**

(25) **amended disclosure shall not be required for conditions and material inaccuracies** of which Buyer is otherwise
   aware, or which are **disclosed in reports provided to or obtained by Buyer or ordered and paid for by Buyer.**
   (4) If any disclosure or notice specified in 6A(1), or subsequent or amended disclosure or notice is Delivered to Buyer after the
   offer is Signed, Buyer shall have the right to cancel this Agreement within **3 Days** After Delivery in person, or **5 Days** After
   Delivery by deposit in the mail, by giving written notice of cancellation to Seller or Seller's agent.
   (5) Note to Buyer and Seller: Waiver of Statutory and Lead Disclosures is prohibited by Law.
   B. **NATURAL AND ENVIRONMENTAL HAZARDS:** Within the time specified in paragraph 14A, Seller shall, if required by Law:
   (i) Deliver to Buyer earthquake guides (and questionnaire) and environmental hazards booklet; **(ii)** even if exempt from the
   obligation to provide a NHD, disclose if the Property is located in a Special Flood Hazard Area; Potential Flooding (Inundation)
   Area; Very High Fire Hazard Zone; State Fire Responsibility Area; Earthquake Fault Zone; Seismic Hazard Zone; and **(iii)**
   disclose any other zone as required by Law and provide any other information required for those zones.
   C. **WITHHOLDING TAXES:** Within the time specified in paragraph 14A, to avoid required withholding, Seller shall Deliver to Buyer or
   qualified substitute, an affidavit sufficient to comply with federal (FIRPTA) and California withholding Law (C.A.R. Form AS or QS).
   D. **MEGAN'S LAW DATABASE DISCLOSURE:** Notice: Pursuant to Section 290.46 of the Penal Code, information about
   specified registered sex offenders is made available to the public via an Internet Web site maintained by the Department of
   Justice at www.meganslaw.ca.gov. Depending on an offender's criminal history, this information will include either the address
   at which the offender resides or the community of residence and ZIP Code in which he or she resides. (Neither Seller nor
   Brokers are required to check this website. If Buyer wants further information, Broker recommends that Buyer obtain
   information from this website during Buyer's inspection contingency period. Brokers do not have expertise in this area.)
7. **CONDOMINIUM/PLANNED DEVELOPMENT DISCLOSURES:**
   A. **SELLER HAS: 7 (or** ☐ _____) **Days** After Acceptance to disclose to Buyer whether the Property is a condominium, or is
   located in a planned development or other common interest subdivision (C.A.R. Form SPQ or SSD).
   B. If the Property is a condominium or is located in a planned development or other common interest subdivision, Seller has **3 (or**

(26) ☐ _____) **Days** After Acceptance to request from the HOA (C.A.R. Form HOA): **(i)** Copies of any documents required by Law;
   (ii) disclosure of any pending or anticipated claim or litigation by or against the HOA; **(iii)** a statement containing the location
   and number of designated parking and storage spaces; **(iv)** Copies of the most recent 12 months of HOA minutes for regular
   and special meetings; and **(v)** the names and contact information of all HOAs governing the Property (collectively, "CI
   Disclosures"). Seller shall itemize and Deliver to Buyer all CI Disclosures received from the HOA and any CI Disclosures in
   Seller's possession. Buyer's approval of CI Disclosures is a contingency of this Agreement as specified in paragraph 14B(3).
8. **ITEMS INCLUDED IN AND EXCLUDED FROM PURCHASE PRICE:**
   A. **NOTE TO BUYER AND SELLER:** Items listed as included or excluded in the MLS, flyers or marketing materials are **not**
   included in the purchase price or excluded from the sale unless specified in 8B or C.
   B. **ITEMS INCLUDED IN SALE:**
   (1) All EXISTING fixtures and fittings that are attached to the Property;
   (2) EXISTING electrical, mechanical, lighting, plumbing and heating fixtures, ceiling fans, fireplace inserts, gas logs and grates,
   solar systems, built-in appliances, window and door screens, awnings, shutters, window coverings, attached floor
   coverings, television antennas, satellite dishes, private integrated telephone systems, air coolers/conditioners, pool/spa

(27) equipment, garage door openers/remote controls, mailbox, in-ground landscaping, trees/shrubs, water softeners, water
   purifiers, security systems/alarms; (If checked) ☐ stove(s), ☐ refrigerator(s); and
   (3) The following additional items: _____.
   (4) Seller represents that all items included in the purchase price, unless otherwise specified, are owned by Seller.
   (5) All items included shall be transferred free of liens and without Seller warranty.
   C. **ITEMS EXCLUDED FROM SALE:** Unless otherwise specified, audio and video components (such as flat screen TVs and
   speakers) are excluded if any such item is not itself attached to the Property, even if a bracket or other mechanism attached to
   the component is attached to the Property; and _____.

Buyer's Initials (_____)(_____)   Seller's Initials (_____)(_____)

Copyright © 1991-2010, CALIFORNIA ASSOCIATION OF REALTORS®, INC.

RPA-CA REVISED 4/10 (PAGE 3 OF 8)

| Reviewed by _____ Date _____ |

EQUAL HOUSING
OPPORTUNITY

FIGURE 5.1 (*Continued*).

Property Address: _____   Date: _____

9. **CONDITION OF PROPERTY: Unless otherwise agreed: (i) the Property is sold (a) in its PRESENT physical ("as-is") condition as of the date of Acceptance and (b) subject to Buyer's Investigation rights; (ii)** the Property, including pool, spa, landscaping and grounds, is to be maintained in substantially the same condition as of the date of Acceptance; and **(iii)** all debris and personal property not included in the sale shall be removed by Seller by Close Of Escrow.

⑈ **(28)**

A. Seller shall, within the time specified in paragraph 14A, DISCLOSE KNOWN MATERIAL FACTS AND DEFECTS affecting the Property, including known insurance claims within the past five years, and make any and all other disclosures required by law.

B. Buyer has the right to inspect the Property and, as specified in paragraph 14B, based upon information discovered in those inspections: (i) cancel this Agreement; or (ii) request that Seller make Repairs or take other action.

C. **Buyer is strongly advised to conduct investigations of the entire Property in order to determine its present condition. Seller may not be aware of all defects affecting the Property or other factors that Buyer considers important. Property improvements may not be built according to code, in compliance with current Law, or have had permits issued.**

10. **BUYER'S INVESTIGATION OF PROPERTY AND MATTERS AFFECTING PROPERTY:**

A. Buyer's acceptance of the condition of, and any other matter affecting the Property, is a contingency of this Agreement as specified in this paragraph and paragraph 14B. Within the time specified in paragraph 14B(1), Buyer shall have the right, at Buyer's expense unless otherwise agreed, to conduct inspections, investigations, tests, surveys and other studies ("Buyer Investigations"), including, but not limited to, the right to: **(i)** inspect for lead-based paint and other lead-based paint hazards; **(ii)** inspect for wood destroying pests and organisms; **(iii)** review the registered sex offender database; **(iv)** confirm the insurability of Buyer and the Property; and **(v)** satisfy Buyer as to any matter specified in the attached Buyer's Inspection Advisory (C.A.R. Form BIA). Without Seller's prior written consent, Buyer shall neither make nor cause to be made: **(i)** invasive or destructive Buyer Investigations; or **(ii)** inspections by any governmental building or zoning inspector or government employee, unless required by Law.

⑈ **(29)**

B. Seller shall make the Property available for all Buyer Investigations. Buyer shall **(i)** as specified in paragraph 14B, complete Buyer Investigations and, either remove the contingency or cancel this Agreement, and **(ii)** give Seller, at no cost, complete Copies of all Investigation reports obtained by Buyer, which obligation shall survive the termination of this Agreement.

C. Seller shall have water, gas, electricity and all operable pilot lights on for Buyer's Investigations and through the date possession is made available to Buyer.

D. **Buyer indemnity and Seller protection for entry upon property:** Buyer shall: **(i)** keep the Property free and clear of liens; **(ii)** repair all damage arising from Buyer Investigations; and **(iii)** indemnify and hold Seller harmless from all resulting liability, claims, demands, damages and costs of Buyer's Investigations. Buyer shall carry, or Buyer shall require anyone acting on Buyer's behalf to carry, policies of liability, workers' compensation and other applicable insurance, defending and protecting Seller from liability for any injuries to persons or property occurring during any Buyer Investigations or work done on the Property at Buyer's direction prior to Close Of Escrow. Seller is advised that certain protections may be afforded Seller by recording a "Notice of Non-responsibility" (C.A.R. Form NNR) for Buyer Investigations and work done on the Property at Buyer's direction. Buyer's obligations under this paragraph shall survive the termination or cancellation of this Agreement and Close Of Escrow.

11. **SELLER DISCLOSURES; ADDENDA; ADVISORIES; OTHER TERMS:**

A. **Seller Disclosures (if checked):** Seller shall, within the time specified in paragraph 14A, complete and provide Buyer with a:
☐ Seller Property Questionnaire (C.A.R. Form SPQ)   **OR**   ☐ Supplemental Contractual and Statutory Disclosure (C.A.R. Form SSD)

B. **Addenda (if checked):**   ☐ Addendum # _____ (C.A.R. Form ADM)
☐ Wood Destroying Pest Inspection and Allocation of Cost Addendum (C.A.R. Form WPA)
☐ Purchase Agreement Addendum (C.A.R. Form PAA)   ☐ Septic, Well and Property Monument Addendum (C.A.R. Form SWPI)
☐ Short Sale Addendum (C.A.R. Form SSA)   ☐ Other _____

⑈ **(30)**

C. **Advisories (If checked):**   ☑ Buyer's Inspection Advisory (C.A.R. Form BIA)
☐ Probate Advisory (C.A.R. Form PAK)   ☐ Statewide Buyer and Seller Advisory (C.A.R. Form SBSA)
☐ Trust Advisory (C.A.R. Form TA)   ☐ REO Advisory (C.A.R. Form REO)

D. **Other Terms:** _____

12. **TITLE AND VESTING:**

A. Within the time specified in paragraph 14, Buyer shall be provided a current preliminary title report, which shall include a search of the General Index. Seller shall within 7 Days After Acceptance give Escrow Holder a completed Statement of Information. The preliminary report is only an offer by the title insurer to issue a policy of title insurance and may not contain every item affecting title. Buyer's review of the preliminary report and any other matters which may affect title are a contingency of this Agreement as specified in paragraph 14B.

⑈ **(31)**

B. Title is taken in its present condition subject to all encumbrances, easements, covenants, conditions, restrictions, rights and other matters, whether of record or not, as of the date of Acceptance except: **(i)** monetary liens of record unless Buyer is assuming those obligations or taking the Property subject to those obligations; and **(ii)** those matters which Seller has agreed to remove in writing.

C. Within the time specified in paragraph 14A, Seller has a duty to disclose to Buyer all matters known to Seller affecting title, whether of record or not.

D. At Close Of Escrow, Buyer shall receive a grant deed conveying title (or, for stock cooperative or long-term lease, an assignment of stock certificate or of Seller's leasehold interest), including oil, mineral and water rights if currently owned by Seller. Title shall vest as designated in Buyer's supplemental escrow instructions. THE MANNER OF TAKING TITLE MAY HAVE SIGNIFICANT LEGAL AND TAX CONSEQUENCES. CONSULT AN APPROPRIATE PROFESSIONAL.

E. Buyer shall receive a CLTA/ALTA Homeowner's Policy of Title Insurance. A title company, at Buyer's request, can provide information about the availability, desirability, coverage, survey requirements, and cost of various title insurance coverages and endorsements. If Buyer desires title coverage other than that required by this paragraph, Buyer shall instruct Escrow Holder in writing and pay any increase in cost.

13. **SALE OF BUYER'S PROPERTY:**

A. This Agreement is NOT contingent upon the sale of any property owned by Buyer.

⑈ **(32)**

OR B. ☐ (If checked): The attached addendum (C.A.R. Form COP) regarding the contingency for the sale of property owned by Buyer is incorporated into this Agreement.

Seller's Initials (_____)(_____)

RPA-CA REVISED 4/10 (PAGE 4 OF 8)

Reviewed by _____ Date _____

CALIFORNIA RESIDENTIAL PURCHASE AGREEMENT (RPA-CA PAGE 4 OF 8)

FIGURE 5.1 (*Continued*).

Property Address: _____   Date: _____

14. **TIME PERIODS; REMOVAL OF CONTINGENCIES; CANCELLATION RIGHTS:** The following time periods may only be extended, altered, modified or changed by mutual written agreement. Any removal of contingencies or cancellation under this paragraph by either Buyer or Seller must be exercised in good faith and in writing (C.A.R. Form CR or CC).

(33)   A. **SELLER HAS: 7 (or ☐ _____) Days** After Acceptance to Deliver to Buyer all Reports, disclosures and information for which Seller is responsible under paragraphs 4, 6A, B and C, 7A, 9A, 11A and B, and 12. Buyer may give Seller a Notice to Seller to Perform (C.A.R. Form NSP) if Seller has not Delivered the items within the time specified.

  B. **(1) BUYER HAS: 17 (or ☐ _____) Days** After Acceptance, unless otherwise agreed in writing, to:
    (i) complete all Buyer Investigations; approve all disclosures, reports and other applicable information, which Buyer receives from Seller; and approve all other matters affecting the Property; and
    (ii) Deliver to Seller Signed Copies of Statutory and Lead Disclosures Delivered by Seller in accordance with paragraph 6A.
    (2) Within the time specified in 14B(1), Buyer may request that Seller make repairs or take any other action regarding the Property (C.A.R. Form RR). Seller has no obligation to agree to or respond to Buyer's requests.
    (3) Within the time specified in 14B(1) (or as otherwise specified in this Agreement), Buyer shall Deliver to Seller either (i) a removal of the applicable contingency (C.A.R. Form CR), or (ii) a cancellation (C.A.R. Form CC) of this Agreement based upon a remaining contingency or Seller's failure to Deliver the specified items. However, if any report, disclosure or information for which Seller is responsible is not Delivered within the time specified in 14A, then Buyer has **5 (or ☐ _____) Days** After Delivery of any such items, or the time specified in 14B(1), whichever is later, to Deliver to Seller a removal of the applicable contingency or cancellation of this Agreement.
    (4) Continuation of Contingency: Even after the end of the time specified in 14B(1) and before Seller cancels this Agreement, if at all, pursuant to 14C, Buyer retains the right to either (i) in writing remove remaining contingencies, or (ii) cancel this Agreement based upon a remaining contingency or Seller's failure to Deliver the specified items. Once Buyer's written removal of all contingencies is Delivered to Seller, Seller may not cancel this Agreement pursuant to 14C(1).

  C. **SELLER RIGHT TO CANCEL:**
    (1) Seller right to Cancel; Buyer Contingencies: If, within time specified in this Agreement, Buyer does not, in writing, Deliver to Seller a removal of the applicable contingency or cancellation of this Agreement then Seller, after first Delivering to Buyer a Notice to Buyer to Perform (C.A.R. Form NBP) may cancel this Agreement. In such event, Seller shall authorize return of Buyer's deposit.

(34)   **(2) Seller right to Cancel; Buyer Contract Obligations:** Seller, after first Delivering to Buyer a NBP may cancel this Agreement for any of the following reasons: **(i)** if Buyer fails to deposit funds as required by 3A or 3B; **(ii)** if the funds deposited pursuant to 3A or 3B are not good when deposited; **(iii)** if Buyer fails to Deliver a notice of FHA or VA costs or terms as required by 3C(3) (C.A.R. Form FVA); **(iv)** if Buyer fails to Deliver a letter as required by 3H; **(v)** if Buyer fails to Deliver verification as required by 3G or 3J; **(vi)** if Seller reasonably disapproves of the verification provided by 3G or 3J; **(vii)** if Buyer fails to return Statutory and Lead Disclosures as required by paragraph 6A(2); or **(viii)** if Buyer fails to sign or initial a separate liquidated damages form for an increased deposit as required by paragraphs 3B and 25. In such event, Seller shall authorize return of Buyer's deposit.
    (3) Notice To Buyer To Perform: The NBP shall: **(i)** be in writing; **(ii)** be signed by Seller; and **(iii)** give Buyer at least **2 (or ☐ _____) Days** After Delivery (or until the time specified in the applicable paragraph, whichever occurs last) to take the applicable action. A NBP may not be Delivered any earlier than **2 Days** Prior to the expiration of the applicable time for Buyer to remove a contingency or cancel this Agreement or meet an obligation specified in 14C(2).

(35)   D. **EFFECT OF BUYER'S REMOVAL OF CONTINGENCIES:** If Buyer removes, in writing, any contingency or cancellation rights, unless otherwise specified in a separate written agreement between Buyer and Seller, Buyer shall with regard to that contingency or cancellation right conclusively be deemed to have: **(i)** completed all Buyer Investigations, and review of reports and other applicable information and disclosures; **(ii)** elected to proceed with the transaction; and **(iii)** assumed all liability, responsibility and expense for Repairs or corrections or for inability to obtain financing.

  E. **CLOSE OF ESCROW:** Before Seller or Buyer may cancel this Agreement for failure of the other party to close escrow pursuant to this Agreement, Seller or Buyer must first Deliver to the other a demand to close escrow (C.A.R. Form DCE).

(36)   F. **EFFECT OF CANCELLATION ON DEPOSITS:** If Buyer or Seller gives written notice of cancellation pursuant to rights duly exercised under the terms of this Agreement, Buyer and Seller agree to Sign mutual instructions to cancel the sale and escrow and release deposits, if any, to the party entitled to the funds, less fees and costs incurred by that party. Fees and costs may be payable to service providers and vendors for services and products provided during escrow. **Release of funds will require mutual Signed release instructions from Buyer and Seller, judicial decision or arbitration award. A Buyer or Seller may be subject to a civil penalty of up to $1,000 for refusal to sign such instructions if no good faith dispute exists as to who is entitled to the deposited funds (Civil Code §1057.3).**

(37) 15. **REPAIRS:** Repairs shall be completed prior to final verification of condition unless otherwise agreed in writing. Repairs to be performed at Seller's expense may be performed by Seller or through others, provided that the work complies with applicable Law, including governmental permit, inspection and approval requirements. Repairs shall be performed in a good, skillful manner with materials of quality and appearance comparable to existing materials. It is understood that exact restoration of appearance or cosmetic items following all Repairs may not be possible. Seller shall: **(i)** obtain receipts for Repairs performed by others; **(ii)** prepare a written statement indicating the Repairs performed by Seller and the date of such Repairs; and **(iii)** provide Copies of receipts and statements to Buyer prior to final verification of condition.

(38) 16. **FINAL VERIFICATION OF CONDITION:** Buyer shall have the right to make a final inspection of the Property within **5 (or _____) Days** Prior to Close Of Escrow, NOT AS A CONTINGENCY OF THE SALE, but solely to confirm: **(i)** the Property is maintained pursuant to paragraph 9; **(ii)** Repairs have been completed as agreed; and **(iii)** Seller has complied with Seller's other obligations under this Agreement (C.A.R. Form VP).

(39) 17. **PRORATIONS OF PROPERTY TAXES AND OTHER ITEMS:** Unless otherwise agreed in writing, the following items shall be PAID CURRENT and prorated between Buyer and Seller as of Close Of Escrow: real property taxes and assessments, interest, rents, HOA regular, special, and emergency dues and assessments imposed prior to Close Of Escrow, premiums on insurance assumed by Buyer, payments on bonds and assessments assumed by Buyer, and payments on Mello-Roos and other Special Assessment District bonds and assessments that are a current lien. The following items shall be assumed by Buyer WITHOUT CREDIT toward the purchase price: prorated payments on Mello-Roos and other Special Assessment District bonds and assessments and HOA special assessments that are a current lien but not yet due. Property will be reassessed upon change of ownership. Any supplemental tax bills shall be paid as follows: **(i)** for periods after Close Of Escrow, by Buyer; and **(ii)** for periods prior to Close Of Escrow, by Seller (see C.A.R. Form SPT or SBSA for further information). TAX BILLS ISSUED AFTER CLOSE OF ESCROW SHALL BE HANDLED DIRECTLY BETWEEN BUYER AND SELLER. Prorations shall be made based on a 30-day month.

Buyer's Initials (_____)(_____)

Seller's Initials (_____)(_____)

RPA-CA REVISED 4/10 (PAGE 5 OF 8)

Reviewed by _____ Date _____

CALIFORNIA RESIDENTIAL PURCHASE AGREEMENT (RPA-CA PAGE 5 OF 8)

FIGURE 5.1 *(Continued)*.

Property Address: _____   Date: _____

(40) **18. SELECTION OF SERVICE PROVIDERS:** Brokers do not guarantee the performance of any vendors, service or product providers ("Providers"), whether referred by Broker or selected by Buyer, Seller or other person. Buyer and Seller may select ANY Providers of their own choosing.

(41) **19. MULTIPLE LISTING SERVICE ("MLS"):** Brokers are authorized to report to the MLS a pending sale and, upon Close Of Escrow, the sales price and other terms of this transaction shall be provided to the MLS to be published and disseminated to persons and entities authorized to use the information on terms approved by the MLS.

(42) **20. EQUAL HOUSING OPPORTUNITY:** The Property is sold in compliance with federal, state and local anti-discrimination Laws.

(43) **21. ATTORNEY FEES:** In any action, proceeding, or arbitration between Buyer and Seller arising out of this Agreement, the prevailing Buyer or Seller shall be entitled to reasonable attorney fees and costs from the non-prevailing Buyer or Seller, except as provided in paragraph 26A.

22. DEFINITIONS: As used in this Agreement:

(44)
  A. **"Acceptance"** means the time the offer or final counter offer is accepted in writing by a party and is delivered to and personally received by the other party or that party's authorized agent in accordance with the terms of this offer or a final counter offer.
  B. **"C.A.R. Form"** means the specific form referenced or another comparable form agreed to by the parties.
  C. **"Close Of Escrow"** means the date the grant deed, or other evidence of transfer of title, is recorded.
  D. **"Copy"** means copy by any means including photocopy, NCR, facsimile and electronic.
  E. **"Days"** means calendar days. However, after Acceptance, the last **Day** for performance of any act required by this Agreement (including Close Of Escrow) shall not include any Saturday, Sunday, or legal holiday and shall instead be the next Day.
  F. **"Days After"** means the specified number of calendar days after the occurrence of the event specified, not counting the calendar date on which the specified event occurs, and ending at 11:59 PM on the final day.
  G. **"Days Prior"** means the specified number of calendar days before the occurrence of the event specified, not counting the calendar date on which the specified event is scheduled to occur.
  H. **"Deliver", "Delivered"** or **"Delivery"**, regardless of the method used (i.e. messenger, mail, email, fax, other), means and shall be effective upon (i) personal receipt by Buyer or Seller or the individual Real Estate Licensee for that principal as specified in paragraph D of the section titled Real Estate Brokers on page 8;
  OR (ii) if checked, ☐ per the attached addendum (C.A.R. Form RDN).
  I. **"Electronic Copy"** or **"Electronic Signature"** means, as applicable, an electronic copy or signature complying with California Law. Buyer and Seller agree that electronic means will not be used by either party to modify or alter the content or integrity of this Agreement without the knowledge and consent of the other party.
  J. **"Law"** means any law, code, statute, ordinance, regulation, rule or order, which is adopted by a controlling city, county, state or federal legislative, judicial or executive body or agency.
  K. **"Repairs"** means any repairs (including pest control), alterations, replacements, modifications or retrofitting of the Property provided for under this Agreement.
  L. **"Signed"** means either a handwritten or electronic signature on an original document, Copy or any counterpart.

(45) **23. BROKER COMPENSATION:** Seller or Buyer, or both, as applicable, agree(s) to pay compensation to Broker as specified in a separate written agreement between Broker and that Seller or Buyer. Compensation is payable upon Close Of Escrow, or if escrow does not close, as otherwise specified in the agreement between Broker and that Seller or Buyer.

24. JOINT ESCROW INSTRUCTIONS TO ESCROW HOLDER:

  A. **The following paragraphs, or applicable portions thereof, of this Agreement constitute the joint escrow instructions of Buyer and Seller to Escrow Holder,** which Escrow Holder is to use along with any related counter offers and addenda, and any additional mutual instructions to close the escrow: 1, 3, 4, 6C, 11B and D, 12, 13B, 14F, 17, 22, 23, 24, 28, 30, and paragraph D of the section titled Real Estate Brokers on page 8. If a Copy of the separate compensation agreement(s) provided for in paragraph 23, or paragraph D of the section titled Real Estate Brokers on page 8 is deposited with Escrow Holder by Broker, Escrow Holder shall accept such agreement(s) and pay out of Buyer's or Seller's funds, or both, as applicable, the respective Broker's compensation provided for in such agreement(s). The terms and conditions of this Agreement not specifically referenced above, in the specified paragraphs are additional matters for the information of Escrow Holder, but about which Escrow Holder need not be concerned. Buyer and Seller will receive Escrow Holder's general provisions directly from Escrow Holder and will execute such provisions upon Escrow Holder's request. To the extent the general provisions are inconsistent or conflict with this Agreement, the general provisions will control as to the duties and obligations of Escrow Holder only. Buyer and Seller will execute additional instructions, documents and forms provided by Escrow Holder that are reasonably

(46)
  necessary to close the escrow.
  B. A Copy of this Agreement shall be delivered to Escrow Holder within **3** business days after Acceptance (or ☐ _____). Escrow Holder shall provide Seller's Statement of Information to Title company when received from Seller. Buyer and Seller authorize Escrow Holder to accept and rely on Copies and Signatures as defined in this Agreement as originals, to open escrow and for other purposes of escrow. The validity of this Agreement as between Buyer and Seller is not affected by whether or when Escrow Holder Signs this Agreement.
  C. Brokers are a party to the escrow for the sole purpose of compensation pursuant to paragraph 23 and paragraph D of the section titled Real Estate Brokers on page 8. Buyer and Seller irrevocably assign to Brokers compensation specified in paragraph 23, respectively, and irrevocably instruct Escrow Holder to disburse those funds to Brokers at Close Of Escrow or pursuant to any other mutually executed cancellation agreement. Compensation instructions can be amended or revoked only with the written consent of Brokers. Buyer and Seller shall release and hold harmless Escrow Holder from any liability resulting from Escrow Holder's payment to Broker(s) of compensation pursuant to this Agreement. Escrow Holder shall immediately notify Brokers: **(i)** if Buyer's initial or any additional deposit is not made pursuant to this Agreement, or is not good at time of deposit with Escrow Holder; or **(ii)** if either Buyer or Seller instruct Escrow Holder to cancel escrow.
  D. A Copy of any amendment that affects any paragraph of this Agreement for which Escrow Holder is responsible shall be delivered to Escrow Holder within **2** business days after mutual execution of the amendment.

Buyer's Initials (_____)(_____)   Seller's Initials (_____)(_____)

RPA-CA REVISED 4/10 (PAGE 6 OF 8)

Reviewed by _____ Date _____

EQUAL HOUSING OPPORTUNITY

FIGURE 5.1 (Continued).

Property Address: _____ Date: _____

25. LIQUIDATED DAMAGES: If Buyer fails to complete this purchase because of Buyer's default, Seller shall
retain, as liquidated damages, the deposit actually paid. If the Property is a dwelling with no more than
four units, one of which Buyer intends to occupy, then the amount retained shall be no more than 3% of
the purchase price. Any excess shall be returned to Buyer. Release of funds will require mutual, Signed
release instructions from both Buyer and Seller, judicial decision or arbitration award. AT TIME OF THE
INCREASED DEPOSIT BUYER AND SELLER SHALL SIGN A SEPARATE LIQUIDATED DAMAGES
PROVISION FOR ANY INCREASED DEPOSIT (C.A.R. FORM RID).

(47)

| Buyer's Initials ____ / ____ | Seller's Initials ____ / ____ |

26. DISPUTE RESOLUTION:

A. **MEDIATION:** Buyer and Seller agree to mediate any dispute or claim arising between them out of this Agreement, or any
resulting transaction, before resorting to arbitration or court action. **Buyer and Seller also agree to mediate any disputes or
claims with Broker(s) who, in writing, agree to such mediation prior to, or within a reasonable time after, the dispute
or claim is presented to the Broker.** Mediation fees, if any, shall be divided equally among the parties involved. If, for any
dispute or claim to which this paragraph applies, any party (i) commences an action without first attempting to resolve the
matter through mediation, or (ii) before commencement of an action, refuses to mediate after a request has been made, then
that party shall not be entitled to recover attorney fees, even if they would otherwise be available to that party in any such
action. THIS MEDIATION PROVISION APPLIES WHETHER OR NOT THE ARBITRATION PROVISION IS INITIALED.
Exclusions from this mediation agreement are specified in paragraph 26C.

(48)

B. **ARBITRATION OF DISPUTES:**
Buyer and Seller agree that any dispute or claim in Law or equity arising between them out of this Agreement or any
resulting transaction, which is not settled through mediation, shall be decided by neutral, binding arbitration. Buyer
and Seller also agree to arbitrate any disputes or claims with Broker(s) who, in writing, agree to such arbitration prior
to, or within a reasonable time after, the dispute or claim is presented to the Broker. The arbitrator shall be a retired
judge or justice, or an attorney with at least 5 years of residential real estate Law experience, unless the parties
mutually agree to a different arbitrator. The parties shall have the right to discovery in accordance with Code of Civil
Procedure §1283.05. In all other respects, the arbitration shall be conducted in accordance with Title 9 of Part 3 of the
Code of Civil Procedure. Judgment upon the award of the arbitrator(s) may be entered into any court having
jurisdiction. Enforcement of this agreement to arbitrate shall be governed by the Federal Arbitration Act. Exclusions
from this arbitration agreement are specified in paragraph 26C.

(49)

"NOTICE: BY INITIALING IN THE SPACE BELOW YOU ARE AGREEING TO HAVE ANY
DISPUTE ARISING OUT OF THE MATTERS INCLUDED IN THE 'ARBITRATION OF DISPUTES'
PROVISION DECIDED BY NEUTRAL ARBITRATION AS PROVIDED BY CALIFORNIA LAW AND YOU
ARE GIVING UP ANY RIGHTS YOU MIGHT POSSESS TO HAVE THE DISPUTE LITIGATED IN A COURT
OR JURY TRIAL. BY INITIALING IN THE SPACE BELOW YOU ARE GIVING UP YOUR JUDICIAL
RIGHTS TO DISCOVERY AND APPEAL, UNLESS THOSE RIGHTS ARE SPECIFICALLY INCLUDED IN
THE 'ARBITRATION OF DISPUTES' PROVISION. IF YOU REFUSE TO SUBMIT TO ARBITRATION
AFTER AGREEING TO THIS PROVISION, YOU MAY BE COMPELLED TO ARBITRATE UNDER THE
AUTHORITY OF THE CALIFORNIA CODE OF CIVIL PROCEDURE. YOUR AGREEMENT TO THIS
ARBITRATION PROVISION IS VOLUNTARY."

"WE HAVE READ AND UNDERSTAND THE FOREGOING AND AGREE TO SUBMIT DISPUTES
ARISING OUT OF THE MATTERS INCLUDED IN THE 'ARBITRATION OF DISPUTES' PROVISION TO
NEUTRAL ARBITRATION."

| Buyer's Initials ____ / ____ | Seller's Initials ____ / ____ |

C. **ADDITIONAL MEDIATION AND ARBITRATION TERMS:**
   (1) **EXCLUSIONS:** The following matters shall be excluded from mediation and arbitration: (i) a judicial or non-judicial
   foreclosure or other action or proceeding to enforce a deed of trust, mortgage or installment land sale contract as
   defined in Civil Code §2985; (ii) an unlawful detainer action; (iii) the filing or enforcement of a mechanic's lien; and
   (iv) any matter that is within the jurisdiction of a probate, small claims or bankruptcy court. The filing of a court
   action to enable the recording of a notice of pending action, for order of attachment, receivership, injunction, or
   other provisional remedies, shall not constitute a waiver or violation of the mediation and arbitration provisions.
   (2) **BROKERS:** Brokers shall not be obligated or compelled to mediate or arbitrate unless they agree to do so in
   writing. Any Broker(s) participating in mediation or arbitration shall not be deemed a party to the Agreement.

27. TERMS AND CONDITIONS OF OFFER:
This is an offer to purchase the Property on the above terms and conditions. The liquidated damages paragraph or the arbitration
of disputes paragraph is incorporated in this Agreement if initialed by all parties or if incorporated by mutual agreement in a counter
offer or addendum. If at least one but not all parties initial such paragraph(s), a counter offer is required until agreement is reached.
Seller has the right to continue to offer the Property for sale and to accept any other offer at any time prior to notification of
Acceptance. If this offer is accepted and Buyer subsequently defaults, Buyer may be responsible for payment of Brokers'
compensation. This Agreement and any supplement, addendum or modification, including any Copy, may be Signed in two or more
counterparts, all of which shall constitute one and the same writing.

(50)

28. TIME OF ESSENCE; ENTIRE CONTRACT; CHANGES: Time is of the essence. All understandings between the parties are
incorporated in this Agreement. Its terms are intended by the parties as a final, complete and exclusive expression of their
Agreement with respect to its subject matter, and may not be contradicted by evidence of any prior agreement or contemporaneous
oral agreement. If any provision of this Agreement is held to be ineffective or invalid, the remaining provisions will nevertheless be
given full force and effect. Except as otherwise specified, this Agreement shall be interpreted and disputes shall be resolved in
accordance with the laws of the State of California. **Neither this Agreement nor any provision in it may be extended, amended,
modified, altered or changed, except in writing Signed by Buyer and Seller.**

(51)

Buyer's Initials (_____)(_____)   Seller's Initials (_____)(_____)

RPA-CA REVISED 4/10 (PAGE 7 OF 8)

| Reviewed by _____ Date _____ |

CALIFORNIA RESIDENTIAL PURCHASE AGREEMENT (RPA-CA PAGE 7 OF 8)

FIGURE 5.1 (Continued).

Property Address: _____ Date: _____

(52) 29. **EXPIRATION OF OFFER:** This offer shall be deemed revoked and the deposit shall be returned unless the offer is Signed by Seller and a Copy of the Signed offer is personally received by Buyer, or by _____ who is authorized to receive it, by 5:00 PM on the third Day after this offer is signed by Buyer (or, if checked,
☐ by _____ ☐AM/☐PM, on _____(date)).
Buyer has read and acknowledges receipt of a Copy of the offer and agrees to the above confirmation of agency relationships.
Date _____ Date _____
BUYER _____ BUYER _____

(53) (Print name) _____ (Print name) _____
_____
(Address)
☐ Additional Signature Addendum attached (C.A.R. Form ASA).

30. **ACCEPTANCE OF OFFER:** Seller warrants that Seller is the owner of the Property, or has the authority to execute this Agreement. **(54)** Seller accepts the above offer, agrees to sell the Property on the above terms and conditions, and agrees to the above confirmation of agency relationships. Seller has read and acknowledges receipt of a Copy of this Agreement, and authorizes Broker to Deliver a Signed Copy to Buyer.
☐ (If checked) **SUBJECT TO ATTACHED COUNTER OFFER (C.A.R. Form CO) DATED:** _____.
Date _____ Date _____
SELLER _____ SELLER _____

(55) (Print name) _____ (Print name) _____
_____
(Address)
☐ Additional Signature Addendum attached (C.A.R. Form ASA).

(56) (____/____) **CONFIRMATION OF ACCEPTANCE:** A Copy of Signed Acceptance was personally received by Buyer or Buyer's
(Initials) authorized agent on (date) _____ at _____ ☐AM/☐PM. **A binding Agreement is created when a Copy of Signed Acceptance is personally received by Buyer or Buyer's authorized agent whether or not confirmed in this document. Completion of this confirmation is not legally required in order to create a binding Agreement. It is solely intended to evidence the date that Confirmation of Acceptance has occurred.**

REAL ESTATE BROKERS:
A. **Real Estate Brokers are not parties to the Agreement between Buyer and Seller.**
B. **Agency relationships are confirmed as stated in paragraph 2.**
C. If specified in paragraph 3A(2), Agent who submitted the offer for Buyer acknowledges receipt of deposit.
D. **COOPERATING BROKER COMPENSATION:** Listing Broker agrees to pay Cooperating Broker (**Selling Firm**) and Cooperating **(57)** Broker agrees to accept, out of Listing Broker's proceeds in escrow: (**i**) the amount specified in the MLS, provided Cooperating Broker is a Participant of the MLS in which the Property is offered for sale or a reciprocal MLS; or (**ii**) ☐ (if checked) the amount specified in a separate written agreement (C.A.R. Form CBC) between Listing Broker and Cooperating Broker. Declaration of License and Tax (C.A.R. Form DLT) may be used to document that tax reporting will be required or that an exemption exists.

Real Estate Broker (Selling Firm) _____ DRE Lic. #_____
(58) By _____ DRE Lic. # _____ Date _____
Address _____ City _____ State _____ Zip _____
Telephone _____ Fax _____ E-mail _____
Real Estate Broker (Listing Firm) _____ DRE Lic. #_____
By _____ DRE Lic. # _____ Date _____
Address _____ City _____ State _____ Zip _____
Telephone _____ Fax _____ E-mail _____

ESCROW HOLDER ACKNOWLEDGMENT:
Escrow Holder acknowledges receipt of a Copy of this Agreement, (if checked, ☐ a deposit in the amount of $ _____),
counter offer numbered _____, ☐ Seller's Statement of Information and ☐ Other _____
_____, and agrees to act as Escrow Holder subject to paragraph 24 of this Agreement, any
supplemental escrow instructions and the terms of Escrow Holder's general provisions if any.

(59) Escrow Holder is advised that the date of Confirmation of Acceptance of the Agreement as between Buyer and Seller is _____.

Escrow Holder _____ Escrow # _____
By _____ Date _____
Address _____
Phone/Fax/E-mail _____
Escrow Holder is licensed by the California Department of ☐ Corporations, ☐ Insurance, ☐ Real Estate. License # _____

(60) **PRESENTATION OF OFFER:** (_____) Listing Broker presented this offer to Seller on _____(date).
Broker or Designee Initials

(61) **REJECTION OF OFFER:** (_____)(_____) No counter offer is being made. This offer was rejected by Seller on_____(date).
Seller's Initials

THIS FORM HAS BEEN APPROVED BY THE CALIFORNIA ASSOCIATION OF REALTORS® (C.A.R.). NO REPRESENTATION IS MADE AS TO THE LEGAL VALIDITY OR ADEQUACY OF ANY PROVISION IN ANY SPECIFIC TRANSACTION. A REAL ESTATE BROKER IS THE PERSON QUALIFIED TO ADVISE ON REAL ESTATE TRANSACTIONS. IF YOU DESIRE LEGAL OR TAX ADVICE, CONSULT AN APPROPRIATE PROFESSIONAL.

This form is available for use by the entire real estate industry. It is not intended to identify the user as a REALTOR®. REALTOR® is a registered collective membership mark which may be used only by members of the NATIONAL ASSOCIATION OF REALTORS® who subscribe to its Code of Ethics.

Published and Distributed by:
REAL ESTATE BUSINESS SERVICES, INC.
a subsidiary of the CALIFORNIA ASSOCIATION OF REALTORS®
525 South Virgil Avenue, Los Angeles, California 90020

Reviewed by _____
Broker or Designee _____ Date _____

REVISION DATE 4/10

CALIFORNIA RESIDENTIAL PURCHASE AGREEMENT (RPA-CA PAGE 8 OF 8)

A list of CAR forms is found on its Web site at http://www.car.org/ or by writing CAR at 525 South Virgil Avenue, Los Angeles, California 90020.

(1) Buyer's Identity

The full and correct names of all parties acquiring an interest in the property should be given, in addition to the name of the party advancing the deposit. This complete list helps establish the parties' rights and obligations and facilitates enforcement against all named individuals. Additionally, it is advisable to include the relationship and status of the buyers. Status includes notations such as husband and wife, single (never married), unmarried (divorced and not remarried), widow, widower, partnership, or corporation.

Capacity to Contract

The broker should confirm the buyer's legal capacity to contract for the purchase of the property. Obviously, minors and incompetents lack capacity. Because corporations and partnerships may have restricted their ability to contract for real estate, the broker should read his or her articles and bylaws. Furthermore, appropriate corporate resolutions and correct procedures must be followed. If a corporation has not yet been formed, promoters should not be allowed to sign in the name of the nonexistent organization, as the seller might then have the power to withdraw from the sale before completion of the incorporation. Finally, powers of attorney must be evaluated for the appropriate legal language and to ensure that the agency has not been revoked by the parties or canceled by the death or incapacity of the principal.

Nominee

Occasionally, the buyer states that he is acting as an intermediary (dummy or strawman) for the real party in interest and desires to be listed as "John Doe or nominee." The courts hold that the term *nominee* denotes a delegation of authority and not an assignment or assignability of an interest. Hence, the nominee receives no contractual rights and may not specifically enforce the contract. *Cisco v. Van Lew (1943) 60 C.A.2d 575.* In some cases, the use of the term assignee (the correct designation) may render the contract illusory and unenforceable. *Rivadell, Inc. v. Raso (1963) 215 C.A.2d 614.* Because of the legal and tax consequences, an attorney should be consulted in drafting this type of clause.

(2) Description

The description required for a deposit receipt is less exacting than the one required for a deed, although it still must enable the courts to identify the property. Street addresses and descriptive names are sufficient, *C.C. 1092,* although it is advisable to include a legal description by reference to a recorded map, metes and bounds, or a government survey designation.

Recorded Map Reference

In residential and other subdivided land, property is commonly designated by reference to a prior recorded map in the county records. For example, "Lot 32 of Block B of the Murphy Tract #48 in the County of _____ State of California, recorded in book 8, page 20, on May 20, 1967."

Metes and Bounds

Property can be described by stating the location and size of its boundaries. This is done by using surveyor's courses and distances and by beginning the description from a known reference point. For example, "Starting at point X, then traveling 129 feet along a line N 52° 22' 18" W, then...."

Government Survey

Property is also described as sections (1 square mile) or portions of a section. The sections are part of a township (36 square miles) designated by reference to intersecting range lines (parallel lines 6 miles apart, running north and south) and township lines (parallel lines 6 miles apart, running east and west). Finally, these coordinates are anchored to one of the three base and meridian locations established in California. A description by government survey might read "SW-1/2 of NE-1/4 of Sec. 18, T2N, R3W, MDB&M."

(3) Agency Confirmation

Disclosure

As Chapter 6 will explain, the agent must disclose whom he or she represents, using a special form. This clause merely confirms the agency relationship and acknowledges receipt of that form.

Potentially Competing Buyer and Seller

This paragraph merely acknowledges that the buyer and seller have competing and therefore conflicting interests. This conflict is especially magnified if only one broker is representing both parties. The paragraph has the parties acknowledging and consenting to the conflict.

Disclosure Confirmation

The confirmation can be done as a separate document (see Chapter 6) which is, in the author's opinion, the preferable method. In such cases, this paragraph would only be an acknowledgment of that information.

[Actually, if the selling broker represents the buyer, then that broker must provide a copy of the confirmation to the seller prior to presenting this offer. That requirement holds true, even though the listing broker should already have given a disclosure to the seller.]

(4) Finance Terms—In General

Some deposit receipts, including the older versions of the CAR forms, used to leave only a large blank space for the brokers to custom draft the financing section. Unfortunately, brokers found this section one of the most difficult in the entire form, and it became one of the more litigated aspects of contract disputes. For a contract to be fully enforceable, the courts require all of the material terms to be stated.

Vague wording, such as "buyer to pay $50,000 down and obtain a loan for the balance," would likely render the contract unenforceable. The nature of all loans has to be fully and completely stated, including the source, time for obtaining the loan, its exact amount, terms of repayment, interest rate, term, and other conditions of the loan. Other factors, such as prepayment provisions, loan fees, points, assumption fees, special FHA or VA (Veterans Administration) clauses, and similar provisions, should also be noted.

Recognizing the difficulty brokers had drafting the financing section, CAR included a series of clauses designed to prompt and guide in the drafting of this part of the deposit receipt. It presents a boilerplate checklist approach, in which the agent or principals fill in the blanks under the appropriate type of financing. Because this section is so important, this text covers each subparagraph.

(4) Finance—Initial Deposit

Initial Deposit

The *Initial Deposit* subparagraph covers the amount of the deposit and how it will be handled. All California brokers are required to specify the form of the deposit. It is the author's opinion that whenever a personal check is accepted the words "subject to collection" should be inserted. If the check is to be held uncashed by the broker, the deposit receipt must so indicate. The 2010 CAR form authorizes the licensee to hold the deposit for up to three days after acceptance before depositing the check into escrow or the broker's trust account (whichever box is checked). Without this wording, the deposit must be deposited or delivered to the named payee by the next business day. If a promissory note is used as the deposit, a notation must be added to the form. It might read "_____–day unsecured promissory note payable to the sellers in the amount of $_____." Promissory notes can create problems of collection and adequacy of consideration in the event of default; therefore, they should be avoided if possible.

Amount of Deposit

Although determination of the amount of the deposit involves significant psychological factors, the amount has added significance in contracts where the liquidated damages equal the amount of the deposit. (See Chapter 4 for the validity of liquidated damages and for rules on retention of deposits over and under 3 percent of the total purchase price.)

Title to Deposit

Whatever the form of the deposit, until the deposit receipt is signed by the seller, forming a contract, the ownership of the deposit and the right to revoke the offer lie with the buyer. *Sarten v. Pomatto (1961) 192 C.A.2d 28.*

Accepting Postdated Checks

A broker accepting a postdated check for the deposit must so indicate on the deposit receipt. If the box indicating the deposit is evidenced by check is marked, there is a misrepresentation of a material fact, for which the broker may be sued. A postdated check is equivalent to a promissory note. *Wilson v. Lewis (1980) 106 C.A.3d 802.*

Management of Deposits

A broker who accepts a deposit with the buyer's offer must manage those funds in accordance with the specific requirements of the real estate commissioner. The deposit receipt states that the deposit, presumably a check, will be held uncashed until the contract is accepted. Then the CAR deposit receipt provides that it must be deposited within three business days to the escrow holder, the broker's trust account, or as otherwise provided.

Often different deposit receipts contain specific instructions or they are silent on provisions for handling the buyer's deposit. Absent specific directions, such as included in this CAR deposit receipt, all funds that are not a check must be placed in the broker's trustee account by the next business day. If the deposit is a check, the broker may hold it uncashed until acceptance of the offer if (1) the check is not negotiable by the broker or if the deposit receipt authorizes the broker to hold the check uncashed and (2) prior to acceptance, the seller is told that the check is being held uncashed. By the next business day after the offer is accepted, the check must be deposited in escrow or a broker's trustee account or given to the seller. However, under written instructions from the seller, the broker may continue to hold the check uncashed pursuant to those instructions. *Regs. 2832.*

(5) Finance—Increased Deposit

Often, the contract provides that the buyers are to increase the deposit after a specified period. Frequently, the increase coincides with the expiration of the contingency period, when the contract becomes unconditional. The balance of the down payment is to be deposited in escrow or a broker's trust account as required by the deposit receipt.

If the contract contains a liquidated damages provision, then the liquidated damages clause must again be reinitialed at the time that the deposit is increased. If the parties fail to reexecute the clause, then the increased portion of the deposit is not available as liquidated damages. If the sellers suddenly find themselves covered by less deposit than imagined, they often look to the broker to cover the difference. Therefore, the broker would be well advised to have the parties reexecute the liquidated damages clause when the deposit is increased. One example of such a form is Figure 5.2 by CAR entitled Receipt for Increased Deposit/Liquidated Damages.

(6) Finance—First Loan

This version of the CAR form assumes (the most common scenario) that the first loan is a new loan from a lender other than the seller.

The other lines specify the terms of the loan. If the buyer will only accept loans without prepayment penalties, the monthly amount should be $_____ "or more." By specifying the maximum interest rate, the buyer is protected in case interest rates spike upward during the contingency period. If rates rise above the specified amount, the buyer is not obligated to proceed with the sale (or the buyer could then try to renegotiate the terms of the sale with the seller).

(7) Finance—Additional Financing Terms

This subparagraph lets the parties write in any additional terms relating to financing. If a different type of loan is intended, it must be explained in detail in other provisions of the deposit receipt or in an attachment. For example, the buyer may be assuming the existing first

FIGURE 5.2 CAR receipt for increased deposit.

CALIFORNIA ASSOCIATION OF REALTORS®

RECEIPT FOR INCREASED DEPOSIT/LIQUIDATED DAMAGES
(C.A.R. Form RID, 7/97)

This Receipt for Increased Deposit relates to the ☐ California Residential Purchase Agreement, or ☐ _____
_____ ("Agreement"), dated _____
on property known as _____ ("Property"),
in which _____ is referred to as Buyer
and _____ is referred to as Seller.
By depositing the sum of _____
Dollars ($ _____) by ☐ cash, ☐ cashier's check, ☐ personal check, or ☐ _____ ,
payable to _____ , Buyer hereby increases the total deposit to
_____ Dollars ($ _____).
Receipt for additional deposit is acknowledged on (Date) _____
Real Estate Broker _____ By _____

THE FOLLOWING LIQUIDATED DAMAGES PROVISION IS HEREBY INCORPORATED IN AND MADE A PART OF THE AGREEMENT.

If Buyer fails to complete this purchase because of Buyer's default, Seller shall retain, as liquidated damages, the deposit actually paid. If the Property is a dwelling with no more than four units, one of which Buyer intends to occupy, then the amount retained shall be no more than 3% of the purchase price. Any excess shall be returned to Buyer. Release of funds will require mutual, Signed release instructions from both Buyer and Seller, judicial decision or arbitration award.

The undersigned have read and acknowledge receipt of a copy of this agreement.

Date _____   Date _____

BUYER _____   SELLER _____

BUYER _____   SELLER _____

SURE TRAC
The System for Success®

Published and Distributed by:
REAL ESTATE BUSINESS SERVICES, INC.
a subsidiary of the California Association of REALTORS®
525 South Virgil Avenue, Los Angeles, California 90020

Reviewed by _____ Date _____   EQUAL HOUSING OPPORTUNITY

RID 7/97 (PAGE 1 OF 1) Print Date

RECEIPT FOR INCREASED DEPOSIT/LIQUIDATED DAMAGES (RID PAGE 1 OF 1)

Source: Reprinted with permission, *California Association of REALTORS®*. Endorsement not implied.

deed of trust, or the seller may be extending a loan to the buyer. The terms of any second loan should be discussed with the same degree of specificity as the first loan. If a special type of financing is involved, such as a wraparound deed of trust, the author suggests that an attachment should be used and that an attorney should probably draft the document. Because the space is small, usually the parties just refer to an attachment, which is "attached to this document as if set out in full," in this space. If seller financing or secondary financing is involved, the parties can attach and use the designated CAR attachments for that purpose.

(8) Finance—Balance and Total Purchase Price

This subparagraph is merely the total of the amounts needed to equal the purchase and not stated elsewhere on this form. By law, the escrow holder must have fully negotiable funds. This means that the day before closing the funds must either be paid by a wire transfer or a California bank's cashier's check. Personal checks must normally be placed in escrow a least three days before closing (up to six days if drawn on out-of-state banks).

Total Purchase Price

This is merely the sum of all the above subparagraphs relating to price. It refers only to the amount paid for the property exclusive of closing costs and loan fees.

(9) Finance—Verification of Down Payment and Closing Costs

This subparagraph sets forth the number of days that the seller has to verify that the buyer does, in fact, have the amount of the deposit and down payment. The major reason for this clause is to allow the seller to be reasonably satisfied that the buyer is presumably qualified. Naturally, if the buyer ultimately breaches the contract the seller can sue. This early warning helps the seller put the property back on the market early if the buyer does not appear qualified.

(10) Finance—Loan Applications

This clause provides the seller seven days (or such days as are stated) to obtain a letter from a lender or mortgage broker that the buyer is prequalified or preapproved for a loan. The clause is commonly misunderstood. It is not a waiver of the financing contingency (meaning if the buyer still cannot obtain the loan within the contingency period stated in another paragraph below the buyer can still cancel the

TABLE 5.1 Types of loan approvals.

	Prequalification	Preapproved	Loan Commitment
Nature	Informal procedure. Lender does not question the validity of any financial information. No credit report done. Some lenders will issue based on information given over the phone.	Formal process. Buyer submits a full written loan application, with supporting data verifying all income and expenses. The lender conducts an independent credit check and verifies the financial data.	Formal process. Besides the formal material for "preapproval" of the buyer, the property is also appraised and evaluated.
Purpose	Letter basically states that the lender "might" make a loan on the stated terms if the property and the borrower check out.	Lender approves the buyer for a specific loan of the stated amount, provided the property appraises correctly and there is a clear title report.	Lender approves both the buyer and the property for the specific loan.
Enforceability	Totally nonbinding on either party. Buyer can go elsewhere. Lender not obligated to make the loan.	Usually, the approval is for a limited time; assumes that there is no change in interest rates and that the property is acceptable.	Usually, without consideration, (e.g., 1/4%) the lender is not obligated to make the loan.
Notes		Preapproval from mortgage companies is of limited value. To be binding, it needs to come from the actual lender who will be making the loan.	Usually, in residential purchases, the lender will honor the loan commitment unless there has been a change in interest rates.

contract). Rather, this clause is merely what some attorneys call a "feel good" letter indicating that the buyer likely has a chance of obtaining a loan. Many buyers and sellers, and even some brokers, confuse prequalification, preapproval and loan commitment, and the enforceability of each. (See Table 5.1.)

(11) Loan Contingency

This paragraph *Loan Terms* states that the buyer's obligation to purchase the property is subject to and conditioned on obtaining the loans specified in the Loans subparagraphs. Provided the buyer acts diligently and in good faith, there is no obligation to purchase the property if the buyer is unable to obtain the desired loan within the specified period.

This subparagraph goes on to state that the deposit, down payment, and closing costs are an obligation of the buyer that is not subject to a contingency. Sometimes the buyer will not have funds for the down payment unless a certain event happens, such as the sale of a currently owned property. In such cases, the payment of the down payment should be made a contingency.

(12) Loan Terms—Contingency Removal

This *Loan Contingency Removal* subparagraph requires the drafter to accept the default time period (17 days) or to state a time to indicate how long the financing contingency remains in effect. Alternatively, they can check a box so that the contingency remains alive and unsatisfied until basically the close of escrow.

If the buyer does not give the loan within the stated time or waive the financing contingency, then the seller may terminate the contract. The provisions of this paragraph control this financing provision, and are not dependent upon the general contingency removal process of contained later in this agreement.

If the buyer waives the contingency and then, for whatever reason, is unable to ultimately obtain financing, the buyer has breached the contract. The buyer can be sued for damages, or more commonly, lose the security deposit. (See Chapter 4 for the validity of liquidated damages and for rules on retention of deposits over and under 3 percent of the total purchase price.)

(13) Loan Terms—No Loan Contingency

This clause means that the buyer is obligated to make the purchase regardless of whether or not the lender will fund the loan. If the interest rates spike and the buyer no longer qualifies for the loan, the buyer is not relieved of the obligation to purchase the property. Without a loan, the buyer would normally be in breach of contract and probably lose the deposit as liquidated damages. This clause is also used if the buyer is paying all cash, because a loan would not be involved.

(14) Finance—Appraisal Contingency and Removal

If this box is checked and the lender's appraisal of the property is less than the amount of the purchase price, the buyer has the option of canceling the contract. Appraisers for lending institutions tend to be on the conservative side. It is not uncommon for an appraisal to be less than the purchase price. Because the buyer is usually responsible for paying all amounts over the appraised value, this clause may save the buyer a serious additional cash amount.

If the buyer is seeking an 80 percent loan on a $500,000 property, the buyer would need $100,000 down. However, if the property only appraised at $480,000, then the 80 percent loan would only be 384,000. In such a situation, the buyer would need $116,000 (20 percent of $384,000) plus $16,000 (100 percent of the amount over the appraised value). In other words, the buyer would need an extra $16,000 down payment.

(15) Finance—All Cash Offer

In the event of an all cash offer, this paragraph requires the buyer to verify that there are or will be sufficient funds to complete the purchase. This reduces the risk of the seller tying up property with an unqualified buyer.

(16) Finance—Buyer Stated Financing

In the event the buyer seeks different financing that specified under "Loans" in this agreement, the seller is not obligated to assist buyer in obtaining that financing. For this reason, it is important to be specific and carefully stated under "Loans" exactly what type of loans the buyer will be seeking. If the buyer does not obtain the desired financing as stated, and does not elect to terminate this contract under the loan contingency agreement, the buyer may be liable for breach of contract if the alternate financing does not materialize.

(17) Allocation of Costs—Introduction

Introductory Paragraph

This section determines who will pay for any reports, inspections, or services. The introductory paragraph refers only to costs of the reports themselves, not to any corrective work recommended by such reports. If no boxes are checked, then by reference to another section in this document, the buyer must pay for any desired reports and inspections. Any results are given to the seller, who has no obligation to take any action. In other words, after ascertaining the findings, the contract is open to negotiation.

Most commonly, the allocation of costs is determined by local county custom. The custom of each county may vary. For example, in one county it may be general practice for the seller to pay for title insurance, whereas in another county the responsibility is traditionally the responsibility of the buyer. However, a contract is a document of negotiation, and the parties are free to agree to any allocation they desire.

Special Situation Because Property Sold "As Is"

In the author's opinion, these paragraphs should also include who will pay for any corrective work recommended by such reports. However, as was explained earlier, the CAR form has the property being sold "as is." As such, unless special boxes are checked in the form, there is normally no actual obligation on the part of the seller to correct most observable defects, and this burden falls to the buyer.

(18) Wood Destroying Pest Inspection

Who Pays for the Report?

Who pays for the pest control report may be of importance to the buyer. Some companies have included wording in their report and agreement that the report is only to be used for the party that ordered it. As to these specific companies, if the seller paid for the report, could the buyer later sue for negligence? To the author's knowledge, this question has not been definitely answered by the courts.

Who Pays for the Work?

Depending on which boxes are checked, the parties have the option of negotiating what work will be done or of having the specified buyer and/or seller paying for the work regardless of amount. By checking boxes, the designated party can incorporate a CAR pest control form that details who will pay for corrective work.

When an allocation of work is recommended, it is common to differentiate between the so-called Section 1 work and Section 2 work. Most reports divide the recommended work between existing, evident infestation (Section 1) and potential, future infestation (Section 2). The repair work recommended under each section can be negotiated separately. Because there is no requirement that the work be completed before close of escrow, the funds for corrective work could be left in escrow. Many lenders require a certificate of noninfestation before close of escrow, and in such cases the clause would have to be modified.

If no box is checked in the introductory paragraph, then the buyer can accept the report, reject it and allow the seller to pay for the work, or face potential termination of the contract. Facing termination of the deposit receipt, the parties then seek to negotiate who will pay for what work. If there can be no agreement, then the purchase contract can be terminated as provided within that paragraph.

In the author's opinion, it is seldom in the best interests of the buyer to agree to pay for the Section 1 and Section 2 work without first having some idea of the cost and extensiveness of such work. If buyers are going to obligate themselves to paying the costs before knowing the nature of the work needed, they should agree to a cap. The clause might read "buyer to pay for all corrective work recommended in Class 1 of the Report up to $5,000. All work required in excess of $5,000 shall be paid by the seller."

Author's Comments on Termite Work

Structural pest control deficiencies, work, and certification are some of the most troublesome areas in the sale of residential property. The pest control certificate assures the buyer that the structure is not infested by termites, plagued by dry rot, or infected with other fungus organisms. The buyer can demand as a condition to the purchase and the close of escrow that the seller furnish a structural pest control certification from a licensed pest control operator. Such certification is necessary because neither the deed nor the deposit receipt contains any implied warranties against such conditions.

Many real estate companies modify the CAR form to incorporate different provisions for the pest control clause. Frequently, it is appropriate to provide that the parties will share the cost of all recommended work or that they will share the cost over and above a specific dollar limit. Other times, it may be appropriate to provide that the seller has the option of doing any work, and if he or she elects not to do the work, then the buyer can either elect to pay for the work or cancel the contract. There are many possible options and solutions to the termite problem, and the CAR clause should not be used without first analyzing it to see if it is, in fact, appropriate for the prevalent situation.

(19) Other Inspections and Reports

One need only look at the litigation to realize that too often buyers fail to conduct adequate investigation into the property. For example, the CAR document, under the wood destroying pest inspection section states that such report shall specifically exclude the roof. It is the author's opinion that a buyer should almost always insist on a roof inspection.

Sewer, septic, and wells generate substantial litigation between residential parties. Often, these clauses and the matter to which they refer seem unimportant until something goes wrong, which is until after close of escrow. The costs to remedy such problems can be very expensive, so the parties would be well advised to give these matters careful consideration.

The buyer needs to thoroughly investigate the property. For example, a permit report is often advisable. If a separate unit, such as a mother-in-law unit or a room addition has been added, it is advisable to check the planning and building departments to determine that all permits have been obtained. Otherwise, a new owner may find that when new work is planned, a city or county could require substantial work or even demolition of certain structures before they will consider issuing any new permits or approvals. Permit reports are only one example of the many types of reports that might be appropriate.

Still, care must be taken to insure that any contingencies are subject to an objective standard of some sort. In one case, the court held that a purchase contract giving the buyer the right to conduct tests and to have "absolute and sole discretion" to purchase the contract during a certain time period of investigation, was not a contract but an unenforceable, invalid option. *Steiner v. Thexton (2008) 163 CA4th 359.*

The CAR has developed an excellent explanatory form for both buyers and sellers explaining the need for disclosure, inspection, and investigation. Using a form such as the Statewide Buyer and Seller Advisory from CAR makes it harder for a party to claim that they were unaware of the need for full disclosure and independent inspections and, in theory, lessens the likelihood of litigation. See Figure 5.3.

(20) Government Requirements and Retrofits

Smoke detectors and water heater bracing are required by law before there can be a transfer of title. This paragraph specifies who shall pay for such reports and work. The second part of the clause deals with retrofit equipment, such as low-flow toilets, special shower heads, weather stripping, or tempered glass. Some properties must be upgraded to meet earthquake retrofit standards. In some homes, such retrofitting can be quite expensive, and the parties may wish to negotiate a cap on the expenses, and should be considered carefully before just checking a box on the allocation of costs.

(21) Escrow and Title

Payment of Escrow Fees

How and who pays the escrow fees is a matter for negotiation between the parties. Many brokers suggest following the "custom" of the county in which the property is located. For example, in the San Francisco Bay area, the buyer typically pays the entire escrow fees in Alameda, San Francisco, and Marin counties. In Santa Clara County,

FIGURE 5.3   CAR statewide buyer and seller advisory.

CALIFORNIA
ASSOCIATION
OF REALTORS®

STATEWIDE BUYER AND SELLER ADVISORY
(This Form Does Not Replace Local Condition Disclosures.
Additional Addenda May Be Attached to This Advisory. See Paragraph 44)
(C.A.R. Form SBSA, Revised 4/07)

Property Address: _____ ("Property").

BUYER RIGHTS AND DUTIES:
- The physical condition of the land and improvements being purchased are not guaranteed by Seller or Brokers.
- You should conduct thorough investigations of the Property personally and with appropriate professionals.
- If professionals recommend further inspections, you should contact qualified experts to conduct such inspections.
- You should retain your own professional even if Seller or Broker has provided you with existing reports.
- You should read all written reports given to you and discuss those reports with the persons who prepared them.
- Your have the right to request that the Seller make repairs, corrections or take other actions based on inspections or disclosures.
- If the Seller is unwilling or unable to satisfy your requests, and you act within certain time periods, you may have the right to cancel the agreement. If you cancel outside these periods, you may be in breach of contract.
- The terms of the purchase agreement and any counter offers and addenda establish your rights and responsibilities.
YOU ARE STRONGLY ADVISED TO INVESTIGATE THE CONDITION AND SUITABILITY OF ALL ASPECTS OF THE PROPERTY. IF YOU DO NOT DO SO, YOU ARE ACTING AGAINST THE ADVICE OF BROKERS.

SELLER RIGHTS AND DUTIES:
- You have a duty to disclose material facts known to you that affect the value or desirability of the Property.
- You are obligated to make the Property available to the Buyer for inspections allowed by the contract.
- This form is not a substitute for completing a Real Estate Transfer Disclosure Statement, if required, and any other property-specific questionnaire or disclosure.
- The terms of the Purchase Agreement and any Counter Offers and Addenda establish your rights and responsibilities.

BROKER RIGHTS AND DUTIES:
- Brokers do not have expertise in all areas and matters affecting the Property or your evaluation of it.
- For most sales of residential properties with no more than four units, Brokers have a duty to make a reasonably competent and diligent visual inspection of the accessible areas of the Property and disclose to you material facts or defects that the inspection reveals.
- Many defects and conditions may not be discoverable by a Broker's visual inspection.
- If Broker gives a referral to another professional, Broker does not guarantee that person's performance. You may select any professional of your own choosing.
- Any written agreement between Broker and Buyer or Seller establishes the rights and responsibilities of those parties.

1. INSPECTIONS: Buyer and Seller are advised that Buyer has the right to obtain various inspections of the Property under most residential purchase agreements. Buyer is advised to have the Property inspected by a professional property inspection service within Buyer's inspection contingency period. A licensed building contractor or other professional may perform these services. The inspector generally does not look behind walls or under carpets, or take equipment apart. Certain items on the Property, such as chimneys and spark arresters, plumbing, heating, air conditioning, electrical wiring, pool and spa, septic system, well, roof, foundation and structural items may need to be inspected by another professional, such as a chimney sweep, plumber, electrician, pool and spa service, septic or well company or roofer. A general physical inspection typically will not test for mold, wood destroying pests, lead-based paint, radon, asbestos and other environmental hazards, geologic conditions, age, remaining useful life or water-tightness of roof, cracks, leaks or operational problems associated with a pool or spa or connection of the Property to a sewer system. If Buyer wants further information on any aspect of the Property, Broker recommends that Buyer have a discussion with the professional property inspector and that Buyer hire an appropriate professional for the area of concern to Buyer. Brokers do not have expertise in these areas. Brokers do not verify the results of any such inspection or guarantee the performance of any such inspector or service. Any election by Buyer to waive the right to a physical inspection of the Property or to rely on somebody other than an appropriate professional is against the advice of Brokers. Not all inspectors are licensed and licenses are not available for all types of inspection activities.

SBSA REVISED 4/07 (PAGE 1 OF 10) Print Date

Buyer's Initials (_____)(_____)
Seller's Initials (_____)(_____)

Reviewed by _____ Date _____

EQUAL HOUSING
OPPORTUNITY

STATEWIDE BUYER AND SELLER ADVISORY (SBSA PAGE 1 OF 10)

Source: Reprinted with permission, *California Association of REALTORS®.* Endorsement not implied.

FIGURE 5.3 *(Continued)*.

Property Address: _____ Date: _____

2. SQUARE FOOTAGE, LOT SIZE AND BOUNDARIES: Buyer and Seller are advised that only an appraiser or land surveyor, as applicable, can reliably confirm square footage, lot size, Property corners and exact boundaries of the Property. Representations regarding these items that are made in a Multiple Listing Service, advertisements, and from property tax assessor records are often approximations, or based upon inaccurate or incomplete records. Fences, hedges, walls or other barriers may not represent actual boundary lines. Brokers have not verified any such representations. Brokers do not have expertise in this area. If Buyer wants information about the exact square footage, lot size or location of Property corners or boundaries, Broker recommends that Buyer hire an appraiser or licensed surveyor to investigate these matters during Buyer's inspection contingency period.

3. SOIL AND GEOLOGIC CONDITIONS: Buyer and Seller are advised that real estate in California is subject to settling, slippage, contraction, expansion, subsidence, earthquakes and other land movement. The Property may be constructed on fill or improperly compacted soil and may have inadequate drainage capability. Any of these matters can cause structural problems to improvements on the Property. Civil or geo-technical engineers are best suited to evaluate soil stability, grading, drainage and other soil conditions. Additionally, the Property may have known or unknown mines, mills, caves or wells. Brokers do not have expertise in this area. If Buyer wants further information, Broker recommends that Buyer hire an appropriate professional. Not all inspectors are licensed and licenses are not available for all types of inspections.

4. GEOLOGIC HAZARDS: Buyer and Seller are advised that California has experienced earthquakes in the past, and there is always a potential of future earthquakes. Damage caused by an earthquake may not be discoverable by Buyer's or Broker's visual inspection. Inspection by a licensed, qualified professional is strongly recommended to determine the structural integrity and safety of all structures and improvements on the Property. If the Property is a condominium, or located in a planned unit development or in a common interest subdivision, Buyer is advised to contact the homeowners association about earthquake repairs and retrofit work and the possibility of an increased or special assessment to defray the costs of earthquake repairs or retrofit work. Buyer is encouraged to obtain and read the booklet entitled "The Homeowners Guide to Earthquake Safety." In most cases a questionnaire within the booklet must be completed by Seller and the entire booklet given to the Buyer if the Property was built prior to 1960. If the Property was built before 1975, and contains structures constructed of masonry or precast (tilt up) concrete walls, with wood frame floors or roof, or if the building has unreinforced masonry walls, then Seller must provide Buyer a pamphlet entitled "The Commercial Property Owner's Guide to Earthquake Safety." Many areas have a wide range of geologic problems and numerous studies have been made of these conditions. Some of this information is available for public review at city and county planning departments. Buyer is encouraged to review the public maps and reports and/or obtain a geologist's inspection report. Brokers do not have expertise in this area. Buyer may be able to obtain earthquake insurance to protect their interest in the Property. Sellers who agree to provide financing should also consider requiring Buyers to obtain such insurance.

5. ENVIRONMENTAL HAZARDS: Buyer and Seller are advised that the presence of certain kinds of organisms, toxins and contaminants, including, but not limited to, mold (airborne, toxic or otherwise), fungi, mildew, lead-based paint and other lead contamination, asbestos, formaldehyde, radon, methane, other gases, fuel oil or chemical storage tanks, contaminated soil or water, hazardous waste, waste disposal sites, electromagnetic fields, nuclear sources, urea formaldehyde, or other materials may adversely affect the Property and the health of individuals who live on or work at the property as well as pets. If Buyer wants further information, Buyer is advised and Broker recommends that Buyer have the Property inspected for the existence of such conditions and organisms, and conditions that may lead to their formation. Not all inspectors are licensed and licenses are not available for all types of inspection activities. Buyer is also advised to consult with appropriate experts regarding this topic during Buyer's inspection contingency period. Brokers do not have expertise in this area. Broker recommends that Buyer and Seller read the booklets titled, "Residential Environmental Hazards: A Guide for Homeowners, Homebuyers, Landlords and Tenants," and "Protect Your Family From Lead In Your Home."

6. MOLD: Buyer and Seller are advised that the presence of certain kinds of mold, fungi, mildew and other organisms, sometimes referred to as "toxic mold" (collectively "Mold") may adversely affect the Property and the health of individuals who live on or work at the Property as well as pets. Mold does not affect all people the same way, and may not affect some people at all. Mold may be caused by water leaks or other sources of moisture such as, but not limited to, flooding, and leaks in windows, pipes and roof. Seller is advised to disclose the existence of any such conditions of which he or she is aware. Buyer should carefully review all of Seller's disclosures for any indication that any of these conditions exist. It is, however, possible that Mold may be hidden and that Seller is completely unaware of its existence. In addition, Mold is often undetectable from a visual inspection, a professional property inspection and even a structural pest control inspection. Brokers do not have expertise in this area. If Buyer wants further information, Broker recommends that Buyer have the Property tested for Mold by an environmental hygienist or other appropriate professional during Buyer's inspection contingency period. Not all inspectors are licensed and licenses are not available for all types of inspection activities.

Buyer's Initials (_____)(_____)
Seller's Initials (_____)(_____)

SBSA REVISED 4/07 (PAGE 2 OF 10)

Reviewed by _____ Date _____

EQUAL HOUSING OPPORTUNITY

STATEWIDE BUYER AND SELLER ADVISORY (SBSA PAGE 2 OF 10)

FIGURE 5.3 (*Continued*).

Property Address: _____ Date: _____

7. WATER INTRUSION: Buyer and Seller are advised that many homes suffer from water intrusion or leakage. The causes of water intrusion are varied, and can include defective construction, faulty grading, deterioration of building materials and absence of waterproof barriers. Water intrusion can cause serious damage to the Property. This damage can consist of wood rot, mold, mildew and even damage to the structural integrity of the Property. The cost of repairing and remediating water intrusion damage and its causes can be very significant. The existence and cause of water intrusion is often difficult to detect. Because you, your Broker or a general home inspector cannot visually observe any effects of water intrusion, Buyer and Seller should not assume that such intrusion does not exist. Broker recommends that Buyer have the Property inspected for water intrusion by an appropriate professional. Brokers do not have expertise in this area.

8. SEPTIC SYSTEM(S): Buyer and Seller are advised that a property may be served by one or more septic systems even though adjoining properties are connected to a sewer line. Buyer and Seller are also advised that some septic tanks and systems may have been abandoned or have leaked into ground water sources. Buyer is advised to contact the appropriate government agency to verify that the Property is connected to a sewer or served by a septic system. If the Property is served by a septic system it may consist of a septic tank, cesspool, pits, leach lines or a combination of such mechanisms ("collectively, System"). No representation or warranty is made by Seller or Broker concerning the condition, operability, size, capacity or future expansion of a System, nor whether a System is adequate for use by the intended occupants of the Property. A change in the number of occupants or the quantity, composition or methods of depositing waste may affect the efficiency of the System. In addition, the amount of rainfall and ground water table may also affect the efficiency of the System. Many factors including, but not limited to, natural forces, age, deterioration of materials and the load imposed on a System can cause the System to fail at any time. Broker recommends that Buyer obtain an independent evaluation of any System by a qualified sanitation professional during Buyer's inspection contingency period. Brokers do not have expertise in this area. Buyer should consult with their sanitation professional to determine if their report includes the tank only, or other additional components of the System such as pits and leach fields. Not all inspectors are licensed and licenses are not available for all types of inspection activities. In some cases, Buyer's lender as well as local government agencies may require System inspection. System-related maintenance costs may include, but not be limited to, locating, pumping or providing outlets to ground level. Brokers are unable to advise Buyer or Seller regarding System-related issues or associated costs, which may be significant. If Buyer and Seller agree to obtain a System inspection, Buyer and Seller are cautioned that the inspection cost may include, but not be limited to, the costs of locating, pumping or providing outlets to ground level.

9. WELL AND WATER SYSTEM(S): Buyer and Seller are advised that the Property may be served by one or more water wells, springs, or private community or public water systems. Any of these private or public water systems may contain bacteria, chemicals, minerals and metals, such as chromium. Well(s) may have been abandoned on the Property. Buyer is advised to have both the quality and the quantity of water evaluated, and to obtain an analysis of the quality of any domestic and agricultural water in use, or to be used at the Property, from whatever source. Water quality tests can include not only tests for bacteria, such as coliform, but also tests for organic and inorganic chemicals, metals, mineral content and gross alpha testing for radioactivity. Broker recommends that Buyer consult with a licensed, qualified well and pump company and local government agency to determine whether any well/spring or water system will adequately serve Buyer's intended use and that Buyer have a well consultant perform an extended well output test for this purpose. Water well or spring capacity, quantity output and quality may change at any time. There are no guarantees as to the future water quality, quantity or duration of any well or spring. If Buyer wants further information, Broker recommends that Buyer obtain an inspection of the condition, age, adequacy and performance of all components of the well/spring and any water system during Buyer's inspection contingency period. Brokers do not have expertise in this area.

10. WOOD DESTROYING PESTS: Buyer and Seller are advised that the presence of, or conditions likely to lead to the presence of, or other infestation or infection of wood destroying pests and organisms may adversely affect the Property. Inspection reports covering these items can be separated into two sections: Section 1 identifies areas where infestation or infection is evident. Section 2 identifies areas where there are conditions likely to lead to infestation or infection. Brokers do not have expertise in this area. If Buyer wants further information, Buyer is advised and Broker recommends that Buyer have the Property inspected for the existence of such conditions and organisms, and conditions that may lead to their formation by a registered structural pest control company during Buyer's inspection contingency period.

11. EASEMENTS, ACCESS AND ENCROACHMENTS: Buyer and Seller are advised that confirming the exact location of easements, shared or private driveways or roadways, and encroachments on or to the Property may be possible only by conducting a survey. There may be unrecorded easements, access rights, encroachments and other agreements affecting the Property that may not be disclosed by a survey. Representations regarding these items that are made in a Multiple Listing Service, advertisements, or plotted by a title company are often approximations, or based upon inaccurate or incomplete records. Brokers have not verified any such representations. If Buyer wants further information Buyer is advised and Broker recommends that Buyer hire a licensed surveyor during Buyer's inspection contingency period. Brokers do not have expertise in this area.

Buyer's Initials (_____)(_____)
Seller's Initials (_____)(_____)

| Reviewed by _____ Date _____ |

SBSA REVISED 4/07 (PAGE 3 OF 10)

STATEWIDE BUYER AND SELLER ADVISORY (SBSA PAGE 3 OF 10)

FIGURE 5.3 (*Continued*).

Property Address: _____ Date: _____

12. EARTHQUAKE FAULT ZONES AND SEISMIC HAZARD ZONES: Buyer and Seller are advised that California Public Resources Code Sections 2622 and 2696 require the delineation and mapping of "Earthquake Fault Zones" along known active faults and "Seismic Hazard Zones" in California. Affected cities and counties must regulate certain development projects within these zones. Construction or development on affected properties may be subject to the findings of a geological report prepared by a registered California geologist. Generally, Seller must disclose if the Property is in such a zone and can use a research company to aid in the process. If Buyer wants further information, Broker recommends that, during Buyer's inspection contingency period, Buyer make independent inquiries with such research companies or with appropriate government agencies concerning the use and improvement of the Property. Brokers do not have expertise in this area. Buyer is advised that there is a potential for earthquakes and seismic hazards even outside designated zones.

13. FIRE HAZARDS: Buyer and Seller are advised that fires annually cause the destruction of thousands of homes. Due to varied climate and topography, certain areas have higher risks of fires than others. Certain types of materials used in home construction create a greater risk of fire than others. If the Property is located within a State Fire Responsibility Area or a Very High Fire Hazard Zone, generally Seller must disclose that fact to Buyer under California Public Resources Code Section 4136 and California Government Code Sections 51178 and 51183.5, and may use a research company to aid in the process. If Buyer wants further information, Broker recommends that, during Buyer's inspection contingency period, Buyer contact the local fire department and Buyer's insurance agent regarding the risk of fire. Brokers do not have expertise in this area. Buyer is advised that there is a potential for fires even outside designated zones.

14. FLOOD HAZARDS: Buyer and Seller are advised that if the Property is located within a Special Flood Hazard Area, as designated by the Federal Emergency Management Agency, or an area of Potential Flooding pursuant to California Government Code Section 8589.3, generally Seller must disclose this fact to Buyer and may use a research company to aid in the process. The National Flood Insurance Program was established to identify all flood plain areas and establish flood-risk zones within those areas. The program mandates flood insurance for properties within high-risk zones if loans are obtained from a federally-regulated financial institution or are insured by any agency of the United States Government. The extent of coverage and costs may vary. If Buyer wants further information, Broker recommends that Buyer consult his or her lender and/or insurance agent during Buyer's inspection contingency period. Brokers do not have expertise in this area. Buyer is advised that there is a potential for flooding even outside designated zones.

15. BUILDING PERMITS, ZONING AND CODE COMPLIANCE: Buyer and Seller are advised that any structure on the Property, including the original structure and any addition, modification, remodel or improvement may have been built without permits, not according to building codes, or in violation of zoning laws. Further, even if such structure was built according to the then-existing code or zoning requirement, it may not be in compliance with current building standards or local zoning. It is also possible that local law may not permit structures that now exist to be rebuilt in the event of damage or destruction. Buyer is advised to check with appropriate government agencies or third party professionals to verify permits and legal requirements and the effect of such requirements on current and future use of the Property, its development and size. If Buyer wants further information Broker recommends that Buyer discuss the issue with an appropriate professional during Buyer's inspection contingency period. Brokers do not have expertise in this area.

16. VIEWS: Buyer and Seller are advised that present views from the Property may be affected by future development or growth of trees and vegetation on adjacent properties and any other property within the line of sight of the Property. Broker makes no representation regarding the preservation of existing views. If Buyer wants further information, Broker recommends that Buyer review Covenants, Conditions and Restrictions, if any, and contact neighboring property owners, government agencies and homeowner associations, if any, during Buyer's inspection contingency period. Brokers do not have expertise in this area.

17. FUTURE REPAIRS, REPLACEMENTS AND REMODELS: Buyer and Seller are advised that replacement or repairs of certain systems or remodels of portions of the Property may trigger requirements that homeowners comply with laws and regulations that either come into effect after Close of Escrow or are not required to be complied with until the replacement, repair or remodel has occurred. Permit or code requirements or building standards may change after Close of Escrow, resulting in increasing costs to repair existing features. In particular, changes to state and federal energy efficiency regulations impact the installation, replacement and some repairs of heating and air conditioning units (HVAC). Federal regulations now require manufacturers of HVAC units to produce only units meeting a new higher Seasonal Energy Efficiency Rating (SEER). This will likely impact repairs and replacements of existing HVAC units. State regulations now require that when installing or replacing HVAC units, with some exceptions, duct work must be tested for leaks. Duct work leaking more than 15 percent must be repaired to reduce leaks. The average existing duct work typically leaks 30 percent. More information is available at the California Energy Commission's website http://www.energy.ca.gov/title24/changeout. Home warranty policies may not cover such inspections or repairs. If Buyer wants further information Broker recommends that Buyer discuss the issue with an appropriate professional during Buyer's inspection contingency period. Brokers do not have expertise in this area.

18. ERRANT GOLF BALLS: Buyer and Seller are advised that if the Property is located adjacent to or near a golf course there is a possibility that golf balls may damage the Property or injure persons or pets on it. Additionally, persons playing golf may enter the Property to retrieve errant golf balls or for other purposes. Broker recommends that Buyer investigate this possibility during Buyer's inspection contingency period. Brokers do not have expertise in this area.

Buyer's Initials (_____)(_____)
Seller's Initials (_____)(_____)

SBSA REVISED 4/07 (PAGE 4 OF 10)

Reviewed by _____ Date _____

STATEWIDE BUYER AND SELLER ADVISORY (SBSA PAGE 4 OF 10)

FIGURE 5.3 (*Continued*).

Property Address: _____ Date: _____

19. SCHOOLS: Buyer and Seller are advised that children living in the Property may not, for numerous reasons, be permitted to attend the school nearest the Property. Various factors including, but not limited to, open enrollment policies, busing, overcrowding and class size reductions may affect which public school serves the Property. School district boundaries are subject to change. Buyer is advised to verify whether the Property is now, and at the Close of Escrow will be, in the school district Buyer understands it to be in and whether residing in the Property entitles a person to attend any specific school that Buyer is interested in. Broker recommends that Buyer contact the local school or school district for additional information during Buyer's inspection contingency period. Brokers do not have expertise in this area.

20. NEIGHBORHOOD NOISE SOURCES: Buyer and Seller are advised that even if the Property is not in an identified airport noise influence area the Property may still be subject to airplanes and other aircraft, commercial or military or both, flying overhead. Other common sources of noise include traffic on streets and highways, trains and general neighborhood noise from people, dogs and other animals. Noise levels and types of noise that bother one person may be acceptable to others. Buyer is advised to satisfy him/herself with regard to any sources of and amounts of noise at different times of day and night. Brokers do not have expertise in this area.

21. PETS AND ANIMALS: Buyer and Seller are advised that the current or previous owner(s) may have had domesticated or other pets and animals at the Property. Odors from animal urine contamination may be dormant for long periods of time and then become active because of heat, humidity or other factors and may not be eliminated by cleaning or replacing carpets or other cleaning. Pet urine and feces can also damage hardwood floors and other floor coverings. Additionally, an animal may have had fleas, ticks and other pests that remain on the Property after the animal has been removed. If Buyer wants further information, Broker recommends that Buyer discuss the issue with an appropriate professional during Buyer's inspection contingency period. Brokers do not have expertise in this area.

22. SECURITY AND SAFETY: Buyer and Seller are advised that state and local Law may require the installation of barriers, access alarms, self-latching mechanisms and/or other measures to decrease the risk to children and other persons of existing swimming pools and hot tubs, as well as various fire safety and other measures concerning other features of the Property. Compliance requirements differ from city to city and county to county. Unless specifically agreed, the Property may not be in compliance with these requirements. Brokers do not have expertise in this area. If Buyer wants further information, Broker recommends that Buyer contact local government agencies about these restrictions and other requirements.

23. RETROFIT: Buyer and Seller are advised that state and local Law may require the installation of operable smoke detectors, bracing or strapping of water heaters, and completion of a corresponding written statement of compliance that is delivered to Buyer. Some city and county governments may impose additional retrofit standards, including, but not limited to, installing low-flow toilets and showerheads, gas shut-off valves, and tempered glass. Brokers do not have expertise in this area. Broker recommends that Buyer and Seller consult with the appropriate government agencies, inspectors, and other professionals to determine the retrofit standards for the Property, the extent to which the Property complies with such standards, and the costs, if any, of compliance.

24. WATER SHORTAGES AND CONSERVATION: Buyer and Seller are advised that the Property may be located in an area that could experience water shortages. The policies of local water districts and the city or county in which the Property is located can result in the occurrence of any or all of the following: **(i)** limitations on the amount of water available to the Property, **(ii)** restrictions on the use of water, and **(iii)** an increasingly graduated cost per unit of water use, including, but not limited to, penalties for excess usage. For further information, Broker recommends that Buyer contact the supplier of water to the Property regarding the supplier's current or anticipated policies on water usage and to determine the extent to which those policies may affect Buyer's intended use of the Property. If the Property is serviced by a private well, Buyer is advised that drought conditions and/or a low water table may make it necessary to arrange, through a private supplier, for delivery of water to the Property. Buyers should contact water truck companies for the costs involved. Brokers do not have expertise in this area.

25. NEIGHBORHOOD, AREA; PERSONAL FACTORS: Buyer and Seller are advised that the following may affect the Property or Buyer's intended use of it: neighborhood or area conditions, including schools, proximity and adequacy of law enforcement, crime, fire protection, other government services, availability, adequacy and cost of any speed-wired, wireless internet connections or other telecommunications or other technology services and installations, proximity to manufacturing, commercial, industrial, airport or agricultural activities or military ordnance locations, existing and proposed transportation, construction, and development, any other source that may affect noise, view, traffic, or odor, wild and domestic animals, other nuisances, hazards, or circumstances, protected species, wetland properties, botanical diseases, historic or other governmentally-protected sites or improvements, cemeteries, conditions and influences of significance to certain cultures and/or religions, and personal needs, requirements and preferences of Buyer.

Buyer's Initials (_____)(_____)
Seller's Initials (_____)(_____)

Copyright © 2004-2007, CALIFORNIA ASSOCIATION OF REALTORS®, INC.
SBSA REVISED 4/07 (PAGE 5 OF 10)

| Reviewed by _____ Date _____ |

EQUAL HOUSING
OPPORTUNITY

STATEWIDE BUYER AND SELLER ADVISORY (SBSA PAGE 5 OF 10)

FIGURE 5.3 (Continued).

Property Address: _____ Date: _____

26. INSURANCE: Buyer and Seller are advised that Buyer may have difficulty obtaining insurance regarding the Property if there has been a prior insurance claim affecting the Property or made by Buyer but unrelated to the Property. Seller is required by C.A.R. Form RPA to disclose known insurance claims made during the past five years. Sellers may not be aware of claims prior to their ownership. If Buyer wants further information, Broker recommends that, during Buyer's inspection contingency period, Buyer conduct his or her own investigation for past claims. Buyer may need to obtain Seller's consent in order to have access to certain investigation reports. If the Property is a condominium, or is located in a planned unit development or other common interest subdivision, Buyer and Seller are advised to determine if the individual unit is covered by the Homeowner Association Insurance. Broker recommends that Buyer consult Buyer's insurance agents during Buyer's inspection contingency period to determine the need, availability and possibility of securing any and all forms of other insurance or coverage or any conditions imposed by insurer as a requirement of issuing insurance. If Buyer takes possession prior to Close of Escrow or Seller remains in possession after Close of Escrow, whether for a limited or extended period of time, Broker recommends that Buyer and Seller each consult with their own insurance agent regarding insurance or coverage that could protect them in the transaction (including but not limited to: personal property, flood, earthquake, umbrella and renter's). Brokers do not have expertise in this area.

27. CALIFORNIA FAIR PLAN: Buyer and Seller are advised that insurance for certain hillside, oceanfront and brush properties may be available only from the California Fair Plan. This may increase the cost of insurance for such properties and coverage may be limited. Broker recommends that Buyer consult with Buyer's own insurance agent during Buyer's inspection contingency period regarding the availability of coverage under the California Fair Plan and the length of time it may take for processing of a California Fair Plan application. Brokers do not have expertise in this area.

28. HISTORICAL DESIGNATION, COASTAL COMMISSION, ARCHITECTURAL, LANDSCAPE, AGRICULTURAL OR OPEN SPACE AND OTHER RESTRICTIONS ON BUILDINGS OR IMPROVEMENTS: Buyer and Seller are advised that the Property may be: **(i)** designated as a historical landmark, **(ii)** protected by a historical conservancy, **(iii)** subject to an architectural or landscaping review process, **(iv)** within the jurisdiction of the California Coastal Commission or other government agency, or **(v)** subject to a contract preserving use of all or part of the Property for agriculture or open space. If the Property is so designated or within the jurisdiction of any such, or similar, government agency then there may be restrictions on Buyer's ability to develop, remove or trim trees or other landscaping, remodel, make improvements to and build on or rebuild the Property. Broker recommends that Buyer satisfy him/herself during Buyer's inspection contingency period if any of these issues are of concern to Buyer. Brokers do not have expertise in this area.

29. 1915 BOND AND MELLO-ROOS COMMUNITY AND OTHER FACILITIES DISTRICTS: Buyer and Seller are advised that the Property may be subject to an improvement bond assessment under the Improvement Bond Act of 1915 and/or a levy of a special tax pursuant to a Mello-Roos community facilities or other district. Seller is generally required to make a good faith effort to obtain a disclosure notice from any local agency collecting such taxes and deliver such notice to Buyers. Brokers do not have expertise in this area.

30. HOMEOWNER ASSOCIATIONS AND COVENANTS, CONDITIONS AND RESTRICTIONS (CC&Rs): Buyer and Seller are advised that if the Property is a condominium, or located in a planned unit development, or in a common interest subdivision there are typically restrictions on use of the Property and rules that must be followed. Restrictions and rules are commonly found in Declarations of Covenants, Conditions and Restrictions (CC&Rs) and other governing documents. Further there is likely to be a homeowner association (HOA) that has the authority to affect the Property and its use. Whether or not there is a HOA, the Property may still be subject to CC&Rs restricting use of the Property. The HOA typically has the authority to enforce the rules of the association, assess monetary payments (both regular monthly dues and special assessments) to provide for the upkeep and maintenance of the common areas, and enforce the rules and assessment obligations. If you fail to abide by the rules or pay monies owed to the HOA, the HOA may put a lien against your Property. The law requires the Seller to provide the Buyer with the CC&Rs and other governing documents, as well as a copy of the HOA's current financial statement and operating budget, among other documents. Buyer is advised to carefully review all HOA documents provided by Seller and the CC&Rs, if any, and satisfy him/herself regarding the use and restrictions of the Property, the amount of monthly dues and/or assessments, the adequacy of reserves, current and past insurance coverage and claims and the possibility of any legal action that may be taken by or against the HOA. The HOA may not have insurance or may not cover personal property belonging to the owner of the unit in the condominium, common interest or planned unit development. See paragraph 26 for further information regarding insurance. Brokers do not have expertise in this area.

31. COMMUNITY ENHANCEMENT AND PRIVATE TRANSFER FEES: Buyer and Seller are advised that some areas or communities may have enhancement fees or user-type fees, or private transfer fees, over and above any stated association fees. Private transfer fees: (A) may last for a fixed period of time or in perpetuity, (B) are typically calculated as a percentage of home's sales price, and (C) may have private parties, charitable organizations or interest-based groups as their recipients. Brokers do not have expertise in this area.

SBSA REVISED 4/07 (PAGE 6 OF 10)

Buyer's Initials (_____)(_____)
Seller's Initials (_____)(_____)

Reviewed by _____ Date _____

EQUAL HOUSING OPPORTUNITY

STATEWIDE BUYER AND SELLER ADVISORY (SBSA PAGE 6 OF 10)

FIGURE 5.3 (Continued).

Property Address: _____ Date: _____

32. GENERAL RECALL/DEFECTIVE PRODUCT/CLASS ACTION INFORMATION: Buyer and Seller are advised that government entities and manufacturers may at any time issue recall notices and/or warnings about products that may be present in the Property, and that these notices or warnings can change. There is no single, all-inclusive source of information on product recalls, defective products or class actions; however, the U.S. Consumer Product Safety Commission (CPSC) maintains a website that contains useful information. If Buyer wants further information regarding the items listed below, Broker recommends that Buyer consult the CPSC website at http://www.cpsc.gov during Buyer's inspection contingency period. The following are examples of recall/defective products/class action information. The information is not exclusive. If Buyer wants further information, Broker recommends that Buyer contact the sources below. Brokers do not have expertise in this area and will not determine if any aspect of the Property is subject to a recall or is affected by a class action lawsuit. (NOTE: While the information below is believed to be current as of the revision date of this form, phone numbers and web addresses may change or be discontinued.)

A. FURNACES: Buyer is advised that the CPSC has issued a warning regarding certain gas-fired horizontal forced-air furnaces that present a substantial risk of fire. The furnaces in question were manufactured from 1983 to 1994 by Consolidated Industries and were marketed under many different brand names. Homes built before 1983 or after 1994 could still have the furnaces in question due to replacements or remodeling. If Buyer wants further information, Broker recommends that Buyer contact CPSC's hotline at (800) 638-2772.

B. WHIRLPOOL MICROWAVE-HOOD COMBINATION: Buyer is advised that Whirlpool Corporation has voluntarily recalled approximately 1.8 million microwave-hood combinations that have been known to overheat and catch fire. The units at issue are installed above ranges and are sold under the Whirlpool, KitchenAid and Kenmore brand names. If Buyer wants further information, Broker recommends that Buyer contact Whirlpool by phone at (800) 785-8897 or at its website, http://www.repair.whirlpool.com.

C. ROOF TILES: Buyer is advised that there is a class action lawsuit concerning certain fire free tiles and quantum panels manufactured and installed by RE-Con Building Products, Inc. from December 1993 to November 1997. If Buyer wants further information, Broker recommends that Buyer call (800) 966-3696 or view the website at http://www.firefreeclaims.com.

D. FIRE SPRINKLER: Buyer is advised that Central Sprinkler Company is recalling 35 million fire sprinkler heads that may be defective. If Buyer wants further information, Broker recommends that Buyer consult the CPSC website at http://www.cpsc.gov or Central Sprinkler Company at (866) 505-8553 or http://www.sprinklerreplacement.com.

E. WATER HEATER: Buyer is advised that certain water heaters manufactured by a variety of companies between 1993 and 1997 may be defective. If Buyer wants further information, Broker recommends that Buyer discuss the issue with an appropriate professional who can determine if the water heater on the Property is defective.

F. ALUMINUM WIRING: Buyer is advised that some properties in California are wired in whole or in part with aluminum wiring which was approved at the time of construction but subsequently determined to be a potential hazard. If Buyer wants further information, Broker recommends that Buyer discuss the issue with an appropriate professional who can determine if the wiring on the Property is defective.

G. GALVANIZED, ABS, POLYBUTELENE AND COPPER PIPE: Buyer is advised that galvanized steel water pipes may corrode and leak after several years and that ABS plastic drain waste and vent pipe may be subject to failure. Buyer is also advised that the adhesive used in the installation of polybutelene pipe has been subject to failure. Additionally, copper pipe installed in slabs may develop leaks as result of reaction to certain soils. If Buyer wants further information, Broker recommends that Buyer discuss the issue with an appropriate professional who can determine if the water pipes and drains on the Property are defective.

H. WATER HEATER GAS CONTROL VALVES: Buyer is advised that the CPSC in cooperation with Robertshaw Controls Company has announced a voluntary recall of approximately 178,000 gas control valves installed on water heaters manufactured between July 2005 and August 2005 with production date codes 5-31 through and including 5-33 under brand names American Proline, Bradford White, GE, GSE, Hotpoint, Jetglas, John Wood, Lochinvar, Premire Plus, Powerflex, Rheem, Richmond, Ruud, Vanguard, Whirlpool and U.S. Craftsman. The CPSC reports that the screws on the valves could break allowing gas to escape from the valves. If Buyer wants further information, Broker recommends that Buyer consult the CPSC website at http://www.cpsc.gov or contact Robertshaw Controls at (888) 225-1071 or http://www.robertshaw.com.

Buyer's Initials (_____)(_____)
Seller's Initials (_____)(_____)

| Reviewed by _____ Date _____ |

EQUAL HOUSING
OPPORTUNITY

STATEWIDE BUYER AND SELLER ADVISORY (SBSA PAGE 7 OF 10)

FIGURE 5.3 *(Continued).*

Property Address: _____ Date: _____

I. ARC-FAULT CIRCUIT BREAKER: Buyer is advised that the CPSC in cooperation with Schneider Electric has announced a voluntary recall of approximately 700,000 Square D Q® and Homeline® AFCI circuit breakers manufactured by Schneider Electric North American Operating Division. The recalled arc-fault interrupter circuit breakers are designed for use in 15 and 20-amp branch circuits; have a blue test button and were manufactured between March 2004 and September 2004. Tests show that these circuit breakers may not provide the arc-fault protection required by the 2001 California Electrical Code, Section 210-21. If Buyer wants further information, Broker recommends that Buyer consult the CPSC website at http://www.cpsc.gov or contact Schneider Electric at (877) 202-9064 or http://www.us.squared.com/recallafci.

33. RENTAL PROPERTY RESTRICTIONS: Buyer and Seller are advised that some cities and counties impose restrictions that limit the rent that can be charged to a tenant, the maximum number of tenants who can occupy the property and the right of a landlord to terminate a tenancy and the costs to do so. If Buyer wants further information, Broker recommends that Buyer investigate the issue with an appropriate government authority during Buyer's inspection contingency period. Brokers do not have expertise in this area.

34. LAND LEASE: Buyer and Seller are advised that certain developments are built on leased land. This means that: (i) Buyer does not own the land, (ii) the right to occupy the land will terminate at some time, (iii) the cost to lease the land may increase at some point in the future, and (iv) Buyer may not be able to obtain title insurance. If Buyer wants further information, Broker recommends that Buyer discuss the issue with an attorney or other appropriate professional. Brokers do not have expertise in this area.

35. HOME WARRANTY: Buyer and Seller are advised that Buyer and Seller can purchase home warranty plans covering certain standard systems of the Property both before and after Close of Escrow. Seller can obtain coverage for the Property during the listing period. For an additional premium, an upgraded policy providing additional coverage for air conditioning, pool and spa and other features can be purchased. Home warranties do not cover every aspect of the Property and may not cover inspections or upgrades for repairs required by state or federal laws. Broker recommends that Buyer review the policy for details. Brokers do not have expertise in this area.

36. INTERNET ADVERTISING: Buyer and Seller are advised that Broker may employ a service to provide a "virtual tour" or Internet marketing of the Property, permitting potential buyers to view the Property over the Internet. Neither the service provider nor Broker has control over who will obtain access to the service or what action such persons might take. Buyer and Seller are advised that Brokers have no control over how long the information concerning the Property will be available on the Internet. Brokers do not have expertise in this area.

37. ESCROW FUNDS: Buyer and Seller are advised that California Insurance Code Section 12413.1 provides that escrow companies cannot disburse funds unless there are sufficient "good funds" to cover the disbursement. "Good funds" are defined as cash, wire transfers and cashiers' or certified checks drawn on California depositories. Escrow companies vary in their definitions of "good funds." Broker recommends that Buyer and Seller ask the escrow company regarding its treatment of "good funds." All drafts and out-of-state checks are subject to waiting periods and do not constitute "good funds" until the money is physically transferred to the escrow holder's account. Brokers do not have expertise in this area.

38. NOTICE OF YOUR "SUPPLEMENTAL" PROPERTY TAX BILL: Buyer and Seller are

advised that pursuant to Civil Code § 1102.6(c), Seller or his or her agent is required to provide the following "Notice of Your 'Supplemental' Property Tax Bill" to the Buyer:

"California property tax law requires the Assessor to revalue real property at the time the ownership of property changes. Because of this law, you may receive one or two supplemental tax bills, depending on when your loan closes.

The supplemental tax bills are not mailed to your lender. If you have arranged for your property tax payments to be paid through an impound account, the supplemental tax bills will not be paid by your lender. It is your responsibility to pay these supplemental bills directly to the Tax Collector.
If you have any questions concerning this matter, please call your Tax Collector's Office."

Although the notice refers to loan closing as a trigger, it is actually the change of ownership which triggers this reassessment. Therefore, the Property can be reassessed even if there is no loan involved in the purchase of the Property. The purchase agreement may allocate supplemental tax bills received after the Close of Escrow to the Buyer. If Buyer wants further information concerning these matters, Broker recommends that Buyer discuss the issue with the County Assessor or Tax Collector. Brokers do not have expertise in this area.

Buyer's Initials (_____)(_____)
Seller's Initials (_____)(_____)

SBSA REVISED 4/07 (PAGE 8 OF 10)

Reviewed by _____ Date _____

EQUAL HOUSING OPPORTUNITY

STATEWIDE BUYER AND SELLER ADVISORY (SBSA PAGE 8 OF 10)

FIGURE 5.3 (*Continued*).

Property Address: _____ Date: _____

39. NON CONFIDENTIALITY OF OFFERS: Buyer is advised that Seller or Listing Agent may disclose the existence, terms, or conditions of Buyer's offer unless all parties and their agent have signed a written confidentiality agreement. Whether any such information is actually disclosed depends on many factors, such as current market conditions, the prevailing practice in the real estate community, the Listing Agent's marketing strategy and the instructions of the Seller.

40. FIRPTA/CALIFORNIA WITHHOLDING: Buyer and Seller are advised that: (i) Internal Revenue Code Section 1445 requires a Buyer to withhold and remit to the Internal Revenue Service 10% of the purchase price if Seller is a non-resident alien, unless an exemption applies. Seller may avoid withholding by providing Buyer a statement of non-foreign status. The statement must be signed by Seller under penalty of perjury and include Seller's tax identification number. Buyer can also avoid the federal withholding requirement if the property price is $300,000 or less, and the Buyer signs an affidavit stating Buyer intends to occupy the property as a principal residence. (ii) California Revenue and Taxation Code Section 18662 requires that a Buyer withhold and remit to the California Franchise Tax Board 3 1/3% of the purchase price unless the Seller signs an affidavit that the property was the Seller's (or the decedent's if a trust or probate sale) principal residence or that the sales price is $100,000 or less or another exemption applies. Exemptions from withholding also apply to legal entities such as corporations, LLCs, and partnerships. Brokers cannot give tax advice. Broker recommends that Buyer and Seller seek advice from a CPA, attorney or taxing authority. Brokers do not have expertise in this area.

41. LIQUIDATED DAMAGES: Buyer and Seller are advised that a liquidated damages clause is a provision Buyer and Seller can use to agree in advance to the amount of damages that a seller will receive if a buyer breaches the agreement. The clause usually provides that a seller will retain a Buyer's initial deposit paid if the Buyer breaches the agreement, and generally must be separately initialed by both parties to be enforceable. For any additional deposits to be covered by the liquidated damages clause, there generally must be another separately signed or initialed agreement. However, if the Property contains from 1 to 4 units, one of which the Buyer intends to occupy, California Civil Code Section 1675 limits the amount of the deposit subject to liquidated damages to 3% of the purchase price. Even though both parties have agreed to a liquidated damages clause, an escrow company will usually require either a judge's or arbitrator's decision or instructions signed by both parties in order to release the Buyer's deposit to the Seller. Buyers and Sellers must decide on their own, or with the advice of legal counsel, whether to agree to a liquidated damages clause. Brokers do not have expertise in this area.

42. MEDIATION: Buyer and Seller are advised that mediation is a process by which the parties hire a neutral person to facilitate discussion and negotiation between the parties with the goal of helping them reach a settlement of their dispute. The parties generally share in the cost of this confidential, non-binding negotiation. If no agreement is reached, either party can pursue further legal action. Under C.A.R. Form RPA-CA; (i) the parties must mediate any dispute arising out of their agreement (with a few limited exceptions, such as matters within the jurisdiction of a small claims court) before they resort to arbitration or court, and (ii) if a party proceeds to arbitration or court without first attempting to mediate the dispute, that party risks losing the right to recover attorney fees even if he or she prevails.

43. ARBITRATION: Buyer and Seller are advised that arbitration is a process by which the disputing parties hire a neutral person to render a decision. Generally, arbitration is faster and less expensive than resolving disputes by litigating in court. The rules are usually less formal than in court, and it is a private process not on the public record. By agreeing to arbitration the parties give up the right to a jury trial and to appeal. Arbitration decisions have been upheld even when arbitrators have made a mistake as to the law or the facts. If the parties agree to arbitration, then any dispute arising out of their agreement (with a few limited exceptions) must be submitted to binding arbitration. Buyer and Seller must weigh the benefits of a potentially quicker and less expensive arbitration against giving up the right to a jury trial and the right to appeal. Brokers cannot give legal advice regarding these matters. Buyers and Sellers must decide on their own, or with the advice of legal counsel, whether to agree to arbitration. Brokers do not have expertise in this area.

Buyer's Initials (_____)(_____)
Seller's Initials (_____)(_____)

| Reviewed by _____ Date _____ |

Copyright © 2004-2007, CALIFORNIA ASSOCIATION OF REALTORS®, INC.
SBSA 4/07 (PAGE 9 OF 10)

STATEWIDE BUYER AND SELLER ADVISORY (SBSA PAGE 9 OF 10)

FIGURE 5.3 (*Continued*).

Property Address: _____ Date: _____

44. LOCAL ADDENDA (IF CHECKED):

The following local disclosures or addenda are attached:

A. ☐ _____

B. ☐ _____

C. ☐ _____

D. ☐ _____

Buyer and Seller acknowledge and agree that Broker: **(i)** does not decide what price Buyer should pay or Seller should accept; **(ii)** does not guarantee the condition of the Property; **(iii)** does not guarantee the performance, adequacy or completeness of inspections, services, products or repairs provided or made by Seller or others; **(iv)** does not have an obligation to conduct an inspection of common areas or areas off the site of the Property **(v)** shall not be responsible for identifying defects on the Property, in common areas, or offsite unless such defects are visually observable by an inspection of reasonably accessible areas of the Property or are known to Broker; **(vi)** shall not be responsible for inspecting public records or permits concerning the title or use of Property; **(vii)** shall not be responsible for identifying the location of boundary lines or other items affecting title; **(viii)** shall not be responsible for verifying square footage, representations of others or information contained in investigation reports, Multiple Listing Service, advertisements, flyers or other promotional material; **(ix)** shall not be responsible for providing legal or tax advice regarding any aspect of a transaction entered into by Buyer or Seller; and **(x)** shall not be responsible for providing other advice or information that exceeds the knowledge, education and experience required to perform real estate licensed activity. Buyer and Seller agree to seek legal, tax, insurance, title and other desired assistance from appropriate professionals.

By signing below, Buyer and Seller acknowledge that each has read, understands and received a copy of this Advisory. Buyer and Seller are encouraged to read it carefully.

Date _____   Date _____

BUYER _____   BUYER _____

(Print name) _____   (Print name) _____

(Address) _____

Date _____   Date _____

SELLER _____   SELLER _____

(Print name) _____   (Print name) _____

(Address) _____

Real Estate Broker (Selling Firm) _____   DRE Lic. # _____

By _____ DRE Lic. # _____   Date _____

Address _____ City _____   State _____ Zip _____

Telephone _____ Fax _____   E-mail _____

Real Estate Broker (Listing Firm) _____   DRE Lic. # _____

By _____ DRE Lic. # _____   Date _____

Address _____ City _____   State _____ Zip _____

Telephone _____ Fax _____   E-mail _____

Published and Distributed by:
REAL ESTATE BUSINESS SERVICES, INC.
a subsidiary of the California Association of REALTORS®
525 South Virgil Avenue, Los Angeles, California 90020

SBSA 4/07 (PAGE 10 OF 10)

Reviewed by _____ Date _____

EQUAL HOUSING OPPORTUNITY

STATEWIDE BUYER AND SELLER ADVISORY (SBSA PAGE 10 OF 10)

the seller traditionally pays the escrow fees. Both parties generally split the escrow charges in Sonoma County. Each county is different. Furthermore, the customs are only guidelines, and the actual division depends on contract negotiations between the parties.

Escrow Company. The escrow provisions are too often left to the broker, although careful deliberation should be given to this important area. The escrow procedures tend to vary significantly between Northern California and Southern California. Generally, the buyer selects the escrow or title company. In practice, the choice is often made by the broker. Either party can select the escrow company, although in practice, the designation is usually made by the broker. In loans covered by the federal Real Estate Settlement Procedures Act of 1974 (RESPA), the seller cannot force the buyer to accept a particular escrow company. In general, RESPA covers most loans for the purchase of a one- to four-family dwelling, owner occupied, made by either (1) a federal bank or savings and loan association or (2) any agency assisted by a government program, such as FHA, VA, or the Department of Housing and Urban Development (HUD). At the state level, developers are prohibited from forcing buyers to use specific companies in which they have an interest. *C.C. 2995.*

Release of Funds. Escrow funds can only be released by agreement of the parties or, in the event of a dispute, by the decision of the arbitrator or judge. The escrow company will not release the funds on the instructions of only one party. This is especially true if there is a dispute over the funds, as often happens when a contract ends because of a contingency or breach. Absent an agreement between the parties, the title company holds the funds until there is a decision of the court or arbitrator.

Payment of Title Insurance

Local custom usually determines who pays for the title report, although the parties may allocate it between themselves in any acceptable manner. This clause relates only to the buyer's California Land Title Association (CLTA) title insurance policy. The buyer obtaining a loan will be required to pay for the lender's American Land Title Association (ALTA) title policy as part of the loan costs.

(22) Other Costs

Introduction

All costs are subject to negotiation, and the decision regarding the various fees can amount to a substantial amount of money. Often, too, the custom for that particular county influences the allocation of these fees. However, even in these situations, nothing is binding, and everything is subject to negotiation.

County Transfer Fees

By custom, the county transfer taxes are often paid by the seller. However, like all fees, the amount is open to negotiation between the parties. The amount of fees can vary from county to county, but are not less than $0.55 per $500 of value.

City Transfer Fees

By custom, city transfer taxes are often split between the parties. However, these fees, like all others in the contract, are subject to negotiation.

Other Fees

The list of other fees can be quite extensive, and further, can vary from type of property within a county to cost differences between counties. "HOA" stands for homeowners' association dues if the sale concerns a condominium or other ownership forms belonging to an association.

Home Warranty

Many brokers recommend plans that "insure" that the property in the home is operational. Theoretically, these plans eliminate many causes of frustration to buyers who purchase their home, only to find overlooked problems. Although these plans do solve many problems, far too many buyers look to these plans to provide full and complete coverage. Agents and buyers relying on such plans should understand their limitations. There have also been cases of warranty companies going bankrupt, and warranties are only as good as the company behind them. This clause provides for waiver of the plan or its use and, if used, who will pay the cost of the plan.

(23) Closing—Possession

This clause, stating whether the buyers will be occupying the property as their principal residence, may seem unimportant. However, any broker who knowingly participates in misleading a seller could perhaps be guilty of fraud. The seller may negotiate differently if he or she believes that the buyers are investors. Additionally, the sellers could conclude that the buyers as investors would have a more difficult time securing financing. Finally, the clause provides evidence for using the 3 percent limit on liquidated damages, if such clause is selected. It is also possible that the clause could be relied upon by a lender, who would then have an independent action if the statement were false.

(24) Closing—Possession Transfer

Although possession normally occurs at close of escrow, the parties may contract for any acceptable time. If an alternative date is used, a lease or rental agreement specifying all terms and conditions is a necessity. Furthermore, special provisions should cover problems that may arise from loss of or destruction to the property. Because of the potential problems that can arise if the transaction falls through, it is the author's opinion that the buyer should rarely be given possession prior to close of escrow.

(25) Statutory Disclosures and Cancellation Rights

Federal and state law requires delivery of a series of advisory notices and disclosure forms including: lead paint disclosures, transfer disclosure statements (TDS), natural hazard disclosure statements (NDH), special tax assessments (including Mello-Roos assessments), and if appropriate, military ordinance disclosures. The seller shall timely deliver these disclosures, while the buyer shall timely acknowledge them. If the seller discovers any material inaccuracies or false representations then the seller is obligated to report them to the buyer (except for anything ordered and paid for by the seller). The buyer then has up to three days after receipt (five days if notified by mail) to terminate the deposit receipt. After the three -or five-day time period, the termination right lapses as if it never existed. Sometimes local ordinances require additional notification forms. As important as these mandatory disclosures are, they are not part of the contract. These paragraphs are merely restating the law about their need and set an obligation that they will be delivered and acknowledged.

Of these many disclosure forms, perhaps the most important is the residential disclosure statement, sometimes referred to as the "Easton" disclosure statement. Basically, this statement notifies the buyer of the condition of the property being sold and the factors affecting its value. This form and the law concerning it are fully discussed in the next chapter of this book.

Natural and Environmental Hazards

The natural hazard statement identifies if the property lies in any extra-hazardous areas such as where there is high risk for earthquake, flood, or fire. If the property is so located, it must be noted on the special disclosure statement mandated by California law.

Data Base Disclosure

The final disclosure indicates that by calling a special phone number, it is possible to find out if any registered sex offenders live in the property's area.

Withholding Tax Disclosure

If the seller is a foreigner and nonresident of the United States, then he or she may be required to have part of the purchase price paid directly to the Internal Revenue Service. The procedure and requirements of this section are discussed in detail in Chapter 6, under "FIRPTA Withholding Statement."

Megan's Law Disclosure

The final disclosure indicates that by calling a special phone number, it is possible to find out if any registered sex offenders live in the property's area.

(26) Condominium/Planned Unit Development Disclosures

If the property is a condominium or planned unit development (PUD), then the seller must provide condominium disclosures about the unit, complex, and association. The type of disclosures and the forms required are mandated by code and must be followed if the property is part of a condominium or PUD.

(27) Items Included and Excluded

Fixtures

Legally, fixtures are automatically included as part of the sale, unless specifically excluded. However, so many problems arise over the classification of fixtures that the CAR clause wisely reiterates that fixtures are included in the sale. Brokers should note CAR's list of fixtures and add or delete items as necessary. The list includes among its items light fixtures, window coverings, television antennas, satellite dishes, private integrated telephone systems, air conditioners, security alarms, and garage door items. Furthermore, the CAR clause states these items shall be sold in "as is" condition, unless warranted elsewhere in this agreement. It might be wise for buyers to add a warranty that all such fixtures shall be in good working order.

Personal Property

The subparagraph "items included" is for listing any personal property included in the sale. Typical items include refrigerators and drapes. Note that the CAR clause requires personal property to be delivered free and clear of any liens and without any warranties of any kind. The author recommends that when representing the buyer, a provision be added that the seller warrants that the included personal property shall be in working order and in the same condition as when this deposit receipt was executed. Not infrequently, litigation arises over what is included in the sale and what is not, so care should be taken in drafting this paragraph and carefully delineating included and excluded items.

(28) Condition of Property

"As Is" with No Warranties

Subparagraph A requires the *buyer* to accept the property "as is," without any express warranties except as provided in the deposit receipt. Some pre-2010 versions of the form do not even use the words as is although the meaning has the same legal effect.

Effect of "As Is." Some brokers and sellers erroneously believe that selling property "as is" will relieve them of all liability. Such clauses only relieve sellers of liability for defects that were not intentionally concealed and only protects against defects that were reasonably observable on a reasonable inspection. *Shapiro v. Hu (1986) 188 C.A.3d 324.* Furthermore, such clauses do not relieve a broker of his or her obligation of inspection.

Potential Exposure for Buyer's Broker. Buying property "as is" without even using the term is potentially confusing and also raises a troubling question. Except for special cases, why would an average buyer wish to purchase property in "as is" condition? Some attorneys have raised the issue that if a buyer does not clearly understand that he or she is purchasing property "as is," might not the broker have a legal liability? This exposure might be especially true if the broker has not explicitly and fully explained the nature of "as is" sales.

The "Local Edition" CAR Form. CAR found that many brokers in Northern California were reluctant to use the new form. Therefore, CAR developed an amended residential purchase agreement called the "local edition." This form meets many of the objects raised by brokers, and even allows modification of the "as is" provision by merely checking a box. However, even if a buyer checked the box, the clause only provides that the roof will not leak, specified built-in appliances shall be in working order, and window and door glass and screens shall be in good condition. Any buyer using the form would probably want to add that the heating, plumbing, and electrical systems will be in working order. Other protections should be added as well.

Not Uncommonly Rewritten. It is not uncommon for some brokers or attorneys representing the buyer to rewrite this section. For example, on an addendum, it might read "Item 9, *Condition of Property*, subparagraphs A and B, and all subparagraphs thereunder, are replaced with the following paragraphs _____." Parties should be careful about modifying or accepting a modified warranty without carefully examining all the ramifications. Many preprinted forms from other organizations have different warranties, and each form should be carefully evaluated and understood. Depending on how the section is rewritten, the clause could provide that the property will be maintained in the same condition as now exists, that the roof will have no leaks, that all appliances will be in good working order, and that there shall be no leaks. Any deficiencies noted on the Real Estate Transfer Disclosure Statement that violate the preceding warranties must be corrected to comply with the warranties of such a rewritten warranty paragraph.

Disclosures

Subparagraph A provides that the seller must disclose known defects, including any insurance claims made within the last five years. Except for the insurance requirement, this obligation is almost a statutory requirement that must be stated in the Real Estate Transfer Disclosure Statement. In the author's opinion, it provides very little that is not already required by law.

"Known" Clause

By using the term "known" to the seller, the author feels the disclosure is further limited. If there is a problem, the buyer must prove that the seller had knowledge about the condition before close of escrow.

Inspections

Items not covered by the warranty of paragraphs above are covered in the "buyer's inspection" and the "suggestion" that the buyer should inspect the property to ascertain its present condition.

Note to Seller

This paragraph merely states that the seller should investigate the property so that seller will have the appropriate information to answer buyer's questions as well as to fill out the statutory disclosure forms.

(29) Buyer's Investigation and Matters Affecting Property

The first paragraph states that the buyer's acceptance of the property's condition is a contingency. For all other situations, buyers often have a misconception that once any defects are found the buyer can *automatically* cancel the contract. A later CAR clause covers contingencies and states that the seller has the option of remedying reasonable deficiencies. If the buyer wants an absolute discretion to terminate the contract if any deficiencies are found, this CAR clause will have to be modified.

Furthermore, the buyer can conduct reasonable investigations and tests of the property's condition. All such tests must be paid for by the buyer (unless otherwise agreed), with the seller given a copy of the reports. Generally, the buyer may not institute any government inspections without the seller's proper written consent. This stops a government agency from having official notice of such problems as mother-in-law units and work done without permits. Before doing any investigation, the buyer must have adequate insurance and is liable for any losses to the seller. The clause also reminds the seller that recording a notice of nonresponsibility will avoid liability for the costs of the tests. Finally, the buyer upon request must give the seller a free copy of all test results.

From the buyer's viewpoint, this inspection is a very important clause and one that is all too often overlooked. Unless the buyer is extremely knowledgeable, he or she should have trained professionals inspect the property. Furthermore, hazardous waste and toxic chemicals should routinely be checked on older properties, as is discussed in later chapters. It is the author's opinion that buyers should almost always have a trained professional or professionals assessing the condition of the property before purchase. The benefit to the seller and broker is that, if the buyer inspects the property and later sues, it becomes difficult to show reliance on statements and disclosure forms provided by the seller.

Buyer's Indemnity

Any inspections or repair work done by the buyer must be done without damaging the property, and the buyer must indemnify the seller for any damages. The seller is reminded that properly posted notices of nonresponsibility provide protection from mechanic's liens. (See Chapter 16 for a discussion of mechanic's liens.)

(30) Disclosures, Addenda and Other Terms

The supplements primarily incorporate any other clauses or entire pages of expanded provisions. Probably the two most commonly used attachments, besides the ones preprinted on the form, are the occupancy agreement and the lease. Figure 5.4 is a sample of a generic addendum, where the parties draft the provision being added or modified.

FIGURE 5.4   CAR addendum.

CALIFORNIA ASSOCIATION OF REALTORS®

ADDENDUM
(C.A.R. Form ADM, Revised 10/01)

No. _____

The following terms and conditions are hereby incorporated in and made a part of the: ☐ Residential Purchase Agreement, ☐ Manufactured Home Purchase Agreement, ☐ Business Purchase Agreement, ☐ Residential Lease or Month-to-Month Rental Agreement, ☐ Vacant Land Purchase Agreement, ☐ Residential Income Property Purchase Agreement, ☐ Commercial Property Purchase Agreement, ☐ other_____,

dated _____, on property known as _____,

in which _____ is referred to as ("Buyer/Tenant")

and _____ is referred to as ("Seller/Landlord").

_____

The foregoing terms and conditions are hereby agreed to, and the undersigned acknowledge receipt of a copy of this document.

Date _____   Date _____

Buyer/Tenant _____   Seller/Landlord _____

Buyer/Tenant _____   Seller/Landlord _____

SURE TRAC
The System for Success®

Published and Distributed by:
REAL ESTATE BUSINESS SERVICES, INC.
a subsidiary of the California Association of REALTORS®
525 South Virgil Avenue, Los Angeles, California 90020

Reviewed by _____ Date _____

EQUAL HOUSING OPPORTUNITY

ADM REVISED 10/01 (PAGE 1 OF 1)   **Print Date**

ADDENDUM (ADM PAGE 1 OF 1)

Source: Reprinted with permission, California Association of Realtors®. Endorsement not implied.

Interim Occupancy Agreement

An occupancy agreement is a lease of the premises by the buyer prior to close of escrow. This leasehold estate can take many forms, most commonly a periodic tenancy, usually for a week-to-week or month-to-month duration. CAR publishes an interim occupancy agreement, a specialized lease form intended for use as an addendum to the CAR deposit receipt. Because the passage of possession also transfers the risk of loss in the event of destruction, specific provisions should be included in the lease requiring the tenant to carry fire insurance in an amount not less than the value of the structure and improvements.

Residential Lease

This form is used when the seller will remain on the property after close of escrow. Problems can arise if the seller refuses to vacate after the specified terms, perhaps because the seller's new property is not ready for occupancy, and the buyer may face a messy eviction process.

(31) Title and Vesting

The seller will timely provide a preliminary title report, to which the buyer can reasonably disapprove within a timely manner. At close of escrow, the buyer will receive an ALTA-R policy (a new form of ALTA-residential policy) or, if not reasonably available, a standard CLTA policy. The title clause covers many important items, some of which can create trouble for the unknowledgeable.

Condition of Title

Brokers and sellers frequently misunderstand the significance of the title clause. Subparagraph B requires title to be free of all liens "except as provided in this agreement." This provision requires the broker to list any and all encumbrances against the property that will not be listed in the title insurance policy; otherwise, the seller may become obligated to transfer title free and clear of those unlisted encumbrances. Among the exclusions from the standard buyer's title insurance policy are liens not of record and conditions discoverable by a physical inspection of the property. This part of the clause should not be ignored.

Other Deposit Receipt Forms. The earlier CAR deposit receipt and many forms still in use state that property is free of liens, encumbrances, easements, restrictions, rights, and conditions, except any listed in the blank space following that clause. Such a clause requires the broker to list all liens and encumbrances to which the property is subject. If the broker writes *none* or *N.A.*, the seller becomes obligated to transfer fully marketable title, free and clear of any liens or encumbrances. Such clear title is a condition few sellers anticipate or are capable of satisfying. Deeds of trust, mortgages, taxes, assessments, judgment liens, mechanic's liens, attachment liens, covenants, conditions, restrictions, nonvisible easements, leases, adverse possession, and numerous other rights may encumber the property. If the land is so encumbered and the exceptions are not noted, the seller (and probably the broker, too) would be liable for damages. Chapter 9 discusses in detail the effect of and damages resulting from unlisted encumbrances.

Selection of Title Company

The deposit receipt states that the buyer will select the title company. The broker usually selects a title company for his or her party, using that company with which the broker is most familiar and has the best relationship. Under RESPA, federal regulations now prohibit the seller, in certain situations, from contracting to choose a title company. Selection of title companies follows the same restrictions as for escrow companies (discussed in more detail in Paragraph 22 "Escrow and Title").

Vesting of Title

The CAR deposit receipt has the buyer taking title as stated in the escrow instructions. An early form of the CAR deposit receipt, as well as many other forms currently in use, requires that the buyer should select the form of holding title at the time that the offer is submitted. At that stage, few buyers possess the knowledge and tax information necessary to make this decision, and, as the broker's primary concern is submitting an offer, far too often the broker suggests a form of vesting. In such situations, the broker runs a serious risk of practicing law without a license. Chapter 11 covers the legal and tax consequences of the major forms of ownership. The author suggests using a clause stating that the manner of holding title shall be designated in the buyer's escrow instructions.

(32) Sale of Buyer's Property

If the box is checked, the clause operates to make this sale conditional on sale of the buyer's existing property. The clause then incorporates another CAR form that discusses if the sellers can continue to market their property and, if so, how to handle any other offers that the seller receives. If the contract is subject to sale of the buyer's property, the author recommends rewriting the clause. For example, if the property must be sold within 60 days, why allow the buyer 60 days to find a buyer? The author prefers giving the buyer 30 days to obtain a fully executed, noncontingent offer with escrow to close within the 60-day period. Therefore, if the buyer does not obtain an offer within 30 days, the buyer is unlikely to find one that is acceptable and can close in such short notice. Figure 5.5 is a sample form commonly used when the purchase is subject to and conditioned upon the prior sale of the buyer's own home.

(33) Time Periods and Contingencies

The deposit receipt contains many contingencies, all related to financing and inspection of the property and documents. The parties sometimes prefer different methods of removing contingencies. For example, some buyers prefer the right to cancel the contract if any deficiencies are found during the pest control inspection. These buyers do not want to provide the seller with the right to correct such problems. These buyers think that they have a better renegotiation strategy if they can cancel the contract. Also, if buyers must pay for corrective work, they want limits on how much work they must correct. It is prudent to analyze the contingency contract and make sure that it fits the current situation. Because this clause is so important, it is worth a careful study by the parties.

Time Periods in This CAR Document

This paragraph in the CAR form lists the periods the buyers and sellers have to satisfy their own conditions. The first subparagraph specifies the time that the seller has to provide the designated disclosures. The second subparagraph provides the time that the buyer has to do the inspections or reviews and object to any findings. The seller has absolutely no obligation to correct any deficiencies notes. The seller can either correct the noted deficiencies, negotiate for an allocation of cost between buyer and seller, or allow the buyer to cancel the contract.

Removal of Contingencies

Different deposit receipts use different methods of removing contingencies. Two types of clauses are in use. In the first method, the active method, the parties must take certain affirmative actions to waive the contingencies. The other method is to have the contingencies automatically waived by passage of time without any action by the parties. It is important to review each deposit receipt to see which method is being used.

Active Method. The active method holds all contingencies are deemed unsatisfied unless specifically and timely waived in writing

FIGURE 5.5   CAR contingency ... of other property.

CALIFORNIA
ASSOCIATION
OF REALTORS ®

**CONTINGENCY FOR SALE OR PURCHASE
OF OTHER PROPERTY**
(C.A.R. Form COP, Revised 11/08)

This is an addendum to the ☐ California Residential Purchase Agreement, ☐ Counter Offer, ☐ Other _____
_____ ("Agreement"), dated _____, on property
known as _____ ("Seller's Property"), between
_____ ("Buyer") and
_____ ("Seller").

A. ☐ (If checked) **SALE OF BUYER'S PROPERTY:**
  1. **(a)** The Agreement is contingent on the close of escrow of Buyer's property, described as: _____
      _____ ("Buyer's Property").
    (b) If Buyer's Property does not close escrow by the earliest of: **(i)** the scheduled close of escrow of Seller's Property; **(ii)** the
      date specified in paragraph A3; or **(iii)** Other ☐ _____, then either Seller, after first
      giving Buyer a Notice to Buyer to Perform (C.A.R. Form NBP), or Buyer may cancel the Agreement in writing.
  2. ☐ (If checked) Buyer's Property is **not** now in escrow and (check boxes as applicable):
    (a) ☐ is not yet listed for sale.
    (b) ☐ is listed for sale with _____ company and is
      offered for sale in the _____ MLS, # _____.
    (c) Buyer shall, within **17 (or** ☐ _____**) Days** After Acceptance, provide Seller with Copies of the contract, escrow
      instructions and all related documents ("Escrow Evidence") for the sale of Buyer's Property showing that Buyer's Property
      has entered escrow.
  3. ☐ (If checked) Buyer's Property **is in escrow** with _____ escrow
      holder, (escrow # _____) scheduled to close escrow on _____ (date). Buyer shall,
      within **5 Days** After Acceptance, deliver to Seller Escrow Evidence that Buyer's Property is in escrow.
  4. If Buyer fails to provide to Seller Escrow Evidence within the time specified in A2(c) or A3, Seller, after first giving Buyer a Notice
      to Buyer to Perform, may cancel the Agreement in writing.
  5. If Buyer's Property is in or enters escrow, Buyer shall give Seller written notice if either party to that escrow gives notice to the
      other of intent to cancel. In such event, either Buyer or Seller may cancel the Agreement in writing.
  6. After Acceptance, Seller shall have the right to continue to offer the Property for sale for Back-up Offers. If Seller accepts a
      written back-up offer:
    (a) **Immediate Right to Notify Buyer to Remove Sale of Property Contingency:** Seller shall have the right to immediately
      give written notice to Buyer to, in writing: **(i)** remove this contingency; **(ii)** remove the loan contingency, if any; **(iii)** provide
      verification of sufficient funds to close escrow without the sale of Buyer's Property; and **(iv)** comply with the following
      additional requirement(s): _____. If Buyer fails to
      complete these actions within **72 (or** ☐ _____**) hours** after receipt of such notice, Seller may then immediately
      cancel the Agreement in writing.
    OR (b) ☐ (If checked) **Delayed Right to Notify Buyer:** Seller shall not invoke the notice provisions in paragraph A6(a): **(i)**
      within the first **17 (or** ☐ _____**) Days** After Acceptance; or **(ii)** (if checked) ☐ during the term of the Agreement.

B. ☐ (If checked) **SELLER'S PURCHASE OF REPLACEMENT PROPERTY:**
  1. The Agreement is contingent on Seller entering a contract to acquire replacement property.
  2. Seller shall, within **17 (or** ☐ _____**) Days** After Acceptance, remove this contingency or cancel the Agreement. If Seller
      does not remove this contingency in writing within that time, Buyer, after first giving Seller a Notice to Seller to Perform (C.A.R.
      Form NSP), may cancel the Agreement in writing.
  3. **(a)** Time periods in the Agreement for inspections, contingencies, covenants and other obligations shall begin: **(i)** as specified
      in the Agreement; **(ii)** (if checked) ☐ the day after Seller delivers to Buyer a written notice removing this contingency; or **(iii)**
      (if checked) ☐ Other _____.
    (b) Buyer and Seller agree that Seller may, by providing Buyer written notice at the time Seller removes this contingency, extend
      the Close Of Escrow date for a maximum of _____ additional Days or until _____ (date).
  4. Even after the expiration of the time specified in B2, Seller retains, until Buyer cancels pursuant to B2, the right to remove in
      writing this contingency or cancel the Agreement. Once Buyer receives Seller's written removal of this contingency, Buyer may
      not cancel pursuant to B2.

**By signing below, Buyer and Seller each acknowledge that they have read, understand, accept and have received a copy of this
Addendum.**

Date_____ Date _____
Buyer _____ Seller _____
Buyer _____ Seller _____

Published and Distributed by:
REAL ESTATE BUSINESS SERVICES, INC.
a subsidiary of the California Association of REALTORS®
525 South Virgil Avenue, Los Angeles, California 90020

Reviewed by _____ Date _____

EQUAL HOUSING
OPPORTUNITY

COP 11/08 (PAGE 1 OF 1)

CONTINGENCY FOR SALE OR PURCHASE OF OTHER PROPERTY (COP PAGE 1 OF 1)

Source: Reprinted with permission, *California Association of Realtors®*. Endorsement not implied.

by the buyer. The bottom line provides that if all contingencies are not timely removed, the seller has the option of canceling the contract. In the author's opinion, this method favors the buyer.

Passive Method The parties will use a passive method of satisfying contingencies (unless the active method is specified). The passive method holds that if the buyer does not give timely notice of disapproval then the contingency is deemed waived and satisfied. In the author's opinion, this method favors the seller over the buyer.

Effect of Contingency Removal

If a buyer's contingency is removed, then the buyer loses all right to object and agrees to continue as without the contingency. This means that the buyer assumes all liability for the repairs to all items to which the seller has not agreed to correct. If the contingency is related to financing, the buyer has become liable to purchase the property regardless of the ability to obtaining financing.

Cancellation of Escrow

If the contract fails to satisfy a condition, the parties must execute mutual instructions to cancel escrow. All funds, less applicable fees and costs, should be returned. However, the parties need to understand that this clause is not self-executing. If there is a good-faith dispute, the clause has little practical value. Even if there is a bad-faith refusal to cancel the escrow, except for a penalty up to $1,000, the clause does not force a reluctant party to cancel the escrow.

Drafting of Contingencies

Drafting of contingencies requires a subjective standard and enough specificity of terms so that a court could enforce the agreement by specific performance. If those objectives are not met, the condition and the entire agreement could fail. For example, in one case, the buyer was to investigate a lot split, but the contingency was subject to the "buyer's sole and absolute discretion." The court ruled such total discretion rendered the contingency invalid. Further, because the deposit was to be refunded if the condition was not satisfied, there was no consideration, so the contract could not qualify as an option. Therefore, the contract was null and void. *Steiner v. Thexton (2008) 163 C.A. 4th 359.* In short, drafting valid contingencies can be technically challenging when one gets creative and excessive.

Satisfaction or Waiver of Contingencies

Because litigation can arise over when and if contingencies have been removed, it is prudent, if not necessary, to carefully document the removal or waiver of contingencies.

(34) Seller's Right to Cancel

This clause gives the buyer the right to cancel the contract if, after giving the buyer the CAR form *Notice to Buyer to Perform*. The timing of the right to cancel depends on the conditions violated, and the subparagraphs specify those rights.

(35) Effect of Buyer's Removal of Contingencies

If and when buyer removes a contingency or cancellation right, such removal shall be deemed to have satisfied or waived such provision. Thereafter, buyer can no longer claim it is a contingency that permits buyer to terminate the contract without liability.

(36) Effect of Cancellation on Deposits

If this agreement is canceled, the parties agree to execute the necessary documents for that cancellation and to notify escrow to release whatever funds is due the other party (less any fees and costs already incurred during that escrow). The clause then reminds the parties of C.C. §1057.3 which provides up to a $1,000 penalty for failure to sign such documents releasing funds in escrow unless a good-faith dispute exists.

(37) Repairs

This clause does not cover who will pay for repairs required by the buyer's inspection reports. Rather, it mandates that any such repairs shall be done in compliance with the applicable laws and ordinances. If the seller agrees to do any work, such work may be done personally or by others hired by the seller. As to any work paid for by the seller, the seller will obtain receipts and give copies to the buyer.

(38) Final Walk Through (Verification)

This clause allows a walk-through inspection before close of escrow. Although this clause is helpful, as worded, any defects or violations are not contingencies. This clause does not provide the right to hold up escrow until a defect is corrected. It just gives rise to damages. Some parties may desire a stronger clause.

(39) Prorations

Prorations can sometimes have a significant effect on the amount of cash a buyer needs to close escrow. The date and allocation of the prorations should be studied carefully, even if the default of close of escrow is used. Normally, all items are prorated as of close of escrow, so the seller makes payment until transfer of title. Thereafter, payment on these ongoing obligations is the buyer's responsibility. In the normal situation, if the seller has prepaid any obligations (such as a full year's insurance premium or property taxes), the buyer must reimburse the seller in escrow for the overpayment. Sometimes prorations are made at a specific date, such as when the buyer assumes occupancy before close of escrow or the seller remains on the property after title transfers.

(40) Selection of Service Providers

This clause is solely for the broker's benefit. It provides that the broker does not guarantee the names of anyone given as a referral nor is the buyer obligated to use those referral sources. It is an attempt to insulate the broker from a lawsuit for negligent referral, although there is some question as to how the courts would treat this provision.

(41) Multiple Listing Service

The broker is granted permission to reveal the price and terms of the sale to the local multiple listing service. Without this clause, publication of the sales terms could result in an invasion-of-privacy suit.

(42) Equal Housing Opportunity

This clause merely states that, as required under the law, the parties are not discriminating on the basis of race, religion, or other constitutionally prohibited practices. It seems to add little to the contract other than to remind the parties about the law.

(43) Attorney Fees

As a general rule in all contract cases, unless the contract provides for attorney's fees, neither party may be awarded attorney's fees. *C.C. 1717.* Hence, without this clause, each party would have to pay their own attorney's fees. This clause provides attorney's fees to the prevailing arbitration or court action. Note that court costs are different from attorney's fees. These costs are generally awarded to the winning party, even without any prior stipulation or contractual agreement.

There are no attorney's fees provisions for mediation. Furthermore, as stated in the mediation paragraph, no prevailing party shall be entitled to attorney's fees unless he or she has first mediated the dispute.

(44) Definitions

The paragraph defines certain terms that are used frequently in the deposit receipt. Far too often the parties overlook this important area of the contract, as many terms used in the deposit receipt have special defined meanings.

(45) Broker Compensation

The paragraph attempts to obligate each party to pay whatever sums are owed the broker under a listing agreement or other separate writing. If the broker is acting solely and exclusively as the buyer's agent, then this reiterates the obligation of the buyer to pay the broker's fee.

(46) Joint Escrow Instructions

This paragraph serves as the nucleus for the lengthy escrow instructions to be prepared by the escrow company. Certain provisions of this agreement present key terms to be incorporated in the escrow. The paragraph also provides that the requirement for the payment of the broker's commission is included in the escrow instructions. The other paragraphs provide the time in which escrow must be opened and that the broker is a party to the escrow for the sole purpose of receiving his commission.

(47) Liquidated Damages

Chapter 4 analyzed in detail the use, problems, and validity of liquidated damages clauses. Basically, the parties may provide for a predetermined amount of damages in the event of the buyer's default. *C.C. 1671 et seq.* (See Chapter 4 for a full discussion.)

In residential purchases, if the parties elect to use this clause, the seller's recovery is limited to the amount of actual damages or the amount of the deposit, whichever is less. However, as a practical matter, few buyers are sophisticated enough to realize that the seller's damages may be less than the deposit; consequently, they often forfeit the entire deposit. In both residential and commercial situations, if the parties do not elect to use this clause, the seller can only recover provable damages through litigation. In either event, the clause contains no provisions for breach by the seller. In such a situation, the buyer must arbitrate or litigate to enforce his or her rights.

(48) Mediation

With a few exceptions, the mediation clause requires the parties to attempt to resolve any conflicts first through nonbinding mediation through a neutral third party. If the person wins their case but has not first gone through mediation before filing a court action or arbitration, then such person is not entitled to attorneys' fees. This clause is operative in every CAR contract, and there is no space for the parties to initial if they desire its provisions.

(49) Arbitration

If the parties have any disputes concerning the agreement or its breach and if the parties check this box, they agree to resolve those issues through binding arbitration. The parties give up their rights to a trial by jury and agree to use an arbitrator. The arbitrator must either be a retired judge or a real estate attorney with five years of experience.

Brokers should be careful about advising their clients to accept this clause; the author thinks that in presenting this clause it could be easy for a broker to be "practicing law without a license." Although the author does not know of any cases yet on this issue, it is possible that advising a client to arbitrate could be construed as giving legal advice.

Arbitration and mediation are discussed in detail in Chapter 2 of this book under "Implementation: Alternative Dispute Resolution." The discussion also includes the author's opinions on the process of arbitration and mediation. Finally, if arbitration is required, the parties may want to consider using the American Arbitration Association (AAA) or the Judicial Arbitration and Mediation Services (JAMS) to settle their dispute.

This clause exempts certain actions from the preceding mediation and arbitration clauses. Some of the most significant exceptions are foreclosure actions, unlawful detainer cases, claims within the probate court jurisdiction, or small claims court jurisdiction.

California law specifies wording and size of type needed for a valid arbitration clause in a residential real estate contract. At least one case in California holds that the Federal Arbitration Act supersedes and controls arbitration clauses. The author feels the reasoning of this case is highly questionable in holding that federal laws preempt state law, but until there is a resolution by the Supreme Court it is hard to know for certain if the state requirements are still required. *Hedges v. Carrigan (2004) 177 C.A.4th 578.* The author recommends still meeting the California code requirements.

Finally, any dispute between the seller and broker will be resolved through mediation and arbitration. However, by so agreeing, the broker is claiming he or she is not a party to the agreement.

(50) Terms and Conditions of Offer

This paragraph states that this is an offer, which the seller can accept in the form of a contract, reject, or counter. Any provisions requiring initials to be effective need both buyer's and seller's initials to be a term of the contract. With only one set of initials, the provision is merely a counteroffer. The parties can use various copies of the deposit receipt, each of which can be considered an original.

(51) Time of Essence: Entire Contract

Time Is of the Essence

The first sentence of the clause states that "time is of the essence." Those words stress the importance of prompt action, stating that failure to perform as required within the specified period amounts to a breach. Without this clause, late performance may be valid if accomplished within a reasonable time. However, even with this clause, promptness may be waived by express agreement or by the parties' conduct. Thus, if a buyer fails to fund on the day set for close of escrow, the seller will have to declare immediately and prove this a material breach, or silence and inaction will allow the buyer a reasonable time (probably a few extra days or more) to fund the escrow. In escrow closing, it is usually difficult to show that a few days' delay is a *material* breach. *Stratton v. Tejani (1982) 137 C.A.11 758.* If the clause has been waived, it can be reinstated only by providing the other party with reasonable opportunity for compliance after proper notice of a demand for compliance. *Pease v. Brown (1960) 186 C.A.2d 425.*

The cases are not always consistent on their treatment in failing to meet a time deadline. In some purchase contracts, where the seller had not changed his or her position, the buyer was allowed extra time. Conversely, for example, in one lease option case, the option expired on a Saturday. The court held that as of Saturday, the option had expired. The court went on to say that deadlines that end on holidays are extended to the next day. For three days' notice and other situations *regulated by statute*, a holiday also includes Saturday and Sunday. *C.C.P. 12a.* However, for *contract deadlines* a different code section applies and Saturdays are not considered a holiday. *C.C.P. § 7. Gans v. Smull, (2003) 111 C.A.4th 985.* So, anyone facing a deadline must analyze all the current cases to gauge the legal effect of how the courts will react to a particular fact pattern that results in a delay.

No Broker Extensions

Older forms provided that the broker could unilaterally extend escrow or other provisions of the contract on notice to the parties. That provision has been eliminated from this edition of the CAR contract because the courts have held such a clause to be inconsistent with (and thus a waiver of) a provision that time is of the essence. *Katemis v. Westerlund (1956) 142 C.A.2d 799.*

Entire Contract, No Oral Understandings

The rest of the clause provides that the written contract signed by the parties represents their entire agreement. All oral agreements and verbal representations are of no force and effect. Any oral representations must be written into and made a part of the contract to be binding. This clause will not relieve a party of liability for fraudulent misrepresentation.

Amendments

This clause requires a written agreement to change any of its provisions. However, as Chapter 4 explained, sometimes an executed oral agreement can modify a written contract. Always have any changes to the contract put in writing and signed by both parties, or these oral understandings may be invalid under the statute of frauds or the requirements of this clause.

Extending Time

It is not uncommon for the parties to extend the time to perform a condition or for the close of escrow. When such extensions are required, the parties need to document the agreement for the extension of time, using the Extension of Time Addendum form.

(52) Offer and Expiration

The clause entitled Expiration of Offer really discusses the time and method of acceptance. Because the deposit receipt is only an offer until it is accepted, the buyer may revoke the offer at any time before acceptance, regardless of the period specified in the form. The general rules of offer and acceptance were examined in detail in Chapter 4.

Form of Acceptance

The CAR clause provides for the *mode* of acceptance. Unless the buyer receives a signed copy of this form personally or by mail before the designated time, the offer expires and may not form the basis of a binding contract. Consequently, *mere* agreement and signature by the seller on the deposit receipt form do not constitute acceptance. The broker should deliver a copy immediately to the buyer, thus forming a binding contract.

(53) Buyer's Signature

All buyers having an interest in the property must execute the deposit receipt. Under the statute of frauds, in most cases only documents signed by the party to be sued may be enforced against that party. *C.C. 1624.*

Signature by Only One Spouse

If spouses are purchasing the property with community property, then both spouses must sign the deposit receipt. See the discussion under "Seller's Signature" for more information on the need for the signature of both spouses.

(54) Acceptance of Offer

This clause states that the seller accepts the offer (although the seller must do so by properly signing the form). It also warrants that the seller either owns the property or has proper authority to sell the real estate.

Counter Offers

The seller can only accept the offer as presented. Any changes in the terms amount to a rejection of the buyer's offer and the submission of a new proposed counter offer. Chapter 4, Contracts and Damages, discusses acceptances and counter offers in details under the section on Acceptance. It is not uncommon for the parties to bounce back and forth, having several levels of counter, counter offers. See Chapter 4, Figures 4.1 and 4.2 for sample counter-offer forms.

(55) Seller's Signature

All sellers having an interest in the property must sign in order to be bound under the statute of frauds. *C.C. 1624.* When the real estate is community property, cases hold that both spouses must sign or the contract is invalid and nonbinding. The cases further hold that the intended buyer cannot sue the spouse who signed the deposit receipt for breach of contract. Nor can the signing spouse be sued for specific performance to force a sale of that spouse's half of the community property. *Droger v. Friedman, Solan & Ross (1991) 228 C.A.3d 301.* Never accept a deposit receipt for the sale of community property without the signature of both spouses.

(56) Confirmation of Acceptance

Because Item 31 (Expiration of Offer) states that acceptance occurs upon receipt of the buyer's offer, the date and time stated form the basis for the formation of the contract. It verifies the time that the contract became binding. The broker should see that the seller receives the signed contract as soon as possible.

(57) Real Estate Broker

In accepting the buyer's offer, the seller also executes a contract with the broker for payment of that broker's commission.

[On default, most listing agreements provide the broker, as the sole commission, receives one-half the amount of deposit remaining after payment of any sales expenses. The seller has no obligation to declare the deposit forfeited. On failure to do so, the broker receives nothing and has no right to try to force the seller to retain the deposit. *Kritt v. Athens Hills Dev. Co. (1952) 109 C.A.2d 642.*]

[If a transaction falls through because of the buyer's default, the buyer's broker can sue the buyer for the full amount of commission that would have been received had the sale been completed. This right of recovery is based on an implied promise or third-party beneficiary theory. *Chang v. Tsang (1991) 1 C.A.4th 1578.* Many buyers suffer from *buyer's remorse* and know the seller will not really force a sale with a specific performance lawsuit. Now, the buyer's broker's threat of a full-commission litigation may save many of these sales. Under this new case, the buyer's broker is actually in a better position than the listing broker. Deposit receipts usually limit the listing broker to one-half of the seller's recovery from the defaulting buyer. Generally, sellers use the liquidated damages clause, so their recovery is limited to the earnest money deposit.]

(58) Broker's Signature: Not Party

The broker's names and not the salesperson's name goes in the space for broker, because the broker must take all listings in his or her name. The listing salesperson, if any, signs on the space after the word "by." This merely confirms the agency relationship stated in Item 47 (Confirmation).

The form is explicit, stating that the party is not signing as a party to the agreement. In the past, most forms, including the older CAR forms, had the broker signing as a party. The primary rationale seemed to be that it somehow helped the broker enforce his or her commission agreement. However, the agreement is really a contract of sale between buyer and seller. When the broker was signing as a party, some courts held that if the broker was involved in the litigation the broker could also be liable for attorney's fees. Although the cases have not been consistent in this area, it appears to be a much wiser practice to keep the broker from signing as a party. The current CAR also adopts this position and keeps the broker signature as a mere confirmation of the nature of his agency role.

(59) Escrow Holder

This paragraph has the escrow acknowledge a copy of the deposit receipt, and, when applicable, any deposits. It also has the escrow agent agree to act as agent (subject to the escrow holder's supplemental instructions).

(60) Presentation of Offer

This paragraph has little legal significance. Rather it offers contemporary evidence of when the broker presented the offer.

(61) Rejection of Offer

This paragraph has little significance, and it makes no legal difference if the seller signs it. If there is no acceptance of the contract, there is no legal reason to sign any document.

DISCLOSURES TO BUYER

The disclosures to the buyer of *residential* property encompass many areas. Disclosures in commercial transactions, while beyond the scope of this chapter, are far less onerous than residential disclosures. For convenience, disclosures are divided into four separate areas: general duty disclosures, residential disclosure statements, natural hazard disclosure statements, and other statutory disclosures.

General Duty Disclosures

Many laws apply general areas of the law and cover other situations including real estate. For example, all participants to a transaction have common laws duties against fraud and misrepresentation. Once a contract exists, an implied covenant of good faith and fair dealing arises. Real estate agents owe the parties an obligation of good faith and fair dealing, in addition to any fiduciary responsibilities that arise because of the agency. If the property contains any hazardous waste or other environmental violations, there must be full disclosure. (All the areas listed in this paragraph are discussed in other chapters of this book.)

If the buyer is the broker's client, such as a buyer's agent, then there is a strong fiduciary duty of utmost good faith and loyalty. It is unclear exactly how far this duty would then go. A 1998 Court of Appeals case held that, "Thus, depending on the circumstances, a broker's fiduciary duty may be much broader than the duty to visually inspect and may include a duty to inspect public records or permits concerning title or use of the property, a duty which is expressly excluded from [code] section 2079." *Field v. Century 21 Klowden-Forest Realty (1998) 63 C.A.4th 18.*

Basically, the seller must disclose anything that can reasonably and foreseeably be likely to affect the value of the property, and that the buyer is unlikely to discover. Thus, the seller's failure to warn of the existence of extremely noisy and bothersome neighbors can violate the seller's requirement of full disclosure. As the court said:

> Whether information has sufficient materiality to affect the value or desirability of residential property is a fact-specific determination [for the jury]. Reputation and history clearly have a significant effect on the value of a piece of property. "George Washington slept here" is worth something, however physically inconsequential that consideration may be. Ill-repute or "bad will" conversely may depress the value of property." ... Failure to disclose a negative fact when it can reasonably be said to have a foreseeably depressing affect on the value of property is tortuous [and makes the seller liable].... [Thus, as in this case] the fact that a neighborhood contains an overtly hostile family who delights in tormenting their neighbors with unexpected noises or unending parties is not a matter which will ordinarily come to the attention of a buyer... If anything, the concept of "let the buyer beware" is an anachronism in California having little or no application in real estate law. *Alexander v. McKnight (1992) 7 C.A.4th 973, 977.*

Residential Disclosure Statements

The seller or a broker would be liable if he or she intentionally misled the buyer or intentionally tried to conceal material facts about the property. However, a 1984 court case, later codified, created new law. It ruled that both sellers and listing brokers have an *affirmative* duty to conduct a reasonable and diligent investigation of the property and to report those findings to the buyer.

Easton Case

In *Easton v. Strassburger (1984) 152 C.A.3d 90,* the listing brokers of residential property noted certain red flags that could be indicative of possible soil problems. The brokers observed netting in the backyard to correct slides, knew that the house was located on filled land, and observed an uneven floor in one room. However, they did not investigate these red flags and instead relied on the seller's statement that the house was in good condition. The listing brokers also failed to disclose these red flags to the buyers. The buyer was liable for intentional concealment and fraud. However, the court ruled that the listing brokers were liable for the buyer's damages, based on a breach of a duty of reasonable investigation and full disclosure. The court found that a duty existed, even though there was no contractual relationship between the listing broker and the buyers, and the buyers were represented by their own broker.

Now Codified

Following *Easton,* the California legislature clarified and codified *Easton's* holding. *C.C. 1102.* Whenever an owner of residential property sells that property, grants a lease with an option to purchase, or trades the property, the owner must provide a *residential disclosure statement.* Furthermore, the listing broker must also conduct his or her own "competent and diligent visual inspection" of the property and report those findings to the buyer. If for any reason the broker cannot make the required inspection, he or she must notify the buyer of that fact and of the buyer's rights to such disclosure.

Exceptions

The duty of brokers and sellers to investigate and disclose the condition of property affirmatively is limited to residential property. There is no such duty for commercial and agricultural property. *Smith v. Richard (1989) 205 C.A.3d 1354.* Furthermore, by statute, certain residential transfers are exempt. The most common exemptions include transfers between spouses, among co-owners, by executors, through trustees under a trustee's sale, and by conveyances under court order.

What Must Be Disclosed

Any material fact about the property that is known or that should be discovered by a diligent inspection and could or may affect the buyer's decision must be reported. This disclosure exceeds just the physical condition of the property. For example, the fact that a murder recently happened on the property must be disclosed because it can affect the value and desirability of property. The statutory duty does not cover inaccessible areas of the property, off-site areas, or public records. However, this statutory duty does not change any existing common law obligations, such as a duty to disclose material facts of which the broker has personal knowledge.

Disclosure Form

The disclosure must be made on a written form using the specific words and questions set forth in the Civil Code. The form is a lengthy statement disclosing the condition of the premises, parts of the residence, soil and land around the home, and other aspects of the property. Chapter 6 contains a copy of the statutory form and is entitled Real Estate Disclosure Statement.

When Presented

The author recommends that the above form be presented to the buyer when the deposit receipt is executed. By delivering the form at this time, the buyer has no option for rescission. If a statement is provided later, the buyer has three days (five if delivery is by mail) to rescind the transaction. If no statement is provided, the buyer can, with some exceptions, rescind anytime before close of escrow. *C.C. 1102.2.*

"As Is" Sales

Some brokers and sellers erroneously believe that selling property "as is" will relieve them of all liability. Such clauses only relieve sellers of liability for defects that were not intentionally concealed and, further, only protect against defects that were reasonably observable upon a reasonable inspection. *Shapiro v. Hu (1986) 188 C.A.3d 324.* Furthermore, such clauses do not relieve a broker of his or her obligation of inspection.

Natural Hazard Disclosure Statements

Nature of the Law

Sellers (and their agents) must certify in a statutory form if property lies in one or more of the special hazard zones. *C.C. 1102.6(c).* The disclosure form specifies if the property is within a special flood hazard zone area, an area of potential flooding, a high fire hazard severity zone, a wildland area that contains substantial forest fire risks, an earthquake fault zone, or a seismic hazard zone. All six of the hazards and areas are specifically defined by statute. If property is within one or more of these areas, there may be limits on developing that property, obtaining insurance, or receiving public assistance following a disaster.

Statutory Form

With a few exceptions, all residential buyers must be given a copy of the disclosure form, the contents of which are specified by statute. (See Figure 5.6). Sellers and agents are liable for the information in the report, unless the information was supplied by public agencies or given in reports prepared by qualified experts. *C.C. 1102.4.* Sellers and agents can list the answers to certain questions as "unknown" if the information is truly unknown, following a reasonable effort to find the answers.

Rescission and Damages

If the disclosure is amended or if it is given after a contract to purchase is signed, the buyer has three days to terminate the contract. The time is extended to five days if the notice to the buyer was sent by mail. Negligently giving a wrong answer or failure to provide the disclosure form when required to do so will not invalidate the sale. Rather, the seller (and if applicable, the broker) will be liable for damages.

Other Statutory Disclosures

Disclosures in General

New laws require new disclosure forms, and frequently old disclosure forms are revised by statute. It is important to use only the latest forms. Some of the more significant disclosure laws are listed in the following sections. Some disclosures require government approved booklets, such as the lead-based paint pamphlet, the earthquake guide, the environmental hazards booklet, and the energy efficiency booklet. Other statutes, while important, cover very specific items, such as compliance with the Smoke Detector Law or disclosures about the existence and safety of any window security bars. Some disclosure requirements may be mandated by local ordinances. For example, many cities and counties have ordinances that require the seller to furnish a 3R Report showing the property's use, occupancy, and zoning. *Govt. C. 38780.*

Lead-Based Paint Warning

For homes built before 1978, the seller must notify the buyer in writing about the required federal disclosures for lead-based paint. *42 U.S.C. 4852d(a)(3).* The disclosure must reveal if the seller has any actual knowledge that lead-based paint was used in the house and how the seller knows of its existence. The seller must also provide

FIGURE 5.6   Natural hazard disclosure statement.

Natural Hazard Disclosure Statement
(C.C. §1102.6c – Statutory Form)

The seller and his or her agent(s) disclose the following information with the knowledge that even though this is not a warranty, prospective buyers may rely on this information in deciding whether and on what terms to purchase the subject property. Seller hereby authorizes any agent(s) representing any principal(s) in this action to provide a copy of this statement to any person or entity in connection with any actual or anticipated sale of the property.

THE FOLLOWING ARE REPRESENTATIONS MADE BY THE SELLER AND HIS OR HER AGENT(S) BASED ON THEIR KNOWLEDGE AND MAPS DRAWN BY THE STATE. THIS INFORMATION IS A DISCLOSURE AND IS NOT INTENDED TO BE PART OF ANY CONTRACT BETWEEN THE BUYER AND THE SELLER.

THIS REAL PROPERTY LIES WITHIN THE FOLLOWING HAZARDOUS AREA(S):

A SPECIAL FLOOD HAZARD AREA (Zone "A") designated by the Federal Emergency Management Agency.
[ ] Yes   [ ] No   [ ] Do Not Know. Information not Available from local jurisdiction

AN AREA OF POTENTIAL FLOODING shown on an inundation map pursuant to Section 8589.5 of the Government Code.
[ ] Yes   [ ] No   [ ] Do Not Know. Information not Available from local jurisdiction

A VERY HIGH FIRE HAZARD SEVERITY ZONE pursuant to Section 51179 of the Government Code. The owner of this property is subject to the maintenance requirements of Section 51182 of the Government Code.
[ ]   Yes   [ ]   No

A WILDLAND AREA THAT MAY CONTAIN SUBSTANTIAL FOREST FIRE RISKS AND HAZARDS pursuant to Section 4125 of the Public Resources Code. The owner of this property is subject to the maintenance requirements of Section 4291 of the Public Resources Code. Additionally, it is not the state's responsibility to provide fire protection services to any building or structure located within the wildlands unless the Department of Forestry and Fire Protection has entered into a cooperative agreement with a local agency for those purposes pursuant to Section 4142 of the Public Resources Code.
[ ] Yes   [ ] No

AN EARTHQUAKE FAULT ZONE pursuant to Section 2622 of the Public Resources Code.
[ ]   Yes   [ ]   No

A SEISMIC HAZARD ZONE pursuant to Section 2696 of the Public Resources Code.
[ ] Yes   [ ] No

THESE HAZARDS MAY LIMIT YOUR ABILITY TO DEVELOP THE REAL PROPERTY, TO OBTAIN INSURANCE, OR TO RECEIVE ASSISTANCE AFTER A DISASTER.

BUYER(S) AND SELLER(S) MAY WISH TO OBTAIN PROFESSIONAL ADVICE REGARDING THOSE HAZARDS.

Seller certifies that the information herein is true and correct to the best of the seller's knowledge as of the date signed by the seller.
Signature of Seller   _____   Date: _____

Agent certifies that the information herein is true and correct to the best of the agent's knowledge as of the date signed by the agent.
Signature of Agent   _____   Date: _____

Buyer certifies that he or she has read and understands this document.
Signature of Buyer   _____   Date: _____

the buyer with an EPA pamphlet. This federal law provides severe penalties for violating its rules and theoretically allows a buyer to rescind a completed sale if the 10-day inspection period required by the disclosures has not been given.

Mello–Roos Assessments

Many counties and entities within the county raise money by forming special districts and issuing bonds to cover capital improvements and local school districts. (These are commonly called *Mello–Roos assessments*.) These bonds and special assessments may be quite substantial and are usually long term. The seller must disclose all such special assessments. *C.C. 1102.6b*.

Environmental Hazards

In residential sales, if the seller has no actual knowledge of any environmental hazards affecting the property, he or she may just provide the buyer with a booklet prepared by the California Department of Real Estate. *C.C. 2079.7*. This booklet briefly describes the risks of environmental hazards and relieves the seller of any further disclosure obligations. The author recommends that the booklet be given out in every transaction as a matter of course. If the seller actually knows of any environmental hazards, they must be disclosed to the buyer.

Death on the Premises

Normally, any death occurring on the property should be disclosed, as it might affect the value of property. However, the legislature has specifically exempted certain disclosures about the death of former occupants. Sellers and brokers need not disclose that a prior occupant had the acquired immunodeficiency syndrome (AIDS), nor disclose any information about the death of a prior occupant that occurred more than three years before the proposed sale. *C.C. 1710.2*. The statute retains liability for intentionally misleading anyone who asks a direct question about AIDS or the deaths of prior occupants.

Subdivisions

Certain properties covered by the Subdivided Lands Act or the Subdivision Map Act require disclosures. Subdivisions are discussed in Chapter 22.

Toxic Mold

The Real Estate Transfer Disclosure Statement (see Figure 6.2 in the next chapter) now asks if the owner is aware of any mold.

Some attorneys are calling mold the biggest real estate problem of the new millennium. At least three types of mold (stachybotrys, penicillium, and aspergillus) can produce serious health problems (such as short-term memory loss, nausea, and asthma). Because these three serious molds only develop in environments of long-term water damage, it is hard for a seller to deny knowledge. In Delaware, a client had a $1 million verdict upheld by the Delaware Supreme Court, and many cases in California have resulted in large verdicts for the buyers. Sellers and brokers should be familiar with the implications of this area.

In 2002, California adopted the *Toxic Mold Protection Act* (*H & SC §26100-26156*), which set forth certain disclosure notice requirements to buyers and tenants of mold-infested structures. However, the act doesn't become operative until six months after the Department of Health Services adopts standards for identifying toxic mold and specifies unsafe limits for those molds. Unfortunately, the department's legislation to develop these guidelines and requirements did not include any funding. It is the author's opinion that this act will probably not become operative for many years.

STUDY QUESTIONS (TRUE–FALSE)

1. The sole function of a deposit receipt is to form the basis of a contract for the sale of real estate.

2. Most deposit receipts follow the language of the standard form deposit receipts.

3. If a broker modifies a provision in the deposit receipt, the parties must initial and date the change, even if all parties sign the contract.

4. If a broker uses the words *or nominee* as one buyer, the contract may be voidable and unenforceable.

5. Until the seller accepts the buyer's offer, the buyer can generally revoke the offer and reclaim the deposit.

6. Normally, if a house is destroyed by fire before close of escrow, the seller assumes all risk of that loss.

7. The liquidated damages clause is unenforceable in California.

8. If the buyer signs a deposit receipt that states that the seller has 48 hours to accept the offer, the buyer may not revoke the offer for 48 hours.

9. Under the CAR deposit receipt, a mere signature of acceptance by the seller does not form a binding contract. A copy of the document must first be delivered to the buyer.

10. It is mandatory that all buyers sign the contract; otherwise, the contract will probably not be enforceable against any nonsigning buyer.

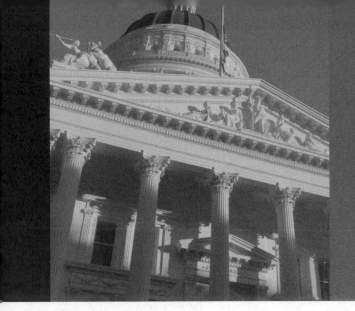

Chapter
6

NATURE OF LISTING AGREEMENTS

Employment Contract

The listing agreement is an employment contract hiring the broker to solicit offers for the seller's property in accordance with the terms and conditions of that agreement. It could be for the sale, exchange, lease, option, or other transfer of an interest in property. For this chapter, it is assumed that all listings are for the sale of property. The listing employs the broker to find a buyer but does not authorize the broker to sell the property or to bind the seller in any sale. Therefore, because a listing is not an offer, a buyer cannot create a contract by offering to buy the property on the exact terms of the listing.

Agency and Contract

The listing creates an agreement bound by contract law. It also establishes a fiduciary relationship governed by **agency** law. The exact responsibilities of a fiduciary relationship are discussed in Chapter 23.

Agency versus Contractual Duties

Agency law differs materially from general contract law and from the requirements to create a contract. Consideration is not necessary to bind a seller to the acts and statements of a broker. *C.C. 2308*. Similarly, a broker may be subject to the duties and responsibilities of an **agent**, but not be entitled to a commission.

Requirements

To be a contract, the listing agreement needs an offer and acceptance, consideration, and the other elements common to all contracts.

Listing Agreements

Additionally, the real estate commissioner imposes certain special requirements on the broker, which, if not met, subjects the broker to disciplinary action.

Commissioner's Regulations

The seller must be given a copy of the listing agreement at the time it is signed. *B.&P.C. 10142.* All exclusive agency and exclusive right to sell listing agreements must contain a specified and definite termination date. *B.&P.C. 10176f.* Absent such a date, an executory listing is voidable by the seller.

Accepting Deposits

Most listing agreements authorize the broker to accept a **deposit** *(earliest money)* with the buyer's offer. Under this clause, the broker accepts the deposit as the seller's agent. Therefore, if the broker loses or misappropriates the deposit, the seller shares liability for the loss.

No Provision

If the listing is silent on this point (which is unusual), then the broker accepts the deposit as the buyer's agent and at the buyer's risk. The seller could obtain the same result by inserting a contract provision that the broker may accept the buyer's deposit only as the buyer's agent.

Responsibility

In any event, whatever the contract provision, the deposit becomes the seller's responsibility on acceptance of the buyer's offer. However, the seller receives title to the deposit only when all the contract provisions have been fulfilled (on transfer of title).

No Rights in Broker

The deposit never becomes the property of the broker, and if it is ever placed in a personal or business account, the broker is guilty of **commingling.** *B.&P.C. 10176e.* Because the broker only holds the deposit in trust, by returning the deposit to the buyer after the seller's acceptance and without the seller's permission, the broker becomes personally liable to the seller for that amount. If any dispute arises between the parties as to their rights in that deposit, the courts, not the broker, should resolve the conflict. Any other course of action may subject the broker to personal liability.

Uncashed Checks as Deposits

Deposits are frequently evidenced by personal checks, which can create potential problems for the broker. If the broker (as the seller's agent) and the buyer agree that the check will be held uncashed as the deposit, the broker's acceptance of the check is payment of the deposit. *Beazel v. Kane (1954) 127 C.A.2d 593.* Without an agreement that the check can be held uncashed, the check will not constitute payment of the deposit until it is honored by the buyer's bank. *Mendiondo v. Greitman (1949) 93 C.A.2d 765.*

Management of Deposits

Once an offer is accepted by the seller, the broker must, by the next business day, either give the check to the seller, deposit it in escrow, or place it in a trustee account. Alternatively, the broker can continue to hold the check uncashed if the listing or other written instructions from the seller so provide, which rarely occurs. *Regs. 2832.*

Appraisals for Listing Price

Brokers must be careful in establishing the listing price. If they advise an incorrect price, they may be held liable for professional malpractice. However, these tort cases are difficult to prove, so the legislature added a new statutory liability for certified **appraisals**. Brokers are liable for appraisals using the words "certified appraisal," "registered appraisal," "licensed appraisal," or other words that are likely to be confused with a certified appraisal. *C.C. 1922.1.*

The standards set by statute include the degree of accuracy and reliability that the appraisal must meet the format and information that can be used, the type of comparable properties allowed, the time all such reports and supporting data must be retained, and the damages recoverable from inaccurate appraisals. The statutes provide that "any person" who is damaged by such an appraisal may recover damages, including attorney's fees.

Therefore, the listing agent would be well advised not to use the term appraisal. The agent should do a competitive market analysis or other evaluation, without calling it an appraisal.

TYPES OF LISTINGS

Open Listing

The **open listing** agreement, made to any number of brokers, promises a commission to the first specific broker, if any, who produces a buyer who is ready, willing, and able to purchase the property on the terms of the listing. Sale of the property automatically terminates all existing open listings, and the seller owes no commissions or notices of termination to the other brokers. The seller also reserves the right to sell the property personally without paying a commission.

Exclusive Agency

The **exclusive agency** listing employs a specific broker as the seller's sole and exclusive agent. The seller maintains the right to sell the property personally without obligation. However, the employed broker is the only authorized agent of the seller, and that broker is entitled to a commission if any broker sells the property. The agency relationship automatically terminates if the owner sells the property before the broker produces a ready, willing, and able buyer, and no notice need be given to the broker. Otherwise, the listing terminates on sale by a broker or on the ending date specified in the listing.

Exclusive Right to Sell

The **exclusive right to sell agency** listing promises the employing broker a commission if anyone, including the owner, sells the property during the listing period. Furthermore, the broker obtains a full commission even if the owner withdraws the property or renders it unmarketable before expiration of the listing period.

SPECIAL LISTING FORMS

An open listing, exclusive agency, or exclusive right to sell are frequently used for special real estate purposes. The most common special purposes are for net listings, option listings, and multiple listings.

Net Listing

A **net listing** agreement entitles a broker to receive a commission only in the amount, if any, that the sales price exceeds the listing price. The net listing specifies the formula to determine the amount of commission, but the actual nature of the agreement may be any of the three standard types of listings discussed earlier. The broker must be careful to disclose the full amount of profit to the seller, or else the broker will violate a fiduciary duty.

Option Listing

The **option listing** grants the broker the right (option) to purchase the seller's property at the price specified in the listing. The listing itself may be any of the standard types of exclusive or open listings. The broker is in a fiduciary relationship of trust and fairness to the seller and must be extremely cautious if exercising the option. *B.&P.C. 10176h.*

Multiple Listing

Multiple listing boards are usually formed by the local real estate board or association of brokers. Such boards pool their listings and will disseminate each listing to all members, inviting their cooperation in the sale of the property for a share of the listing broker's commission. Because of antitrust laws, any type of listing, including open listings, can be submitted to the multiple listing service. *C.C. 1087.* Furthermore, any broker, whether or not a member of the local real estate board, must be allowed full access to the multiple listing service. *Marin Co. Bd. of Realtors, Inc. v. Palsson (1976) 16 C.3d 920.*

BROKER'S RIGHT TO COMPENSATION

Amount by Agreement

A broker's compensation is usually a percentage of the selling price, customarily 5 to 7 percent, although the amount is entirely subject to negotiation and agreement between the parties. However, care must be taken to avoid violations of federal antitrust law by price fixing within the industry.

All listings on one- to four-family owner-occupied homes must contain a provision immediately under the clause, establishing the amount of commission and that the commission is negotiable. In 10-point bold type, the provision must state "Notice: The amount or rate of real estate commission is not fixed by law. It is set by each broker, individually, and may be negotiated between seller and broker." Furthermore, the amount of commission may not be preprinted in the form. It must be written in by the broker. *B.&P.C. 10147.5.*

Problems

An agent establishes rights to a commission by proving that he or she is a licensed broker or salesperson who has a written agreement to obtain a commission and has complied with all the requirements of that contract. Most litigation focuses on whether the broker was the *procuring cause* producing a *ready, willing, and able buyer* and on sales to broker-introduced buyers after the end date of the listing agreement.

Writing Mandatory

Unless the broker's right to a commission exists in writing, the broker is not entitled to any commission from the principal. C.C. *1624.* Generally, even if the seller intentionally misleads the broker into operating under an oral listing, it is the broker who suffers the consequences and receives no compensation. *Augustine v. Trucco (1954) 124 C.A.2d 229.*

Except between Brokers

Agreements between cooperating brokers to share a commission are exempt from the statute of frauds requirement and may be enforced as oral agreements.

Except Tort Interference

If a third-party intentionally induces a seller to breach the broker–principal relationship, the broker can collect a commission from the third party under the tort of *interference with a prospective advantage.* This rule applies even if the broker–seller relationship operates under an unenforceable oral agreement, because it is based on tort and not on contract theories. *Buckaloo v. Johnson (1975) 14 C.3d 815.*

Procuring Cause

In certain situations, the broker must prove that the broker was the **procuring cause** of the sale, that is, that the sale resulted directly and proximately from the broker's personal efforts. The broker must have introduced a qualified buyer who, through an unbroken chain of events or negotiations, either purchased or offered to purchase the seller's property. If the broker introduced the parties during the listing period and, through an unbroken chain, the sale is consummated after expiration of the listing period, the broker will still be entitled to a commission. *Strout Western Realty Agency, Inc. v. Lewis (1967) 255 C.A.2d 254.* Conversely, if there is a good-faith break in the chain of negotiations, if the parties later consummate a sale, the broker will not be the procuring cause. *Nelson v. Mayer (1954) 122 C.A.2d 438.*

Conspiracy

If the parties intentionally break the chain and postpone execution of the sale until after expiration of the listing period, they have committed a civil conspiracy. The broker may collect the full commission by suing the seller in contract or the buyer in tort. *California Auto Court Assn. v. Cohn (1950) 98 C.A.2d 145.*

Safety Clause

The question of procuring cause arises only if the broker has not otherwise earned a commission under the listing agreement. Generally, this occurs when the owner claims credit for sale under a general or exclusive agency listing, between competing brokers for the same commission, or when the **safety clause** requires the broker to be the procuring cause. Under exclusive right to sell agreements, the broker earns a commission regardless of who is the procuring cause.

Ready, Willing, and Able Buyer

Most listing agreements provide that the broker must produce a buyer who is *ready, willing, and able* to purchase the property on the exact terms of the listing or on other terms acceptable to the seller. Once the broker has done so, according to most agreements, the broker has earned the commission. If the seller refuses to sell or interjects new and unacceptable terms to a sale, the broker has still earned the compensation.

Sale Required

Occasional listings contain a *no deal, no commission* clause, which provides that the broker earns a commission only if the property is actually sold. In such cases, unless the ready, willing, and able buyer actually purchases the property, the broker earns no compensation.

Safety Clause

The safety clause provision found in most listings provides that, if anyone found by the broker during the listing period buys the property during a specified period after the expiration of the listing, the broker still receives a commission. The broker must usually supply the names of prospective buyers to the seller within a specified number of days after the listing period.

Two Commissions Possible

The seller could be liable for two commissions if, during that listing period, another broker sold the property to a prospective client of the prior broker. To avoid this possibility, the owner should specifically exclude from the new listing anyone contacted by the first broker. The old CAR listing forms contained such a clause protecting the owner from the possibility of owing two commissions. The new form contains no such exception if the broker timely supplied the seller a written list of names of prospective purchasers.

SPECIAL COMMISSION SITUATIONS

Withdrawal Requires Commission

If the owner withdraws the property from sale or renders it unmarketable during the term of the usual exclusive right to sell listing, the broker is entitled to the full commission based on the listing price. In one case, the seller listed a property for $85,000, promising to pay the broker 6 percent of the actual selling price and recognizing that the listing price would probably be higher than the final sale price. Before the broker produced a buyer, the owner, without justification, withdrew the property from the market. The court awarded the broker $5,500, or 6 percent of the $85,000 listing price. *Blank v. Borden (1974) 11 C.3d 963.*

Default by Buyer

If the buyer **defaults** on the contract, the seller is not obligated to sue for damages or specific performance. If the seller elects to sue for the buyer's breach, any recovery generally entitles the broker to the full commission. If the owner does not sue but retains the deposit for damages, then under the CAR and most other deposit receipts, the broker is entitled to one-half the deposit on default by the buyer and declared forfeiture of the deposit by the seller. The broker's total recovery is limited to an amount equal to one-half the deposit. *Chapman v. Gilmore (1963) 221 C.A.2d 506.*

Seller's Option

As with any breach, the seller is not obligated to declare the deposit forfeited. If the seller does not claim the deposit, no liability to the broker is incurred for any commission. *Kritt v. Athens Hills Dev. Co. (1952) 109 C.A.2d 506.*

Probate Sales

Originally, all probate sales and most probate listings required the cumbersome and time-consuming process of court confirmation. However, most wills drafted since 1978 allow executors who elect to probate estates under the Independent Administration of Estates

Act (IAEA) to avoid court approval and confirmation. Unless there are specific objections of interested parties to that particular probate estate, such sales are handled much the same as any other ordinary real state sale. Thus, executors have the options of two forms of sale of probate real estate.

Traditional Method

All exclusive right-to-sell listings require court approval and are usually limited to 90 days. If a listing is signed before court approval, it is not valid until confirmed. All sales must be confirmed by the court, in a court process involving open bidding. (See Figure 6.1.) If the broker's sale is approved, he or she generally receives a full commission as set by the court. If the court accepts a higher bid at the confirmation hearing, the broker's commission, if any, is set by local court rules and state law. *Prob.C. §10161–10168.*

Independent Administration of Estates Act

To use the Independent Administration of Estates Act ("IDEA") process, the decedent's will must specifically authorize used of the IDEA and also allow executors the right to sell property. Most wills written today allow both actions. Executors can list property on the multiple listing service, and successfully sell probate property without court approval. Executors must first provide notice of the proposed sale to the heirs, beneficiaries, and others who have requested special notice. If no one objects within 15 days after receiving the advance notice, the executor can proceed without court approval. If there is an objection, then the sale must be confirmed by the court in a hearing similar to the traditional method. *Prob. C. 10510 et seq.* The required "notice of proposed action" procedure is generally handled by attorneys for the estate. The author's experience has been that executors selling residential property rarely receive any objections and can proceed without court confirmation.

Disallowed Commission

Regardless of the type of probate, the court will not allow a broker to receive a commission from a probate sale if the broker will have any interest in the property or the entity purchasing the property. *Prob.C. §10160.5.*

After Expiration of Listing

Normally, any work done by the broker after expiration of the listing agreement is at the broker's risk. However, if the seller urges and encourages the broker's work beyond the termination period, the seller is estopped from raising the defense of the statute of frauds, and the

FIGURE 6.1 Report of Sale and Order Confirming Sale of Real Property.

DE-260/GC-060

ATTORNEY OR PARTY WITHOUT ATTORNEY (Name, State Bar number, and address):	FOR COURT USE ONLY

TELEPHONE NO.:   FAX NO. (Optional):

E-MAIL ADDRESS (Optional):

ATTORNEY FOR (Name):

SUPERIOR COURT OF CALIFORNIA, COUNTY OF

STREET ADDRESS:

MAILING ADDRESS:

CITY AND ZIP CODE:

BRANCH NAME:

☐ ESTATE ☐ CONSERVATORSHIP ☐ GUARDIANSHIP OF

(Name):

☐ DECEDENT ☐ CONSERVATEE ☐ MINOR

REPORT OF SALE AND PETITION FOR ORDER CONFIRMING SALE OF REAL PROPERTY
☐ and Sale of Other Property Sold as a Unit

CASE NUMBER:

HEARING DATE AND TIME: DEPT.:

1. **Petitioner** (name of each):

    is the ☐ personal representative ☐ conservator ☐ guardian of the estate of the decedent, conservatee, or minor
    ☐ purchaser (30 days have passed since the sale) (Attach supporting declaration (Prob. Code, § 10308(b).)

    and **requests** a court order for (check all that apply):

    a. confirmation of sale of the estate's interest in the real property described in Attachment 2e
    b. ☐ confirmation of sale of the estate's interest in other property sold as a unit as described in Attachment 2c.
    c. ☐ approval of commission of (specify):   % of the amount of: $
    d. additional bond ☐ is fixed at: $ ☐ is not required.

2. **Description of property sold**

    a. Interest sold: ☐ 100% ☐ Undivided (specify):   %
    b. ☐ Improved ☐ Unimproved
    c. ☐ Real property sold as a unit with other property (describe in Attachment 2c).
    d. Street address and location (specify):

    e. Legal description is affixed as Attachment 2e.

3. **Appraisal**

    a. Date of death of decedent or appointment of conservator or guardian (specify):
    b. Appraised value at above date: $
    c. Reappraised value within one year before the hearing: $ ☐ Amount includes value of other property
    sold as a unit. (If more than one year has elapsed from the date in item 3a to the date of the hearing, reappraisal is required.)
    d. Appraisal or reappraisal by probate referee ☐ has been filed ☐ will be filed
    ☐ has been waived by order dated:

4. **Manner and terms of sale**

    a. Name of purchaser and manner of vesting title (specify):

    b. ☐ Purchaser is the ☐ personal representative ☐ attorney for the personal representative.
    c. Sale was ☐ private ☐ public on (date):
    d. Amount bid: $ Deposit: $
    e. Payment ☐ Cash ☐ Credit (specify terms on Attachment 4e.)
    f. ☐ Other terms of sale (specify terms on Attachment 4f.)
    g. ☐ Mode of sale specified in will. ☐ Petitioner requests relief from complying for the reasons stated in Attachment 4g.
    h. ☐ Terms comply with Probate Code section 2542 (guardianships and conservatorships).

Page 1 of 2

Form Adopted for Mandatory Use
Judicial Council of California
DE-260/GC-060 [Rev. January 1, 2006]

**REPORT OF SALE AND PETITION FOR ORDER
CONFIRMING SALE OF REAL PROPERTY**
(Probate—Decedents' Estates and Guardianships and Conservatorships)

Probate Code, §§ 2540, 10308
www.courtinfo.ca.gov

American LegalNet, Inc.
www.USCourtForms.com

FIGURE 6.1 *(Continued).*

DE-260/GC-060

☐ ESTATE ☐ CONSERVATORSHIP ☐ GUARDIANSHIP OF	CASE NUMBER:
(Name):	

5. Commission
- a. ☐ Sale without broker
- b. ☐ A written ☐ exclusive ☐ nonexclusive contract for commission was entered into with *(name):*
- c. ☐ Purchaser was procured by *(name):*
  a licensed real estate broker who is not buying for his or her account.
- d. ☐ Commission is to be divided as follows:

6. Bond
- a. Amount before sale: $ ☐ none.
- b. Additional amount needed: $ ☐ none.
- c. ☐ Proceeds are to be deposited in a blocked account. Receipts will be filed. *(Specify institution and location):*

7. Notice of sale
- a. ☐ Published ☐ Posted as permitted by Probate Code section 10301 ($5,000 or less)
- b. ☐ Will authorizes sale of the property
- c. ☐ Will directs sale of the property

8. Notice of hearing
- a. Special devisee:
  - (1) ☐ None.
  - (2) ☐ Consent to be filed.
  - (3) ☐ Written notice will be given.
- b. Special notice:
  - (1) ☐ None requested.
  - (2) ☐ Has been or will be waived.
  - (3) ☐ Required written notice will be given.
- c. Personal representative, conservator of the estate, or guardian of the estate:
  - (1) ☐ Petitioner (consent or notice not required).
  - (2) ☐ Consent to be filed.
  - (3) ☐ Written notice will be given.

9. Reason for sale *(need not complete if item 7b or 7c checked)*
- a. ☐ Necessary to pay
  - (1) ☐ debts
  - (2) ☐ devise
  - (3) ☐ family allowance
  - (4) ☐ expenses of administration
  - (5) ☐ taxes
- b. ☐ The sale is to the advantage of the estate and in the best interest of the interested persons.

10. Formula for overbids
- a. Original bid: $ _____
- b. 10% of first $10,000 of original bid: $ _____
- c. 5% of (original bid minus $10,000): $ _____
- d. Minimum overbid (a + b + c): $ _____

11. Overbid. Required amount of first overbid *(see item 10):* $ [_____]

12. Petitioner's efforts to obtain the highest and best price reasonably attainable for the property were as follows *(specify activities taken to expose the property to the market, e.g., multiple listings, advertising, open houses, etc.):*

13. Number of pages attached: ____

Date:

_____
(TYPE OR PRINT NAME OF ATTORNEY)

▶ _____
(SIGNATURE OF ATTORNEY*)
* (Signature of all petitioners also required (Prob. Code, § 1020).)

I declare under penalty of perjury under the laws of the State of California that the foregoing is true and correct.

Date:

_____
(TYPE OR PRINT NAME OF PETITIONER)

▶ _____
(SIGNATURE OF PETITIONER)

DE-260 GC-060 [Rev. January 1, 2006]

REPORT OF SALE AND PETITION FOR ORDER CONFIRMING SALE OF REAL PROPERTY
(Probate—Decedents' Estates and Guardianships and Conservatorships)

Page 2 of 2

broker may recover the commission by producing a ready, willing, and able buyer. *Kraemer v. Smith (1960) 179 C.A.2d 52.*

Buckaloo v. Johnson
14 C.3d 815 (1975)

[Mrs. Benioff, the seller, placed a For Sale–Contact Your Broker sign on her Dark Gulch property, intending the sign to serve as an open listing. Mr. Buckaloo, the plaintiff, was the broker who informed and interested the buyer, Mrs. Arness, in the property. Mrs. Arness bought the property without the services of broker Buckaloo, who then sued the owner for his commission under breach of contract. He also sued the buyers and others in tort for intentional interference with a prospective business advantage.

Buckaloo could obtain no commission from the seller because there was no written agreement, and the statute of frauds prohibits any broker from enforcing an oral listing agreement. Furthermore, the For Sale sign could not constitute a written document under the very liberal statute of frauds.]

MOSK, JUSTICE. However, plaintiff included in his complaint a cause of action not dependent on compliance with the Statute of Frauds: intentional interference with prospective economic advantage. This is a tort theory of recovery, rather than contract, and is based on interference with a "relationship" between parties irrespective of the enforceability of the underlying agreement. The nature of the tort does not vary with the legal strength, or enforceability, of the relation disrupted. The actionable wrong lies in the inducement to break the contract or to sever the relationship so disrupted, whether it is written or oral, enforceable or not enforceable.

The principles of liability for interference with contract extend beyond existing contractual relations, and a similar action would lie for interference with relations that are merely prospective or potential. [Both the tort of interference with contract relations and the tort of interference with prospective contract or business relations involve basically the same conduct on the part of the **tortfeasor**. In one case the interference takes place when a contract is already in existence, in the other, when a contract would, with certainty, have been consummated but for the conduct of the tortfeasor.]

One doctrine requires certain kinds of contracts to be in writing and finds expression in the Statute of Frauds. The other doctrine holds that a party who suffers the loss of an advantageous relationship or of a contract should recover his damages from a malicious interloper. Can one so damaged through the loss of an oral contract prevail despite noncompliance with the Statute of Frauds? The court concluded that the complaint stated a cause of action notwithstanding the lack of a valid contract, because the essence of the tort contemplates, basically, the

continued

disruption of a relationship, not necessarily the breach of a contract. Contracts that are voidable by reason of the Statute of Frauds, formal defects, lack of consideration, lack of mutuality, or even uncertainty of terms still afford a basis for a tort action when the defendant interferes with their performance.

The mere fact that a prospective economic relationship has not attained the dignity of a legally enforceable agreement does not permit third parties to interfere with performance. This of course does no violence to traditional contract principles because the third party, a stranger to the economic relationship, was not the party whom the contract principle was designed to affect. Thus the cases are clear that a prospective purchaser may not induce a seller bound under an oral agreement to breach that agreement and sell to him at a price that necessarily excludes the broker.

Less obvious perhaps, but nonetheless actionable, are the circumstances in which the purchaser, with full knowledge of the economic relationship between broker and seller, intentionally induces the latter to violate the terms of the relationship and seek refuge in the unenforceability of the contract. As the New Jersey court noted, however, in order to successfully maintain this cause of action it must be shown that the interloper received pecuniary benefit in the way of a reduced selling price resulting from the exclusion of the broker's commission.

Finally, we note the elements of the tort itself. In the real estate brokerage context, these are: (1) an economic relationship between broker and vendor or broker and vendee containing the probability of future economic benefit to the broker, (2) knowledge by the defendant of the existence of the relationship, (3) intentional acts on the part of the defendant designed to disrupt the relationship, (4) actual disruption of the relationship, and (5) damages to the plaintiff proximately caused by the acts of the defendant.

[The case is reversed and remanded to the trial court for a jury to determine whether the elements of the tortfeasor's interference exist.]

ANALYSIS OF CALIFORNIA ASSOCIATION OF REALTORS®, LISTING AGREEMENT

The numbers appearing before the headings in this section correspond with the circled boldface numbers on Figure 6.2.

(1) Name of Seller

The names of all parties selling an interest in the property should be given. This complete list helps establish the parties' rights and

FIGURE 6.2   Cal Assoc Realtors Listing Agreement.

CALIFORNIA
ASSOCIATION
OF REALTORS®

RESIDENTIAL LISTING AGREEMENT
(Exclusive Authorization and Right to Sell)
(C.A.R. Form LA, Revised 10/02)

1. **EXCLUSIVE RIGHT TO SELL:** _____ (1) (2) _____ ("Seller")
    hereby employs and grants _____ (3) _____ ("Broker")
    beginning (date) _____ and ending at 11:59 P.M. on (date) _____ (4) _____ ("Listing Period")
    (5) exclusive (6) irrevocable right to sell or exchange the real property in the City of _____
    County of _____, California, described as: _____
    _____ ("Property").

2. **ITEMS EXCLUDED AND INCLUDED:** Unless otherwise specified in a real estate purchase agreement, all fixtures and fittings that
    are attached to the Property are included, and personal property items are excluded, from the purchase price.
    ADDITIONAL ITEMS EXCLUDED: _____
    ADDITIONAL ITEMS INCLUDED: _____ (8) _____
    Seller intends that the above items be excluded or included in offering the Property for sale, but understands that: (i) the purchase
    agreement supersedes any intention expressed above and will ultimately determine which items are excluded and included in the sale;
    and (ii) Broker is not responsible for and does not guarantee that the above exclusions and/or inclusions will be in the purchase agreement.

3. **LISTING PRICE AND TERMS:**
    A. The listing price shall be: _____ (9) _____
        _____ Dollars ($ _____).
    B. Additional Terms: _____ (10) _____
        _____.

4. **COMPENSATION TO BROKER:**
    **Notice: The amount or rate of real estate commissions is not fixed by law. They are set by each Broker
    individually and may be negotiated between Seller and Broker (real estate commissions include all
    compensation and fees to Broker).** (11)
    A. Seller agrees to pay to Broker as compensation for services irrespective of agency relationship(s), either ☐ _____ percent
        of the listing price (or if a purchase agreement is entered into, of the purchase price), or ☐ $ _____,
        AND _____ (12) _____, as follows:
    (13)   (1) If Broker, Seller, cooperating broker, or any other person procures a buyer(s) who offers to purchase the Property on the
            above price and terms, or on any price and terms acceptable to Seller during the Listing Period, or any extension.
            (2) If Seller, within _____ calendar days **(a)** after the end of the Listing Period or any extension, or **(b)** after any cancellation
            of this Agreement, unless otherwise agreed, enters into a contract to sell, convey, lease or otherwise transfer the Property
    (14)   to anyone ("Prospective Buyer") or that person's related entity: **(i)** who physically entered and was shown the Property during
            the Listing Period or any extension by Broker or a cooperating broker; or **(ii)** for whom Broker or any cooperating broker
            submitted to Seller a signed, written offer to acquire, lease, exchange or obtain an option on the Property. Seller, however,
            shall have no obligation to Broker under paragraph 4A(2) unless, not later than **3 calendar days** after the end of the Listing
            Period or any extension or cancellation, Broker has given Seller a written notice of the names of such Prospective Buyers.
    (15)   (3) If, without Broker's prior written consent, the Property is withdrawn from sale, conveyed, leased, rented, otherwise
            transferred, or made unmarketable by a voluntary act of Seller during the Listing Period, or any extension.
    B. If completion of the sale is prevented by a party to the transaction other than Seller, then compensation due under paragraph
        4A shall be payable only if and when Seller collects damages by suit, arbitration, settlement or otherwise, and then in an amount
    (16)   equal to the lesser of one-half of the damages recovered or the above compensation, after first deducting title and escrow
        expenses and the expenses of collection, if any.
    C. In addition, Seller agrees to pay Broker: _____ (17) _____.
    D. (1) Broker is authorized to cooperate with and compensate brokers participating through the multiple listing service(s)
        ("MLS"): **(i)** in any manner; **OR (ii)** (if checked) by offering MLS brokers: either ☐ _ (18) _ percent of the purchase
    (19)   price, or ☐ $ _____.
        (2) Broker is authorized to cooperate with and compensate brokers operating outside the MLS in any manner.
    E. Seller hereby irrevocably assigns to Broker the above compensation from Seller's funds and proceeds in escrow. Broker may
    (20) submit this agreement, as instructions to compensate Broker pursuant to paragraph 4A, to any escrow regarding the Property
        involving Seller and a buyer, Prospective Buyer or other transferee.
    F. (1) Seller represents that Seller has not previously entered into a listing agreement with another broker regarding the Property,
        unless specified as follows: _____
        (2) Seller warrants that Seller has no obligation to pay compensation to any other broker regarding the Property unless the
    (21)   Property is transferred to any of the following individuals or entities: _____

        (3) If the Property is sold to anyone listed above during the time Seller is obligated to compensate another broker: **(i)** Broker is
        not entitled to compensation under this agreement; and **(ii)** Broker is not obligated to represent Seller in such transaction.

LA REVISED 10/02 (PAGE 1 OF 3)   Print Date

Seller acknowledges receipt of a copy of this page.
Seller's Initials (_____)(_____)

Reviewed by _____ Date _____

EQUAL HOUSING
OPPORTUNITY

Source: Reprinted with permission. *California Association of REALTORS®.* Endorsement not implied.

FIGURE 6.2 *(Continued)*.

Property Address: _____ Date: _____

(22) 5. **OWNERSHIP, TITLE AND AUTHORITY:** Seller warrants that: **(i)** Seller is the owner of the Property; **(ii)** no other persons or entities have title to the Property; and **(iii)** Seller has the authority to both execute this agreement and sell the Property. Exceptions to ownership, title and authority are as follows: _____

(23) 6. **MULTIPLE LISTING SERVICE:** Information about this listing will (or ☐ will not) be provided to the MLS of Broker's selection. All terms of the transaction, including financing, if applicable, will be provided to the selected MLS for publication, dissemination and use by persons and entities on terms approved by the MLS. Seller authorizes Broker to comply with all applicable MLS rules. MLS rules allow MLS data to be made available by the MLS to additional Internet sites unless Broker gives the MLS instructions to the contrary.

(24) 7. **SELLER REPRESENTATIONS:** Seller represents that, unless otherwise specified in writing, Seller is unaware of: **(i)** any Notice of Default recorded against the Property; **(ii)** any delinquent amounts due under any loan secured by, or other obligation affecting, the Property; **(iii)** any bankruptcy, insolvency or similar proceeding affecting the Property; **(iv)** any litigation, arbitration, administrative action, government investigation or other pending or threatened action that affects or may affect the Property or Seller's ability to transfer it; and **(v)** any current, pending or proposed special assessments affecting the Property. Seller shall promptly notify Broker in writing if Seller becomes aware of any of these items during the Listing Period or any extension thereof.

(25) 8. **BROKER'S AND SELLER'S DUTIES:** Broker agrees to exercise reasonable effort and due diligence to achieve the purposes of this agreement. Unless Seller gives Broker written instructions to the contrary, Broker is authorized to order reports and disclosures as appropriate or necessary and advertise and market the Property by any method and in any medium selected by Broker, including MLS and the Internet, and, to the extent permitted by these media, control the dissemination of the information submitted to any medium. Seller agrees to consider offers presented by Broker, and to act in good faith to accomplish the sale of the Property by, among other things, making the Property available for showing at reasonable times and referring to Broker all inquiries of any party interested in the Property. Seller is responsible for determining at what price to list and sell the Property. **Seller further agrees to indemnify, defend and hold Broker harmless from all claims, disputes, litigation, judgments and attorney fees arising from any incorrect information supplied by Seller, or from any material facts that Seller knows but fails to disclose.**

(26) 9. **DEPOSIT:** Broker is authorized to accept and hold on Seller's behalf any deposits to be applied toward the purchase price.

10. **AGENCY RELATIONSHIPS:**
   A. **Disclosure:** If the Property includes residential property with one-to-four dwelling units, Seller shall receive a "Disclosure Regarding Agency Relationships" form prior to entering into this agreement.
   B. **Seller Representation:** Broker shall represent Seller in any resulting transaction, except as specified in paragraph 4F.
   C. **Possible Dual Agency With Buyer:** Depending upon the circumstances, it may be necessary or appropriate for Broker to act as an agent for both Seller and buyer, exchange party, or one or more additional parties ("Buyer"). Broker shall, as soon as practicable, disclose to Seller any election to act as a dual agent representing both Seller and Buyer. If a Buyer is procured directly by Broker or an associate licensee in Broker's firm, Seller hereby consents to Broker acting as a dual agent for Seller and such Buyer. In the event of an exchange, Seller hereby consents to Broker collecting compensation from additional parties for services rendered, provided there is disclosure to all parties of such agency and compensation. Seller understands and agrees that: **(i)** Broker, without the prior written consent of Seller, will not disclose to Buyer that Seller is willing to sell the Property at a price less than the listing price; **(ii)** Broker, without the prior written consent of Buyer, will not disclose to Seller that Buyer is willing to pay a price greater than the offered price; and **(iii)** except for (i) and (ii) above, a dual agent is obligated to disclose known facts materially affecting the value or desirability of the Property to both parties.
   D. **Other Sellers:** Seller understands that Broker may have or obtain listings on other properties, and that potential buyers may consider, make offers on, or purchase through Broker, property the same as or similar to Seller's Property. Seller consents to Broker's representation of sellers and buyers of other properties before, during and after the end of this agreement.
   E. **Confirmation:** If the Property includes residential property with one-to-four dwelling units, Broker shall confirm the agency relationship described above, or as modified, in writing, prior to or concurrent with Seller's execution of a purchase agreement.

(27)

(28) 11. **SECURITY AND INSURANCE:** Broker is not responsible for loss of or damage to personal or real property, or person, whether attributable to use of a keysafe/lockbox, a showing of the Property, or otherwise. Third parties, including, but not limited to, appraisers, inspectors, brokers and prospective buyers, may have access to, and take videos and photographs of, the interior of the Property. Seller agrees: **(i)** to take reasonable precautions to safeguard and protect valuables that might be accessible during showings of the Property; and **(ii)** to obtain insurance to protect against these risks. Broker does not maintain insurance to protect Seller.

(29) 12. **KEYSAFE/LOCKBOX:** A keysafe/lockbox is designed to hold a key to the Property to permit access to the Property by Broker, cooperating brokers, MLS participants, their authorized licensees and representatives, authorized inspectors, and accompanied prospective buyers. Broker, cooperating brokers, MLS and Associations/Boards of REALTORS® are not insurers against injury, theft, loss, vandalism or damage attributed to the use of a keysafe/lockbox. Seller does (or if checked ☐ does not) authorize Broker to install a keysafe/lockbox. If Seller does not occupy the Property, Seller shall be responsible for obtaining occupant(s)' written permission for use of a keysafe/lockbox.

(30) 13. **SIGN:** Seller does (or if checked ☐ does not) authorize Broker to install a FOR SALE/SOLD sign on the Property.

(31) 14. **EQUAL HOUSING OPPORTUNITY:** The Property is offered in compliance with federal, state and local anti-discrimination laws.

(32) 15. **ATTORNEY FEES:** In any action, proceeding or arbitration between Seller and Broker regarding the obligation to pay compensation under this agreement, the prevailing Seller or Broker shall be entitled to reasonable attorney fees and costs from the non-prevailing Seller or Broker, except as provided in paragraph 19A.

(33) 16. **ADDITIONAL TERMS:** _____
_____
_____

(34) 17. **MANAGEMENT APPROVAL:** If an associate licensee in Broker's office (salesperson or broker-associate) enters into this agreement on Broker's behalf, and Broker or Manager does not approve of its terms, Broker or Manager has the right to *cancel* this agreement, in writing, within 5 days after its execution.

18. **SUCCESSORS AND ASSIGNS:** This agreement shall be binding upon Seller and Seller's successors and assigns.

Seller acknowledges receipt of a copy of this page.
Seller's Initials (_____)(_____)

Reviewed by _____ Date _____

EQUAL HOUSING OPPORTUNITY

Source: Reprinted with permission. *California Association of REALTORS®*. Endorsement not implied.

FIGURE 6.2 (*Continued*).

Property Address: _____   Date: _____

19. **DISPUTE RESOLUTION:**

   A. **MEDIATION:** Seller and Broker agree to mediate any dispute or claim arising between them out of this agreement, or any resulting transaction, before resorting to arbitration or court action, subject to paragraph 19B(2) below. Paragraph 19B(2) below applies whether or not the arbitration provision is initialed. Mediation fees, if any, shall be divided equally among the parties involved. If, for any dispute or claim to which this paragraph applies, any party commences an action without first attempting to resolve the matter through mediation, or refuses to mediate after a request has been made, then that party shall not be entitled to recover attorney fees, even if they would otherwise be available to that party in any such action. THIS MEDIATION PROVISION APPLIES WHETHER OR NOT THE ARBITRATION PROVISION IS INITIALED.

   B. **ARBITRATION OF DISPUTES:** (1) Seller and Broker agree that any dispute or claim in Law or equity arising between them regarding the obligation to pay compensation under this agreement, which is not settled through mediation, shall be decided by neutral, binding arbitration, including and subject to paragraph 19B(2) below. The arbitrator shall be a retired judge or justice, or an attorney with at least 5 years of residential real estate law experience, unless the parties mutually agree to a different arbitrator, who shall render an award in accordance with substantive California Law. The parties shall have the right to discovery in accordance with Code of Civil Procedure §1283.05. In all other respects, the arbitration shall be conducted in accordance with Title 9 of Part III of the California Code of Civil Procedure. Judgment upon the award of the arbitrator(s) may be entered in any court having jurisdiction. Interpretation of this agreement to arbitrate shall be governed by the Federal Arbitration Act.
   (2) **EXCLUSIONS FROM MEDIATION AND ARBITRATION:** The following matters are excluded from mediation and arbitration hereunder: (i) a judicial or non-judicial foreclosure or other action or proceeding to enforce a deed of trust, mortgage, or installment land sale contract as defined in Civil Code §2985; (ii) an unlawful detainer action; (iii) the filing or enforcement of a mechanic's lien; and (iv) any matter that is within the jurisdiction of a probate, small claims, or bankruptcy court. The filing of a court action to enable the recording of a notice of pending action, for order of attachment, receivership, injunction, or other provisional remedies, shall not constitute a waiver of the mediation and arbitration provisions.

   "NOTICE: BY INITIALING IN THE SPACE BELOW YOU ARE AGREEING TO HAVE ANY DISPUTE ARISING OUT OF THE MATTERS INCLUDED IN THE 'ARBITRATION OF DISPUTES' PROVISION DECIDED BY NEUTRAL ARBITRATION AS PROVIDED BY CALIFORNIA LAW AND YOU ARE GIVING UP ANY RIGHTS YOU MIGHT POSSESS TO HAVE THE DISPUTE LITIGATED IN A COURT OR JURY TRIAL. BY INITIALING IN THE SPACE BELOW YOU ARE GIVING UP YOUR JUDICIAL RIGHTS TO DISCOVERY AND APPEAL, UNLESS THOSE RIGHTS ARE SPECIFICALLY INCLUDED IN THE 'ARBITRATION OF DISPUTES' PROVISION. IF YOU REFUSE TO SUBMIT TO ARBITRATION AFTER AGREEING TO THIS PROVISION, YOU MAY BE COMPELLED TO ARBITRATE UNDER THE AUTHORITY OF THE CALIFORNIA CODE OF CIVIL PROCEDURE. YOUR AGREEMENT TO THIS ARBITRATION PROVISION IS VOLUNTARY."

   "WE HAVE READ AND UNDERSTAND THE FOREGOING AND AGREE TO SUBMIT DISPUTES ARISING OUT OF THE MATTERS INCLUDED IN THE 'ARBITRATION OF DISPUTES' PROVISION TO NEUTRAL ARBITRATION."

   | Seller's Initials _____ / _____ | Broker's Initials _____ / _____ |

20. **ENTIRE CONTRACT:** All prior discussions, negotiations and agreements between the parties concerning the subject matter of this agreement are superseded by this agreement, which constitutes the entire contract and a complete and exclusive expression of their agreement, and may not be contradicted by evidence of any prior agreement or contemporaneous oral agreement. If any provision of this agreement is held to be ineffective or invalid, the remaining provisions will nevertheless be given full force and effect. This agreement and any supplement, addendum or modification, including any photocopy or facsimile, may be executed in counterparts.

By signing below, Seller acknowledges that Seller has read, understands, accepts and has received a copy of this agreement.

Seller _____   Date _____

Address _____ City _____ State _____ Zip _____

Telephone _____ Fax _____ E-mail _____

Seller _____   Date _____

Address _____ City _____ State _____ Zip _____

Telephone _____ Fax _____ E-mail _____

Real Estate Broker (Firm) _____

By (Agent) _____   Date _____

Address _____ City _____ State _____ Zip _____

Telephone _____ Fax _____ E-mail _____

SURE TRAC
The System for Success™

Published by the
California Association of REALTORS®

Source: Reprinted with permission. *California Association of REALTORS®*. Endorsement not implied.

obligations and facilitates enforcement against all named individuals. See the discussion under number 37 on the need to list both spouses if community property is being listed.

Capacity to Contract

If there is any question, the broker should confirm the seller's legal capacity to contract for the sale of the property. Obviously, minors and incompetents lack capacity. Because corporations and partnerships may have restricted their ability to contract for real estate, the broker should read their articles and bylaws. Furthermore, appropriate corporate resolutions and correct procedures must be followed. Finally, powers of attorney must be evaluated for the appropriate legal language and to ensure that the agency has not been revoked by the parties or canceled by the death or incapacity of the principal.

(2) Name of Broker

Because a salesperson lacks authority to list property in his or her own name, the broker's name must be used. If the broker operates a business under a fictitious name, a *dba* (doing business as) should be included after the name.

(3) Commencement Date

Although sound drafting principles dictate the need for a commencement date, its absence is neither fatal nor grounds for discipline by the real estate commission. If this date is omitted, the contract is presumed effective on the date that the listing is signed.

(4) Termination Date

All exclusive listing contracts must have a definite and set termination date; otherwise, the broker will be subject to disciplinary action by the real estate commissioner. *B.&P.C. 10176f.* If the property has already been sold or if the broker has fully performed all duties required, he or she is still entitled to the commission despite having violated the real estate law. However, if the contract is still executory and not fully performed by the broker, the seller can rescind the contract. *Lewis & Queen v. Ball & Sons (1957) 48 C.2d 141.*

(5) Exclusive Right to Sell

This contract grants the agent an exclusive right to sell the owner's property. The broker earns the commission, as defined later in the document, if the property is sold during the listing term. It does not matter whether the sale occurs through the efforts of a real estate broker or by the actions of the owner.

(6) Irrevocable Right

The broker promises to use due diligence in finding a buyer, thereby creating a bilateral contract. *Herz v. Clark's Market (1960) 179 C.A.2d 471.* Consequently, the seller owes the broker a full commission by unjustly and prematurely terminating the listing or rendering the property unmarketable. *Blank v. Borden (1974) 11 C.3d 963.*

Rescission

Unless the broker uses due diligence in attempting to secure a purchase, there is a failure of consideration. If the seller first notifies the broker of a rescission, the seller may then sell the property personally or through another broker without obligation to pay a commission to the original broker. *Coleman v. Mora (1968) 263 C.A.2d 137.* However, if the seller fails to notify the broker of intent to rescind, the seller waives any breach by the broker. *C.C. 1689.* The seller would then be liable for a full commission to the broker who sells the property, even if the broker failed to use due diligence. *Carlsen v. Zane (1968) 261 C.A.2d 399.*

Other Methods of Termination

The listing agreement is a contract to employ an agent. If the seller dies before the broker produces a buyer, the agreement is automatically terminated by law. *C.B. Webster Real Estate v. Richard (1971) 21 C.A.3d 612.* Because the listing is also a contract, it can be terminated by any of the methods available for termination of contracts.

(7) Description of Property

The description need only be sufficient to locate the property from the document. A legal description or a description of the detail required in a deed is not necessary. However, it is advisable to include both the street address, if applicable, and, if available, a legal description from the deed or title policy.

(8) Items Excluded and Included

Personal property included in the sale (which in residential property typically includes such items as carpets and drapes) should be listed. Any fixtures not included in the purchase should also be listed here on the appropriate line.

(9) List Price

This paragraph states the listing price in dollars. The main difficulty here is establishing the correct and valid reasonable listing price. Usually, the price is established through a competitive market analysis, appraisal, or broker evaluation of the circumstances of sale. If the listing price is below fair market value, the broker would do well to consider having a letter or other written documentation that the seller knows that the listing price is different from the current value.

(10) Terms of Sale

The listing must state the specific and detailed terms that the seller will accept. Failure to do so creates problems if the broker must sue to collect the commission. Generally, brokers fill in this section with a simple clause like "all cash to the seller."

However, if there are any special terms, they should be noted. If FHA and VA loans are acceptable, the broker should specify the number of points that the seller will pay. In the case of conventional loans, the seller's obligation for prepayment penalties should be stated. If there is to be an assumption, with the seller carrying secondary financing, the specific terms of the purchase money financing should be given. A description of this purchase money loan should include the amount of monthly payments, interest rates, prepayment clauses, impound (if any), and other such terms of the loan. If the seller has a low tax basis in the property, he or she may request or need tax sheltering through an installment sale or qualified trade for like property.

(11) Notice: Commission Negotiable

All listings on one- to four-family owner-occupied dwellings must contain specific wording indicating that the commission is negotiable. Furthermore, the amount of the commission must be written in by hand. *B.&P.C. 10147.5.*

(12) Commission: Amount

The commission is set either as a percentage of the sales price, which is the most common method, or as a flat fee. The appropriate commission blank is filled in and is the total compensation that can be earned by the broker.

(13) Commission: Sale

Subparagraph 4(a)(1) states that the broker earns a commission when the seller is presented with an acceptable offer to buy the property. The subparagraph does not require completion of the sale, only a valid, acceptable offer. If there are contingencies in the contract, presumably those conditions would have to be satisfied before the commission is earned. This is an exclusive right to sell because the clause provides a commission is earned even if the buyer is produced by the seller or any other person during the effective period of the listing.

(14) Commission: Safety Clause

Subparagraph 4(a)(2) is called a *Safety Clause*. It allows the broker to earn the full commission if the property is sold during the safety period, usually 90 days after the termination of the listing to anyone with whom the broker has negotiated (procuring cause). To qualify, the broker must notify the seller in writing, before the termination date of the listing, of those prospective buyers with whom he or she claims the right to a future commission.

The earlier CAR forms protected the seller from paying two commissions. The new form provides that the original listing broker is entitled to a full commission if a later broker sells the property to one of the listed prospective purchasers. Paragraph 4(f) allows and requires the seller to list any prior brokers who might have a right to compensation because of their safety clause.

See Figure 6.3 for the California Association of Realtors form notifying the seller of potential buyers who have either shown an interest in or made an offer on the listed property, and for whom a sale to one of them during the safety period would require a commission to the real estate broker.

(15) Commission: Withdrawal from Sale

Subparagraph 4(a)(3) permits the broker to recover the *full* commission if the seller renders the property unmarketable or withdraws it from sale during the listing period. *Blank v. Borden (1974) 11 C. 3d 963.*

Higher Fee

Some listing agreements, including older versions of the CAR exclusive listing, allow the broker to write in and set the amount of the commission in the event that the seller withdraws the property from sale. Occasionally, brokers specified a higher commission here, to attempt to discourage the seller from breaching. There is some question as to the legality of inserting a higher commission here, on the theory that it may amount to an invalid penalty. Brokers would be well advised in such situations to keep the commission the same or less than the original commission for a sale.

(16) Commission: Buyer Default

If the buyer defaults and the seller recovers any damages, the broker is entitled to a percent of the net damages recovered. The broker may receive the full commission amount specified earlier or one-half of the net recovery, whichever is less. This clause only applies if the seller collects damages. The wording cannot be used to force the seller to

FIGURE 6.3   CAR Notice of Prospective Buyers.

CALIFORNIA ASSOCIATION OF REALTORS®

NOTICE OF PROSPECTIVE BUYERS/TRANSFEREES
(C.A.R. Form NPB, 4/09)

1. **NOTICE OF PROSPECTIVE BUYERS/TRANSFEREES:** This notice is being provided to you as required by the Residential Listing Agreement (Exclusive (RLA), Agency (RLAA) or Open (RLAN))(or if checked), ☐ Commercial, Residential and Vacant Land Listing Agreement, ☐ Exclusive Authorization for Vacation Rental, ☐ Manufactured Home Listing Agreement, ☐ Lease Listing Agreement, ☐ Business Listing Agreement (the 'Listing Agreement'), between _____ _____ ("Seller/Landlord"), and _____ ("Broker") for the property described as _____ ("Property").

2. **LISTING PERIOD:** The Listing Agreement commenced on _____ and was scheduled to expire on, or was extended to, _____ ("Listing Period").

3. **COMPENSATION AGREEMENT:**
   A. Seller/Landlord has agreed to pay Broker the compensation provided for in the Listing Agreement if within the specified time after the Listing Period or any extension, or after any cancellation of the Listing Agreement unless otherwise agreed, Seller/Landlord enters into a contract to sell, convey, lease or otherwise transfer the Property to anyone ("Prospective Buyer/Transferee") or that person's related entity who during the listing period or any extension (i) Physically entered and was shown the Property by Broker or a cooperating broker, or (ii) Submitted to Seller/Landlord a signed written offer to acquire, lease, exchange or obtain an option on the Property.
   B. The obligation above only applies if Broker has provided to Seller/Landlord a list of Prospective Buyers/Transferees no later than 3 calendar days after the end of the Listing Period or any extension or cancellation.

4. **LIST OF PROSPECTIVE BUYERS/TRANSFEREES:**

NAME	BROKER/AGENT	DATE OF OFFER
_____	_____	_____
_____	_____	_____
_____	_____	_____
_____	_____	_____
_____	_____	_____
_____	_____	_____

   ☐ If checked see attached list of Prospective Buyers/Transferees

5. **NOTIFYING NEW BROKER:**
   Seller/Landlord is advised to provide this Notice to any broker Seller/Landlord intends to relist with. Failure to do so may obligate Seller/Landlord to pay two commissions.

6. **DATE OF NOTICE:**
   This Notice of Prospective Buyers/Transferees is being provided to Seller/Landlord on _____ (Date).

   Real Estate Broker (Firm) _____ DRE License # _____
   By (Agent) _____ DRE License # _____ Date _____
   Address _____ City _____ State _____ Zip _____
   Telephone _____ Fax _____ E-mail _____

   I acknowledge receipt of a copy of this Notice of Prospective Buyers/Transferees.

   Seller/Landlord _____ Date: _____

   Seller/Landlord _____ Date: _____

Published and Distributed by:
REAL ESTATE BUSINESS SERVICES, INC.
a subsidiary of the California Association of REALTORS®
525 South Virgil Avenue, Los Angeles, California 90020

Reviewed by _____ Date _____

EQUAL HOUSING OPPORTUNITY

NPB 4/09 (PAGE 1 OF 1)

NOTICE OF PROSPECTIVE BUYER/TRANSFEREES (NPB PAGE 1 OF 1)

Source: Reprinted with permission. *California Association of REALTORS®*. Endorsement not implied.

sue for damages, as it only allows a commission if and when the seller recovers any net proceeds.

(17) Additional Compensation

Any additional payments to the broker can be listed here. Typical examples might include a bonus if the property is sold within a set number of days or could include broker-incurred costs (such as postage and printing costs). Some offices may require a set fee to accept certain listings.

(18) MLS Fee Compensation

This clause allows brokers to cooperate with other brokers on the multiple listing service (MLS) and to share the commission as the brokers agree. Alternatively, by checking the boxes, the seller can specify that the cooperating broker only receive a specific percentage or dollar amount of the total commission.

(19) Cooperate with Other Brokers

This clause allows brokers to cooperate with other brokers who are not members of the MLS and to share the commission as the brokers agree.

(20) Commission: Assignment

This subparagraph grants the broker an assignment of the seller funds in escrow. This clause gives the broker certain rights in the funds and provides greater leverage in the event of a dispute or litigation. However, there is a question if the seller must execute escrow instruction before title or escrow companies will honor the clause. The author has found that if a dispute arises few sellers will cooperate to assist the broker.

(21) Prior Broker's Claim

This clause requires the seller to designate any other brokers who might have an obligation to a commission. If the seller puts "none" in the subparagraph and there is another broker with a right to commission, the seller has broken a *warranty*.

Exception: Another Broker

The second part of the clause provides an exception to avoid a situation in which a second broker, having a prior right to the commission, also claims compensation. A typical example could arise if a prior listing expired and the prior broker claimed the commission under the *safety clause* above.

This sentence states that a sale by a second broker with a superior right to payment prevents the listing broker from also demanding a commission. Thus, the seller is saved the expense of a double commission.

(22) Title

The title paragraph provides a warranty for the broker's benefit that all sellers are listed as owners unless they are noted as an exception. If there are none, as is usually the case, the term "none" should be written. Further, it should be noted that they have the right to sell such real estate.

(23) Multiple Listing Service

This clause allows the broker to place the property on the local multiple listing service (MLS), to employ subagents, and to disclose the terms and price of the final sales price. Some brokers attempt to sell the property in-house without listing it on the MLS, in which case the "will not" box would be checked. It is generally in the seller's best interest to place the home on the MLS promptly, unless the house is unusually expensive or there is a particular reason to avoid wide exposure. Recognizing new technology, the clause also allows the broker to place the property on the internet of the MLS rules so allow.

It is also possible to modify the clause if the property is not to be listed on the MLS. The seller could add a provision providing that for a time period, such as the first week, the property will not be listed on the MLS. After that first week, if the property has not been sold, it will be placed on the MLS.

(24) Seller's Warranties to Broker

Here the seller represents that there are no delinquencies, liens, bankruptcies, litigation, or proposed assessments, except those specifically indicated in writing. This clause is important to the broker because the broker will be making statements to potential buyers about the property's existing liens, potential encumbrances, and general marketability based upon the seller's representations. Even after execution of the listing agreement, if the seller learns of a change affecting the warranties the broker must be notified.

(25) Broker's and Seller's Duties

The broker agrees to use due diligence to find a buyer and, if authorized, to advertise the property. This clause makes the contract a *bilateral* agreement, with each side making promises to the other party. The seller agrees, besides the other terms of the listing, to act in good faith.

Indemnify Broker

The subparagraph also has the seller indemnify and defend the broker in any lawsuit from any claims or damages arising from incorrect information given by the seller. As helpful as this clause is, the provision may not be quite as broad as it seems. Because the broker has an independent duty to inspect and report on the condition of the property, the courts will ultimately have to decide on the legal validity of this clause. As to other misstatements and nondisclosures by the seller, the clause is probably valid, assuming that the broker has not knowingly or negligently participated in the misstatements or nondisclosure. However, the clause is of highly questionable validity when it attempts to relieve the broker from his or her own negligent acts and is probably invalid to the extent that it seeks to relieve the broker for intentional or reckless conduct. *C.C. 1668.*

(26) Acceptance of Deposit

Absent this clause, the broker has no authority to accept a deposit on behalf of the seller. Few sellers object to this clause. Indeed, because it is preprinted on the form, rarely do sellers know that they have a right not to authorize acceptance by the broker. Some sophisticated sellers authorize the broker to accept the deposit only as the agent of the buyer.

(27) Agency Relationship

This paragraph states that the broker is an agent of the seller. In some circumstances, the broker may also act as an agent of the buyer. In such cases, the broker will timely notify the seller in the manner provided by law.

Representation in an Exchange

This second part of the clause allows the broker to act as a dual agent in a trade, commonly called a tax-free exchange. Absent full disclosure to and approval from the seller, the broker may not represent more than one party in a trade. This clause authorizes the broker to represent all the parties to a trade and to collect a commission from each.

(28) Security and Insurance

This clause protects the broker if anyone is injured on the property, while doing marketing, sales, or other authorized activities. Further, it acknowledges that the broker maintains no insurance that offers such protection. Finally, the buyer must protect his own valuables and personal property.

(29) Lockbox

The broker is authorized to install a lockbox on the door containing a key to the property if the seller initials the "yes" box. The seller is notified that not all brokers showing the property may be insured and that the seller should consider appropriate insurance.

(30) For Sale Sign

This clause records the seller's decision about allowing a For Sale sign to be placed on the property.

(31) Equal Housing Opportunity

This clause reiterates the federal law (Fourteenth Amendment, *Jones v. Alfred Mayer Co.*, and the Civil Rights Acts of 1964 and 1968); the state law (Unruh Civil Rights Act and the Rumford Fair Housing Law); and the Real Estate Commission's regulations (*Regs. 2780*).

(32) Attorney Fees

As a general rule, in all contract cases, unless the contract provides for attorney's fees, neither party may be awarded attorney's fees. *C.C. 1717.* Hence, without this clause each party would have to pay their own attorney's fees. This clause provides attorney's fees to the prevailing arbitration or court action. Note that court costs are different from attorney's fees. These costs are generally awarded to the winning party, even without any prior stipulation or contractual agreement.

There is no attorneys' fees provision for mediation. Furthermore, as stated in the mediation paragraph, no prevailing party shall be entitled to attorney's fees unless he or she has first mediated the dispute.

(33) Additional Terms

Any repairs to be made, limitation on the amount of termite work to be paid for by the seller, special provisions for the transfer of possession, rental agreements, and other relevant provisions that affect the listing agreement should be listed.

(34) Management Approval

Even though this contract is signed by the seller and a representative of the broker, the broker (through his agents) has five days in which to reject the listing. If the broker exercises this "condition subsequent," the listing agreement becomes null and void.

(35) Dispute Resolution

Mediation

The mediation clause requires the parties to attempt to resolve any conflicts first through *nonbinding* mediation through a neutral third party. If the parties do not first mediate before filing a court action or arbitration, then such parties are not entitled to attorney's fees if they prevail in their action. This clause has some limited exceptions, including foreclosure actions, unlawful detainer cases, and claims within the probate court jurisdiction. This clause is operative in every CAR contract, and there is no space for the parties to initial if they desire its provisions.

Arbitration

If the parties have any disputes concerning the agreement or its breach, and if the parties initial this clause, they agree to resolve those issues through *binding* arbitration. The parties give up their rights to a trial by jury and agree to let a retired judge or qualified attorney act as arbitrator.

Brokers should be careful about advising their clients to accept this clause; the author thinks that in presenting this clause it could be claimed that a broker was "practicing law without a license." A broker is encouraging a client to give up numerous legal remedies and rights in favor of arbitration. Although the author does not yet know of any cases on this issue, it is possible that advising a client to arbitrate could be construed as giving legal advice.

Care must be taken so that either both sides initial or neither side initials the arbitration clause. There is no mutuality of remedy requirement. If only one side signs, then that one party can be forced into arbitration. In a listing, if only the owner signs the arbitration clause and a dispute arises, the broker has the election of either arbitration or litigation. Conversely, the owner can only litigate and cannot force the broker into arbitration. *Grubb & Ellis Co. v. Bello (1993) 19 CA4th 231.*

Arbitration and mediation are discussed in detail in Chapter 2 of this book under "Implementation: Alternative Dispute Resolution." The discussion also includes the author's opinions on the process of arbitration and mediation.

Exclusions

There are some limited exceptions to arbitration and mediation, including claims within the probate court jurisdiction or small claims court jurisdiction.

(36) Entire Agreement

This agreement states that all side agreements, oral understandings, and other representations not written and part of this listing form are void. The provision that the written agreement expresses the party's entire agreement is generally valid and binding, except as to fraud.

Finally, the clause states that the buyer has received, read, and understood the contract. It creates a presumption of delivery of a copy of the listing at the time of its execution, as required under the real estate law. *B.&P.C. 10142.* A violation of this statute does not invalidate the listing, although it subjects the broker to disciplinary action. *B.&P.C. 10176, 10177; Summers v. Freeman (1954) 128 C.A.2d 828.*

(37) Sellers' Signatures

The signatures of all sellers are generally essential to a claim for commission. Under the statute of frauds, only sellers who execute the listing generally bear any responsibility for payment of the commission, and parties who have not signed the agreement generally have no obligation for payment of the commission. *C.C. 1624.*

One Signature: Spouse

If only one spouse signs a listing, the validity of that listing varies depending on how title is held. If the property is *community property*, both spouses must sign for the listing to be valid. Neither spouse, alone, can sell or contract to sell community property. Neither spouse is liable for damages, nor can the signing spouse be forced to sell his or her half of the property. *Droeger v. Friedman, Sloan & Ross (1991) 54 C.3d 26.* Never accept a listing for the sale of community property without the signature of both spouses.

If the property is held as *tenants in common* or as *joint tenants*, the result is different. Generally, if only one spouse signs the listing, then liability for the commission extends only to that signing spouse. *Angell v. Rowlands (1978) 85 C.A.3d 536.* The courts also hold that a nonsigning spouse generally cannot grant oral approval to sign the listing in his or her name. The spouse must sign to be liable. *Tamimi v. Bettencourt (1966) 243 C.A.2d 377.*

(38) Broker Signatures

Only brokers can contract with the seller, so either the broker signs the forms or a salesperson executes the form on behalf of the broker. A salesperson would sign "Ted Gordon Broker, by Joe Salesman."

OTHER DOCUMENTS REQUIRED

Residential Disclosure Statement

A broker is required to conduct a "reasonably competent and diligent visual inspection of the accessible areas" of residential property. Furthermore, the broker is required to disclose the findings of that inspection to the buyer, as well as any other known or discovered facts that could "materially affect the value or desirability of the property," *C.C. 2079*, which is based in large part on the case of *Easton v. Strassburger (1984) 152 C.A.3d 90*. Chapter 5 discussed the purpose of the disclosure statement in more detail. The information in the form is mandated by statute and is reproduced as Figure 6.4.

FIRPTA Withholding Statement

The Internal Revenue Code requires the buyer to withhold part of the selling price and remit that amount to the Internal Revenue Service (IRS) instead of to the seller. *I.R.C. 1445*. These statutes are called FIRPTA (Foreign Investment in Real Property Tax Act of 1980), and they require buyers to withhold 10 percent of the sales price of any property. Additionally, another 3.3 percent must be withheld for the state of California. *R.&T.C. 18805*. The 10 percent federal and 3.3 percent state amounts must be withheld, unless:

1. *The seller is a U.S. citizen or resident.* If the seller certifies under penalty of perjury that he or she is a U.S. citizen or resident (Certificate of Non-Foreign Status), then no withholding is required. Even if the affidavit is false, as long as the buyer relies upon it in good faith, no withholding is required.

2. *The buyer's residence is valued under $300,000.* If the property's sales price does not exceed $300,000, and if the buyer will use the property as his or her family's residence, then the 10 percent withholding is not required. A buyer should sign a statement of residential use.

3. *The qualifying statement applies.* If the seller is a foreigner and does not qualify under exemption 2, the seller should apply for a waiver. The IRS will issue the certificate if it is satisfied that no taxes will be due on the sale (i.e., no gain is realized) or an agreement has been reached with the IRS for payment of the taxes due.

If the property is sold for nothing down or for less than 13.3 percent down and withholding is required, the buyer must still withhold the full amount, even if the funds are the buyer's own money. If the seller pays the required taxes, there is no liability to the buyer, even if the tax was not withheld during the sale. *I.R.C. 1463*.

FIGURE 6.4   Residential Disclosure Statement.

CALIFORNIA ASSOCIATION OF REALTORS®

REAL ESTATE TRANSFER DISCLOSURE STATEMENT
(CALIFORNIA CIVIL CODE §1102, ET SEQ.)
(C.A.R. Form TDS, Revised 10/03)

THIS DISCLOSURE STATEMENT CONCERNS THE REAL PROPERTY SITUATED IN THE CITY OF _____
_____, COUNTY OF _____, STATE OF CALIFORNIA,
DESCRIBED AS _____.
THIS STATEMENT IS A DISCLOSURE OF THE CONDITION OF THE ABOVE DESCRIBED PROPERTY IN COMPLIANCE
WITH SECTION 1102 OF THE CIVIL CODE AS OF (date) _____. IT IS NOT A WARRANTY OF ANY
KIND BY THE SELLER(S) OR ANY AGENT(S) REPRESENTING ANY PRINCIPAL(S) IN THIS TRANSACTION, AND IS
NOT A SUBSTITUTE FOR ANY INSPECTIONS OR WARRANTIES THE PRINCIPAL(S) MAY WISH TO OBTAIN.

I. COORDINATION WITH OTHER DISCLOSURE FORMS

This Real Estate Transfer Disclosure Statement is made pursuant to Section 1102 of the Civil Code. Other statutes require disclosures,
depending upon the details of the particular real estate transaction (for example: special study zone and purchase-money liens on
residential property).

Substituted Disclosures: The following disclosures and other disclosures required by law, including the Natural Hazard Disclosure
Report/Statement that may include airport annoyances, earthquake, fire, flood, or special assessment information, have or will be made
in connection with this real estate transfer, and are intended to satisfy the disclosure obligations on this form, where the subject matter
is the same:

☐ Inspection reports completed pursuant to the contract of sale or receipt for deposit.
☐ Additional inspection reports or disclosures: _____
_____

II. SELLER'S INFORMATION

The Seller discloses the following information with the knowledge that even though this is not a warranty, prospective
Buyers may rely on this information in deciding whether and on what terms to purchase the subject property. Seller hereby
authorizes any agent(s) representing any principal(s) in this transaction to provide a copy of this statement to any person or
entity in connection with any actual or anticipated sale of the property.

**THE FOLLOWING ARE REPRESENTATIONS MADE BY THE SELLER(S) AND ARE NOT THE
REPRESENTATIONS OF THE AGENT(S), IF ANY. THIS INFORMATION IS A DISCLOSURE AND IS NOT
INTENDED TO BE PART OF ANY CONTRACT BETWEEN THE BUYER AND SELLER.**

Seller ☐ is ☐ is not occupying the property.

A. The subject property has the items checked below (read across):

☐ Range	☐ Oven	☐ Microwave
☐ Dishwasher	☐ Trash Compactor	☐ Garbage Disposal
☐ Washer/Dryer Hookups		☐ Rain Gutters
☐ Burglar Alarms	☐ Smoke Detector(s)	☐ Fire Alarm
☐ TV Antenna	☐ Satellite Dish	☐ Intercom
☐ Central Heating	☐ Central Air Conditioning	☐ Evaporator Cooler(s)
☐ Wall/Window Air Conditioning	☐ Sprinklers	☐ Public Sewer System
☐ Septic Tank	☐ Sump Pump	☐ Water Softener
☐ Patio/Decking	☐ Built-in Barbecue	☐ Gazebo
☐ Sauna		
☐ Hot Tub	☐ Pool	☐ Spa
☐ Locking Safety Cover*	☐ Child Resistant Barrier*	☐ Locking Safety Cover*
☐ Security Gate(s)	☐ Automatic Garage Door Opener(s)*	☐ Number Remote Controls ____
Garage: ☐ Attached	☐ Not Attached	☐ Carport
Pool/Spa Heater: ☐ Gas	☐ Solar	☐ Electric
Water Heater: ☐ Gas	☐ Water Heater Anchored, Braced, or Strapped*	
Water Supply: ☐ City	☐ Well	☐ Private Utility or
Gas Supply: ☐ Utility	☐ Bottled	Other_____
☐ Window Screens	☐ Window Security Bars ☐ Quick Release Mechanism on Bedroom Windows*	

Exhaust Fan(s) in _____ 220 Volt Wiring in _____ Fireplace(s) in _____
☐ Gas Starter _____ ☐ Roof(s): Type: _____ Age: _____ (approx.)
☐ Other: _____
Are there, to the best of your (Seller's) knowledge, any of the above that are not in operating condition? ☐ Yes ☐ No. If yes, then
describe. (Attach additional sheets if necessary): _____
_____

(*see footnote on page 2)

TDS REVISED 10/03 (PAGE 1 OF 3) Print Date

Buyer's Initials (_____)(_____)
Seller's Initials (_____)(_____)

Reviewed by _____ Date _____

EQUAL HOUSING OPPORTUNITY

REAL ESTATE TRANSFER DISCLOSURE STATEMENT (TDS PAGE 1 OF 3)

Source: Reprinted with permission. *California Association of REALTORS®*. Endorsement not implied.

FIGURE 6.4 *(Continued)*.

Property Address: _____   Date: _____

B. Are you (Seller) aware of any significant defects/malfunctions in any of the following? ☐ Yes ☐ No. If yes, check appropriate space(s) below.

☐ Interior Walls ☐ Ceilings ☐ Floors ☐ Exterior Walls ☐ Insulation ☐ Roof(s) ☐ Windows ☐ Doors ☐ Foundation ☐ Slab(s) ☐ Driveways ☐ Sidewalks ☐ Walls/Fences ☐ Electrical Systems ☐ Plumbing/Sewers/Septics ☐ Other Structural Components

(Describe: _____

_____

_____

_____)

If any of the above is checked, explain. (Attach additional sheets if necessary.): _____

_____

_____

_____

*This garage door opener or child resistant pool barrier may not be in compliance with the safety standards relating to automatic reversing devices as set forth in Chapter 12.5 (commencing with Section 19890) of Part 3 of Division 13 of, or with the pool safety standards of Article 2.5 (commencing with Section 115920) of Chapter 5 of Part 10 of Division 104 of, the Health and Safety Code. The water heater may not be anchored, braced, or strapped in accordance with Section 19211 of the Health and Safety Code. Window security bars may not have quick release mechanisms in compliance with the 1995 edition of the California Building Standards Code.

C. Are you (Seller) aware of any of the following:

1. Substances, materials, or products which may be an environmental hazard such as, but not limited to, asbestos, formaldehyde, radon gas, lead-based paint, mold, fuel or chemical storage tanks, and contaminated soil or water on the subject property .... ☐ Yes ☐ No

2. Features of the property shared in common with adjoining landowners, such as walls, fences, and driveways, whose use or responsibility for maintenance may have an effect on the subject property .... ☐ Yes ☐ No

3. Any encroachments, easements or similar matters that may affect your interest in the subject property .... ☐ Yes ☐ No

4. Room additions, structural modifications, or other alterations or repairs made without necessary permits .... ☐ Yes ☐ No

5. Room additions, structural modifications, or other alterations or repairs not in compliance with building codes .... ☐ Yes ☐ No

6. Fill (compacted or otherwise) on the property or any portion thereof .... ☐ Yes ☐ No

7. Any settling from any cause, or slippage, sliding, or other soil problems .... ☐ Yes ☐ No

8. Flooding, drainage or grading problems .... ☐ Yes ☐ No

9. Major damage to the property or any of the structures from fire, earthquake, floods, or landslides .... ☐ Yes ☐ No

10. Any zoning violations, nonconforming uses, violations of "setback" requirements .... ☐ Yes ☐ No

11. Neighborhood noise problems or other nuisances .... ☐ Yes ☐ No

12. CC&R's or other deed restrictions or obligations .... ☐ Yes ☐ No

13. Homeowners' Association which has any authority over the subject property .... ☐ Yes ☐ No

14. Any "common area" (facilities such as pools, tennis courts, walkways, or other areas co-owned in undivided interest with others) .... ☐ Yes ☐ No

15. Any notices of abatement or citations against the property .... ☐ Yes ☐ No

16. Any lawsuits by or against the Seller threatening to or affecting this real property, including any lawsuits alleging a defect or deficiency in this real property or "common areas" (facilities such as pools, tennis courts, walkways, or other areas co-owned in undivided interest with others) .... ☐ Yes ☐ No

If the answer to any of these is yes, explain. (Attach additional sheets if necessary.): _____

_____

_____

_____

_____

Seller certifies that the information herein is true and correct to the best of the Seller's knowledge as of the date signed by the Seller.

Seller_____   Date _____

Seller_____   Date _____

Buyer's Initials (_____)(_____)
Seller's Initials (_____)(_____)

TDS REVISED 10/03 (PAGE 2 OF 3)

Reviewed by _____ Date _____

☖ EQUAL HOUSING OPPORTUNITY

REAL ESTATE TRANSFER DISCLOSURE STATEMENT (TDS PAGE 2 OF 3)

FIGURE 6.4   *(Continued)*.

Property Address: _____   Date: _____

III. AGENT'S INSPECTION DISCLOSURE
(To be completed only if the Seller is represented by an agent in this transaction.)

THE UNDERSIGNED, BASED ON THE ABOVE INQUIRY OF THE SELLER(S) AS TO THE CONDITION OF THE PROPERTY AND BASED ON A REASONABLY COMPETENT AND DILIGENT VISUAL INSPECTION OF THE ACCESSIBLE AREAS OF THE PROPERTY IN CONJUNCTION WITH THAT INQUIRY, STATES THE FOLLOWING:

☐ Agent notes no items for disclosure.

☐ Agent notes the following items: _____

_____

_____

_____

_____

Agent (Broker Representing Seller) _____   By _____   Date _____
　　　　　　　　　　　　　　　(Please Print)　　　　　　　　　　　　　(Associate Licensee or Broker Signature)

IV. AGENT'S INSPECTION DISCLOSURE
(To be completed only if the agent who has obtained the offer is other than the agent above.)

THE UNDERSIGNED, BASED ON A REASONABLY COMPETENT AND DILIGENT VISUAL INSPECTION OF THE ACCESSIBLE AREAS OF THE PROPERTY, STATES THE FOLLOWING:

☐ Agent notes no items for disclosure.

☐ Agent notes the following items: _____

_____

_____

_____

Agent (Broker Obtaining the Offer) _____   By _____   Date _____
　　　　　　　　　　　　　(Please Print)　　　　　　　　　　　　　(Associate Licensee or Broker Signature)

V. BUYER(S) AND SELLER(S) MAY WISH TO OBTAIN PROFESSIONAL ADVICE AND/OR INSPECTIONS OF THE PROPERTY AND TO PROVIDE FOR APPROPRIATE PROVISIONS IN A CONTRACT BETWEEN BUYER AND SELLER(S) WITH RESPECT TO ANY ADVICE/INSPECTIONS/DEFECTS.

I/WE ACKNOWLEDGE RECEIPT OF A COPY OF THIS STATEMENT.

Seller _____ Date _____   Buyer _____ Date _____

Seller _____ Date _____   Buyer _____ Date _____

Agent (Broker Representing Seller) _____   By _____   Date _____
　　　　　　　　　　　　　(Please Print)　　　　　　　　　　　　　(Associate Licensee or Broker Signature)

Agent (Broker Obtaining the Offer) _____   By _____   Date _____
　　　　　　　　　　　　　(Please Print)　　　　　　　　　　　　　(Associate Licensee or Broker Signature)

SECTION 1102.3 OF THE CIVIL CODE PROVIDES A BUYER WITH THE RIGHT TO RESCIND A PURCHASE CONTRACT FOR AT LEAST THREE DAYS AFTER THE DELIVERY OF THIS DISCLOSURE IF DELIVERY OCCURS AFTER THE SIGNING OF AN OFFER TO PURCHASE. IF YOU WISH TO RESCIND THE CONTRACT, YOU MUST ACT WITHIN THE PRESCRIBED PERIOD.

A REAL ESTATE BROKER IS QUALIFIED TO ADVISE ON REAL ESTATE. IF YOU DESIRE LEGAL ADVICE, CONSULT YOUR ATTORNEY.

THIS FORM HAS BEEN APPROVED BY THE CALIFORNIA ASSOCIATION OF REALTORS® (C.A.R.). NO REPRESENTATION IS MADE AS TO THE LEGAL VALIDITY OR ADEQUACY OF ANY PROVISION IN ANY SPECIFIC TRANSACTION. A REAL ESTATE BROKER IS THE PERSON QUALIFIED TO ADVISE ON REAL ESTATE TRANSACTIONS. IF YOU DESIRE LEGAL OR TAX ADVICE, CONSULT AN APPROPRIATE PROFESSIONAL.

This form is available for use by the entire real estate industry. It is not intended to identify the user as a REALTOR®. REALTOR® is a registered collective membership mark which may be used only by members of the NATIONAL ASSOCIATION OF REALTORS® who subscribe to its Code of Ethics.

SURE▪TRAC
The System for Success®

Published and Distributed by:
REAL ESTATE BUSINESS SERVICES, INC.
a subsidiary of the California Association of REALTORS®
525 South Virgil Avenue, Los Angeles, California 90020

Reviewed by _____ Date _____

EQUAL HOUSING OPPORTUNITY

TDS REVISED 10/03 (PAGE 3 OF 3)

REAL ESTATE TRANSFER DISCLOSURE STATEMENT (TDS PAGE 3 OF 3)

Source: Reprinted with permission. *California Association of REALTORS®.* Endorsement not implied.

California's Onerous Withholding

Beginning in 2003, any individual that sells non-exempt property in California will have to pay the state 3.33 percent of the gross proceeds within 23 days from close of escrow. R&TC 18662. One way California is reducing its large deficit is through this new, accelerated tax collection method. The collection process only applies to individuals (not artificial entities like corporations, partnerships, or irrevocable trusts). The statute exempts primary residences, tax-free (*§1031*) exchanges, involuntary conversions, some foreclosures, property under $100,000, and sales resulting in a tax loss. All other property is subject to this withholding tax. While there is no disclosure form for this withholding, a broker representing a seller subject to this tax, should strongly consider advising the seller of this provision.

The abhorrent effect of basing the tax on the gross proceeds is that if the property merely results in a small taxable gain for the taxpayer, he or she must still pay the entire 3.33 percent of the gross proceeds. If the person purchased property one year ago for $1,000,000, and then sold it today for $1,000,500, that person would only owe capital gains tax on $500. However, they would still have to pay the state $33,316.50 dollars (3.3% × $1,000,500). Then, when that person files an income tax return, he or she can seek a refund of almost all of the withheld money. Of course, the person receives the refund without interest, and the State was able to use the money to help balance its budget for that year. Since 2007, residents can elect to file form 593-E and have tax withheld on the capital gains at California's highest tax rate. For example, if you sell property worth $500,000 and your basis is $400,000 your capital gains are $100,000. For an individual, California's highest tax rate is 9.3 percent, so total withholdings would be $9,300 ($100,000 × 9.3%). Tax-free (*§1031*) exchanges will probably become far more popular.

Agency Disclosure Statement

Beginning in 1988, a new law governed brokers involved in the sale of one- to four-family residential property, leases for more than one year of such property, or the sale of a mobile home. In such transactions, the broker must provide clients with a written disclosure of the broker's agency relationship. The disclosure statement must follow the form specified by statute. It states whether the agent is exclusively representing the buyer, the seller, or both parties and then defines the nature and duties of each agency representation. Dual agents are forbidden from disclosing information about the price to the other party without full consent. *C.C. 2373*. With the exception of the prohibition on discussing price, the statute and forms are designed for disclosure of the agency relationship and do not alter the normal rules of agency. *C.C. 2382.*

Two Forms

Basically, two forms are involved. The first is called an Agency Disclosure Addendum, or, more commonly, simply Disclosure Regarding Real Estate Agency Relationships. Figure 6.5 is a copy of the front of the form. The back merely contains a verbatim copy of the appropriate statute. In brief, this form states the responsibilities of an agent, telling how those duties vary by representing a seller, by representing a buyer, and by representing both parties. The second form is a short document called an Agency Confirmation Statement, or simply a Confirmation form. (See Figure 6.6.) This document merely states (confirms) whom the agent is representing. Sometimes the second form is included as part of another form, such as a deposit receipt, although the author believes it is better business practice to retain the two separate forms.

When Presented

The first form, the disclosure form, is presented by the listing agent before accepting the listing. Then, as soon thereafter as practical, but not later than immediately prior to presenting any contracts of sale, the listing agent presents the seller with the confirmation statement. The agent representing the buyer presents the disclosure form and confirmation forms as soon as the buyer becomes "serious" and not later than immediately before signing an offer.

Brokers need to be diligent and careful to provide the agency forms at the proper time. Failure to present the agency disclosure form at the time a listing is signed waives the broker's right to commission. The one exception where an agent would not lose the commission appears to be when the seller is of such sophistication to have "sufficient knowledge concerning the information obtained in the disclosure form." *Huijers v. DeMarrais (1992) 11 C.A.4th 676.* Listing brokers need to provide the disclosure form twice: at the time of the listing and when an offer is given to the seller.

Sales of Mobile Homes

Sales of mobile homes involve separate paperwork and requirements from normal home sales. The sales requirements differ if the home is personal property or real property. Mobile homes are ordinarily personal property. However, the mobile home becomes real property if four requirements are met: a building permit is obtained, the home rests on a permanent foundation, a certificate of occupancy is obtained, and a document of affixation to land is recorded.

FIGURE 6.5   Agency Disclosure Addendum.

CALIFORNIA ASSOCIATION OF REALTORS®	**DISCLOSURE REGARDING REAL ESTATE AGENCY RELATIONSHIP** **(As required by the Civil Code)** **(C.A.R. Form AD, Revised 11/09)**

When you enter into a discussion with a real estate agent regarding a real estate transaction, you should from the outset understand what type of agency relationship or representation you wish to have with the agent in the transaction.

SELLER'S AGENT

A Seller's agent under a listing agreement with the Seller acts as the agent for the Seller only. A Seller's agent or a subagent of that agent has the following affirmative obligations:
To the Seller: A Fiduciary duty of utmost care, integrity, honesty and loyalty in dealings with the Seller.
To the Buyer and the Seller:
    (a) Diligent exercise of reasonable skill and care in performance of the agent's duties.
    (b) A duty of honest and fair dealing and good faith.
    (c) A duty to disclose all facts known to the agent materially affecting the value or desirability of the property that are not known to, or within the diligent attention and observation of, the parties. An agent is not obligated to reveal to either party any confidential information obtained from the other party that does not involve the affirmative duties set forth above.

BUYER'S AGENT

A selling agent can, with a Buyer's consent, agree to act as agent for the Buyer only. In these situations, the agent is not the Seller's agent, even if by agreement the agent may receive compensation for services rendered, either in full or in part from the Seller. An agent acting only for a Buyer has the following affirmative obligations:
To the Buyer: A fiduciary duty of utmost care, integrity, honesty and loyalty in dealings with the Buyer.
To the Buyer and the Seller:
    (a) Diligent exercise of reasonable skill and care in performance of the agent's duties.
    (b) A duty of honest and fair dealing and good faith.
    (c) A duty to disclose all facts known to the agent materially affecting the value or desirability of the property that are not known to, or within the diligent attention and observation of, the parties.
An agent is not obligated to reveal to either party any confidential information obtained from the other party that does not involve the affirmative duties set forth above.

AGENT REPRESENTING BOTH SELLER AND BUYER

A real estate agent, either acting directly or through one or more associate licensees, can legally be the agent of both the Seller and the Buyer in a transaction, but only with the knowledge and consent of both the Seller and the Buyer.
In a dual agency situation, the agent has the following affirmative obligations to both the Seller and the Buyer:
    (a) A fiduciary duty of utmost care, integrity, honesty and loyalty in the dealings with either the Seller or the Buyer.
    (b) Other duties to the Seller and the Buyer as stated above in their respective sections.
In representing both Seller and Buyer, the agent may not, without the express permission of the respective party, disclose to the other party that the Seller will accept a price less than the listing price or that the Buyer will pay a price greater than the price offered.
The above duties of the agent in a real estate transaction do not relieve a Seller or Buyer from the responsibility to protect his or her own interests. You should carefully read all agreements to assure that they adequately express your understanding of the transaction. A real estate agent is a person qualified to advise about real estate. If legal or tax advice is desired, consult a competent professional.
Throughout your real property transaction you may receive more than one disclosure form, depending upon the number of agents assisting in the transaction. The law requires each agent with whom you have more than a casual relationship to present you with this disclosure form. You should read its contents each time it is presented to you, considering the relationship between you and the real estate agent in your specific transaction.
This disclosure form includes the provisions of Sections 2079.13 to 2079.24, inclusive, of the Civil Code set forth on page 2. Read it carefully.
I/WE ACKNOWLEDGE RECEIPT OF A COPY OF THIS DISCLOSURE AND THE PORTIONS OF THE CIVIL CODE PRINTED ON THE BACK (OR A SEPARATE PAGE).

Buyer/Seller/Landlord/Tenant_____ Date _____

Buyer/Seller/Landlord/Tenant_____ Date _____

Agent _____ DRE Lic. # _____
                      Real Estate Broker (Firm)
By _____ DRE Lic. # _____ Date _____
      (Salesperson or Broker-Associate)

AGENCY DISCLOSURE COMPLIANCE (Civil Code §2079.14):
• When the listing brokerage company also represents Buyer/Tenant: The Listing Agent shall have one AD form signed by Seller/Landlord and a different AD form signed by Buyer/Tenant.
• When Seller/Landlord and Buyer/Tenant are represented by different brokerage companies: (i) the Listing Agent shall have one AD form signed by Seller/Landlord and (ii) the Buyer's/Tenant's Agent shall have one AD form signed by Buyer/Tenant and either that same or a different AD form presented to Seller/Landlord for signature prior to presentation of the offer. If the same form is used, Seller may sign here:

_____ _____   _____ _____
  Seller/Landlord   Date   Seller/Landlord   Date

Published and Distributed by:
REAL ESTATE BUSINESS SERVICES, INC.
a subsidiary of the California Association of REALTORS®
525 South Virgil Avenue, Los Angeles, California 90020

AD REVISED 11/09 (PAGE 1 OF 2) PRINT DATE

Reviewed by _____ Date _____

EQUAL HOUSING OPPORTUNITY

DISCLOSURE REGARDING REAL ESTATE AGENCY RELATIONSHIP (AD PAGE 1 OF 2)

Source: Reprinted with permission. *California Association of REALTORS®*. Endorsement not implied.

FIGURE 6.5 *(Continued)*.

CIVIL CODE SECTIONS 2079.13 THROUGH 2079.24 (2079.16 APPEARS ON THE FRONT)

2079.13 As used in Sections 2079.14 to 2079.24, inclusive, the following terms have the following meanings:
(a) "Agent" means a person acting under provisions of title 9 (commencing with Section 2295) in a real property transaction, and includes a person who is licensed as a real estate broker under Chapter 3 (commencing with Section 10130) of Part 1 of Division 4 of the Business and Professions Code, and under whose license a listing is executed or an offer to purchase is obtained. **(b)** "Associate licensee" means a person who is licensed as a real estate broker or salesperson under Chapter 3 (commencing with Section 10130) of Part 1 of Division 4 of the Business and Professions Code and who is either licensed under a broker or has entered into a written contract with a broker to act as the broker's agent in connection with acts requiring a real estate license and to function under the broker's supervision in the capacity of an associate licensee. The agent in the real property transaction bears responsibility for his or her associate licensees who perform as agents of the agent. When an associate licensee owes a duty to any principal, or to any buyer or seller who is not a principal, in a real property transaction, that duty is equivalent to the duty owed to that party by the broker for whom the associate licensee functions. **(c)** "Buyer" means a transferee in a real property transaction, and includes a person who executes an offer to purchase real property from a seller through an agent, or who seeks the services of an agent in more than a casual, transitory, or preliminary manner, with the object of entering into a real property transaction. "Buyer" includes vendee or lessee. **(d)** "Dual agent" means an agent acting, either directly or through an associate licensee, as agent for both the seller and the buyer in a real property transaction. **(e)** "Listing agreement" means a contract between an owner of real property and an agent, by which the agent has been authorized to sell the real property or to find or obtain a buyer. **(f)** "Listing agent" means a person who has obtained a listing of real property to act as an agent for compensation. **(g)** "Listing price" is the amount expressed in dollars specified in the listing for which the seller is willing to sell the real property through the listing agent. **(h)** "Offering price" is the amount expressed in dollars specified in an offer to purchase for which the buyer is willing to buy the real property. **(i)** "Offer to purchase" means a written contract executed by a buyer acting through a selling agent which becomes the contract for the sale of the real property upon acceptance by the seller. **(j)** "Real property" means any estate specified by subdivision (1) or (2) of Section 761 in property which constitutes or is improved with one to four dwelling units, any leasehold in this type of property exceeding one year's duration, and mobile homes, when offered for sale or sold through an agent pursuant to the authority contained in Section 10131.6 of the Business and Professions Code. **(k)** "Real property transaction" means a transaction for the sale of real property in which an agent is employed by one or more of the principals to act in that transaction, and includes a listing or an offer to purchase. **(l)** "Sell," "sale," or "sold" refers to a transaction for the transfer of real property from the seller to the buyer, and includes exchanges of real property between the seller and buyer, transactions for the creation of a real property sales contract within the meaning of Section 2985, and transactions for the creation of a leasehold exceeding one year's duration. **(m)** "Seller" means the transferor in a real property transaction, and includes an owner who lists real property with an agent, whether or not a transfer results, or who receives an offer to purchase real property of which he or she is the owner from an agent on behalf of another. "Seller" includes both a vendor and a lessor. **(n)** "Selling agent" means a listing agent who acts alone, or an agent who acts in cooperation with a listing agent, and who sells or finds and obtains a buyer for the real property, or an agent who locates property for a buyer or who finds a buyer for a property for which no listing exists and presents an offer to purchase to the seller. **(o)** "Subagent" means a person to whom an agent delegates agency powers as provided in Article 5 (commencing with Section 2349) of Chapter 1 of Title 9. However, "subagent" does not include an associate licensee who is acting under the supervision of an agent in a real property transaction.

2079.14 Listing agents and selling agents shall provide the seller and buyer in a real property transaction with a copy of the disclosure form specified in Section 2079.16, and, except as provided in subdivision (c), shall obtain a signed acknowledgement of receipt from that seller or buyer, except as provided in this section or Section 2079.15, as follows: **(a)** The listing agent, if any, shall provide the disclosure form to the seller prior to entering into the listing agreement. **(b)** The selling agent shall provide the disclosure form to the seller as soon as practicable prior to presenting the seller with an offer to purchase, unless the selling agent previously provided the seller with a copy of the disclosure form pursuant to subdivision (a). **(c)** Where the selling agent does not deal on a face-to-face basis with the seller, the disclosure form prepared by the selling agent may be furnished to the seller (and acknowledgement of receipt obtained for the selling agent from the seller) by the listing agent, or the selling agent may deliver the disclosure form by certified mail addressed to the seller at his or her last known address, in which case no signed acknowledgement of receipt is required. **(d)** The selling agent shall provide the disclosure form to the buyer as soon as practicable prior to execution of the buyer's offer to purchase, except that if the offer to purchase is not prepared by the selling agent, the selling agent shall present the disclosure form to the buyer not later than the next business day after the selling agent receives the offer to purchase from the buyer.

2079.15 In any circumstance in which the seller or buyer refuses to sign an acknowledgement of receipt pursuant to Section 2079.14, the agent, or an associate licensee acting for an agent, shall set forth, sign, and date a written declaration of the facts of the refusal.
2079.16 Reproduced on Page 1 of this AD form.
2079.17 **(a)** As soon as practicable, the selling agent shall disclose to the buyer and seller whether the selling agent is acting in the real property transaction exclusively as the buyer's agent, exclusively as the seller's agent, or as a dual agent representing both the buyer and the seller. This relationship shall be confirmed in the contract to purchase and sell real property or in a separate writing executed or acknowledged by the seller, the buyer, and the selling agent prior to or coincident with execution of that contract by the buyer and the seller, respectively. **(b)** As soon as practicable, the listing agent shall disclose to the seller whether the listing agent is acting in the real property transaction exclusively as the seller's agent, or as a dual agent representing both the buyer and seller. This relationship shall be confirmed in the contract to purchase and sell real property or in a separate writing executed or acknowledged by the seller and the listing agent prior to or coincident with the execution of that contract by the seller.
(c) The confirmation required by subdivisions (a) and (b) shall be in the following form.

_____**(DO NOT COMPLETE. SAMPLE ONLY)**_____ is the agent of (check one): ☐ the seller exclusively; or ☐ both the buyer and seller.
(Name of Listing Agent)

_____**(DO NOT COMPLETE. SAMPLE ONLY)**_____ is the agent of (check one): ☐ the buyer exclusively; or ☐ the seller exclusively; or
(Name of Selling Agent if not the same as the Listing Agent)   ☐ both the buyer and seller.

(d) The disclosures and confirmation required by this section shall be in addition to the disclosure required by Section 2079.14.

2079.18 No selling agent in a real property transaction may act as an agent for the buyer only, when the selling agent is also acting as the listing agent in the transaction.

2079.19 The payment of compensation or the obligation to pay compensation to an agent by the seller or buyer is not necessarily determinative of a particular agency relationship between an agent and the seller or buyer. A listing agent and a selling agent may agree to share any compensation or commission paid, or any right to any compensation or commission for which an obligation arises as the result of a real estate transaction, and the terms of any such agreement shall not necessarily be determinative of a particular relationship.

2079.20 Nothing in this article prevents an agent from selecting, as a condition of the agent's employment, a specific form of agency relationship not specifically prohibited by this article if the requirements of Section 2079.14 and Section 2079.17 are complied with.

2079.21 A dual agent shall not disclose to the buyer that the seller is willing to sell the property at a price less than the listing price, without the express written consent of the seller. A dual agent shall not disclose to the seller that the buyer is willing to pay a price greater than the offering price, without the express written consent of the buyer. This section does not alter in any way the duty or responsibility of a dual agent to any principal with respect to confidential information other than price.

2079.22 Nothing in this article precludes a listing agent from also being a selling agent, and the combination of these functions in one agent does not, of itself, make that agent a dual agent.

2079.23 A contract between the principal and agent may be modified or altered to change the agency relationship at any time before the performance of the act which is the object of the agency with the written consent of the parties to the agency relationship.

2079.24 Nothing in this article shall be construed to either diminish the duty of disclosure owed buyers and sellers by agents and their associate licensees, subagents, and employees or to relieve agents and their associate licensees, subagents, and employees from liability for their conduct in connection with acts governed by this article or for any breach of a fiduciary duty or a duty of disclosure.

Copyright © 1991-2009, CALIFORNIA ASSOCIATION OF REALTORS®, INC.
AD REVISED 11/09 (PAGE 2 OF 2)

Buyer's Initials (_____)(_____)
Seller's Initials (_____)(_____)

| Reviewed by _____ Date _____ |

🏠 EQUAL HOUSING OPPORTUNITY

DISCLOSURE REGARDING REAL ESTATE AGENCY RELATIONSHIP (AD PAGE 2 OF 2)

Source: Reprinted with permission. *California Association of REALTORS®.* Endorsement not implied.

FIGURE 6.6 Agency Confirmation Statement.

CALIFORNIA
ASSOCIATION
OF REALTORS ®

CONFIRMATION OF REAL ESTATE AGENCY RELATIONSHIPS
(As required by the Civil Code)
(C.A.R. Form AC, Revised 04/08)

Subject Property Address _____

The following agency relationship(s) is/are hereby confirmed for this transaction:

LISTING AGENT: _____
is the agent of (check one):   (Print Firm Name)

❏ the Seller/ Landlord exclusively; or

❏ both the Buyer/Tenant and Seller/Landlord

SELLING AGENT: _____
(if not the same as Listing Agent)   (Print Firm Name)

is the agent of (check one):

❏ the Buyer/Tenant exclusively; or

❏ the Seller/Landlord exclusively; or

❏ both the Buyer/Tenant and Seller/Landlord

I/WE ACKNOWLEDGE RECEIPT OF A COPY OF THIS CONFIRMATION.

Seller/Landlord _____ Date _____

Seller/Landlord _____ Date _____

Buyer/Tenant _____ Date _____

Buyer/Tenant _____ Date _____

Real Estate Broker (Selling Firm) _____

By _____ Date _____

Real Estate Broker (Listing Firm) _____

By _____ Date _____

A REAL ESTATE BROKER IS QUALIFIED TO ADVISE ON REAL ESTATE. IF YOU DESIRE LEGAL ADVICE,
CONSULT YOUR ATTORNEY.

Published and Distributed by:
REAL ESTATE BUSINESS SERVICES, INC.
a subsidiary of the California Association of REALTORS®
525 South Virgil Avenue, Los Angeles, California 90020

Reviewed by _____ Date _____

EQUAL HOUSING
OPPORTUNITY

CONFIRMATION REAL ESTATE AGENCY RELATIONSHIPS (AC PAGE 1 OF 1)

Source: Reprinted with permission. *California Association of REALTORS®*. Endorsement not implied.

Personal Property

To begin, the licensee cannot even sell a mobile home unless it is at least one year old. Furthermore, the home must either be registered with the Department of Motor Vehicles (DMV) or the Department of Housing and Community Development (HCD) for at least one year. Thus, a vehicle may be one year old but not be registered for a year, in which case it is illegal for a broker to sell that mobile home. *B.&.P.C. 10131.6.* Second, the mobile home must be in a residential mobile home park or on a lot properly zoned for mobile homes with at least a one-year right of occupancy. Any sale or advertising must be in conformity with all rules and lease terms of the mobile home park. *C.C.798.70* and *798.75.* A variety of reporting and other statutory requirements must be met for the agent selling mobile homes.

Real Property

If the mobile home is affixed and part of the real property, the complex requirements affecting mobile homes that are personal property do not apply. The home is not licensed with the DMV or the HCD, and it is sold the same as any other real property. If the new purchaser will remain in the mobile home park, the park agreement may require the manager's prior approval, and the broker needs to be familiar with all such agreements.

Sale of Condominiums

The seller of a condominium or planned unit development must provide prospective purchasers with a series of additional disclosure documents about the unit. These documents include the covenants, conditions, and restrictions bylaws; articles of incorporation; any age requirements; financial statements; and association dues and charges. Civil Code 1368 sets forth the exact documents needed. However, because most sellers are unaware of these requirements, it generally falls to the broker to make sure that the disclosures are made.

STUDY QUESTIONS (TRUE–FALSE)

1. The listing agreement employs and authorizes the broker to sell the property for the listed amount.

2. A broker who does not have a contractual relationship with a party may still owe certain fiduciary duties.

3. After accepting a deposit, a broker must deposit it in a business account within a certain period or face disciplinary action.

4. The exclusive agency listing provides that the listing broker will receive a commission if anyone other than the owner sells the property.

5. If a seller intentionally and knowingly misleads a broker to sell property with only an oral listing, the broker can recover the commission by proving the oral contract.

6. The broker must always be the procuring cause of the sale to be entitled to a commission.

7. A listing agreement is a bilateral contract; consequently, if the seller unjustly withdraws the property from sale, the broker may receive the full commission.

8. The real estate commissioner requires that all listing agreements have a commencement date stated in the document.

9. Under the CAR listing agreement, the broker earns a commission by producing a ready, willing, and able buyer.

10. Generally, if only the wife signs a listing agreement, the broker may have trouble collecting a commission.

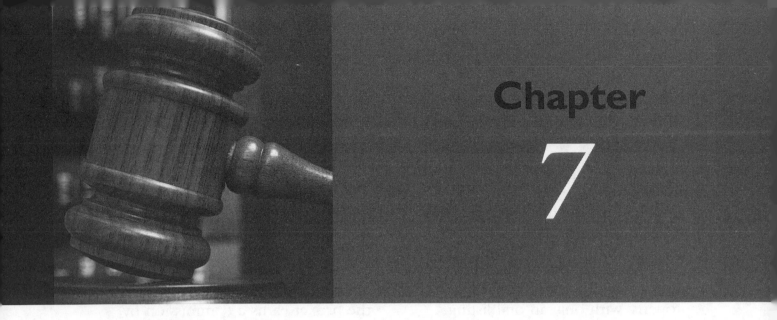

Chapter

7

NATURE OF EASEMENTS

Definition and Nature

An **easement** is a nonpossessory right to use another's land. It transfers a mere *use* of someone's land for specific, limited purposes, but, unlike a lease, it passes no rights of possession. The easement holder does not own the land or even have the right to possess the property to the exclusion of others. Rather, the easement holder has the right, which may be shared with others, to *use* someone else's land for the easement holder's benefit. The most common easement is a **right-of-way**, which gives the easement holder the nonrevocable right to cross another's land for the purposes stated in the easement. Such rights, of course, diminish the rights of the landowner, who may not use the property to interfere with the easement holder's rights.

Types of Easements

Easements are generally categorized as *appurtenant* or as *in gross*, depending on whether they benefit a specific parcel of property or a particular individual.

Easement Appurtenant

An **easement appurtenant** is attached to and part of the land of the easement holder. Thus, it requires at least two separately owned parcels of property. The first, which is burdened by the easement (e.g., it has a right-of-way across it), is called the **servient tenement**. The other property, which enjoys the use and benefit of the easement, is called the **dominant tenement**.

Nonpossessory Interests

Easement in Gross

An **easement in gross** has no dominant estate, as it belongs to an individual rather than to a parcel of property. Thus, the only land involved is the servient estate, the property burdened by the easement. A typical example of this type of easement is a public utility easement owned by a utility company.

Purpose of Easement

Easements generally permit the use of another's land. These easements are sometimes categorized as *affirmative easements*. For example, if an individual has a right-of-way across another's land, that is called an affirmative easement. Infrequently, one encounters a **negative easement**. Under a negative easement, the easement holder prohibits the owner of land burdened by the easement from using the land in a certain way. Negative easements usually prohibit a landowner from building on part of the property. If an individual is prohibited from building more than a one-story home, the easement is negative. (Negative easements are seldom used today, as covenants, subdivision restrictions, and other vehicles are preferred.)

View Easements A typical example of a negative easement is an easement prohibiting anyone from blocking that owner's view. Many states still allow uses to acquire this "negative easement," but California does not permit such easements. No matter how glorious a property owner's view, there is no right to that view except by contract or by local ordinance. Most subdivision tracts since the 1950s have covenants, conditions, and restrictions ("CC&Rs") providing height limits on structures and limitations on blocking views. Other owners in the subdivision can enforce these restrictions. Additionally, some local zoning ordinances prohibit buildings and trees from blocking views. Perhaps the most famous ordinance is in Washington, DC, where no building in the city can be taller than the United States capital. Another typical example is the Tiburon, California's ordinance against trees above a specified height. *Kucera v. Lizza (1997) 59 CA4th 1141.*

Profit á Prendre

In certain situations a special easement, called a **profit á prendre**, is created. This easement grants the owner the right to enter and remove the resources from another's land. It is an easement with a power to consume. Typical examples are easements granting the right to enter and cut timber, mine coal, or drill for oil.

CREATION OF EASEMENTS

Grant and Reservation

Of the several methods of creating easements, the simplest is by express grant or reservation. In a grant, an instrument expressly granting another person rights in his land is executed by the landowner. (See Figure 7.1 for a grant of an easement.) Alternatively, the landowner transferring property can reserve (or hold back) an easement for personal use. The retained easement arises through a reservation in the granting instrument.

Implied Easements

Easements may also be created by implication of the law. They are called **implied easements** because they are not created by the express intentions of the parties. These easements are either easements by necessity or easements by implication. If a grantor conveys part of his property, retaining the parcel that now becomes landlocked, so that there is absolutely no access to the streets, then the grantor may ask for an easement by necessity across the property previously granted. The grantor must take action to create the easement. Conversely, if the grantor transfers property that benefits from an obvious, existing, and reasonable use of the grantor's land, then the new owner may force an easement by implication. The new owner claims the easement under the theory that any preexisting use across the grantor's land was granted by implication and included with the grant of the property. See Table 7.1 for a detailed summary and comparison of the two easements.

FIGURE 7.1   Grant of Easement.

[Recording Data and Parcel Number]

Grant Of Easement
And Maintenance Agreement

This Grant of Easements and Road Maintenance Agreement ("Agreement") is made by and between John and Mary Jones, husband and wife (collectively "the Joneses") and Peter Smith, a single man ("Smith").

Recitals

The parties to this Agreement are owners of land located in Contra Costa County, California. The Joneses owns approximately 8.53 acres and commonly known as 1234 Able Street, Walnut Creek, California, and identified more fully as Exhibit "A," attached to this Agreement (the "Jones Property"). Smith owns approximately 0.76 acres immediately adjacent to (and sharing a coterminous border with) the northerly side of the Jones Property. The property owned by Smith is more fully identified as Exhibit "B," attached to this Agreement (the "Smith Property")

The Jones desire to grant an easement for ingress and egress across their property in consideration for Smith improving and paying for the payment of easement area, after which both properties will share equally in the cost of maintenance of that roadway easement. Therefore, the parties agree as follows:

Agreement

1.   Grant of Easement. The Jones hereby grant a nonexclusive easement (the "Easement") for ingress and egress over an area lying fifteen feet in width along the western boundary of the Jones Property, and described shown more fully on the diagram of the Jones Property, attached as Exhibit "C" to this Agreement.

2.   Purpose and Scope of Easement. The easement is limited to ingress and egress to or for use of the Smith Property. The Easement does not allow parking vehicles nor any other use except reasonable ingress and egress. The parties acknowledge that the Smith Property is a single-family residence and the Jones Easements are specifically limited to use of the Smith Property as a single-family residence. Neither party may obstruct, impede or interfere with the other's reasonable use of the Easements. The Joneses expressly reserve the right to likewise utilize the Easements for ingress and egress to or from any point within the Jones Property and to use the Easement in any lawful manner that does not interfere with the purpose of the Easement.

3.   Easement Appurtenant. The Easement is appurtenant to and for the benefit the Smith Property while burdening the Jones Property.

4.   Road Improvements. As part of the consideration for the Easement, Smith shall pay all costs of initial improvement and construction of a paved roadway across the entire width and length of the Easement. The roadway's surface shall consist of a 1-inch bituminous asphalt mat, sloped outward enough to carry surface drain-water to the left shoulder, and have an aggregate base of no less than 2 inches compacted CL5 (Class 5). All construction and material shall be in accordance with the plans and specifications attached as Exhibit "D" to this Agreement. Construction shall begin not later than 30 days from the date of execution of this Agreement, and be completed not later than 60 days thereafter. Smith agrees to minimize the impact upon the Jones Property during improvement on the Easement, and further to protect large trees from removal if at all possible.

5.   Road Maintenance. The parties agree to equally pay the reasonable costs associated with annual maintenance of the paved roadway on the Easements. [The Agreement may include

FIGURE 7.1   (*Continued*).

provisions how request for money shall be made, when payment is due, and what remedies are available if payment is not timely made.]

6.   <u>Easement Runs With The Land</u>. The grant of the Easement shall run with the land and be binding on and inure to the benefit of the parties hereto, their respective heirs, successors and assigns.

7.   <u>Other Provisions</u>. [The Agreement may include provisions for indemnification of each other for injuries caused by the one of the parties. It may also require insurance coverage and naming each party was a named insured. Commonly, agreements include an attorney's fee provision. Jones may reserve the right to require Smith, at Joneses' expense, to remove and relocate and rebuild the Easement if Jones determines that the existing Easement location interferes with future development of Jones Property. The agreement may require no action, liens, deeds of trusts or other encumbrances be placed on the property that would or could impair the easement.]

Dated: _____   [Signature] John Jones, Grantor: _____
Dated: _____   [Signature] May Jones, Grantor: _____
Dated: _____   [Signature] Peter Smith, Grantee: _____

[Notary]

TABLE 7.1   Types of Implied Easements.

	Easement by Necessity	Easement by Implication
Nature	Arises when there is a conveyance of part of a tract of land of such nature and extent that the part conveyed or retained is shut off from access to roads by the land from which it is severed or by the land of strangers.	Arises when the owner of two adjacent lots sells one of them. He impliedly reserves all apparent and visible easements across the land that are necessary for the reasonable use of the retained lot.
Need	Strict necessity.	Reasonable necessity.
Assumptions	That grantor conveys all rights necessary for beneficial use of that parcel and retains all rights necessary for beneficial use of the retained land.	Implied understanding exists that burdens and correlative advantages shall continue as before the separation of title.
Rationale	Rests on public policy that land not be rendered unfit for occupancy by lack of access.	Rests on the implied intentions of the parties.
Essential elements	Relation of grantee–grantor exists; dominant and servient estates are under some common ownership at time of conveyance; and necessity for way exists at time of conveyance.	Before separation of title, there must have been use giving rise to the easement so long continued and so obvious as to show that it was intended as permanent; also, easement must be reasonably necessary for enjoyment of the land granted.

Easement by Prescription

A third method of acquiring an easement is by prescriptive use. This method is similar to the acquisition of land by adverse possession, except that mere use, rather than possession, is required. Also, no taxes need be paid as an element to acquiring an easement by prescription. The easement is acquired against the consent of the landowner by open and notorious use of the property in a hostile manner, under a claim of right or color of title, for five consecutive years.

Notorious Use

The claimant must *actually, openly, and notoriously* use the landowner's property. Simply stated, the use must not be concealed. It must be such that the landowner could acquire knowledge of the use if he reasonably inspected his property. It does not require **actual notice** to the owner. Indeed, an absentee owner could conceivably never acquire actual notice of the adverse use. The law only requires **constructive notice**: the use is of such visibility that a reasonable person making reasonable inspections of the property will discover the use.

Hostile Use

To be hostile, the use must be made without the owner's consent. Because the owner has not granted permission for the use, it is deemed against (adverse to) his interests. To prevent someone from acquiring an easement by prescription, an owner need only grant consent to that use. The four most common methods of granting consent (thereby destroying acquisition of an easement by prescription) follow.

1. *By license.* The easiest method of granting consent is through a license: a revocable, nontransferable, and personal right to use one's property. Because it is not an interest in the land, it need not be written, although a written instrument is desirable because it proves consent.

2. *Record statutory notice.* The second and easiest method of granting permission is to record in the county recorder's office a *notice of consent* in the form prescribed by Civil Code 813. This method is also conclusive and guaranteed to prevent anyone from acquiring an easement by prescription. (See Figure 7.2).

3. *Posting general signs.* Traditionally, posting notices that permission is revocable at any time or that the land is private property has been held sufficient to prevent acquisition of easement by prescription. *Jones v. Tierney-Sinclair (1945) 71 C.A.2d 366.* However, it is risky to rely on such signs, because they are not conclusive. The signs are merely one of the factors of evidence to be considered. *Pratt v. Hodgson (1949) 91 C.A.2d 401.*

FIGURE 7.2   Recorded (Notice of Consent).

> ### NOTICE OF CONSENT TO USE LAND
> (Civil Code §813)
>
> I give notice that pursuant to Section 813 of the California Civil Code that:
>
> I am the owner of record of the real property commonly known as [a ranch at 2130 Davidson Road] in the City of _____, County of _____, State of California, more particularly described as _____ [legal description] _____.
>
> I am consenting to the use of my property by the general public for the following purposes: _____ _____.
>
> I am granting my consent permissively only, and such consent may be revoked at any time in accordance with the provisions of Civil Code 813.
>
> Executed on this ___ day of _____, 20__, in the City of _____, County of ____, State of California.
>
> _____
> Ted H. Gordon, Owner
>
> [Note: Must be recorded in each county in which the property is located.]

FIGURE 7.3   Posted Sign (Notice of Consent).

> RIGHT TO PASS BY PERMISSION, AND SUBJECT TO CONTROL OF OWNER.
> SECTION 1008, CIVIL CODE.
>
> _____
>
> [Note: This sign must be posted at each entrance to the property, or at intervals of 200 feet or less along the perimeter of the land.

4. *Statutory sign.* A method authorized by code and guaranteed to prevent anyone from acquiring an easement by prescription is to post signs that state "Right to pass by permission and subject to control of owner under Civil Code 1008." Such signs must be posted at the entrance to the property or at intervals of not more than 200 feet along the perimeter of the property. (See Figure 7.3.)

Claim of Right or Color of Title

Use of the property must be made either under a claim of right or under a color of title. Under a claim of right, the intruder must know that he is using the property without the owner's permission. Courts have also held it sufficient that the claimant mistakenly believes that he has the right to the land when, in fact, he has no such right. A person using the property under a color of title holds a defective instrument that purports to grant a right to use the land when, in fact, it does not grant such a right. Additionally, the claimant must, in good faith, rely on the defective instrument and believe that he is entitled to use the land.

If an individual has a forged deed, an invalid court order, or some other instrument that leads the person to believe that he has the right to use of the property, any occupancy is under a **color of title**. Conversely, if there is no written instrument purporting to grant the right to use the property, any occupancy is under a **claim of right**. If an individual began using part of another's driveway for a right-of-way, knowing that the property was not his, such use would be by claim of right.

Five Years' Continuous Use

Finally, the claimant must have used the land continuously for five consecutive years. However, *continuous use* does not require *constant use*. The occupant must make only ordinary use of the property with similar frequency as would a reasonable owner of similar property.

USE, MAINTENANCE, AND REPAIR OF EASEMENTS

By the Terms of the Easement

The terms of an agreement creating an easement often dictate the duties of repair and maintenance. In such cases, the document controls the rights and duties of the parties.

Statutory Duty of Repair

If there is no such agreement, or if the agreement is silent on the subject of maintenance, then the owner of the easement (i.e., the dominant estate) has an affirmative duty to maintain the easement in good repair. *C.C. 845.* The servient owner generally has no duty to contribute toward the costs of maintenance, although the servient owner must permit the easement owners reasonable access to make all necessary repairs and maintenance.

A person receiving an easement to a neighbor's property should try to put in the grant an agreement that both parties will share equally in the costs of repair and maintenance. Otherwise, the dominant owner of the easement will have full responsibility for repairs and maintenance.

Limited Rights of Improvement

As a general rule, the easement owner may make only limited improvements to the easement, provided such improvements do not change the nature of the easement or materially increase the burden on the servient estate. Thus, a pipeline easement usually permits the owner to change the pipe, but not to lay additional pipe.

Interference with Easement Use

An easement is a property right. Anyone who interferes with that easement (including the owner of the property on which the easement lies) is liable for damages. In some cases, the easement owner can also seek an injunction ordering removal of the acts or things that restrict easement use.

In one case, a neighbor used a 25-foot strip of an owner's land as an area for trucks to turn around. Because the owner refused to grant an easement or to authorize use of the land, the neighbor used it without permission. After seven years of use, the owner constructed a building that interfered with the previous use by the neighbor's trucks. The neighbor went to court and established an easement by prescription. The court further awarded damages against the owner for blocking what was an easement and issued an injunction ordering the owner to remove that portion of the building interfering with the easement. *Warsaw v. Chicago Metallic Ceiling, Inc. (1984) 35 C.3d 564.* Therefore, it is important that owners either prevent others from extensively using their property or that they grant them permission to do so. Otherwise, owners may find themselves in the unfortunate position of being unable to build on their property because to do so would obstruct the easement. Alternatively, owners may be forced to pay damages for interference with an easement.

TERMINATION OF EASEMENTS

Common Methods of Termination

Easements may be terminated by several methods, including the same procedures by which they can be created. Thus, an easement may be extinguished by a written release. The easement may also be extinguished by merger if the dominant and servient tenements are acquired by the same person. (Because an easement is an interest in the land of *another*, common ownership terminates an easement.) An easement can also be lost by prescription. If the servient owner uses the easement in a manner inconsistent with that easement (e.g., fences off a driveway easement) continuously for five years, the easement will be lost.

Nonuse Generally Does Not Terminate

Generally, mere nonuse of an easement will not affect the easement unless the easement was acquired by prescription. If the easement was so acquired, then five years of continuous nonuse will extinguish it. *C.C. 811.4.* However, if the nonuse is coupled with an intent by the owner to abandon that easement, the easement may be terminated by abandonment.

Termination by Estoppel

The easement may be lost by the doctrine of **estoppel**. If the conduct of the easement owner reasonably indicates relinquishment of all rights to the easement, and the servient owner reasonably acts to his detriment on that conduct, the easement is extinguished. For example, if A, the dominant owner, declares that he will no longer use the easement right-of-way, and relying thereon, B, the servient owner, constructs a house on that pathway, then the easement is terminated.

Destruction and Misuse

Another method of losing an easement is by destruction of the servient estate. Generally, mere misuse or excessive use will not terminate the easement. The normal remedy is an injunction and/or damages, although at least one California case has held misuse to be grounds for termination of an easement.

APPLY THE LAW

Crimmins v. Gould
149 C.A.2d 383 (1957)

[The plaintiff owned a pathway called McCormick Lane, on which Lot 1 and four other parcel owners held an easement of right-of-way for ingress and egress. Parcel 2 never had any easement rights in the lane. Defendants acquired Parcels 1 and 2 and extended the easement in two directions to connect with Watkins Avenue. Defendants then formally dedicated to the city of Atherton both extensions to the easement and subdivided lots 1 and 2 into 29 residential parcels. Plaintiff sued to enjoin the 29 lot owners' use of his pathway and to extinguish Parcel 1's easement rights for misuse. Defendants tried to defend the suit in part by claiming that termination of Parcel 1's easement rights was an inappropriate remedy and that the plaintiff's pathway was acquired by the public by implied dedication by adverse use. Defendants lost and appealed.]

APPLY THE LAW

continued

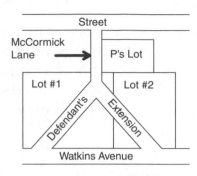

BRAY, JUSTICE. The land [McCormick Lane, which was owned by the plaintiff] was used by others not connected with the properties surrounding the lane. The Atherton police patrolled it occasionally. Sightseers and those who thought the lane was a public street would drive in and out. Groups would drive to the orchard end for a picnic or to park. Necking couples drove in. Atherton installed guard rails on each side of the lane and has maintained them since. The town installed an electric street light at midpoint in the lane. Chuckholes in the lane were repaired from time to time by the town just as any other street would be repaired. On learning of the new subdivision, plaintiff notified defendants that the lane was not to be connected to the subdivision. Since the connection was made in 1954, the use of the lane and the wear and tear have greatly increased.

The lane never became a public way. Such use of it as was made by the public was permissive only. The small amount of improvement and repair made by the town did not constitute an adverse use or an acceptance by the town of the lane as a public way. These are only two methods by which private property may become a public way other than by purchase: (1) By an offer of dedication by the owner and a formal acceptance by a public authority or long continued use by the public itself. This did not exist here. (2) Where no express offer of dedication is made by the owner, by long continued adverse use by the public. In such event, offer of dedication by the owner is presumed. The evidence showed no such situation here.

Defendants contend that the use by the public of McCormick Lane was such as to give rise to the presumption that a use by other than the owner is adverse and not permissive. The sporadic use by the public of McCormick Lane is not the type of use required.

The evidence clearly shows that Parcel 2 neither by grant nor prescription acquired any right to use McCormick Lane. The small use of it made by the owners or occupants of Parcel 2 over the years until recently was not an adverse one. The most serious question in the case is whether the easement of ingress and egress to and from the lane appurtenant to

Parcel 1 was lost by the attempted change in use. Plaintiff concedes that the change from orchard to residential estates did not extinguish the easement. It is the acts of defendants in extending McCormick Lane to Watkins Avenue, dedicating it as a public street, and in allowing the owners of Parcel 2 to connect with McCormick Lane as extended, a public street, which runs across Parcel 2 and connects with Watkins Avenue, which plaintiff claims extinguished the easement of Parcel 1. Defendants thereby attempted to use the easement appurtenant to Parcel 1 for the benefit of all owners in Parcel 2 and the public generally. This caused the court to declare the easement abandoned by misuse.

APPLY THE LAW

continued

In cases involving extraordinary or excessive use, all parties in the instant case agree that the servient owner is entitled to an injunction.

However, here the question is not the propriety of an injunction but rather the propriety of an extinguishment. There do not seem to be any California cases on extinguishment for excessive use by nondominant property where the right given to the dominant estate was by grant. But there are a number of out-of-state cases. The general rule is that misuse or excessive use is not sufficient for abandonment or forfeiture, but an injunction is the proper remedy. But where the burden of the servient estate is increased through changes in the dominant estate, which increase the use and subject it to use of nondominant property, a forfeiture will be justified if the unauthorized use may not be severed and prohibited.

The California cases holding that injunctive relief is a proper remedy of the servient owner for unauthorized or excessive uses of an easement do not hold that it is the exclusive remedy. As hereafter pointed out, an injunction could not grant plaintiff real relief where defendants have attempted to tie two public streets in to their easement.

Certainly here the situation that defendants deliberately brought about is *incompatible with* the nature or exercise of the easement.

The right to an easement is not lost by using it in an unauthorized manner or to an unauthorized extent, unless it is impossible to sever the increased burden so as to preserve to the owner of the dominant tenement that to which he is entitled. Yet [it can still] impose on the servient tenement only that burden that was originally imposed on it without the obligation attempted to be imposed on it by alterations. The rule is especially applicable where the servitude is not materially increased. Such a misuser does not authorize the owner of the servient estate to prevent a further use of the easement for erecting obstructions, or by restraining the owner of the easement by force or violence. The proper remedy being an action for damages; or for an injunction if the remedy at law is inadequate.

[The court then defined how an injunction was totally inadequate, especially because the defendant's sections of the lane had been dedicated

continued

to the public and, therefore, could not be limited in use. Furthermore, if the easement were extinguished by putting a fence across the lane at its old end, above the two extensions added by defendants, defendants would still have a means of access to Watkins Avenue. They would be deprived only of direct access to the other street.

Normally, misuse of an easement is remedied by damages or an injunction. However, in those rare cases in which the misuse is severe and caused by changes in the dominant estate, so that it is impossible to compensate the servient estate by damages or by enjoining the gross misuse, the easement may be terminated. Here the dominant estate was subdivided into many parcels and used by both the subdivision owners and by the public, who was not even related to the dominant estate. Termination was the only acceptable remedy. Therefore, the judgment is affirmed, and the easement is extinguished.]

LICENSES

Definition

Licenses are traditionally defined as personal, revocable, and nonassignable permission to perform acts on another's land. In other words, the license makes lawful acts that would otherwise constitute trespass.

Revocable at Will

Because no consideration is given for the license, the owner may revoke permission at any time. If an owner authorizes a neighbor to camp on the property, for example, the neighbor has a license. However, if, when the neighbor arrives with a sleeping bag, the owner locks the gate, the owner has automatically revoked permission, and the license is terminated.

Nontransferable

Additionally, the license is personal to the individual to whom it was granted. Because it is merely a personal privilege and not an interest in land, any attempted transfer automatically terminates the license.

Written or Oral

Because licenses are not considered an interest in land, there is no requirement under the statute of frauds that they be in writing. Indeed, most licenses are oral. Occasionally, however, a license may arise without any express agreement whatsoever. See Figure 7.4 for a sample of a written license.

FIGURE 7.4   License.

License Agreement

This License ("Agreement") is made June 10, 2010, between Ted Gordon, "Licensor," (called "Gordon") and John Jones, "Licensee." (called "Jones" in this Agreement).

Recitals

This Agreement is entered into based on the following facts. Gordon owns the property at 123 Maple Street, San Francisco, California ("the Property") and Jones wishes permission to walk across the northwest 5 feet of the property, immediately adjacent to the property line, and described more fully on the attached Exhibit "A," and referred to in this Agreement as the "License Area." Gordon is willing to allow Jones a license to use the License Area as provided in this Agreement.

Agreement

Gordon gives Jones a revocable license to walk across the License Area to reach the sidewalk on Market Street, in San Francisco, and for no other purpose. This license is temporary, nonassignable, nonexclusive, and may be revoked at any time. This is a license as defined by the California Civil Code and not a grant of an easement or any other type of interest in the Property. Further, Jones may only use the license in such manner as will not interfere with Gordon's use of the Property.

Jones shall indemnify and hold harmless Gordon against any claims arising out of the activities upon and uses of the License Area, and shall provide _____ insurance in the amount of $____, as evidenced by a certificate insuring this obligation in form and amount acceptable to Gordon, with the Gordon as an additional insured.

This Agreement is governed by California law. All notices shall be personally delivered or mailed by first class mail, certified receipt requested, addressed to that party, which receipt need not be signed for. If any party to this agreement institutes legal action, the prevailing party will be entitled to reasonable attorney's fees. This Agreement represents to full and complete agreement of parties and there are no other oral understanding or side agreements covering the subject of this Agreement.

Dated: _____   Licensor (Signature): _____

Dated: _____   Licensee (Signature): _____

May Be Implied

Implied consent to a license arises when an owner would normally speak out or take action against certain conduct if he objected to it. The owner's silence or inaction implies consent to the conduct. For example, in the *Zellers* case, which follows, because the owner did not object to his neighbor's dumping fill on his property, and because a reasonable person would object to the unwanted dumping of dirt, the owner's silence was taken by the courts as implied consent.

Irrevocable License

Although a license is generally revocable, nonassignable, and personal—and, therefore, unlike an easement—in certain circumstances it may become irrevocable and assignable. As such, it becomes a *license coupled with an interest* in land, which for all practical purposes is an *easement*. Indeed, one leading authority describes an irrevocable license as an easement. *3 Powell on Real Property, 526.5T.*

Creation of an Irrevocable License

Generally, the license becomes irrevocable only when the individual detrimentally relies on the license and expends time and money in improvements, under circumstances such that the grantor knew or should have known that the licensee would expend such time or money in such reliance. Under these circumstances the courts may find any revocation inequitable, and they will make the license irrevocable. Thus, if an owner gave a neighbor the right to use a dirt road across a property and, in reliance, the neighbor paved the road, the owner might be estopped from revoking the neighbor's right to use the road.

APPLY THE LAW

Zellers v. State of California
134 C.A.2d 270 (1955)

[Plaintiff and defendant owned adjacent tracts of land. Defendant was grading his land and obtained written permission to dump his fill in certain specified portions of plaintiff's land. The fill, however, was placed on areas outside the locations provided for in the contract and that defendant had no permission to fill. Plaintiff knew of this unauthorized dumping, but took no action until the project was three-fourths completed and over 20,000 cubic yards of earth had been dumped. She then sought to prevent defendant from continuing to dump fill on her land.

Evidence established that defendant willfully dumped the fill on areas for which he had no permission; this amounted to a form of trespassing. The main issue is whether plaintiff's failure to make a timely and reasonable objection now gives rise to an irrevocable license, under which defendant may continue dumping fill on the authorized portions of plaintiff's land.]

WHITE, JUSTICE. An implied license is one which is presumed to have been given from the words, acts or passive acquiescence of the party authorized to give it. Such a license must be established by proof, and it is not to be inferred from equivocal declaration or acts of the owner of the land.

The consent from which a license arises may be manifested by the conduct of any kind. The manifestation may consist in the use of language. Such conduct may consist of acts indicative of consent by the actor to the use of his land by another, or it may consist in the failure to take reasonable action when inaction may reasonably lead to an inference of consent.

We cannot say that as a matter of law the evidence was insufficient to support the findings that the appellant's [plaintiff's] conduct conferred an implied license with regard to the fill here in question. Judgment affirmed. [An irrevocable license arises, permitting defendant to continue dumping his fill on plaintiff's land.]

DEDICATION OF PROPERTY

Nature and Definition

Dedication is a gift of private property by the owner to the public. The intent of the donor may be express or implied. The gift may be made through formal statutory procedures, *Subdivision Map Act, Gov.C. 66410 et seq.,* or through the informal (and often implied) nonstatutory method known as common law dedication. Finally, the gift may be either of the entire fee simple ownership interest in the land or of an easement.

Offer and Acceptance

In all cases, there must be an unequivocal offer of dedication by the donor, either through express contractual terms or by implied conduct. Furthermore, the public or the appropriate government agency must expressly or impliedly accept the offer of dedication.

Common Law and Statutory Dedication

Statutory dedication requires substantial compliance with the procedures of the Subdivision Map Act. Any deviation requires meeting the separate requirements of the simplified common law procedure (see Table 7.2).

TABLE 7.2   Types of Dedication.

Common Law Dedication		When Effective	
Express	Implied	Voluntary	Compulsory
By deed; sale of lots by reference to areas given to public use (which do not meet the requirements of the Subdivision Map Act).	Occasionally by owner's conduct; usually by use by the public (in the case of easements) for less than five years (plus repairs, maintenance, or improvements by the public); or use by the public for five years. Severely limited since 1971 by *C.C. 1009.*	Voluntarily recording a subdivision map or plot plan indicating an intent to dedicate areas to the public, plus formal public acceptance, all in accordance with the Subdivision Map Act.	Dedicating property under the Subdivision Map Act, because such dedication is imposed as a condition precedent to the approval of the subdivider's permit [*Assoc. Home Bldrs. v. Walnut Creek (1971) 4 C.3d 633*].

Special Rules for Implied Easements

Before 1971, any open and notorious use of another's land by the public, continuously for the prescriptive five-year period, amounted to a dedication, if the owner expressly or implied consented. The implied consent (*offer*) generally arose from the owner's passive acceptance of the public's or the government's repairs, maintenance, or improvements during the five-year period of use by the public. *Gion v. Santa Cruz (1970) 2 C.3d 29.* Consequently, owners have been reluctant to permit the public to use their property for fear of losing it by implied dedication. After the *Gion* case, a special statute was enacted to provide protection for owners. *C.C. 1009.* The provisions of this statute are as follows:

1. *Recorded notice of consent.* If an owner records a statement of consent to public use in the form authorized by *C.C. 813* and permits the public reasonably open access to a property, the public cannot obtain an easement by dedication, and an individual may not acquire an easement by prescription.

2. *Posted sign of consent.* If an owner posts at each entrance to the property or at intervals of not more than 200 feet along the perimeter of the property signs containing the wording of *C.C. 1008*, there can be no dedication of an easement or acquisition of an easement by prescription.

3. *General protection.* Even in the absence of recording a statutory notice or posting a sign containing the code wording, easements by dedication (except for property along the coast) are severely restricted. The public may not acquire an easement unless the owner has made an irrevocable offer of dedication in writing or unless the government makes improvements or repairs during the public's five-year use of the property.

However, in addition to the three protections offered previously, the statute creates two exceptions. The public may acquire an easement by dedication by five years of continuous and notorious use in two situations.

1. *Governmental improvements.* If a government agency makes visible improvements or repairs in such a manner as to give constructive notice to the owner of the public use, then the public may still acquire an easement by dedication. To prevent the dedication, within the five-year period, the owner must make reasonable efforts to block the use and maintenance of or repairs to the property.

2. *Coastal property.* For property located within 1,000 yards of the Pacific Ocean or any of its bays or harbors, mere use by the public for five years will amount to a dedication, unless the owner recorded the statutory notice, posted the statutory sign, or entered into an agreement with a government agency for public use of the property.

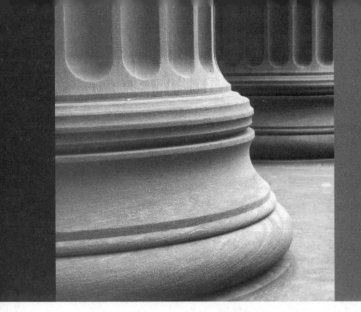

Chapter
8

CLASSIFICATION OF ESTATES

Characteristics of an Estate

Estate is a legal term used to define the degree of a person's ownership interest in property. As discussed in Chapter 1, the estate consists of a bundle of rights, which society allows and enforces. Thus, no rights in property are absolute. The estate is a measure of the quantity and quality of the interests included in the bundle of rights that make up the estate. Estates are often classified by their duration, quality, time of enjoyment, and number of tenants.

Duration of an Estate

Duration is the most important characteristic of an estate. If the estate's duration is potentially indefinite or is measured by the length of someone's life, it is classified as a **freehold estate**. Freehold estates include fee simple estates, life estates, and their future interests. All other estates are known as **nonfreehold estates** or **leasehold estates**. In lay terms, these estates are leases; they include tenancy for years, tenancy for period to period, tenancy at will, and tenancy at sufferance. All leases have a fixed or determinable duration, or their duration continues until one party gives the appropriate legal notice of termination.

Quality of an Estate

Quality refers to the absoluteness or certainty of the estate's duration. An estate subject to contingencies terminates on the happening of the condition. The estate's duration is uncertain, because the

Estates in Land

contingency may occur at any time, thereby ending the estate before its natural termination date. At the other extreme, an estate may be totally free of any conditions or limitations. Such an estate is called a **fee simple absolute**.

If an estate is given to a person only so long as liquor is not sold on the premises, it is a **conditional estate**. It could last forever (if no liquor is sold) or terminate tomorrow if the condition is violated. Conversely, most homes purchased by grant deeds contain no restrictions of any nature and are considered absolute grants of fee title.

Court Construction of Ambiguities

The courts abhor forfeitures of estates and are reluctant to find a condition in an estate. This is roughly analogous to jurors' reluctance to find a criminal guilty of murder when punishment must be the death penalty. Thus, whenever there is any ambiguous language in the grant, the courts will first try to find a simple covenant between landowners. If the language of the grant cannot be so construed, the courts next look for a fee simple subject to a condition subsequent. If the language is clear and convincing, the courts will find the condition subsequent. The courts then look for a waiver or any other legal reasons why the condition can no longer be enforced. Only if the wording of the condition and the conduct of the parties leaves no other alternative will the courts find a breach of the condition causing a forfeiture of the estate.

Estate's Time of Enjoyment

The time of enjoyment differentiates between present and future interests. A present interest entitles the owner to all rights of possession to the exclusion of others. A future interest will or may provide the owner with the right to possession at some time in the future.

A fee simple absolute estate theoretically lasts forever and never terminates. It is of infinite duration. Every other estate's duration is or may be less than infinite. Therefore, every lesser estate must be only part of a fee simple absolute estate. When the lesser estate terminates, the property must go somewhere. This other interest, which offers the right to possession and control only at a later date, is called a **future interest**. Every estate other than a fee simple absolute estate creates a future interest.

Number of Owners

Any number of persons may own any estate or interest in property. If the estate is held by only one person, it is called **ownership in severalty**. Co-ownership is usually limited to joint tenancy, tenancy in common, or community property (unless special entities, such as trusts, corporations, or partnerships, are included).

FREEHOLD ESTATES

Nature of Freehold Estates

The terms *freehold* and *nonfreehold* derive from the types of estates men could own in feudal England. A serf was a nonfree man, bound to his lord. The only estate he could own was a lease—hence, the name *nonfreehold estate*. A free man, a property owner, could own both fee simple estates and life estates—hence, the name *freehold estates*. California recognizes only three types of freehold estates: *fee simple absolute*, **fee simple subject to condition subsequent**, and **life estates**. (See Table 8.1.) Before 1983, a fourth estate existed, called a *fee simple determinable estate;* however, such estates have been abolished and changed to *fee simple subject to condition subsequent estates*.

Fee Simple Absolute Estates

The fee simple absolute estate is the greatest or largest estate permitted at law. When people buy or sell land, they generally purchase or convey a fee simple absolute estate. Indeed, the layperson typically equates ownership of land with a fee simple absolute estate. This estate is presumed by law in every grant of real estate in California unless specific words of limitation are used or

TABLE 8.1 Freehold Estates.

Present Interest (Estate)	Words to Create	Future Interest (Estate)	Action to Create Future Interest
Fee simple absolute	To, Grant to, To____ and his/her heirs	None (no future interest)	Not applicable
Fee simple subject to condition subsequent (fee simple defeasible)	Upon the condition that; But if; As long as; Until	Power of termination	Optional power that must be timely exercised by grantor
Life estate	To____ for life	Reversion	None; automatically reverts to grantor
	To____ for life, then to____	Remainder	None; automatically arises in a third person

unless the grantor owned a lesser estate at the time of conveyance. No particular words are needed to create this estate. It is called a *fee* estate because of its potentially indefinite duration. Furthermore, it is a *simple* estate, because it carries no limitations on its inheritability. Finally, it is an *absolute* estate because it is unconditional and therefore incapable of divestment. Of course, fee simple absolute estates can be and usually are subject to other restrictions, such as zoning ordinances and building codes. However, this broad range of controls has no effect on title to the estate and is not found in the deed.

Fee Simple Defeasible Estates

Occasionally, fee estates are granted subject to a condition that, if violated, could lead to loss of the estate. These estates are called **defeasible**, which simply means the estates are capable of being defeated by a condition. Unless the estate is defeated due to the violation of the condition, the owner possesses about the same rights and privileges as the holder of a *fee simple absolute* estate. These infrequently created estates usually arise as a means of private-land control or regulation over the land being transferred. For example, when Leland Stanford granted land to Stanford University, he did so on the condition that no liquor would be sold on that property. Since 1983, all conditional fee estates are *fee simple subject to condition subsequent* estates. Before 1983, an additional defeasible estate called *fee simple determinable* existed. (See Figure 8.1.)

FIGURE 8.1   Types of Estates.

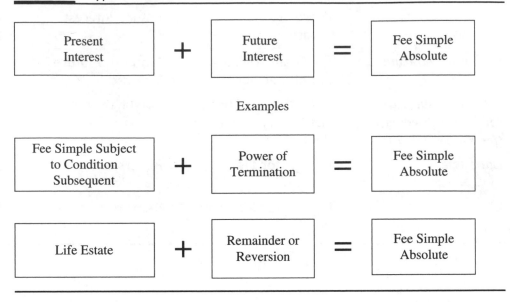

Determinable Estates before 1983

Until 1983 California recognized fee simple determinable estates. These estates used the words "until," "so long as," or "during" in the condition. A typical example is "to Ted so long as he sells no liquor." If the condition was violated, the estate was *automatically* terminated. These estates were abolished beginning in 1983. All existing fee simple determinable estates are now fee simple subject to condition subsequent estates. *C.C. 885.020.*

Fee Simple Subject to Condition Subsequent

Since 1983, any estate granted in fee but containing a condition that, if violated, could lead to termination of the estate is called fee simple *subject to condition subsequent*. These estates are typically created with such words as "but if," "upon the condition that," "until," "so long as," or "during." A typical example is "to Ted but if he sells liquor, then back to grantor." The future interest arising from this estate is called a **power of termination**. (Before 1983, the future interest was also sometimes called a **right of reentry**.)

Forfeiture Only if Timely Act

The key distinguishing characteristic of these conditional estates is that, on violation of the condition, the grantor (1) must declare the forfeiture, (2) in a timely period, (3) while the condition is valid. The grantor who fails to timely act has waived the right to object, and the grantee ceases to be bound by that condition. Furthermore, statutes establish somewhat complex periods after which a condition expires. Most commonly, this is 30 years after the condition's creation. *C.C. 885.030.* Chapter 14 discusses these limitations in more detail.

Life Estate

A life estate is one whose duration is measured by and limited to the life or lives of one or more persons. Thus, a grant to A *for life* creates an estate whose duration is equal to the life of A. When A dies, the estate automatically ends. Occasionally, the measuring life is that of a person other than the life tenant, as would be created by a grant to A *for the life of B.* Called an *estate pur autre vie,* this estate's duration is equal to the life of B. Thus, if A dies before B, the estate has not terminated, and A's heirs will inherit an estate measured by the remaining life of B. On termination of the life estate, the future interest can either revert to the grantor (reversion) or arise in a third person (remainder). Life estates (see Figure 8.2) normally arise in estate planning situations. However, their use and importance have diminished because of increasing reliance by attorneys on trusts and because of their limited tax advantages. *I.R.C. 2036.*

Use Today

Life estates have diminished in popularity with the rise of living (revocable) trusts, which allows for greater and more complex control over assets. Life estates are still used occasionally for family planning, and sometimes as a means of making gifts that might later qualify the property owner for MediCal (California's version of Medicaid). The theory is by making a gift to your children or others, the future interest usually is worth little and the gift tax can be small or sheltered with the

FIGURE 8.2   Future Interests of Life Estates.

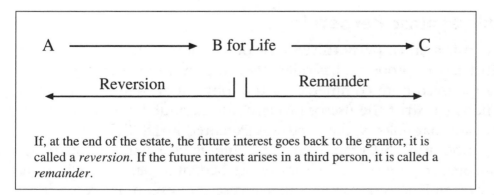

If, at the end of the estate, the future interest goes back to the grantor, it is called a *reversion*. If the future interest arises in a third person, it is called a *remainder*.

$1,000,000 lifetime gift tax exclusion. (Federal estate taxes had some negative tax consequence, but on small estates the impact was immaterial.) Further, the property owner is guaranteed use of the property during his, her, or their lifetime. Then, if the statutory time period has passed (currently five years), MediCal might not count the life estate as an asset. The law was recently changed so allow MediCal to consider such interests, but there is still a question if they will do so. Still, life estates are not overly common today.

Contingent Life Estates

As with any transfer of property, the life estate can be made subject to a condition. (Conditions are discussed later in this chapter.) For example, the author had a case where the parent wanted to grant a life estate, but didn't want the son to marry. Because California doesn't allow retractions on marriage, title couldn't read, "to son for life, unless he marries." However, by changing the wording slightly, the client achieved her objective. The deed read, "Mother to son for life as long as he is single." Life estates with conditions can allow for some fairly sophisticated family planning. The cost of having an attorney prepare a deed is very small in relation to the cost of drafting a revocable trust.

Rights and Duties of Life Tenant

The owner of a life estate enjoys almost all the benefits and rights of a holder of a fee simple absolute estate, except that the life tenant may not commit waste. Generally, the courts construe as waste any act that significantly decreases the value of the future interest. *C.C. 818.* Absent such waste, the life tenant can enjoy, lease, mortgage, or transfer his interest at will. However, any such encumbrance or conveyance cannot exceed the term of the life estate. Because of the uncertainty and possibility of a premature death, the life tenant frequently finds a limited market for sale or encumbrance of his life estate.

Rule against Perpetuities

The **rule against perpetuities**, one of the most complex rules in the entire law of property, basically seeks to prevent property from being removed from commerce for too long. Because future interests generally restrict the use of property for extended periods (e.g., in the case that follows, the deed was executed in 1878, although the litigation arose 80 years later), the rule against perpetuities holds that property must vest within prescribed time periods. The time limit, simply stated, requires that future interests must vest within

21 years after the death of someone who was alive on the effective date of the grant, or 90 years. *Prob.C. 21205.* It is not important to understand the rule, only to realize that certain highly complex requirements must be satisfied in creating or analyzing fee estates with conditions. An attorney should definitely be consulted. If the rule is violated, the entire future interest is void, and the grantee holds a fee simple absolute.

APPLY THE LAW

Alamo School District v. Jones
182 C.A.2d 180 (1960)

[In 1878, Mary Jones deeded property to a school district subject to the right to purchase it back should the land ever cease to be used for school purposes. The school wanted to use it now, some 80 years later, for other purposes and hence brought an action for declaratory relief. The school district (respondents) alleged, and the trial court so found, that the conditions in the deed did not reserve a future interest in the property. All that was created was a personal covenant, an option to purchase, which terminated on the grantor's death. The grantor's heirs (appellants) appealed.]

DUNIWAY, JUSTICE. There were three types of future interest in the grantor recognized at common law: the reversion, the possibility of reverter, and the right of entry for condition broken. Each is recognized in California. Does the deed create or reserve any of those interests?

Reversion [from Life Estate]

Civil Code, Section 768, defines a reversion as "the residue of an estate left by operation of law in the grantor or his successors commencing in possession on the determination of a particular estate granted." The deed before us conveys a fee simple. A reversion can exist only when the estate conveyed is less than a fee simple, the classic example being a reversion arising from the granting of a life estate.

Possibility of Reverter [from Old Fee Simple Determinable; since 1983, a Fee Simple Subject to Condition Subsequent]

A possibility of reverter is created when the duration of an estate is limited by a measure of its life additional to that inherent in the estate itself. A fee simple is perpetual. Thus, a possibility of reverter is created by the conveyance of a fee simple that is to last "until" a named event or "during" a period limited by such an

continued

event or "as long as" a certain state of facts continues. Any expression conveying the same idea is sufficient. A classic example is "to A in fee simple until St. Paul's falls," or "as long as St. Paul's stands."

The rule is technical and is based on the idea that duration of the estate is limited, so that when the event upon which it is limited occurs, the estate of the grantee ipso facto terminates, there being thus a "reverter" to the grantor. It is called a "possibility of reverter" because the event upon which the limitation depends may never occur. In the meantime, the grantee has a fee simple estate. Nothing in the deed indicates an automatic reversion of the granted estate when the property is "abandoned for school purposes."

Right of Re-Entry [from Fee Simple Subject to Condition Subsequent]

The question whether the deed creates such a right is more difficult. In classical theory, it was distinguished from the possibility of reverter by the fact that it was not a limitation upon the estate granted (not a measure of its duration) but a condition upon the occurrence of which the granted estate could be cut off by re-entry of the grantor. An example of such a condition would be one of a fee simple "upon condition that, if St. Paul's falls, the estate shall terminate." The effect is not to terminate the estate automatically, as a reservation does, but to give the grantor a right of re-entry. The estate terminates only if the right is exercised.

However, nothing in the present deed says that the estate granted is conditional upon such use, or that the estate is subject to termination for breach of the condition.

Contingent Option

The language used is the customary language of an option; the grantor is given a contingent right to purchase. Appellants [defendants] lay great stress upon the words "subject to," contending that these words import a condition. No doubt they may, in a particular case, but we see no basis for giving them this effect when they are considered in connection with the balance of the language to which they are merely introductory. We hold that the deed created only a contingent option in the grantor, and not a true future interest, i.e., not a reversion, not a possibility of reverter, and not a right of entry for breach of condition

APPLY THE LAW

continued

subsequent. Our code recognizes no other future interest in a grantor.

We are assisted in coming to the foregoing conclusion by certain rules of construction. The Civil Code provides: "A grant is to be interpreted in favor of the grantee, except that a reservation in any grant is to be interpreted in favor of the grantor." Another section states: "A fee simple title is presumed to be intended to pass by a grant from real property, unless it appears from the grant that a lesser estate was intended." A third section provides: "A condition involving a forfeiture must be strictly interpreted against the party for whose benefit it is created." The deed purports on its face to grant a fee, and it is so construed.

The grantor has merely a right or power to terminate the estate of the grantee and retake the same if there is a breach of condition. The policy of the law is to construe language limiting the use of the land as creating covenants personal to the grantor and not assignable, rather than as creating conditions subsequent.

There is another good reason why the contingent option should be construed as personal to the grantor. If so construed, it would have to be exercised during her lifetime and consequently would be valid rather than void under the rule against perpetuities. An interpretation that gives effect is preferred to one that creates a void interest. Judgment affirmed. [The school owns the property in fee simple absolute and may do with it as it wishes.]

NONFREEHOLD ESTATES

Nature of Tenancy

A leasehold is an estate in land, and as such it differs from all other uses of land. It is the only relationship that transfers exclusive right to possession, as opposed to the mere privilege to use the land.

Comparison to Other Relationships

The occupant of a hotel room is a licensee because of the extensive control (rights to enter for inspection, maid service, etc.) retained by the management. A true tenant would have exclusive possession free from disturbance by the landlord. Similarly, for example, the right to erect billboards and signs on property is generally treated as an easement because it does not pass exclusive rights to possession of the property.

Importance of Differentiation

The significance of the differentiation among licenses, easements, profits, and leases relates to the remedies and procedures for breach. A true tenant under an oral or written lease may be removed only by strict statutory eviction procedures, whereas, for example, a license may normally be revoked at will without notice.

Eviction Procedure

The procedure for eviction of a tenant is discussed in detail in Chapter 13. Basically, the procedure requires service of a three-day notice to quit or pay rent, followed by an unlawful detainer court action, and, finally, eviction by the sheriff.

Strict Adherence Required

Any deviation from the specific procedural requirements of the California codes will nullify an eviction action. A wrongful eviction can subject the landlord to civil and even criminal action.

Types of Tenancies

The only four types of leasehold estates are: the estate for years, the periodic tenancy, the estate at will, and the estate at sufferance. (See Table 8.2.) The terms *tenancy* and *estate* are used interchangeably in describing leasehold interests.

Estate for Years

An **estate for years** is a tenancy of a fixed duration: a definite and ascertainable period of a year, or any fraction or multiple thereof. Thus, a lease for seven days qualifies as an estate for years since it has definite beginning and ending dates and hence a definite period. Because an ending date is specified, the tenancy terminates automatically and without notice at the end of the set period.

Periodic Tenancy

A **periodic tenancy** continues indefinitely for successive periods until terminated by proper notice. The covenants, conditions, and terms of the prior period carry over into each successive period. The distinguishing characteristics of this tenancy are its definite beginning date and the known duration of the period (e.g., month to month), with a totally undeterminable ending period.

TABLE 8.2 Nonfreehold Estates.

	Estates for Years	Estates from Period to Period	Estates at Will	Estates at Sufferance
Characteristics	Fixed term—a fraction or multiple of a year. Definite beginning and end dates. Fixed conditions.	Indefinite term. Definite beginning date and length of period. Conditions carry over from period to period.	No specified term or conditions. Original entry with permission under void contract or lease.	No term at all. Original entry with permission, but current occupancy without consent or authorization.
Duration	Fixed term—accurately stated or computable at time lessee takes possession.	Indefinite term, continuing for successive periods of time until terminated.	No duration except statutory minimum of 30 days for notice purposes.	No duration.
Limitations on term	Must be in writing if for more than one year; term not to exceed 99 years for city lots.	City lots presumed to be month to month unless otherwise stated in writing.	Acceptance of rent creates an estate from month to month or as agreed.	Acceptance of rent creates an estate from month to month or as agreed.
Termination	Automatically terminates at end of term.	By 30-day notice or per lease terms.	By 30-day notice; no longer may be terminated at will.	No notice. But must be by court action as "self-help" is forbidden.
Creation	By oral agreement if less than one year; otherwise, by written lease.	Presumed by law; by agreement; by accepting rent at end of fixed lease term.	Taking possession while negotiating a lease, or under void lease or contract.	Remaining in possession at end of lease term.

Notice to Terminate

Whereas a tenancy for years terminates automatically, the periodic tenancy can be terminated only on proper notice. This notice must be given in a time span equal to the number of days of the period. Thus, a week-to-week tenancy requires a seven-day notice to terminate, whereas a month-to-month tenancy necessitates 30 days' advance notice. (However, when the tenant has lived in the property one year or more, a 60-day notice is required.) (See Chapter 13 for more information.)

When Notice Is Given

The law provides that notice to terminate may be given at any time during the tenancy. For example, a month-to-month tenant who pays rent on the first of each month can give the 30-day notice on the tenth of the month. In this case, the tenancy would terminate on the tenth day of the next month.

Tenancy at Will

Tenancy at will is unique and rarely encountered. The traditional concept has been modified by statute. Traditionally, the estate was one of unknown duration, capable of being terminated at the will, whim, and desire of either party. It elevated what would otherwise have been trespassing into a respected, but tenuous, estate. The tenancy at will differs from a license, in that a license is a mere permission to use the premises *under* the owner, whereas the tenant at will has exclusive right to possession *superior* to that even of the landlord. In both the license and the tenancy at will, either party at common law could terminate the interest *at will* without notice to the other party.

Changed by Statute

Statute has greatly modified the traditional at-will tenancy. It may no longer be terminated at will without notice. Instead, the landlord must now give the tenant 30 days' advance notice as the means of terminating the estate. *C.C. 789.* Furthermore, such tenancies usually arise when an individual occupies another's land with permission, frequently pending lease negotiations, or under a void lease or contract. By definition, no express agreement exists as to the nature and amount of rent; this is why it does not qualify as a periodic tenancy.

Tenancy at Sufferance

A **tenancy at sufferance** occurs when a tenant who was lawfully in possession remains in possession without the owner's consent after the termination of the tenancy or contractual right to occupancy. Typically, such a tenancy arises when the lessee remains on the premises after the end of the lease. At common law, the landlord could either remove the tenant as a trespasser or elect to treat him or her as a tenant under a new tenancy.

Eviction

Statutes have greatly modified the landlord's first option regarding **eviction**. Although the tenant may be considered a type of trespasser, and as such need not be given advance notice, the tenant must nevertheless be evicted through court action, almost always through unlawful detainer action. *C.C.P. 1161.1.* By using this option, the landlord can recover the *reasonable value* of the use of the premises; in addition, if demand for return of the premises has been ignored, the landlord may additionally have the reasonable value amount increased. *C.C. 3345.*

Accept Rent

Alternatively, the landlord may accept rent from the occupant, converting the possession into a periodic tenancy. *C.C. 1945.* Even if the landlord does not accept rent, a consent by implication to continued occupation by the tenant may have created a tenancy at will. If so, 30 days' notice is required to terminate a tenancy at will. *C.C. 789.* Thus, the landlord must act promptly to evict a tenant as a trespasser or tenant at sufferance if the inaction is not to be construed as implied acceptance of a new tenancy. *Cowell v. Snyder (1911) 15 C.A. 634.*

Advantages of a Written Lease

In all the tenancies discussed thus far, an informal oral agreement is perfectly valid, binding, and enforceable unless the statute of frauds requires a writing. Such a writing is necessary only when the lease term is greater than one year, *C.C. 1091,* or when the end date of a less than one-year term ends more than one year from the date of its making. *C.C. 1624.* A landlord should probably always demand a written lease, even in the case of a month-to-month tenancy. The elements of proof at trial are thereby made easier; the statute of limitations is extended from two to four years; numerous items such as attorney's fees and continuation on breach can be included in the lease; finally, a lease is one screening technique to eliminate unworthy tenants.

APPLY THE LAW

Covina Manor, Inc. v. Hatch
133 C.A.2d Supp. 790 (1955)

[While defendant was employed by plaintiff, he was given oral permission to occupy one of plaintiff's houses. Upon termination of their relationship, plaintiff demanded possession of the premises, served a three-day notice to quit or pay rent, and instigated an unlawful detainer action. Contrary to plaintiff's assertion that possession was under a license, defendant alleged that occupancy was pursuant to a tenancy at will. Therefore, defendant further claimed that 30-day notice must be given to terminate the estate. Because it was not given, defendant claims the unlawful detainer action is premature and will not lie.]

PATROSSO, JUSTICE. A tenancy at will is an estate that simply confers a right to the possession of the premises leased for such indefinite period

APPLY THE LAW
continued

as both parties shall determine such possession shall continue. The tenant at will is in possession by right with consent of the landlord whether express or implied, and he does not begin to hold unlawfully until the termination of his tenancy. His estate is a leasehold, and he holds in subordination to title of the landlord. A permissive occupation of real estate, where no rent is reserved or paid and no time agreed on to limit the occupation, is a tenancy at will.

It is equally well settled that one who enters upon land by permission of the owner under a void parol contract or under a void lease, or pending unexecuted negotiations for a written lease, is a tenant at will. Thus, whether we accept the testimony to the effect that defendants were granted oral permission to occupy the premises without specification as to time or rent, or whether we accept entry under a verbal agreement (invalid under the statute of frauds) that the property was conveyed in consideration of services to be rendered, the status of the defendants was that of tenants at will.

The preceding discussion serves to dispose of plaintiff's argument that defendants were mere licensees. A license is an authority to do a particular act or series of acts upon the land of another and conveys no estate in the land, whereas a tenancy at will is the permissive right to occupy and enjoy the premises and creates an estate in tenancy. The test, whether an agreement for the use of real estate is a license or a lease, is whether the contract gives *exclusive possession* of the premises against the world, including the owner, in which case it is a lease, or whether it merely confers a privilege to occupy under the owner, in which case it is a license, and this is a question of law arising out of the construction of the instrument. Here, under the evidence, defendant's occupation of the premises was exclusive even as against the plaintiff. The judgment is reversed. [Thirty days' statutory notice must be given to first terminate the estate before an unlawful detainer action can be brought.]

STUDY QUESTIONS (TRUE–FALSE)

1. Ownership in severalty means that only one person owns the property.

2. A grant to B *as long as it is used for commercial purposes* is an example of a fee simple subject to condition subsequent estate.

3. All fee simple estates are absolute estates that create no future interests in property.

4. In the life estate of *A to B for the life of* X, when X dies, B owns the estate free and clear.

5. In the life estate of *A to B for the life of* X, if B dies before X, the estate goes to B's heirs at law for the duration of X's life.

6. The key distinctions between a lease and a license are the amount of control exercised by the owner of the land and the right to exclusive possession, as opposed to mere use of the property.

7. A lease from January 1 to January 31 is a periodic tenancy.

8. A periodic tenancy *generally* continues automatically and indefinitely 30 days at a time until terminated by 30 days' notice.

9. In California, a tenancy at will is an estate that can be terminated by either party at any time.

10. The statute of frauds holds that only written leases can be enforced by lawsuits.

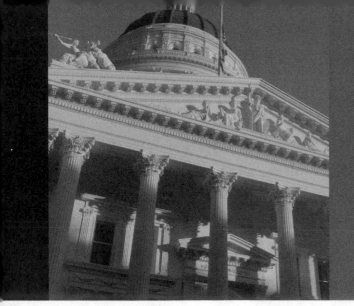

Chapter 9

NATURE AND TYPES OF DEEDS

Nature of Deeds

A **deed** is an instrument used to transfer title to real estate. It is the document most often used to convey an interest in land, although contracts of sale (land sales installment contracts), and court orders can also accomplish a transfer of title. Depending on the type of deed used, the law may imply certain warranties or guarantees about title (see Table 9.1).

Grant Deeds

A **grant deed** (see Figure 9.1) is the most common form of deed used in California. Every grant deed contains two implied warranties of title, unless these provisions are expressly modified or eliminated. *C.C. 1113.* The **grantor** warrants not to have previously conveyed the same interest to someone else and not to have previously encumbered the property. These warranties against previous transfers and encumbrances do not warrant that the grantor owns the property or that title is free of all encumbrances. If one of the warranties is breached, the **grantee** has a variety of options, including rescission of the transaction or damages for breach of warranty. These warranties are excluded from deeds used to convey a gift, to transfer an interest less than fee simple, or to pass title at a judicial sale. *In re Estate of Porter (1903) 138 C. 618.* Additionally, all **grants** of real estate are presumed to be of fee simple unless the deed clearly states differently. *C.C. 1105.*

Voluntary Transfers of Property

Quitclaim and Related Deeds

A **quitclaim deed** (see Figure 9.2) contains no warranties whatsoever. It is commonly used to clear title when the grantor has no real interest to convey. For example, if a married woman acquires separate property, the law presumes it to be community property until proved otherwise. To clear title of any community interest, the husband would execute a quitclaim deed to the wife, although he owned no interest in the property. Most deeds executed by government officials (such as sheriff's deeds) contain no warranties and are similar to a quitclaim deed. Also, quitclaim deeds are commonly used to convey less than fee simple estates and interests in land.

Warranty Deeds

Warranty deeds are rarely encountered in California, although they are widely used in many other states. These deeds contain broad warranties guaranteeing that there are no encumbrances of any nature against the property and that no one will disturb the peaceful, quiet possession of the grantee. Furthermore, the grantor agrees to defend the warranties in a lawsuit or otherwise. The widespread use of title insurance has eliminated the need for the use of warranty deeds in California.

Originally No Other Warranties

Until recently, a deed contained no other warranties, except those written in the deed or implied by statute. In one court case, the plaintiff brought suit because the house purchased was on filled land, which settled, damaging the home. The court denied recovery from

TABLE 9.1   Comparison of Types of Deeds.

	Grant Deed	Quitclaim Deed	Warranty Deed
Words of conveyance	Grant or other words of similar intent.	Right, title and interest; or to remise, release and quitclaim.	Grant to ... and warrant that....
Number of warranties	Contains two warranties implied by statute.	Contains no warranties, or even implications that grantor owns an interest in the property.	Contains six warranties expressly stated in the deed.
Nature of warranties	That grantor has not conveyed the same estate and that the interest conveyed is free from encumbrances done, made, or suffered by the grantor, or any person claiming under him.	Not applicable.	That grantor has title to interest conveyed and can transfer it; that no encumbrances exist; that grantor will defend against any conflicting claims and compensate for any loss arising therefrom.
Limitations on warranties	Applies only to grants of fee simple or life estate, provided deed contains no words of limitation. Applies only to grantor personally; does not cover defects caused by predecessors in title.	Not applicable.	No limitations unless stated in the deed. Some covenants run with the land.
After-acquired title	Passes by statute.	Does not pass.	Passes by warranties in deed.
Use in California	Extensively used to pass title to fee simple estates.	Commonly used, but usually only to clear title or prevent clouds on title.	Rarely used, because title insurance provides greater coverage and financial protection.

the defendant contractor because neither the warranty against encumbrances nor the warranty of title had been breached, and no other implied warranties were involved in the sale. *Gustafson v. Dunman, Inc. (1962) 204 C.A.2d 10.*

Warranty in New Homes

In 1974, the California Supreme Court extended the doctrine of merchantability, ruling that in newly constructed housing there is an implied warranty of quality and fitness. *Pollard v. Saxe &*

FIGURE 9.1 Grant Deed.

When Recorded Mail To, And Mail Tax Statements To:

Mr. & Mrs. John Buyer
123 Jones Street
San Rafael, CA 94903

Assessor's Parcel Number

123-44-5678

Grant Deed

Documentary Transfer Tax of $_____
  [ ] Computed on full value of property conveyed, or
  [ ] Computed on full value less value of liens and encumbrances
     remaining at time of sale
Property lies in
  [ ] Unincorporated area, or
  [ ] Within the City of _____.
The Above Declarations Are Made By
The Undersigned Grantor(s)

FOR GOOD AND VALUABLE CONSIDERATION, The Receipt Of Which Is Hereby Acknowledged:

TED H. GORDON

Does Hereby Grant To:

JOHN BUYER and JOAN BUYER, Husband and Wife, as Joint Tenants

The Following Described Real Property In The State Of California, County Of *Marin*, City Of *San Rafael,*

> *Lot #1 of Block A, as shown on that certain map entitled "Tract 12345,"
> and filed for record on January 15, 1990, as Book 123 in Page 567, in the
> Official Records of the County of Marin, State of California.*

Date: *January 3, 2004*   */s/ TED H. GORDON*

(Notary)

FIGURE 9.2   Quitclaim Deed.

Quitclaim Deed

Documentary Transfer Tax of $_____
  [ ] Computed on full value of property conveyed, or
  [ ] Computed on full value less value of liens and encumbrances
     remaining at time of sale
Property lies in
  [ ] Unincorporated area, or
  [ ] Within the City of _____.
The Above Declarations Are Made By
The Undersigned Grantor(s)

FOR GOOD AND VALUABLE CONSIDERATION, The Receipt Of Which Is Hereby Acknowledged:

TED H. GORDON

Does Hereby Grant To:

JOHN BUYER and JOAN BUYER, Husband and Wife, as Joint Tenants

The Following Described Real Property In The State Of California, County Of
Marin, City Of San Rafael,

*Lot #1 of Block A, as shown on that certain map entitled "Tract 12345,"
and filed for record on January 15, 1990, as Book 123 in Page 567, in the
Official Records of the County of Marin, State of California.*

Date: *January 3, 2004*   */s/ TED H. GORDON*

(Notary)

Yolles Dev. Co. (1974) 12 C.3d 374. This doctrine, although it may help a new-home buyer remedy defects in construction, is separate and different from the warranties of title existing in grant deeds. Under the *Pollard* decision, the buyer of property in Gustafson might have been able to recover if he had given the builder prompt notice of the defect caused by the settling.

Warning to Brokers

Many deposit receipts, including the old CREA (now called CAR) form, state that title is to be free from all liens and encumbrances except those listed. The broker must be extremely cautious to check title and to list documents of record and taxes due but not yet of record.

Evans v. Faught
231 C.A.2d 698 (1965)

APPLY THE LAW

[Defendants leased part of their property and a right-of-way to the county to construct a building. Plaintiff later purchased the property, after personally inspecting the land. Two years later, he paid the county $5,500 to terminate its lease, then sued the seller (defendant) for breach of the implied warranty in the grant deed against encumbrances. Defendant claimed that he was not liable for breach because plaintiff had actual knowledge of the unrecorded lease to the county before buying the property and had personally inspected the property and had seen the county building and the road leading to it.

Under *C.C. 1173*, a grant deed, absent specific provisions to the contrary, contains two implied warranties: (1) that the grantor has not previously conveyed the estate and (2) that the property is free from all encumbrances. The courts have construed encumbrances to include only those encumbrances that affect title and have held that encumbrances that affect physical condition are not covered by grant deed warranty.]

MOLINARI, JUSTICE. There are two kinds of encumbrances, that is, those that affect title and those that affect only the physical condition of the property. A mortgage or other lien is an illustration of the former, and a public road or right-of-way is an example of the latter. The distinction between the two is that an encumbrance affecting title is one that is usually of a temporary character and capable of removal. An encumbrance affecting the physical condition of the property consists of a servitude [burden] imposed upon the land that is visible to the eye and that affects not title, but only the physical condition of the property.

continued

If the encumbrance is one affecting title, the covenant against encumbrances is broken at the time of the transfer and the vendor's prior knowledge or notice of the encumbrance is immaterial. However, if the alleged encumbrance consists of a physical burden upon the land, permanent in character and of an open and notorious nature, which affects only the physical condition of the property, it is not an encumbrance under Section 1113, and the covenant is not therefore broken at the time of transfer. The rationale of the rule, insofar as it concerns visible physical burdens upon the land, is that in the absence of an express agreement, the buyer is presumed to have contracted to accept the land subject to physical encumbrances of an open and notorious nature.

The building and the road leading to it were not encumbrances within the meaning of Section 1113 because they unquestionably constituted physical burdens upon the land of an open and notorious nature. Accordingly, plaintiff was presumed to have contracted to accept the land subject to such physical encumbrances.

The important question is the effect of the unrecorded lease. An unrecorded lease that is binding upon a purchaser of real property is a limitation affecting title because it obviously is a right or interest in land that subsists in a third person to the diminution of the value of the land. The plaintiff's knowledge of the existence of the lease prior to the execution of the conveyance is not a bar to an action for breach of covenant because he was entitled to rely upon the covenant in the deed made subsequent to the acquisition of such knowledge.

Suffice it to say, the fact that plaintiff was presumed to accept whatever physical encumbrances were on the land does not compel the conclusion that he was willing to accept title subject to the limitations and conditions imposed by the lease.

The Damages

The usual measure of damages for breach of a covenant against encumbrances is the amount the covenantee actually expends in removing the encumbrance, not exceeding the value of the property at the time of the breach.

This rule refers to such encumbrances as may be satisfied by the payment of money (e.g., mortgages and other liens), but is not applicable to encumbrances that cannot be extinguished at the will of the owner by the payment of any sum (e.g., easements or restrictions on the use of land). In the latter instance, the applicable rule is that the damages are based upon the natural and proximate consequences to the plaintiff of the existence and continuance of the encumbrance. Compensation is estimated by the amount that the existence of the encumbrance reduces the market value of the land.

A lease encumbrance falls in the latter category because it is not such as may be satisfied and extinguished at the will of the owner by the payment of money. The instant lease could only be extinguished with consent of the lessee. The amount paid in the present case was such as was arrived at and agreed to by plaintiff and the County after negotiation. Accordingly, the proper measure of damages should have been the amount by which the existence of the lease reduced the market value of the land at the time the conveyance was made, and not the sum paid by plaintiff to the County to extinguish the lease. [That amount was allowed, however, because of a procedural technicality.] The judgment is affirmed. [Plaintiff–buyer cannot recover, although normally he would have been entitled to the damages caused by the lease.]

REQUIREMENTS FOR A VALID DEED

Basic Requirements

To be valid, a deed must meet seven requirements. If any of the requirements is lacking, the deed will be void and of no effect. The seven requirements for a valid deed are as follows:

1. Written document
2. Signature of competent grantor
3. Grantee capable of holding title
4. Description of property
5. Operative words of conveyance
6. Delivery
7. Acceptance

Consideration Not Required

Consideration is not essential to the validity of a deed, although it is usually present. Property may easily be given by gift or inheritance, for which there is no consideration. However, if the deed lacks consideration, the grantee is not a bona fide purchaser for value entitled to the protections of the recording act. Furthermore, if the gift is to defraud creditors or results in the grantor's being rendered insolvent, creditors may bring appropriate action to set the transaction aside.

Recording Not Required

The deed need not be acknowledged or recorded. However, unless the deed is acknowledged it may not be recorded; if it is not recorded, the grantee has no protection against a bona fide purchaser in good faith for value. By gaining the protection of the recording statutes (discussed in full in Chapter 14), the grantee's interest will be superior to almost everyone else's interest, which comes after that grantee.

Acknowledgment

An acknowledgment is a formal declaration by a person authorized by statute to verify that the person who executes the instrument is, in fact, the one named. Most acknowledgments are taken before **notary publics**, who are people licensed to acknowledge instruments for payment.

Competent Grantor

A grantor, the one who will execute the deed, must have legal capacity to sign the deed. Minors are incapable of executing deeds, and any conveyance by a minor is totally void and of no effect. *C.C. 25.* Thus, if a minor signs a deed to real property, the document is worthless and conveys no title whatsoever. If a minor owns real estate, it must be transferred through a legally appointed guardian.

Additionally, the grantor should sign the deed in exactly the same name as that in which title was acquired, or it will not impart constructive notice. *C.C. 1096.* An identical signature is essential to complete the chain of title on the public records. Thus, if Mary Jones through marriage changes her name to Mary Smith, she should sign the deed as "Mary Smith, who acquired title as Mary Jones."

Agent Signing

If an agent signs the deed for the grantor under a power of attorney, the power of attorney must be notarized and recorded to provide a complete chain of title on the public records. The attorney should execute the deed as "Joe Seller, by Ted Gordon, under power of attorney."

Using Powers of Attorney

Great care must be used in drafting **powers of attorney**, for these documents are strictly and severely construed by the courts. Many forms for power of attorney available in stationery stores were printed out of state and authorize the agent to *sell* the real estate. However, in California the power to *sell* does not include the power to *convey.* Thus, someone using one of those forms could sign only the deposit receipt, not the deed. *Delano v. Jacoby (1892) 96 C. 275.*

Competent Grantee

The grantee must be an existing legal person. All living people and most business organizations, except unincorporated associations, may hold title. Minors and incompetents may own real estate, although they may convey any such real estate only through a guardian or conservator.

Adequate Property Description

The property conveyed must be described specifically enough to enable a qualified surveyor to determine its location. A street address or a name description, such as "The Gordon Ranch," although not preferred, is legally sufficient. Most descriptions are by metes and bounds, by the government survey system, or by reference to a recorded map.

Words of Conveyance

The deed must include operative words of conveyance indicating that the grantor immediately intends to transfer an interest in property. Words such as "grant," "convey," and "transfer" are sufficient.

Legal Delivery

Legal **delivery** is the most difficult and frequently litigated issue involving the validity of deeds. (Delivery in this case is a legal concept, not a reference to physical delivery.) A deed is not valid until delivered. Legal delivery is the *irrevocable* and *unconditional intent* of the grantor to divest himself *immediately* of an interest in real estate.

Example of Nondelivery

Assume A executes a deed in favor of B, telling B that he will give the deed to him only if B marries A's daughter. B asks to see the deed, so A hands it to him for inspection. B, who now holds a properly signed deed, refuses to return it to A. The deed is invalid because it was not legally delivered. A did not intend to divest himself immediately of title; he merely parted with physical possession to allow B to examine the deed. Mere physical delivery is not legal delivery.

Example of Delivery

If A made out a deed to B and gave that deed to C to hand deliver to B, and C refused to deliver the deed, there would still have been legal delivery. Even though B does not have physical possession, the grantor intended to divest himself immediately of an interest in real estate when he gave the deed to C.

Presumptions on Delivery

The law presumes that the deed has been properly delivered if the grantee has physical possession of the deed or if the deed has been recorded. Conversely, if the deed is in the grantor's possession, it is presumed to be an undelivered deed. Either presumption can be overcome with evidence to the contrary.

Acceptance

Finally, the deed must be accepted by the grantee. Acceptance is seldom a problem, and it is usually presumed in transfers beneficial to the grantee.

WILLS AND INTESTACY

Types of Wills

A will is an instrument by which a person directs the disposition of his or her estate on death. California recognizes only three types of wills.

Witnessed Will

Most wills are **formal wills**, also called **witnessed wills**. Generally, they are drafted by attorneys because they are valid only if executed in accordance with strict statutory policy. *Prob.C. 50.* The will must be in writing, and the testator must sign at the end of the will in the presence of at least two witnesses, both or all of whom also sign, acknowledging that the testator declared the document to be his or her will.

Statutory Wills

In 1983, California abolished the almost never used *oral will (nuncupative wills),* and the codes allowed an entirely new type of will, called a **statutory will**, a special preprinted, preapproved form of will specified by statute. If a person is willing to accept one of the two approved forms, he need only check the appropriate boxes, sign the will, and have two witnesses sign where indicated on the form. The statutory will does not allow any extra clauses to be added or any existing clauses to be modified. However, it is adequate for individuals whose testamentary desires exactly follow the codified will plan and who do not desire any sophisticated tax planning. *Prob.C. 56.3.*

Holographic Wills

Holographic wills are handwritten and signed by the testator. No witnesses are needed, and there is no prescribed form. Originally, the will had to be entirely in the testator's own handwriting, although new statutes and case law require that only the "material provisions" must be in the testator's handwriting. The author strongly suggests that, unless a person is knowledgeable of the many common will

TABLE 9.2 Transfer of Property on Death.

	Testate	Intestate
Community property	Decedent's share all passes as directed in will.	Decedent's share all goes to the surviving spouse.
Separate property	Decedent's share all passes as directed in will.	One-half to spouse, one-half to child; or one-third to spouse, two-thirds to children. If no children, one-half to spouse, one-half to parents.

provisions, including executor's powers, guardianship requirements, fiduciary bonds, and similar provisions, another will form should be used.

Intestacy

If a person dies **intestate** (without a will) or if part of the will is invalid, leaving undisposed property, the affected property passes by the laws of intestate succession (see Table 9.2).

Community Property

All community property passes to the surviving spouse, regardless of any children or other heirs. *Prob.C. 201.*

Separate Property

Separate property passes by a defined statutory scheme, according to the following schedule:

1. One-half to surviving spouse; one-half to child
2. One-third to surviving spouse; two-thirds equally to children
3. All to children if there is no surviving spouse
4. One-half to surviving spouse; one-half to parent, if there are no children
5. All to collaterals (aunts, uncles, cousins), only if there are no parents, brothers, sisters, nephews, nieces, children, grandchildren, or surviving spouse

Terminology Used with Wills

Terminology is important to understanding wills and intestacy. **Testate** describes a person who dies leaving a will; *intestate* means one who dies without leaving a will. The **testator** is one who makes a will. The **executor** is the person appointed by the will to act as representative for the estate. The corresponding person appointed by the court in an intestate estate is called the *administrator*. A **devise** is a gift of real estate by will. A **bequest** is a gift of personal property by will, which, if it is money, is called a **legacy**. **Ambulatory** refers to the fact that because a will has no legal effect until the testator's death, it may be freely amended or revoked during the testator's lifetime. An amendment to a will is called a **codicil**.

Escheat

If a person has no heirs at law capable of taking title to property through intestate succession, then the property passes to the state of California through a process called **escheat**. Appropriate publication and filings are made, and if no one claims the estate within five years, the decedent's net estate is ultimately transferred to the attorney general. The state is the permanent owner.

LAND SALES CONTRACTS

Definition

A **land sales contract** is known by many names, including installment land contract, contract of sale, real property sales contract, or simply installment contract. Whichever name is used, it refers to a contract for the purchase of real estate where the seller (**vendor**) retains title until the buyer (**vendee**) makes a specific amount of periodic installment payments. Although the required condition is usually full payment of the purchase price, it could be any agreed on amount paid or any other specified condition. The code defines a contract of sale as one *that does not require conveyance of title within one year from the date of formation of the contract. C.C. 2985.*

The seller retains *legal* title as security for the payment of the purchase price or fulfillment of other stated conditions. The buyer, until transfer of legal title, holds *equitable* title to the property. As such, the buyer has the right to receive legal title on satisfaction of the stated terms and conditions of the installment contract.

Seller's Right and Duties

The seller, as the legal owner, is entitled to possession of the property, although one of the terms of the installment contract usually passes possession to the buyer. A buyer should always check to ensure that the contract transfers the right to possession of the property. Without such wording, possession remains with the seller.

Similarly, the legal owner is responsible for taxes, although such obligation is often shifted to the buyer. Absent fraud, the seller need not own legal title at the time a land sales contract is executed. However, the seller must be able to pass title at the time stated in the contract. Within certain distinctly defined limitations, the seller may transfer or encumber limited interest in the property. *C.C. 2985.1, 2985.2.* Specific statutes provide penalties for any seller who misappropriates or improperly handles the buyer's payments. *C.C. 2985.3, 2985.4.*

Buyer's Rights and Duties

The contract normally gives the buyer the right to possession, the obligation for taxes, and the responsibility for destruction to the property. Unless prohibited by contract, the buyer can normally sell or encumber equitable interest in the property. However, because of the limited nature of the interest, the buyer may find it difficult to find a buyer or lender interested in the property. On residential property, the buyer can also prepay a loan, except the parties can agree to prohibit it during the first year. *C.C. 2985.6.*

Reasons for Demise

The once widely used installment land sales contract is seldom used today and has been described by a leading authority as "legally obsolete." *48 Cal.L.R. 775.* However, the contract was saved from extinction by its use in Cal-Vet loans and as a means of acquiring low-interest loans during periods of high, rising interest rates.

The primary reason for the increased unpopularity of the land sales contract is the courts' steady removal of the vast protections available to the seller, at the expense of the buyer, in the event of a default. Removing a defaulting buyer's interest in the property may prove more expensive and take longer, depending on the circumstances, than the procedures available with conventional financing.

Land sales contracts have gained short spurts of relatively recent acceptance as a means of creative financing. In 1974, the California Supreme Court ruled that lenders could not accelerate their loans under a **due-on-sale** clause for a sale under a land sales contract unless the lender could demonstrate jeopardy to security. Following this ruling, land sales contracts gained some popularity. Then the 1978 *Wellencamp* decision allowing outright sales of property without acceleration seemed to suggest an end to land sales contracts. However, in November 1982, *Wellencamp* was overruled by new federal legislation that specifically authorizes a lender to treat a sale under a land sales contract as any other sale. Thus, a lender can accelerate under a land sales contract as effectively as for a "straight" sale. Except for sales that can be hidden from lenders so that they cannot accelerate loans because they do not know about the sales, it appears that land sales contracts should be only infrequently, if not rarely, used in California.

Trustee's Sale

Some title company land sales contain wording similar to that in a deed of trust, purporting to give the seller the right to foreclose by trustee's sale in the event of a default. However, the author is not aware of any California appellate courts that have yet ruled on the validity of such a provision. Such documents must be considered susceptible to lengthy judicial action and should probably be avoided.

Advantages and Disadvantages to Seller

The major advantages of land sales contracts to the seller are that the buyer's interest can be expeditiously and inexpensively terminated if the contract is not of record and the buyer is not willing to engage in litigation. The contract may provide a means of selling property without paying an assumption fee or facing an acceleration of an existing loan.

The major disadvantage to the seller is that, because most buyers record the land sales contract, the seller must clear title, usually by a quiet title action. Such an action is both expensive and time consuming; if the buyer is under a legal disability (e.g., if a minor or an incompetent) or is hiding from service, the lawsuit becomes far more difficult. If the buyer created any mechanic's liens or other third-party interests in the property, those interests may have to be resolved in court. Finally, if the buyer's payments exceed the seller's damages, the seller will actually have to refund overpayments to the defaulting buyer.

Advantages and Disadvantages to Buyer

The major advantages to the buyer include the possibility of recovery of part of the payments over the amount of the seller's damages, the possibility of purchasing the property with an existing loan without facing an increase in the interest rate, and the fact that a **judgment lien** will not attach to the buyer's equitable title.

The disadvantages to the buyer are numerous. Probably the most significant are the difficulty in obtaining financing from lenders because of the unattractive security, the possible prohibitions against assignments by the contract terms, and the possibility that the seller may not have title even after all payments have been made. Also, liens against the seller may seriously affect the buyer. For example, if the buyer is given notice of a judgment lien against the seller, any payments then made to the seller are at the buyer's risk, because the seller is not entitled to them.

APPLY THE LAW

Honey v. Henry's Franchise Leasing Corp.
64 C.2d 801 (1966)

[Plaintiff purchased property from defendant for $135,000 under a land sales contract. After the buyer had paid a total of $33,450, he defaulted on the contract. The trial court, under these facts, entered judgment for the seller quieting title on the condition that the seller return to the defendant buyer the amount his payments exceeded the rental value of the property during the buyer's occupancy. The issue on appeal is whether the defaulting buyer is entitled to any refund of his payment and, if so, what amount.]

TRAYNOR, JUSTICE. Even a willfully defaulting vendee may recover the excess of his part payments over the damages caused by his breach. We agree with defendant's contention that the trial court erred in measuring its damages under this rule by the rental value of the property while plaintiff was in possession instead of by the loss of the benefit of defendant's bargain. Because the trial court found that the fair market value of the property at the time of the trial was $90,000, defendant contends that the difference between the contract price of $135,000 and the fair market value of the property exceeded plaintiff's part payments of $33,450.

The rule of the *Freedman* case [an earlier decision by this court] precludes penalties and forfeitures by denying the vendor the right on the vendee's default to retain both the property and any payments that have been made in excess of the actual damages caused by the default. The *Freedman* case, however, did not restrict the right of a vendor to realize the benefit of his bargain.

Because rules precluding forfeitures and antideficiency legislation have put the latter type of contract substantially on a par in many respects with mortgages and deeds of trust, amicus curiae [an adviser to the judge] suggests that the law governing those security devices should

APPLY THE LAW

continued

be adopted with appropriate modifications in determining the remedies for breaches of installment contracts.

The value of the property to the seller is ordinarily the market value of the property at the date of the breach. This rule presupposes that the vendee is free to use or dispose of the property on that date. Accordingly, if the vendee has interfered with the vendor's freedom in this respect, by retaining possession or asserting an interest in the property, the vendor may include any additional damages caused thereby in the amount necessary to give him the benefit of his bargain.

In the present case, defendant repossessed some of the property before trial, and it is impossible to determine from the record whether the value of all of the property at the time of the trial was equal to its value at the time of the breach plus any consequential damages that may have been incurred. Accordingly, the judgment is reversed with directions to retry the issue of damages only and to enter the appropriate judgment.

[Therefore, defendant buyer is entitled to a refund based on whatever amount, if any, his total payments exceeded the seller's actual damages. However, the seller's damages are not calculated by using the fair rental value of the property, because that measure applies only to rescission. When the seller selects a quiet title action, his damages are calculated as the difference between the contract purchase price and the value of the property at the date of breach, plus any other provable damages sustained because of the buyer's breach.]

STUDY QUESTIONS (TRUE–FALSE)

1. Grant deeds contain the implied warranty that the property is fit for the purpose for which it is sold.

2. Use of a deed warrants ownership of an interest.

3. A deed does not require consideration to be valid.

4. A deed signed by a minor is totally void and of no validity whatsoever.

5. If A gives a deed to his sister just before undergoing surgery, telling her to keep the deed unless he survives the operation, the deed is invalid because of lack of delivery.

6. Insane persons and minors are incapable of owning real estate in their own name.

7. If the signature on a holographic will cannot be easily read, witnesses are required to make the will valid.

8. If a husband dies intestate with six children, his wife will receive all their community property, even if it was the only property owned by the husband.

9. A defaulting buyer under a land sales contract may recover the amount of his payments that exceed the seller's actual damages.

10. The seller retains title and also the right to possession unless and until transferred by the terms of the contract.

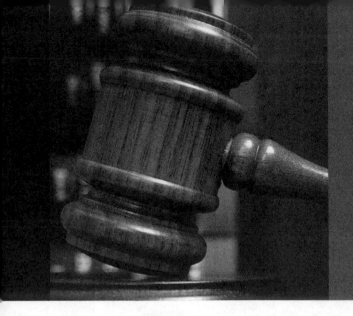

10

NATURE OF ADVERSE POSSESSION

Definition

Adverse possession is a method of acquiring title to another's property without that owner's consent. *C.C. 1007.* The claimant need only pay the taxes and occupy the property in a notorious and adverse manner for five consecutive years under a claim of right or color of title. Once these requirements are met, the claimant automatically becomes the new and lawful owner of the property.

Perfecting Marketability

Even though passage of title is automatic, title is still not marketable. To become marketable, the adverse possessor's title must be ascertainable from a search of the county records. There must be a recorded document of title, usually either a quitclaim deed from the owner or a judgment of quiet title action executed by a judge.

Use of Adverse Possession

The public usually associates adverse possession only with vacant, uncultivated property miles from civilization. In fact, adverse possession has numerous applications today even in urban communities. It will not work against public property; adverse possession is applicable only to private property.

The rationale for adverse possession rests on the doctrine that property should not be removed from use for excessive periods. An owner who does not care enough about the property to observe and object to another's possession of it deserves to lose it. When the possessor first appears, only the owner has the right to evict the trespasser.

Involuntary Transfers of Property

But the statute of limitations for trespass is five years; after five years, the owner loses the right to evict the possessor. Thus, no person has the right to dispossess the trespasser, who, having paid the taxes and met the requirements of the law, becomes the owner.

Comparison to Easement by Prescription

Adverse possession and easement by prescription have many of the same elements and similar legal justification, but each concept involves entirely different rights (see Table 10.1). The key differences are that an easement by prescription does not require payment of taxes, and it only grants the right to use the property. Adverse possession transfers exclusive possession of the property and requires payment of taxes.

Thus, in one case, two landowners were mistaken as to their common boundaries. One owner used 15 feet of the neighbor's property as his own, believing it to be his own, for growing trees and shrubs and for laying a sidewalk. Because the use existed over five years, the court held that this mistaken property owner acquired an easement by prescription over that 15-foot strip for growing shrubs and maintaining a sidewalk. Because taxes were not paid, adverse possession was not possible. *Gilardi v. Hallam (1981) 120 C.A.3d 647.*

REQUIREMENTS OF ADVERSE POSSESSION

Basic Requirements

The claimant must meet all five elements of adverse possession before acquiring title to the property: (1) notorious occupation of the property, (2) hostility to the owner, (3) occupation under a claim of right

TABLE 10.1 Nature of adverse possession and easement by prescription.

	Adverse Possession	Easement by Prescription
Rights Acquired	Right to title (possession) of land; ownership	Right to mere use of the land
Elements	Notorious possession	Notorious use (not possession)
	Hostile to owner	Hostile to owner
	Under claim of right or color of title	Under claim of right or color of title
	Continuous possession for five years	Continuous use for five years
	Payment of taxes	
Payment of taxes	Must be paid; One of the elements	No payment of taxes
Nature of proof	Generally greater to establish possession	Generally lesser to establish use

or color of title, (4) occupation for five continuous years, and (5) payment of all taxes levied against the property.

Notorious Occupation

The first requirement is that the claimant must actually, openly, and notoriously occupy the property. The occupancy must be such that the owner could discover the possession on a reasonable inspection of the property. That the true owner is miles away and lacks actual notice is immaterial, as long as the possession is such that the owner could discover it with due diligence. The question of what acts constitute ownership of sufficient magnitude to provide notice depends on the facts of each particular case.

Hostile (Adverse) Possession

Secondly, the possession must be adverse or hostile to the owner. Any possession without the owner's consent or permission is hostile because it is adverse to the owner's interests.

Effect of Adverse Possession

Adverse possession describes the effects of lapse of time in the creation of a new estate and the extinguishment of an existing property interest. When the occupier first takes possession, the owner has a cause of action for trespassing. However, after the statute of limitations (five years) has run out, the one person who could evict the occupier—the owner—is barred from doing so. Thus, the occupier has exclusive right to possession (and therefore to title).

Owner Must Have Right to Possession

For a claimant to acquire title against an owner, that owner must have a present right to bring a cause of action against the occupant–trespasser. One cannot claim adverse possession against the owner of a future interest, because that future-interest holder has no present right to possession and hence no right to bring a trespass action against an occupant. An exception is that adverse possession can run against a future owner if possession has already begun against the owner of a present interest, who thereafter creates a future interest in the land.

Claim of Right or Color of Title

The third element is that the possession must be made under either a claim of right or a color of title. If the possessor acts in good faith and claims the land because of defective document, then occupation is under a *color of title*. Typically, defective instruments include forged deeds, rescinded judicial decrees, community property deeds without a spouse's signature, and other documents appearing to transfer title without having the legal validity to do so. Conversely, as with the old squatter's rights, if the possessor occupies the land knowing it is not his, possession is by *claim of right*. Even if the possessor mistakenly believes he owns the property, as long as he does so without reliance on a written document, possession is also classified as a claim of right.

The importance of the distinction between claim of right and color of title concerns the amount of property that can be claimed and the type of occupation necessary to acquire that property. The possessor must possess and use the property in a similar manner as would an owner of that property. However, the type of occupation required under a claim of right is more demanding than that required under a color of title. Furthermore, occupation under a color of title gives the possessor the right to claim all the area described in the defective instrument. Conversely, under claim of right, an adverse possessor can claim only the property physically and factually occupied (see Table 10.2).

Five Years' Continuous Possession

The fourth requirement is that the property must have been continuously possessed for five consecutive years. However, continuous possession does not require constant possession. The occupant must make only such ordinary possession of the property with such frequency as would a reasonable owner of similar property.

TABLE 10.2   Comparison of claim of right and color of title.

	Claim of Right	Color of Title
Nature	Occupant knows that he or she has no rights to title or mistakenly believes he or she has right to occupancy.	Occupant believes that he or she has right to occupancy because of a defective instrument.
Document involved	No.	Yes.
Property acquired	Only that which is actually occupied.	Property actually and constructively occupied. Entire property may be acquired although claimant occupies only a portion.

Abatement during Disability

Because adverse possession is based on the right of the legal owner to bring action against the occupant, if the owner is under a legal disability at the time the occupation begins, the five years cannot begin to run until the earlier of (1) the owner's recovery from the disability or (2) 20 years. *C.C.P. 328.* Disabilities include minority, insanity, and imprisonment for less than life.

Payment of Taxes

Finally, the occupant must pay all taxes against the property during the five-year period. It is immaterial that the true owner may also pay the taxes and assessments levied against the property. The attorney general's office has ruled that anyone who requests a tax statement for a parcel or property must receive such a statement. *Ops.Cal.Atty.Gen. 59–70.* The payment must be made during each of the five years; failure to pay the assessment during a single year defeats a claim to adverse possession. *Southern Land Co. v. McKenna (1929) 100 C.A. 152.*

Priority in Payment

If taxes were assessed against the adverse claimant, it is immaterial whether the true owner of the property paid first. However, if the claimant does not have taxes assessed in his or her name, then the claimant must pay the taxes before the owner makes payment. *Carpenter v. Lewis (1911) 161 C. 484.*

West v. Evans
29 C.2d 414 (1946)

[Pursuant to a divorce decree, wife Melinda acquired a three-quarter interest in the family home as tenant in common with her ex-husband, James. Under the same decree, James moved out, and Melinda lived on the property with her adopted son, West, plaintiff herein. Melinda gave West a deed to the entire property (although she only owned three-quarters), which he duly recorded. Six years later, West married and moved out, leaving Melinda the sole occupant until her death. During probate, West claimed the entire property, three-quarters by deed and the other quarter by adverse possession. Defendants (James's heirs) claimed that the quarter interest could not be acquired by adverse possession because the possession was not open and notorious and additionally because the possession was not hostile. The latter contention was based on the theory that West was a cotenant, and possession by one cotenant is possession by all cotenants. All other elements of adverse possession were met.]

EDMUNDS, JUSTICE. To establish title by adverse possession, the claimant must establish five elements in connection with his occupancy of the property. (1) Possession must be actual occupation under such circumstances as to constitute reasonable notice to the owner. (2) Possession must be hostile to the owner's title. (3) The holder must claim the property as his own, either under color of title or claim of right. (4) Possession must be continuous and uninterrupted for five years. (5) The possessor must pay all the taxes levied and assessed upon the property during the period. Unless each of these elements is established by the evidence, the plaintiff has not acquired title by adverse possession.

Actual possession means a subjection to the will and dominion of the claimant. It is established not alone by the assertion of title. It must be coupled with acts of ownership that proclaim to the world and bring notice to the owner, that a right [is] claimed in the land over which the claimant is seeking to exercise dominion. But in the present case, there was no change in possession at any time after the date of the interlocutory [divorce] decree. Melinda continued to live on the property until her death in 1944, and West occupied it with her until his marriage in 1937. To the public generally, and to the heirs of James, after the date of the interlocutory decree when the cotenants [heirs] acquired title, there was no indication of any change in possession from Melinda.

The testimony of West conclusively negates his claim that, at any time prior to 1944, he had actual possession of the property. From 1917

continued

until the date of her death in 1944, Melinda stayed in her home. During the 20 years following 1917 he lived with her. Upon his marriage in 1937 he "moved off gradually." Referring to that time he declared: "She didn't want anybody to live with her and she didn't care to live with any of her relatives." She said, "This is my home and I want to stay right here."

The evidence conclusively establishes that for many years West paid the taxes on the property, but such payment is not an act of ownership equivalent to possession. The payment of taxes is an additional requirement for the acquisition of title by adverse possession.

The exclusive occupancy by a cotenant is deemed permissive; it does not become adverse until the tenant out of possession has had either actual or constructive notice that the possession of the cotenant is hostile to him. West argues that the recordation of the deed in 1931 constitutes such notice. However, the recordation of a deed purporting to convey the entire property in land to a tenant in possession is not independent of any other facts, notice to his cotenant of the adverse character of the grantee's possession. The only act upon which West can rely to give the notice of his claim of ownership is the recordation of the deed in 1931, and such recordation alone is not sufficient for that purpose. The evidence is undisputed and it does not show the elements that the law requires for establishing such title. The judgment is reversed. [West did not acquire title by adverse possession.]

CONDEMNATION (EMINENT DOMAIN)

Nature and Definition

Eminent domain is the power of the state to acquire private property for public use upon payment of just compensation. Although the terms eminent domain and **condemnation** are frequently used synonymously, eminent domain refers to a right or power of the state, whereas condemnation is a proceeding through which the state acquires property by eminent domain.

Inverse Condemnation

True acts under the police power only regulate property and require no payment to the owner. Hence, governments naturally favor exercise of the police power where applicable. However, as discussed later in this chapter, a regulation can be so severe as to amount to a taking. Even a regulation that temporarily restricts property, such as a building moratorium, may entitle the owner to damages for the period of the taking. *First Lutheran Etc. Church v. County of Los Angeles (1987) 482 U.S. 304.* The disguised condemnation would entitle the owner to compensation under an inverse condemnation action. It is called *inverse* because it is initiated by the owner, and it forces the condemning agency to compensate the owner.

The mere passage of a restricted ordinance does not automatically amount to a taking. The property owner must first *exhaust* the administrative remedies. In other words, the property owner must first apply for all governmental permits or relief from the oppressive ordinance; once no other remedies are available, then the property owner can show that he or she was damaged and entitled to compensation. *First Lutheran Etc. Church v. County of Los Angeles (1987) 482 U.S. 304.*

Dedication as Disguised Condemnation

It is not uncommon for governmental agencies to grant building permits or other approval for property development on the condition that the owner dedicate a portion of his or her property to the public or pay a fee to offset other governmental needs. For example, in one recent case, the California Coastal Commission only allowed a beachfront property owner to construct a home on the condition the owner grant an easement across the property to the public. Such conditions are no longer valid unless the condition or required grant is directly related to minimizing the impact of the property's development. *Nollan v. Calif. Coastal Commission (1987) 483 U.S. 825.* The Court held such unrelated conditions that amounted to a taking of the property for which the government must compensate the owner.

Legal scholars are uncertain as to just how far the Supreme Court will go to restrict the power of governments to require a landowner to dedicate a part of his or her property as a condition for obtaining a building permit. In the *Nollan* case, the Court required an essential nexus between a county's conditions for a building permit and the builder's development. Otherwise, the conditions for the building permit amount to a taking for which the developer must be compensated. A more recent case went further and required both an essential nexus and a rough proportionality. The Court then stated that there is no "precise mathematical calculation required, but the city must make some sort of individualized determination that the required dedication is related both in nature and extent to the impact of the proposed development." *Dolan v. City of Tigard (1994) 512 U.S. 687.* The burden of proof has shifted to the government to show that the condition for the permit is proportional. Cities and counties will have a much more difficult time requiring builders to donate part of their land in exchange for a building permit. The government must prove that specific problems will be caused by the development and that the land or funds demanded of the developer are roughly proportional to the cost of correcting or reducing the problem.

Distinction from Police Power

Condemnation is totally separate and distinct from the exercise of **police power**. Traditionally, zoning and police power applications amount to a mere *regulation* of property, for which no compensation need be paid to the owner. Eminent domain, conversely, is the actual taking of property, for which the owner must be fully and fairly compensated (see Table 10.3.)

Difficulty in Application

Theoretically, the distinction between regulation and taking is clear. However, in practice, it is often difficult to differentiate between them. Regulations that severely affect a property's value fall into a gray area where only the courts can make the final determination. The courts have adopted numerous approaches. Traditionally, they required a physical invasion of the property before they would find a taking. When the invasion theory failed to cover new complexities, the courts used a diminution-of-value approach. If and when government action rendered the property almost worthless or significantly

TABLE 10.3 Comparison of eminent domain and police power.

	Eminent Domain	Police Power
Action	Taking private property	Mere regulation of property
Purpose	To take property and use it for the general welfare	To prevent use in a manner detrimental to the general welfare
Examples	Condemnation actions	Zoning, building codes, setback lines
Compensation paid	Yes	No

diminished in value, a taking had occurred. Many courts today tend to ignore the reduction in value as a criterion if the prohibited use was one that amounted to a quasi-nuisance to the community. Each case must be decided on its own merits.

The exact definition of a taking is somewhat uncertain at this time because the U.S. Supreme Court broke its 50 years of silence and issued several cases beginning in 1987 on condemnation. Although the Court did not define a taking, it suggested that a taking might perhaps ultimately be defined as a regulation that denies an owner all economic use of his or her property. But the Supreme Court then went on to suggest that perhaps even a total regulation may be justified to protect public safety. Unfortunately, even this vague wording arose in another context, so all definitive definitions of a taking will have to wait for future clarification from the courts.

It appears, however, that the definition of a taking is broad. The U.S. Supreme Court upheld a Hawaiian land reform law requiring the breakup of large private landholdings and the forced redistribution to small homeowners. The Hawaiian government could condemn the property of large landowners, acquire title, and then sell the property in small parcels to individual homeowners. The Court was untroubled by the fact that the property would ultimately be transferred to private beneficiaries. The decision went on to state that, "the court long ago rejected any liberal requirement that condemned property be put into use for the general public." The government does not have to actually use the property. "It is only the taking's purpose, and not its mechanics, that must pass scrutiny" under the Fifth Amendment. *Hawaii Housing Authority v. Midkiff (1984) 467 U.S. 229.*

APPLY THE LAW

Nollan v. California Coastal Commission
483 U.S. 825; 107 S.Ct. 2389 (1987)

[The Nollans owned a beachfront lot in Ventura County, California. They wanted to replace their dilapidated bungalow on their land with a three-bedroom house, and they applied for a permit from the California Coastal Commission. The commission would only grant the permit if the Nollans would dedicate an easement across their land for the public to have greater access to the beach. The Nollans thought this condition was an unlawful *taking* of their property, which was illegal under the Fifth Amendment to the U.S. Constitution. The trial court agreed and issued an order (called a writ of mandamus) removing the dedication and granting the permit. On appeal,

continued

the Court of Appeal reversed the lower court and allowed the dedication requirement. The court held that, even though the dedication significantly reduced the value of the Nollan's property, it did not deprive them of all use of the land. Therefore, the appeals court held the condition did not amount to a taking.

The California Supreme Court refused to hear the appeal, but the U.S. Supreme Court accepted the case].

SCALIA, JUSTICE. Had California simply required the Nollans to make an easement across their beachfront available to the public on a permanent basis in order to increase public access to the beach, rather than conditioning their permit to rebuild their house on their agreeing to do so, we have no doubt there would have been a taking.

To say that the appropriation of a public easement across a landowner's premises does not constitute the taking of a property interest but rather "a mere restriction on its use" is to use words in a manner that deprives them of all their ordinary meaning. Indeed, one of the principal uses of the eminent domain power is to assure that the government be able to require conveyance of just such interests, so long as it pays for them.

Perhaps because the point is so obvious, we have never been confronted with a controversy that required us to rule upon it, but our cases' analysis of the effect of other governmental action leads to the same conclusion. We have repeatedly held that, as to property reserved by its owner for private use, "the right to exclude [others is] one of the most essential sticks in the bundle of rights that are commonly characterized as property."

We observed that where governmental action results in "a permanent physical occupation" of the property, by the government itself or by others, our cases uniformly have found a taking to the extent of the occupation, without regard to whether the action achieves an important public benefit or has only minimal economic impact on the owner. "We think a permanent physical occupation has occurred, for purposes of that rule, where individuals are given a permanent and continuous right to pass to and fro, so that the real property may continuously be traversed, even though no particular individual is permitted to station himself permanently upon the premises."

Given, then, that requiring uncompensated conveyance of the easement outright would violate the Fourteenth Amendment, the question becomes whether requiring it to be conveyed as a condition for issuing a land use permit alters the outcome. We have long recognized that land use regulation does not effect a taking if it "substantially advances legitimate state interests" and does not "deny an owner economically viable use of his land." However, a use restriction may constitute a "taking" if not reasonably necessary to the effectuation of a substantial government purpose. Our cases have not elaborated on the standards for determining what constitutes a "legitimate state interest" or what type of connection between the regulation and the state interest satisfies the requirement that the former substantially advance the latter. They have made clear, however, that a broad range of governmental purposes and regulations satisfies these requirements.

The Commission argues that a permit condition that serves the same legitimate police-power purpose as a refusal to issue the permit should not be found to be a taking if the refusal to issue the permit would not constitute a taking. We agree. Thus, if the Commission attached to the permit some condition that would have protected the public's ability to see the beach notwithstanding construction of the new house—for example, a height limitation, a width restriction, or a ban on fences—so long as the Commission could have exercised its police power to forbid construction of the house altogether, imposition of the condition would also be constitutional.

The Commission claims that the condition at issue here is reasonably related to the public need or burden that the Nollans' new house creates or to which it contributes. We can accept, for purposes of discussion, the Commission's proposed test as to how close a "fit" between the condition and the burden is required, because we find that this case does not meet even the most untailored standards. The Commission's principal contention to the contrary essentially turns on a play on the word "access."

The Nollans' new house, the Commission found, will interfere with "visual access" to the beach. That in turn (along with other shorefront development) will interfere with the desire of people who drive past the Nollans' house to use the beach, thus creating a "psychological barrier" to "access."

Rewriting the argument to eliminate the play on words makes clear that there is nothing to it. It is quite impossible to understand how a requirement that people already on the public beaches be able to walk across the Nollans' property reduces any obstacles to viewing the beach created by the new house. It is also impossible to understand how it lowers any "psychological barrier" to using the public beaches, or how it helps to remedy any additional congestion on them caused by construction of the Nollans' new house. We therefore find that the Commission's imposition of the permit condition cannot be treated as an exercise of its land use power for any of these purposes. Our conclusion on this point is consistent with the approach taken by every other court that has considered the question, with the exception of the California state courts.

APPLY THE LAW

continued

continued

The Commission may well be right that it is a good idea, but that does not establish that the Nollans (and other coastal residents) alone can be compelled to contribute to its realization. Rather, California is free to advance its "comprehensive program," if it wishes, by using its power of eminent domain for this "public purpose." If the Commission wants an easement across the Nollans' property, it must pay for it.

Reversed.

CONDEMNATION GUIDELINES

Limitations on Condemnation

The right of all governments to take private property for public good on just compensation is inherent. The statutes limiting the exercise of eminent domain are liberal and general in nature. *C.C.P. 1230.010–1273.060.* Basically, three requirements must be met: The taking must be for the public good, it must be necessary for the proposed public use, and just compensation must be paid. *C.C.P. 1240.030.*

Finally, there is one additional requirement. Proposition 99, passed by the California votes in 2008, holds that governments cannot acquire homes under eminent domain for the intent of transferring it to a private person. However, the proposition contains exceptions, perhaps the most important of which are exceptions for public health, public safety, emergencies, and restricting crime. In the author's opinion, these exceptions and the fact that most condemnation is of non-residential property, makes this proposition less onerous and all encompassing than is often believed.

For the Public Good

The requirement that any condemned property be taken for the public good is further defined by statute. Any use authorized by statute is presumed to be in the public interest, which is specifically defined to include social, environmental, economic, and aesthetic purposes. *C.C.P. 1240.010.* All agencies must adopt a resolution that the condemnation action is for public necessity. If the resolution is made by a state or local government agency taking property within its borders, then that determination is conclusive unless gross abuse of discretion or bribery can be proved. *C.C.P. 1245.244, 1245.270.* Finally, the particular property must be suitable and necessary for the proposed purpose for which it is condemned.

Just Compensation

The condemning agency must pay the owner the fair market value of the property, exclusive of any value attributable to the project for which the property is condemned and without any consideration of the effect of the condemnation action on the value of the property. *C.C.P. 1263.330.* However, just compensation is not indemnification for all losses sustained by the property owner because of the taking. As a general rule, the property owner is not compensated for moving expenses (with some exceptions), attorney's fees, witness fees, court costs, and appraisal fees. Since 1976, the owner of a business may obtain compensation for loss of goodwill to the extent that it could not have been reasonably avoided. *C.C.P. 1263.510.*

Amount of Compensation

The amount of just compensation is usually calculated by one or more traditional appraisal techniques: the cost method (determination of today's replacement cost less depreciation); the market comparison method (valuation by comparison to the selling prices of similar properties); and the capitalization of income method (the property's effective net income over time capitalized to a present-value figure by a determined interest rate).

Condemnation Procedure

Most condemnation actions are settled by negotiation and stipulation between the owner and the condemning agency. If they proceed to trial, all questions of law are decided by the judge; the sole and exclusive function of a jury is to determine the amount of compensation to be paid to the property owner. In such a trial, neither party has the burden of proof on the issue of the property's value.

ADDITIONS AND SUBTRACTIONS BY WATER

Nature of the Problem

When land borders on a stream, river, lake, or ocean, the action of the water can affect the size of the land. Water tends to erode a person's property by carrying off portions of the land. Frequently, these deposits are carried by the water and deposited on another's land. Similarly, a person's land could grow by recession of the water. If a stream dried up, land would now extend where water once lay. Depending on how a person's land grew, he may be able to claim the enlargement to his property as a new boundary.

Gradual Gain of Land

If a person's land grew from the slow, almost imperceptible, deposits carried by water, then a person owns the enlargement to his or her property. The process of adding the land by deposits is called accretion, and the land so added is called alluvium. Similarly, if the water recedes by slow, almost imperceptible, degrees, enlarging a person's land, he or she owns the newly added land. Additions from receding water are called reliction.

Sudden Removal of Land

If a person loses a considerable and distinguishable part of his land by a sudden and violent action of the water, it is called avulsion. In such cases, the owner can reclaim his or her land from the new location within one year from the date of loss.

STUDY QUESTIONS (TRUE–FALSE)

1. Adverse possession applies only to vacant or abandoned land.

2. Payment of taxes by an adverse claimant is sufficient notice to an owner that the possessor is claiming the property adversely.

3. Even though the claimant has met all the requirements for adverse possession, the ownership is unmarketable until perfected by a quitclaim deed from the owner or a judgment of quiet title.

4. The time for adverse possession does not begin to run until the owner has actual notice of the claimant's occupation of the property.

5. Possession under a claim of right requires the occupant to have a defective or invalid document purporting to grant certain rights of possession.

6. The occupant must occupy the property almost every day of the year to acquire title by adverse possession.

7. If the owner pays taxes on the property, a claimant cannot acquire title by adverse possession.

8. Condemnation is the lay term for eminent domain.

9. An owner who wins a condemnation case against the government is not reimbursed for appraiser's or attorney's fees.

10. No matter how severe the regulation of property, no compensation is due the owner under the exercise of police power.

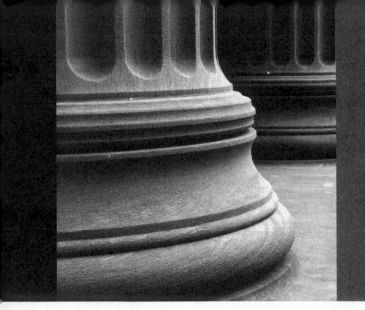

CO-OWNERSHIP

Types of Co-ownership

An estate in real property may be owned by one or more persons. If the property is solely owned, it is called *ownership in severalty*. The word severalty denotes a "state of being separate." It means that the real estate is owned by one individual, alone and separate from anyone else. If two or more persons hold title, it is a form of *joint ownership,* also known as *co-ownership*. The **Civil Code** recognizes only five types of joint ownership: joint tenancy, tenancy in common, community property, community property with right of survivorship, and tenancy in partnership. Other forms of joint ownership operate as a deviation or combination of the four forms or as a special tax form of ownership.

Nature of Co-ownership

Joint ownership can exist in any estate, although the owners must have concurrent ownership interests in the identical estate. For example, two owners of a present interest or a future interest would be considered co-owners. However, an owner of a present interest and an owner of a future interest would not qualify as joint owners. Similarly, the owner of the surface land of property and a separate owner of the subsurface land would not be joint owners. Each co-owner of an estate holds a percentage of the total estate, without an exclusive right to any specific portion of it.

Joint Ownership

JOINT TENANCY

Nature of Joint Tenancy

Joint tenancy is essentially ownership of property by two or more individuals with right of survivorship. On death, the interest of the deceased joint tenant vests with the surviving joint tenants. One exception is recognized: A joint tenant who murders a co-owner may not receive property through that joint tenancy. Because a corporation has a potentially indefinite duration at law, it may not hold property in joint tenancy. The rationale is that because, at law, a corporation may never die, no right of survivorship would be possible.

Example

If A, B, and C held property in joint tenancy, on the death of C, A and B would each own an undivided one-half interest in joint tenancy. If A then died, B would own the entire estate in severalty.

Survivorship

Survivorship is the right of surviving joint tenants to receive the decedent's interest in the property, free of probate. It is accomplished by a legal fiction that each tenant holds title to the entire estate. Thus, on the death of one tenant that interest is immediately and automatically eliminated. Because a deceased joint tenant owns no interest after death, there is nothing to be disposed of by will or intestacy. Hence, any inclusion of joint tenancy property in a will is meaningless and of no force and effect (provided at least one joint tenant survives to receive the property).

Any judgment lien, deed of trust, or other lien against that deceased joint tenant's interest in property is extinguished on death. Because there is nothing to pass through probate, no interests can attach. The remaining joint tenants receive the title unencumbered by the decedent's liens. Thus, in one case, a father and daughter owned property in joint tenancy. A creditor of the father had a judgment lien against the father's interest in the property. The creditor essentially becomes a gambler in such case. If the debtor is the surviving joint tenant, then the lien attaches to the entire property. If, as in this case, the judgment dies first, the creditor loses his lien. When the father died, the daughter took the property free and clear of the judgment lien. *Ziegler v. Bonnel (1942) 52 C.A.2d 217.* When husbands and wives own property in joint tenancy, the effect is different because most debts are community property debts for which both spouses have a liability.

Still Requires Action

Although a decedent's interest in joint tenancy property passes automatically on death to the surviving joint tenants, it is not a recognized transfer of public record. To be marketable and salable, the decedent's interest must be removed from the public records. The removal requires two steps. First, the deceased tenant's death must be established by recording a copy of the death certificate. Second, the surviving joint tenants must record an affidavit stating that they are the same surviving tenants named in the deed. Only when these documents have been recorded will the transfer be perfected, insurable by a title company, and salable to others (see Figure 11.1).

Severance

During the lifetime of the joint tenancy, it can easily be severed at the whim and will of any joint tenant or by the involuntary transfer of a joint tenant's interest. When one joint tenant transfers his share, the grantee takes title as tenant in common to the other joint tenants. However, even though the joint tenancy is severed as to that one joint tenant, the remaining joint tenants (if there are more than one) continue to hold among themselves in joint tenancy.

Example

If A, B, and C held property in joint tenancy, and C transferred his or her share to X, then A and B would hold as joint tenants between themselves. If A died, his or her one-third interest would go to B. However, both A and B would hold as tenants in common to X.

FIGURE 11.1   Affidavit of death of joint tenant.

**When Recorded Mail To, And
Mail Tax Statements To:**

Mrs. Alice Survivor
123 Jones Street
San Rafael, CA 94903

Assessor's Parcel Number

123-44-5678

Affidavit - Death of Joint Tenant

I, THE UNDERSIGNED, having been duly sworn, and being of legal age, hereby certify under penalty of perjury, as follows:

1. That JOE DECEDENT has died, and attached hereto is a certified copy of the death certificate.

2. That JOE DECEDENT was named as one of the parties in that joint tenancy deed dated January 10, 1989, which was executed by JOE SELLER, in favor of JOE DECEDENT and ALICE SURVIVOR, husband and wife, recorded as instrument number 765453 on January 10, 2005, in the official records of Marin County, California.

3. That the property described in the above joint tenancy deed was situated in the City of San Rafael, County of Marin, State of California, and described as:

    Lot #1 of Block A, as shown on that certain map entitled "Tract 12345," and filed for record on January 15, 1990, as Book 123 in Page 567, in the Official Records of the County of Marin, State of California.

Date: *January 3, 2005*   *TED H. GORDON*

(Notary)

X could will his or her share, and on his or her death it would not pass to A and B, just as A and B's interests would never pass to X.

Example

An agreement inconsistent with the nature and requirements of joint tenancy will terminate the tenancy. For instance, an agreement between husband and wife joint tenants that on the death of either one of them the property will go to their children changes the joint tenancy into a tenancy in common. *McDonald* v. *Morly (1940) 15 C.2d 409.*

Four Unities

Traditionally, the creation of a joint tenancy required the existence of the four common-law unities of title, time, interest, and possession. The unity of *time* required that the joint tenants acquire their property at the same time. Unity of *title* demanded that the owners receive their ownership from the same deed or instrument. Unity of *interest* indicated that each owner must have the same amount and type of interest in property. Finally, unity of *possession* held that all owners must have the same, equal, undivided right to possession of the entire property. However, California has relaxed the requirement. The issue of unities rarely arises and then usually for a determination of whether a joint tenancy is terminated rather than created (see Table 11.1).

TABLE 11.1   The four unities.

	Common-Law Requirements	Current California Requirements
Time	Each tenant must acquire his interest at exactly the same time. A tenant may only deed to himself and another through a "strawman."	All tenants must be named in one deed or integrated document. A tenant may directly deed to himself and another as joint tenants without using a "strawman."
Title	Each tenant must acquire his ownership from the exact same instrument. No direct deeding; must use a "strawman."	All tenants must be named in one deed or integrated document. Direct deeding is possible.
Interest	Each tenant must hold exactly the same type and amount of ownership interest. One tenant cannot own a one-quarter interest, while the other owns three-quarters.	Each tenant must hold the same type of interest. As to the portion of the property held in joint tenancy, those tenants must hold equal interests. The same tenant could also own a different tenancy interest. Thus A could hold one-half the property as a tenant in common, and the other one-half could be held between A and B, one-quarter each, as joint tenants.
Possession	Each tenant must have an equal, undivided, and identical right to possession.	The tenants may have different rights to possession (e.g., a lease) if all tenants agree and there is no intent to sever the tenancy.

Creation of Joint Tenancy Today

To create a joint tenancy today in California, it is generally necessary only to state in the transfer that the grantees are to hold title "as joint tenants." "A transfers to X and Y with right of survivorship" is insufficient to create a joint tenancy. Rather, X and Y will each have a life estate with a remainder in fee contingent upon survival. *Froelich Motor Co. v. Kohler Estate (1966) 240 C.A.2d 897.*

Riddle v. Harmon
102 C.A.3d 542 (1980)

[A wife terminated title to joint tenancy she held with her husband, the plaintiff. She severed the title by deeding from herself as a joint tenant to herself as a tenant in common. She then made a will disposing of her half-interest in the property. Shortly thereafter she died, and her husband sued the executor of the estate, the defendant, claiming such direct deeding from herself to herself failed to sever the tenancy. The trial court agreed that deeding through a strawman was needed, even in the year 1979. The executor appealed.]

POCHE, JUSTICE. The basic concept of joint tenancy is that it is one estate that is taken jointly. Under the common "Law," four unities were essential to the creation and existence of an estate in joint tenancy: interest, time, title, and possession. [The joint tenants must have acquired their interest at the same time, by the same instrument, which grants them an equal interest with an undivided right to possession of the entire property.] If one of the unities was destroyed, a tenancy in common remained.

Severance of the joint tenancy extinguishes the principal feature of that estate, the right of survivorship. This "right" is a mere expectancy that arises only upon success in the ultimate gamble—survival—and then only if the unity of the estate has not theretofore been destroyed by voluntary conveyance by partition proceedings, by involuntary alienation under an execution, or by any other action that operates to sever the joint tenancy.

An indisputable right of each joint tenant is the power to convey his or her separate estate by way of gift or otherwise without the knowledge or consent of the other joint tenant and to thereby terminate the joint tenancy. If a joint tenant conveys to a stranger [often called a "strawman"] and that person reconveys to the same tenant, then no revival of the joint tenancy occurs because the unities are destroyed. The former joint tenants become tenants in common.

At common law, one could not create a joint tenancy in himself and another by a direct conveyance. It was necessary for joint tenants to acquire their interests at the same time (unity of time) and by the same conveyancing instrument (unity of title). So, in order to create a valid

APPLY THE LAW
continued

joint tenancy where one of the proposed joint tenants already owned an interest in the property, it was first necessary to convey the property to a disinterested third person, a "strawman," who then conveyed the title to the ultimate grantees as joint tenants. This remains the prevailing practice in some jurisdictions. Other states, including California, have disregarded this application of the unities requirement as one of the obsolete subtle and arbitrary distinctions and niceties of the feudal common law, and allow the creation of a valid joint tenancy without the use of a strawman.

By amendment to its Civil Code, California became a pioneer in allowing the *creation* of a joint tenancy by direct transfer. A joint tenancy conveyance may be made from an owner to himself and others. Accordingly, in California, it is no longer necessary to use a strawman to *create* a joint tenancy.

The "two-to-transfer" notation stems from the English common law feoffment ceremony with livery of seisin. If the ceremony took place upon the land being conveyed, the grantor (feeoffor) would hand a symbol of the land, such as a lump of earth or a twig, to the grantee (feeoffee). In order to complete the investiture of seisin it was necessary that the feeoffor completely relinquish possession of the land to the feeoffee. [According to the court it was not until 1845 that a statute permitted the English to transfer fee ownership by deed. The physical act of passing dirt (seisin) grew out of the illiterate society where people could not conceptualize the fact that mere "rights" and just "things" could be transferred.] One could not be both grantor and grantee in a single transaction. Handing oneself a dirt clod is ungainly. Just as livery of seisin has become obsolete, so should ancient vestiges of that ceremony give way to modern conveyancing realities.

We discard the archaic rule that one cannot [transfer to] oneself. We reject the rationale because it rests on a common law notion whose reason for existence vanished about the time that grant deeds and title companies replaced colorful dirt clod ceremonies as the way to transfer title to real property. One joint tenant may unilaterally sever the joint tenancy without the use of an intermediary device. The judgment is reversed. [The joint tenancy was severed, so the wife's interest could pass by her will.]

TENANCY IN COMMON

Nature of Tenancy

Tenancy in common is merely ownership by two or more people without the right of survivorship. Each tenant owns an undivided interest in the right to possession of the premises, but no other unities or requirements must be met. Each party can freely will the interest on death, and there are no requirements as to how or when the property was acquired or held or as to what the proportionate shares of each individual are in the land.

Creation

Tenancy in common is created by express agreement between the parties, by a statement in the instrument that title shall be held as tenants in common, or by acquisition of any property by two or more individuals (who are not husband and wife) where the exact nature of the tenancy is not stated. Whenever an attempted joint tenancy fails between two people who are not married, they hold title as tenants in common.

Rights of Tenants

In California, each cotenant has certain common rights as to that tenancy. Indeed, basic rights to possession and contribution are the same, whether the tenant is a joint tenant or a tenant in common.

Right to Possession

Each tenant has an equal right to possession of the entire premises. One tenant may not claim exclusive occupancy of the entire property, nor may one tenant lease or otherwise convey an interest granting exclusive occupancy of the premises. The only interest one cotenant may grant—without, of course, the concurrence of all other cotenants—is a nonexclusive right to possession in common with the other cotenants.

Right to Contribution

A cotenant has a right to expect the other tenants to contribute their prorata share for any ordinary repairs or costs of maintaining the property. If payment is not made, the tenant is given an equitable lien against the other tenants' interest in the property, which can be foreclosed upon. *Calkins* v. *Steinbach (1884) 66 C.177.* However, a cotenant has no right of contribution for improvements to the property unless all other cotenants have agreed to the expenditures for those improvements. *Higgins* v. *Ova (1928) 204 C. 231.*

Right to Sell and Mortgage

Each tenant can sell, lease, mortgage, or otherwise encumber his or her interest in joint-tenancy property without the knowledge or approval of the other cotenants. *Thompson* v. *Thompson (1963) 218 C.A.2d 804.* Of course, the deed or other encumbrance only affects that one cotenant's interest. However, banks and other individuals rarely grant loans or purchase property without the consent and involvement of all owners.

Common Problems

The three most common problems faced by cotenants are probably the following:

1. *Unanimous consent to sell.* Because each tenant owns his or her own interest in the property, all joint owners must sign the deed to transfer title. Technically, less than all the owners could sell their interest and transfer title, but as a practical matter, what buyer would purchase less than the entire property? Thus, one co-owner can, and frequently does, stop a sale desired by all other tenants.
2. *Unanimous consent to mortgage.* Similarly, one tenant can generally stop a refinance or other loan on the property by refusing to sign. Lenders almost always require the signatures of all parties.
3. *Unanimous consent on major decisions.* Technically, a violation of the fiduciary duties to other cotenants can be resolved in court. However, such a procedure is expensive, takes an unreasonable amount of time, and often provides inadequate compensation and remedies to the other parties. Additionally, the courts do not always agree that a reluctant tenant has breached a fiduciary duty. The courts hold that cotenants need not always approve capital improvements and other management decisions desired by the other cotenants.

Solution: The Cotenancy Agreements

The solution to most of the problems faced by cotenants is a well-drafted **cotenancy** agreement. These documents generally have all cotenants agree not to sell, lease, partition, mortgage, or otherwise encumber their interest without the consent of the other cotenants. Often, these agreements provide that all cotenants will participate in a sale or refinance of the property on the approval of a specified percentage of co-owners. Such agreements often include provisions for failing to pay each co-owner's share of contributions, when and how improvements and repairs are to be made, the effect of bankruptcy of a co-owner, and the management of the property. Any such cotenancy agreement should specifically waive the right to partition the property.

Such agreements are valid between the parties, but they do not bind any bona fide purchasers or encumbrancers without notice. Therefore, either the agreement or a memorandum of that agreement should be recorded.

COMMUNITY PROPERTY

Origin of Community Property

California is one of only eight community property states in the nation. The concept of community property for all those states originated in Mexican law, although each state now has its separate version of community property principles.

Nature

The basic theory of community property is that husband and wife are like partners; therefore, any property acquired during their marriage by the labor or skill of one of them belongs to them both. It is immaterial if one spouse contributes no or nominal property to the marriage; because they are equal *partners,* the law assumes that the earning spouse is able to make those contributions only because of the responsibilities assumed by the other spouse.

Domestic Partnerships

There are two types of domestic partnerships in California. The first is when two adults of the same sex have chosen to live together, share each others lives, registered as domestic partners with the Secretary of State. There are a few other minor technicalities. The second type of domestic partners is seniors of the opposite sex (where at least one of them is age 62 or older and eligible for Social Security). They must make the same commitments and have filed with the Secretary of State. *Family. C. §297.*

The Family Law Code says domestic partners shall have "the same rights, protections, and benefits, and shall be subject to the same responsibilities, obligations, and duties" and traditional spouses that are married. *Family. C. 297.5.* For purposes of this book, it is not relevant whether or not domestic partnerships have exactly and completely all of the same rights as married partners. Rather, it is important to recognize that the community property law provisions as well as the rights on death are applicable to couples in both marriage and in domestic partnerships.

Management and Control

Before 1977, the husband had management and control over the community property. Since 1977, both spouses have generally had equal rights over the community property. *C.C. 5125, 5127.* The four most important exceptions to the equal management rule are the following:

1. All transfers or encumbrances on real property require both spouses' signatures.
2. Neither spouse alone can make a gift of community property.
3. If one spouse operates or manages a business (e.g., a real estate business or dry cleaner), the other spouse has no rights of management or control over that business. However, the nonmanaging spouse has the right to object to a sale or mortgage of substantially all the business's assets.
4. Neither spouse alone can transfer or encumber furniture or furnishings in the family home or the other spouse's clothes.

Separate Property

Any property owned before marriage or acquired by one spouse during marriage by gift or inheritance is considered separate property. *C.C. 5107, 5108.* The rationale is that in either case no community skill or effort was involved. Similarly, any income, rents, or profits acquired from that property without community effort and any property purchased with those funds remain separate property. Also, any earnings or accumulation of one party while living separate and apart from the other spouse is the separate property of that party. *C.C. 5118.*

Community Property

The law presumes that any property not held before marriage or acquired during marriage by gift or inheritance is community property. *C.C. 5110.* If there is a question as to the nature of property owned by married people, it is presumed to be community property. In addition, several categories of property are specifically held to be community in nature.

Acquisitions

Anything acquired or purchased with community property is community property. Thus, if one spouse buys stock during marriage from money derived from his earnings, the stock is community property.

Improvements to Separate Property

Whenever community property is used to improve separate property, part of that community property becomes mixed *(commingled)* with the separate property. This situation typically arises when a spouse uses community property skills or money in the operation or management of a business owned before marriage. When an allocation between separate and community property becomes necessary in the event of death or divorce, the courts generally use one of two formulas.

Community Property Residual

When the court finds that the increase in value of the business from the time of marriage to the time of allocation is due mainly to the personal services of one spouse, it allocates a fair rate of return (usually 7 percent) to the original investment and treats that amount as separate property. The remainder of the increase in value is considered to be community property. *Pereira v. Pereira (1909) 156 C. 1.*

Separate Property Residual

If the court finds that the personal services of a spouse played a minor role in the increase in value, then the value of the property or efficiency of the business was the major factor resulting in the increase in value. In such situations, the court allocates a reasonable value to the personal services as community property. The balance of the increase in value is separate property. *Van Camp v. Van Camp (1921) 53 C.A. 17.*

Credit

Credit is property. Anything purchased on credit, where the lender relied for collateral primarily on the earning power of either spouse or upon the community assets, is community property.

Commingling

If separate property is commingled (mixed) with community property to such an extent that it cannot be separated or traced to its source as separate property, it will all become community property. In effect, improvements to separate property involve commingling.

Division of Community Property

The parties may divide community property between themselves for a variety of purposes. Generally, however, a division occurs only on divorce or death.

Dissolution of Marriage

Because each spouse has an equal interest in the community property, on dissolution (divorce), the community property must be divided equally. However, the court may provide for an unequal division if it finds that one party deliberately squandered or misused community property for that one spouse's benefit. Finally, the court may award all the community property to one spouse if the net value of that community property is less than $5,000 and the other spouse cannot be found. *C.C. 4800.*

Death

Upon the death of a spouse, the deceased spouse's half of the community property passes by the provisions of the will or, if there is no will, then by the rules of intestacy (see Table 11.2). See Table 11.3 for an comparison of the types of ownership. There are also tax advantages on death when holding title as community property (see Table 11.4).

Secretive Transfers

If property standing in the name of one spouse alone is, in fact, community property, and if that property is transferred without the other spouse joining in the deed or executing a quitclaim deed, the transaction may be set aside. The entire transaction may be rescinded if action is taken while the conveying spouse is alive and within the period of the statute of limitations. If recovery is not sought until after the conveying spouse's death, then the other spouse can recover only one-half of the property. The rationale is that the conveying spouse's transfer is considered tantamount to a testamentary disposition of that spouse's one-half interest in the property.

Statute of Limitations

The statute of limitations for conveyances, encumbrances, and gifts of real property is five years. *C.C.P. 318.* When the community property is recorded and held in the name of one spouse alone, a special one-year statute of limitations applies. *C.C. 5127.* When fraud is involved, the period is the longer of the ordinary statute of limitations or three years from the date of the discovery of the fraud. *C.C.P. 338.4.*

Protection for Transferee

Whenever one spouse is conveying property standing in his or her name alone, because of the presumption that all property acquired during marriage is community property, a broker or third party should demand that the other spouse either sign the deed or execute a quitclaim deed to the conveying spouse.

TABLE 11.2 Comparison of joint ownership (Non-Tax).

	Joint Tenancy	Tenancy in Common	Community Property	Community Property with Right of Survivorship
Definition	Property held by two or more people, with right of survivorship (as though they collectively constitute one person).	Property held by two or more people, who each own an undivided interest, without the right of survivorship.	Property held in common by husband and wife as a kind of marital partnership.	Property held in common by husband and wife as a kind of marital partner-ship, but with right of survivorship.
Creation	Traditionally, by meeting the four unities of title, time, interest, and pos-session, plus an unequivo-cal intention to create a joint tenancy.	By expressly so stating; or any property acquired by unmarried persons that fails as joint tenancy or fails to state the nature of the tenancy.	By expressly so stating; or any property acquired by married people that fails as joint tenancy or that fails to state the nature of the tenancy.	By expressly so stating plus spouse must sign the deed verifying acceptance of this form of title.
Presumption	No. Never presumed.	Yes, if not husband and wife.	Yes, if married.	No. Never presumed.
Unities	Time (created at the same time) Title (created by same deed) Interest (equal) Possession (undivided).	Possession (undivided).	Not applicable.	Not applicable.
Ownership	Each tenant is fictionally deemed the owner of the whole; thus there is only one title to the property.	Each tenant owns a sepa-rate legal title to his interest.	Each spouse owns one-half interest, although there is only one title.	Each spouse owns one-half interest, although there is only one title.

(Continued)

TABLE 11.2 (*Continued*)

	Joint Tenancy	Tenancy in Common	Community Property	Community Property with Right of Survivorship
Conveyance	A transfer by one tenant severs the joint tenancy as to that tenant's interest, but does not affect the continuation of the joint tenancy of any two or more other joint tenants.	Each tenant's interest is a separate title that can be conveyed separately by its owner.	Title cannot be transferred separately; both spouses must join in the conveyance.	Title cannot be transferred separately; both spouses must join in the conveyance.
Purchaser	Will be a tenant in common with the other owner(s).	Will be a tenant in common with the other owner(s).	Not applicable, as one spouse cannot convey separately.	Not applicable, as one spouse cannot convey separately.
Death of one party	Estate passes unalterably to the other joint tenant(s) outside of probate and free from debts of that deceased joint tenant.	Estate passes through probate per decedent's will or by intestacy, if any is left after paying decedent's debts.	Estate passes as directed by will; otherwise, all to surviving spouse. Goes through probate, except spouse may elect to take outside of probate.	Estate passes automatically to surviving spouse. No probate, and not passing by provisions in will.

TABLE 11.3   Comparison of joint ownership (Tax).

	Joint Tenancy	Tenancy in Common	Community Property
Tax basis on death	Deceased's interest only acquires free stepped-up basis to fair market value on date of death or executor's alternate valuation date.	Deceased's interest only acquires free stepped-up basis to fair market value on date of death or executor's alternate valuation date.	Entire property receives free stepped-up basis to fair market value on date of death or executor's alternate valuation date.
	If there is a written agreement that the property was really community property, both halves will receive a stepped-up basis. *Rev. Rule 87-98.*		
Amount included in decedent's estate	Entire property, less percentage attributable to survivor's contribution. If community property and can so prove, both halves will receive stepped-up basis. *Rev. Rule. 87-98.*	Decedent's separate interest (percentage by deed). No contribution determination.	Only half the property is included. It is assumed that each contributed proportionately, so no tracing of amounts or percentages involved.

TABLE 11.4   Transfers upon death.

	Community Property	Separate Property
With a will (testate)	Deceased spouse's half passes to the heirs named in the will.	Entire property passes to the heirs named in the will.
Without a will (intestate)	Entire property passes to surviving spouse. (Survivor already owns one-half and now receives decedent's half.) None passes to children or other heirs.	Half passes to spouse, half to child. If more than one child, then one-third to spouse and two-thirds equally to children. If no children, then one-half to spouse and one-half to decedent's parents.

Andrade Development Co. v. Martin
138 C.A.3d 330 (1982)

APPLY THE LAW

[The buyer, Andrade, entered into a contract to purchase property owned by Arnold Martin and his wife, Ardismae. It was community property, and the deed so indicated. The contract of sale was contained in the escrow instructions, which only the husband executed. Even though the escrow instructions and contract of sale had a signature line for the wife, she refused

continued

to sign. The buyer, Andrade, sued, seeking specific performance as to the husband's one-half interest, or alternatively for damages. The wife cross-complained, seeking to cancel the entire contract because it lacked her signature.]

COLOGNE, JUSTICE. [The controlling statute is Civil Code 5127, which reads in part, that except for transfers to certain trusts and except for situations in which one spouse is incompetent.]

Either spouse has the management and control of the community real property but both spouses either personally or by duly authorized agent must join in executing any instrument by which community real property or any interest therein is leased for a longer period than one year, or is sold, conveyed, or encumbered, provided however that the sole lease, contract, mortgage, or deed of either spouse, holding the record title to community real property to a lessee, purchaser, or encumbrancer, in good faith without knowledge of the marriage relation, shall be presumed to be valid. No action to avoid any instrument mentioned in this section, affecting any property standing of record in the name of either spouse alone, executed by the spouse alone, shall be commenced after expiration of one year from the filing of record of such instrument in the recorder's office.

The history of this provision reveals the evolution of women's more equal status under California Community Property Law. The section as it now reads gives either spouse the management and control of the community real property but requires both to join in executing any instrument by which the community real property is sold.

The issue before us is: what is the effect of a husband's execution of escrow instructions that purport to sell the community property of husband and wife where the wife does not sign the document?

We believe the nonconsenting spouse should be fully protected in such efforts to dispose of community real property. We hold the contract is subject to a timely action during the marriage to avoid it, a corollary of which is no specific performance or damages are recoverable as to any part of the effort to dispose of the community real property. Any effort to dispose of this property will adversely affect the spouse's interests. Disposal of community property or partition of the spouse's interests should be allowed only where the spouse consents or where a court sitting in equity can provide an equitable result as in dissolution or probate proceedings.

It is true that there is also no express provision in our statutes to cover the situation where the wife sues after the husband's death. The decisions holding that recovery in such case is limited to one-half the property must rest, ultimately, upon the theory that the husband had the right, at his death, to give away one-half by will, and that his gift

APPLY THE LAW

continued

could be viewed as the equivalent of a provision by will. But this theory cannot justify a similar result where the wife brings her action during the marriage. The husband has no right, prior to death, to give away any of the community property without the wife's consent; and the gift cannot be regarded as the equivalent of a will because the time for effective exercise of the power of testamentary disposition has not yet arrived.

Damages for breach of contract might be appropriate under general contract principles if the title were in the husband's name alone and he led the buyer to believe he was able to convey good title. Under the stipulated facts, that is not the case here as there was clear indication in the contract that the wife was a necessary party, and no representation was made that the husband spoke for her or would deliver her consent.

It is appropriate to note what we are not dealing with. First, we are not dealing with the case where the property has not been found to be community property. Many cases deal with property held by husband and wife but that is not identified as community property; for example, a sale of real property held by husband and wife in joint tenancy. The court applied general contract principles about binding nonsigning parties without reference to section 5127 or the status of the property as community property. Here, the property was held as community property and section 5127 must be applied.

Second, we are not dealing with the sale to a purchaser who acquires the interest in good faith without knowledge of the marriage relationship. Here, Andrade signed escrow instructions that identified the Martins as husband and wife, so he knew of their relationship.

Third, we are not dealing with transfers of community property interest followed by the death of the transferor spouse where a court of equity construes the contract to be an effort to effect testamentary disposition of the husband's interest in community property.

Fourth, we are not dealing with the seller's bad faith in attempting to avoid an obligation that might suggest equitable remedies.

Fifth, we are not dealing with transfers that are part of divorce proceedings and with respect to which a court, sitting in equity, can order a division of community property under its jurisdiction.

The judgment is affirmed [and Andrade cannot force specific performance against all or half of the community real property, nor are they entitled to any damages].

COMMUNITY PROPERTY WITH RIGHT OF SURVIVORSHIP

Beginning in July 2001, California created a new form of property ownership between spouses called community property with right of survivorship. This ownership provides the benefits of both community property and joint tenancy. It provides that community property shall pass on death directly to the surviving spouse through right of survivorship. The property will not be probated; it will pass automatically. However, like joint tenancy, the survivor will still need to record proof of death and notification of the transfer. The entire property will receive the very important tax benefits of community property. (Both halves of the community property will receive a free step-up tax basis.)

To create this new form of ownership, the spouses must sign a deed that includes the words "community property with right of survivorship." Unlike all other deeds, the grantee(s) must sign the deed verifying acceptance of this form of title. *C.C. 682.1(a).*

OTHER FORMS OF JOINT OWNERSHIP

Many Forms

Numerous forms of joint ownership are available besides joint tenancy, tenancy in common, and community property. Only the more common alternatives are covered in this section. For example, trusts and planned unit developments are not discussed.

General Partnerships

A **partnership** is a continuing business enterprise operated by two or more people as co-owners for a profit. *Corp. C. 15006.* The profit requirement limits partnerships to business and investment undertakings. Although it is not required, it is always advantageous to reduce a partnership agreement to writing. If there is no writing, then the California version of the Uniform Partnership Act governs the rights and duties of the partners. Absent an agreement to the contrary, all partners are equally liable for partnership debts, have an equal interest in the partnership property, and hold equal rights in management decisions. Thus, a 90 percent partner would have the same vote as a 10 percent partner because voting is by number of partners without an agreement and not in proportion to ownership interests.

Limited Partnership

Limited partnership consists of one or more general partners, who have unlimited partnership liability and exclusive rights of management and one or more limited partners. A limited partner has no voice in the basic management, but also has no personal liability greater than his investment. *Corp.C. 15501 et seq.* The limited partner's interest is so similar in effect and power to the ownership of stock in a corporation that a permit must be obtained from the corporation commissioner or an exemption must exist under the Corporate Securities Law. By law, a limited partnership exists only after a partnership agreement or certification of that agreement is recorded.

Joint Venture

A **joint venture** is similar to a partnership, except that it is created for a single business transaction or series of individual transactions. A partnership contemplates operation of a continuing business enterprise for an unlimited or fixed period, broader in operation and duration than that of a joint venture. Nevertheless, the two entities are similar enough that joint ventures are governed by the general rules of partnerships. *Zeibak v. Nasser (1938) 12 C.2d 1.*

Corporations

Corporations are a separate legal entity for all purposes. Owners merely hold shares of stock in their corporation, but the corporation owns all property and controls daily management functions. Corporations begin with filing of articles of incorporation with the secretary of state and thereafter enjoy a perpetual existence, undisturbed by the death of any of the shareholders.

Subchapter-S Corporation

A **subchapter-S corporation** functions exactly the same as a normal corporation, except that for federal income tax purposes the owners elect to be taxed as if they were a partnership. Certain size limitations and other restrictions are set on some of the corporation's operations.

Limited Liability

One of the advantages of a corporation is its *limited* liability. If the corporation does something wrong, only the corporation, and not the officers, directors, or shareholders, has any liability. However, this protection is commonly misunderstood, especially in small corporations. A true corporation will protect against contract obligations but rarely against tort actions. If a person who is a member of the corporation does something wrong, he personally may be sued as well as the corporation. Thus, it is difficult to imagine a situation in which a one-person corporation would provide any additional protection to the shareholder–officer. Because of the tax ramifications and the possible limitations on the corporation's limited liability, an attorney should be consulted before a corporation is formed. The court summarized those situations in which others besides the corporation may have a liability.

> Directors and officers of a corporation are not rendered personally liable for its torts merely because of their official position, but may become liable if they directly ordered, authorized or participated in the tortious conduct. Personal liability, if otherwise justified, may rest upon a "conspiracy" among the officers and directors to injure third parties through the corporation. Shareholders of a corporation are not normally liable for its torts, but personal liability may attach to them through application of the "alter ego" doctrine, or when the shareholder specifically directed or authorized the wrongful acts. Wyatt v. Union Mortgage Co. (1979) 24 C.3d 773, 785.

Limited Liability Company

Limited liability companies allow entities to enjoy limited liability like a corporation, while retaining the preferential tax treatment of a partnership. In order to prevent businesses from filing in the other 46 states that already permit limited liability companies, California passed its own version of the statutes in October 1994. *Corp. C. 17000 et seq.* It may be that these entities will become one of the most popular methods of jointly owning property.

Creation and Operation

A limited liability company is created by filing *Articles of Organization* with the secretary of state. Most entities define their business relationship and procedures with an *Operating Agreement*. This agreement follows no set form and usually defines such matters as management procedures, buy–sell provisions, indemnification programs, voting rights, and benefits of members. The entity must be exempt or otherwise qualify under the corporate securities laws.

Taxation

The main purpose of limited liability companies over corporations is the benefit of being taxed like a partnership. However, California's laws are so flexible that the entities can fail to qualify for this tax benefit if the founders are not careful. All limited liability companies should be formed with the advice and assistance of a qualified attorney and tax advisor. Interests in a limited liability company are personal property somewhat similar to shares of stock. As such, individuals cannot transfer their interest and qualify for a tax-free exchange under *I.R.C. § 1031.*

Syndications

Real estate **syndications** consist of numerous individuals who pool their financial resources to acquire real estate. The syndicate itself is not a legal entity, and the underlying form of ownership is usually a limited partnership or a limited liability company, although it may be a general partnership, a corporation, or a trust. The Real Estate Syndication Act, *B.&P.C. 10250 et seq.,* was repealed in 1977; the corporation commissioner now regulates the formation and sale of syndicates in California.

Real Estate Investment Trusts

The Internal Revenue Code in 1960 specifically authorized the formation of a **real estate investment trust (REIT)** to hold property. *I.R.C. 856–858.* The specific code requirements are detailed, but some of the major provisions require the trust to have more than 100 beneficial investors and to receive 95 percent or more of its gross income from investments; 75 percent or more of such net income must be from real estate investments. REITs are more popular under the new tax laws because their income is portfolio income and not subject to passive activity restrictions.

Condominiums

Condominiums involve separate ownership of individual units (interests in space) with ownership as tenants in common of common areas. *C.C. 783* and *C.C. 1350 et seq.* The occupant owns a unit, secures the financing, and receives an individual tax bill. Condominium plans and covenants, conditions, and restrictions (**C.C.&R.s**) must exist and be recorded. Any condominium project having two or more units qualifies as a subdivision and is regulated as such. *B.&P.C. 11004.*

Cooperatives

All units in a cooperative project are owned by a separate entity, usually a corporation. *B.&P.C. 11003.2.* The residents normally occupy their premises under a lease, with concurrent stock ownership in the corporation. Before 1977, a single, blanket deed of trust existed against the entire project, and taxes were assessed against the project as a whole. Consequently, if a tenant failed to pay the taxes of mortgage indebtedness, others must cover that obligation or risk being in default. Since 1977, lenders have been permitted to make loans to individual owners, using the individual's stock or membership certificate as collateral. *Fin.C. 1236, 7153.4.* Consequently, cooperatives formed after 1977 are approximately equivalent in marketing and financing to condominiums.

Common Interest Developments

Common interest developments are condominiums, cooperatives, and other specially defined projects that contain separately owned units or areas plus shared common areas. *C.C. 1351.* Although the types of separately owned units may vary, each project has enough similarities for many laws to apply equally to all such units. All common interest developments are managed by an incorporated or unincorporated association. Condominium associations are called *homeowner's associations.*

Great care must be taken in evaluating and investigating the soundness, operation, and makeup of the association and the development. All attorneys hear horror stories about associations where the officers run the association so rigidly that life becomes unpleasant for some members. One legal commentator called these officers "little Hitlers." Financially, even though bylaws or other documents state that the association may not raise its dues, statutes provide that an association must pay its existing obligations. Therefore, it can raise regular assessments up to 20 percent over last year's amount and can impose special assessments up to 5 percent of the fiscal year's expenses without a vote. The amounts can be increased even if a simple majority of a quorum favors the increase. *C.C. 1366.* Because a quorum is at least 50 percent of the owners, it is mathematically possible for 26 percent of the owners to approve these increases.

Before a common interest development or an owner can sue to enforce the bylaws or other governing documents, the parties must first try to resolve their disagreement through alternate dispute resolution, *C.C. 1354,* which was discussed in Chapter 2.

Unless both sides agree, the ADR attempt is nonbinding and of no force or effect. The dispute will still have to be settled through the courts. Still, it is a procedural step that must be satisfied before litigation.

STUDY QUESTIONS (TRUE–FALSE)

1. Joint tenants can only will their share of the property, and any will that they execute can have no effect whatsoever on any other joint tenant's interest.

2. Either one of two joint tenants can break a joint tenancy, even if the other tenant objects to the dissolution of that joint tenancy.

3. If A, B, C, and D own property in joint tenancy, and A transfers her interest to R, then B, C, D, and R own title in joint tenancy.

4. If two brothers take title as *A and B jointly*, they hold title in joint tenancy.

5. Whenever two or more individuals, not husband and wife, take title jointly, title is presumed to be held as tenants in common.

6. A joint venture is approximately equivalent to a general partnership for a limited and single purpose or project.

7. If a husband transfers property standing in his name alone and the property is, in fact, community property, the wife may share in the proceeds but may not set aside the sale.

8. A wife dies intestate, leaving only a community property estate, a husband, and three children. The husband receives one-third of the property, and the children inherit the rest.

9. If a wife during a marriage inherits $40,000 from her mother-in-law, it is community property.

10. If the husband purchases with his earnings an insurance policy on his life, naming his mother as beneficiary, the policy is nevertheless community property.

CHAPTER SUPPLEMENT REAL ESTATE SYNDICATIONS

Nature of Syndications

Syndication is a sophisticated investment vehicle for two or more people to buy property. It is also a frequently misunderstood concept. Syndication is not an *entity* like a limited partnership, limited liability company, or corporation, although it commonly utilizes one of those vehicles to hold title. Rather, syndication is a *process* of acquiring, holding, and then selling property or other assets.

Usually, the syndicator finds suitable property, and convinces other to pool their investment and buy that property. Typically the syndicator is a broker (or uses the services of a broker) to acquire and manage the property for the investors. Ultimately and generally years later, the property is sold and the proceeds divided according to the limited partnership or limited liability company documents. The syndicator takes fees and/or a percentage of proceeds for these services.

By pooling their investment, members are able to buy bigger properties that theoretically have larger and more stable returns. Additionally, a knowledgeable syndicator conceivably better able to professionally mange that property while also relieving investors of that burden. Even after paying the syndicator's fees, the investors should hypothetically receive larger returns than if they purchased property themselves and attempted to manage it.

Normally, if several individuals were to purchase property, they would probably do so as tenants in common. Each would help manage the property and own a percentage share according to their investment. One of the distinguishing features of syndication is centralized management by the syndicator, although the investors may retain certain limited voting rights on major decisions.

Regulations for Syndicators

License Requirements

To sell shares in a security (which is what syndications are), the person must be a broker-dealer licensed under the California Department of Corporations. Real estate brokers forming real estate syndications of not more than 100 people are exempt from licenses under the corporate securities law, and instead are governed by the California Department of Real Estate. *Corp. C. 25206.*

Education and Financial Qualifications

Additionally, for larger syndications the syndicator is covered under the rules of the Department of Corporation, which requires the syndicator (called a "sponsor" in the regulations) to meet certain educational and financial qualifications. Syndicators must have at least two years of real estate experience in the type of property involved (four years in some cases). Further, the syndicator's net worth must be the greater of $100,000 or 5% of the total amount of securities sold in the last year plus 5% of the amount of this offering. *10 Cal. Code Reg. 260.140.111.1, .2.*

Regulated by the Department of Corporations

Because the major decisions are made by someone other than the investor, the syndication is considered a security. As such, in many ways it is much like stock in a corporation, and the Department of Corporations treats the interests similarly. The U.S. Supreme Court defines a security as a "scheme [that] involves an investment of money in a common enterprise with profits to come solely from the efforts of others." *S.E.C. v. W. J. Howey Co.* (1946) 328 U.S. 293, 301. California's definition of a security is even broader and does not necessarily require an expectation of profits. Syndication clearly counts as securities and is covered under the law. Investors expect profits because of the efforts of others, and not just from the property.

Recession for Unregistered Securities

As a security, investors have very important protections. If the security should have been registered and was not eligible for an exemption from qualification, the investor has a right of rescission. A rescission is a process where the investor returns his or her interest in the syndication, and the syndicator is forced to return the investor's money, plus interest at 10%, less any income received as distributions. *Corp. C. 25503.* The statute of limitations is short: the earlier of two years from the date of purchase or one year after discovering the securities violation. *Corp. C. 25507.* Because most syndicators in their written materials state the securities are not registered, the practical effect is a one-year statute of limitations.

A rescission is designed to unwind the transaction and theoretically return each party to the position they were in prior to the transaction. In effect, if the syndication is not registered or exempt from registration, the syndicator becomes a guarantor of the syndication's success during the period within the statute of limitations.

If the syndication is profitable and successful, everybody is happy and there is no problem. However, if poor economic times, bad investment decisions, or mismanagement results in losses or less than expected returns, investors are unhappy. This dissatisfaction can turn to litigation, and rather than the investor bearing the risk of loss, the syndicator pays the price for failing to follow the securities law. With so much at stake, it is easy to understand why securities law is so important to syndications. After the statute of limitations for rescission has run, the investor is limited to ordinary civil liability for negligence or other appropriate common law remedies.

California Regulation

The Corporate Commissioner is charged with preventing any sale of securities that are: (1) not "fair, just, and equitable," (2) where the issuer "intends to transact its business fairly and honestly," and (3) that securities and the method of issue will not "work a fraud upon the purchaser." *Corp. C. 25140(b)*. To make this determination, the syndicator must file a lengthy and sometimes expensive registration form with the Department of Corporations. Smaller offerings can avoid this expensive process by carefully adhering to the requirements for an exemption from qualification.

For smaller syndications, the Commissioner usually requires a legend condition on these securities restricting its transferability. Thus, if an investor wanted to sell his or her interest in the syndication, there would be certain limitations on how that interest could be marketed, in addition to any limitations the syndicator might have placed during the initial purchase documents.

Public and Private Syndication

Syndications are usually classified as public or private offerings. A public syndication means the syndication can offer interests to the public at large, and often does so through advertising.

Conversely, private syndications are done through special exemptions allowing only a certain, limited number of qualified individuals to receive offers to participate in the investment. Statistically, most real estate syndications are private offerings, and as such they are sold under one of the securities exemptions. As such, they avoid the expense and time of qualifying the syndication. They also avoid the strict limitations on syndicator's compensation. *10 Cal. Code reg. 260.140.110.1 et seq.*

Typical Syndication Process

While the process below is typical of many syndications, there is no requirement that formation follow in the exact order listed below. It is not uncommon for some of these steps to be interchanged or placed in a different order. However, the author finds the process below in the order presented is the most common process he has encountered.

Tie Up the Property

Assuming the syndicator has found a desirable property at a reasonable price, the syndicator must then obtain a binding right to buy that property if and when investors can be found. Sometimes the property is secured with an option to buy, but most often the property is bound by a deposit receipt. This contract to purchase the property is subject to the right to transfer that contract to an entity to be formed (such as a limited partnership or limited liability company). Further, the contract usually includes a condition subsequent making the purchase subject to obtaining financing and obtaining investors. Generally the syndicator also opens escrow in his or her name.

Prepare a Private Placement Memorandum

The syndicator (often with the help of an attorney) prepares a *private placement memorandum*. This lengthy document details the property, estimates the future growth and disbursements, discusses how much the syndicator will be paid, estimates the potential risks of the investment, and provides other informative information about the potential investment. Many people mistakenly believe the purpose of the private placement memorandum is for the investors; its true purpose is to protect the syndicator. By laying out as many risks as possible and discussing various profit scenarios, the syndicator is informing the investors of probable outcomes. This makes it harder for investors to sue the syndicator if the investment turns sour. The syndicator can point to the private placement memorandum and claim the investor was informed of the risks when he or she invested and therefore should not now be allowed to complain.

Obtain Securities Exemption or Qualification

Usually the syndicator believes he or she has people that can be approached to purchase the syndication while still meeting the California securities exemption. If not, an attorney advises the syndicator on the qualification procedure with the Department of Corporations.

Most private syndications rely on the "non-public offering" exemption. For the exemption there must: (1) be less than 35 investors, with spouses counted as only one investor (2) all of whom have a pre-existing business or person relationship with the syndicator or its related people, (3) are purchasing the interest for their own investment and not for resale, and (4) the offer has not included any public advertising. *Corp. C. 25012(f)*. Some syndicators routinely file the exemption notice with the Corporate Commissioner, others feel that because the failure to file does not affect the availability of the exemption there is no need to file. *Corp. C. 25012(f)*. The syndicator will be sure to approach only those people who qualify as investors, and who cumulatively do not exceed 35 people. Most of these non-public securities are offered only to California residents so as to come within an exemption of the U.S. securities law (or are modeled after other available exemptions from full qualification).

Find Investors and Execute Subscription Agreements

In finding suitable investors, syndicators has these potential investors fill out a *subscription agreement*. The subscription agreement asks investors questions to verify that they meet the securities exemption or qualification requirements. The document also forms a binding contract obligating the investor to purchase an interest in the syndication.

Form the LLC or LP

Now the attorney forms the limited partnership ("LP") or the limited liability company ("LLC"). There are tax and management decisions why one entity may be preferred over the other form. Sometimes this entity is prepared and formed all at one time when the private placement memorandum is drafted, the securities exemption is determined, and the subscription agreements written. If so, the entity is initially formed as an empty shell with the syndicator as the sole investor.

Obtain Financing and Assign Deposit Receipt

Secure whatever loans will be required, and receive the money from the investors for interests in the LLC or LP. Satisfy all the conditions of the deposit receipt, including the due diligence review and perform other necessary investigations. The deposit receipt or agreement to purchase the property is assigned to the new entity. Although technically, the entity could be a corporation or general partnership, for tax reasons and matters of management, the vehicle is almost always a limited liability company or limited partnership.

Finally, Close Escrow

The LLC or LP now closes escrow and owns the property.

Management by Syndicator

Usually, the syndicator manages the property for the fees specified in the private placement memorandum and LLC or LP agreement. Syndicators of private placements are not bound by the fee limitations required in California regulations for public syndications. *10 Cal. Code reg. 260.140.110.1 et seq.* Therefore, anyone investing in a private syndication needs to pay particular attention to the total fees and types of costs charged by syndicators.

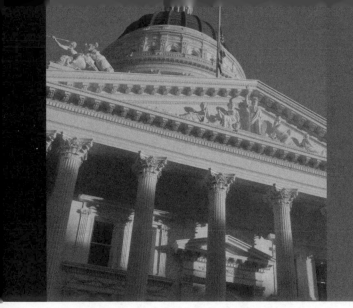

DUTY OWED TO PEOPLE ON THE OWNER'S PROPERTY

General Liability

Whenever someone enters someone else's land, the landowner owes that individual some form of duty. In the case of a trespasser, it may be merely the duty to refrain from intentionally injuring that person. For example, landowners are liable for injuries to trespassers caused by intentionally shooting at them with the intent of only scaring those trespassers away. At the other extreme, if the landowner invites a business person into his home, he owes that individual a duty of protection. Before 1968, the duty was fixed by arbitrary classifications of status, which were removed after the 1968 California Supreme Court ruling in *Rowland v. Christian 69 C.2d 108.* However, even though the categories of individuals on the land have been abolished, the old classifications are important, as they provide some guidelines as to the quality of care owed an individual.

Law Before 1968

Before 1968 an individual who entered someone else's land was classified as a **trespasser**, a **licensee**, or an **invitee**, and the duties owed to each were entirely different.

Trespasser

A trespasser is one who enters upon another's land without the owner's consent. The owner always owes a duty to abstain from any

Landowner's Liability for Injuries

intentional or wanton injuries to that trespasser. Furthermore, if the owner knows or should know about that trespasser, he or she is further obligated to warn the trespasser about any dangerous artificial conditions on the premises. If trespassers frequent a limited area of the owner's property such as a path across railroad tracks, the owner assumes a further duty to discover the trespassers and avoid injuring them. Finally, if the trespassers are likely to be children, and the cost of protecting the children is small in comparison with the foreseeability of risk to the children, then, under the attractive nuisance doctrine, the owner has a special duty to keep the premises safe for those children–trespassers.

Ancient English law and even the law of the Old West allowed landowners to shoot first and ask questions later. The rise of the middle class and the urbanization of America caused society to reverse its priorities and to elevate human rights over property rights. A typical example was discussed in Chapter 1, where First Amendment rights (free speech on privately owned shopping center property) took priority over the rights of private property. The laws concerning trespassers follow in the same parameters. Many people are still amazed when the newspapers carry stories about a trespasser intent on burglary who is wounded by a spring gun or other weapon. The trespasser sues and recovers thousands of dollars for injuries from the landowner.

Licensee

A licensee is someone who enters land with consent for a nonbusiness purpose. A social guest is authorized entry, and the guest's purpose is social, having no connection with a mutual business endeavor. Also, by case law, government employees (such as police, firefighters, and building inspectors) are also held to be licensees. The duty approximates that toward a known trespasser, in that the owner need only avoid willful or wanton injury and, in some cases, warn of any definitely known hazard. There is no obligation to make the premises safe or to discover and correct any defects, under the theory that such guests should not expect the owner to improve the property above its normal condition enjoyed by that owner.

Invitee

When expressly or impliedly invited to enter another's land for mutual business, a person qualifies as an invitee. The owner owes the invitee an affirmative duty to make the premises safe and to discover and correct any unsafe conditions on the property. Typical invitees include customers entering a business establishment and employees or servants of property owners.

Problems with Old Law

California was one of the first states to abolish the classifications of trespasser, licensee, and invitee. Juries need no longer struggle over the often difficult task of classification of status.

Example

Under the old law, a person entering a bar to use the toilet was a licensee, *Kneiser v. Balasco-Blackwood Co. (1913) 22 C.A. 205*, whereas a person entering a gas station solely to use a pay telephone was an invitee. *Lehman v. Richfield Oil Corp. (1913) 121 C.A.2d 261*. A person who entered a bar to use the toilet but was induced to buy a drink first and then injured was a licensee. *Kneiser v. Balasco-Blackwood Co. (1913) 22 C.A. 205*. However, if the person first used the toilet and then bought a drink, he or she was an invitee. *Braun v. Vallade (1917) 33 C.A. 279*.

New Rule

In 1966, the law was changed. Juries need now only analyze the facts under the general tort rules of foreseeability. A landowner is now required to use ordinary care to prevent injury to anyone who comes on the land. However, although the owner owes a reasonable duty to everyone, that duty varies depending on the nature of the individual's purpose for entering the land, the probability of that person's being injured, and the foreseeability of that person's being expected to visit the land.

Exceptions for Recreational Licenses

To encourage landowners to open their property to the public for recreational activities, a special statute reduces a landowner's liability for injury to these people. Individuals entering with permission for hunting, fishing, hiking, sightseeing, or other recreational activities must accept the property in as-is condition, with the landowner owing them only the slightest duty of care. *C.C. 846.*

End Result

The new rules under *Rowland v. Christian* greatly enlarge the duties now owed to licensees and trespassers, providing far greater protection for both. The net effect of the new process generally equals the result reached under the old classification theory for invitees or represents a moderately higher duty of care. The new rule has only a slight effect on invitees because the old rule already afforded them a high degree of protection.

Freed from the difficult categorization requirements, juries are now permitted a more flexible approach to a landowner's liability. However, as one court stated:

> The term invitee has not been abandoned, nor have trespasser and licensee. In the minds of the jury, whether a possessor of the premises has acted as a reasonable man toward the plaintiff, in view of the probability of injury to him, will tend to involve the circumstances under which he came upon the defendant's land; as well as whether the condition itself presented an unreasonable risk of harm, in view of the foreseeable use of the property. In turn that reinvolves the degree to which those on the property could be expected to be there, and the use they could be expected to make of the premises. In this, there is a wide difference between a trespasser, who actually may be forbidden the use of the property, and an invitee, invited or urged to be there. *Beauchamp v. Los Gatos Golf Course (1969) 273 C.A.2d 20, 25.*

DUTY OWED TO PEOPLE OFF THE OWNER'S PROPERTY

General Rule

Generally, the landowner has no duty to or liability for injuries to people outside the land. Therefore, absent a specific ordinance, statute, or exception to the general rule, a landowner has no liability for the condition of the sidewalks or streets in front of his or her property.

Exceptions for Adjoining Property

However, if the owner exercises *control* over **adjoining** property, the landowner may become liable for injuries arising on that land. To be liable, the owner must have control over the land and the risk of injury must be foreseeable. Both of these questions are issues for the jury and depend on the facts of each case. Thus, in one case, an owner was liable for people attacked on a vacant lot next to that owner's store. The owner encouraged patrons to park on the vacant land and exercised other types of control. *Southland Corp. v. Superior Court (1988) 203 C.A.3d 656.*

Exceptions for Sidewalks

Sidewalks are a common problem for landowners. An owner is liable for the repair and maintenance of the sidewalks in front of the property. If the owner fails to make the repairs, the city or county can do so and charge the owner for the cost. *Sty.Hy.C. 5610.* However, this statutory duty extends only to the *cost of repair* and excludes liability for injuries to third persons. *Jones v. Deeter (1984) 152 C.A.3d 798.*

Generally, an owner only becomes liable for injuries on adjoining sidewalks if that owner *modified* the sidewalk for private use or created a *dangerous* condition. Typical examples of modifying property for private use would include building a wooden driveway with loose planks or constructing a streetlight with a defective bulb. Examples of the creation of a dangerous condition include temporary situations such as seeping oil, debris, and even slippery pieces of meat left on the sidewalk.

APPLY THE LAW

Rowland v. Christian
69 C.2d 108 (1968)

Peters, Justice. Plaintiff appeals from a summary judgment for defendant Nancy Christian in this personal injury action. In his complaint plaintiff alleged that about November 1, 1963, Miss Christian told the lessors of her apartment that the knob of the cold water faucet on the bathroom basin was cracked and should be replaced; that on November 20, 1963, plaintiff entered the apartment at the invitation of Miss Christian; that he was injured while using the bathroom fixtures, suffering severed tendons and nerves of his right hand; and that he incurred medical and hospital expenses. He further alleged that the bathroom fixtures were dangerous, that Miss Christian was aware of the dangerous condition, and that his injuries were proximately caused by the negligence of Miss Christian.

APPLY THE LAW

continued

One of the areas where this court and other courts have departed from the fundamental concept that a man is liable for injuries caused by his carelessness is with regard to the liability of a possessor of land for injuries to persons who have entered upon that land. It has been suggested that the special rules regarding liability of the possessor of land are due to historical considerations stemming from the high place that land has traditionally held in English and American thought, the dominance and prestige of the landowning class in England during the formative period of the rules governing the possessor's liability, and the heritage of feudalism.

The departure from the fundamental rule of liability for negligence has been accomplished by classifying the plaintiff either as a trespasser, licensee, or invitee and then adopting special rules as to the duty owed by the possessor to each of the classifications. Generally speaking a trespasser is a person who enters or remains upon land of another without a privilege to do so; a licensee is a person like a social guest who is not an invitee and who is privileged to enter or remain upon land by virtue of the possessor's consent; and an invitee is a business visitor who is invited or permitted to enter or remain on the land for a purpose directly or indirectly connected with business dealings between them.

Although the invitor owes the invitee a duty to exercise ordinary care to avoid injuring him, the general rule is that a trespasser and licensee or social guest are obligated to take the premises as they find them. The possessor of the land owes them only the duty of refraining from wanton or willful injury. The ordinary justification for the general rule is based on the theory that the guest should not expect special precautions to be made on his account, and that if the host does not inspect and maintain his property the guest should not expect this to be done on his account.

Whatever may have been the historical justification for the common distinctions, it is clear that those distinctions are not justified in the light of our modern society and the complexity and confusion that have arisen. A man's life or limb does not become less worthy of protection by the law nor a loss less worthy of compensation under the law because he has come upon the land of another without permission or with permission but without a business purpose. Reasonable people do not ordinarily vary their conduct depending upon such matters. To focus upon the status of the injured party as a trespasser, licensee, or invitee in order to determine the question of whether the landowner has a duty of care is contrary to our modern social mores and humanitarian values. The common law rules obscure rather than illuminate the proper considerations that should govern determination of the question of duty.

continued

We decline to follow and perpetuate such rigid classification. The proper test to be applied to the liability of the possessor of land is whether in the management of his property he has acted as a reasonable man in view of the possibility of injury to others. Although the plaintiff's status as a trespasser, licensee, or invitee may in the light of the facts given have some bearing on the question of liability, the status is not determinative.

We assume the defendant Miss Christian was aware that the faucet handle was defective and dangerous, that the defect was not obvious, and that plaintiff was about to come in contact with the defective condition. Under the undisputed facts she neither remedied the condition nor warned the plaintiff about it. The judgment is reversed [and the plaintiff is entitled to recovery for his injuries].

LIABILITY OF LANDLORD FOR INJURIES

General Background

When a person leases his property to another, the **landlord** has transferred the exclusive right to possession to the tenant. However, unlike the old common law, the landlord can still be held liable for certain injuries. This section deals with the liability of the landlord (as opposed to the liability for the owner of property) when other people are injured.

Common Law Rule

At common law, the landlord generally transferred a nonfreehold estate in land and the tenant assumed all liability for the condition of the premises and any injury to the tenants. The courts slowly eroded this absolute protection, and began allowing exceptions. The most common were if a landlord contractually or voluntarily repaired the premises, operated the common areas, maintained an existing nuisance or safety violation, or had notice of certain types of undisclosed but hazardous conditions.

The Modern Law Looks to Foreseeability

The 1968 *Rowland v. Christian* case abolished the old trespasser–licensee–invitee classification and instead adopted the general tort liability of foreseeability of injury to others. The courts have (somewhat inconsistently) expanded the doctrine to landlords. They seem subject to the same type of balancing of the equities as tenants. The courts seem to weigh the foreseeability of the injury to the cost of repairs that would have avoided the dangerous condition and to the amount of control the landlord has over the dangerous condition.

Semi-Public Leases

Special obligations and liability can apply for landlords who lease their property for semi-public use. The typical example is a landlord leasing a movie theater or auditorium that he knows will be used by the public.

Four Major Areas of Exposure

A landlord's liability most often involves four major areas of exposure, although these four sections are not the only areas of landlord liability.

Landlord Contractually or Voluntarily Repairs

The landlord becomes liable if he contractually agrees in the lease to repair the premises and keep them habitable, or voluntarily repairs the premises. If the landlord agrees in the lease to assume responsibility for repairs of dangerous conditions, he becomes liable for negligently failing to make those repairs. Even when there is no obligation on the landlord for making those repairs, if the landlord makes the repairs negligently, he can be held liable for ordinary negligence.

Common Area

Landlords retain control over common areas and are responsible for their condition. Typical common areas include elevators and hallways.

Existing Nuisance or Public Safety Violation

The landlord is also liable if there was an existing nuisance on the property or if there is a violation of public safety laws.

Landlord Has Knowledge of Dangerous Condition

The landlord may have some exposure from defects in the condition of the premises, and in some cases, from the acts of others. Cases holding a landlord liable for the condition of the property arise where the landlord actually knows of a dangerous condition but does not make it known to the tenant. For the tenant, the condition must not be apparent or the tenant is given constructive notice of its condition. The second category, injury caused by third parties, relies heavily on the foreseeability of the harm to a tenant balanced against the burden and cost to the landlord.

1. *Caused by another tenant.* The California Supreme Court ruled that if a landlord knew of another tenant's dangerous temperament or the keeping of a vicious dog, the landlord must take reasonable steps to protect other tenants or evict the troubling tenant. In one case, a residential landlord had six notices that a particular tenant was dangerous and failed to act. When that tenant injured another resident of the apartment, the landlord was held liable. *Madhani v. Cooper (2003) 106 C.A.4th 412.* Unfortunately, determining what is "reasonable" and "foreseeable" involves questions of fact that must be decided on a case-by-case basis.

2. *Caused by a stranger.* If a stranger injures a tenant while on the premises, the landlord may be liable in some circumstances. This type of case mostly involves strangers committing criminal acts, such as rape or other physical harm. While these cases are not consistent, it seems that the landlord is liable if (a) it was foreseeable that this type of injury could have occurred, (b) it could have been avoided by certain action by the landlord, and (c) the costs of such action are not unduly burdensome. *Valencia v. Michaud (2000) 79 C.A.4th 741.* Generally, the landlord must have had some notice of previous occurrences of similar violent crime in that particular building and such crime must have been avoidable through the exercise of reasonable cost and effort.

NUISANCES

Definition

A **nuisance** (now codified) is "anything which is injurious to health, or is indecent or offensive to the senses, or an obstruction to the free use of property, so as to interfere with the comfortable enjoyment of life or property." *C.C. 3479.*

Nature

Basically, a nuisance is an unreasonable use of one's property. It follows from the general nature of all property rights in a democracy. Generally, a landowner may use property as he or she so desires, to the extent that it does not unreasonably deprive or interfere with the use of another's property (see Table 12.1.).

Classification

A few nuisances, called *nuisances per se*, are classified as such by statute or case law. All other nuisances are *nuisances per incident*; they must be proved as such on a case-by-case basis.

TABLE 12.1 Comparison of nuisance and trespass.

	Nuisance	Trespass
Invasion	Physical or intangible	Physical only
Type of invasion	Usually intangible (noise, smoke, odor, etc.) or tangible invasion of airspace (encroachments)	Usually physical objects (people or things) on the land
Cause of action	Invasion of person's interest in *use and enjoyment* of land	Invasion of person's interest in exclusive *possession* of land
Elements	Showing of both *unreasonable conduct* and *material injury*	Showing only of *intentional* unauthorized entry
Balancing the equities	Yes (except nuisance per se)	No
Tort	Intentional, negligent, or strict liability	Intentional only

Per-Incident Nuisance

The per-incident category, to which almost all nuisances belong, includes those operations that become offensive only because of their manner of operation (as in the principal case) or because of their location (e.g., a garbage dump in a residential neighborhood).

Public and Private Nuisances

Nuisances may be either public or private (see Table 12.2.).

Environmental Use

Most public nuisances affect the environment and are now covered by increasingly effective environmental legislation. However, the public

TABLE 12.2 Comparison of public and private nuisances.

	Public Nuisance	Private Nuisance
Invasion	Invasion of common public rights that affects the entire community or a large group of people (although not necessarily equally)	Interference with one individual's use of his property alone, or in a greater degree or kind than the injury suffered by the public
Right to bring action	Any public body; private individual only if it is a private nuisance to him	Only the individual(s) directly affected
Remedies	Criminal indictment, civil action for abatement	Self-help; civil suit for damages and injunction
Statute of limitations	Not applicable	Applicable and may bar recovery

nuisance doctrine is still useful for obstructions of public ways, activities that create fire or health hazards, unreasonable restraints on traffic, and operation of offensive businesses (such as houses of prostitution). The private nuisance doctrine remains a powerful weapon against individuals interfering with reasonable enjoyment of another's property, as in the principal case.

Remedies for a Nuisance

A variety of remedies is available for a nuisance. Injunction is the remedy generally sought. The plaintiff obtains a court order directing the removal of the offending structure, cessation of the injurious conduct, or prevention of the building or creation of a nuisance. The plaintiff may also request damages for an injunction and usually does so as an alternative or additional remedy. Finally, in certain situations, as when a tree branch encroaches on another's land, the plaintiff can adopt a self-help remedy, removing the nuisance on his own without court assistance.

Injunction for Per Se Nuisances

If the nuisance is classified as per se, the plaintiff can seek and obtain an injunction before or while the activity or structure is being developed. The rationale is that because the act or building is automatically declared a nuisance by statute, the injunction should issue at any time.

Injunction for Per-Incident Nuisances

However, most nuisances are per incident, in which case the court will not issue an injunction, if at all, until after the act or structure is completed. Until it is finished or in operation, the courts are unable to judge whether, because of the circumstances, the act or structure is, in fact, a nuisance.

Balancing the Equities

Once the court finds a per-incident nuisance, it may then *balance the equities* before it will consider the issuance of an injunction. The court balances the harm that would be suffered by the plaintiff in ordering the nuisance removed as against the social utility to the defendant public or property owners in allowing the nuisance to continue. If the court finds the harm suffered is slight in comparison with the severe and inequitable harm caused by ordering the nuisance removed, the court generally refuses to issue an injunction to abate the nuisance.

Example

In one case, the court found that the foundation of a building encroached less than two inches on the plaintiff's land, that the cost to move the building would be substantial, and that the harm to the property owner by the loss of a few inches of property was insignificant. Under those facts, the court refused to issue an injunction and instead awarded a few hundred dollars as damages.

Limitation on Use

The doctrine of balancing the equities is not used in certain situations. If the nuisance was intentionally created, as opposed to an innocently created mistake, an injunction will issue regardless of the relative harms. A balancing is also not applicable to a serious nuisance or a substantial encroachment. Finally, unless the plaintiff can establish a serious harm by the nuisance's continuance, as opposed to a mere benefit from its removal, the injunction will not issue.

APPLY THE LAW

Gelfand v. O'Haver
33 C.2d 218 (1948)

Carter, Justice. Plaintiffs obtained an injunction restraining defendants from maintaining a nuisance by unreasonable and injurious methods of operating their music studio. Defendants operate a music studio in an area in the City of Los Angeles where the zoning ordinance permits the operation of such a business. Plaintiffs are the occupants of neighboring buildings. The court found that the studio is conducted in a residence building without soundproofing or adapting it for such [music school business] use, and that in so doing [defendants] have caused persons to sing and rehearse and practice on musical instruments daily from early hours of the morning to late hours of the night.

Defendants contend that there is no evidence to establish a nuisance justifying injunctive relief, for there is no evidence that the studio is operated in a manner different from others in the city and that such evidence is necessary under the Code of Civil Procedure. That section provides "any use expressly permitted [within that zone shall not] be deemed a nuisance without the evidence of the employment of unnecessary and injurious methods of operation."

Prior to the addition of that section to the Code, the law was settled that a person could enjoin certain conduct as a nuisance even though the business was conducted in a district zoned to permit business of the type [for] which complaint was made and defendant was making an effort to operate his business in a careful and efficient manner. In the light of that rule the manifest purpose of the adoption of [the Code] section was to eliminate injunctive relief where the business is operated in its appropriate zone and

continued

the only showing is an injury and nuisance to the plaintiff in such operation. He must show more, namely, that the defendant employed "unnecessary and injurious methods" in the operation of the business.

But that does not mean that the only evidence that will establish an unnecessary and injurious method of operation is a failure to pursue the methods customarily and usually employed in other similar businesses in the vicinity. While such evidence may be relevant to that issue, we see no reason why it should be indispensable.

For illustration, if the defendant's plant is emitting more of these annoying things than other plants in the same business of equal output are emitting, there is something wrong with the equipment and management of the defendant's plant and the smoke, odors, gases, smudges, and noises are unnecessary and unreasonable. Further, if devices or more efficient management would reduce the smoke, odors, gases, smudges, noises, and vibrations at a reasonable expense, it is the duty of the defendant to secure such devices or management, and, if it fails to do so, the smoke, noises, etc., emitting from its plant may be regarded as unnecessary and unreasonable.

In support of the findings of the employment of unnecessary and injurious methods of operation used for the studio as a residence; that nothing was done to soundproof it or adapt it to the operation of the business; that the windows were left open permitting free flow of the sound; and that the noise emanated from the studio night and day. That is plainly sufficient to support the finding and to satisfy the requirement that there be evidence of the employment of unnecessary and injurious methods of operation. The judgment is therefore affirmed. [The injunction is valid. Defendants are prohibited from operating their business in violation of that injunction.]

TREES

General Problems

Problems often arise between neighbors over who owns the trees between their property or over what rights a landowner has to cut off an encroaching tree limb. The ownership of a tree depends on the location of its trunk; the right to cut down overhanging branches depends on the ownership of the tree.

Ownership of Trees

If the trunk of a tree rests entirely on someone's land, the tree belongs exclusively to that person. It is immaterial to ownership that some of the limbs or roots may extend onto a neighbor's land. *C.C. 833*. However, if the trunk rests on the boundary line between two adjacent properties, the tree is a *line tree*. Each adjacent property owner of a line tree is a tenant in common with the other owner.

Rights of Tree Owner

The sole owner of a tree can generally cut, trim, or remove a tree at will, regardless of a neighbor's reaction. However, if two or more property owners have ownership interests in a tree, such as a line tree, then neither can cut or alter that tree without the other's consent. If two owners cannot agree on a certain action against a commonly owned tree, the only remedy is through use of the courts.

Right to Cut Neighbor's Overhanging Branches

If a neighbor owns a tree, the branches of which overhang someone else's land, that landowner has a right to cut off those offending branches. The same rule applies to tree roots that extend on another's land. The right only allows the landowner to cut back the branches or roots to the property line. Furthermore, the branches or roots cannot be trimmed if doing so would create a hazard, such as causing the tree to die and become unsafe. However, provided the circumstances and the trimming are reasonable, the landowner can cut back the branches to the property line without advance notice or court approval. If the landowner is concerned as to what is reasonable, he or she can obtain a court order mandating the neighbor to cut back the tree branches and roots. *Booska v. Patel (1994) 24 C.A.4th 1786.*

FENCES

Obligation to Pay

An owner has no duty to erect and maintain a fence, unless the land has been fenced under an obligation imposed by statute (e.g., because of animals or a swimming pool) or is bound by CC&Rs or other private covenants. However, once the decision has been made to fence in the land, the owner is then bound to pay one-half the cost of erecting such fence, or if the fence has already been erected, then to pay the neighbor one-half the cost of such fence. *C.C. 841.*

Spite Fences

If it can be proved that someone's fence is over 10 feet high and was erected to annoy a neighbor, then the fence must be reduced to

10 feet in height under the spite fence statutes. All fences over 10 feet are presumed to be spiteful. *C.C. 841.4.* The cases are unclear whether a maliciously erected fence under 10 feet can be abated.

Fence Mistakenly on Neighbor's Property

A not uncommon dispute arises between neighbors when one neighbor builds a fence on what he or she thinks is the property line. Years later, it is discovered that the fence lies entirely on the other's property, and that neighbor now wants ownership of that strip of land. Usually, the defending neighbor tries to block ownership to the strip of land by claiming either an easement by prescription, adverse possession or a boundary line agreement.

This seems to be an evolving area of law where cases are not yet entirely consistent. The prevailing trend seems to find that the mere erection of a fence does not grant the other neighbor an easement by prescription. The courts hold that to grant such an easement would be tantamount to ownership, or at the very least exclusive rights, in contrast to a typical easement that ripens into a non-exclusive use. *Silacci v. Abramson (1996) 45 C.A.4th 558.* Therefore, this line of cases holds that no easement by prescription arises.

Because the other party did not pay taxes (the tax bills are prepared on the basis of the legal description in the deed), there is no right to ownership by adverse possession. Finally, because the boundary was not in dispute when the fence was built, most courts find that there is no basis for the doctrine of boundary line by agreement. There was no implied agreement to settle the boundary line at the fence because the parties didn't know the boundary line was in question.

ENCROACHMENTS

Nature and Definition

An **encroachment** is that part of a building or other structure that extends onto the land or airspace of a neighbor's property. The encroachment may either be a trespass or a nuisance, depending on the type of interference involved (see Table 12.3.).

Remedies

The normal **remedy** is an injunction ordering the removal of the offending encroachment. However, when the encroachment was unintentional, the injury was slight, and the hardship to remove it would be severe, the court may balance the equities. Instead of

TABLE 12.3   Types of encroachments.

	Trespass	Nuisance
Encroachment	On the land	In the airspace
Example	Building, fence	Overhanging balcony
Statute of limitations	Three years from date trespass begins	Not applicable; considered a continuous action, giving rise to a new action each day
Remedy	Injunction, damages	Injunction, damages

issuing an injunction, the court may order only that damages be awarded. In one famous case in which the encroachment was less than four inches and the cost of removing the offending wall would have exceeded $6,800, an owner was awarded $200. Any such balancing is discretionary with the court and available only when the encroachment resulted from an unintentional act and innocent mistake.

STORM DAMAGE

Property owners can be liable to downhill neighbors for mud slides, water runoff, and other types of storm damages. The heavy storms bracketing California in the early 1980s have increased the importance of such laws. Although the exact rules relating to storm damage are complex and beyond an introductory text, the basic rules are easily summarized. The California Supreme Court clarified the law in two cases.

Creating Dangerous Conditions

Up until 1966, California followed the common law rule that if an owner left his land in its natural condition, he was not liable for water damage to downhill owners. However, if the uphill owner changed the natural flow of discharge water, then he was liable for any damages caused by that water. However, in 1996, the California Supreme Court changed the common law rules to one of reasonableness. *Keys v. Romley (1966) 64 C.2d 396.*

Basically, the unreasonable owner loses, unless both parties are reasonable, in which case the downhill owner wins. So, if the uphill owner was reasonable but the downhill owner was unreasonable, then the uphill owner wins. Conversely, if the uphill owner was unreasonable while the downhill owner was reasonable, the downhill owner wins. If both owners acted reasonably, then following the old common law, the downhill owner would win.

Failure to Correct Dangerous Conditions

Before 1981, an owner of totally unimproved land that remained in its natural condition could not be liable for storm damage resulting from water runoff or landslide damage. Then the Supreme Court held that a landowner could be negligent for failing to exercise reasonable care to improve property to prevent damage to a neighbor's land. Owners of improved or unimproved land would be well advised to periodically inspect their parcels. If they discover or could have discovered on reasonable investigation a dangerous condition that they unreasonably fail to correct, they will generally be liable for damages to neighboring property.

LATERAL AND SUBJACENT SUPPORT

Nature and Development

Within certain limitations, a property owner is entitled to have land supported by **adjacent** surface land (**lateral support**), as well as supported from below by the underlying earth (**subjacent support**). At common law, anyone who excavated property, irrespective of whatever care and skill were used, was held absolutely liable for any and all damage done to neighbors' unimproved property. However, the demands of urbanization and industrialization have required procedures for excavation and development of property freed from the ancient doctrine of strict liability. To meet these requirements, California adopted a complex combination of common law and statutory provisions.

Lateral Support

At common law, a person who excavated and caused damage to a neighbor's land by removing that neighbor's lateral support was absolutely liable for the damage. It was immaterial how skillfully the excavation was accomplished; strict liability did not depend on negligence. However, strict liability applied only to land in its natural condition. If buildings were on the land, the excavator–landowner was liable only for damage to them resulting from negligent excavation. If the damage to the land only resulted because of the weight of the structures, the excavator was freed from the strict liability for his damages. To encourage excavation, the legislature

TABLE 12.4   Liability for lateral support.

Depth of Excavation	Reasonable Notice Required	Special Requirements	Landowner's Liability to Adjacent Property
Outside C.C. 832 (common law rules)	No	Neighbor must be given right to enter excavator's land to protect his property.	Strict liability for damage to land. Liable only for negligent damages to or because of structures.
Any depth, and neighbor's land unimproved	Yes	Neighbor must, if desired, be given up to 30 days' advance notice to protect his property. Common law right to enter excavator's land to protect his property.	Liable only for negligent excavation.
Greater than walls or foundations of neighbor's buildings, but equal to or less than nine feet	Yes	Neighbor must, if desired, be given up to 30 days' advance notice to protect his property, plus a license to enter excavator's land to protect his property.	Liable only for negligent damage to land; no liability for damage to buildings.
Greater than nine feet, and neighbor's foundations deeper than nine feet	Yes	Provided excavator is given, if needed, a license to enter neighbor's land to protect it, then excavator must at his own expense support neighbor's buildings.	Strict liability for all damage to neighbor's land and buildings (except for minor settlement cracks).

passed a special statute protecting an excavating landowner from strict liability (see Table 12.4.).

Limitations of the Statute

Civil Code 832 protects an excavating landowner from the strict liability of common law if the requirements of the statute are met and provided that damage is not the result of negligent excavation. However, the statute has its limits. If the damage is to a nonadjacent landowner or if the landowner fails to comply with the code provisions, the common law rules of strict liability apply. *Wharam v. Investment Underwriters, Inc. (1943) 58 C.A.2d 346.* Furthermore, the code protections cover only the owner (freehold or leasehold) of property. Thus, a nonowner, such as a professional excavator, is bound by the ordinary rules of negligence, but not the common law or code section liabilities. Finally, government agencies are bound by rules of eminent domain and not by rules of tort liability.

Subjacent Support

Subjacent support, excluded from statutory coverage, is governed by the common law rules of support. *Marin Mun. Water Dist. v. N.W. Pac. R.R. Co. (1967) 253 C.A.2d 83.* Basically, the owner is entitled to absolute support for the land in its natural condition. To the extent that building or other improvements caused or contributed to the subsidence, that underground excavating owner would be liable only for damage to the structures caused by negligence.

Eminent Domain by State

In a 1970 case involving the Bay Area Rapid Transit District, the California Supreme Court ruled that when the state, or one of its subdivisions, excavates in such a manner as to damage private property, the state is absolutely liable. This strict liability is imposed under the doctrine of condemnation, holding that the damage amounts to a *taking* of private property. Hence, the statutory relief provided by C.C. 832 is inapplicable between the state and private parties. *Holtz v. Sup. Ct. (1970) 3 C.3d 296.*

STUDY QUESTIONS (TRUE–FALSE)

1. Under the former California law, people entering on another's land were classified as trespassers, invitees, or licensees, with the highest duty owed to licensees.

2. All trespassers are owed the same duty.

3. A licensee and a trespasser have greater protection under the new law than they were afforded under the former classification theory.

4. Generally, a person making no alterations or repairs to the sidewalk in front of a house has no liability for injuries to others from defects in the sidewalk.

5. A nuisance requires an actual physical invasion of property to be actionable.

6. An owner who builds a house that accidentally but unquestionably encroaches one foot on a neighbor's property can be forced to move the building.

7. An owner has an absolute and unqualified right to cut back to the property line any encroaching branches of a neighbor's tree.

8. If a neighbor refuses to pay half the cost of a common fence, an owner can erect any style of wood fence to any height and his neighbor cannot object.

9. A trespass is an encroachment on the land, whereas a nuisance is an encroachment of the airspace.

10. Whenever an owner digs a hole for a swimming pool and that hole causes a neighbor's soil to slide into the hole, damaging that neighbor's building, the landowner is liable.

Chapter 13

LIMITATIONS ON LANDLORD'S REMEDIES

Originally No Limitations

In ancient times and at common law, once a tenant entered into one of the four types of leasehold estates discussed in Chapter 8 and then breached one of the conditions or failed to pay rent, the landlord could easily evict that tenant. The landlord could remove anyone wrongfully in possession of premises, provided only reasonable force was used. If the tenant failed to pay rent, the landlord resorted to self-help remedies designed to evict the tenant, such as threats of violence, changing the locks on the doors, or other methods not requiring resort to the courts.

Modern Restrictions

Although some landlords still threaten tenants with physical removal for nonpayment of rent or violation of other lease provisions, the landlord is legally helpless and unable to evict the tenant through any procedure other than court action. A landlord who uses extrajudicial remedies to evict a tenant is guilty of **forcible detainer**, a criminal offense. Furthermore, the landlord is civilly liable for unlawful entry and may further be sued for tort damages for emotional distress suffered by the tenant. *Dalusio v. Boone (1969) 71 C.2d 484.*

Violation Does Not Terminate Lease

A mere violation of a lease provision, including nonpayment of rent, does not terminate the **lease**. The tenancy continues, unless the landlord elects to timely declare it terminated by a three-day notice. Once

Leases and Eviction

the lease is terminated, and only then, the landlord may proceed to evict through an **unlawful detainer** action.

Jordan v. Talbot
55 C.2d 597 (1961)

TRAYNOR, JUSTICE. Plaintiff was a tenant in the defendant's apartment house. The lease provided that the lessor had a right of re-entry upon the breach of any condition in the lease and a lien upon all personal effects, furniture, and baggage in the tenant's apartment to secure the rents and other charges. Plaintiff paid rent for eight months. After she was two months in arrears in rent, defendant, without her consent and during her temporary absence, unlocked the door of her apartment, entered and removed her furniture to a warehouse, and refused to allow her to reoccupy the apartment. Thereupon plaintiff filed this action for forcible entry and detainer and for conversion of her furniture and other personal property.

The jury returned a verdict of $6,500 for forcible entry and detainer and for conversion and $3,000 punitive damages. Plaintiff appeals from an order granting defendant's motion for a new trial. Plaintiff contends that there is no evidence that he violated the Code of Civil Procedure.

Re-Entry is not a Defense to Forcible Entry

In defining forcible entry the Code of Civil Procedure refers to "every person," thereby including owners as well as strangers to the title. Under the Code of Civil Procedure the plaintiff "shall only be required to show, in addition to forcible entry or forcible

continued

detainer complained of, that he was peaceably in the actual possession at the time of the forcible detainer." Nowhere is it stated that a right of re-entry is a defense to an action for forcible entry or detainer.

Nor can such a defense be implied from the historical background or purpose of the statute. [The original forcible entry and detainer statute, enacted in England in 1381, provided only criminal sanctions for its breach. The purpose of the statute was to preserve the peace by preventing disturbances that frequently accompanied struggles for the possession of land.]

The action of forcible entry and detainer is a summary proceeding to recover possession of premises forcibly or unlawfully detained. The injury in such cases is confined to the actual peaceable possession of the plaintiff and the unlawful or forcible ouster or detention by defendant, the object of the law being to prevent the disturbance of the public peace by the forcible assertion of a private right.

The lease herein is silent as to the method of enforcing the right of re-entry. In any event, a provision in the lease expressly permitting a forcible entry would be void as contrary to the public policy. Regardless of who has the right to possession, orderly procedure, and preservation of the peace require that the actual possession shall not be disturbed except by legal process.

Guilty of Forcible Entry

[The Civil Code] prohibits an entry by means of breaking open doors or windows. Defendant violated this section when he unlocked plaintiff's apartment without her consent and entered with the storage company employees to remove her furniture, even though there was no physical damage to the premises or actual violence.

The statute was intended to prevent bloodshed, violence, and breaches of the peace, too likely to result from wrongful entries into the possession of others; and it would be absurd to say, that to enable a party to avail himself of its provision, there must have occurred precisely the evil that it was the object of the law to prevent.

Guilty of a Forcible Detainer

The Code of Civil Procedure provides that a person is guilty of a forcible detainer if he "by force or by menaces and threats of violence, unlawfully holds and keeps possession of any real property, whether the same was acquired peacefully or otherwise." In the present case, there is evidence that the apartment was withheld by force and menace and that such withholding was unlawful.

continued

Not Authorized to Enter Home

The provision in the lease granting defendant a lien does not specify a means of enforcement. Even if the lease had authorized a forcible entry, it would be invalid as violating the policy of the forcible entry and detainer statutes. Because the policy of these sections is the preservation of the peace, the rights thereunder may not be contracted away; thus, defendant's right of re-entry and his lien on personal property in the apartment did not justify his entry into the apartment.

Not Convert Goods

Defendant stored most of the items removed from plaintiff's apartment in a warehouse in plaintiff's name. The items that the warehouseman had difficulty removing were stored in the lessor's basement and held for the plaintiff. The lessor did not use any of the plaintiff's belongings or make any claim to ownership. [Therefore, there was no conversion. The plaintiff was guilty only of forcible entry and detainer, for which he must pay damages.]

EVICTION PROCESS

Regulated by Statute

The eviction process is regulated almost totally by statute. The detailed procedure mandated by the Civil Code and the Code of Civil Procedure must be scrupulously followed. Because unlawful detainer actions severely curtail many of the defendant's normal rights, any intentionally or carelessly omitted procedure or deviation from Code requirements may be grounds for complete dismissal of the unlawful detainer action.

Steps in Eviction

The three major steps that must be followed for eviction are (1) terminating the lease by serving the tenant a three-day notice for cause or a 30-day notice without cause; (2) filing, serving, and winning an unlawful detainer action; and (3) physical eviction by the sheriff. (See Table 13.1 for a summary of the eviction process and the time it requires.)

TABLE 13.1   Minimum number of days in eviction process.

Day of Month	Event	Notes
	I. Pretrial	
	(Ignores Holidays–Assumes no delays)	
Day 1	Rent due	Rent is delinquent at midnight.
Day 2	Serve three-day notice to "Quit or Pay Rent"	Personal service is best.
Day 5	Last day to pay rent and cure default	If rent not paid, lease is terminated.
Day 6	File Unlawful Detainer Action	Action filed in court. Summons and complaint served on tenant. Personally serve so today is date of service.
Day 11	Last day for tenant to file "Answer to Complaint" with court	If tenant does not answer, landlord files default and obtains judgment and writ of execution and gives to sheriff. If tenant answers, landlord files "At Issue Memorandum" with court asking for first available date for trial.
	II. Trial	
Trial day	Court trial	Usually a "short cause" matter, requiring 15 minutes to two hours. It generally takes about one to three weeks (sometimes months) for trial date. Following trial, the judge issues a judgment for landlord. (If tenant failed to answer complaint on day 11, landlord can immediately apply for a judgment by default and avoid trial.) Landlord has clerk issue writ of execution.
	III. After Court Judgment	
	(Ignores Holidays–Assumes no delays)	
Day 1	Writ given to Sheriff	Landlord delivers the writ of execution to sheriff.
Day 2	Sheriff serves 5-day notice on tenant	Assumes sheriff immediately serves the writ, which never happens.
Day 7	Eviction	Sheriff physically removes tenant from premises if he or she has not already vacated.

IV. Legal Method Of Counting Days

1. *Exclude first day.* The day any legal document is served is excluded and not counted in any computations. C.C.P. 12.

2. *Count unless last day a holiday.* Count off the next three full days, in which the tenant has to pay rent or whatever time person has to do any obligation. If the last day falls on a holiday, the last day is extended until the next business day. *C.C.P. 12a.* A day does not end until 11:59 that night. *Gov. C. 6806.* Holidays are Saturday, Sunday, and state traditionally defined holidays. *C.C.P. 10, 12a, 12b.*

3. *Next day take action.* After the elapsed days, action can be taken. For example, if three days has passed for nonpayment of rent, on the next day the complaint for unlawful detainer can be filed with the court and served. (If that day is a weekend, remember that the courts will be closed until Monday.)

Termination of Tenancy

The first step toward eviction is the termination of the lease, for until the lease is terminated, an unlawful detainer action will not be permitted. The method of termination depends on the nature of the tenancy involved and on the reason for the termination.

No Termination Notice

If the lease has expired by its own terms (e.g., at the end of a one-year lease or any other estate for years), the tenancy has automatically ended and no notice needs to be given. The landlord may immediately file an unlawful detainer action and serve it on the tenant without any advance notice. *C.C.P. 1161.1.*

Thirty-Day Notice to Terminate Tenancy

A landlord desiring to terminate a periodic tenancy *without* cause must serve, at any time during the month, a 30-day notice. Without the notice, the tenancy will automatically be renewed at the end of each period. *C.C. 1946, 791.* (See Figure 13.1.) If rent is payable on the first of each month, and the 30-day notice is served on April 15,

---

FIGURE 13.1   Thirty-day notice.

Thirty-Day Notice

[If the tenant has been living in the property one year or longer, then whenever the terms Thirty-Day or 30-day appears, change the words to Sixty-Day or 60-day before using the notice.]

To: John Jones, Tenant
    Subtenants and Occupants in Possession

You are hereby notified pursuant to Civil Code Section 1946 that your month-to-month lease on the premises you now rent, commonly known as 1234 Clay Street, Apartment #7, in City, State, is hereby terminated 30 days from the date this is served on you, to wit _____, 20_____.

You are required to deliver up possession of your premises to Ted Gordon, landlord, at 999 XYZ Street, City, State on or before the end of the said 30-day period.

This notice is intended as a 30-day notice terminating your above stated tenancy, and failure to peacefully deliver possession with that 30-day period will result in the institution of legal action against you.

Dated: _____   Ted Gordon
                                               Landlord/ Owner

the tenant will owe only half a month's rent when paying rent on May 1. *Wheeler v. Bainbridge (1948) 84 C.A.2d Supp. 849.*

Aside from for a few minor exceptions, if the tenant has resided in the property for one year or longer, then it instead requires a 60-day notice to terminate the tenancy. However, the tenant can still use a 30-day notice to terminate his or her tenancy. *C.C. 1946.1(b).* Finally, a landlord can use a 30-day notice if the property is in escrow and being sold to a person who plans to live in it for at least a year.

Thirty-day Notice to Change Tenancy Provisions

The 30-day (or 60-day) termination notice discussed above should not be confused with a somewhat similar notice, also called a 30-day notice (used to change the terms of a tenancy). *C.C. 827.* (See Figure 13.2). Frequently, a landlord serves a 30-day change-in-tenancy notice, indicating that in 30 days the rent will increase or other terms will change. A tenant who remains in possession after the time the new terms take effect is bound by those new terms. *C.C. 827.*

Beginning in 2001, a new notice period is needed to raise the rent on residential tenancies under month-to-month or lesser periodic tenancies. If, cumulatively, all rent increases within a one-year period will exceed 10 percent, then 60-days advance notice is required to

FIGURE 13.2   Thirty-day notice to change tenancy terms.

<u>**Thirty-Day Notice**</u>
<u>**To Change Terms Of Tenancy**</u>

[If the change in terms increases the rent by 10% over a one-year period, then whenever the terms Thirty-Day or 30-day appears, change the words to Sixty-Day or 60-day before using the notice.]

To: John Jones, Tenant
    Subtenants and Occupants in Possession

You are hereby notified that your tenancy premises you now rent, commonly known as 1234 Clay Street, Apartment #7, in City, State, is changed as follows: _____.

This change shall take place 30 days from the date this notice is served on you, or on _____, whichever date is the latest.

All of the other terms and conditions of your lease remain unchanged, and in full force and effect.

Dated: _____   Ted Gordon
                                                       Landlord/ Owner

raise the rent. If the total rent increases are ten percent or less, then a 30-day notice will suffice. Thus, if a landlord raised the rent 5 percent in March 2001 and 3 percent in September 2001, then a 3 percent raise in February 2002 would require 60-days notice. This special 60-day notice is required. Landlords must be careful to use current thirty-day notice forms or risk the possibility of making an error. *C.C. §827(b)*.

Three-Day Notice

A landlord desiring to terminate any tenancy for *cause* must first serve a **three-day notice**. *C.C.P. 1161*. The notice must be served on the tenant and on any subtenant occupying the premises. If the subtenant is not named, the judgment does not apply to that subtenant. *Kwock v. Bergren (1982) 130 C.A.3d 596.* This notice is required even if the lease provides that such notice is waived. *Jordan v. Talbot (1961) 55 C.2d 597.* If the tenant cures the default stated in the notice (e.g., by paying rent) within the three-day period, the breach is cured without penalty as if the default had never occurred. *C.C. 1161.5.* (See Figure 13.3.)

Stated in the Alternative

The three-day notice must be stated in the alternative: to cure the default within three days (e.g., by payment of rent) *or* to quit the premises. Failure to state the notice in the alternative invalidates the notice. *Hinman v. Wagon (1959) 172 C.A.2d 24.* One exception is that the notice need not be stated in the alternative if the breach is incurable, such that any attempt at alternative action would be meaningless. However, landlords would be prudent always to state such notice in the alternative, because the penalty for an improper notice is the dismissal of the unlawful detainer action.

Landlord Sign the Notice

Federal law requires that "debt collectors" give 30-days notice before enforcing a consumer debt. *Fair Debt Collection Practices Act, 15 UCS 1692g*. Federal cases from another state seem to hold that attorneys, property managers and others might have to provide this notice when giving a three-day notice. Until a California cases rules on this issue, landlords would be well advised to sign their own three-day notice in residential tenancies. By signing their own notice, landlords would be exempt even if the *Fair Debt Collection Practices Act* were to apply. *California Real Property Journal, 1999, Vol. 17, No. 2, pg. 16*. Conversely, a tenant might raise this issue as a defense to a residential unlawful detainer action.

FIGURE 13.3   Three-Day Notice.

Three-Day Notice

To: John Jones, Tenant
      Subtenants and Occupants in Possession

You are hereby notified pursuant to the Code of Civil Procedure, Section 1161, that you are delinquent in rent on the premises you now lease, commonly known as 1234 Clay Street, Apartment #7, in City, State, in the amount of $_____, for the period from _____, 20_____ to _____, 20_____.

You are further notified that within three days from the date of service on you, to wit: _____, 20_____, you must either pay the due and owning amounts or quit possession of those premises and deliver up that possession to Ted Gordon, landlord, at 999 XYZ Street, City, State. You may make payment to me at that address between 9 A.M. and 5 P.M. Failure to do so will result in legal proceedings for unlawful detainer being filed against you to recover possession of the premises and up to $600 statutory penalty, plus rents and damages.

You are also notified that the landlord hereby declares a forfeiture of your lease if the delinquent rent is not paid within the three-day period.

Dated: _____   Ted Gordon
                                                                          Landlord/ Owner

---

Unlawful Detainer Action

The second step in the eviction process is court action. Landlords naturally select unlawful detainer actions, *C.C.P. 1159–1179a*, because they are the most inexpensive, safe, and expedient method available. An unlawful detainer action differs from a normal civil suit and offers several advantages over it.

Shortened Response Time

The defendant (tenant) has only five days to respond to (answer) an unlawful detainer complaint, whereas a normal summons permits 30 days before a pleading or appearance is required. *C.C.P. 1167.* This 25-day saving is material to a landlord whose tenant is not paying rent and is possibly judgment proof. Additionally, many tenants are unable to respond appropriately within the short five-day time limit, so a judgment by default is obtained.

Calendar Priority

Unlawful detainer actions have calendar (docket) preference over all other civil actions. *C.C.P. 1179a.* Most civil cases take from three months to one year under the current fast-track system to come to trial, during which time the delinquent tenant would remain in possession of the premises. Most unlawful detainer actions, because of their docket priority over other civil actions, are heard within three to six weeks.

No Cross-Complaints

The tenant is prevented from asserting a cross-complaint or filing a counterclaim. The only material issue is the lawful right to possession. In residential leases, the tenant can raise, as an affirmative defense, the issue of breach of the warranty of habitability or of retaliatory eviction. These defenses are not available in commercial leases. A tenant cannot raise the defense of **fraud**, for example, because, even if fraud is proved, it will not preserve the tenant's right to possession—the only issue of importance in unlawful detainer actions. The tenant has to raise any issues unrelated to possession, such as fraud, in an ordinary and separate lawsuit. *Nork v. Pac. Coast Medical Ent., Inc. (1977) 73 C.A.3d 410.*

Statutory Damages

At its discretion, the court may add statutory damages up to $600 in addition to the rent awarded if it determines that the tenant acted in bad faith or maliciously. *C.C.P. 1174.* Thus, if the judge finds that $800 back rent is due and owing, he or she may award the landlord a judgment in the amount of $1,400. Some judges frequently impose the maximum $600 fine; others are extremely reluctant to impose such a penalty.

Optional Stay of Execution

If the defendant loses the case and appeals the decision, the judge has discretion over whether to withhold stay of sentence. *C.C.P. 1177.* In most civil cases, it is mandatory that a judge delay imposition of sentence (i.e., eviction) until the appeals are completed.

Eviction by the Sheriff

Once the judgment is awarded to the landlord, it must be enforced; the judgment itself is not self-executing. The judgment entitles the landlord to a writ of execution, also known as a **writ of possession** or a writ of restitution, which authorizes the sheriff to begin the eviction process. First, the sheriff serves a formal five-day notice of eviction, either by personal service or by posting a copy on the premises and mailing a copy to the defendant. *C.C.P. 1174; 488.310.*

Only in the unusual event that the tenant has not vacated the premises within the five-day period specified in the notice does the sheriff physically evict.

Writ of Immediate Possession

If the defendant resides outside the state or has departed from the state and cannot, after due diligence, be found in California, or has concealed himself or herself to avoid service of the summons, then the landlord may, after filing an unlawful detainer action, also file a motion for immediate possession. After a hearing, the sheriff would be authorized to issue a **writ of immediate possession**. *C.C.P. 1166a*. To take advantage of this remedy, the plaintiff must post a bond with the court to cover the defendant's damages, should the defendant ultimately prevail in the unlawful detainer action.

Defense Strategy

As a defense, many attorneys advise their clients to vacate the premises voluntarily. This abandonment automatically changes the lawsuit into an ordinary civil action for damages. *C.C. 1952.3*. As such, the lawsuit loses its priority and must await its regular turn on the civil docket. The threat of $600 statutory damages is eliminated, and the tenant may file an ordinary crosscomplaint. The increased exposure to the landlord in time, expense, and risk often permits the tenant to achieve a far more advantageous settlement.

Special Tenancies

Other tenancy situations are subject to extensive legislation. All questions regarding these rentals and evictions require an understanding of the special statutes covering these occupancies. Some of the special situations include the following:

Mobile Home Tenancies

Residential mobile home parks are governed by a comprehensive set of statewide statutes called the *Mobilehome Residency Law. C.C. 798 et seq*. These statutes govern the landlord–tenant relationship and the creation, nature, and termination of any tenancies within the park. For example, tenancies cannot be less than one year, unless requested by the tenant. Tenants must be given a 60-day notice before the rent can be increased. Management may require the right to approve any buyers of a mobile home if the purchaser will remain in the park. Management can only terminate a tenancy for certain stated, statutory reasons, and then only upon giving 60 days' notice. These are a few of the many statutes governing mobile home parks that must be reviewed when dealing with mobile homes.

Section 8 Housing

Section 8 housing is a program of federal assistance to low-income recipients in rental units provided by landlords who wish to participate in the government program. The name "section 8," while commonly used today, has no real meaning. The name was derived from section 8 of the original bill that authorized such assistance. Basically, landlords are either an owner of large projects where at least 20% of the unit is dedicated to low-income housing, or they are landlords who voluntarily agree to accept a section 8 participant as a tenant in one or more units in their building. Any landlord whose unit or units are habitable enough to meet the HUD requirements can voluntarily agree to accept section 8 tenants. *42 USC 1437f.*

The County or administrative agency qualifies the tenant through a rigorous income and asset test. Once the tenant is found in need of federal assistance, the participant (or the participant and his or her family) receives a voucher for section 8 housing. The tenant must still find a vacant section 8 unit. In some jurisdictions, many units are available, whereas in other areas there may be a wait of a year or more.

The participant will then pay rent (normally up to but not more than 30% of their income). The government agrees to pay the remainder of the rent, which amount is usually lower than the fair market rent. The tenant obtains housing within his or her means, and the landlord obtains a tenant whose rent is partially guaranteed. If the landlord operates a HUD approved project where at least 20% of the units are low-income tenants, there are also tax benefits for the project owner. However, section 8 tenants do have certain rights superior to those under state law, including the right to be evicted only upon 60-days notice and then for only specified reasons.

Domestic Violence Termination

There is a very minor and limited exception allowing tenants subjected to domestic violence or stalking to terminate a lease early. *C. C.1846.7.*

LANDLORD–TENANT RELATIONSHIP

Governed by Law

Whenever a leasehold estate is created, a landlord–tenant relationship arises. It is frequently accompanied by a written lease, although sometimes there is only an oral agreement. Infrequently, the relationship develops by implication of the law without any express agreement. However, in all situations, the California codes and case law govern the rights and responsibilities of the parties. The control may be comprehensive and strict, as in residential leases, or limited to specific provisions, as in large industrial leases.

Governed by Contract

Within the parameters established by law, the parties are free contractually to expand or restrict their rights and duties. However, while the parties may waive certain provisions of the law, there are other areas where any attempted waiver is void as against public policy. Consequently, it is important in analyzing the landlord–tenant relationship to review any existing leases.

The lease provisions must be checked against the code sections to determine which clauses are valid and which are not. In some matters, the laws favor the tenant, such as the rights available if the dwelling is uninhabitable. In other areas, the law favors the landlord, such as the right to prohibit distribution of tenant newsletters in apartment complexes. *Golden Gateway Center v. Golden Gateway Tenants Assn. (1999) 73 C.A.4th 908.*

No Standard Form Lease

If a standard form lease existed, it would be an ideal model from which to analyze each provision, clause by clause, as a means of explaining the landlord–tenant relationship. Unfortunately, no single lease is recognized or even used as a model for other leases. Thousands of different forms exist, with as many variations as there are combinations of different clauses. Further, if a residential lease is negotiated in one of the major languages used in California (defined by statute), then the lease document must also be written in that language. *C.C. 1632.* Probably the two most commonly used "standardized" forms are the CAR residential lease and the AIREA (American Industrial Real Estate Association) commercial lease.

CAR Residential Lease

Certain organizations publish form leases that are standardized to their particular needs. The largest California group to publish a lease form is the California Association of REALTORS® (CAR). This form was created by a joint committee of the California Association of REALTORS® and the California Bar Association. (See Figure 13.4.)

FIGURE 13.4 Flexibility where goes.

CALIFORNIA
ASSOCIATION
OF REALTORS ®

**RESIDENTIAL LEASE OR
MONTH-TO-MONTH RENTAL AGREEMENT**
(C.A.R. Form LR, Revised 11/08)

Date _____, _____ ("Landlord") and
_____ ("Tenant") agree as follows:

1. PROPERTY:
   A. Landlord rents to Tenant and Tenant rents from Landlord, the real property and improvements described as: _____ ①
   _____ ("Premises").
   B. The Premises are for the sole use as a personal residence by the following named person(s) **only:** _____ ②
   _____
   C. The following personal property, maintained pursuant to paragraph 11, is included: _____
   _____ or ☐ (if checked) the personal property on the attached addendum.

2. TERM: The term begins on (date) _____ ③ _____ ("Commencement Date"), **(Check A or B):**
   ☐ **A. Month-to-Month:** and continues as a month-to-month tenancy. Tenant may terminate the tenancy by giving written notice
   at least 30 days prior to the intended termination date. Landlord may terminate the tenancy by giving written notice as
   provided by law. Such notices may be given on any date.
   ☐ **B. Lease:** and shall terminate on (date) _____ at _____ ☐ AM/ ☐ PM.
   Tenant shall vacate the Premises upon termination of the Agreement, unless: **(i)** Landlord and Tenant have extended this
   agreement in writing or signed a new agreement; **(ii)** mandated by local rent control law; or **(iii)** Landlord accepts Rent from
   Tenant (other than past due Rent), in which case a month-to-month tenancy shall be created which either party may
   terminate as specified in paragraph 2A. Rent shall be at a rate agreed to by Landlord and Tenant, or as allowed by law. All
   other terms and conditions of this Agreement shall remain in full force and effect.

3. RENT: "Rent" shall mean all monetary obligations of Tenant to Landlord under the terms of the Agreement, except security deposit.
   A. Tenant agrees to pay $ _____ per month for the term of the Agreement.
   B. Rent is payable in advance on the **1st (or ☐** _____ ④ _____ **) day** of each calendar month, and is delinquent on the next day.
   C. If Commencement Date falls on any day other than the day Rent is payable under paragraph 3B, and Tenant has paid one full
   month's Rent in advance of Commencement Date, Rent for the second calendar month shall be prorated based on a 30-day
   period.
   D. PAYMENT: Rent shall be paid by ☐ personal check, ☐ money order, ☐ cashier's check, or ☐ other _____,
   to (name) _____ (phone) _____ at (address)
   _____ , (or at any other location
   subsequently specified by Landlord in writing to Tenant) (and ☐ if checked, rent may be paid personally, between the hours of
   _____ and _____ on the following days _____). If any payment is
   returned for non-sufficient funds ("NSF") or because tenant stops payment, then, after that: (i) Landlord may, in writing, require
   Tenant to pay Rent in cash for three months and (ii) all future Rent shall be paid by ☐ money order, or ☐ cashier's check.

4. SECURITY DEPOSIT:
   A. Tenant agrees to pay $ _____ ⑤ _____ ⑥ _____ as a security deposit. Security deposit will be
   ☐ transferred to and held by the Owner of the Premises, or ☐ held in Owner's Broker's trust account.
   B. All or any portion of the security deposit may be used, as reasonably necessary, to: **(i)** cure Tenant's default in payment of Rent (which
   includes Late Charges, NSF fees or other sums due); **(ii)** repair damage, excluding ordinary wear and tear, caused by Tenant or by a
   guest or licensee of Tenant; **(iii)** clean Premises, if necessary, upon termination of the tenancy; and **(iv)** replace or return personal
   property or appurtenances. **SECURITY DEPOSIT SHALL NOT BE USED BY TENANT IN LIEU OF PAYMENT OF LAST
   MONTH'S RENT.** If all or any portion of the security deposit is used during the tenancy, Tenant agrees to reinstate the total security
   deposit within five days after written notice is delivered to Tenant. Within 21 days after Tenant vacates the Premises, Landlord shall:
   (1) furnish Tenant an itemized statement indicating the amount of any security deposit received and the basis for its
   disposition and supporting documentation as required by California Civil Code § 1950.5(g); and **(2)** return any remaining
   portion of the security deposit to Tenant.
   ⑦ **C. Security deposit will not be returned until all Tenants have vacated the Premises and all keys returned. Any security
   deposit returned by check shall be made out to all Tenants named on this Agreement, or as subsequently modified.**
   ⑧ **D.** No interest will be paid on security deposit unless required by local law.
   ⑨ **E.** If the security deposit is held by Owner, Tenant agrees not to hold Broker responsible for its return. If the security deposit is held
   in Owner's Broker's trust account, **and** Broker's authority is terminated before expiration of this Agreement, **and** security deposit
   is released to someone other than Tenant, **then** Broker shall notify Tenant, in writing, where and to whom security deposit has
   been released. Once Tenant has been provided such notice, Tenant agrees not to hold Broker responsible for the security
   deposit.

5. MOVE-IN COSTS RECEIVED/DUE: Move-in funds made payable to _____
   shall be paid by ☐ personal check, ☐ money order, or ☐ cashier's check.

Category	Total Due	Payment Received	Balance Due	Date Due
Rent from _____ to _____ (date)				
*Security Deposit				
Other _____				
Other _____				
Total				

*The maximum amount Landlord may receive as security deposit, however designated, cannot exceed two months' Rent for
unfurnished premises, or three months' Rent for furnished premises.

LR REVISED 11/08 (PAGE 1 OF 6) Print Date

Tenant's Initials (_____)(_____)
Landlord's Initials (_____)(_____)

Reviewed by _____ Date _____

EQUAL HOUSING
OPPORTUNITY

RESIDENTIAL LEASE OR MONTH-TO-MONTH RENTAL AGREEMENT (LR PAGE 1 OF 6)

FIGURE 13.4   (*Continued*).

Premises: _____ Date: _____

6. **LATE CHARGE; RETURNED CHECKS:**
    A. Tenant acknowledges either late payment of Rent or issuance of a returned check may cause Landlord to incur costs and expenses, the exact amounts of which are extremely difficult and impractical to determine. These costs may include, but are not limited to, processing, enforcement and accounting expenses, and late charges imposed on Landlord. If any installment of Rent due from Tenant is not received by Landlord within **5 (or ☐ _____) calendar days** after the date due, or if a check is returned, Tenant shall pay to Landlord, respectively, an additional sum of $ _____ or _____% of the Rent due as a Late Charge and $25.00 as a NSF fee for the first returned check and $35.00 as a NSF fee for each additional returned check, either or both of which shall be deemed additional Rent.

    (10)

    B. Landlord and Tenant agree that these charges represent a fair and reasonable estimate of the costs Landlord may incur by reason of Tenant's late or NSF payment. Any Late Charge or NSF fee due shall be paid with the current installment of Rent. Landlord's acceptance of any Late Charge or NSF fee shall not constitute a waiver as to any default of Tenant. Landlord's right to collect a Late Charge or NSF fee shall not be deemed an extension of the date Rent is due under paragraph 3 or prevent Landlord from exercising any other rights and remedies under this Agreement and as provided by law.

7. **PARKING: (Check A or B)**
    ☐   A. Parking is permitted as follows: _____ (11) _____
    _____.
    The right to parking ☐ is ☐ is not included in the Rent charged pursuant to paragraph 3. If not included in the Rent, the parking rental fee shall be an additional $ _____ per month. Parking space(s) are to be used for parking properly licensed and operable motor vehicles, except for trailers, boats, campers, buses or trucks (other than pick-up trucks). Tenant shall park in assigned space(s) only. Parking space(s) are to be kept clean. Vehicles leaking oil, gas or other motor vehicle fluids shall not be parked on the Premises. Mechanical work or storage of inoperable vehicles is not permitted in parking space(s) or elsewhere on the Premises.
    OR ☐   B. Parking is not permitted on the Premises.

8. **STORAGE: (Check A or B)**
    ☐   A. Storage is permitted as follows: _____ (12) _____
    The right to storage space ☐ is, ☐ is not, included in the Rent charged pursuant to paragraph 3. If not included in the Rent, storage space fee shall be an additional $ _____ per month. Tenant shall store only personal property Tenant owns, and shall not store property claimed by another or in which another has any right, title or interest. Tenant shall not store any improperly packaged food or perishable goods, flammable materials, explosives, hazardous waste or other inherently dangerous material, or illegal substances.
    OR ☐   B. Storage is not permitted on the Premises.

9. **UTILITIES:** Tenant agrees to pay for all utilities and services, and the following charges: _____ (13) _____
    except _____, which shall be paid for by Landlord. If any utilities are not separately metered, Tenant shall pay Tenant's proportional share, as reasonably determined and directed by Landlord. If utilities are separately metered, Tenant shall place utilities in Tenant's name as of the Commencement Date. Landlord is only responsible for installing and maintaining one usable telephone jack and one telephone line to the Premises. Tenant shall pay any cost for conversion from existing utilities service provider.

10. **CONDITION OF PREMISES:** Tenant has examined Premises and, if any, all furniture, furnishings, appliances, landscaping and fixtures, including smoke detector(s).
    (Check all that apply)
    ☐   A. Tenant acknowledges these items are clean and in operable condition, with the following exceptions: _____ (14) _____
    _____.
    ☐   B. Tenant's acknowledgment of the condition of these items is contained in an attached statement of condition (C.A.R. Form MIMO).
    ☐   C. Tenant will provide Landlord a list of items that are damaged or not in operable condition within **3 (or ☐ _____) days** after Commencement Date, not as a contingency of this Agreement but rather as an acknowledgment of the condition of the Premises.
    ☐   D. Other:_____.

11. **MAINTENANCE:**
    A. Tenant shall properly use, operate and safeguard Premises, including if applicable, any landscaping, furniture, furnishings and appliances, and all mechanical, electrical, gas and plumbing fixtures, and keep them and the Premises clean, sanitary and well ventilated. Tenant shall be responsible for checking and maintaining all smoke detectors and any additional phone lines beyond the one line and jack that Landlord shall provide and maintain. Tenant shall immediately notify Landlord, in writing, of any problem, malfunction or damage. Tenant shall be charged for all repairs or replacements caused by Tenant, pets, guests or licensees of Tenant, excluding ordinary wear and tear. Tenant shall be charged for all damage to Premises as a result of failure to report a problem in a timely manner. Tenant shall be charged for repair of drain blockages or stoppages, unless caused by defective plumbing parts or tree roots invading sewer lines.
    B. ☐ Landlord ☐ Tenant shall water the garden, landscaping, trees and shrubs, except: _____ (15) (16) _____
    _____.
    C. ☐ Landlord ☐ Tenant shall maintain the garden, landscaping, trees and shrubs, except: _____
    _____.
    D. ☐ Landlord ☐ Tenant shall maintain _____
    E. Tenant's failure to maintain any item for which Tenant is responsible shall give Landlord the right to hire someone to perform such maintenance and charge Tenant to cover the cost of such maintenance.
    F. The following items of personal property are included in the Premises without warranty and Landlord will not maintain, repair or replace them: _____.

Tenant's Initials   (_____)(_____)
Landlord's Initials (_____)(_____)

Reviewed by _____ Date _____

RESIDENTIAL LEASE OR MONTH-TO-MONTH RENTAL AGREEMENT (LR PAGE 2 OF 6)

FIGURE 13.4 (*Continued*).

Premises: _____ Date: _____

12. **NEIGHBORHOOD CONDITIONS:** Tenant is advised to satisfy him or herself as to neighborhood or area conditions, including schools, proximity and adequacy of law enforcement, crime statistics, proximity of registered felons or offenders, fire protection, other governmental services, availability, adequacy and cost of any wired, wireless internet connections or other telecommunications or other technology services and installations, proximity to commercial, industrial or agricultural activities, existing and proposed transportation, construction and development that may affect noise, view, or traffic, airport noise, noise or odor from any source, wild and domestic animals, other nuisances, hazards, or circumstances, cemeteries, facilities and condition of common areas, conditions and influences of significance to certain cultures and/or religions, and personal needs, requirements and preferences of Tenant.

13. **PETS:** Unless otherwise provided in California Civil Code § 54.2, no animal or pet shall be kept on or about the Premises without Landlord's prior written consent, except: _____

14. ☐ **(If checked) NO SMOKING:** No smoking is allowed on the Premises. If smoking does occur on the Premises, **(i)** Tenant is responsible for all damage caused by the smoking including, but not limited to, stains, burns, odors and removal of debris; **(ii)** Tenant is in breach of this Agreement; **(iii)** Tenant, Authorized Guests, and all others may be required to leave the Premises; and **(iv)** Tenant acknowledges that in order to remove odor caused by smoking, Landlord may need to replace carpet and drapes and paint entire premises regardless of when these items were last cleaned or replaced. Such actions and other necessary steps will impact the return of any security deposit.

15. **RULES/REGULATIONS:**
   A. Tenant agrees to comply with all Landlord rules and regulations that are at any time posted on the Premises or delivered to Tenant. Tenant shall not, and shall ensure that guests and licensees of Tenant shall not, disturb, annoy, endanger or interfere with other tenants of the building or neighbors, or use the Premises for any unlawful purposes, including, but not limited to, using, manufacturing, selling, storing or transporting illicit drugs or other contraband, or violate any law or ordinance, or commit a waste or nuisance on or about the Premises.
   B. **(If applicable, check one)**
      ☐ 1. Landlord shall provide Tenant with a copy of the rules and regulations within _____ days
      or _____ .
      OR ☐ 2. Tenant has been provided with, and acknowledges receipt of a copy of the rules and regulations.

16. ☐ **(If checked) CONDOMINIUM;PLANNED UNIT DEVELOPMENT:**
   A. The Premises is a unit in a condominium, planned unit development, common interest subdivision or other development governed by a homeowners' association ("HOA"). The name of the HOA is _____. Tenant agrees to comply with all HOA covenants, conditions and restrictions, bylaws, rules and regulations and decisions. Landlord shall provide Tenant copies of rules and regulations, if any. Tenant shall reimburse Landlord for any fines or charges imposed by HOA or other authorities, due to any violation by Tenant, or the guests or licensees of Tenant.
   B. **(Check one)**
      ☐ 1. Landlord shall provide Tenant with a copy of the HOA rules and regulations within _____ days
      or _____ .
      OR ☐ 2. Tenant has been provided with, and acknowledges receipt of, a copy of the HOA rules and regulations.

17. **ALTERATIONS; REPAIRS:** Unless otherwise specified by law or paragraph 29C, without Landlord's prior written consent, **(i)** Tenant shall not make any repairs, alterations or improvements in or about the Premises including: painting, wallpapering, adding or changing locks, installing antenna or satellite dish(es), placing signs, displays or exhibits, or using screws, fastening devices, large nails or adhesive materials; **(ii)** Landlord shall not be responsible for the costs of alterations or repairs made by Tenant; **(iii)** Tenant shall not deduct from Rent the costs of any repairs, alterations or improvements; and **(iv)** any deduction made by Tenant shall be considered unpaid Rent.

18. **KEYS; LOCKS:**
   A. Tenant acknowledges receipt of (or Tenant will receive ☐ prior to the Commencement Date, or ☐ _____):
      ☐ _____ key(s) to Premises,   ☐ _____ remote control device(s) for garage door/gate opener(s),
      ☐ _____ key(s) to mailbox,   ☐ _____,
      ☐ _____ key(s) to common area(s), ☐ _____.
   B. Tenant acknowledges that locks to the Premises ☐ have, ☐ have not, been re-keyed.
   C. If Tenant re-keys existing locks or opening devices, Tenant shall immediately deliver copies of all keys to Landlord. Tenant shall pay all costs and charges related to loss of any keys or opening devices. Tenant may not remove locks, even if installed by Tenant.

19. **ENTRY:**
   A. Tenant shall make Premises available to Landlord or Landlord's representative for the purpose of entering to make necessary or agreed repairs, decorations, alterations, or improvements, or to supply necessary or agreed services, or to show Premises to prospective or actual purchasers, tenants, mortgagees, lenders, appraisers, or contractors.
   B. Landlord and Tenant agree that 24-hour written notice shall be reasonable and sufficient notice, except as follows, 48-hour written notice is required to conduct an inspection of the Premises prior to the Tenant moving out, unless the Tenant waives the right to such notice. Notice may be given orally to show the Premises to actual or prospective purchasers provided Tenant has been notified in writing within 120 days preceding the oral notice that the Premises are for sale and that oral notice may be given to show the Premises. No notice is required: **(i)** to enter in case of an emergency; **(ii)** if the Tenant is present and consents at the time of entry or **(iii)** if the Tenant has abandoned or surrendered the Premises. No written notice is required if Landlord and Tenant orally agree to an entry for agreed services or repairs if the date and time of entry are within one week of the oral agreement.
   C. ☐ **(If checked)** Tenant authorizes the use of a keysafe/lockbox to allow entry into the Premises and agrees to sign a keysafe/lockbox addendum (C.A.R. Form KLA).

20. **SIGNS:** Tenant authorizes Landlord to place FOR SALE/LEASE signs on the Premises.

21. **ASSIGNMENT; SUBLETTING:** Tenant shall not sublet all or any part of Premises, or assign or transfer this Agreement or any interest in it, without Landlord's prior written consent. Unless such consent is obtained, any assignment, transfer or subletting of Premises or this Agreement or tenancy, by voluntary act of Tenant, operation of law or otherwise, shall, at the option of Landlord,

Tenant's Initials (_____)(_____)
Landlord's Initials (_____)(_____)

Reviewed by _____ Date _____

LR REVISED 11/08 (PAGE 3 OF 6)

RESIDENTIAL LEASE OR MONTH-TO-MONTH RENTAL AGREEMENT (LR PAGE 3 OF 6)

FIGURE 13.4 (Continued).

Premises: _____ Date: _____

terminate this Agreement. Any proposed assignee, transferee or sublessee shall submit to Landlord an application and credit information for Landlord's approval and, if approved, sign a separate written agreement with Landlord and Tenant. Landlord's consent to any one assignment, transfer or sublease, shall not be construed as consent to any subsequent assignment, transfer or sublease and does not release Tenant of Tenant's obligations under this Agreement.

(29) 22. **JOINT AND INDIVIDUAL OBLIGATIONS:** If there is more than one Tenant, each one shall be individually and completely responsible for the performance of all obligations of Tenant under this Agreement, jointly with every other Tenant, and individually, whether or not in possession.

23. ☐ **LEAD-BASED PAINT (If checked):** Premises was constructed prior to 1978. In accordance with federal law, Landlord gives and Tenant acknowledges receipt of the disclosures on the attached form (C.A.R. Form FLD) and a federally approved lead pamphlet.

(30) 24. ☐ **MILITARY ORDNANCE DISCLOSURE:** (If applicable and known to Landlord) Premises is located within one mile of an area once used for military training, and may contain potentially explosive munitions.

25. ☐ **PERIODIC PEST CONTROL:** Landlord has entered into a contract for periodic pest control treatment of the Premises and shall give Tenant a copy of the notice originally given to Landlord by the pest control company.

26. ☐ **METHAMPHETAMINE CONTAMINATION:** Prior to signing this Agreement, Landlord has given Tenant a notice that a health official has issued an order prohibiting occupancy of the property because of methamphetamine contamination. A copy of the notice and order are attached.

27. **MEGAN'S LAW DATABASE DISCLOSURE:** Notice: Pursuant to Section 290.46 of the Penal Code, information about specified registered sex offenders is made available to the public via an Internet Web site maintained by the Department of Justice at www.meganslaw.ca.gov. Depending on an offender's criminal history, this information will include either the address at which the offender resides or the community of residence and ZIP Code in which he or she resides. (Neither Landlord nor Brokers, if any, are required to check this website. If Tenant wants further information, Tenant should obtain information directly from this website.)

28. **POSSESSION:**

    A.   Tenant is not in possession of the premises. If Landlord is unable to deliver possession of Premises on Commencement Date, such Date shall be extended to the date on which possession is made available to Tenant. If Landlord is unable to deliver **(31)** possession within **5 (or ☐ _____) calendar days** after agreed Commencement Date, Tenant may terminate this Agreement by giving written notice to Landlord, and shall be refunded all Rent and security deposit paid. Possession is deemed terminated when Tenant has returned all keys to the Premises to Landlord.

    B.   ☐ Tenant is already in possession of the Premises.

29. **TENANT'S OBLIGATIONS UPON VACATING PREMISES:**

    A.   Upon termination of this Agreement, Tenant shall: **(i)** give Landlord all copies of all keys or opening devices to Premises, including any common areas; **(ii)** vacate and surrender Premises to Landlord, empty of all persons; **(iii)** vacate any/all parking and/or storage space; **(iv)** clean and deliver Premises, as specified in paragraph C below, to Landlord in the same condition as referenced in paragraph 10; **(v)** remove all debris; **(vi)** give written notice to Landlord of Tenant's forwarding address; and **(vii)** _____.

(32)   B.   All alterations/improvements made by or caused to be made by Tenant, with or without Landlord's consent, become the property of Landlord upon termination. Landlord may charge Tenant for restoration of the Premises to the condition it was in prior to any alterations/improvements.

(33)   C.   **Right to Pre-Move-Out Inspection and Repairs: (i)** After giving or receiving notice of termination of a tenancy (C.A.R. Form NTT), or before the end of a lease, Tenant has the right to request that an inspection of the Premises take place prior to termination of the lease or rental (C.A.R. Form NRI). If Tenant requests such an inspection, Tenant shall be given an opportunity to remedy identified deficiencies prior to termination, consistent with the terms of this Agreement. **(ii)** Any repairs or alterations made to the Premises as a result of this inspection (collectively, "Repairs") shall be made at Tenant's expense. Repairs may be performed by Tenant or through others, who have adequate insurance and licenses and are approved by Landlord. The work shall comply with applicable law, including governmental permit, inspection and approval requirements. Repairs shall be performed in a good, skillful manner with materials of quality and appearance comparable to existing materials. It is understood that exact restoration of appearance or cosmetic items following all Repairs may not be possible. **(iii)** Tenant shall: **(a)** obtain receipts for Repairs performed by others; **(b)** prepare a written statement indicating the Repairs performed by Tenant and the date of such Repairs; and **(c)** provide copies of receipts and statements to Landlord prior to termination. Paragraph 29C does not apply when the tenancy is terminated pursuant to California Code of Civil Procedure § 1161(2), (3) or (4).

(34) **(35)** **(36)** 30. **BREACH OF CONTRACT; EARLY TERMINATION:** In addition to any obligations established by paragraph 29, in the event of termination by Tenant prior to completion of the original term of the Agreement, Tenant shall also be responsible for lost Rent, rental commissions, advertising expenses and painting costs necessary to ready Premises for re-rental. Landlord may withhold any such amounts from Tenant's security deposit.

31. **TEMPORARY RELOCATION:** Subject to local law, Tenant agrees, upon demand of Landlord, to temporarily vacate Premises for a reasonable period, to allow for fumigation (or other methods) to control wood destroying pests or organisms, or other repairs to Premises. Tenant agrees to comply with all instructions and requirements necessary to prepare Premises to accommodate pest **(37)** control, fumigation or other work, including bagging or storage of food and medicine, and removal of perishables and valuables. Tenant shall only be entitled to a credit of Rent equal to the per diem Rent for the period of time Tenant is required to vacate Premises.

32. **DAMAGE TO PREMISES:** If, by no fault of Tenant, Premises are totally or partially damaged or destroyed by fire, earthquake, accident or other casualty that render Premises totally or partially uninhabitable, either Landlord or Tenant may terminate this Agreement by giving the other written notice. Rent shall be abated as of the date Premises become totally or partially uninhabitable. **(38)** The abated amount shall be the current monthly Rent prorated on a 30-day period. If the Agreement is not terminated, Landlord shall promptly repair the damage, and Rent shall be reduced based on the extent to which the damage interferes with Tenant's reasonable use of Premises. If damage occurs as a result of an act of Tenant or Tenant's guests, only Landlord shall have the right of termination, and no reduction in Rent shall be made.

(39) 33. **INSURANCE:** Tenant's or guest's personal property and vehicles are not insured by Landlord, manager or, if applicable, HOA, against loss or damage due to fire, theft, vandalism, rain, water, criminal or negligent acts of others, or any other cause. **Tenant**

Tenant's Initials   (_____)(_____)
Landlord's Initials (_____)(_____)

LR REVISED 11/08 (PAGE 4 OF 6)

| Reviewed by _____ Date _____ |

RESIDENTIAL LEASE OR MONTH-TO-MONTH RENTAL AGREEMENT (LR PAGE 4 OF 6)

FIGURE 13.4 (*Continued*).

Premises: _____ Date: _____

is advised to carry Tenant's own insurance (renter's insurance) to protect Tenant from any such loss or damage. Tenant shall comply with any requirement imposed on Tenant by Landlord's insurer to avoid: **(i)** an increase in Landlord's insurance premium (or Tenant shall pay for the increase in premium); or **(ii)** loss of insurance.

(40) 34. **WATERBEDS:** Tenant shall not use or have waterbeds on the Premises unless: **(i)** Tenant obtains a valid waterbed insurance policy; **(ii)** Tenant increases the security deposit in an amount equal to one-half of one month's Rent; and **(iii)** the bed conforms to the floor load capacity of Premises.

(41) 35. **WAIVER:** The waiver of any breach shall not be construed as a continuing waiver of the same or any subsequent breach.

36. **NOTICE:** Notices may be served at the following address, or at any other location subsequently designated:
Landlord: _____ Tenant: _____

(42)(43)(44) _____ _____
_____ _____

(45) 37. **TENANT ESTOPPEL CERTIFICATE:** Tenant shall execute and return a tenant estoppel certificate delivered to Tenant by Landlord or Landlord's agent within 3 days after its receipt. Failure to comply with this requirement shall be deemed Tenant's acknowledgment that the tenant estoppel certificate is true and correct, and may be relied upon by a lender or purchaser.

(46) 38. **TENANT REPRESENTATIONS; CREDIT:** Tenant warrants that all statements in Tenant's rental application are accurate. Tenant authorizes Landlord and Broker(s) to obtain Tenant's credit report periodically during the tenancy in connection with the modification or enforcement of this Agreement. Landlord may cancel this Agreement: **(i)** before occupancy begins; **(ii)** upon disapproval of the credit report(s); or **(iii)** at any time, upon discovering that information in Tenant's application is false. A negative credit report reflecting on Tenant's record may be submitted to a credit reporting agency if Tenant fails to fulfill the terms of payment and other obligations under this Agreement.

39. **MEDIATION:**
A. Consistent with paragraphs B and C below, Landlord and Tenant agree to mediate any dispute or claim arising between them out of this Agreement, or any resulting transaction, before resorting to court action. Mediation fees, if any, shall be divided equally among the parties involved. If, for any dispute or claim to which this paragraph applies, any party commences an action without first attempting to resolve the matter through mediation, or refuses to mediate after a request has been made, then that party shall not be entitled to recover attorney fees, even if they would otherwise be available to that party in any such action.

(47) **B.** The following matters are excluded from mediation: **(i)** an unlawful detainer action; **(ii)** the filing or enforcement of a mechanic's lien; and **(iii)** any matter within the jurisdiction of a probate, small claims or bankruptcy court. The filing of a court action to enable the recording of a notice of pending action, for order of attachment, receivership, injunction, or other provisional remedies, shall not constitute a waiver of the mediation provision.

C. Landlord and Tenant agree to mediate disputes or claims involving Listing Agent, Leasing Agent or property manager ("Broker"), provided Broker shall have agreed to such mediation prior to, or within a reasonable time after, the dispute or claim is presented to such Broker. Any election by Broker to participate in mediation shall not result in Broker being deemed a party to this Agreement.

(48) 40. **ATTORNEY FEES:** In any action or proceeding arising out of this Agreement, the prevailing party between Landlord and Tenant shall be entitled to reasonable attorney fees and costs, except as provided in paragraph 39A.

41. **C.A.R. FORM:** C.A.R. Form means the specific form referenced or another comparable from agreed to by the parties.

42. **OTHER TERMS AND CONDITIONS;SUPPLEMENTS:** ☐ Interpreter/Translator Agreement (C.A.R. Form ITA);
☐ Keysafe/Lockbox Addendum (C.A.R. Form KLA); ☐ Lead-Based Paint and Lead-Based Paint Hazards Disclosure (C.A.R. Form FLD)

(49) _____
_____
_____

The following ATTACHED supplements are incorporated in this Agreement: _____
_____
_____

43. **TIME OF ESSENCE; ENTIRE CONTRACT; CHANGES:** Time is of the essence. All understandings between the parties are incorporated in this Agreement. Its terms are intended by the parties as a final, complete and exclusive expression of their Agreement with respect to its subject matter, and may not be contradicted by evidence of any prior agreement or contemporaneous oral agreement.

(50) If any provision of this Agreement is held to be ineffective or invalid, the remaining provisions will nevertheless be given full force and effect. Neither this Agreement nor any provision in it may be extended, amended, modified, altered or changed except in writing. This Agreement is subject to California landlord-tenant law and shall incorporate all changes required by amendment or successors to such law. This Agreement and any supplement, addendum or modification, including any copy, may be signed in two or more counterparts, all of which shall constitute one and the same writing.

44. **AGENCY:**
(51) **A.** **CONFIRMATION:** The following agency relationship(s) are hereby confirmed for this transaction:
Listing Agent: (Print firm name) _____ is the agent of (check one): ☐ the Landlord exclusively; or ☐ both the Landlord and Tenant.
Leasing Agent: (Print firm name) _____ (if not same as Listing Agent) is the agent of (check one): ☐ the Tenant exclusively; or ☐ the Landlord exclusively; or ☐ both the Tenant and Landlord.
B. **DISCLOSURE:** ☐ (If checked): The term of this lease exceeds one year. A disclosure regarding real estate agency relationships (C.A.R. Form AD) has been provided to Landlord and Tenant, who each acknowledge its receipt.

45. ☐ **TENANT COMPENSATION TO BROKER:** Upon execution of this Agreement, Tenant agrees to pay compensation to Broker as specified in a separate written agreement between Tenant and Broker.

Tenant's Initials (_____)(_____)
Landlord's Initials (_____)(_____)

LR REVISED 11/08 (PAGE 5 OF 6)

Reviewed by _____ Date _____

EQUAL HOUSING
OPPORTUNITY

RESIDENTIAL LEASE OR MONTH-TO-MONTH RENTAL AGREEMENT (LR PAGE 5 OF 6)

FIGURE 13.4 (*Continued*).

Premises: _____ Date: _____

52 **46.** ☐ **INTERPRETER/TRANSLATOR:** The terms of this Agreement have been interpreted for Tenant into the following language: _____. Landlord and Tenant acknowledge receipt of the attached interpretor/translator agreement (C.A.R. Form ITA).

47. **FOREIGN LANGUAGE NEGOTIATION:** If this Agreement has been negotiated by Landlord and Tenant primarily in Spanish, Chinese, Tagalog, Korean or Vietnamese, pursuant to the California Civil Code, Tenant shall be provided a translation of this Agreement in the language used for the negotiation.

48. **OWNER COMPENSATION TO BROKER:** Upon execution of this Agreement, Owner agrees to pay compensation to Broker as specified in a separate written agreement between Owner and Broker (C.A.R. Form LCA).

49. **RECEIPT:** If specified in paragraph 5, Landlord or Broker, acknowledges receipt of move-in funds.

53 Landlord and Tenant acknowledge and agree Brokers: **(a)** do not guarantee the condition of the Premises; **(b)** cannot verify representations made by others; **(c)** cannot provide legal or tax advice; **(d)** will not provide other advice or information that exceeds the knowledge, education or experience required to obtain a real estate license. Furthermore, if Brokers are not also acting as Landlord in this Agreement, Brokers: **(e)** do not decide what rental rate a Tenant should pay or Landlord should accept; and **(f)** do not decide upon the length or other terms of tenancy. Landlord and Tenant agree that they will seek legal, tax, insurance and other desired assistance from appropriate professionals.

Tenant agrees to rent the Premises on the above terms and conditions.

Tenant **54 55** _____ Date _____
Address _____ City _____ State _____ Zip _____
Telephone _____ Fax _____ E-mail _____

Tenant _____ Date _____
Address _____ City _____ State _____ Zip _____
Telephone _____ Fax _____ E-mail _____

☐ **GUARANTEE:** In consideration of the execution of this Agreement by and between Landlord and Tenant and for valuable consideration, receipt of which is hereby acknowledged, the undersigned ("Guarantor") does hereby: **(i)** guarantee unconditionally to Landlord and Landlord's agents, successors and assigns, the prompt payment of Rent or other sums that become due pursuant to this Agreement, including any and all court costs and attorney fees included in enforcing the Agreement; **(ii)** consent to any changes, modifications or alterations of any term in this Agreement agreed to by Landlord and Tenant; and **(iii)** waive any right to require Landlord and/or Landlord's agents to proceed against Tenant for any default occurring under this Agreement before seeking to enforce this Guarantee.

56

Guarantor (Print Name) _____
Guarantor _____ Date _____
Address _____ City _____ State _____ Zip _____
Telephone _____ Fax _____ E-mail _____

Landlord agrees to rent the Premises on the above terms and conditions.

Landlord _____ Landlord _____

Address _____

Telephone _____ Fax _____ E-mail _____

REAL ESTATE BROKERS:
A. Real estate brokers who are not also Landlord under this Agreement are not parties to the Agreement between Landlord and Tenant.
B. Agency relationships are confirmed in paragraph 44.
C. **COOPERATING BROKER COMPENSATION:** Listing Broker agrees to pay Cooperating Broker (Leasing Firm) and Cooperating Broker agrees to accept: **(i)** the amount specified in the MLS, provided Cooperating Broker is a Participant of the MLS in which the Property is offered for sale or a reciprocal MLS; or **(ii)** ☐ (if checked) the amount specified in a separate written agreement between Listing Broker and Cooperating Broker.

Real Estate Broker (Listing Firm) _____ DRE Lic. # _____
By (Agent) _____ DRE Lic. # _____ Date _____
Address _____ City _____ State _____ Zip _____
Telephone _____ Fax _____ E-mail _____

Real Estate Broker (Leasing Firm) _____ DRE Lic. # _____
By (Agent) _____ DRE Lic. # _____ Date _____
Address _____ City _____ State _____ Zip _____
Telephone _____ Fax _____ E-mail _____

THIS FORM HAS BEEN APPROVED BY THE CALIFORNIA ASSOCIATION OF REALTORS® (C.A.R.). NO REPRESENTATION IS MADE AS TO THE LEGAL VALIDITY OR ADEQUACY OF ANY PROVISION IN ANY SPECIFIC TRANSACTION. A REAL ESTATE BROKER IS THE PERSON QUALIFIED TO ADVISE ON REAL ESTATE TRANSACTIONS. IF YOU DESIRE LEGAL OR TAX ADVICE, CONSULT AN APPROPRIATE PROFESSIONAL.

This form is available for use by the entire real estate industry. It is not intended to identify the user as a REALTOR®. REALTOR® is a registered collective membership mark which may be used only by members of the NATIONAL ASSOCIATION OF REALTORS® who subscribe to its Code of Ethics.

Published and Distributed by:
REAL ESTATE BUSINESS SERVICES, INC.
a subsidiary of the California Association of REALTORS®
525 South Virgil Avenue, Los Angeles, California 90020

LR REVISED 11/08 (PAGE 6 OF 6)

Reviewed by _____ Date _____

EQUAL HOUSING OPPORTUNITY

RESIDENTIAL LEASE OR MONTH-TO-MONTH RENTAL AGREEMENT (LR PAGE 6 OF 6)

Source: Reprinted with permission. California Association of REALTORS®. Endorsement not implied.

AIEA Commercial Lease

The most commonly used commercial lease form in California is the American Industrial Real Estate Association (**AIREA**) lease form. However, many large corporations have their own forms, and many businesses and property owners have custom lease forms drawn up by their own attorneys. Shopping centers frequently have attorneys draft special leases for their use. Still, because of the high cost of drafting lease forms, the AIREA form seems to be the most commonly used commercial lease form in California.

Most industrial leases are either *net* or *gross* leases, or a variation of one of those leases. Simply stated, a gross lease means the tenant pays one flat sum as rent, and the landlord pays all expenses. In a net lease, the tenant pays a base rent plus a percentage of the operating expenses and taxes on the property. A common variation of the net lease is the so-called "net, net, net" or "triple net" lease. Here the tenant traditionally pays a base rent, plus the costs of maintenance and repairs, taxes and insurance on the building. However, these terms are not legal terms, the types of leases vary considerably, and one cannot always rely on the name given to the lease.

CAR Lease Analyzed

For simplicity, this book uses the CAR residential lease form as a guide to analyze the provisions frequently encountered in residential leases. Certain self-explanatory clauses not worthy of review will be ignored. Conversely, frequently encountered clauses not found in the CAR form are discussed. The numbers preceding each heading correspond to the circled numbers on the lease agreement.

ANALYSIS OF A LEASE

(1) Lease and Demise

The lease has a dual character in law. It is both a **conveyance** of an estate in land and a contract for the possession of property in consideration of rent. Therefore, the courts have applied both the rigid property law concept and the liberal contract construction when interpreting the lease provisions. Clearly, contract analysis, with its more modern and reasonable rules, emerges as the dominant trend in today's courts and in recent legislation.

(2) List of Occupants

As a general rule, anyone not listed on the lease or occupying the premises as a subtenant has no obligation to pay rent. Furthermore, restricting the occupancy gives the landlord more control over the premises and makes it easier to serve everyone an eviction.

(3) Term

Depending on which box is checked, the tenancy shall be month to month or for a fixed term. If the tenancy is for a set term and the tenant remains (holds over) after the term, the tenancy shall be a month-to-month tenancy at the same terms.

(4) Rent Payment

Rent is the consideration for the lease. It should be carefully detailed in clause 3 of the CAR lease. This lease form states that rent is due and payable in advance on the first of each month or other appropriate period. Absent such a provision, rent is ordinarily due at the end of the lease period. *C.C. 1947.* By checking the Installment option, the total rent for the entire period of the tenancy is included. Thus, in a one-year lease at $1,000 per month, the total rent would be $12,000.

Nonapportionable

Additionally, rent is nonapportionable. The entire sum is due on the first day of each month rather than accruing on a daily basis. Without a specific provision in the lease or a wrongful termination by the landlord, the tenant is not entitled to a partial refund of rent by vacating before the end of the term. *Friedman v. Isenbruck (1952) 111 C.A.2d 335.*

Rent Controls

Normally, a landlord may charge whatever rent the market permits. However, rent control laws may limit and control the amount of rents and frequency of rent increases. At the federal level, rent controls arose during and after World War II and again in 1971 under President Nixon and the Economic Stabilization Act of 1970. Fourteen California communities enacted rent control ordinances following termination of the federal act. In 1976, the California Supreme Court upheld the validity of rent control laws. Since then, those cities and counties that have adopted rent control ordinances follow one of two types. The first type restricts the amount of increases during occupancy and even when the property is vacant. The second type only restricts rental increases during a tenancy and allows the landlord to raise the rent to any amount during a vacancy. Most local ordinances also restrict a landlord's right to evict a tenant to the criteria stated in the legislation. Anyone owing or renting property in a city or county that has a rent control ordinance and that covers the type of unit involved needs to comply with these laws.

Statewide Rent Control Limitations

In compromise legislation between tenant groups and landlord associations, California adopted statewide limits on residential rent control. (The law is known as the Costa–Hawkins Rental Housing Act and is found in *C.C. 1954.50 et seq.*) In those 14 cities and counties that have rent control, some units will be protected by local rental control ordinances and others will be covered by the statewide rent control law. Since January 1, 1999, the statewide law has prevented any local rent controls from applying to *covered* units.

Covered Units

Except for leases entered into before 1996, there are no longer any rent controls on single-family residences and individual condominiums. For other units, such as apartments, there are rent "vacancy decontrols." In other words, in cases where the tenant vacates an apartment voluntarily or is evicted for nonpayment of rent, the unit becomes lawfully vacant. On such units, the landlord can charge the new tenant any amount of rent. Units that are not lawfully vacant remain under rent control. Therefore, existing tenants who remain in their apartments after January 1, 1999, remain under local ordinances.

Other Exemptions

The statewide rent control statute governs what units can be subject to controls on *rents*. It places no restrictions on that part of local ordinances that provides *eviction protection*. Publicly assisted housing is exempt from all phases of local rent control ordinances. Certain designated subleases, assignments, and specified substandard rentals with long-standing deficiencies are exempt from rent control. Cities without rent control cannot adopt rent control ordinances. Finally, with some limited exceptions, commercial property is exempt from all local rent controls. *C.C. 1954.27.*

(5) Advance Deposits

Technically, there are several types of deposits, each with a different purpose. The classification of the deposit determines its purpose. Thus, a cleaning deposit may not be used by the landlord as and for a security deposit. There are four traditional types of deposits.

Bonus Deposit

This deposit is actually a fee given by the tenant in consideration of and for the execution of the lease by the landlord. Upon signing the lease, the landlord has earned the fee, unless the landlord later breaches the lease. This deposit seldom appears on modern lease forms, except for rare situations where demand for housing far exceeds available supply.

Security Deposit

These funds are held by the landlord as a deposit to ensure faithful performance by the tenant of the terms of the lease. Traditionally, the **security deposit** could be offset to secure the breach of *any* term, covenant, or condition of the lease. However, recent statutory language has limited this deposit in both residential and commercial leases to secure only defaults in the payment of rent, repair for damages to the premises caused by the tenant, and cleaning the premises when the tenant leaves. The lease must specifically provide that the deposit can be used for rental defaults, repairs, or cleaning. *C.C. 1950.5e, 1950.7c.* Presumably, therefore, the security may not be used for any other purpose, although the landlord could certainly seek judicial recovery for damages sustained from the breach of any other term in the lease.

Cleaning Deposit

The cleaning deposit is a fund to cover the landlord's cost of cleaning the premises after the tenant vacates.

Last Month's Rent

This sum is a prepayment of the last month's rent, to be held by the landlord and applied toward or as the last month's rent.

(6) Amounts of Advance Deposits

Before January 1, 1978, there was no restriction on the amount of advance deposits required, if any, or their designation. The landlord generally accepted the maximum deposit the market would bear and classified that deposit in the manner deemed most advantageous. After 1978, statutes limited the amount of deposits that could be collected in residential tenancies.

Residential Limits

The law limits the amount a landlord can collect as an advance deposit for the rental of residential property that will be actually occupied by the tenant. All advance payments, which specifically include prepaid rent, cleaning deposits, and security deposits, cannot cumulatively exceed two months' rent for unfurnished residential property or three months' rent for furnished units. *C.C. 1950.5c.*

Exceptions

Three exceptions are recognized to the monetary limitations. First, in leases over six months, a special exemption may be available. The second exception provides that, if the tenant requests and the landlord agrees, a specified fee or charge may be imposed for structural, decorative, furnishing, or other similar alterations to the unit, provided the sum is not for cleaning or repairing, for which the landlord may charge the previous tenant. *C.C. 1950.5c.*

Screening Fees

As another exception to the total amount of charges a tenant may face, landlord is allowed to charge a fee to screen prospective tenants. Such fees cannot exceed $30 and typically cover the cost of a credit report or other verification form. *C.C. 1950.6.* Any landlord performing a credit check, should know there are certain obligations imposed when the reports suggest an identify theft issue could be involved. *C.C. 1985.20.3.*

Nonresidential Leases Unrestricted

The preceding limitations apply only to residential property occupied by the tenant. All other leases are totally unrestricted in amount and classification of deposits.

(7) Refund of Advance Deposits

As a general rule, the landlord must promptly refund any unused security or cleaning deposit or be liable for specified penalties. The landlord can retain only that amount of the deposit reasonably necessary to compensate for defaults in the payment of rents, repairing damages caused by the tenant, or cleaning the premises. In residential and commercial leases, the sum deducted for cleaning cannot include deductions for ordinary wear and tear. *C.C. 1950.5e, 1950.7.*

Time Limits and Wording

Within three weeks after the tenant vacates the premises, the landlord must return to the tenant any unused portions of the cleaning and security deposits along with an itemized statement showing the amount of and the reasons for any sums retained by the landlord. In commercial leases, if the lease permits, return of any unused deposit can be extended for up to 30 days if part of the deposit was retained by the landlord for damages. Since 2004, the list must be supported by copies of invoices, receipts, or other documents substantiating the actual payment by the landlord (unless the total deductions are less than $125). *C.C. 1950.5(g)(4).* Any bad-faith retention by the landlord can subject him to a penalty of up to 200% of the amount of the security deposit plus any actual damages suffered by the tenant. *C.C. 1950.5k*. Additionally, it is unlawful for residential leases even to state that a security deposit is nonrefundable.

The Supreme Court increased the penalty for landlords who in bad faith withhold the deposit. They lose their right to withhold damages from the tenant's deposit. Instead, such landlords must return the tenant's entire deposit and sue in a separate action for any damages suffered. *Granberry v. Islay Investments (1995) 9 C.4th 738.*

(8) Interest on Deposit

No state law requires the landlord to pay interest on the deposits. A few local communities have ordinances that require the landlord to credit part of the interest to the tenant. This clause provides that the deposit shall not earn interest unless required by local ordinance.

(9) Management of Advance Deposits

The security deposits are held by the landlord for the benefit of the tenant; therefore, the tenant has priority over any creditors of the landlord except a trustee in bankruptcy. In residential leases, the tenant's claim shall have priority even over a trustee's claim. *C.C. 1950.5d*. However, no definitive cases seem to have resolved the issue of whether a landlord may commingle the deposit with personal funds. *22 Hastings L.J. 1373,1379–1381.*

The CAR lease clause 4E focuses mostly on holding the broker not responsible for return of the deposit when it is under the control of the owner.

(10) Late Charges

Late charges on rent are upheld if the amount charged is reasonable and related to the administrative costs and loss of interest on the funds. What amount is reasonable can only be determined by the facts of a case at the time of trial. Consequently, many attorneys, including the author, ignore late charges in an eviction procedure unless those charges are minor. Otherwise, if the courts find the amount unreasonable, they are disallowed. If disallowed, then the landlord asked too much in the three-day notice and complaint, and the entire unlawful detainer action is invalid. This clause sets a $25 fee for a "bounced check" plus an additional sum specified in the lease if the rent is late.

(11) Parking

This clause designates whether the tenant shall have parking and, if so, it is included in the base rent or at an extra cost. Finally, it defines the tenant's responsibilities in using the parking spaces.

(12) Storage

Some apartment complexes provide storage areas for the tenants. If storage facilities are provided, this clause defines the rights and costs of such storage. The clause defines the type of goods that can be stored in such facilities, which is helpful in the event the tenant violates the provisions and causes damages.

(13) Utilities

In residential buildings, the landlord has a duty to ensure that the property is habitable for human occupation, which includes the availability of basic utilities. However, the landlord is not obligated to pay for these utilities. Because many utilities are master metered, the landlord pays the bill and seeks reimbursement from the tenant. In commercial property, the tenant sometimes has the obligation to provide and bring in utilities, as well as pay the monthly costs. Utilities are freely negotiable in commercial leases.

In those situations in which the tenant's premises are not separately metered, the landlord must provide the written notification of how the utility bills for that unit will be calculated. *C.C. 1940.9.*

Where the utilities are separately metered, the utilities can only charge the tenant if the utilities bill is unpaid. They may not seek payment from the landlord or future tenants. *Pub. Util.C. 10009.6.*

(14) Condition of Premises

The tenant needs to inspect and enumerate any defects in the premises carefully. Otherwise, on vacancy, the tenant can be charged for the condition of the premises over and above normal wear and tear. Too often furniture, fixtures, and premises in previously poor condition are charged to the tenant, because the tenant failed to note the damage to the premises at the beginning of the tenancy. Unless the tenant can prove the initial condition of the premises, it may be difficult to defend against claims by the landlord.

If the premises are in good condition, it is helpful for the landlord to have documented evidence to that fact. Otherwise, if the tenant is evicted, the tenant could try to raise an affirmative defense of substandard premises. If the tenant signed a document verifying the condition of the premises, it becomes far harder for the tenant to claim a violation of the **warranty of habitability**.

(15) Maintenance and Fitness (Habitability)

Under ancient law, a landlord generally assumed no obligations or warranties as to the condition of the premises, their fitness for use, or their repair and maintenance. It was strictly caveat emptor, with the tenant assuming all the risk and, absent fraud, accepting the premises as is. However, modern statutes and case law have divided leases into two categories and created separate duties for residential and commercial property.

Commercial Property

Absent fraud, a landlord has almost no noncontractual obligations regarding the fitness of commercial property. As to such premises, the old law of caveat emptor prevails. The landlord has no duty to make the property fit for the tenant's intended purpose or to repair and maintain the premises. *Glenn R. Sewell Sheet Metal, Inc. v. Loverde (1969) 70 C.2d 666.* The landlord's only obligation remains for premises (1) for which the landlord maintains control (e.g., common hallways); (2) that violate building codes or other government ordinances and for which the tenant has not contractually assumed the obligation; or (3) for which the landlord has contractually assumed the obligation by a provision in the lease.

Residential Property

The second category of property is residential premises. Because of the public policy needs of a community to provide adequate housing for its residents, special implied warranties (by statute and case law) impose duties of fitness and repair on the landlord.

Statutory Duty of Habitability

The Civil Code (sections 1941 et seq.) imposes a statutory duty of habitability, requiring the landlord to maintain and repair *residential* property. If the property is uninhabitable (as defined in *C.C. 1941.1*), then the tenant may deduct up to one month's rent to repair the deficiencies if the:

1. Tenant has not contributed substantially to the uninhabitable condition.
2. Tenant has not used this remedy more than twice within the last 12 months.

3. Landlord has been given reasonable notice and opportunity to repair the deficiencies. The amount of advance notice varies with the circumstances, although 30 days is presumed reasonable in all cases.

Any attempted waiver of the tenant's statutory rights by a provision in the lease is void as against public policy, although its requirements may be effectively circumvented by a provision requiring the tenant to maintain and repair the premises as part of the consideration for the lease.

Common Law Duty of Habitability

In addition to the above statutory duty, there is a nonwaivable common law warranty of habitability in all *residential* leases. *Green v. Superior Court (1974) 10 C.3d 616.* The statutory warranty was legislation born of compromise between tenant groups, landlord associations, and Realtors®; for that reason, it is weak and narrow in scope. The common law warranty, conversely, was created by the courts and is a strong, effective warranty.

The exact parameters of habitability have not yet been established by the courts. The *Green* case defined uninhabitable dwellings as those not in "substantial compliance with those applicable buildings and house code standards that materially affect health and safety." Later cases have held that if a building fails to meet standards enumerated in the statutory duty, even if the tenant does not use the "repair and deduct remedy," the property is uninhabitable. *Knight v. Hallsthammer (1981) 29 C.23d 46, 58.* One case even held that failure to provide security guards pursuant to a rental agreement was a breach of the implied warranty of habitability. *Secretary of Housing & Urban Dev. v. Layfield (1979) 88 C.A.3d Supp. 28.*

Although a tenant may not vacate the premises for a violation, he may raise this issue as a defense to an unlawful detainer action, or he may use it as an offset to the amount of rent claimed by the landlord. Damages for breach of common law warranty are calculated at trial by the somewhat nebulous determination of the difference between the fair market value of the premises (defined as contract rent) and the value of the premises as provided with the defects. The warranty cannot be waived by the tenant's continued living in the uninhabitable premises or by the tenant being unaware of the uninhabitable condition before moving in. The breach cannot be waived even if the landlord has not had a reasonable opportunity to repair the condition. Thus, a new owner buying the property immediately becomes subject to any claims existing against the previous owner. *Knight v. Hallsthamner (1981) 29 C.3d 46.*

If the court finds the landlord has not substantially complied with building and housing code standards that materially affect health and safety, the tenant will win. If the tenant pays the overdue rent determined by the court within five days, the lease continues with the tenant in possession as if no breach had occurred. If payment made by the tenant is not timely, the landlord can recover possession of the premises. *C.C. 1174.2.*

Additional Protection for Residential Property

If the premises are uninhabitable, it is unlawful for a landlord to collect or demand rent. A violation makes a landlord liable for all the tenant's damages and attorney's fees, plus punitive damages not to exceed $5,000. *C.C. 1942.4.* Furthermore, if a tenant raises the warranty of habitability defense in an unlawful detainer action, at time of trial the premises will be presumed to be uninhabitable. By shifting the burden to the landlord, the tenant will find it much easier to win.

In both the above situations, the premises will be deemed uninhabitable, if either (1) the premises violate the provisions of the Civil Code or (2) the landlord has taken over 60 days, without good cause, to correct any written deficiencies noted by a public housing official and not caused by the tenant. *C.C. 1942.3.*

Alternative Protection

A new and powerful approach for tenants of substandard residential dwellings, which is just beginning to be selectively enforced in a few cities throughout the state, is a tax code provision. On proper application to the district attorney, owners of those dwellings will not be allowed to claim interest deductions, depreciation, taxes, or amortization expenses for state income tax purposes. *R.&T.C. 24436.5.* Finally, tenants can have a receiver appointed by the court to take possession of the management and rents from the property and to make improvements at the landlord's expense. *H.&S.C. 17980.7.*

(16) Retaliatory Eviction

In residential leases, if a landlord significantly increases rent, changes the lease, or evicts a tenant merely because the tenant exercised rights of fitness and habitability or complained to a governmental agency about the dwelling's habitability, the eviction is void and illegal. *C.C. 1942.5.* The court can award the tenant damages up to $2,000 for **retaliatory eviction**. The residential tenant is protected only if rent is current and warranty has not been used within the last year. Furthermore, the protection is good only for six months. The landlord may safely raise the rent after six months without consequences. The landlord can even serve a 30-day notice of termination within the 180-day period as long as the effective date of the change or termination is after the six-month period.

In commercial leases, there are no statutory restrictions against retaliatory eviction except for constitutionally prohibited discrimination, such as race or religion.

(17) Neighborhood Conditions

Tenants have filed lawsuits alleging that they were unaware of the condition of the neighborhood, the crime rate, nearness of government facilities, and nuisances from noise and odors. This clause attempts to help insulate the landlord by shifting the responsibility to the tenant. How effective such a clause would be in court is questionable. It might help on some issues that the tenant is clearly responsible for investigating. Others, such as a vicious animal on the premises or a rape in the garage would be a question of fact. This clause would probably offer little protection to the landlord.

(18) Pets

Normally, a landlord can restrict or prohibit tenants from having pets or may charge an additional fee for those pets. Only federally subsidized housing for the elderly requires a landlord to allow pets. A landlord cannot prohibit guide dogs for the blind and certain other pets for handicapped individuals.

(19) Rules and Regulations

This clause attempts to regulate the tenant's conduct. In large complexes and other buildings with rules, the tenant must follow those document requirements. The clause also adds that the tenant shall act lawfully, prudently, and constructively toward the unit and any other tenants. Although the lease speaks only in terms of the tenant's obligations, the landlord owes the tenant certain implied-in-law obligations of undisturbed possession. If the landlord unreasonably interferes with the tenant's peaceful possession, the tenant may treat the landlord's acts as a breach of the covenant of quiet enjoyment, which amounts to an eviction.

(20) Condominium and Planned Unit Development

If this box is checked, then the premises are part of a condominium and planned unit development. The tenant agrees to abide by their rules and regulations and to reimburse the landlord for any fines or costs imposed because of a violation of their rules and regulations.

(21) Alterations

The tenant is forbidden to make alterations without prior written consent. The list of prohibited alterations includes painting, changing the locks, adding television reception equipment, or attaching fixtures.

(22) Keys and Locks

This paragraph designates the number of keys the tenant receives and is responsible for returning. It also informs the tenant if the locks have been rekeyed after the previous tenant vacated. The tenant has the right to rekey the locks but must promptly provide the landlord with copies and pay any costs of retooling the locks.

(23) Covenant of Quiet Enjoyment

Every lease is an implied covenant of quiet enjoyment. *C.C. 1927.* This warranty of peaceful possession applies only to the landlord and offers no defense against strangers or other tenants. A breach of this covenant constitutes either an actual or a constructive eviction. An actual eviction occurs when the tenant is physically removed or ousted from all or part of the premises by the landlord or someone with paramount title. A constructive eviction results from a substantial interference with the tenant's beneficial use and enjoyment of all or part of the premises to such an extent as to render them unfit or unsuited for the tenant's use. Examples of constructive evictions include harassment of the tenant, extensive and unwarranted repairs, and the landlord's failure to make vitally necessary repairs.

Remedies

Constructive eviction, unlike actual eviction, requires the tenant to vacate the premises within a reasonable time or be deemed to have waived the breach. When there is a total eviction, the tenant may abandon the premises, surrendering possession thereof to the landlord, and thereby terminate all obligation for rent. A partial eviction permits the tenant to use the premises rent free during the period of the ouster on the theory that the landlord cannot apportion the wrong. *Giraud v. Milvich (1938) 29 C.A.2d 543.*

(24) Entry

In a residential lease, a landlord has only a very limited right of entry into a tenant's premises, *C.C. 1954,* which rights may not be waived. The landlord may enter dwellings only for an emergency (such as a fire), to make necessary or agreed repairs, to show the premises to a prospective tenant or purchaser, after an abandonment by tenant, or by court order and for no other purposes. Additionally, entry for repairs can be made only during the normal daylight working hours unless the tenant consents at the time of entry. Furthermore, this entry must generally be preceded by reasonable notice, which in all cases is presumed to be a minimum of 24 hours. Finally, the landlord may not abuse the right of access or use it to harass tenants. Entry in commercial leases usually depends on the rights granted in the lease.

(25) Right of Reentry

The CAR lease does not contain the so-called *self-help* clause common to some older lease forms. This clause provides that the landlord can reenter and take possession of the premises upon default, but it is now void as against public policy. Any such entry would be an unlawful entry and detainer. The landlord would be liable for all damages caused by a wrongful eviction. *Jordan v. Talbot (1961) 55 C.2d 597.* Such acts are also a misdemeanor. *Penal C. 418.*

Broadly Interpreted

Forcible entry and unlawful detainer include the obvious situations where a landlord changes the locks on a door or hires thugs to threaten the tenant, as well as less obvious attempts to remove the tenant. In certain instances, heavy fines may be involved. A landlord who intentionally turns off a tenant's utilities, changes the locks on the door, or unlawfully removes a tenant's personal property is liable for damages, including the tenant's attorney's fees plus $100 per day in punitive damages. *C.C. 789.3.*

(26) Signs

The tenant grants the landlord permission to place For Rent signs on the premises.

(27) Assignment and Sublease

Assignments and subleases have significant differences, especially as to the remaining liability of the tenant.

Nature of Assignment and Sublease

An assignment occurs when the tenant transfers the entire interest in the property. Any lesser transfer leaves that tenant with a right of reentry on breach and is a sublease. If Ted has six years left on a 5,000-square-foot lease, and he transfers the premises for five years, Ted creates a sublease. Similarly, if Ted transfers 4,000 square feet for six years, a sublease arises.

Liability under Assignment

Under an assignment, the assignee pays rent directly to the landlord. Tenants commonly and incorrectly believe that, once they assign the lease, they have no further liability. The original tenant remains fully liable for the rent and other obligations not performed by the new assignee. This rule holds true even if the landlord consents to the assignment and the assignee agrees to assume the lease obligations. *Peiser v. Mettler (1958) 50 C.2d 594.*

Liability under Sublease

In a sublease, the new tenant pays rent directly to the original tenant, who then makes payment directly to the landlord. The original tenant remains primarily liable for the rent and other lease obligations.

(28) Right to Assign and Sublease

Restrictions on assignments and subleases can differ between residential and commercial leases. Commercial leases are governed by comprehensive requirements specified in the statutes. *C.C. 1995.010–1995.340.* The basic rules are noted subsequently. If the lease absolutely prohibits transfer or only allows it with the landlord's consent, which can be unreasonably withheld, there is a special rule if the tenant breaches the lease. The landlord cannot use the "continuation of a lease" remedy (discussed in paragraph 23).

Lease Silent or Allows

If the lease is silent on the subject, the tenant may assign or sublease at will and without the landlord's consent. Any clauses restricting assignment or sublease are strictly construed against the landlord. Thus, a clause restricting assignment would not prohibit sublease.

Absolute Prohibition

Landlords can absolutely prohibit all assignments and subleases. Most residential leases, like the CAR lease, completely prohibit all transfers. Few commercial leases contain such an absolute ban.

Transfer if Landlord Consents

Most commercial leases allow a transfer only with the landlord's prior consent. If there is no requirement on the type of consent required, then the landlord cannot unreasonably withhold such consent. Landlords may be arbitrary and unreasonable in withholding or granting consent, provided the lease reserves such rights to the landlord.

The courts might require the landlord to act in good faith. Based on this uncertainty, most leases specify reasonable standards that must be met before a transfer. Many such leases also contain a provision giving the landlord some or all of any rental increases resulting from the assignment or sublease. Generally, most clauses granting the landlord right to rental increases are valid unless found excessive and unconscionable. *Ilkhchooyi v. Best (1995) 37 C.A.4th 395.* However, in such situations, for the clause to be valid in commercial leases, the lease itself must "clearly state" the amount to be charged. *C.C. 1950.8.*

(29) Joint and Individual Obligations

When there is more than one tenant, each is jointly and individually liable for the *entire* amount of the rent and any other obligations under the lease. Assume Ted and Bob are tenants and default on the lease, incurring a $5,000 obligation. The landlord can sue either Ted or Bob or both for the $5,000. If the landlord obtains a $5,000 judgment against Ted and Bob, the landlord can collect the full $5,000 against just Ted. Ted would then have to bring a separate lawsuit against Bob for reimbursement ("contribution") for Bob's $2,500 half of the obligation. Or, assume five people decide to rent an apartment, and, then one of the tenants leaves. Another tenant unofficially takes the departing tenant's place. The departed tenant is still liable under the lease. Tenants should carefully understand their rights when co-signing a lease.

(30) Various Disclosure Notices

Lead-based paint, military ordinance, and database disclosures are mandated by law if they are applicable to the property. Pest control notifies and obligates a tenant to cooperate with on-going pest control maintenance. The database concerns the so-called "Megan's Law" disclosure about proximity to the residences of registered sexual offenders.

Federal law requires the landlord to provide the tenant notice if the property was built before 1978. The notice includes a disclosure plus a booklet called the "Disclosure of Information on Lead-Based Paint and/or Lead-Based Paint Hazards." The tenant must acknowledge receiving both of these items. The warning statement, in part, provides that "Houses built before 1978 may contain lead-based paint. Lead from paint, paint chips, and dust can pose health hazards if not managed properly. Lead exposure is especially harmful to young children and pregnant women." *24 C.F.R. 35.88.*

(31) Possession

This clause deals with situations in which the landlord is unable to deliver possession of premises on the date that the lease is to commence. It states that the commencement date will just be extended until the landlord can offer the premises. After a five-day delay (or whatever number of days has been specified in the lease), the tenant has the option of terminating the lease.

From the tenant's perspective, the CAR lease makes no difference between circumstances beyond the landlord's control and those within its control. Furthermore, if the tenant must terminate the lease, all that the tenant receives is return of the prepaid rent and security deposits. There is no provision for damages.

(32) Tenant's Obligations upon Vacating Premises

The obligations upon vacating mostly reiterate existing laws and provide a helpful incentive to encourage and remind the tenant of his or her obligations. However, the clause does impose some additional provisions not required by code. The tenant is obligated to have carpets and drapes professionally cleaned, leave a forwarding address, and have all fixtures become the property of the landlord.

(33) Pre-Move Out Inspection

Landlords must give tenants a written notice that they have the right to request an initial inspection of their apartment before they move out. If the tenant requests such an inspection, they can be present, and it must be at least two weeks before the end of the tenancy. Then, the landlord must provide the tenant with an itemized list of deficiencies in the form required by the Civil Code. *C.C. 1950.5(b)*. In the words of the statute, the purpose of the inspection is to allow the tenant to "remedy identified deficiencies" so as "to avoid deductions from the security" deposit. *C.C. 1950.5(f)*. See Figure 13.5 for a copy of a notice advising the tenant of their pre-inspection rights.

(34) Breach of Contract and Early Termination
Landlord's Remedies upon Breach

If the tenant breaches the lease by failing to pay rent or otherwise to perform all the lease conditions, the landlord has two possible options: to terminate the lease, suing the tenant for damages; or, if the lease contains the appropriate clause, to continue the lease in effect, and sue the tenant for damages as they occur.

Termination of the Lease

If the tenant abandons the property while in violation of a lease provision or if the landlord ends the lease because of a breach by the tenant, the lease is automatically terminated. The landlord then sues the tenant for damages authorized by the Civil Code. *C.C. 1951.2*. The landlord receives one or more of four types of damages.

FIGURE 13.5 Tenant's right to pre-inspection.

Vacating Tenant's Right to Request an Initial Inspection

Dear Tenant:

Should you wish, you have the right to ask for an initial inspection of your rental property unit ("your premises") before your lease ends, including the right to be there at this initial inspection. If you so request, I or my agent will arrange this inspection at least two weeks before the end of your lease.

Such an inspection would notify you of what deficiencies are in the condition of your premises that would have to be corrected for you to receive a full refund of your security deposit. California Civil Code 1950.5 allows me to deduct for repair and cleaning that exceeds ordinary wear and tear, or as otherwise allowed in Civil Code 1950.5(b).

If you request an initial inspection, you may, but you need not be present. I will give you at least 48 hours' advance written notice of the time of the inspection, unless we otherwise agree in writing to an alternate, mutually convenient time. Following such an initial inspection, I will provide you with a list of deficiencies so you will have an opportunity to "remedy identified deficiencies, in a manner consistent with the rights and obligations of the parties under the rental agreement, in order to avoid deductions from the security" deposit. The itemized statement will also include a copy of Civil Code 1950.5(b) and (d), and it will be given to you immediately after the inspection. If you are not there, I will leave your copy on your premises.

If you want an initial inspection, so notify me in writing at my address at _____. You are not required to have an initial inspection. If I do not hear from you, you will have waived this inspection, and my duties under Civil Code 1950.5(f) are discharged.

Sincerely,

The landlord is first entitled to the unpaid rent due at the time of the termination, plus interest.

Second, the landlord may recover the amount of rent that accrues from the date of termination to the date of a court judgment, plus interest. That post-termination amount must be reduced by any sum that could have been avoided had the landlord acted reasonably to mitigate damages.

Third, if the lease contains a provision paraphrasing the wording of *C.C. 1951.2,* the landlord is also entitled to an additional measure of damages. Most leases now contain the specified wording, although the CAR lease form does not. The landlord is entitled to collect the total amount of rent that accrues from the date of a court judgment to the date that the lease would ordinarily expire, discounted to a present value, plus interest. That amount must be further reduced by any sums that the landlord could have avoided by reasonable efforts to mitigate damages. The discount rate applied is the one in effect for the Federal Reserve Bank in San Francisco at the time of the judgment, plus 1 percent.

Finally, the landlord is entitled to any other amounts necessary to compensate for damages proximately caused by the tenant's default and reasonably foreseeable at the time of the breach.

Continuation of the Lease

Under certain conditions, the landlord may elect not to terminate the lease or to collect damages as provided in the previous paragraphs. Rather, the landlord may keep the lease in full force and effect and collect rent from the tenant as it becomes due. *C.C. 1951.4.*

The landlord may use this election only if the lease contains an express covenant providing for continuation of the lease after the tenant's breach. The CAR lease does not contain such wording, although most other lease forms permit this election. Finally, this alternative may be used only if the lease provides the tenant with a reasonable right to assign or sublet the lease. Landlords almost never select this alternative.

Statutory Damages

In unlawful detainer actions where the tenant has intentionally and maliciously remained on the premises without paying or curing the default, the court has the optional and discretionary power to add an additional statutory award up to $600 as a punitive measure against the tenant. *C.C.P. 1175b.* Many judges are extremely reluctant to impose such a penalty. Small claims court awards are further limited in that any judgment cannot exceed the jurisdictional limit of $5,000.

(35) Abandonment

Sometimes tenants vacate the premises before the end of the lease, usually owing money and leaving no notice of their whereabouts. The landlord then faces the obligation of establishing the fact that the tenant has in fact abandoned the premises and is not just temporarily absent.

The landlord may prove abandonment by any judicially accepted method, including a new and simplified statutory procedure. *C.C. 1951.3.* The code method requires that the tenant be 14 days' delinquent in rent under circumstances that lead the landlord reasonably to believe that the tenant has abandoned the premises. Then the landlord serves or mails a form notice of abandonment. *C.C. 1951.* Unless the tenant pays all or part of the rent or responds in writing that the premises have not been abandoned, there has been a conclusive abandonment. After 15 days (18 days if the notice is served by mail, which most are), there is abandonment, and the landlord can then change the locks. This is faster than an unlawful detainer action in such situations, and the landlord can still sue for damages.

(36) Disposing of Abandoned Personal Property

If the residential tenant abandons the premises, leaving personal property behind, the landlord may dispose of that property safely, expeditiously, and without liability in the manner provided by code. *C.C. 1980–1991.* The code method does not preclude other reasonable methods of disposition. *C.C. 1981.* However, because the penalty and liability of the landlord are so great for wrongful disposition, it is suggested that the landlord use only the code procedure.

Notice and Storage

The landlord first gives written notice (in the form specified by *C.C. 1984–1985*) to the tenant or anyone else he believes to have an ownership interest. Then he stores the property, using reasonable care. Unless the property is reclaimed (by paying all reasonable storage costs) within 18 days after the mailing of the notice, the landlord may dispose of the property in the manner provided by the code.

Sale or Disposition

After proper notice, the property may be sold or destroyed without further notice or liability if its total value is less than $300. *C.C. 1988.* Otherwise, it must be sold at a public sale. The proceeds of the sale are applied first to pay the cost of the sale and then costs of storage. The balance, if any, is then paid to the tenant or owner, if it is claimed within 30 days. Otherwise, it is paid to the county treasurer. *C.C. 1988.*

Residential Leases

Landlords must turn over to the tenant the tenant's personal property upon receipt of the reasonable storage and handling costs. This procedure only applies to situations where the landlord receives a written request within 18 days from the date the tenant vacates the premises.

Commercial Tenancies

Commercial leases are governed by an entirely different set of procedures. *C. C.1993.*

(37) Temporary Relocation

The tenant agrees to temporarily vacate the premises, remove whatever possessions are there (including food and medicines), and find a place to live during pest control work. The tenant agrees to undertake all these problems for a credit equal to the cost of renting the premises on a daily basis. Tenants may wish to consider amending this clause to include and require the cost of obtaining temporary housing and the storage or loss of their food and possessions.

(38) Damages to Premises

If the premises are totally or partially destroyed by no fault of the tenant, either party can elect to terminate the lease. If it is not terminated, then the landlord must repair the premises. The rent would then be reduced equal to the reasonable loss of use of the premises. If the tenant or one of the tenant's guests caused the destruction, then only the landlord has the right to terminate the lease. Additionally, the tenant must pay the full amount of normal rent.

Some tenants may want to question such a clause and provide different options depending on whether or not the loss is covered by the landlord's insurance. They may also want provisions on how quickly the landlord must rebuild the premises. Tenants may also feel that a mere reduction in rent may not compensate them for the severe inconvenience of rebuilding part of the property.

(39) Insurance

The landlord's normal insurance policy does not cover the tenant's possessions, and this clause reminds the tenant to obtain such insurance. Without such an insurance policy, the tenant would often be unprotected for damage to personal property.

(40) Waterbeds

The tenant may only have a waterbed upon obtaining valid insurance, increasing the security deposit, and not exceeding the load-bearing capacity of the floor.

(41) Antiwaiver

Antiwaiver clauses state that a landlord's failure to promptly enforce any one clause shall not amount to a waiver of the right to do so in the future. Without such a clause, the law states that, once the tenant has breached a covenant, the landlord must act promptly if he desires to terminate the lease. Otherwise, any conduct inconsistent with the termination and with knowledge of the breach could be construed as a ratification of the lease and the tenancy. If the tenant breaches a continuous covenant, each successive act is a new violation offering the landlord an independent right of termination. Thus, the failure to prosecute one breach is not a waiver of future violations. Although antiwaiver clauses can be waived, *Salton Comm. Services Dist. v. Southard (1967) 256 C.A.2d 526*, such clauses create a strong presumption, usually upheld, that the landlord did not intend to waive the breach by not enforcing one of the rights promptly. *Karbelning v. Brothwell (1966) 244 C.A.2d 333.*

Rent during Breach

If there is no antiwaiver clause, the acceptance of rent by the landlord, with full knowledge of the breach, is a waiver of that breach. Once an unlawful detainer action has been filed, a residential landlord cannot accept partial rent without waiving the default. In commercial leases, the landlord can accept partial rent even after an unlawful detainer action has been filed provided the tenant is first given actual notice that the partial rent does not cure the default. *C.C.P. 1161.1(c).*

(42) Notices

This clause provides the address at which a party may be served. If proper service is made to that address, that party is charged with notice and service.

(43) Manner of Service

The CAR lease does not contain special provisions regarding service or a clause modifying the normal statutory requirements. Some leases do modify the normal methods of service.

Statutory Requirements

Without a specific lease clause, notice to terminate (*C.C. 1946*), to modify (*C.C. 827*), or to give the three-day notice (*C.C.P. 1161*) must be written and personally served on the tenant. If the tenant is not at the home or usual place of business, then the notice may be served by leaving a copy of the notice with a person of suitable age and discretion at either place and by mailing a copy to the tenant's residence. If neither of the preceding methods is possible, then service may be accomplished by posting a copy of the notice on the property, leaving a copy with a competent person if such a person can be found, and mailing a copy to the tenant. *C.C.P. 1162.* Notice of termination may also be sent by certified or registered mail. *C.C. 1946.*

Contractual Modification

A lease can provide that all notices may be sent by registered, certified, or regular mail. If the lease so provides, the parties are bound by that manner of service, and the notice is effective once so sent. Thus, the mere refusal of a party to accept a letter from the mail carrier would not invalidate such service. *Hignell v. Gebala (1949) 90 C.A.2d 61.*

(44) Notice Period

The CAR lease does not modify the normal notice periods, as do some leases. The parties have contractual freedom to select any period not less than seven days for serving notices to modify or terminate a tenancy. *C.C. 1946, 827.* Where there is no provision in the lease, the period for a month-to-month tenancy is thirty days. *C.C. 1946, 827.* Notice of termination (i.e., the 30-day notice) may be given at any time during the month. Once given, rent is due and payable only up to and including the day of termination (i.e., the thirtieth day). *C.C. 1946.*

(45) Tenant Estoppel Certificate

Lenders generally require landlords to provide a statement from each tenant before they will grant any loans on the property. Also, anyone interested in buying the property would want to know the current condition of the leases. These statements are commonly called estoppel certificates. They confirm the terms of the lease and that it is still in existence and often include the amounts of any deposits and prepaid rents. This clause requires the tenant to supply such a statement when asked.

(46) Credit Check

This clause grants the landlord the right to check a tenant's credit, but the landlord must be very careful to do so in a manner that does not violate a tenant's right to privacy or serve as a form of discrimination. The evaluation of the report must be reasonably limited to tenant's ability to comply with the lease terms and rental amounts and not unfairly affect minority or handicapped applications.

If any employer obtains a credit report that can affect employment, that employer must provide the employee or applicant with written notice of any adverse information or action taken. *C.C. 1785.20a.* The statute seems limited to employers, but a landlord might be well advised to follow its provisions.

If a landlord is considering a more extensive investigation, such as personal interviews with others or checking prior references, he or she should study the Investigative Consumer Reporting Agencies Act. *C.C. 1786.10 et seq.*

(47) Mediation

Except for unlawful detainer actions, mechanic's liens, and a few other matters, the mediation clause requires the landlord and tenant to attempt to resolve any conflicts first through nonbinding mediation through a neutral third party. In certain circumstances, the broker can elect also to adopt mediation. If the person wins his or her case, but has not first gone through mediation before filing a court action, then such person is not entitled to attorney's fees. This clause is operative in every CAR lease, and there is no space for the parties to initial if they desire its provisions. Mediation is discussed in detail in Chapter 2 of this book under "Implementation: Alternative Dispute Resolution." The discussion also includes the author's opinions on the process of mediation.

(48) Attorney Fees

The court costs awarded the winning party, *C.C.P. 1021–1035*, should not be confused with attorney's fees, which are awarded only through contractual provisions. *C.C.P. 1021*. In landlord–tenant cases, attorney's fees are recoverable only if the lease provides for their award to the winning party.

Dual Coverage

Additionally, those lease provisions that allow only for attorney's fees to the landlord are automatically expanded by statute to include the tenant if the tenant is the successful party. *C.C. 1717*. Thus, unilateral lease provisions are bilateral, providing that a tenant, if the prevailing party, can recover attorney's fees and court costs from the landlord as part of the judgment.

(49) Other Terms–Exculpatory Clause

A lease can and sometimes does incorporate any number of different provisions, including a so-called "exculpatory clause."

An exculpatory clause is a provision that insulates the landlord against any liability for damages or injuries sustained by the tenant or guests while on the premises. It is an attempt to have the tenant contractually assume the landlord's liability. This clause is common to many leases, although it is not found in the CAR form.

Without an exculpatory clause, the party who has possession and control of a portion of the property is liable for injuries on that section of the premises. Thus, a landlord generally has no tort liability for areas under a tenant's control and possession unless there is (1) fraudulent concealment, (2) covenant to repair, (3) statutory duty to repair, or (4) voluntary repairs negligently done. Similarly, a landlord would have a duty to inspect and repair those areas in which possession is retained, such as hallways, stairs, and other common areas.

Restrictions on Use

Exculpatory clauses are void and of no effect in residential leases. *Henrioville v. Marin Ventures, Inc. (1978) 20 C.3d 512.* In other leases, these clauses are still valid. *C.C. 1953a5.* However, they are severely construed against the landlord and offer no protection to the landlord against willful acts and affirmative negligence. *C.C. 1668.*

(50) Entire Contract and Modification

This clause, among its other provisions, states that the lease represents the entire and total contract between the parties and that there are no side agreements or oral understandings between the parties. If the landlord has made any promises to the tenant, they must be in writing or the tenant may be precluded from providing them in court.

Modification of a Lease

The law provides that a written contract can be modified by another written contract; by an executed oral agreement; or, if the contract does not prohibit oral modifications, by an oral agreement supported by new consideration. *C.C. 1698.* Oral contracts may be modified by any of those three methods or, additionally, by a written agreement unsupported by consideration. *C.C. 1697.*

Example

In one case involving a written lease, a landlord orally reduced the tenant's rent from $675 per month to $300 and accepted $300 for many months. Later, after the tenant had defaulted on the payments, the landlord sued for $675 per month for the unpaid rent and $375 per month for those months in which the tenant paid only $300. The court held that the $300 per month constituted payment in full as to those months because the acceptance amounted to an executed agreement. However, for those months for which no rent was collected, the entire $675 was due because there was neither a written contract nor an executed oral agreement. *Stoltenberg v. Harveston (1934) 1 C.2d 264.*

(51) Agency

This clause confirms who the broker represents, assuming that a broker is involved, which is necessary for the broker's protection and meeting statutory requirements.

(52) Interpreter and Translator

Many tenants leasing residential property are unable to read and understand English, especially in a technical document. This clause evidences that the tenant had the clause read to them and they fully understood its provisions. Furthermore, if the tenancy was negotiated in Spanish, then the tenant must be given a copy of the lease written in Spanish.

(53) Broker's Disclaimers

The disclaimers in this clause are designed to protect the broker. However, they provide a useful reminder to the parties as to the limitations of the broker's advice and role. Although the clause attempts to insulate the broker from a lawsuit, the courts still hold the broker to the required duties and obligations and responsible for their own torts.

(54) Tenant's Signature

All tenants should sign the lease. Under the statute of frauds, in most cases concerning leases over a year, only documents signed by a tenant may be enforced against that party. *C.C. 1624.* There are exceptions, and certain actions may be brought against people residing in the property without a signed lease.

(55) Discrimination

Almost no leases today specify any form of unconstitutional discrimination. However, if the landlord or his agents discriminate in practice or effect on the basis of race, color, creed, religion, or national origin, they violate federal laws. *Jones v. Alfred Mayer Co. (1968) 392 U.S. 3601* and *42 U.S.C. 3601 et seq. (Civil Rights Act of 1968).* The California statute is broader and prohibits discrimination on the basis of sex, race, color, religion, ancestry, national origin, disability, medical condition, marital status, or sexual orientation. *C.C. 51-2 (Unruh Civil Rights Act) and H.&S.C. 35720 et seq. (Rumford Fair Housing Act).* Further, and except as provided otherwise by federal statutes as to rentals the landlord may not ask about immigration or citizenship status. *C.C. 1940.3* Discrimination cases can be prosecuted by a private attorney, the state of California through the Fair Employment Practices Commission, or the federal government through HUD.

Americans with Disability Act

Another completely separate set of laws prohibits discrimination based on disabilities. The federal statute is called the Americans with Disabilities Act (usually just called the "ADA"), *42 USC §§12101-12213, 29 CFR 1630,* and the California act, as part of the Unruh Act, *C.C. 54.1.* Under these acts, the disabled have a right to both equal treatment and equal opportunity. So, for example, the courts have held a tenant who suffered from a disease making it difficult for him to walk long distances is entitled to a parking space close to his apartment regardless of the landlord's typical parking policy. In another example, a person who because of a disability needed a dog or cat for companionship is entitled to keep such an animal despite a landlord's "no pets" policy. Existing buildings can be modified (usually at tenant expense) to meet a disabled person's needs, and new building are often constructed meeting the architectural standards of the American National Standards Institute.

Other Discrimination

Numerous forms of discrimination are illegal, including discrimination on the basis of sex, blindness, physical handicaps, having children, and, perhaps, any blatant arbitrary discrimination. For example, it is unlawful to discriminate against two unmarried people living together. *Smith v. Fair Employment and Housing Com'n (1996) 12 C.4th 1143.* Similarly, a landlord cannot discriminate against a prospective tenant just because that person is on welfare. *Gilligan v. Jamco Dev. Corp. (1997) 108 F.3d 246.*

Most landlords will grant a lease to a husband and wife when only one spouse works, if that person's income qualifies financially for that lease. It would then be illegal to discriminate against an unmarried couple and require both people to qualify individually financially for the lease. *Hess v. Fair Employment and Housing Commission (1982) 138 C.A.3d 232.* However, the landlord can use income qualifications if they are reasonable and applied fairly in a nondiscriminatory manner. A requirement that tenants earn at least three times the amount of rent was held reasonable, even though it disproportionately affected women. *Harri's v. Capital Growth Investors XIV (1991) 52 C.3d 1142.*

(56) Guarantee

If a third party is guaranteeing the tenant's payment and faithful performance of the lease, then this clause would be checked and signed by the person guarantying the lease.

STUDY QUESTIONS (TRUE–FALSE)

1. If a tenant has not paid rent for one month, the landlord may change the lock on the door and sue the tenant for back rent.

2. A three-day or 30-day notice is always required to terminate a tenancy.

3. A three-day notice stating, "You have three days to quit the premises" is valid if written and personally served on the tenant.

4. Almost all landlords use the unlawful detainer action, because it reduces the time to respond to a summons to five days and has priority on the court calendar.

5. A tenant may always assign his or her interest in a lease if that lease contains no specific prohibition against assignments.

6. A student who rents an apartment that is substandard and in violation of the housing code may, on proper notice, refuse to pay any further rent until the premises are brought up to code.

7. If the lease provides the landlord with the right to inspect the premises at any time, she may do so as long as she does not abuse the privilege.

8. If the lease does not specifically provide for attorney's fees, the winning party to a lawsuit may not recover the cost of an attorney.

9. A student renting an unfurnished apartment for $300 per month may not be required to pay more than $600 in cleaning fees and security deposits.

10. If a student pays a $400 nonrefundable cleaning fee and it costs only $360 to clean the apartment, the manager must refund the $40 within three weeks or be liable for a penalty up to $800 plus actual damages.

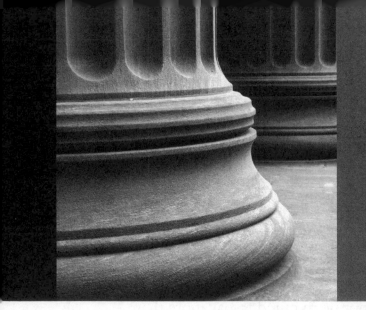

Chapter

14

NATURE AND EFFECT OF RECORDING

Recording Optional

Recording a deed or other instrument is optional, though highly advisable. An unrecorded instrument is fully valid between the parties, and, as between those parties, recording imparts no additional validity to the document.

Effect of Recording

The primary importance of recording is to provide constructive notice of the recorded document to subsequent purchasers and encumbrancers. *C.C. 1213.* Recording also establishes priorities between deeds and other recorded documents. The general rule is that an instrument obtains its priority as of the date of its recording. *C.C. 1214.* Recording also creates a presumption that the document was legally delivered. Additionally, certain instruments (such as **homesteads** and judgment **liens**) must be recorded before they become valid.

Constructive Notice

Constructive notice is a legal fiction. The law conclusively presumes that once an instrument is properly recorded, anyone who later acquires an interest in that property has notice of the instrument and its contents. This notice is imputed even if the person is totally ignorant of the document's existence.

Limited Notice

Constructive notice is given to purchasers and encumbrancers. Thus, an excavator who digs on a property, damaging an underground pipe,

Recording System

has not had constructive notice of that pipe's existence simply because an easement had been recorded. As one court stated, "It is sometimes said that the record of a deed is constructive notice to all the world. This is too broad and unqualified an enunciation of the doctrine. It is constructive notice only to those who are bound to search for it." *Mt. States Tel. & Tel. Co. v. Kelton (1955) 285 P.2d 168.*

Recording Requirements

Only written instruments affecting an interest in property may be recorded by paying the appropriate fee at the county recorder's office in which the property is located. The instrument must also be acknowledged and, where applicable, the appropriate documentary transfer tax fees are imposed by the city or county.

Acknowledgment

Except for a few exceptions (e.g., **lis pendens**, **notice of default**, and **judgments**), all documents must be acknowledged before they can be recorded. An **acknowledgment** is a formal declaration by a person authorized by statute (such as a judge, a military officer, or a notary) that the person who signed his name to the instrument is, in fact, that very person. It verifies the identity of the person executing the instrument, without making any statement about the validity of the instrument itself. Most verifications are taken by notaries, people licensed by the state to acknowledge instruments for a fee (see Figure 14.1). The actual form for the notary is prescribed by statute. *C.C. 1189.*

Preliminary Change of Ownership Report

When you file a document that potentially changes ownership (or the equivalent of ownership) to property, your annual property taxes may

FIGURE 14.1   Acknowledgment.

Acknowledgment

State of California   )

County of _____) ss

On __<<date>>__ , before me, __<<Name of Notary>>__ , a Notary Public in and for the State of California, personally appeared, _____ , proved to me on the basis of satisfactory evidence) to be the person(s) whose name(s) is/are subscribed to the within instrument, and acknowledged to me that he/she/they executed the same in his/her/their authorized capacity(ies) and that by his/her/their signature(s) on the instrument the person(s), or the entity upon behalf of which the person(s) acted, executed the instrument.

I certify under PENALTY OF PERJURY under the laws of the State of California that the foregoing paragraph is true and correct.

Witness my hand and official seal.

                                                    _____
                                                    Notary Signature

go up. Under Proposition XIII, property taxes are normally increased to 1% of the sales or transfer value of the property (unless the transfer is exempt from a property tax increase). To provide the necessary information to the county to determine if property taxes will be increased because of the transfer, the recorder requires the transferor to file a Preliminary Change of Ownership Report A copy of the Preliminary Change of Ownership Report is included in Chapter 17.

Transfer Tax Stamps

Regardless of whether or not your annual property taxes will be increased, many transactions are subject to a one-time fee called Documentary Transfer Tax. To determine if this fee can be assessed, most counties require that a recorded document that potentially changes ownership also file a Transfer Tax Affidavit (sometimes called an Affidavit of Documentary Transfer Tax) as part of the requirements to record a document. See Figure 14.2.

Basically, both an Affidavit of Documentary Transfer Tax as well as a Preliminary Change of Ownership Report must be filed before the recorder will record a document involving transfer of title. There are two exceptions when an Affidavit of Documentary Transfer Tax is not required. Thee first exception is when the sales price or other information on consideration paid is already contained the Proposition XIII

FIGURE 14.2   Transfer tax affidavit.

Transfer Tax Affidavit

NOTICE: ANY MATERIAL MISREPRESENTATION OF FACT IN THIS AFFIDAVIT IS A MISDEMEANOR UNDER THIS COUNTY'S REAL PROPERTY TRANSFER TAX ORDINANCE. ANY PERSON WHO MAKES SUCH A MISREPRESENTATION IS SUBJECT TO PROSECUTION FOR SUCH OFFENSE.

1. <u>Location of Property.</u>
     Street Address: _____   Lot _____, Block _____
     Describe document(s) to be recorded: _____

2. <u>Is This a Foreclosure or a Trustee Sale?</u>   ☐ Yes   ☐ No
     (If yes, complete this section, if no, proceed to #3)

     A. Is the Transferee the foreclosing Beneficiary or Mortgagee   ☐ Yes   ☐ No
     B. Is the Transferee foreclosing a Senior Loan   ☐ Yes   ☐ No
     C. If no, enter the amount(s) of Senior Loan(s) and proceed to #6 $_____

3. <u>Is This a Lease?</u>   ☐ Yes   ☐ No
     (If yes, complete this section, if no, proceed to #5)

     A. Is remaining term of lease including renewal options equal or greater than 35 years?
        (If yes, complete section #6, if no, then no transfer tax and proceed to #4)   ☐ Yes   ☐ No
     B. If yes, submit a copy of lease or summary of its terms
     C. If yes, consideration or value of leasehold Interest $_____
     D. Enter amount on line 6A for tax calculation

4. <u>Is This a Gift in Whole or in Part?</u>   ☐ Yes   ☐ No
     (If yes, complete this section, if no, proceed to #5)

     A. If yes, fair market value of property interest $_____
     B. If yes, Name of Transferor (Donor):   _____
     C. If yes, Name of Transferee (Donee):   _____
     D. If yes, Donor sign paragraph below and then proceed to section #7

     Please be aware that certain gifts in excess of $13,000 per calendar year may trigger a Federal Gift Tax. In such cases, the Transferor (donor) may be required to file Form 709 (Federal Gift Tax Return) with the Internal Revenue Service. Please also be aware that Information stated on this document may be given and used by governmental agencies, including the Internal Revenue Service. I, as the Transferor (Donor), declare under the penalty of perjury, that I have read the aforementioned paragraph and acknowledge that a Federal Gift Tax may be triggered.
                                                        (Signature of Donor): _____

5. <u>Do You Content That No Transfer Tax Is Due for a Reason Not Explained Above?</u>   ☐ Yes   ☐ No
     (If yes, complete this section, if no, proceed to #6)

     A. If yes, explain fully (1) the nature of this transaction, and (2) the reason why you contend no transfer tax is due. (Use additional papers if necessary and attach copies of records or documents (i.e., tax returns, entity formation documents, etc.) supporting your claim.

     _____
     _____

FIGURE 14.2 *(Continued).*

6. <u>Taxable Transactions</u>

(Complete the following and calculate the tax due)

A. Consideration Paid $_____

(Including the value of any lien or encumbrance thereon at time of transfer)

B. Fair Market Value $_____

C. Tax Due (Apply local country transfer tax, which can vary between counties) $_____

7. <u>Contact Information</u>

A. Name of Person to Contact: _____   Phone: _____

B. Mailing Address: _____

I DECLARE OR AFFIRM UNDER PENALTY OF PERJURY THAT THE FOREGOING IS TRUE AND CORRECT.

Name of Transferee: _____   Signature of Transferee: _____

Executed (Signed) in the City of _____, County of _____, State of _____

Date of Execution: _____

NOTICE: ANY MATERIAL MISREPRESENTATION OF FACT IN THIS AFFIDAVIT IS A MINDEMEANOR UNDER THIS COUNTY'S REAL PROPERTY TRANSFER TAX ORDINANCE. ANY PERSON WHO MAKES SUCH A REPRESENTATION IS SUBJECT TO PROSECUTION FOR SUCH OFFENSE.

Preliminary Change of Ownership Report. The second exception is for transfers that are exempt from a Proposition XIII property tax increases. Thus, transfers (such as conveyances between spouses, the $1 million child exemption, and the other many exceptions covered in detain in Chapter 17) are except from both property tax increases and documentary transfer taxes.

Originally, the State of California imposed a documentary transfer tax, but they abandoned such taxes, and the cities and counties immediately adopted the tax. Most cities or counties impose the same tax rate as the old state tax: $1.10 per $1,000 of value or consideration given, over and above liens remaining on the property at the time of sale. *R.&T.C. 11911.* Chartered cities can set their own tax rate. For example, the city of San Rafael charges $2.55 per $1,000 of sales price. The tax is paid by the person transferring the interest in the property. *R.&T.C. 11912.*

Bona Fide Purchaser

A **bona fide purchaser (BFP)**, or encumbrancer, is someone who pays value for an interest in property in good faith and without actual or constructive notice of any prior adverse interests. The status of a BFP achieves importance because a BFP who first records the document receives interest free, clear, and unburdened by any prior unrecorded claims in the property.

No Notice

Notice may be actual or constructive. *C.C. 18.* Actual notice is simply notice or information about a fact derived from a person's five senses. The person who hears or observes something has actual notice about that thing. Constructive notice may be the notice imparted by law from the recording of a document. Additionally, constructive notice may be the type of notice a person would receive when undertaking a reasonable investigation on discovering any fact that a reasonable person would investigate. Because a reasonable person would normally inspect property, an owner is presumed to have knowledge of an adverse possessor living on that property even if the owner never, in fact, visited the land.

Priorities

Priorities become important when there are conflicting claims or interests in the same property. Assume that A sells the property to B and then immediately sells the same property (fraudulently, of course) to C. A then vanishes to another state. A problem of priorities arises as to who owns the property, B or C. Or, assume that the owner, A, executes a deed of trust in favor of B, who records a lien. Later C, a judgment creditor, records a lien against A's property. Would B or C have the prior, superior lien?

Determining Priority

Priority depends on whether the conflicting documents are recorded because different priority rules exist for unrecorded instruments. Priority also requires ascertaining whether either of the conflicting claimants is a BFP or encumbrancer because BFPs have certain priority rights.

Document Must Be Indexed

A document is not deemed recorded until it has been accepted by the county recorder, processed, and indexed. Once the document is indexed, the public can find notice of the recording. It is this indexing that sets the day at which the document provides constructive notice and not the date on which the recorder accepts the instrument. *Lewis v. Superior Court (1994) 30 C.A.4th 1850.*

Title Insurance

In general, most of the purchasers and encumbrancers are protected against conflicting claims by **title insurance**. Title companies research the recorded documents and issue their policy of title insurance based on their review of the record. This policy of title insurance protects the owner or encumbrancer for the period of ownership of the property or lien. (Title insurance is discussed more fully in Chapter 22.)

GENERAL PRIORITIES

Unrecorded Documents

Unrecorded documents are fully effective and binding between the parties. Under common law, the first document in time between two otherwise equal instruments is the first in priority. The rationale is that, once the owner has conveyed an interest, that same interest cannot be conveyed to anyone else. Thus, if A sold property to B, who did not record, and then later sold property to C, who also did not record, B would own the property. C would have no interest in the property but would have a valid lawsuit against A, assuming that A could be found.

Effect of Recording

California established recording statutes that revised the common law rules of priorities. The first BFP who records has priority, free and clear of any prior unrecorded claims in the property. An unrecorded deed is not enforceable against a subsequent BFP who first records. The purpose of the statutes is to encourage prompt recording, thereby reducing the possibility of fraud by providing a means of notice to anyone else who is interested in the property. Thus, if A sold property to B, who did not record, and one year later sold the same property to C, a BFP who immediately recorded, C would be the owner of the property, unencumbered by any claim of B. *C.C. 1214.*

Race–Notice Recording Statute

California has what is known as a race–notice recording statute, which specifies that the first person to record without notice of conflicting claims has priority. Race refers to the race to be the first to record. Notice relates to the second requirement that the person must not have actual or constructive notice of any adverse interests in the property.

Effect of Improper Recording

Only properly recorded documents provide constructive notice. Thus, if A sells to B, who records a deed that is not acknowledged, and later A sells the same property to C, a BFP who records, C would prevail and have priority over B.

Curative Statute

By statute, any defectively recorded instrument will impart constructive notice after one year. *C.C. 1207.* Thus, in the previous example, if the sale to C occurred over one year after the sale to B, then B would win. B would have priority because he or she was the first to record, and C could not be a BFP, because she would have constructive notice of B's claim.

Effect of Notice

To obtain priority, the first person to record must not have notice of a conflicting claim in the property.

Actual Notice

If A sold property to B, who recorded a defectively executed deed, and then two weeks later A sold the same property to C, who inspected the county records and saw the defective deed, then B would win. B's interest has priority because C has actual notice of B's claim, a circumstance that prevents C from being a BFP.

Constructive Notice

A person is charged with those facts that a reasonably prudent person would investigate and discover. Thus, if A sold property to B, who did not record but lived on the property, and later A sold the property to C, who recorded, then B would win. C would be charged with the knowledge of B's living on the property and, thus, could not obtain priority. A reasonably prudent person would view the property and by reasonable inquiry discover B's existence.

Chain of Title

The term **chain of title** refers to a chronological history of all documents affecting title to a certain property. To be part of the chain of title, an instrument must be properly recorded so that it may be discovered by a search of the title using the grantor–grantee index of the county recorder. If the document cannot be found by this method, it is said to be a wild document, which does not impart constructive notice. Thus, if A sold to B, who did not record, then B sold to C, who did record, and then A sold to D, who recorded, D would have priority. D could not find any prior grant from A to B because B did not record, and D would have no means or reason to look for C, because C could not be traced to A in the grantor–grantee index. This assumes that D is a BFP, who by definition would have no actual or constructive notice of C's rights.

Transferee of a Bona Fide Purchaser

Once a BFP has priority over other interests, that BFP can transfer that interest to someone else, and that transferee would take the same priority held by the transferor. Thus, if A sold to B, who did not record, and then sold to C, a BFP who did record, C would have priority. C could give title as a gift to D, who may not be a BFP, who would take the same priority that C held. The reason is obvious. C's interest would not be very valuable or salable if the transferee might be subject to prior conflicting claims that had not been valid against C. (One exception exists. If the transferee was already in the title chain and subject to prior claims, then, in this limited exception, the prior owner–transferee would take subject to claims existing against him when he first held an interest in the title.)

APPLY THE LAW

In Re Duncombe
143 B.R. 243 (Bankruptcy C.D. Cal. 1992)

[A federal bankruptcy stops a foreclosure sale if notice of that bankruptcy is recorded before the foreclosure deed. A particular strong-arm section of the federal bankruptcy law allows a bankruptcy trustee to obtain the status of a BFP, even if he or she had notice of prior claim. Because bankruptcy law waives the normal state rule that prior notice prevents a person from being a BFP, it can truly be a race to the recorder's office.]

BUFFORD, JUDGE. This case involves a real race to the county recording office to record a deed under the recording act, the bane of all first year law students.

The race began with the fall of the hammer at the foreclosure sale of debtor Damon Duncombe's Inglewood home at approximately 11:00 A.M. on December 12, 1991. The sale took place at the main entrance to the Moss Building in Tarzana, California, the location of the offices of the foreclosure trustee under Duncombe's deed of trust. The participants in the race were Duncombe and William Little, who made the winning bid at the foreclosure sale.

The race routes for the two runners were quite different, but both ended at the Los Angeles County recorder's office in the Hall of Administration in downtown Los Angeles. The debtor's route led first to the bankruptcy court's chapter 13 filing office in downtown Los Angeles to file this chapter 13 bankruptcy case. The debtor then had to proceed to the Hall of Administration to record a notice of the bankruptcy filing.

Little's route to the recorder's office was somewhat more direct. His designated runner James Lee first had to obtain the foreclosure deed. Lee was informed that the deed would be sent to be recorded in the next several days. Lee was able to obtain the deed the same day only after explaining that Little had previously lost just this kind of race, and that it was extremely important to obtain the deed right away. After a quick lunch at a fast food outlet nearby, Lee returned and had to wait until approximately 3:00 P.M. to obtain the deed. By then afternoon traffic on the freeway had built up, and it was 4:01 before he was able to record the deed at the Hall of Administration.

APPLY THE LAW
continued

In the meantime, the debtor's route to the recorder's office posed difficulties as well. After the sale was completed, Duncombe headed directly to the Federal Building, where the chapter 13 filing office is located. When he finally found the building, there was no parking available. It took him ten minutes to walk back to the federal building [from his parking spot], and another ten minutes to find the chapter 13 office. By this time it was almost 1:00, and the line to get into the chapter 13 filing office was very long. He waited nervously in line for 45 minutes before it was his turn at the front.

By now it was almost 2:00, and Duncombe still had not had lunch. Someone told him that there was a cafeteria on the third floor, and he went there and got a quick lunch. It was almost 3:20 when be began the several-block walk to the county recorder's office. He arrived there shortly after 3:00, and recorded his notice of filing of his bankruptcy case at 3:21 P.M. Fortunately for Duncombe, Lee did not arrive until 40 minutes later.

Having won the race to the recorder's office, Duncombe now claims that the transfer of the property in the foreclosure sale is avoidable under the Bankruptcy Code. Little claims that the bankruptcy trustee's bona fide purchaser status (through which the debtor claims his entitlement) is defeated by constructive notice of the sale. [Little claims that because Duncombe attended the foreclosure sale he had actual notice of Little's purchase.]

This case is governed by the California recording, which provides: "Every conveyance of real property…is void as against any subsequent purchaser…of the same property…in good faith and for a valuable consideration, whose conveyance is first duly recorded …"

This is a typical race–notice recording statute. Under a race–notice recording act, the party who wins the race to the courthouse to record a conveyance of real property obtains superior title unless the winner has notice of the conveyance to the second finisher in the race.

Here Little lost the race to the county recording office. Duncombe filed this bankruptcy case and recorded notice before Little recorded his trustee's deed. Thus, the foreclosure sale is subject to avoidance [being set aside and declared void] under the Bankruptcy Code. Under this provision, a bankruptcy trustee has the status of a hypothetical bona fide purchaser as a matter of law. Neither actual nor constructive notice to the trustee (or to the debtor standing in the shoes of the trustee) defeats this status.

continued

While acceptance of the highest bid may complete a foreclosure sale, it is recordation of the sale, rather than its consummation, that perfects the transfer of property against the trustee in bankruptcy. For the following reasons, the Court finds that a foreclosure sale is subject to avoidance under a race–notice recording and the "strong arm" provision of the Bankruptcy Code. If the foreclosed-out owner files a bankruptcy case and records it prior to the recordation of the foreclosure deed, [he will prevail] even though the purchaser has acted diligently in recording his foreclosure deed. [Duncombe wins, the foreclosure sale is voided, and the property becomes an asset in the bankruptcy case.]

[California passed *C.C. 1058.5* to circumvent the holding of this case. The new law holds that if the trustee's deed is recorded within 15 days from the trustee's sale the deed shall be deemed perfected retroactive as of 8 A.M. on the date of sale. However, the validity of this new law is in doubt. One line of cases holds that the new law is effective. *In re Garner (1997) 208 B.R. 698.* The older line of cases holds that state law cannot change Federal law, and the *Duncombe* case in this book is still valid. *In re Sanders (1996) 198 B.R. 326.* This line of cases holds that if the debtor files bankruptcy before recordation of the trustee's deed the bankruptcy's automatic stay prevents any valid trustee's sale.]

SPECIAL PRIORITIES

Mechanic's Liens

Mechanic's liens are an exception to the general rule that the first to record without notice has priority. These liens may begin as off-the-record interests that can be superior to the claims of BFPs and encumbrancers who first record. The reason is that mechanic's liens obtain their priority as of the date work commences on a project. *C.C. 3134.* Among themselves, all mechanic's liens are of equal priority, relating and attaching to the project at its commencement. For example, assume that work on a project began January 1, and on January 10, a deed of trust was recorded. Then on February 1, A, a laborer, dug a foundation. Finally, on February 15, B, a carpenter, built the walls. Both A and B could have mechanic's liens before the deed of trust. Both liens would obtain their priority as of January 1 when work commenced on the project and would be of equal rank with each other.

The date when work commenced on a project is a factual question to be determined in each case. The courts hold that commencement requires some actual, visible alteration to the land or the delivery of materials to the site. Thus, the preparation of architectural plans does not qualify as commencement.

Time Limits

However, to be valid, mechanic's liens must be recorded within specified times from the date the contractor, laborer, or supplier did work or supplied material to the project. A general contractor must record a lien within 60 days, and all other mechanics have 30 days in which to record their liens, if a notice of completion has been filed. If no notice of completion was filed, then all mechanics have 90 days after the actual completion of the project in which to file their liens. (See the section on mechanic's liens in Chapter 16 for other requirements as to filing and enforcing mechanic's liens.)

Judgment Liens

Once a judgment is recorded, it becomes a lien on all nonexempt real property of the judgment debtor in that county for 10 years unless it is extinguished earlier or renewed for another 10 years. Judgment liens have different priorities as to deeds of trust and other encumbrances (discussed later). However, as to other judgment liens, each lien takes its priority as of the date of recordation. Furthermore, if the debtor later acquires new real estate in the county where the lien is recorded, those liens automatically attach to the after-acquired property. All existing judgment liens attach as of the date that the property is acquired, but between themselves each lien keeps its priority. *C.C.P. 697.380[g]*.

Junior to Prior Liens

Because a judgment lienor did not pay value for the lien, he is not a BFP or encumbrancer. Therefore, any existing lien, whether recorded or unrecorded, known or unknown to the judgment creditor, takes priority over the judgment lien. *Livingston v. Rice (1955) 131 C.A.2d 1*. For instance, if A holds an unrecorded second deed of trust against a property and B holds an unknown and unrecorded deed to one-half the land, both A's and B's claims will be superior to a later recorded judgment lien by C.

Superior to Most Later Claims

As a general rule, once the judgment is recorded, it becomes a lien as of that date and obtains its priority on the date of recordation. *Gov.C. 27326*. Except for statutory exceptions, such as taxes and assessments, all later recorded interests are **junior liens** to the judgment lien.

Future Advances under Deed of Trust

Sometimes recorded **deeds of trust** provide that the lender may or must make additional future advances (loans) to the borrower and that these future advances shall be secured by the existing deed of trust. If another lien arises between the time that the deed of trust was recorded and the time of the future advance, a question of priorities arises between the new lien and the future advance.

Obligatory Advances

If under the terms of the deed of trust the lender must make additional advances to the **trustor**, then any such further loans will obtain the priority of the deed of trust.

Optional Advances

If the lender has the option of whether or not to make future advances, such future advances will have the priority of the deed of trust only if the lender has no actual notice of an intervening claim. Therefore, anyone considering a loan to a person having property subject to a deed of trust with optional advances should personally advise the lender of the new loan, both by telephone and with a confirming letter.

LIS PENDENS

Nature

Lis pendens is Latin for "litigation pending" (see Figure 14.3). It informs the world that a lawsuit affecting title to the property is pending and that any judgment obtained in that litigation will obtain priority as of the date of the lis pendens. The lis pendens is not a condition for the filing of an action; however, without the constructive notice afforded by its recordation, subsequent BFPs or encumbrancers will take the property free and clear of the judgment. *C.C.P. 409.*

Purpose

At common law, anyone who acquired an interest in real estate during the pendency of a lawsuit took the property subject to that judgment. This harsh rule was necessary to prevent transfer of property during the litigation, thereby defeating the power of the court to render an enforceable judgment. When it became impractical to force a BFP or an encumbrancer to check all the courts in a district for pending litigation, the doctrine of lis pendens developed. It put the burden on the plaintiff in litigation, if he wanted to protect himself, to record the lis pendens, thereby giving constructive notice of his lawsuit.

FIGURE 14.3 Lis pendens.

Name of Attorney
Street Address
City, State, Zip Code
Telephone Number

SUPERIOR COURT OF THE STATE OF
CALIFORNIA, COUNTY OF _____

Names of All)	
Plaintiffs,)	
)	
Plaintiffs,)	
)	Number of Case
v.)	
)	
Names of All)	
Defendants,)	
)	NOTICE OF PENDENCY OF ACTION
Defendants.)	(Lis Pendens)
_____)	

NOTICE is hereby given that in the above entitled court, under the above stated case number, the plaintiff has commenced an action which affects and concerns the title of real property.

This action is now pending, the object of which is: [to force the defendants named above to transfer title to plaintiffs under a contract of sale executed between the above named parties].

The real property affected by the above action is located in the City of _____, County of _____, State of California, described as follows: _____.

EXECUTED on this _____ day of _____, 20____, in the City of —————, County of —————, State of California.

_____
Signature

Use by Some Attorneys

Some attorneys automatically file a lis pendens whenever they file a suit affecting title to real estate. The recordation guarantees constructive notice. Additionally, the lis pendens clouds title, often inhibiting the marketability of the property and enhancing the leverage for an early settlement of the lawsuit.

The right to file a lis pendens is absolutely privileged. By filing it in a lawsuit, a person avoids becoming subject to a cross-complaint for slander of title, interference with prospective economic advantages, or other such torts. Only rarely, after completion of the lawsuit, could a landowner become subject to a claim for malicious prosecution. A landowner's only immediate remedy is to expunge the lis pendens by posting a bond. For the above reasons, lis pendens is a popular tool in litigation affecting title to property. *Wood Court II Ltd. v. McDonald (1981) 119 C.A.3d 245.*

Release by Bond

Recognizing the potential for abuse, the legislature provided a means for expunging the cloud from title while still protecting the parties to a lawsuit. The lis pendens may be released by the posting of a bond, the exact amount of which is determined by the courts. *C.C.P. 409.2.* The bond is seldom the amount of the suit. In one case, a $10,000 bond was held adequate for a suit alleging damages of $670,000. *Howden-Goetzl v. Superior Court (1970) 7 C.A.3d 135.* If the court finds that the lis pendens was filed in bad faith, has little likelihood of success, or does not affect title or possession to the property, the court may expunge the lis pendens without the posting of a bond.

APPLY THE LAW

Patten–Blinn Lumber Co. v. Francis
166 C.A.2d 196 (1958)

[A church hired a general contractor, John Francis, paying him in advance for all materials and supplies. However, Francis used part of the funds to pay other debts, so that one of the materialmen, the plaintiff, was never paid. Plaintiff was unable to sue the general contractor because of a discharge in bankruptcy. Therefore, he was forced to file a lawsuit and to try to foreclose on his mechanic's lien. A statute, now *C.C. 3145*, requires that for the lien to remain valid a lawsuit to begin foreclosure must be commenced within 90 days of the filing of the mechanic's lien. Thereupon, a lis pendens must be filed to provide notice of the court action, for the mechanic's lien to retain its recording priority against bona fide purchasers and encumbrancers. The trial court found that notice was not given as required, and it therefore barred plaintiff from foreclosing his mechanic's lien. The issue on appeal is whether the failure to timely record a lis pendens should prohibit foreclosure of the mechanic's lien as against a party to the lawsuit, a person who obviously has actual knowledge of the existence of the lien.]

APPLY THE LAW

continued

WHITE, JUSTICE. A lis pendens is the filing for record with the recorder of a notice of the pendency of a suit involving the title to or right of possession of real property. It is the mode substituted by the Legislature for the constructive notice to all the world of the pendency of such an action, which formerly arose upon the institution of the suit. Thus, a purchaser or encumbrancer of property, instead of being required to examine all the suits pending in the courts to ascertain whether any of them relate to or affect the real estate he is negotiating about, has now only to examine the notices of lis pendens filed in the recorder's office.

The purpose of the Legislature was thus to furnish the most certain means of notifying all persons of the pendency of the action, and thereby warning them against attempting to acquire a legal or equitable interest in the property concerning which the suit was brought. Also, it binds such persons as might acquire any interest in the property in controversy after the recording of the notice by any judgment that might be secured affecting such property. This is all that the Legislature intended.

The provisions in Section 1198.1 that no lien shall be binding for more than 90 days unless proceedings be commenced in a proper court within that time to enforce the same is the same as when enacted in 1872. And certainly in 1872 there was little extra burden imposed upon those who had to determine whether the lien, because an action was commenced, continued in existence beyond 90 days. In those days, the county clerk's office was probably across the hall, or downstairs, from the recorder's office, providing a quick and easy way to determine whether an action had been filed.

It was not until 1929 that the Legislature provided that such courts should have jurisdiction over mechanic's liens foreclosure. This move, together with the great growth of our State and the increased number of municipal courts, puts the statute in question in a different light than it appeared when enacted originally in 1872.

The purchaser of property or lender on property in Los Angeles County, to protect himself against a pending action to foreclose a mechanic's lien, must search the records in 16 different municipal courts. These 16 separate municipal courts are located within a radius of some 30 miles from the Hall of Records in downtown Los Angeles. He would then have to cover a total distance of well over 200 miles, and it would undoubtedly take him at least two days to make the necessary search.

To us it seems clear that the Legislature was not concerned with giving additional notice to a party to the action, who already has notice by service of the complaint upon him. The Legislature was concerned solely with extending to purchasers or encumbrancers the protection afforded

continued

by requiring the filing of the notice before constructive notice is deemed given. It was not for the protection of the parties to the action, who already have notice of the pendency of the lien, the claim made by it, and the action seeking to foreclose the same. We are satisfied that the purpose of a notice of lis pendens under the mechanic's lien law is to perform its usual office, to give constructive notice, nothing more.

Judgment reversed. [Plaintiff–materialman may foreclose his mechanic's lien to collect his bills, even though the church will then be paying twice for the same services.]

RECORDING LIMITS

Problem

Many times, title to real estate is clouded by old documents, such as unexercised options, deeds of trust paid off but not reconveyed, expired options, and unperformed contracts of sales. These types of old, recorded instruments have no validity, but their existence often hampers marketability of property. Often the only way to clear such documents was through expensive and time-consuming quiet title actions. In 1983, the law set up time limits for all existing and newly recorded liens. After a specified period, the document will have no recording effect. *C.C. 882.020 et seq.* The period specified by statute can be extended by filing a notice of intent to preserve interest.

Periods

The most significant periods need not be memorized; rather, their existence should be recognized. Whenever a deed of trust, option, or other lien on property is recorded, it is advisable also to record a notice of intent to preserve interest. The periods of greatest importance are as follows:

1. *Deeds of trust.* A deed of trust or mortgage becomes unenforceable and unforecloseable 10 years after the date of the last payment, if that payment can be ascertained from the public record. If the final payment cannot be fixed from the record, then the instrument becomes unenforceable 60 years after the date of recordation. A notice of intent to preserve interest, recorded within the preceding periods, extends the date another 10 years. Existing loans are allowed as an exception to the new laws until 1988.

2. *Unexpired options.* An option to purchase expires six months after its stated termination date. If no ending date is specified, then the

option expires six months after it is recorded. Because of this short survival period, any option created should have a definite, specified termination date.

3. *Powers of termination.* All future interests from fee simple estates are called powers of termination. They expire 30 years from the date of recordation unless extended another 30 years by a notice of intent to preserve interest.

STUDY QUESTIONS (TRUE–FALSE)

1. Unless a deed is recorded, it is not valid.

2. If X sold his or her property to A, who did not record, and then sold it to B, who did record, as between A and B, B would win.

3. If X, a grantee, records a deed that is not notarized, it will not impart constructive notice until one year has passed.

4. If a father gives his son property by a grant deed, and the son properly records, the son will have the full protection of the recording laws.

5. If A buys property in which she knows that B claims prior title, as long as B's deed is not recorded and A never sees the deed, as between A and B, A will win.

6. If A sold to X, who did not record his deed but lived on the property, and then A sold to Y, who properly recorded, generally X would win between X and Y.

7. If A digs the foundation for a house, is not paid, and files a mechanic's lien before B, who paints the house and files a mechanic's lien, A's lien will be superior to B's lien.

8. A promptly recorded abstract of judgment becomes a lien on all nonexempt property in that county owned by the judgment debtor for a period of 10 years.

9. A lis pendens prevents anyone from further encumbering or transferring an interest in property until the conclusion of the lawsuit.

10. A lawsuit does not give constructive notice to the world unless a lis pendens is filed.

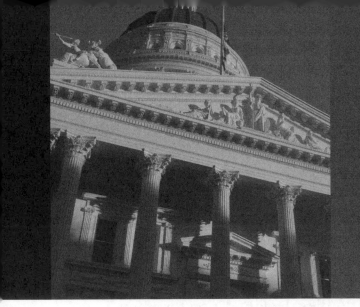

SECURITY AND OBLIGATION

Nature of Security

The typical security transaction arises out of a loan of money. To secure and guarantee payment, the lender requires a specific parcel of property to be held as security. If the borrower defaults on the promissory note, the lender can have the secured property sold and use the proceeds to satisfy the outstanding debt. This security interest in real property is known as a lien. In California, voluntary liens are usually deeds of trust, although they may be mortgages.

Security Separate from Obligation

The deed of trust or mortgage is completely separate and independent from the obligation that it secures. Although a debt can exist without security (e.g., an unsecured note), a security cannot exist without a debt. The deed of trust or mortgage is generally valid and enforceable only to the extent that a valid lawsuit can be brought under the promissory note. *Coon v. Shry (1930) 209 C. 612.* The single exception is a deed of trust that by statute remains enforceable even when the statute of limitations has run on the underlying promissory note. By statute, a deed of trust can still be foreclosed even if the statute of limitations renders the underlying note unenforceable.

Nature of Obligation

Almost all deeds of trust and mortgages are security for promissory notes. However, anything capable of being reduced to monetary value may be secured by a lien.

Mortgages and Deeds of Trust

Promissory Note

A **promissory note** is an unconditional written promise to pay someone a sum of money at a specified future date. Like contracts, all promissory notes are assignable. However, an assignee can never take better title than the transferor. To meet commercial needs, most notes are **negotiable instruments**. A negotiable document is one that in many ways approximates the transferability of money; it is freely transferable.

Negotiable Instruments

Promissory notes that are in writing, signed by the maker, with an unconditional promise to pay a certain sum of money, on demand or at a fixed date, to the bearer or another specified individual are negotiable promissory notes. A person who accepts a negotiable promissory note from another in good faith, and for consideration, and without notice of any defenses is a **holder in due course**. Such a **transferee** takes the note free from personal defenses that the maker may have against the original payee, such as lack of consideration, prior payment, setoff, or fraud in the inducement.

Assume that Mike executed a negotiable note for $8,000 in favor of Larry. Furthermore, assume that Larry owes Mike $5,000 on a totally unrelated debt. When the note becomes due, Mike could tender $3,000 as payment in full, because he could offset the $5,000 due him. *Comm. C. 3306.* If, before payment, Larry *assigned* the note to Aaron, Mike could still tender the $3,000 to Aaron as payment in full. An assignee can have no better rights than the assignor. *C.C. 1459.* However, if Larry had *negotiated* the note to Aaron, who was a holder in due course, Aaron would take the note free from any personal defenses, like setoff. *Comm. C. 3305.* Larry would then need to pay the full $8,000. Thus, a holder in due course can actually have more rights than the transferor.

Classification of Notes

Promissory notes are frequently classified according to their repayment schedule. **Straight notes** are those whose entire principal is due at the end of the term; interest, if any, is usually payable periodically throughout the term of the note. **Installment notes** require periodic payments of principal and interest throughout the term of the note. The most common amortization schedules for installment real estate loans are listed below.

Level Payment Notes

This is the note most commonly used for real estate loans, especially first deeds of trust. In the level payment method, the total monthly payment is always the same, although the amounts of each payment allocated to principal and interest vary throughout the term of the note. Many schedules exist; generally, the initial payments are allocated largely to reduction of interest. Thus, on long-term notes, many lenders are willing to permit prepayment after five or six years, because most of the note's total interest has by then been paid. (See Figure 15.1.)

These notes can be identified by terminology defining the note as "installment note—interest included" or sometimes just "level payment" note. The note, itself, contains the words "principal and interest payable in installment of $_____ per month. ... Each payment shall be credited first on interest then due and the remainder on

FIGURE 15.1   Diagram of level payment & of constant reduction principle.

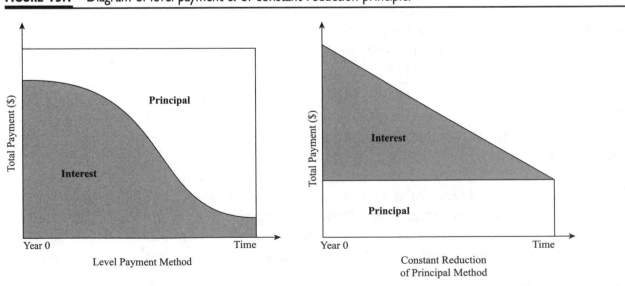

principal; and interest shall then cease upon the principal so credited." (See Figure 15.2.)

On a $2,000,000 loan at 8% for 30 years, the borrower would owe $14,675.29 per month. He or she would owe this same amount on the first day of the loan when the entire $2 is outstanding as well as on the last payment when the principal is almost completely repaid.

FIGURE 15.2 Promissory note.

PROMISSORY NOTE
(Secured Installment Note, Interest Included)

$300,000.00
June 1, 2004

FOR VALUE RECEIVED and herein acknowledged, we, jointly and severally, promise to pay to XYZ BANK, or order, at 123 Jones Street, San Francisco, California, the principal sum of THREE HUNDRED THOUSAND DOLLARS ($300,000.00).

Interest Rate. Unpaid principal shall bear interest from the date of this Note at the rate of Nine percent (9%) per annum. Each payment shall be credited first on interest then due, and the remainder to principal, and, the interest shall thereupon cease upon the principal so credited.

Installment Payments. Beginning on July 1, 2004, and the first of every month thereafter, the Borrowers shall pay the sum of TWO THOUSAND FOUR HUNDRED THIRTEEN DOLLARS AND NINETY-TWO CENTS ($2413.92), until the above principal sum and the interest thereon have been fully paid.

Prepayment. The Borrowers may prepay any part or all of the principal of the note at any time or times, without penalty.

Acceleration. Should default be made in the payment of any installment of principal or interest when due, or any time in default, the entire amount of principal and accrued interest, at the election of the holder, shall immediately become due and payable.

Due-On-Sale. In the event the Borrowers-Trustors agree to sell, transfer, or convey their interest in the real property or any part thereof or any interest therein, without the prior written consent of the Beneficiary, the Beneficiary may at its option declare all outstanding sums immediately due and payable. The terms "Trustors," "Borrowers," and "Beneficiary" include their successors.

Attorneys' Fees. If action is instituted on this note, the Borrowers promise to pay such sum as the court may adjudge for attorneys' fees.

Security. This note is secured by a deed of trust to ABC TITLE COMPANY, as Trustee.

Miscellaneous Provisions. Failure or delay in exercising any right or option in this Note given to the holder, shall not constitute a waiver of any such right or option or a waiver of any other right or option under this Note. All paragraph headings are for convenience only, and not to be considered a part of this Note in interpreting or enforcing any of its terms.

JOHN BUYER   JOAN BUYER

One highly disadvantageous way of calculating interest from the perspective of the borrower is the "rule of 78," a method sometimes used on automobiles and other personal property. Such method is illegal for use in real estate loans. *15 USC 1615.*

Unequal Payment—Constant Reduction

In this method, the amount of each monthly payment varies, decreasing consistently with the constant reduction of principal. The amount of the outstanding principal determines the amount of interest included in each payment. These notes are usually called "installment notes—interest extra." They are not common for real estate loans, although they may infrequently be used on junior deeds of trust. Each time the borrower makes a payment, the amount of principal is reduced. Because interest is only charged on the outstanding balance due, the amount of interest decreases each month. Thus, the monthly payment is similarly decreased.

Unequal Payment—Adjustable Rate Loans

These loans are generally considered a cross between a level payment note and a constant reduction loan. Basically, the note begins as a level payment note, which each payment being exactly the same amount. Then, at predetermined times, the interest rate increases (although occasionally it may decrease as well depending on the formula or index used to determine the amount of change). When the rate changes, the loan is "recast," meaning it is recalculated as a level payment note at the new interest rate.

Some loans do not adjust the amount of interest, but keep the payment the same regardless of the interest rate. In such cases, the borrower typically pays at the lower initial rate, but such payment is not enough to fully pay off the real amount due at the new interest rate. As such, the unpaid amount of interest is added to and increases the amount of principal. (See "negative amortization" below.)

Adjustable rate loans are a defined by statute and heavily regulated on first deeds of trust on one-to-four family owner-occupied residences. By California law, such loans rates cannot change more often then every six months, nor greater than ¼ percent per adjustment, and overall may not increase more than 2.5 percent during the life of the loan. *C.C. 1916.5.* Unfortunately, most banks and saving and loans are regulated by federal law. Federal law allows far more flexibility than California statutes and authorizes many more varieties of adjustable rate loans.

Unequal Payment—Balloon

A **balloon payment** is defined by statute as any payment that is at least twice the amount of the smallest installment. *B.&P.C. 10244.* No real estate loan (except a purchase money loan) with a term less than three years, and no loan on an owner-occupied dwelling (except a purchase money loan) of less than a six-year term, may include a balloon payment if (1) it is secured by a first deed of trust under $20,000, or (2) it is secured by a second deed of trust under $10,000. *B.&P.C. 10240.*

Except for a minor exception, all balloon notes dated after 1983, taken back by a seller and secured by a deed of trust on an owner-occupied dwelling, do not become due until after giving the borrower 90 days' advance notice. The notice must be in writing containing specified information notifying the borrower of the upcoming due date. Finally, the notice can't be delivered more than 150 days prior to the loan's due date. *C.C. 2924i.* If the notice is not given, the loan is not invalid. Rather, the loan does not become legally due until 90-day after the proper notice is given.

Unequal Payment—Negative Amortization

Negative amortization means not all the interest due on a loan is paid. The unpaid amount of each monthly payment is merely added to the principal, making the principal grow larger and larger each month. The biggest danger of these loans occurred in the 1970s and 1980s in adjustable rate mortgages where the principal amount grew to more than the value of the real estate securing those loans. Borrowers were stuck with loans greater than the value of their property. Frequently, such loans were secured by "purchase money deeds of trust," so the borrower had no personal liability. The abuses and losses lead the government to enact legislation controlling some of the more egregious abuses.

All balloon notes dated after July 1, 1983, taken back by a seller and secured by a deed of trust on an owner-occupied dwelling do not become due until after giving the borrower 60 days' advance written notice of the upcoming due date. Even if the maturity date has passed, the note is not due and therefore cannot be foreclosed until 60 days after giving notice. *C.C. 2966.* On nonseller-originated balloon notes made after January 1, 1984, the notice period is 90 days. *C.C. 2924i.*

COMPARISON OF MORTGAGES AND DEEDS OF TRUST

Deed of Trust

The deed of trust is a three-party security device by which the owner of property (trustor) **transfers title** in **trust** to a third party (**trustee**) to hold as security for the repayment of a debt to the lender (**beneficiary**). The trustee has the statutory and contractual power to sell the property at a private sale through an expedient summary procedure in the event of a default in the repayment of the note. (See Figure 15.3.)

The trustee is often named without agreeing to so serve. Many forms distributed by title companies and lenders have their names preprinted on the form. The beneficiary can change the trustee at

FIGURE 15.3 Deed of trust.

Assessor's Parcel Number
    123-44-5678

<u>Short Form Deed of Trust</u>

This Deed of Trust, is made this <u>1st</u> day <u>January</u>, <u>2004</u>, by and between <u>John Buyer</u>, called Trustor, <u>XYZ Title Company</u>, called Trustee, and <u>ABC Bank</u>, called Beneficiary.

Secured Property. The Trustor hereby irrevocably transfers to the Trustee, in Trust, with power of sale, the following described real property in the State of California, County of <u>Marin</u>, City of <u>San Rafael</u>:

> Lot #1 of Block A, as shown on that certain map entitled "Tract 12345," and filed for record on January 15, 1990, as Book 123 in Page 567, in the Official Records of the County of Marin, State of California.

Assignment of Rents. Together with all rents and profits from such property, as provided by the provisions relating thereto and incorporated herein.

Obligations Secured. This trust is made for the purpose of securing: (1) the Trustor's performance of each and every provision of this instrument incorporated herein by reference, and (2) payment of the promissory note executed simultaneously herewith, and any extensions thereof, in the principal sum of <u>$300,000</u> executed by the Trustor in favor of the Beneficiary or order.

Fictitious Recordings. All of the provisions, numbered (1) to (20), of those deeds of trust, recorded in blank, in the Official records of the county recorder where the secured property is recorded, as noted below opposite the name of such county, is incorporated herein and made a part hereof, as if set forth in full in this document. The county is stated, followed by the book and page of the blank instrument's recording that is incorporated herein.

Alameda	123	456	Humboldt	123	444	Sonoma	123	888
Alpine	231	323	Los Angeles	999	333	Sutter	333	666
Butte	333	454	Marin	333	777	Ventura	456	823
Contra Costa	456	888	Orange	555	333	Yolo	765	333
Fresno	999	454	Sacramento	666	543	Yuba	888	965

Notice of Default. The undersigned requests copies of any Notice of Default and of any Notice of Sale under this Deed of Trust.

_____ /s/ John Buyer

(Notary)

FIGURE 15.4   Reconveyance of deed of trust.

Recording Requested By And:
When Recorded Mail To:
            Mr. & Mrs. John Jones
            1008 Stanton Court
            Orinda, California 94563
Assessor's Parcel Number
            266 - 850 -007 -16

Full Reconveyance of Deed of Trust

Ted Gordon, as duly appointed Trustee under the Deed of Trust described below, received written request and instructions from the hold of that Deed of Trust to execute a reconveyance since all amount amounts secured by that deed of trust have been paid and the Deed of Trust is sent for cancellation.

Therefore, based on the foregoing, I Ted Gordon, as trustee execute this reconveyance to Mr. & Mrs. John Jones, the Trustors, and do so without express or implied warranties of any kind.

The Deed of Trust being reconveyed was originally executed by Mr. & Mrs John Jones, as Trustors, and recorded in the official records of Contra Costa County, on August 23, 1995, in book 8247 at Page 1684, as Instrument Number 185-112766. The Deed of Trust was securing property described as Lot 111, Map of Tract 419, filed on February 7, 1977 in Map Book 166, on Page 624, of the official records of Contra Costa County.

This reconveyance is executed on this 15th day of June, 2010, in the city of Orinda, County of Alameda.

_____

[Notary]   Ted Gordon, Trustee

any time and without the trustee's consent by recording a substitution of trustee.

When the deed of trust is fully paid off, the lender directs the trustee to record a Full Reconveyance of Deed of Trust. (See Figure 15.4.) This form clears title and evidences complete satisfaction of the debt.

Mortgage

The **mortgage** is seldom used by lenders in California. A mortgage is a two-party instrument by which the lender (**mortgagee**) obtains a lien on the owner's (**mortgagor's**) property. On default of the obligation, the lender must enforce the lien through cumbersome and time-consuming court action. (See Table 15.1 for comparison of mortgages and deeds of trust.)

TABLE 15.1   Comparison of deeds of trust and mortgages.

	Deeds of Trust	Mortgage
Definition	A contract by which title to the property is conveyed to a trustee as security for the repayment of a loan.	A contract by which property is hypothecated (pledged without delivery) for the repayment of a loan.
Parties	Trustor (borrower, debtor) Trustee (holder of title) Beneficiary (lender, creditor)	Mortgagor (borrower, debtor) Mortgagee (lender, creditor)
Title	Pass to trustee ("bare legal title")	Remains with mortgagor.
Statute of limitations	Ten years from due date stated on the recorded documents, else 60 years from date of recordation	Action to foreclose is barred when the statute of limitations (usually four years) has run on the original debt.
Foreclosure methods	Either as a deed of trust (trustee's sale) or as a mortgage (judicial sale)	Only judicial foreclosure is available.
Foreclosure procedure	Instituted by (1) recording a notice of default, (2) period to reinstate, (3) after 90 days, publishing once a week for three weeks, (4) trustee's sale and issuance of trustee's deed; average time about four months	Instituted by (1) filing a complaint, a lawsuit to foreclose, (2) mortgagor may reinstate up to court decree, (3) court judgment ordering sale, (4) judicial sale. If a deficiency judgment is sought, there are two more steps: (5) one-year equity of redemption, (6) issuance of sheriff's deed. Average time six to 18 months for court decree of sale.
Owner's rights after sale	None; trustor has no rights after trustee's sale	If a deficiency judgment is sought, the mortgagor has one-year statutory right-of-redemption period in which to repurchase the property. By paying rent, the mortgagor may live on the property for that one year.
Deficiency judgment	None (unless foreclosed as a mortgage and not a purchase money instrument)	Yes, if property sold for less than judgment and not a purchase money instrument.

CLAUSES COMMON IN PROMISSORY NOTES AND DEEDS OF TRUST

Acceleration Clauses

Most promissory notes and deeds of trust contain an **acceleration clause**. On default of a payment or other violation of a condition, this provision permits the lender at his option to declare the entire amount of outstanding principal and interest immediately due and payable. Three basic types of violations trigger an acceleration clause.

Default of Payment Clause

A default in the payment of principal, interest, taxes, insurance, or any other specified sum provides the lender with the right to accelerate a loan with a default of payment clause. On default, the lender may sue for the entire unpaid balance of the note, without having to wait for each periodic payment to fall due before being able to file suit.

Due-on-Sale Clause

The due-on-sale clause, also known as an **alienation provision**, provides the lender with the right to accelerate and declare due and payable the entire unpaid balance of a loan on the sale of the secured property. Thus, unless the new buyer was paying off the existing loan, the lender had the power to coerce the terms of any assumption or transfer of title. If a buyer was unwilling to assume the loan at the new prevailing interest rate, the lender merely accelerated and called in the loan.

In a period of easy money, when interest rates are low, most new buyers obtain new loans to pay off existing lenders. Buyers do not want to assume loans with higher interest rates. Conversely, during periods of rising interest rates and tight money, lenders do not want to be locked into low-interest-rate loans. Therefore, these lenders call in their loan on sale. They will not permit the new buyer to assume the old loan or take the property subject to the existing financing.

The enforceability of due-on-sale clauses has been one of the more frequently litigated issues in recent times. Over the years, such clauses have had a varied history of enforcement. Since 1986, when the transition period of the *Garn Bill* expired, the law has been well settled and definitive.

If there is no due-on-sale clause in the loan, it may be freely transferred. Whenever a loan contains a due-on-sale clause, the lender may enforce that provision upon transfer, unless the loan is on a home. Certain sales of owner-occupied residences are exempt, as are specified transfers under deeds of trusts. For more information, see Table 15.2, which is designed as a reference and summarizes many of the detailed provisions of the *Garn Bill*, including the type of transfers that are covered, the exempt conveyances, and the problems with junior financing.

TABLE 15.2   Enforceability of due-on-sale clauses.

Provision	Applicable Rule ("Garn Bill")
	I. Basic Rule
Basic rule	Any sale or transfer of property secured by a loan containing a due-on-sale clause is enforceable at the option of the lender, unless the transfer is exempt under the home exemption.
Transfers	The definition of a "sale or transfer" that triggers a due-on-sale clause is broadly defined to cover almost every type of transfer. *12 CFR 591.2(b)*. It includes sales, deeds, installment sales, options contracts, even leases over three years in duration. The broad definition in the *Garn Bill* even includes the refinancing of junior deeds of trust.
Exemptions	The *Garn Bill* lists certain exemptions applicable to transfers of homes, a residence occupied by the borrower. When one of those exemptions occurs (listed in Part II below), the lender many not activate the due-on-sale clause. Thus, any transfer other than a home that fits one of the exemptions allows the lender to call its loan. *12 CFR 591.5(b)(1)*.
	II. Exemptions (not a "transfer" for due-on-sale purposes)
Death to relative	If the borrower dies and the residence that he occupied passes to a relative who will also occupy the home, the lender cannot accelerate the loan.
To spouse or children	If the borrower transfers property to a spouse or to children who will occupy the home, the lender cannot accelerate the loan. The exemption also includes conveyances to a spouse pursuant to a divorce when the spouse will occupy the home. (The exemption does not include transfers from children to parents.)
Death of joint tenant	If a joint tenant borrower who lives in his home dies, the transfer to the other surviving joint tenants is exempt. The surviving joint tenants do not need to occupy the property.
To some trusts	A transfer into a trust that does not affect the owner's rights of occupancy or change the owner's ratio of ownership excludes the lender from accelerating the loan. (The owner must notify the lender prior to the transfer.)
Other transfers	The creation of junior deeds of trust on owner-occupied homes is exempt. (See Article III below.) Leases not more than three years in length and without granting an option to purchase are exempt. The last exemption is for liens from purchase money loans for household appliances.
	III. Foreclosure and Refinancing Junior Deeds of Trust
Basic rule	The definition of "transfers" is so broad as to include the creation of junior deeds of trust or the foreclosure of a junior lien. *12 CFR 591.2(b)*. The Federal Home Loan Bank Board regulations exempt as a transfer the creation of a junior lien, provided the loan is on the borrower's owner-occupied home.

TABLE 15.2 *(Continued)*.

Provision	Applicable Rule ("Garn Bill")
New junior loans	Most due-on-sale clauses also prohibit further encumbrances on the property, so that a lender under a first deed of trust can declare the entire loan due and payable if the borrower adds additional financing to the secured property. Usually, the lender will use the junior lien as leverage to increase the interest rate on the senior loan, rather than declare the loan due and payable. There is one exception. If the secured property is a home occupied by the borrower, the lender cannot accelerate the loan because of junior financing. *12 CFR 591.5(b)(1)(i).*
Foreclosure	The foreclosure of any junior lien on any type of property permits the senior lien to declare his lien also due and payable. Thus, if a holder of a second deed of trust forecloses his loan, the purchaser at that sale could be forced to also pay off the first deed of trust. More likely, the lender of the first would demand an increase in the interest rate. There is no exception for owner-occupied residences.

Due-on-Encumbrance Clause

The due-on-sale clause often includes the placing of additional liens on the property within the definition of a transfer. Such clauses are called **due-on-encumbrance clauses**. California law (before the *Garn Bill*) prohibited a lender from accelerating a loan merely because a borrower placed another deed of trust on the property, unless the lender could demonstrate that the junior lien jeopardized the lender's.

Assignment of Rents Clause

An **assignment of rents clause** entitles the lender to any rents and profits from the property on default. The lender accepts the property's income as additional security.

Late Charges Clause

Notes often include a provision that allows the lender to impose a fee or charge for a late payment. The lender is prohibited from charging a late fee until the lender has provided the borrower with 10 days' notice or has notified the borrower on the monthly billing statement that the fee will be imposed after 10 days. *C.C. 2954.5.* In all cases, the amount must be reasonable to be valid.

Prepayment Clause

A **prepayment clause** permits the borrower to repay the loan early. Without this clause, the borrower is prohibited from prepaying any or all of the loan without the lender's approval. By code, most loans under $100,000 secured by a deed of trust include a statutory right to prepay the loan at any time by also paying all accrued interest. *C.C.2954.9*. Many institutional lenders and certain governmentally backed or guaranteed loans must also provide for the unqualified right of prepayment. When the loan is prepaid, the trustor only owes the amount then due, not interest that would have been due on future payments.

Or-More Clause

The simplest type of prepayment clause is the **or-more clause**. It allows the borrower to repay any or all of the loan at any time without a penalty. The prepayment provision in the note would be worded "in payment of $_____ or more."

Prepayment Fees

Certain loans, such as residential loans, limit the amount a lender can charge as a prepayment fee. However, it is always wise to insist on a prepayment clause and to consider negotiating the maximum of the prepayment fee. Loans for commercial real estate apparently allow any reasonable fee. In one case, the court upheld a penalty fee equal to 50 percent of the loan amount. The early payment resulted in the seller's (lender's) loss of installment sale tax treatment, which was the reason for the large penalty. *Williams v. Fassler (1980) 110 C.A.3d 7.*

Residential Loans

Many residential loans contain "5-year, 20 percent prepayment penalties" because such fees are the maximum allowed under California law. *C.C. 2954(b)*. Such loans provide that there can be no prepayment penalty after the first five years. During the first five years, up to 20 percent of the original principal amount can be prepaid in any one year without penalty. The prepayment fee on the amount over 20 percent cannot exceed the equivalent of six months' interest on that balance. *C.C. 2954(b)*. For example, on a $100,000 loan bearing interest at 10 percent per annum, the borrower could prepay $20,000 during the second year without penalty. The penalty fee on the remaining $80,000 could not exceed $4,000.

The Federal Home Loan Bank Board (FHLBB) regulated prepayment penalties, prohibiting their use while exercising a due-on-sale clause in deeds of trust secured by owner-occupied dwellings. *12 C.F.R. 3445*. All other prepayment clause provisions are a matter of contract between the lender and the borrower. *12 C.F.R. 555.15*. Because the *Garn–St. Germain Act* made it clear that federal preemption applied, lenders seem no longer limited by California law, which limited residential prepayment penalties to five years and not more than six months' interest penalty.

Governmental Loans

Most governmentally backed loans and many institutional loans contain regulations limiting the amount of any prepayment penalty. For example, FHA loans contain a limited prepayment penalty, whereas VA and Cal-Vet loans allow no prepayment penalty.

Wraparound Deeds of Trust

The **wraparound deed of trust** is known by a variety of names, including all-inclusive, overlapping, and hold harmless deed of trust. Generally, the all-inclusive deed of trust arises as a purchase money instrument taken back by the seller. The amount of the loan includes (wraps around) the existing first deed of trust on the property, as well as other existing loans. The seller uses the proceeds from the wraparound loan to pay off the existing encumbrances on the property. Thus, the wraparound loan includes, but is junior to, existing loans. The *Garn Bill* holds that such transfers justify acceleration, so wraparounds will be less frequently used.

Example

If the seller lists a property, which has a $25,000 first deed of trust, for $50,000 in an ordinary sale, the buyer would pay $50,000 to the seller. The down payment might be $5,000, with the remaining $45,000 in the form of a loan from a savings and loan association. In a wraparound situation, the buyer would pay the same $5,000 down. The $45,000 balance would be an all-inclusive deed of trust. The property would still be burdened by the $25,000 first deed of trust, whose payments the seller would continue to make from the payments received toward the $45,000 purchase money second deed of trust.

Blanket Deed of Trust

A **blanket deed of trust** is simply a deed of trust that secures more than one parcel of property. It is commonly found on subdivided land.

Future Advances Clause

If a deed of trust contains a **future advances** clause, the lender may make additional loans that will be secured by the existing deed of trust. Without such a provision, any additional loan, even after the promissory note has been almost completely paid off, is not secured by the deed of trust. When the deed of trust provides for obligatory (mandatory) future advances by the lender, they automatically retain the same priority as the original deed of trust. Conversely, optional (discretionary) advances made by the lender retain the same priority as the original deed of trust only over prior liens of which the lender has no actual (personal) knowledge.

Partial Release Clause

A **partial release clause** in a deed of trust provides for the release of certain parts or parcels of property from the security of the deed of trust. Property so released is completely free and clear of that deed of trust.

Subordination Agreements

A **subordination agreement** permits a reduction in the deed of trust's recording priority. One party agrees to place a deed of trust in a lower or junior position to a later (and otherwise inferior or junior) deed of trust. Then, the later deed of trust actually becomes senior to the earlier deed of trust.

DISCLOSURE AND LIMITS ON FINANCE CHARGES

Usury

Nature of Usury Laws

The law carefully regulates and limits the amount of interest a lender can charge. Unless the parties specify that the loan will be interest free, interest at the rate of 7 percent per annum, uncompounded, is always presumed and added to any loan. *C.C. 1914, 1916-1.* The parties are free to contract for any rate that does not exceed the maximum rate set by law. Before 1979, the maximum rate, 10 percent per annum, was easy to determine. In November 1979, California passed Proposition 2, which set three separate maximum rates. A loan will fall into one of four categories that determine the rate to be used. The four categories could be conveniently labeled consumer loans, business loans, exempted loans, and legislative regulation. The rates are as follows:

1. *Consumer loans.* Loans that "are primarily for personal, family, or household purposes" may not exceed 10 percent per annum. One of the uncertainties of this section concerns the word *primarily* and whether the courts will ultimately adopt a mathematical approach to this problem. There is an exemption for real estate

loans "which are primarily for the purchase, construction, or improvement of real property." These real estate loans are exempt from the 10 percent consumer loan classification. Most attorneys feel the loan-use requirement must be strictly construed. Thus, a loan to refinance a consumer's home would be limited to the 10 percent rate unless the proceeds were used primarily for purchase, construction, or improvement of real estate.

2. *Commercial loans.* Any loan used for a nonconsumer-defined purpose is limited to the greater of (a) 10 percent per annum or (b) 5 percent over the rate charged by the Federal Reserve Bank of San Francisco. The exact rate used by the Federal Reserve Bank and the date on which the rate is fixed are carefully defined in detail in the statutes.

3. *Unregulated loans.* Certain loans are unregulated, and the lenders may charge any interest desired. These unregulated loans fall into three categories:

    a. *Institutional lenders.* Certain lenders are exempt from the usury statutes. The most common exemptions apply to institutional lenders, such as banks, savings and loan associations, and insurance companies, and to special regulated lenders like credit unions and personal finance companies.

    b. *Real estate brokers.* All loans made or arranged through real estate brokers and secured entirely or partially by real property are exempt from regulation. Thus, any loan in which the broker acts as an agent for the borrower or the lender is exempt; also, any loan made by the broker from his or her own funds is exempt. *C.C. 1916.1.* In one case, a broker loaned money at 250 percent interest, and the court reluctantly held the loan was not usurious. *Garcia v. Wetzel (1984) 159 C.A.3d 1093.* (Such a loan might be attacked as an unconscionable contract.) The broker's exemption applies only to brokers and not to salespersons. A broker can make a secured real estate loan at 25 percent interest, but if a salesperson makes the same loan, the salesperson will be guilty of usury. *People v. Asuncion (1984) 152 C. A. 3d 422.*

    c. *Purchase money loans.* All loans made as part of the sale, in which the seller carries back part of the purchase price with a deed of trust on the property, are exempt from the usury laws. The reason is that the law considers such transactions to be an extension of credit, rather than a loan.

4. *Legislative regulation.* Under Proposition 2, the legislature is given the authority to regulate the classes of exempt lenders as well as the rates that they may charge. Now statutes, in addition

to constitutional amendments, can regulate the categories of exempt lenders or place rate limits on these lenders. There is considerable speculation that if real estate brokers abuse their exempt status the legislature may regulate their interest rate limits.

Effect of Usury

Under the state law, if the loan is usurious, after raising the usury claim the borrower is relieved from obligation to pay any future, unpaid interest. He needs only to repay the principal. The lender forfeits any and all future amounts of interest due under the loan. The lender can only collect the outstanding principal payment without any interest. Furthermore, the borrower can recover all interest (not just the usurious amount) paid in the last two years. Additionally, if the lawsuit is brought within one year of a usurious payment, the borrower will be awarded three times the amount of usurious interest paid within that one-year period. *C.C. 1916-3.* Finally, in extreme cases, the lender can be charged with the felony of loan sharking.

Federal Truth in Lending Law

Since 1969, most real estate loan transactions have been governed by the **Federal Truth in Lending Act**, Title I of the Federal Consumer Protection Act. *15 U.S.C. 1601 et seq.* The act is implemented through Regulation Z under the direction of the Federal Reserve System. Basically, the act requires full disclosure in meaningful terms of the true costs of credit. It requires documents stating the annual percentage rate (APR), amount of down payment, loan terms, and monthly payment. It is a disclosure statute, making no attempt to regulate or limit the costs of that credit.

Real Estate Loans Covered

Truth in lending disclosure documents are required for real estate loans:

1. Made to an individual (as opposed to a corporation or partnership);
2. Whose proceeds are used primarily for personal, family, or household purposes? A business loan is not covered, even though the borrower's residence is used as collateral.
3. By a lender (creditor) who has already made 25 loans of any type, or five loans secured by real estate, within the last calendar year. Thus, a creditor making only one loan is not covered by the Truth in Lending Act, even though it is to an individual for domestic purposes. Only creditors are responsible for the disclosure. Real estate brokers and other arrangers of credit are no longer responsible for the disclosure. *12 C.F.R. 226.2(a)(17).*

Rescission Rights

Besides the full disclosure requirements, Regulation Z has separate provisions that provide certain real estate loans and some credit transactions with a special three-day right of rescission. Generally, deeds of trust on a consumer's residence are covered under the rescission provisions, with the major exceptions of *first* deeds of trust given to purchase the residence. Because the exception is limited to purchase money first deeds of trust, a loan granted for a refinance and a second deeds of trust used in the purchase of a residence would both require the right of rescission. Even if the recession rights are inapplicable, the disclosure sections still apply.

If the loan is covered by rescission rights, the borrower can cancel anytime within three days after receiving the disclosure documents. The exact form of the recession notice that must be provided with the loan is found in Appendix G of Regulation Z and is shown in Figure 15.5. The time for rescission can be extended up to three years after the loan is made is no such documents are provided to the borrower. If the loan is so cancelled, the borrower is not obligated to pay any costs nor incur any obligations. For a true emergency, the borrower can waive the three-day recession right. *12 CFR 226.15.*

Real Property Loan Law

Because of the many abuses and excessive loan charges imposed on secured real estate loans, the legislature enacted the Real Property Loan Act. *B.&P.C. 10240 et seq.* The act limits the amount of fees, charges, and commissions that may be charged on small loans secured by real estate. It further places limits on the use of balloon payments in notes. The act regulates the finance charges only on loans under $30,000 secured by a first deed and loans under $20,000 secured by a junior deed of trust, which are negotiated by a real estate broker. *B.&P.C. 10245.* However, the broker must provide a broker's loan statement for all brokered loans, regardless of amount. However, for residential loans created after 1997, this disclosure statement can often be met by a RESPA (Real Estate Settlement Practices Act) disclosure statement. *B.&P.C. 10240.* However, subprime loans (discussed later in this chapter) require a special form. *10 Code of Regs 2944.* Further, nontraditional and subprime mortgages require a special additional form. *10 Code of Regs 2844.*

Loan Applications

The laws, rules, and regulations governing loan processing and closing of loan applications include both state and federal laws. They

FIGURE 15.5   Three-day recession notice (Reg. Z).

G-8-RESCISSION MODEL FORM
(When Adding a Security Interest)
[From Appendix G of Truth in Lending—Regulation Z]

1. Your Right to Cancel.

You have agreed to give us a [mortgage/lien/security interest] [on/in] your home as security for your existing open-end credit account. You have a legal right under federal law to cancel the [mortgage/lien/security interest], without cost, within three business days after the latest of the following events:

  (1) the date of the [mortgage/lien/security interest] which is _____ ; or
  (2) the date you received your Truth-in-Lending disclosures; or
  (3) the date you received this notice of your right' to cancel the [mortgage/lien/security interest].

If you cancel the [mortgage/lien/security interest], your cancellation will apply only to the [mortgage/lien/security interest]. It will not affect the amount you owe on your account. Within 20 calendar days after we receive your notice of cancellation, we must take the necessary steps to reflect that any [mortgage/lien/security interest] [on/in] your home has been cancelled. We must also return to you any money or property you have given to us or to anyone else in connection with this increase.

You may keep any money or property we have given you until we have done the things mentioned above, but you must then offer to return the money or property. If it is impractical or unfair for you to return the property, you must offer its reasonable value. You may make the offer at your home or at the location of the property. Money must be returned to the address shown below. If we do not take possession of the money or property within 20 calendar days of your offer, you may keep it without further obligation.

How to Cancel.

If you decide to cancel the [mortgage/lien/security interest], you may do so by notifying us, in writing, at [creditor name and business address].

You may use any written statement that is signed and dated by you and states your intention to cancel, or you may use this notice by dating and signing below. Keep one copy of this notice no matter how you notify us because it contains important information about your rights.

If you cancel by mail or telegram, you must send the notice no later than midnight of (date) _____ (or midnight of the third business day following the latest of the three events listed above). If you send or deliver your written notice to cancel some other way, it must be delivered to the above address no later than that time.

I WISH TO CANCEL.

_____   _____
Customer Signature   Date

---

define how loan applications must be processed, prohibit certain forms of discrimination against property locations or types of borrowers, and control the approval process. Different agencies, such as the FHA, or secondary loan markets, such as the Federal National

Mortgage Association (Fannie Mae), have their own regulations that must be followed. The following paragraphs highlight a few of the frequently encountered problems in this area.

Appraisal Reports

People who pay for an appraisal report as part of a loan application are entitled to a copy of that report. Before 1993, applicants often had difficulties obtaining information about these reports required by lenders. *B.& P.C. 11423.*

Processing Time

A very helpful statute for anyone applying for an institutional loan on a one- to four-family residence is the Federal Consumer Credit Protection Act. The bank or savings and loan association must process a completed loan application within 30 days. If it cannot or if it declines to make the loan, the lender must provide a full written report of its reasons. *15 U.S.C. 1691(d)(1).*

False Loan Information

Applicants who submit false financial information or other incorrect information on a loan application can face serious consequences. If the false information is proven to be fraudulent, the lender is not limited by anti-deficiency statutes. Further, if the loan application is made to a bank or other lender insured by the Federal Deposit Insurance Corporation (FDIC), the federal government could intervene if a loss was involved. *U.S. v. 3814 N.W. Thurman St. (1999) 164 F.3d 1191.*

Sale of Loan

Once the loan is funded and completed, it is often sold to Fanny Mae, Freddie Mac, or other institutions in the secondary market. In these loan sales, the servicing may be handled by yet another institution. The borrower has no say in these matters and only hears about it by letter from a new servicing agent. By law, both the old lender and the new lender are required to send letters about the transfer, *RESPA, 12 U.S.C. 2605,* which preempts C.C. *2937.* Con artists sometimes send notices to borrowers indicating there has been a transfer and then fraudulently keep whatever sums are sent. Borrowers should never accept assignment without a letter from both the old and the new lender. Borrowers cannot be charged a late fee for 60 days from the transfer if the payment is sent to the old lender.

Private Mortgage Insurance

Private mortgage insurance (often called PMI) protects the lender if the borrower defaults. In a foreclosure sale, the property may bring only 75 to 85 percent of its appraised value. This insurance protects the lender against the upper end of the loan that might otherwise be unprotected. When lenders make a conventional loan over 80 percent of value, they often require PMI. A lender cannot require private mortgage insurance on conventional loans executed after March 1995, if the loan-to-value ratio is 75 percent or less. *C.C. 2954.7.* Thus, if a home later appreciates in value so that the ratio is below 75 percent, borrowers can later terminate this insurance. This California statute only covers conventional loans and has no impact on government loans. Consequently, FHA loans have a type of insurance the borrower must maintain. FHA's general policy is not to release such insurance regardless of the loan-to-value ratio.

Impound Accounts

Lenders frequently require borrowers to make monthly payments to the lender equal to one-twelfth of the amount of property taxes and property insurance. The lender then makes the annual payment for the borrower and in this way insures that the taxes and insurance are paid. This practice was so abused that California law now makes most impound accounts voluntary. Impound accounts can only be demanded for FHA or VA loans, conventional loans over a 90 percent loan-to-value ratio, or loans where the borrower has paid two consecutive tax installments late. *C.C. § 2954.* RESPA restricts the amount of impound accounts on federal loans. *12 U.S.A. 2609.* In one case, a borrower requested that, as allowed by law, his impound account be terminated, and the lender refused; the jury awarded the borrower $750,000 in punitive damages. *Kirk v. Source One Mortgage Services Corp. (1996) 46 C.A.4th 483.*

Real Property Securities Dealers

Since 1989, most brokers who make or arrange mortgage loans will be required to prepare a disclosure statement called a Lender/Purchaser Disclosure Statement. *B.&P.C. 10232.4.* This disclosure is made to almost all noninstitutional lenders and note purchasers.

Predatory Lending Law

Reacting to the increasing number of people paying such exorbitant interest rates and finance charges on secured loans that they lose their homes, the legislature passed the Predatory Lending Law. *Fin. C. 4970-4978.8.* This complex law regulates certain consumer loans under $250,000 that are made after July 2002. To be covered, the loan must be secured by a deed of trust on the borrower's primary home (a one-to-four family, owner-occupied residence), where either the interest rate or the total finance charge exceeds statutory limits. Covered loans have many restrictions, including the requirements that a covered loan cannot have a prepayment penalty after three years, that any junior loans must not have negative amortization, or that any loan of five years or less must be fully amortized. Most importantly, anyone making such a loan must "reasonably believe" that the consumer can make the payments from other than the equity in their home.

Subprime Loans

The huge losses and high numbers of foreclosures beginning in 2006 was largely a result of subprime loan, and of all the states in the nation, California was impacted the most. Subprime loans can loosely be defined as loans made to high-risk borrowers that probably would not have qualified under the more traditional requirements.

A high debt-to equity ratio means there is little equity in the property, and borrowers with a low credit score statistically are far more likely to default. Further, such subprime loans were often "stated loans" (also called "no documentation loans") because the borrower did not have to verify and prove their income nor amount of other debt. The lender relied on whatever figures the borrower wrote down without verifying those figures.

One reason so many lenders made such loans was the lack of effective regulations prohibiting such practices and because of the higher interest rate that could be charged to borrowers. Lenders making these loans and mortgage brokers originating such loans made large profits on these loans. Figures vary, but many believe as many of 20% or more of all subprime borrowers were ultimately unable to repay their mortgage and went into default. The abuses and amount of excessive loans is one of the many reasons credited for the recession of 2008–2010.

In 2001, California had attempted to regulate predatory lender with *Fin Code* 4970-4979.8. Among other provisions, it provides that at the time of making a loan the lender must reasonably believe the borrower will have the ability to repay the loan. A borrower is presumed to be able to repay the loan if "at the time the loan is consummated, the consumer's total monthly debts, including amounts owed under the loan, do not exceed 55 percent of the consumer's [verified] monthly gross income." *Fin Code 4973(f)*.

How a person could repay a loan using *gross* income and not *net* income and having 54.9% debt seems questionable, and the inability of this code section to limit the predatory lending of the mid 2000s is perhaps self-evident. The California codes also seek to limit negatively amortized loans, but because of federal preemption, California was forced to exempt first deeds of trust. Thus, there is really little effective restrictions on negative amortization and many other loan abuses. *Fin Code 4973(c)*.

The federal law preempts most state laws when it comes to regulating lending practices, especially because it controls first deeds of trust. As such, any effective legislation will have to originate at the federal level. One potential source of these federal controls is Federal Reserve's amended Regulation Z. The amended regulation covers all first deeds of trust made after September 2009 by banks, savings and loans, mortgage loan brokers, and other institutional lenders. The regulation, among its provisions, requires that lenders must have a *reasonable belief* that borrowers can repay the loan before making it, and that borrowers must document their claims of monthly income. *12 C.F.R. 226.34(a)(4).*

It is the author's belief subprime loans and first deed of trusts will be an area of growing concern and of considerable regulation in the upcoming years.

DEFICIENCY JUDGMENTS

Nature of Deficiency

When the proceeds of the sale of property foreclosed under a mortgage or deed of trust are insufficient to satisfy the amount due on that mortgage or deed of trust, the amount (balance) then due the lender is called a *deficiency*. Only under certain specified circumstances may the lender sue the borrower for this deficiency. (See Table 15.3.)

Example

The amount due on a deed of trust was $63,000, and the property foreclosed to satisfy that amount brought only $55,000 at the trustee's sale. The lender is still owed $8,000. However, if the deficiency resulted from foreclosure of a *purchase money* deed of trust, no deficiency (recovery against the borrower) is allowed.

TABLE 15.3   Right to deficiency judgment.

	Deed of Trust	Mortgage
Method(s) of foreclosure	Can be foreclosed by trustee's sale, the traditional method, or by court action (like a mortgage).	Can only be foreclosed by court action.
Deficiency judgment	No deficiency judgment when foreclosed by trustee's sale. Deficiency judgment allowed in court foreclosure if not a purchase money instrument.	Deficiency judgment allowed if not a purchase money instrument.

Restrictions on Deficiency Judgments

A **deficiency judgment** is never possible for a deed of trust foreclosed by a power of sale (**trustee's sale**). However, a deed of trust foreclosed like a mortgage (by court action) and a mortgage permit a deficiency judgment (action against the debtor personally) if they are not *purchase money* instruments. By statute, certain residential loans obtained by fraud are exempt. This exemption is discussed later in the chapter. Also, loans that are subordinated to construction loans may permit deficiency judgments in certain situations.

Purchase Money Instruments

A purchase money deed of trust or mortgage is defined by Section 580b of the Code of Civil Procedure. To the layperson, anytime money is used in the purchase of property it is considered purchase money. However, at law, to be purchase money, the funds must be used toward the property's acquisition, and the loan must be one of two types recognized by law. (See Table 15.4.) The following are the two purchase money loans:

1. *Front seller.* A promissory note given by the buyer to the seller for part of the purchase price and secured by the property being purchased is purchase money. In effect, the seller has extended credit to the buyer and secured that credit by the seller's own property. Because real dollars do not physically change hands, this type of purchase money loan is often called a soft *money* loan. The nature of the property involved is immaterial. It could be raw land or commercial, industrial, or residential property.

TABLE 15.4   Types of purchase money instruments.

	Soft Money	Hard Money
Lender	Seller	Third person
Borrower	Buyer	Buyer
Effect	Extension of credit by seller to buyer for purchase of seller's property	Loan of money (real dollars) by third person to buyer for purchase of seller's property
Dollar limitations	None: amount of money immaterial	None: amount of money immaterial
Property limitations	None: any type of property (e.g., raw land, commercial, or residential)	Only one- to four-family owner-occupied dwelling in which buyer actually resides

2. *From third person.* A promissory note is given by the buyer to a third party for part of the purchase price and secured by the property being purchased, which property is a one- to four-family dwelling that will be occupied by the purchaser. Thus, the loan must be from someone other than the seller, and it must actually be used for all or part of the purchase of property. These loans are often called *hard money* loans.

Examples of Purchase Money Deeds of Trust

Purchase money deeds of trust (PMDTs) are just another way of saying "nonrecourse" financing. The following do *not* qualify as PMDTs; therefore, the borrower would be liable for any deficiency.

1. A loan to refinance a homeowner's residence is not purchase money because the proceeds are not used to purchase the home. Thus, one of the costs of refinancing involves loss of the antideficiency protection.

2. A loan to remodel a homeowner's residence or to add a swimming pool is not purchase money because the proceeds are not used to purchase all or part of the home. *Allstate S.&L. Assn. v. Murphy (1979) 98 C.A.3d 761.* Conversely, a construction loan to finance the building of the residence would be purchase money.

3. A loan to purchase a five-unit motel in which the borrower lived would not be purchase money because the loan becomes hard money on property over four units. If the property was a fourplex, the loan would be purchase money. Also, if the seller (not the lender) received the promissory note secured by the five-unit motel, it would be soft money purchase money.

Purpose of Deficiency Statutes

Deficiency legislation was passed in California during the Depression to protect homeowners (hard money) and to protect buyers who purchased property from sellers at overvalued prices and secured the property by a deed of trust or mortgage (soft money). However, a deficiency judgment is also allowed on nonpurchase money mortgages and deeds of trust that are foreclosed by court action. The rationale is that if the property is sold for an unreasonably low price the debtor is protected by the one-year period of redemption. During this period, the debtor can repurchase the property at the price for which it was sold at the foreclosure sale. Sellers accepting purchase money deed of trust face risks that to some extent can be minimized. (See Table 15.5.)

TABLE 15.5 Risks of PMDTs to sellers.

Risks to Purchase Money Deeds of Trust (PMDT) Holder	Possible Methods to Help Minimize the Risks

I. NONTAX CONSIDERATIONS

No Deficiency Judgment. No deficiency judgment is allowed after foreclosing a PMDT. Therefore, if there is insufficient equity in the property, the note may be worthless.

1. Be sure there is sufficient downpayment so that the loan is well secured by the property.
2. Be sure the buyer has sufficient resources and income to make the payments on the first and second deeds of trust. (Qualify the buyer as would any other lender, including income statements, net worth, proof of employment, proof of savings accounts and the like.)
3. Be sure the buyer has a past history of financial responsibility ("credit character") indicative of a desire to meet the current loan payments. (Qualify the buyer with acceptable TRW or other credit company reports.)

Insufficient Equity. If the senior lien forecloses, the PMDT holder will be wiped out if there is insufficient equity in the property.

1. Solution 1-3 above.
2. Record a "Notice of Delinquency" to receive advance notice of a delinquency that has not ripened into a foreclosure.
3. Prepare the second deed of trust so that it is salable in the secondary market so that it can, if ever needed, be more easily sold. (For example, FANNIE MAE, through qualified lenders, will purchase PMDT if the FANNIE MAE note and deed of trust form is used, and the underwriting eligibility criteria (of property and borrowers) are met.

I. TAX CONSIDERATIONS

Other Sales Incorporated. Other un-related installment sales may be used to calculate the gain, which could make this sale unprofitable.

1. Installment tax reporting allows the seller to spread the taxable gain over the term of the loan instead of reporting the entire gain in the year of sale. However, unless the property is the taxpayer's principal resident or business property under $150,000, there may be serious tax problems. The law provides complex rules determining the gain, including the calculations of all installment debts of the taxpayer.

(Continued)

TABLE 15.5   *(Continued)*.

Risks to Purchase Money Deeds of Trust (PMDT) Holder	Possible Methods to Help Minimize the Risks
	2. Check with a CPA before executing any installment sales, especially if you have other installment sales in process on other transactions.
Interest Rate Too Low. The interest rate on the PMDT is too low. If the rate is less than 9% per annum, the IRS may recalculate (rewrite) the loan for tax purposes, "imputing" an interest rate of 9%. If the "Applicable Federal Rate" (AFT) is less than 9%, then you and the IRS can use the lower AFR rate.	1. Charge at least 9% interest (or the AFR interest rate, if less than 9%). Special rules exist for loans over $2.8 million, and many other situations. *IRC 1274.* Maximum interest rate must virtually be 110% of the "Applicable Federal Rate," a rate which fluctuates monthly. Otherwise the IRS will "impute" a rate equal to 120% of the AFR. It is not nearly as important now, since all income is taxed as ordinary income and capital gains of lesser importance.
	2. Sale of taxpayer's principal residence, and sales of real estate worth less than $250,000 are some of the exceptions from the above rules.
Mortgage Greater Than Basis. If the buyer is assuming or taking "subject to" an existing deed of trust, there will be taxable gain to the extent the debt exceeds the taxpayer's basis.	1. Sell the property for all cash, when there is a "mortgage over basis" problem. *(Tax Reg 15A.453-1b3i, e)*
	2. Understand the nature of the problem. For example, assume property sells for $300,000: $15,000 down, $30,000 PMDT, and the buyer assumes a $255,000 first deed of trust. Assuming the seller's tax basis is $120,00, the seller will have $135,000 capital gains (255,000–$120,000).
If Accelerated Depreciation Involved. If the property was depreciated under the old tax laws using accelerated depreciation, there will be "recapture" problems.	1. Make sure the deposit is large enough to cover closing costs and tax consequences.
	2. See a CPA or attorney before executing the deposit receipt.

Exemption for Fraudulent Loans

In recent years, the courts and the legislature have found it inequitable that purchasers obtained loans through fraud and then shielded themselves from any liability because of the deficiency statutes. If the borrower secures the loan by fraud, then the tender may sue for actual damages (plus punitive damages up to 50 percent of the actual damages) in a separate suit, without violating the one-action or antideficiency statutes. However, the same statute exempts loans under $150,000 on owner-occupied residences from fraud lawsuits. *C.C.P. 726.* Typical examples of fraud include cases where a borrower fraudulently claims that he or she intends to live on the property or fraudulently misstates the annual property income.

Bargioni v. Hill
59 C.2d 121 (1963)

[Before 1963, hard money purchase money loans involved secured loans from third persons for the purchase of any type of real estate. Since that date, two additional requirements were added. The secured property being purchased must be one- to four-family dwellings, and the purchaser must reside in that property. This case arose before the new statute. Therefore, the loan discussed in this case would not be purchase money today because a large apartment was involved. However, if a four-plex was acquired today under the facts of this case, it would be purchase money.

Almost all hard money purchase money loans involve actual loans of cash, which physically transfers during escrow. The issue in this case is whether the term loan is to be broadly interpreted or narrowly construed. The plaintiff, a real estate broker, received his commission from the sale as a promissory note executed by the buyer, the defendant, and secured by the purchased property. The Court had to consider whether this commission arrangement, in effect, amounted to a loan of the broker's commission to the buyer to purchase the property.]

TRAYNOR, JUSTICE. Defendant purchased a motel and executed a $5,000 note to plaintiff, who had acted as broker in the transaction. The note was secured by a junior trust deed on the motel. Defendant defaulted on the note and plaintiff sued for the balance due, the security having been lost through a private sale under a senior trust deed. The trial court entered judgment for the amount due. Defendant appeals.

Defendant also contends that plaintiff's recovery is barred by Section 580b of the Code of Civil Procedure, which provides that no deficiency judgment shall lie after any sale of real property "under a deed of trust or mortgage given to secure payment of the balance of the purchase price of real property." This section compels a purchase money mortgagee to assume the risk that the security is inadequate.

The purposes are to discourage land sales that are unsound because the land is overvalued and, in the event of a depression in land value, to prevent the aggravation of the downturn that would result if defaulting purchasers lost the land and were burdened with personal liability. These purposes are served by relieving the purchaser of

continued

personal liability to any person who finances the purchase and takes as security a trust deed or mortgage on the property purchased, provided the financier intended the loan to be used to pay all or part of the purchase price.

The trial court found that the parties did not intend that plaintiff's commission be part of the purchase price of the motel. This finding is not supported by the evidence. Plaintiff was employed by the seller, plaintiff's brother, to act as broker in the sale of the motel, and plaintiff in turn associated another broker. A written agreement of the sale was signed by the buyer and seller and both brokers, under which the purchase price was set at $310,000, and the seller was to pay the broker's commissions, which amounted to $10,000.

Thereafter, however, defendant agreed to pay the brokers' commissions, and the purchase price was correspondingly reduced to $300,000 net to him from the sale. He also knew that the seller was obligated to pay the brokers' commissions of $10,000, and that the seller had agreed to finance the purchase on these terms.

Thus, in accepting defendant's note in payment of the commission, plaintiff extended credit that otherwise would have been extended by the seller. That credit was necessary to the consummation of the sale. The only reasonable inference that can be drawn from this evidence is that plaintiff intended to and did partially finance the purchase. Because his note was secured by a deed of trust on the motel, his recovery is barred by Section 580b.

Judgment reversed [and the broker cannot recover his commission or sue defendant personally for that amount].

FORECLOSURE PROCESS AND PROCEDURE

When the trustor of a deed of trust is in default, the beneficiary can enforce the obligation only through **foreclosure** proceedings. The beneficiary has the option of either judicial or nonjudicial proceedings. If the beneficiary is reserving the rights to a deficiency judgment or attempting to foreclose a nonmonetary obligation, he or she must foreclose judicially, as if it was a mortgage. In all other cases, the beneficiary forecloses by a trustee's sale. This nonjudicial remedy is used today in nearly all normal foreclosure situations. To protect trustors of foreclosed property, the law provides special protection against unconscionable contracts of sale and, in the case of residential property, statutes impose especially strict rules regulating any attempted sale.

Nature of Trustee's Foreclosure

Unless the lender sees a deficiency judgment, almost all California deed of trust are foreclosed by a **nonjudicial process**. The loans are foreclosed and sold by a private trustee's sale. This contrasts to a **judicial foreclosure,** which is accomplished by a lawsuit in the courts.

General Procedure

The private sale follows certain well-defined procedures established by law. Additionally, before foreclosing any deed of trust, the deed of trust itself must be reviewed. If the small print imposes any additional terms for foreclosure, then those terms, too, must be followed.

The "normal" foreclosure process consists of out four steps: record the notice of default, wait the three-month period of reinstatement, publish the notice of sale, and hold the trustee's sale. The requirements of each step are carefully controlled by statute.

Two Classes of Loans

In response to the subprime meltdown in California, the beginning in late 2008, the State created two classes of loans. The first category involves loans: (1) secured by owner-occupied residences, (2) that were made during 2003 through 2007. These five years represent approximately the time frames that so many subprime loans were made and that result in an extraordinarily high percentage of foreclosures. For simplicity, in this book the author will refer to this first category loans as "Crisis Period Loans." These Crisis Period Loans have special requirements in addition to the normal foreclosure process. These additional requirements will exist through 2012. The second class of loans is to all other loans including Crisis Period Loans after 2012. These loans follow the normal foreclosure procedures.

The special requirements for Crisis Period Loans are in response to a fiscal problem in California as well as a political crisis. Most of the statutory provisions are "sunset," meaning they expire at specified times, all on or before the end of 2012. It is possible that circumstance may entice the legislature to extend the time period or to modify the requirements and special wording used in some of the foreclosures. Always check the latest laws.

Trustee's Foreclosure Process

Pre-foreclosure Evaluation for Crisis Period Loans

Before a lender can foreclose a Crisis Period Loan the lender must first contact the borrower. It is only after 30 days from the first contact (or one month after trying with due diligence to find the borrower) that the lender can begin foreclosure. The statute says, the borrower or its agent "shall contact the borrower in person or by telephone in order to assess the borrower's financial situation and explore options for the borrower to avoid foreclosure." *C.C. 2923.5.* This special 30-day provision does not apply to any loans except Crisis Period Loans.

The exact meaning these requirements in unclear and its parameters have not been litigated in court. It definitely means the parties must explore other financial alternatives to foreclosure. Further, the lender must "advise the borrower that he or she has the right to request a subsequent meeting and, if requested, the mortgagee, beneficiary, or authorized agent shall schedule the meeting to occur within 14 days." The statute *suggests* an appropriate workable solution might be a five-year interest rate reduction, or boost the loan term period to 40 years, or defer part of the principal, However, nowhere does the statute specify the lender must grant any special concessions or withhold foreclosure if the borrower is unable to meet his, her, or their financial obligations. As once critic said, at the very least, the statute "buys the borrower an extra month" and in some cases something may be worked out.

Notice of Default

The first step in the actual foreclosure process is to record a notice of default on the form prescribed by statute. *C.C. 2924.* (See Figure 15.6.) Generally, the foreclosure is handled by a professional foreclosure company, because the procedural requirements are somewhat complex, and the total fees are limited by statute. Within 10 business days after recording the notice, a copy must be sent to the trustor, at the last known address, and to anyone else who recorded a request for special notice.

Within 30 days after recording the notice, a copy must be sent to everyone of record having a junior deed of trust or junior lease. *C.C. 2924b.* Thus, the only advantage to a junior lien holder of recording a request for special notice is slightly less than 20-day advance notice. (See Figure 15.7 for a sample request for special notice.)

Right to Reinstate

Any time the beneficiary declares a default for an installment payment and accelerates and declares the entire outstanding balance of the loan due and payable, the trustor has a statutory right of reinstatement.

FIGURE 15.6 Notice of default.

Notice of Default
[Consumer Notice Required by C.C. §2924c(b)(1)]

IMPORTANT NOTICE

IF YOUR PROPERTY IS IN FORECLOSURE BECAUSE YOU ARE BEHIND IN YOUR PAYMENTS, IT MAY BE SOLD WITHOUT ANY COURT ACTION, and you may have the legal right to bring your account in good standing by paying all of your past due payments plus permitted costs and expenses within the time permitted by law for reinstatement of your account, which is normally five business days prior to the date set for the sale of your property. No sale date may be set until three months from the date this notice of default may be recorded (which date of recordation appears on this notice). This amount is _____ as of _____[date]_____ and will increase until your account becomes current.

While your property is in foreclosure, you still must pay other obligations (such as insurance and taxes) required by your note and deed of trust or mortgage. If you fail to make future payments on the loan, pay taxes on the property, provide insurance on the property, or pay other obligations as required in the note and deed of trust or mortgage, the beneficiary or mortgagee may insist that you do so in order to reinstate your account in good standing. In addition, the beneficiary or mortgagee may require as a condition to reinstatement that you provide reliable written evidence that you paid all senior liens, property taxes, and hazard insurance premiums.

Upon your written request, the beneficiary or mortgagee will give you a written itemization of the entire amount you must pay. You may not have to pay the entire unpaid portion of your account, even though full payment was demanded, but you must pay all amounts in default at the time payment is made. However, you and your beneficiary or mortgagee may mutually agree in writing prior to the time the notice of sale is posted (which may not be earlier than the end of the three-month period stated above) to, among other things, (1) provide additional time in which to cure the default by transfer of the property or otherwise; or (2) establish a schedule of payments in order to cure your default; or both (1) and (2).

Following the expiration of the time period referred to in the first paragraph of this notice, unless the obligation being foreclosed upon or a separate written agreement between you and your creditor permits a longer period, you have only the legal right to stop the sale of your property by paying the entire amount demanded by your creditor.

To find out the amount you must pay, or to arrange for payment to stop the foreclosure, or if your property is in foreclosure for any other reason, contact:

_____ (Name of beneficiary or mortgagee)
_____ (Mailing address)
_____ (Telephone)

If you have any questions, you should contact a lawyer or the governmental agency which may have insured your loan.

Notwithstanding the fact that your property is in foreclosure, you may offer your property for sale, provided the sale is concluded prior to the conclusion of the foreclosure.

Remember, **YOU MAY LOSE LEGAL RIGHTS IF YOU DO NOT TAKE PROMPT ACTION.**

- - - - -

FIGURE 15.6   (*Continued*).

[Required by C.C. §2924(a)(1)]

Notice is given to you by this document stating that I, the person signing this notice below, am the agent for _____ Title Company, the Trustee under that deed of trust executed by you as Trustor(s), and _____ Bank as Beneficiary, and _____ Title Company as Trustee, on _____[date]_____. For convenience, the aforesaid deed of trust shall sometimes be called "that Deed of Trust" in this notice. That Deed of Trust was recorded on _____[date]_____ as Instrument Number _____, in reel _____ and image _____, in the official records of _____ County, California. That deed of trust is security for the property described as _____.

That Deed of Trust is security for an obligation which has been breached, which breach or breaches are described as follows: _____.
Because of that breach or breaches, the Beneficiary, _____ Bank, declares that all sums secured by that Deed of Trust are hereby declared immediately due and owing and the Beneficiary elects to sell or causes to be sold the property described above to satisfy that obligation.

[Paragraph added for loans made in years 2003 through 2007
that are secured by owner-occupied residential property]
[Required through year 2012 by C.C. §2923.5(j)]

As required by California Civil Code 2923.5, the Beneficiary, _____ Bank, declares that it has contacted you, the Trustor, to evaluate and assess your financial situation, and has explored options for you to avoid foreclosure in the manner specified by statute. [or the Beneficiary has tried with due diligence to contact you, the borrower, as required by this statute, or you have surrendered the property to beneficiary, or its authorized agent.]

Anytime after recording, the notice of default until five business days before the actual sale, the trustor can cure the default by paying only the amount of installments in arrears plus certain statutory costs and fees. *C.C. 2924c.* On such payment, the acceleration is voided, and the loan is considered current as if the default never occurred. For example, on a $100,000 loan, the trustor in default of two $500 monthly payments could cure the default by paying $1,000 plus fees and costs. The trustor would not be obligated to pay the entire $100,000 balance declared due and payable because of acceleration. Once reinstated, the trustee records a *notice of rescission*.

Notice of Sale

Once the three-month period of reinstatement has passed, the trustee can set the date for a sale. *C.C. 2924f.* (See Figure 15.8 for a sample Notice of Sale.)

Additionally, a special statute was enacted effective June 15, 2009, and it extends the 90-day right to reinstate period to 180-day right to

FIGURE 15.7 Request for special notice of default.

Recording Requested By:

Ted Gordon
1234 Jones Street
San Francisco, CA 94111

When Recorded Mail To:

Ted Gordon
1234 Jones Street
San Francisco, CA 94111

Assessor Parcel No:
145-987-07-2

Request for Notice of Default and Sale
(Pursuant to Civil Code 2924)

As provided by the California Civil Code, the undersigned requests a copy of (1) any Notice of Default, and (2) any Notice of Sale, to the deed of trust named below.

The deed of trust to which notice is requested is for that instrument executed on December 15, 2010, in which Peter Smith is the Trustor, XYZ Bank is the beneficiary, and ABC Title Company is the Trustee, and which instrument was recorded on December 15, 2010, in the Official Records of county of Marin, State of California, in Reel 9087, and Image 297.

Notice is to be mailed to:

Ted Gordon
1234 Jones Street
San Francisco, CA 94111

NOTICE. A copy of any notice of default and of any notice of sale will be sent only to the address contained in this recorded request. If your addresses changes, a new request must be recorded.

Dated: _____   [Signature] Ted Gordon, _____

[Notary]

reinstate for Crisis Period Loans. This extra 90-day extension is limited to first deeds of trust that qualify as Crisis Period Loans. There are a few minor exceptions. *C.C. 2923.52.* This special provision expires at the end of 2010 December 31, 2010.

Because the notice must be published at least once a week for three weeks, the sale date must be at least three weeks after publication. Three weeks before the sale, notice must also be sent to anyone who received a copy of the notice of default, and the notice must be posted

FIGURE 15.8   Notice of trustee's sale.

Recording Requested By And:

When Recorded Mail To:

    XYZ Title Company

    888 Fifth Avenue

    San Rafael, CA 94563

Assessor's Parcel Number

    266 - 850 -007 -1

NOTICE OF TRUSTEE'S SALE OF PROPERTY

YOU ARE IN DEFAULT UNDER A TRUST DEED DATED MAY 2, 2000. UNLESS YOU TAKE ACTION TO PROTECT YOUR PROPERTY, IT MAY BE SOLD AT A PUBLIC SALE. IF YOU NEED AN EXPLANATION OF THE NATURE OF THE PROCEEDING AGAINST YOU, YOU SHOULD CONTACT A LAWYER.

NOTICE IS HEREBY GIVEN that:

1. <u>Property to Be Sold</u>. The property to be sold is a single-family residence commonly known as 123 Jones Street, Corte Madera, California, and more particularly known as Marin County Assessor's Parcel Number 266-850-007-1. (For convenience, this property is sometimes called "the Property" in this notice.)

2. <u>Date, Time and Location of Sale</u>. The sale will be held on Monday, June 30, 2010 at 3:30 p.m., at the main entrance to the City Hall, at 12345 Third Street, in San Rafael, California, which is in the same county in which the Property is located.

3. <u>Name, Address and Telephone of Trustee</u>. The person who will be conducting the sale is Joe Agent, whose street address is XYZ Title Company, at 888 Fifth Avenue, in San Rafael, California, and whose telephone number is (415) 111-1111.

4. <u>Trustors and Obligation</u>. The Trustors are Robert and Jane McMasters, husband and wife, who obtained a loan from the beneficiary, XYZ Bank, and which loan was secured by a deed of trust on the Property. That deed of trust was executed on May 2, 2000 and recorded on the same date in the official records of Marin County in Reel 3456 at Image 344. (For convenience, this deed of trust is sometimes called "the Deed of Trust" in this notice.)

5. <u>Notice of Default Recorded</u>. As required by statute, a duly executed notice of default was recorded on August 1, 2010 in the official records of Marin County in Reel 3556 at Image 104.

6. <u>Nature of Sale</u>. The Property will be sold at a public auction to the highest bidder, for cash, in U.S. currency (and/or the cashier's certified or other checks specified in Civil Code Section 2924h), which is all due and payable at the time of sale. The sale is made under and by the terms of the power of sale in the Deed of Trust.

7. <u>Sale Without Warranties</u>. The sale of the Property is made in "as is" condition, without warranties of any kind, including no warranties regarding title, possession or encumbrances.

8. <u>Notice as Ordered by Beneficiary</u>. This notice is given under written orders received by the Trustee from the Beneficiary.

FIGURE 15.8   (*Continued*).

---

9. <u>Amount Due</u>. On November 6, 2010, when this notice was first published, the total unpaid balance under the promissory note secured by the Deed of Trust on the Property, plus reasonable estimated costs, expenses and advances, totaled $453,678.

10. <u>No Buyer Options Notice Required</u>. The Trustee declares that this loan that is secured by the Deed of Trust on the Property was not made between 2001 through 2007, and therefore no statement need be made about contracting the borrower to assess the borrower's financial situation and to explore options for the to avoid foreclosure pursuant to Civil Code §2923.5.

Note that paragraph title are for convenience only, and not to be considered a part of this notice, or used to construe any of the notice's meaning.

Dated: November 6, 2010   XYZ Title Company, Trustee

                                                          Signed by: <u>Joe Agent</u>

[Notary]

---

on the property. Finally, notice must be recorded 14 days before the sale.

It should be noted that those persons acquiring a junior lien after the notice of default has been recorded are not protected nor provided notice by recording a request for special notice. Because they did not receive a copy of the notice of default, they are not entitled to a copy of the notice of sale. The situation is best handled by direct contact with the trustee or beneficiary conducting the foreclosure.

If the deed of trust secures the trustor's home and arose out of an obligation subject to the Unruh Act (which covers certain consumer contracts), special additional notice provisions are required. *C.C. 2924f.* During this period, the owner has the right to pay off the full amount of the outstanding loan principal plus costs, interest, and damages. This right is called the equity of redemption and, if exercised, it extinguishes the loan and stops the foreclosure proceeding.

Trustee's Sale

The sale is held in the county where the property is located. It is held by public auction and goes to the highest bidder. Each person must bid cash or the equivalent, except for the foreclosing beneficiary, who can credit-bid the amount of his loan. *C.C. 2924g,h.* Only the foreclosing beneficiary can (and always does) bid based on the outstanding balance of the deed of trust. The full amount due is almost always bid. Junior lien holders cannot credit-bid the amount of their loan.

They, too, must bid cash, which is logical because the senior beneficiary would not wish any "paper" from a lienor in an even lower position.

Provided that the trustee announces at the time set for sale that the sale has been postponed, the law is fairly liberal in granting the trustee up to three postponements. The trustee can also have one additional delay if he or she reasonably believes that the trustor has filed for bankruptcy. Any additional delays must be preceded by republishing the notice of the sale.

A common question arises when the trustor tenders only part payment. Technically, if the beneficiary accepts it, clearly stating acceptance is without waiving any right to enforce the default, such payment will have no effect on the foreclosure. However, to avoid any problems of proof concerning the issue of prejudice or defenses of waiver or estoppel, many attorneys advise their clients to refuse anything less than full payment.

Judicial Foreclosure

A mortgage is foreclosed by judicial action. Although mortgages are seldom encountered in California, deeds of trust are foreclosed judicially "like a mortgage" if the lender is seeking a deficiency judgment. In judicial foreclosures, the steps are to file a lawsuit, reinstate until trial, obtain a judgment of foreclosure at trial, issue a judgment ordering foreclosure, and have the sheriff sell the property. If a deficiency judgment was requested, the trustor has a one-year period of redemption (three months if no deficiency results from the sale).

File Lawsuit

Judicial foreclosure is initiated by filing a lawsuit in the superior court in the county in which the property is located. A complaint is filed with the county clerk and then served on all necessary parties. Usually, a lis pendens is recorded to provide constructive notice to any subsequent purchasers or encumbrancers that their rights will be subject to the outcome of the litigation.

Generally, an attorney prepares the complaint and, in deciding whom to name as defendants, orders a foreclosure guarantee report or a litigation guarantee report from a title company. These title reports show who has to be joined in the lawsuit. Anyone left out of the lawsuit is not affected by the foreclosure. Thus, if a junior lienor is not named, that lien is not extinguished by the court action. *Carpenter v. Brenham (1870) 40 C. 221.* Similarly, if only two of three co-owners are named, only two-thirds of the property can be foreclosed and sold.

Right to Reinstate and Equity of Redemption

Until the time of the court judgment ordering sale of the property, the debtor can reinstate the loan by paying the delinquent installments plus interest and costs. Because a contested foreclosure action may take six months to two years to get to court, the debtor has ample opportunity to cure the default. The debtor also has an equitable right of redemption to terminate the foreclosure by paying the full outstanding loan amount plus costs, interest, and damages. This equitable right is seldom used, because the right to reinstate also runs to the time of judgment.

Trial and Court Judgment

If the trustor fights the foreclosure rather than allowing a judgment by default, a trial is held. The judge alone hears the facts and issues a judgment ordering a foreclosure sale of the property. The trustor who also wants a deficiency judgment so notifies the court, which then orders a one-year right of redemption to the sale.

Sale of Property

The court issues a judgment ordering a foreclosure sale of the property. The judgment creditor then takes the judgment to the sheriff to execute (levy) on the property. The sheriff holds a sale of the property to the highest bidder. A bidder need not pay all cash at the sale. The bidder can deposit the greater of $5,000 or 10 percent of the bid price at the sale and deposit the balance within 10 days. *C.C.P. 701.590(c)*. Two types of levy procedures are possible, depending on whether the creditor sought a deficiency judgment.

1. *No deficiency judgment sought.* If the creditor has not sought a deficiency judgment, then the sheriff follows the normal levy procedure. The levy process (execution on the judgment) cannot begin until 120 days after the debtor (mortgagor or trustor) has been notified of the levy. Then, another 20 days of publication of notice of the sale must occur. C.C.P. *701.540-701.545*. The minimum time from the filing of the lawsuit until the sale is 150 days plus the time it takes to get to trial. A default judgment can often be heard within 7 to 15 days, whereas a contested case can take four to 18 months or longer to get to trial. Once the sheriff sells the property, the sale is final. There is no redemption period, and the sheriff issues a deed to the purchaser.

2. *Deficiency judgment sought: Redemption period.* If the creditor applied to the court for a deficiency judgment, then the sheriff follows a special levy process. This process is similar to the process required by the old foreclosure laws existing before July 1983. The sale must be advertised as prescribed by statute for 20 days. At the sale, the purchaser receives only a *certificate of sale*, not a *deed*. Within one year after the sale (three months if no deficiency occurs at the sale), the debtor (and only the debtor or a successor in interest) can redeem the property by paying the purchase price plus set fees. Furthermore, if the property is a home, the debtor can live on the property. The redemption only applies to the debtor or a successor in interest. If the property is not redeemed during the redemption period, then the sheriff issues a deed to the purchaser. *C.C.P 729.010.* Thus, although there is no 120-day waiting period before beginning the levy, there is a one-year redemption period following the sale (reduced to three months if there is no deficiency).

Sale of Residential Property in Foreclosure

The legislature was concerned about distressed homeowners who were ignorant of their rights in foreclosure and unknowledgeable about the significant increase in their equity due to inflation. Therefore, the legislature enacted a series of bills that regulate the sales and, in some cases, loans made by homeowners while their property is in foreclosure or during a specified period after that event. For example, one statute provides anyone selling a principal residence while subject to an outstanding notice of default must sign a home *equity sales contract*. It also permits the seller to rescind the transaction without penalty within five business days of signing the contract. *C.C. 1695–1695.12.* Another statute provides that homes may be sold while in foreclosure to an unconscionable disadvantage and allows the homeowner to rescind the transaction anytime within two years. *C.C. 1695.13–1695.14.*

EFFECTS OF FORECLOSURE ON OTHER EXISTING DEEDS OF TRUST

General Rule

When property is encumbered by several liens and one of those liens is foreclosed, the status and validity of the remaining liens depend on their priority in relation to the foreclosed lien. Generally, the foreclosure of a senior lien extinguishes all junior liens, whereas the foreclosure of a junior lien has no effect on a senior encumbrance.

Notice of Delinquency

The beneficiary of a junior loan on a one- to four-family residence and for junior loans under $300,000 on any kind of property can have the trustor sign a notice of delinquency. Once properly executed and recorded, it is sent to the senior lender. For the duration of the notice, the senior lender would then have to provide notice whenever the trustor is more than four months in delinquency, even if the lender is not yet going to begin foreclosure. *C.C. 2924e.*

Effect of Junior's Foreclosure

The foreclosure of a second deed of trust has no effect on the validity of the first deed of trust. The purchaser at the foreclosure sale buys the property subject to the first deed of trust. The rationale is that when the junior deed of trust became a lien the property was already burdened by the first deed of trust and, consequently, the junior lienor should not be able to grant a greater interest than he already owned. (However, under the Garn Bill, such sales appear to be transfers, which would allow a lender to exercise a due-on-sale clause in a senior deed of trust.)

Effect of Senior's Foreclosure

By the same logic, when the owner of the first deed of trust obtained a lien, the property was free of any junior liens, and the owner should therefore be able to offer the property at a foreclosure sale in the condition it was in when it was obtained. Because a foreclosure of a senior lien extinguishes all junior liens, holding junior deeds of trust can be very risky; this is why their interest rates are so much higher than first deeds of trust.

Exception If Owner Purchases

One exception to the rule that foreclosure of the first deed of trust eliminates junior liens is when (as in the principal case) the purchaser, at a foreclosure sale, is the owner of the property. In such a rare situation, all junior liens discharged by the foreclosure reattach to the property.

Options for Junior Lienor

Because the foreclosure of a senior lien eliminates all junior encumbrances, the rights and remedies of a junior lienor are strongly related to and frequently dependent on the actions of the senior lien and the value of the property. The holder of a second deed of trust has several options when the first deed of trust goes into default or foreclosure, but the junior holder must take action to protect his or her interest. The trustee's sale conclusively terminates any interest of junior lienors in the property. (The only person to have any interest in the property after the sale would be the trustor, and then only if the property is judicially foreclosed on a nonpurchase money instrument, at which a deficiency judgment is sought.)

Depending on the circumstances and the value of the property over and above the lien, the astute junior lienor may be able to minimize losses or even salvage the investment. If the property has no significant value over and above the amount of the senior lien being foreclosed, then there is nothing the junior can do except take a tax write-off on the lien. Assuming that there is or may be some value in the property above the total of the senior lien, then the junior has four options.

1. *Reinstate.* Within the three-month reinstatement period, the junior could advance the funds to bring the senior deed of trust current, thereby curing the default. *C.C. 2876.* When the property is worth more than the junior lien, one of the junior's best alternatives is to cure the senior and foreclose the junior lien. If the junior did not obtain a waiver from the senior lender when he or she placed the loan, the senior may call its loan due and payable on foreclosure of the property. Even worse, if the junior is required to pay off the senior loan before maturity, the senior lender may also require a prepayment penalty. *Pacific Trust Co. v. Fidelity Federal Savings (1986) 184 C.A.3d 817.*

2. *Do nothing.* The junior can allow the foreclosure sale to occur and hope that there will be surplus funds. If so, they will be paid to the junior lienors in order of priority (even if their loans are not yet otherwise due). If there are no surplus proceeds, the junior may sue the trustor personally for the deficiency if the deed of trust is a nonpurchase money loan. This "do-nothing" remedy is followed when the junior lacks or refuses to expend more funds to protect the loan.

3. *Junior can bid.* If the property is worth significantly more than the amount of the junior lien, the junior often bids for the property at the senior's trustee sale. The foreclosing senior lien must be paid in cash. The junior lienor then acquires the property and its equity unless someone bids even more (including enough to pay off the junior lien with cash).

4. *Junior can foreclose.* Because a default of the senior lien is considered a default of the junior lien, the junior lienor could foreclose simultaneously with the senior. In practice, this option is almost never selected because it offers no real benefits.

TRANSFER OF SECURED PROPERTY

Right to Transfer

Even though title to property encumbered by a deed of trust technically rests with the trustee, the law recognizes the security instrument as a lien. The true owner of the property, the trustor, is free to sell, give, or otherwise transfer the encumbered property at will and without the consent of the beneficiary. *C.C. 864, 865.* However, if the transfer is made without the consent of the beneficiary, he or she may be able to accelerate the loan and declare the entire balance immediately due and payable. The ability of the lender to demand full payment depends on the existence of a due-on-sale clause in the note. The *Garn Bill.*

Effect of Transfer on Debt

When the property is transferred, the grantee receives title subject to all existing liens and encumbrances of notice. Furthermore, if the grantee assumes the loan or accepts it under a *novation* (see later section on this topic), then, to the extent a deficiency judgment is permitted by law, the grantee will be personally liable for payment of the loan.

Subject To

If the grantee takes the property only subject to the loan, then only the property remains liable for the loan. Furthermore, the original owner retains a contingent personal liability on the loan, because his name is still on the promissory note. The new owner accepts no personal liability for payment under the note, because she never agrees personally to assume any obligations.

Assumption

Under an **assumption**, the new owner agrees to accept and assume a personal obligation to make payment on the promissory note. In the event of a default, the property is first foreclosed. If there is a deficiency, the new owner is personally liable to the extent that a deficiency judgment is permitted. Furthermore, if the new owner is unable to satisfy the deficiency, the old owner, who also signed the note promising to pay, becomes liable for payment as a surety.

It is a common misconception among sellers that once a buyer assumes their loan they have no further liability. This belief is fostered, in part, by ignorance and in part by the rarity of cases in which sellers are actually sited because of a deficiency remaining after foreclosure of the property and recourse to the buyer. However, it is important to know the buyer. Even if sellers have no personal liability because a purchase money deed of trust is involved, a default could have a negative effect on their credit.

Liability Requires Deficiency Judgment

The new grantee personally assuming the loan has no personal liability if the law does not permit a deficiency judgment. Furthermore, if the old owner was insulated from a deficiency judgment, then the new owner retains that protection and freedom from personal liability.

Novation

For the old owner to be released from any personal liability under the promissory note, the lender and new owner must execute a novation. In this agreement, the lender specifically releases the old owner and substitutes the new owner.

STUDY QUESTIONS (TRUE–FALSE)

1. In a deed of trust, the lender is called the trustor and the borrower is called the beneficiary.

2. An acceleration clause permits a lender to charge a late fee for a tardy loan payment.

3. Due-on-sale clauses are always enforceable by lenders whenever one transfers property.

4. A blanket deed of trust covers parcels exempt by a partial release clause.

5. Regulation Z limits the amount of interest a lender can charge on a one- to four-family owner-occupied residence.

6. The first step in nonjudicial foreclosure is to record a notice of default.

7. Generally, foreclosure of a senior lien extinguishes all junior liens.

8. When a deed of trust on any type of property is foreclosed by a trustee's sale, a deficiency judgment is never possible.

9. If A borrows $500,000 from a bank to purchase a five-unit apartment building, it would be a purchase money deed of trust.

10. If the seller takes back a $1,000,000 deed of trust for a shopping center, he has accepted a soft money purchase money deed of trust.

Chapter 16

NATURE OF INVOLUNTARY LIENS

Creation

An **involuntary lien** is a lien created by a creditor without the consent or participation of the property owner. The most common involuntary liens created by individuals are the attachment lien, the judgment lien, the execution lien, and the mechanic's lien. They arise by the creditor's unilaterally recording or filing the appropriate documents. All but the mechanic's lien arise only in the course of a lawsuit. The unsecured creditor seeks to protect an interest and secure payment by specific assets of the debtor. The mechanic's lien, conversely, arises before the filing of a lawsuit. It is created by the unpaid mechanic who has worked on or supplied materials for improvements to property and who now wants a security interest in that improved property.

Effect of Lien

The lien is only a charge on real estate, affecting title only. Until the lien is actually enforced by foreclosure, the debtor's possession in the property remains unchanged. If and when the lien is foreclosed and the property is sold, the foreclosure and sale procedure is somewhat similar to a foreclosure sale of a mortgage by judicial action.

ATTACHMENT LIENS

Nature

An **attachment lien** is a temporary action, collateral to a pending lawsuit. The unsecured creditor seeks to attach and claim a security interest in the debtor's property, so that if the creditor ultimately

Involuntary Liens

wins a judgment in a lawsuit, there will be certain assets from which to obtain payment.

Terminology

If a third person holds possession of the property, the procedure is technically called a **garnishment**. Although, technically, only attachment of property in the debtor's possession is called an attachment, garnishment is also frequently called attachment, and in this chapter the term will be used in the broader sense.

Old Attachment Law

Before 1971, it was a simple procedure to obtain an attachment. The creditor merely filed an appropriate declaration and form declaring that the lawsuit involved an express or implied contract for the payment of money. Then, without any notice whatsoever to the debtor, the court clerk issued a **writ of attachment**. The writ was forwarded to the sheriff, who attached whatever property he could find. With the exception of real estate, attachment deprived the debtor of the right to use any attached property during the term of the attachment.

Declared Unconstitutional

As a matter of course, many attorneys automatically filed for and obtained prejudgment attachments securing possible judgments. This deprived the debtor of the property's use, which often forced the settlement of an otherwise defensible lawsuit to retain control of the property. Recognizing the lack of advance notice, the absence of a hearing, and the attachment of many exempt assets, the California Supreme Court in 1971 declared California's prejudgment attachment statutes unconstitutional. *Randone v. Appellate Department (1971) 5 C.3d 536.*

Current Statutes

In 1972, California passed entirely new attachment statutes to meet the new constitutional requirements of such statutes. Since 1972, the statutes have undergone various revisions, the most current being those found in *C.C.P. 481.010–492.090.*

Limitations on Use of Attachments

The new statutes exempt the necessities of life, restrict the individuals against whom **attachments** will lie, and generally require prior notice and a judicial hearing. Basically, prejudgment attachments may be issued only (1) against individuals engaged in a trade, business, or profession; (2) for obligations due under an express or implied contract; (3) if the amount claimed (exclusive of costs, interests, and attorney's fees) is reasonably calculated to be over $500; and (4) if the property attached, with some exceptions, is not exempt or used for personal or family needs. *C.C.P. 483.010.*

As a practical matter, **prejudgment attachment** liens can be rarely used against individuals unless there is a clear business purpose involved. Thus, in one case, an 86-year-old woman contracted to sell one of her five parcels of real estate to the plaintiff. The transaction was never consummated, and the woman sold the property to someone else. The plaintiff then sued, claiming breach of contract, and tried to file an attachment lien against the other four parcels of real estate. The court held no attachment would issue, because the contract did not arise out of the woman's trade, business, or profession. The court went on to state that even if the woman had been a real estate broker she would have been selling her own properties for her own account and, therefore, not acting within her trade, business, or profession. *Nakasone v. Randall (1982) 129 C.A.3d 757.*

Procedure to Obtain Attachment

There are two procedures for obtaining a prejudgment attachment. The first and most common method requires a judicial hearing of which the defendant has at least 20 days' advance notice. Furthermore, the court must find legitimate grounds for the attachment's issuance. *C.C.P. 484.010–484.110.* Second, and only if great, irreparable harm would result to the plaintiff by waiting for a hearing, an attachment may issue by an **ex parte** order without notice to the defendant. *C.C.P. 485.010–485.540.* Under either procedure the plaintiff, showing the potential for great harm, may obtain a protective order preventing the defendant from transferring any assets, except in the ordinary course of business, until a court hearing. *C.C.P. 486.010 et seq.*

Attachment of Real Estate

Special rules exist for the attachment of real estate because the prejudgment lien does not deprive the debtor of possession of property. All nonexempt real property (including leasehold estates over one year) may be attached. *C.C.P. 487.010.* Unless extended by the court, the lien will expire on discharge, release, or at the end of three years, whichever occurs first. If the plaintiff wins the lawsuit and obtains a judgment, the attachment becomes merged into the judgment. However, the priority of the judgment is determined by the date of the prejudgment attachment.

JUDGMENT LIENS

Nature

Once a final judgment has been rendered in a case, awarding a fixed sum of money damages, that judgment may be recorded. Once recorded, the judgment becomes a lien on all real estate owned by the judgment debtor and on any real estate subsequently acquired during the lien's existence. The judgment creditor can then foreclose the lien and force a sale of any real estate to which the judgment lien attached. Alternatively, the judgment creditor can wait until the property is sold and be paid out of escrow.

Final Judgment Required

For such a judgment to be final, one of two events must occur. Either the original case must be concluded in all respects and the time for appeal must have passed, or all appeals must be resolved. *C.C.P. 1049.* The appeal period is 60 days after entry of the judgment.

Specified Money Judgment Needed

The judgment or court order must be for a fixed and ascertainable amount of money damages. A special exemption exists for recorded decrees for spousal support (alimony) or for child support. Support judgments become a lien for the stated amount and for all future installments when and as they mature and become due. *C.C.P. 697.350.*

Interest Rate

All judgments earn interest at the rate of 10 percent per annum, uncompounded. *C.C.P. 685.010.* The legislature has the right to change the interest rate to any amount under 10 percent, but not less than

7 percent. A $10,000 judgment would accrue $1,000 interest per year, whether in the first or the fifteenth year, because interest is uncompounded.

Recorded to Be a Lien

Once the judgment is final, an abstract of that judgment must be recorded before it becomes a lien. *C.C.P. 697.310.* On request, the county clerk will automatically issue an **abstract of judgment**, a one-page summary of the court judgment and the amounts due (see Figure 16.1).

Effective Territory

The abstract may be recorded in any or all California counties in which the creditor wants to create a lien. The creditor can create liens anywhere in California, even if the debtor does not own property in that county.

Available Equity to Be Effective

As Chapter 18 will explain, judgment liens only attach to the amount of equity in excess of the homestead amount. A 1997 case holds that the excess amount is determined at the time the judgment lien is recorded and not when it is enforced. *In re Jones (1997) 106 F.3d 923.*

Assume that an owner had a home worth $200,000 on which he owed $125,000 secured by a deed of trust. That person would have $75,000 equity in the home. If he had recorded a family homestead worth $75,000, there would be no surplus equity over and above the homestead amount. If a creditor recorded a judgment lien at that time, it would not attach to the home because there was no surplus equity. Thus, years later, if the home appreciated in value so that there was surplus equity, the lien still would not attach to the property. The lien was ineffective at the time it was recorded and so could not later be effective. In this situation, a judgment creditor would be well advised not to record a judgment lien until there was surplus equity in the home.

Property Attached

The judgment lien attaches to all nonexempt real estate owned or later acquired during the life of the judgment lien by the judgment debtor in the county in which it is recorded. Judgments will reach a present or future, vested or contingent, or legal or equitable interest in real property. *C.C.P. 697.340.* The judgment lien will not attach to rents, a lease having an unexpired term of less than two years, or the interest of a beneficiary under a trust.

FIGURE 16.1 Abstract of judgment.

ATTORNEY OR PARTY WITHOUT ATTORNEY (*Name, address, state Bar number, and telephone number*):
Recording requested by and return to:

☐ ATTORNEY FOR   ☐ JUDGMENT CREDITOR   ☐ ASSIGNEE OF RECORD

SUPERIOR COURT OF CALIFORNIA, COUNTY OF

STREET ADDRESS:

MAILING ADDRESS:

CITY AND ZIP CODE:

BRANCH NAME:

PLAINTIFF:

DEFENDANT:

FOR RECORDER'S USE ONLY

CASE NUMBER:

ABSTRACT OF JUDGMENT—CIVIL AND SMALL CLAIMS

☐ **Amended**

FOR COURT USE ONLY

1. The ☐ judgment creditor ☐ assignee of record
   applies for an abstract of judgment and represents the following:
   a. Judgment debtor's

   ⌐ Name and last known address ¬

   ⌊ ... ⌋

   b. Driver's license no. [last 4 digits] and state: ☐ Unknown
   c. Social security no. [last 4 digits]:   ☐ Unknown
   d. Summons or notice of entry of sister-state judgment was personally served or
      mailed to (<u>name and address</u>):

2. ☐ Information on additional judgment debtors is shown on page 2.

3. Judgment creditor (*name and address):*

4. ☐ Information on additional judgment creditors is shown on page 2.

5. ☐ Original abstract recorded in this county:
   a. Date:
   b. Instrument No.:

Date:

_____
(TYPE OR PRINT NAME)

▶

_____
(SIGNATURE OF APPLICANT OR ATTORNEY)

6. Total amount of judgment as entered or last renewed:
   $

7. All judgment creditors and debtors are listed on this abstract.

8. a. Judgment entered on (*date):*
   b. Renewal entered on (*date):*

9. ☐ This judgment is an installment judgment.

[SEAL]

This abstract issued on (*date):*

10. ☐ An ☐ execution line ☐ attachment lien
    is endorsed on the judgment as follows:
    a. Amount: $
    b. In favor of (*name and address):*

11. A stay of enforcement has
    a. ☐ not been ordered by the court.
    b. ☐ been ordered by the court effective until
       (*date):*

12. a. ☐ I certify that this is a true and correct abstract of
       the judgment entered in this action.
    b. ☐ A certified copy of the judgment is attached.

Clerk, by _____, Deputy

Form Adopted for Mandatory Use
Judicial Council of California
EJ-001 [Rev. January 1, 2008]

ABSTRACT OF JUDGMENT—CIVIL AND SMALL CLAIMS

Page 1 of 2
Code of Civil Procedure §§ 488.480, 674.700.190

American Legalnet. Inc.
www.FormsWorkflow.com

FIGURE 16.1 (*Continued*).

PLAINTIFF:	CASE NUMBER:
DEFENDANT:	

JUDGMENT IS ENTERED AS FOLLOWS BY: ☐ **THE COURT** ☐ **THE CLERK**

4. ☐ **Stipulated Judgment.** Judgment is entered according to the stipulation of the parties.

5. **Parties.** Judgment is
   a. ☐ for plaintiff (*name each*):

   and against defendant (*names*):

   ☐ Continued on Attachment 5a.

   b. ☐ for defendant (*name each*):

c. ☐ for cross-complainant (*name each*):

   and against cross-defendant (*name each*):

   ☐ Continued on Attachment 5c.

   b. ☐ for cross-defendant (*name each*):

6. **Amount.**
   a. ☐ Defendant named in item 5a above must pay plaintiff on the complaint:

(1) ☐ Damages	$
(2) ☐ Prejudgment interest at the annual rate of %	$
(3) ☐ Attorney fees	$
(4) ☐ Costs	$
(5) ☐ Other (*specify*):	$
(6) **TOTAL**	$

   c. ☐ Cross-defendant named in item 5c above must pay cross-complainant on the cross-complaint:

(1) ☐ Damages	$
(2) ☐ Prejudgment interest at the annual rate of %	$
(3) ☐ Attorney fees	$
(4) ☐ Costs	$
(5) ☐ Other (*specify*):	$
(6) **TOTAL**	$

   b. ☐ Plaintiff to receive nothing from defendant named in item 5b.
       ☐ Defendant named in item 5b to recover costs $
           ☐ and attorney fees $

   d. ☐ Cross-complainant to receive nothing from cross-defendant named in item 5d.
       ☐ Cross-defendant named in item 5d to recover costs $
           ☐ and attorney fees $

7. ☐ Other (*specify*):

Date: ☐ _____
                               JUDICIAL OFFICER

Date: ☐ Clerk, by_____, Deputy

(SEAL)

CLERK'S CERTIFICATE (*Optional*)

I certify that this is a true copy of the original judgment on file in the court.

Date:

Clerk, by_____, Deputy

Page 2 of 2

JUD-100 [New January 1, 2002]   **JUDGMENT**

Covers Only Nonexempt Property

The lien covers only nonexempt real property interests owned by the judgment debtor. It will not attach to property exempt because of a homestead or to personal property. The lien will attach to whatever real estate interests are owned by the debtor, including that share of joint tenancy property.

Covers After-Acquired Property

The judgment lien attaches to any nonexempt real property acquired by the judgment debtor after creation of the lien, provided the lien has not expired. Attachment to after-acquired property is automatic, requiring no action whatsoever by the creditor. Thus, if judgment debtor A buys a building, the judgment lien will automatically attach to it.

Duration of Lien

The judgment is valid for 10 years from the date of its entry. *C.C.P. 697.310.* Hence, the judgment lien is valid from the date of its recordation until the expiration of the 10-year period from the date of the judgment's entry. For example, if the judgment is recorded seven years after entry of the judgment, the lien would be valid for only three years. If the judgment is unsatisfied at the end of 10 years, it may be renewed for another 10-year period at the discretion of the court. The court normally grants such extensions.

General Priority

Judgment liens generally obtain their priority among competing creditors as of the date of their recordation. Generally, any lien or encumbrance recorded after the judgment is junior to that judgment. There are certain exceptions, such as for tax liens or other liens given priority by statute. (For more detail, see Chapter 17.)

Priority to After-Acquired Property

All judgment liens, regardless of their date of recordation, attach automatically to any after-acquired property as of the date that the property is acquired. These liens on the after-acquired property derive their priority as of the date that they attach to the new property, the date of acquisition. Because all such existing judgment liens attach equally, between themselves, their priority is as of the date that they were first recorded. *C.C.P. 697.380(g).*

Assume that Ted owned Blackacre, which had two judgments recorded against it, one by Jane on May 1993 and the other by Ken on June 1993. Then on March 4, 1994, Ted acquired Blueacre by gift. Jane's and Ken's liens would attach to Blueacre automatically on

March 4, 1993; as to any other liens that would later arise against Blueacre, the judgment liens would have a March 4, 1994, priority date. As between the two liens, because Jane's lien was the first recorded, it would have priority over Ken's lien, both on Blackacre and on Blueacre.

APPLY THE LAW

Halvey v. Bank of America
43 C.A.2d 532 (1941)

[Robert E. Hopkins & Company owned a parcel of real estate in Los Angeles County. Because Hopkins was unable to pay his real property taxes, the property was sold to the state. Sale to the state is a bookkeeping entry in the tax assessor's office, and the owner has five years from that date to redeem the property before it is deeded to the state. During this period of redemption, Bank of America recorded a judgment against Hopkins & Co. that became a judgment lien on that Los Angeles property. The issue in this case is whether the judgment lien attaches to the judgment debtor's right of redemption.

A judgment does not attach to all property but only that property specified by law. Under the law existing before 1983, the liens only reached vested interests in real property. Since July 1983, a new statute allows judgment liens to reach present or future, vested or contingent, or legal or equitable interest in real property.]

CONWAY, JUSTICE. The judgment lien created by the recordation of an abstract of judgment is purely statutory, because no such right existed under the common law.

The courts of this state have on many occasions passed upon the extent or limitation of a judgment lien. Upon the recordation of an abstract of judgment with the county recorder, the judgment or decree becomes a lien upon all the real property of the judgment debtor in such county owned by him at the time, or that he may afterwards acquire. The statutory lien of a judgment upon the real estate of the judgment debtor can attach only property in which such debtor has a vested legal interest. A judgment lien will not attach except to a vested interest of the judgment debtor in the real property.

An examination of the authorities discloses a vast difference in the classes of property and interests therein that will support judgment liens, homesteads, and levies under execution. Property interests of any and every kind, whether real or personal, and every interest therein are subject to seizure under attachment or levy on execution, unless exempt from execution. While many classes of property may be taken on execution, only two classes are subject to the lien of a judgment—real property owned by the debtor at the time of docketing and real property that he may afterward acquire.

Although any interest in real property, legal or equitable, may be seized and sold under execution, only real property actually owned by the judgment debtor will support a judgment lien. A mere equitable interest in real property acquired under a contract of purchase is not considered real property.

It has been held that an estate for years in real property is not such an interest as will carry a judgment lien.

The right to redeem carries no vested interest in the land. It is therefore ordered that the judgment be reversed. [Under pre-1983 law, the judgment lien has no effect on and does not attach to the right to redeem during the five-year sale-to-the-state period.]

APPLY THE LAW

continued

EXECUTION LIENS

Nature of Writ of Execution

A judgment is not self-executing. To enforce the judgment, an order is needed directing the sheriff to seize and sell certain of the debtor's nonexempt assets. Such an order is called a writ of execution. The actual physical seizure is called a levy.

Creation of an Execution Lien

The mere issuance of a writ of execution has little effect on the property. Once the sheriff enforces the writ by seizing the property, a lien is created and attaches to the property. The lien's priority is normally the date of the levy. However, if the creditor had an earlier lien, such as a judgment lien, the execution lien assumes the earlier lien's priority. In other words, the earlier lien merges into the execution lien.

Enforcement of the Lien

Once a levy of execution is issued under a writ of execution, it creates a lien on that property for two years. Thus, if the property is later transferred or further encumbered, the lien keeps its priority as of its date. The creditor then has the sheriff sell the property through the normal process of posting and publishing notice of the sale as prescribed by statute and then deeding it to the person who is the highest bidder at an auction-type sale. *C.C.P. 701.510 et seq.* Since July 1983, sales have been final, and the debtors (former property owners) no longer have a one-year right of redemption. The minimum time required to hold a sale, once the execution process is begun, is slightly more than 140 days.

Because a sale wipes out all junior liens and as junior lienors no longer have a right of redemption, their only remedy to protect their equity is to redeem from the senior lien before the foreclosure sale. Then, the junior lien acquires all the rights of the senior lien (called subrogation). *C.C. 2904.*

MECHANIC'S LIEN

Definition and Nature of Lien

A mechanic's lien is a security interest given to a mechanic who improves a specific parcel of property. The unpaid mechanic obtains security against the property, including improvements, to ensure payment. The rationale for mechanic's liens is that the property has increased in value because of the mechanic's labor or supplies; hence, it is only fair that the property stand as security for the debt to that property. These liens have no relationship to a lawsuit and arise long before any action would be filed in court. Only mechanics may obtain a mechanic's lien (see Figure 16.2).

Definition of Mechanic

Any mechanic who works on or supplies materials for the improvement of real estate is entitled to a lien on that property to assure and secure payment. *C.C. 3109–3153.* The term mechanic encompasses almost everyone who improves the property. There are four categories of mechanics.

Original Contractor

The original contractor is any contractor who has a direct contractual relationship with the owner. *C.C. 3095.* They are known in the construction industry as general contractors or prime contractors. Under the statutory definition, there may be more than one original contractor. A person who only supplies labor and materials to the owner, even if under a direct contract, is not a contractor, but a laborer or materialman.

Subcontractor

Subcontractors are contractors who have no direct contractual relationship with the owner. *C.C. 3104.* Their contracts are with the original contractor.

Laborer

A laborer is any employee who physically labors on or performs skills or services for the improvement of the property. *C.C. 3089.*

FIGURE 16.2 Mechanic's lien.

Mechanic's Lien

NOTICE TO ALL CONCERNED, that I, _____, hereby allege and claim a lien upon the land and improvements described in this document.

Demand. The amount claimed, due and owing, after all deductions for credits and setoffs, is _____ dollars

Location of Property. The property against which the lien is claimed, is commonly known as _____ Street, in the City of _____, County of _____, State of California, and more particularly described as _____.

Owner of Property. The owner, or reputed owner, of the property against which the lien is claimed is _____.

Benefit's Rendered. Labor, services, equipment or materials were furnished for the benefit of the above described property, the general of which consist of _____.

Employer or Contact With. The above described labor, services, equipment, or materials, were furnished to the or under employment by _____.

EXECUTED on _____, 20____, in the City of _____, County of _____, State of California.

_____
Claimant

Verification

Notary

Materialman

The materialman is anyone who supplies materials or equipment actually used in or consumed by the property improvements. *C.C. 3090.*

Procedures to Obtain a Lien

The mechanic's lien is available only if certain requirements are met and prescribed procedures followed within specific time limits. If any one of these deadlines is missed or if any requirement is lacking, the lien is extinguished. For example, a mechanic sent notice of the mechanic's lien by first-class mail instead of by certified or registered mail. Even though the owner received the notice, the court held that the mechanic's lien was invalid for failure to follow the exact statutory procedure. *IGA Aluminum Products v. Manufacturer's Bank (1982) 130 C.A.3d 699.*

FIGURE 16.3   Preliminary 20-day notice.

Preliminary 20-Day Notice

To: Joe Owner

This is to give you notice that I, Ted Gordon, of 5678 Rockridge Street, San Francisco, CA, will furnished lumber, labor, and equipment more fully described on Exhibit "A" to this notice, and that the estimated total price the lumber, labor, and equipment so furnished is $8,329 all of which will be delivered to or furnished at your property at 1234 California Street, San Francisco, California, pursuant to the contract between us which you signed on June 4, 2009. As required by California Civil Code §3097(c) the following notice is provided.

NOTICE TO PROPERTY OWNER

If bills are not paid in full for the labor, services, equipment, or materials furnished or to be furnished, a mechanic's lien leading to the loss, through court foreclosure proceedings, of all or part of your property being so improved may be placed against the property even though you have paid your contractor in full. You may wish to protect yourself against this consequence by (1) requiring your contractor to furnish a signed release by the person or firm giving you this notice before making payment to your contractor, or (2) any other method or device that is appropriate under the circumstances. Other than residential homeowners of dwellings containing fewer than five units, private project owners must notify the original contractor and any lien claimant who has provided the owner with a preliminary 20-day lien notice in accordance with Section 3097 of the Civil Code that a notice of completion or notice of cessation has been recorded within 10 days of its recordation. Notice shall be by registered mail, certified mail, or first-class mail, evidenced by a certificate of mailing. Failure to notify will extend the deadlines to record a lien.

Date: *August 8, 2009*   Signed: *Ted Gordon*

Preliminary Twenty-Day Notice

Except for original contractors and for laborers working for wages, all mechanics must serve a preliminary 20-day notice as a prerequisite for eligibility to file a mechanic's lien. *C.C. 3097.* (See Figure 16.3.) This notice must be served within 20 days of furnishing labor, equipment, or materials, and copies must be served to the owner, the original contractor, and any construction lenders. If the notice contains incorrect or incomplete information or if it is not served within the 20-day period, the mechanic forfeits the right to file a mechanic's lien for that work or material. *C.C. 3114.* However, if the person does other work for that job site and timely serves a 20-day notice, a mechanic's lien for that other, later work may be filed.

Recording Lien

The mechanic must then record his lien with the county recorder of the county in which the property is located. If the owner has recorded a notice of completion (or a notice of cessation of labor), the original contractor has 60 days and all other mechanics have 30 days to record their mechanic's liens. However, if no such notices have been recorded, then all mechanics, including the original contractor, have 90 days in which to record their liens. Failure to file within these periods, which operates like a statute of limitation, prevents one from obtaining a mechanic's lien. *C.C. 3115, 3116.*

File Lawsuit

Once the mechanic's lien has been filed, a complaint to foreclose must be filed with the court within 90 days or the lien is extinguished. *C.C. 3144.* If there has been an extension of credit between the parties, then certain circumstances may allow this period to be extended up to one year. Even though the lien may become unenforceable for failure to file a lawsuit within the required period, in some cases it may be possible to sue on the original debt in other types of lawsuits. *Potts v. Grover (9th Cir. 1979) 608 F.2d 1279.* However, a person with a mechanic's lien should meet the deadline and not rely on potential remedies.

Trial within Two Years

Finally, the complaint must be prosecuted and brought to trial within two years of its filing, or the judge may dismiss the complaint and eliminate the mechanic's lien. *C.C. 3147, 3148.*

Various Remedies for a Mechanic

An unpaid mechanic has several different remedies, most of which can be pursued simultaneously, although any recovery under one method must be credited toward recovery from any other procedure.

Mechanic's Lien

The mechanic can file a mechanic's lien against the property, foreclose on that lien, and have the property sold to satisfy the claim. *C.C. 3109–3153.*

Lawsuit in Contract

The individual who expressly or impliedly contracted for supplies and labor can be sued by the mechanic. *C.C. 3152.* The lawsuit most often would be brought by the general contractor, who is usually the contracting party. Furthermore, unless a written contract provides otherwise, the owner must pay all the undisputed amount within 30 days of demand. If an amount is in good faith truly disputed, the owner can only withhold 150 percent of the disputed amount. All other amounts under the contract must be paid to the contractor. *C.C. 3260.1.*

Stop Notice

The mechanic can file a stop notice with and against any person holding unexpended construction funds, thereby forcing that party to pay over to the mechanic the amount of the claim up to the extent of any remaining funds. *C.C. 3156–3175.*

Attach Performance Bond

If a performance **bond** has been posted, the mechanic can file and proceed directly against that bond. *C.C. 3085, 3096.*

Attach Contractor's Bond

If the person with whom the mechanic has contracted to provide supplies and labor is a licensed contractor, then limited recovery can be had against the contractor's licensing bond. *B.&P.C. 7071.6 et seq.*

Protections for Owner

Besides the obvious security afforded by a well-drawn contract with a financially secure and reliable contractor, the owner has several other methods of protecting against mechanic's liens.

Record Contract and Post Bond

The owner may, and usually does, require the general contractor to record the construction contract and post a performance bond. By code, the contract recordation gives all mechanics actual notice of its contents, thereby limiting all liens to and for supplies and labor specified in the contract. Additionally, if the performance bond is equal to 50 percent of the contract price, the liens may not exceed the price stated in the recorded contract. Finally, if the bond is recorded before commencement of the work, the owner's liability is limited to the amount of unpaid funds due the general contractor, leaving the bond and the general contractor liable for the balance of the claim. *C.C. 3235, 3236.*

Delayed Payment

Another common protection is to withhold a portion of the funds, usually 10 to 20 percent, until 35 days after the notice of completion is recorded. Because all mechanic's liens, except those of the general contractor, must be recorded by that time, the owner has knowledge of all liens before completing payment. It is generally advisable to appoint a third person, such as an engineer or architect, to make the final determination of when the project is completed for purposes of recording a notice of completion. In most cases, payment cannot be delayed more than 45 days after completion without meeting stringent requirements specified by statute.

Amortized Payment

Finally, the owner may pay the contractor in installments, withholding each partial payment until the contractor has furnished definite proof that all materialmen's bills and laborers' wages have been paid for that segment of the work. For example, it may be agreed that the first installment, equal to 15 percent of the contract price, shall be paid on completion of the foundation.

Posting Bond

If a mechanic's lien has already been filed, as in the principal case, the owner may release the property by filing a bond equal to one and one-half times the disputed claim. *C.C. 3143.*

Waivers From Mechanics

If you know all the subcontractors, materialmen, and laborers, a property owner can have them sign a waiver and release before making payment. In that manner, the property can help protect the property. However, that is often impracticable as the original contractor frequently hires subcontractors directly and usually without consulting the owner.

One partial solution is to have the original contractor sign a waiver. Any well-worded release will do. (See Figure 16.4 for sample of a simplified waiver for the general contractor.)

FIGURE 16.4   Waiver of Mechanic's lien by general contractor.

Unconditional Waiver And Release Upon
Final Payment For General ("Original") Contractor

(Waiver of Right to Mechanic's Lien)

The undersigned has been paid in full for all labor, services, equipment or material furnished to *Ted Gordon, Owner*, on the job of *Ted Gordon*, located at *123 Jones Street, San Francisco, California*, and does hereby waive and release any right to a mechanic's lien, stop notice, or any right against a labor and material bond on the job, except for disputed claims for extra work in the amount of $ *Zero Dollars*.

Dated: _____

/s/ Signed, by General Contractor

The waiver for anyone else is far more complicated because any waiver will be invalid unless the mechanic uses the form mandated by the civil code. Any other form is invalid and of no force and effect. If the proper notice is not timely given within the statutory time, the mechanic may not file a mechanic's lien, and conversely, the property owner need not fear such a lien. Which form an owner uses depends on the circumstances requiring the waiver.

The first decision is to determine if the release is for a *progress payment* or for a *final payment*. A **progress payment** means the only part of the work is covered and the release will only apply to that part of the work. The progress release will not stop a mechanics' lien for anything arising before or after the progress period.

Secondly, the statutory releases distinguish between *conditional* and *unconditional* releases. A **conditional release** arises when the claimant releases the property from a mechanics lien in exchange for payment. The release is only valid if and when the claimant is paid for his or her services. If for some reason no payment is made or if the check is not honored by the bank, the waiver never takes effect and the claimant can still file a mechanic's lien. Conversely, an **unconditional release** is used when the claimant has already been paid and the right to a mechanics' lien is being immediately waived. The release is valid without any conditions that must occur before it is effective.

Thus, there are four releases for claimants who are not the original contractor. There is a release for a progress payment that is conditional (Figure 16.5), a progress payment that is unconditional (Figure 16.6), a final payment that is conditional (Figure 16.7) and a final payment that is unconditional (Figure 16.8).

Construction Defect Lawsuits

The owner can always sue the builder or contract on a breach of contract action. Such litigation is slow and expensive, but new laws give it more teeth. Beginning in 2003, anyone suing on a defectively built or designed residential property must first give notice. The builder, contractor, subcontractor, product manufacturer, or design professional who did the defective work must be given notice and a chance to correct the work before there is a lawsuit. For the consumer, the statute requires the builder to provide a minimum one-year warranty covering over 40 defined areas of the residence, in areas of water, structure, soil, fire protection, plumbing, and other areas. A typical listed area is the one that states that a "structure shall be constructed so as to materially comply with the design criteria for earthquake and wind load resistance, as set forth in the applicable government building codes, regulations, and ordinances in effect at the time of original construction." *C.C. 896.*

FIGURE 16.5   Release for progress payment—conditional.

Conditional Waiver And Release
Upon Progress Payment
Cal. Civil Code §3262(d)(1)

Upon receipt by the undersigned of a check from [maker of check] in the sum of $ _____ , payable to [payee or payees of check] and when the check has been properly endorsed and has been paid by the bank upon which it is drawn, this document shall become effective to release any mechanics' lien, stop notice, or bond right the undersigned has on the job of [owner] located at [job description] to the following extent. This release covers a progress payment for labor, services, equipment, or material furnished to [your customer] through [date] only and does not cover any retentions retained before or after the release date; extras furnished before the release date for which payment has not been received; extras or items furnished after the release date.

Rights based upon work performed or items furnished under a written change order which has been fully executed by the parties prior to the release date are covered by this release unless specifically reserved by the claimant in this release.

This release of any mechanics' lien, stop notice, or bond right shall not otherwise affect the contract rights, including rights between parties to the contract based upon a rescission, abandonment, or breach of the contract, or the right of the undersigned to recover compensation for furnished labor, services, equipment, or material covered by this release if that furnished labor, services, equipment, or material was not compensated by the progress payment.

Before any recipient of this document relies on it, that party should verify evidence of payment to the undersigned.

Dated: _____   Signed: _____

If the defect causes damages and is not one of the over 40 listed items, then the residential owner may immediately sue without giving advance notice or following the detailed procedure required by statute. *C.C. 897*. The statutes go on to give certain protections to third-party inspectors and generally limits causes of action for construction defects to 10 years from date of construction.

This was compromise legislation between the builders and the consumers. Opinions vary considerably as to how much these new statutes will actually help the consumer. The author feels it will be of material benefit to homeowners facing a problem caused by a small builder. Large builders may prefer litigation, where they can cross-complain against subcontractors and others and hope another party's insurance company will pay all or part of the cost. In any event, if the

FIGURE 16.6   Release for progress payment—unconditional.

Unconditional Waiver And Release
Upon Progress Payment
Cal. Civil Code §3262(d)(2)

[Print the following notice in at least as large a type
as the largest type otherwise used in the document:]

NOTICE: THIS DOCUMENT WAIVES RIGHTS UNCONDITIONALLY
AND STATES THAT YOU HAVE BEEN PAID FOR GIVING UP THOSE
RIGHTS. THIS DOCUMENT IS ENFORCEABLE AGAINST YOU IF YOU
SIGN IT, EVEN IF YOU HAVE NOT BEEN PAID. IF YOU HAVE NOT
BEEN PAID, USE A CONDITIONAL RELEASE FORM.

The undersigned has been paid and has received a progress payment in the
sum of $_____ for labor, services, equipment, or material furnished
[Your Customer] on the job of [Owner] located at [Job Description] and
does hereby release any mechanics' lien, stop notice or bond that the
undersigned has on the above referenced job.

This release covers a progress payment for labor, services, equipment, or
material furnished to [your customer] through [date] only and does not
cover any retentions retained before or after the release date; extras
furnished before the release date for which payment has not been received;
extras or items furnished after the release date.

Rights based upon work performed or items furnished under a written
change order which has been fully executed by the parties prior to the
release date are covered by this release unless specifically reserved by the
claimant in this release.

This release of any mechanics' lien, stop notice, or bond right shall not
otherwise affect the contract rights, including rights between parties to the
contract based upon a rescission, abandonment, or breach of the contract,
or the right of the undersigned to recover compensation for furnished labor,
services, equipment, or material covered by this release if that furnished
labor, services, equipment, or material was not compensated by the progress
payment.

Dated: _____   Signed: _____

alleged defect is one of the over 40 listed items, the new statutes will
control the procedure.

Required Protection in Contract

If an owner hires a contractor whose employee is injured by a violation of a labor laws, the owner may be liable. An exception applies for

FIGURE 16.7   Release for final payment—conditional.

Conditional Waiver And Release
Upon Final Payment
Cal. Civil Code §3262(d)(3)

Upon receipt by the undersigned of a check from _____ in the sum of $_____ payable to _____ and when the check has been properly endorsed and has been paid by the bank upon which it is drawn, this document shall become effective to release any mechanic's lien, stop notice, or bond right the undersigned has on the job of job of [owner] located at [job description].

This release covers the final payment to the undersigned for all labor, services, equipment, or material furnished on the job, except for disputed claims for additional work in the amount of $_____. Before any recipient of this document relies on it, the party should verify evidence of payment to the undersigned.

Dated: _____   Signed: _____

---

work on an owner's residence where he or she lives, for work on a farm, or for work where the contract includes sufficient funds for the contractor to comply with all relevant laws. Otherwise, the owner should protect himself by listing in the contract all of the requirements mandated by the labor code, including stating the worker's compensation insurance policy number, the contractor's state income tax number, the automobile insurance policy number. If not, and the employee is injured and the contractor lacks fund to cover that injury, the owner may be liable. *Labor C. § 2810.*

Other Owner Protections

If the work is for a home improvement, various additional protections are available for the owner. For example, any contract over $500 must be in writing to be enforceable. *B.&P.C. 7159.* The contract has to describe the work, the payment, and the scheduling. Furthermore, the contractor cannot ask for an advance payment greater than the lesser of $1,000 or 10 percent of the contract price. Finally, the owner can recover any sums paid to an unlicensed contractor. *B. & P.C. 7031(b).*

Notice of Nonresponsibility

When the person who orders the work on the property is a tenant or other person who owns less than fee title, only a limited property

FIGURE 16.8   Release for final payment—unconditional.

Unconditional Waiver And Release
Upon Final Payment
Cal. Civil Code §3262(d)(4)

[Print the following notice in at least as large a type
as the largest type otherwise used in the document:]

NOTICE: THIS DOCUMENT WAIVES RIGHTS UNCONDITIONALLY
AND STATES THAT YOU HAVE BEEN PAID FOR GIVING UP THOSE
RIGHTS. THIS DOCUMENT IS ENFORCEABLE AGAINST YOU IF YOU
SIGN IT, EVEN IF YOU HAVE NOT BEEN PAID. IF YOU HAVE NOT
BEEN PAID, USE A CONDITIONAL RELEASE FORM

The undersigned has been paid in full for all labor, services, equipment, or material furnished to [Your Customer] on the job of [Owner] located at [Job Description] and does hereby waive and release any right to a mechanic's lien, stop notice, or any right against a labor and material bond on the job, except for disputed claims for extra work in the amount of $ _____.

Dated: _____   Signed: _____

---

interest is subject to a mechanic's lien. *C.C. 3128.* The owner's property interest is subject to the same mechanic's lien, unless, on learning of the work, the owner promptly notifies the mechanics and assumes no liability for the improvements. Specifically, to exempt the property, the owner must post and record a notice of **nonresponsibility** within 10 days after receiving actual or constructive knowledge of the actual commencement of the work. *C.C. 3129.*

Constructive notice is that notice that will put a reasonable owner on notice or cause a reasonable owner to investigate a property and discover that a tenant is having work done on the property. The owner is not required to have actual notice. Thus, if a plumbing truck is parked outside an apartment building for a reasonable period while the owner is on vacation, the law imputes constructive notice to that absent owner. Under those facts, a reasonable owner will investigate what the truck is doing in front of the building.

Only Property Liable

Failure to properly post and record a notice of nonresponsibility subjects the property, but not the owner personally, to liability.

Effect of Lease Provision

The common lease clause that provides that the landlord's interest will be subject to any mechanic's liens for work ordered by the tenant does not prevent mechanics from filing liens against the landlord's interest. *Ott Hardware Co. v. Yost (1945) 69 C.A.2d 593.* The landlord's only protection is to file a notice of non-responsibility.

States Shingle Co. v. Kaufman
227 C.A.2d 830 (1964)

FRIEDMAN, JUSTICE. The sole question on appeal is whether this material-man's lien foreclosure action is barred by failure to commence it in "a proper court" within the 90-day period [after recording the mechanic's lien, as required by the Civil Code].

Plaintiff supplied building materials to Friedli, a general contractor, for use in constructing a building on defendants' property in El Dorado County. The materials were used in construction of the building, but plaintiff was never paid. Plaintiff filed a claim of lien in the office of the El Dorado County Recorder. Exactly 90 days later, plaintiff filed this action.

Actions for recovering possession, quieting title, or enforcing liens upon real estate shall be commenced in the county where the land is located. Such actions shall be tried in that county, subject to the court's power to transfer actions. Municipal courts have original jurisdiction over construction lien foreclosure actions within the limits of their monetary jurisdiction.

There is no municipal court in El Dorado County where defendants' land is situated. Hence, the present suit should have been filed in the El Dorado Superior Court. For some undisclosed reason, plaintiff filed this action in Alameda rather than El Dorado County, thus creating the question on appeal—whether the suit was commenced in "a proper court" within the 90-day period. Additionally, although there are municipal courts in Alameda County that had monetary jurisdiction, plaintiff saw fit to file this action in the superior rather than municipal court.

A lis pendens was recorded in El Dorado County. Eleven months later, the action was transferred to the El Dorado Superior Court. Defendants filed an answer, raising the special defense that the action had not been timely filed. Judgment of foreclosure was entered. Defendants appealed.

The precise language of the statute is that the lien does not bind the property beyond 90 days unless the action is commenced within that time. In light of that language, the apparent statutory objective is to "unbind" the property at the end of 90 days, permitting owners, buyers, encumbrancers and title insurance companies to deal freely with the

APPLY THE LAW

continued

property in reliance upon expiration of the limitation period. Even though a lien claim may have been filed, the foreclosure suit may never be forthcoming. Persons dealing with the property are entitled to rely upon the record. They should not face the burden of examining court filings in superior or municipal courts in 57 California counties other than that in which the construction work has occurred.

We conclude that the present foreclosure action was not commenced in or transferred to a proper court within 90 days after filing of the lien claim; hence, foreclosure is barred by the 90-day period of limitations.

However, failure to recover upon the lien does not preclude a personal judgment against any person liable. Judgment reversed. [The mechanic's lien is extinguished for failure to file in the proper court within the prescribed 90-day period.]

STUDY QUESTIONS (TRUE–FALSE)

1. Prejudgment attachments are a popular method of securing an attachment on a debtor's property.

2. Only general contractors and subcontractors may obtain mechanic's liens against the owner's property.

3. The mechanic must notify the owner and others of the right to a potential mechanic's lien within 20 days of furnishing the work or materials to obtain a mechanic's lien.

4. The mechanic must record a mechanic's lien within 90 days after the filing of the notice of completion or lose the right to file a mechanic's lien.

5. Generally, even though a mechanic's lien has been properly and timely filed, a mechanic may lose it unless an action is filed in court to foreclose it within 90 days of recordation.

6. If the mechanic loses a mechanic's lien because of tardy filing, no other effective remedy is available.

7. Unless the owner records a notice of nonresponsibility within 10 days of acquiring actual or constructive notice of work ordered by his tenants, the building may be liable for work not ordered.

8. When the court issues a judgment against a debtor, the judgment automatically becomes a lien on all nonexempt real estate owned in the county by the debtor.

9. A judgment is valid only for 10 years unless renewed for another 10 years.

10. Regardless of their dates of creation, all judgments attach equally, automatically, and simultaneously to all after-acquired property.

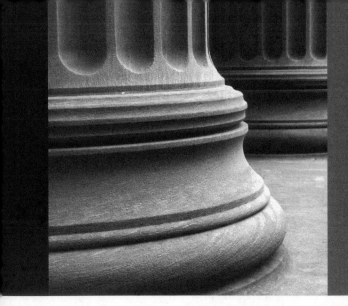

Chapter

17

NATURE OF TAXES AND TAXABLE PROPERTY

Nature and Types of Taxes

Numerous taxes are levied by the many branches of federal, state, and local governments. This chapter discusses only real property taxes, the most important source of revenue for local government. The power to tax is inherent in the government, and the only constitutional limitation appears to be the requirement that the tax be equal in its burdens and uniform in its application.

Effect of Nonpayment

If property taxes are not paid when due, they become a lien on real property. If the taxes remain unpaid, the property can ultimately be foreclosed and sold at a tax sale. The proceeds of that sale will first be applied to the tax debt; the balance, if any, will be paid to the ex-property owner.

Exempt Property

Certain property is wholly or partially exempt from taxation. This is a consideration in preparing the county assessment roles of taxable property.

Government Property

Federally owned property and all property owned by state and local governments is exempt from taxation, whether or not the property is used in a governmental or proprietary manner.

Property Taxes

Welfare Institutions

Property of churches, schools, hospitals, charities, and other welfare organizations is exempt, provided that the property is used exclusively for its religious, educational, charitable, or welfare purposes; that such operations are not conducted for profit; and that no earnings are used to benefit any private individual.

Exemptions

Certain taxable property containing family living units obtains limited tax exemptions, the most common being the open-space exemption, the veteran's exemption, and the **homeowner's exemption**.

Open-Space Exemption

Under the Williamson Act, *Gov.C. 51200 et seq.*, certain farmland and open space property is assessed at its current use value rather than its fair market value. Most counties require a minimum of 50 to 100 acres of land before they will accept it for a Williamson Act contract. Under the contract, the owner must agree to maintain the property in its current use for at least 10 years. Each year, the contract automatically renews for a full 10-year period until the owner gives 10 years' advance notice of intent to cancel. In the past, owners were frequently able to terminate their contracts early on paying an agreed fee to the county. A recent court decision now blocks this premature termination procedure except in unusual circumstances. *Sierra Club v. City of Hayward (1981) 28 C.3d 840.* Williamson Act contracts are still popular, but less in demand for property that may become developable within a 10-year period.

Veteran's Exemption

The veteran's exemption is available to certain California veterans or, if the veteran is deceased, then to the spouse, widowed mother, or pensioned parents. It amounts to $40 off the normal tax bill. (Before July 1, 1978, under the old taxing system, it was $1,000 off the assessed value.) For a claimant to qualify, the total fair market value of personal and real property (without any deductions for deeds of trust or other encumbrances) must not exceed $20,000 ($40,000 if married). *Cal. Const. Art. XIII, Sec. 1–1/4.* The veteran may not receive both the veteran's exemption and the homeowner's exemption on the same property. The claimant could take the homeowner's exemption on a principal residence and, assuming qualification for both exemptions, the veteran's exemption on other real estate owned.

If the veteran is disabled and has household income under $24,000, there is a different exemption, called the disabled veteran's exemption. Beginning in 2005, the disabled exemption amount is $150,000. *R.&T.C. §205.5.*

Homeowner's Exemption

A homeowner actually residing on the premises of a dwelling used as a principal residence on March 1 of the previous year qualifies for the homeowner's exemption. The deduction is $70 off the normal tax bill (prior to July 1, 1978, it was $1,750 off the assessed value). *R.&T.C. 218.* To qualify, the dwelling must be a single-family residence, a unit in a duplex, or a condominium. The unit must be actually occupied by the claimant; the premises cannot be rented, vacant, or under construction on the lien date.

TAX COLLECTION PROCESS

Due Dates

Real property taxes are payable in two installments, due on November 1 and February 1, although the entire tax may be paid when the first installment is due. The first installment becomes delinquent on December 10 and the second installment on April 10. If the delinquency date falls on a weekend or legal holiday, that date is extended to the next business day. The dates are easily remembered by using the mnemonic phrase "No Darn Fooling Around"—November 1, December 10, February 1, and April 10. (See Table 17.1.)

Lien if Not Paid

If the installments are not paid when due, they become a lien against the property on January 1 immediately preceding the fiscal year for

TABLE 17.1 Important tax dates.

January 1	Taxes become a lien
February 1	Second installment of taxes due
April 10	Second installment of taxes delinquent
June 8	Delinquent tax list published
June 30	Last day of fiscal year
	Delinquent property sold to the state
July 1	Beginning of fiscal year
	Assessor completes assessment roll
September 1	Tax rate determined by the year
November 1	First installment of taxes due
December 10	First installment of taxes delinquent

which they are levied. Thus, if the November 2009 first installment and/or the February 2010 second installment are delinquent, they become a lien on the property as of January 1, 2009.

Tax-Defaulted Property

If the delinquent taxes and penalties remain unpaid, then sometime between the delinquency date of April 10 and the deadline of June 30 the property is considered tax-defaulted property. This is only a book-keeping entry that starts the five-year redemption period running: The assessor merely stamps a notation of the nature and amount of the delinquency. The taxpayer's possession and use of the property are entirely undisturbed. Beginning in 2005, the five-year period is reduced to three years for commercial property.

Redemption

The taxpayer then has five years to redeem the property by paying all delinquent taxes and penalties. Besides a one-time penalty of 6 percent per delinquent installment, plus certain minimal bookkeeping charges, a 1 percent per month redemption penalty is also incurred. If the property is redeemed (and it may be redeemed in installments of 20 percent or more per year), the effect is as if there had never been any delinquency.

Subject to Power of Sale

If the property is not redeemed, then at any time after the five-year period the property may be transferred to the state. The county tax collector actually executes a deed to the state. On recordation and delivery to the state, the land is called tax-defaulted property subject to power of sale. The owner is divested of all rights in the property, which is then sold at public auction. If remaining in possession until the auction, the taxpayer may be liable for rental payments.

Transfer Free and Clear

The deed to the state conveys title free and clear of any private liens. The only encumbrances to which the property may be bound are certain special tax or assessment liens, easements, and recorded restrictions. *R.&T.C. 3520.*

State Issues New Deed

The deed from the state to the new purchaser is a new title, rather than a title derived from the former owner. Consequently, the new owner could receive better title than was held by the original owner.

Excess Sums of Sale

Any sums received over and above the amount of delinquent taxes and penalties are paid to the original owner, who now has no personal liability for payment of property taxes. Thus, even if the proceeds of the sale are insufficient to pay the taxes, the original owner's tax liability is eliminated.

APPLY THE LAW

Weston Inv. Co. v. State of California
31 C.2d 390 (1948)

[Before 1988, California used different terminology for failure to pay real property taxes. The process was exactly the same, only the names were different. Instead of calling real estate "tax-defaulted property," the parcel was called "sold to the state." There was no actual sale, only a bookkeeping entry, but the terminology and the effect of this bookkeeping entry were questioned.

Shortly after the "sale," what is now called "tax-defaulted property," the United States condemned that property, and deposited $252,800 with this court as fair compensation. Defendant, the state of California, claimed both the amount of taxes due and the penalties for nonpayment of property taxes. Plaintiff paid both charges under protest from the condemnation fund and sued the state to recover the amount claimed as redemption penalties. The court found for plaintiff, and defendant state of California appealed.]

GIBSON, JUSTICE. Defendants contend that delinquent and redemption penalties are a part of the tax, and that all are a lien on the property. They argue, therefore, that plaintiff is personally liable for the redemption

APPLY THE LAW

continued

penalties, and that, inasmuch as the condemnation fund deposited by the government takes the place of the real property, it is subject to the lien of the tax, including all penalties.

There can be no question that delinquent penalties are a part of the tax and that together with the tax they become a lien on the real property, and plaintiff does not dispute that the lien for taxes and delinquent penalties is attached to the fund. Plaintiff contends, however, that redemption penalties are not a part of the tax obligation. [Rather, these are] charges imposed for the exercise of the right to redeem property that has been sold to the state for taxes and that where the title of the United States intervenes no redemption right ever accrues. Therefore, there is no basis for the imposition of redemption penalties.

When a property owner is in default in payment of his tax obligations, the statute imposes delinquent penalties in order to encourage voluntary payment of the tax. If the delinquency persists, the property is "sold" to the state as a preliminary step in the actual enforcement of the tax lien against the land. The "sale," that occurs "by operation of law and declaration of the tax collector" starts the running of the five-year period at the expiration of which the state may acquire legal title. Redemption penalties are imposed as a condition of being relieved from the consequences of the sale. The taxpayer is not required to redeem and it is entirely optional with him whether to take advantage of the privilege given him by law to redeem the land or let the state keep it.

The provisions of the Revenue and Tax Code that deal with the subject of redemption do not make the redemption penalties a part of the tax obligation to be secured by the lien. Although the statutes provide that the delinquent penalty "attaches to" the taxes, there is no similar provision with respect to the redemption penalty.

When, after the lapse of the five-year period, the property is sold at public auction, redemption penalties are not included in the amount of the minimum bid that a purchaser from the state is required to offer. This fact indicates that redemption penalties were not intended to be regarded as part of the taxes. If property is deeded to the state at the expiration of five years, the statute provides that the deed shall recite that the property was sold to the state for non-payment of delinquent taxes that were a lien on the real property and the amount for which the property was sold. Redemption penalties are not included in this amount, which covers only taxes, delinquent penalties, and costs of sale.

The statutory scheme, when considered as a whole, clearly indicates that redemption penalties are merely what the name implies—charges for the exercise of the privilege of redeeming sold property. The property in question having been acquired by the United States prior to the tax sale, no right to redeem ever came into existence, and plaintiff was under no

continued

liability to pay penalties imposed solely as a condition to the exercise of a privilege that he never had.

The judgment is affirmed. [Plaintiff may recover any amount he paid as tax penalties.]

TAXING PROCEDURE

Proposition 13

Proposition 13 on the June 1979 ballot (the Jarvis–Gann Initiative) added the controversial Article XIIIA to the California Constitution. It provides for radical reductions in property taxes as well as significant limitations on the addition of any taxes at the state and local levels. Even though the U. S. Supreme Court recently upheld the constitutionality of Proposition 13, it may be amended by future propositions. Local services are starting to suffer such serious cutbacks that the people of California might consider amendments to Proposition 13.

Another issue about Proposition 13 is seldom raised and has not been addressed in any of the lawsuits. Homeowners move on the average every five to seven years, whereas large corporate buildings are often sold every 20 to 40 years. The result transfers a greater tax burden on residential owners, the opposite of what was intended by the original backers of Proposition 13. Although there appears to be little interest now, in the future a serious attempt might be made to adjust the manner of calculating taxes on commercial property. California's bond rating is now the lowest in the nation, and banks may force future legislatures to consider the politically unpopular decision of revising Proposition 13.

Tax Limits

Since Proposition 13, property taxes are limited to 1 percent of the real property's full cash value ($1 per $100). The effect of Proposition 13 is to place a 1 percent of value limitation on real estate, as well as on personal property. However, exceptions can permit the tax rate to be above the 1 percent limit. Because of exceptions to Proposition 13, a person needs to see the actual tax bill to determine the true charges against property. The most common exceptions to the 1 percent limit are, Mello-Ross assessments, post-November 2000 school bonds, voter approved new assessments, and pre July 1978 bonds.

Mello-Ross Assessments

The California Supreme Court ruled that Proposition 13 applied to "ad valorem" taxes and not to "special taxes." These special assessments tax every parcel of property with a flat tax unrelated to the value of the property (such as $200 per parcel) and are exempt from Proposition 13. Special taxes are generally imposed according to statutes commonly called *Mello-Ross Assessments*. To help finance improvements, most communities in California have established Mello-Ross Districts (also known as Community Facilities Districts). Special assessments are designed to improve or benefit only certain property, not the general public. For example, a school district was allowed to set up a special assessment district to pay for lighting and other improvement to its facilities. *Howard Jarvis Taxpayer's Assn. v. Whittier Union H.S. Dist. (1993) 15 C.A.4th 730.*

Post November 2000 School Bonds

Proposition 39 was passed by the voters in the November, 2000 election. It allows new property taxes that will be used for schools to be passed by a special 55 percent majority vote. A statute that became effective upon the passage of Proposition 39, capped property taxes at $60 per $100,000 of assessed value. These assessments are expected to become common and popular with school districts.

Voter-Approved Assessments

Since July, 1978, voters have been able pass a new ad valorem tax on property if that tax is approved by 66 2/3 percent of the voters. However, this supermajority vote is so difficult to obtain, that few assessments are approved.

Pre-July 1978 Bonds

The 1 percent limit may be increased to cover any pre-July 1978 voter-approved bonds. Because bonds are often for 30 years or more, some of them may still be applicable to property.

Value Roll-Back to 1975

For calculation of taxes, the value shown on the assessor's records for the fiscal year 1975 to 1976 is deemed to be the true value of the property for that year. However, because the majority of property is not reappraised each year, most properties will benefit from this because their 1975 appraisal value actually represents an appraisal made years earlier. For any property sold, transferred, or significantly repaired since March 1975, the base value is the value as of the date of that transfer, sale, or repair. *R.&T.C. 110.1.*

Inflation Factor Increase

Once the base amount is established, the statute provides that the value of the property will be tied to the consumer price index, to consider inflation. Property assessments cannot then increase more than 2 percent per year unless the property is sold, transferred, or newly constructed. In the event of such sale or new construction, the assessor would appraise the property at its new full cash value. After such reappraisal, which becomes a new base amount, the property value is then limited to the base plus the maximum 2 percent annual inflationary increase. By liberally interpreting the new act, the State Board of Equalization instructed county assessors to add 2 percent a year to the 1975 value as a retroactive inflation factor. Thus, for example, if a property was not sold between 1975 and 1978, its full cash value for the 1978 to 1979 fiscal year was its 1975 value increased by 2 percent per year for three years.

Change of Ownership

The law provides that a new base amount shall be established and property shall be newly appraised at its full cash value upon a change in ownership. Such changes include both recorded and unrecorded transfers of legal or equitable title, except transfers of legal title under deeds of trust and similar instruments. To minimize some of the hardships brought about by transfers of title, the legislature has specifically included, among its exceptions, transfers that will not result in reassessment. *R.&T.C. 61–65.* The following are the most important exceptions:

1. Any transfer between spouses. Such conveyances include creating or terminating a joint interest, transfers on death, and divisions by divorce.

2. Change of title between cotenants that does not change their percentage of ownership interest. Such transfers include changing of title from tenants in common to joint tenants.

3. Most creations and transfers of joint tenancy interests and many terminations of joint tenancy interest. Whenever a grantor creates or transfers a joint tenancy interest while remaining as a joint tenant, the property is not reappraised. When a joint tenant dies or transfers his entire interest exclusively to the joint tenants who originally created the tenancy, there is no reevaluation. Any other transfer requires a total or partial reevaluation.

    If A, B, and C create a joint tenancy, there will be no effect. When B and C die, there will be no effect, because their interest passes to an original joint tenant. When A finally dies, the entire property will be reappraised. If X, Y, and Z hold as joint tenants and Z transfers a half-interest to M, there will be no effect, because Z remains a joint tenant. However, if Z transfers the entire interest to M, then one-third of the property will be reevaluated. Thus, two-thirds of the property will remain at the original valuation, whereas one-third will be reappraised to its current full cash value.

4. Most estate-planning trusts and life estates where the grantor retains a present interest or significant control over the trust. Also covered are transfers to a partnership or corporation controlled by the grantor.

5. All transfers of a lease where the remaining lease term (including potential options) is less than 25 years.

6. All transfers of security interests, such as a transfer to or a reconveyance from a trustee under a deed of trust.

7. Any transfers or sales after November 4, 1987, from a parent to a child are exempt if the sale or transfer is either the parent's principal residence, or if it is the first $1,000,000 of other property transferred from the parent. This special exemption arose as Proposition 58, which was passed by the voters in 1986.

8. Homeowners age 55 or older who have not used the exemption previously have a special carryover value. If they purchase a new home of equal or lesser value in the same county within two years of transfer, their new home will have the same assessed value as their own home. The new home will not be the normal one 1 percent of the purchase price. *R.&T.C. 69.5.*

Generally, a conveyance causes a reassessment of the entire property. However, if only a portion of the property or if only one cotenant's proportionate interest is sold, then only that portion or interest is reappraised. Thus, a sale of one unit in a condominium results in a re-evaluation of that unit and a transfer of a tenant in common's 20 percent interest causes only that 20 percent to be reappraised. The balance of the property retains its old value.

To assist the assessor in recognizing reassessment situations, the recorder requires a Preliminary Change of Ownership Report to be filed when recording a deed or other transfer document. The report basically lists the major exemptions from reassessment and provides financial information for transfers that will require a tax reevaluation. The two-page statewide form defined by statute is shown in Figure 17.1. *R.&TC. 480.4.* However, each county can and does adopt its own form based on the statewide form. It is best to use the local county form in recording a deed.

FIGURE 17.1   Preliminary change of ownership report.

Preliminary Change Of Ownership Report

To Be Completed by Transferee Prior to Transfer of Subject Property Per §480.3 of the Revenue and Taxation Code.
(Form Prescribed in R.&T.C. §480.4)

SELLER (Transferor):	For Assessor's Use Only
BUYER (Transferee):	
A.P. #(s):	Recorded Book, _____
Address **(If Improved)**:	Page, _____
Mail Tax Information To:	Date: _____
Name:	Document No. _____
Address:	

A lien for property taxes applies to your property on January 1 of each year for the taxes owing in the following fiscal year, July 1 through June 30. One-half of these taxes is due November 1, and one-half is due February 1. The first installment becomes delinquent on December 10, and the second installment becomes delinquent on April 10. One tax bill is mailed before November 1 to the owner of record. If this transfer occurs after January 1 and on or before December 31, you may be responsible for the second installment of taxes due February 1.

The property which you acquired may be subject to a supplemental tax assessment in an amount to be determined by the (name of county) County Assessor. For further information on your supplemental roll tax obligation, please call the (name of county) County Assessor at (phone number).

Part I: Transfer Information:

A.   Was this transfer solely between husband & wife, addition of a spouse, death of a spouse, divorce settlement, etc.?   ☐ Yes   ☐ No

B.   Was this transaction only a correction of the name(s) of the person(s) holding title to the property (for example, a name change upon marriage)?   ☐ Yes   ☐ No

C.   Was this document recorded to create, terminate, or reconvey a lender's interest in the property?   ☐ Yes   ☐ No

D.   Is this transaction recorded only as a requirement for financing purposes or to create, terminate, or reconvey a security interest (e.g. cosigner)?   ☐ Yes   ☐ No

E.   Was this document recorded to substitute a trustee under a deed of trust, mortgage, or other similar document?   ☐ Yes   ☐ No

F.   Did this transfer result in the creation of a joint tenancy in which the seller (transferor) remains as one of the joint tenants?   ☐ Yes   ☐ No

G.   Does this transfer return property to person who created the joint tenancy? (Original transferor)?   ☐ Yes   ☐ No

H.   Is this transfer of property:

   1.   to a trust for the benefit of the grantor, or the grantor's spouse?   ☐ Yes   ☐ No

   2.   to a revocable trust by the transferor?   ☐ Yes   ☐ No

   3.   to a trust from which the property reverts to the grantor within 12 years?   ☐ Yes   ☐ No

I.   If this property is the subject of a lease, is the lease for a term of less than 35 years including written options?   ☐ Yes   ☐ No

J.   Is this a transfer from parents to children or from children to parents?   ☐ Yes   ☐ No

K.   Is this a transaction to replace a principal residence by a person 55 years 55 years of age or older?   ☐ Yes   ☐ No

L.   Is this transaction to replace a principal residence by a person who is severely disabled as defined by Revenue and Taxation Code Section 69.5?   ☐ Yes   ☐ No

   Within the same county. ☐ Yes ☐ No

M.   Is this transfer solely between domestic partners currently registered with the Secretary of State?   ☐ Yes   ☐ No

* If you checked yes to J,K or L, you may qualify for a property tax reassessment exclusion, which may result in lower taxes on your property. Failure to file a claim results in reassessment of the property.

*IF YOU HAVE ANSWERED "YES" TO ANY OF THE ABOVE QUESTIONS EXCEPT J, K OR L, PLEASE SIGN AND DATE, OTHERWISE COMPLETE THE BALANCE OF THE FORM.

FIGURE 17.1 (Continued).

Preliminary Change of Ownership Report, Page Two 2.

PART II: OTHER TRANSFER INFORMATION
A. Date of transfer if other than recording date _____
B. Type of transfer. Please check appropriate box.

  ❏ Purchase ❏ Foreclosure ❏ Gift ❏ Gift or Exchange ❏ Merger, Stock or Partnership Acquisition

  ❏ Contract of Sale - Date of Contract _____

  ❏ Inheritance - Date of Death _____   ❏ Other: Please Explain: _____

  ❏ Creation of Lease   ❏ Assignment of Lease   ❏ Termination of a Lease   ❏ Sale/Leaseback

  ❏ Date Lease Began _____   ❏ Original Term in Years (Including Written Options) _____

  ❏ Remaining Term in Years (Including Written Options) _____
C. Was only a partial interest in the property transferred?   ❏ Yes ❏ No
  If Yes, Indicate the Percentage Transferred _____ %

PART III: PURCHASE PRICE AND TERMS OF SALE
A. Cash Down Payment or Value of Trade or Exchange (Excluding Closing Costs)   Amount $_____
B. First Deed of Trust @ ___ % Interest for ___ Years. Pymts./Mo. = $___ (Prin. & Interest Only) $_____

  ❏ FHA (__ Discount Points)   ❏ Fixed Rate   ❏ New Loan

  ❏ Conventional   ❏ Variable Rate   ❏ Assumed Existing Loan Balance

  ❏ VA (__ Discount Points)   ❏ All Inclusive D.T. ($___ Wrapped)   ❏ Bank or Savings & Loan

  ❏ Cal-Vet   ❏ Loan Carried by Seller   ❏ Finance Company

  Balloon Payment   ❏ Yes   ❏ No   Due Date _____   Amount $_____
C. Second Deed of Trust @ ___ % Interest for ___ Years. Pymts./Mo. = $___ (Prin. & Interest Only) $_____

  ❏ Bank or Savings & Loan   ❏ Fixed Rate   ❏ New Loan

  ❏ Loan Carried by Seller   ❏ Variable Rate   ❏ Assumed Existing Loan Balance

  Balloon Payment   ❏ Yes   ❏ No   Due Date _____   Amount $_____
D. Other Financing. Is there other financing not Covered in (b) or (c) above? ❏ Yes ❏ No $_____

  ❏ Bank or Savings & Loan   ❏ Fixed Rate   ❏ New Loan

  ❏ Loan Carried by Seller   ❏ Variable Rate   ❏ Assumed Existing Loan Balance

  Balloon Payment   ❏ Yes   ❏ No   Due Date _____   Amount $_____
E. Was an Improvement Bond Assumed by the Buyer? ❏ Yes ❏ No   Amount $_____
F. Total Purchase Price (or Acquisition Price, if Traded or Exchanged, Including Real Estate Commissions if Paid)

  Total Items A through E | $ |
G. Property Purchased ❏ Through a Broker ❏ Direct from Seller ❏ From a Family Member ❏ Other ___
  If Purchased Through a Broker, Provide Broker's Name and Phone Number: _____
  Please Explain Any Special Terms, Seller Concessions, Or Financing and Any Other Information That Would
  Help the Assessor Understand the Purchase Price and Terms of Sale. _____

PART IV: PROPERTY INFORMATION
A. Type of Property Transferred:

  ❏ Single-Family Residence   ❏ Agricultural   ❏ Timeshare

  ❏ Multiple-Family Residence (No. of Units: ____) ❏ Co-Op/ Own-Your-Own   ❏ Manufactured Home

  ❏ Commercial/ Industrial   ❏ Condominium   ❏ Unimproved Lot

  ❏ Other (Description): _____
B. Is This Intended as Your Principal Residence?   ❏ Yes   ❏ No
  If Yes, Enter Date of Occupancy _____ 19___ or Intended Occupancy _____ 19__
C. Is personal property included in the purchase price (i.e. furniture, farm equipment, machinery, etc.)
  (Other than a manufactured home subject to local property tax)?   ❏ Yes   ❏ No
D. Is a manufactured home included in the purchase price   ❏ Yes   ❏ No
  If Yes, How Much of the Purchase Price is Allocated to the Manufactured Home? $_____
  If Yes, Enter the Value of the Personal Property Included in the Purchase Price. $_____ (Attached List)
E. Does the Property Produce Income?   ❏ Yes   ❏ No   If Yes, the Income is From: _____
F. What Was the Condition of the Property At the Time of Sale: ❏ Good ❏ Average ❏ Fair ❏ Poor
  Please explain the physical condition of the property and provide any other information (such as restrictions,
  etc.) that would assist the Assessor in Determining the Value of the Property. _____

I certify that the foregoing is true, correct, and complete to the best of my knowledge and belief.
Signed: _____   Date: _____
      (NOTE: The Assessor may contact you for further information.)

Newly Constructed Property

The act provides that any newly constructed property necessitates a new base year and a reappraisal to its full cash value. The term **newly constructed** is defined in the statutes as (1) a new physical addition to the property, (2) an alteration that changes a use of the property, or (3) a rehabilitation or renovation equivalent to a new improvement. However, if the property was destroyed by a disaster and timely rebuilt to its equivalent condition before the destruction, such rebuilding will not be considered a new construction. If there has been new construction, only that portion of the property that was newly constructed will be reappraised. The value of the remaining property remains unchanged. *R.&T.C. 61.*

Senior Citizen Legislation

Senior citizens (age 62 or older) may qualify for special tax advantages. If they have only low or moderate income, they may have their property taxes postponed. *R.&T.C. 20601.* Instead of paying the taxes annually, the state places a tax lien on the property, which is enforced when the owner dies or sells the property. There are other complicated circumstances in which the postponed taxes may become due. Low-income seniors can qualify for assistance from the state to actually pay part of the property taxes. *R.&T.C. 20501.*

Over 55 or Disabled Carryover Basis

Older Californians (age 55 or older) and disabled citizens were often afraid to sell their homes because of the big increase in property taxes. If people qualify, they may retain (or carry over) their low property tax basis to their new house.

Six requirements apply to the carryover provision. First, the person must be over age 55 or disabled when the home is sold. For married couples or co-owners, at least one person must be over 55 or disabled and the other spouse or owner must also live in the property. Second, the value of the new home cannot be more than the value of the old home. In other words, the person can't buy a amore expensive home. The property must be of the same or lesser value. Third, the exemption can only be used once. Fourth, the new home must be bought or built within two years of the sale of the old house. The two-year period can be before or after the sale of the old home. Fifth, the person claiming the carry over exemption must be eligible for the homeowners exemption or the disabled veteran's exemption. Finally, the new home must be in the same county as the old home. Alternatively, the person can move to another county if that county is one of the few that has voted to accept a carryover tax basis from other counties. *R.&T.C. 69.5.*

CALCULATION OF TAXES

Taxes before July 1978

Under the old California laws, the first step in calculating taxes was for the assessor to appraise the property and set its fair market value. Next, the assessor determined the assessed value of the property, which was one-fourth of the appraised value. Then, any special exemption, such as the homeowner's exemption or veteran's exemption, was subtracted from the assessed value. Finally, the tax rate was multiplied by the net assessed value to determine the total property taxes due from the property owner.

Taxes since July 1978

Under the new tax system, the assessor determines the current full cash value, which is the base year full cash value increased by not more than 2 percent per year since that base year. The gross amount of property taxes is 1 percent of that full cash value. From this tax figure, the assessor deducts any exemptions, and the result is the property owner's tax bill.

Sample Tax Calculations

To calculate the 2003 tax bill, assume that the house was worth $80,000 in March 2000. In March 2000, the house was worth $90,000, and in March 2003, $100,000.

2000 Value under the New Law

Assuming that the property was owned and lived in before March 2000 until the present without any sale, transfer of interest, or major improvements, then the total tax bill would be $778. Take the March 2000 value ($80,000) and increase it 2 percent per year for three years; the full cash value in 2003 would then be $84,896. One percent of that amount is $848. The $70 homeowner's exemption reduces the property tax bill to $778.

2003 Value under the Old Law

Under the tax law before July 1, 2003, the property taxes due for 2003 would have been $2,720.25 (assuming a tax rate equal to last year's San Francisco tax rate of $1.170 per $100 of assessed value). The assessor derives the assessed value by taking one-fourth of the $100,000 2003 fair market value, or $25,000. That value is further reduced by the $1,750 homeowner's exemption, leaving a net assessed value of $23,250. Finally, that net figure is multiplied by $0.1170, the tax rate, to derive a total tax due of $2,720.25.

Tax on House Sold in 2003 under the New Method

Assume that the same house was sold in March 2002 for $90,000. Under the new tax rate, the 2003 taxes would be $848. Take $90,000 as the 2002 base year value and add 2 percent, making the 2003 value $91,800. One percent of that amount is $918. Subtract the $70 homeowner's exemption for a total tax due of $848.

PRIORITY OF TAX LIENS

Normal Priority Rules Inapplicable

Whenever there are both a tax lien and another lien, it is important to be able to determine priorities. The normal rule that priority is established as of the date of recording does not often apply to taxes. To avoid confusion in establishing priorities for tax liens, one should determine whether

1. The delinquent tax is one that creates a lien on the property and, if so, when and by what procedure. Delinquent state and federal taxes can become a lien only by statutory enactments.
2. The liens involved are federal tax liens, state tax liens (including the liens of cities, counties, and other political subdivisions), or private liens (such as deeds of trust, homesteads, and judgment liens).
3. The liens are either of the same class (e.g., county property taxes versus city street assessments) or of different classes (such as state versus federal). If they are of the same class, one must determine whether the liens arise from the same or different taxing organizations.

Priority over Private Liens

Generally, state tax liens are superior to private liens, regardless of the date of the private lien's creation. *R.&T.C. 2192.1.*

Importance to Lenders

Because tax liens are superior before deeds of trust, any foreclosure sale for that superior lien provides the buyer with title free and clear of the prior deed of trust. *R.&T.C. 3712.* Therefore, most deeds of trust provide that the beneficiary may foreclose immediately to protect the interest if the trustor becomes delinquent on real property taxes or assessments.

Priority to Federal Tax Liens

Among federal, state, and private liens, priority depends on the normal rules of recording, with the first to record being the superior lien

U.S. v. Estate of Romani (1998) 523 U.S. _____ and *26 U.S.C. 6323.* However, a private lien must be definite in amount and perfected against a specific property to gain priority. Thus, a mortgage might be superior to a federal tax lien, whereas attorney's fees provided for foreclosure could be junior to the federal lien if those fees were not definite in amount at the time of filing the tax lien.

Priority between Tax Deeds

All state tax deeds, as the principal case stated, are equal in priority to each other. *R.T.C. 3900.* Although this rule applies to tax deeds from separate taxing agencies, it remains uncertain whether the same rule applies to successive tax liens of the same taxing agency.

APPLY THE LAW

Bd. Supervisors v. Lenergan
27 C.3d 855 (1980)

[On June 6, 1978, the California voters passed Proposition 13 (the Jarvis–Gann Initiative), which added Article XIIIA to the California Constitution and revolutionized the method of taxing property. However, the initiative contained many ambiguities that had to be resolved by the courts.

The constitution holds that the tax on personal property cannot be higher than the tax on real property. The Constitution also provides that, although the tax for real estate will be determined each year, the tax for personal property will be taxed at last year's secured rate. The 1 percent limitation of Proposition 13 held that the 1978 to 1979 secured tax rolls would be 1 percent. The question was whether the 1 percent limit would also apply to the 1978 to 1979 unsecured rolls, or whether they would be taxed at the 1977 to 1978 (prior year's) rate, unaffected by the 1 percent rule. Much of the confusion stemmed from the fact that Proposition 13 did not distinguish between the secured and unsecured rolls.]

MOSK, JUSTICE. Unless otherwise provided by the State Constitution or Federal law, all property in California is taxable "in proportion to its full value." Property is defined comprehensively to include "all matters and things, real, personal, and mixed, capable of private ownership." Real property, or real estate, is in turn defined to include: (a) The possession or ownership of land, (b) minerals, quarries, and standing timber of the land, and (c) improvements. Personal property comprises all other property.

The Legislature may classify personal property for differential taxation, but the tax per dollar of full value shall not be higher on personal property than on real property in the same taxing jurisdiction. The assessor of each county has a duty to prepare an assessment roll listing all taxable property within the county. For this purpose, all

APPLY THE LAW

continued

property is classified as either secured or unsecured. The "secured roll" is that part of the roll containing property, the taxes on which are a lien on real property sufficient, in the opinion of the assessor, to secure payment of the taxes. The remainder of the roll is the "unsecured roll."

Whether a tax on property is a lien against real property is determined by statute. Every tax on real property is a lien against property assessed. Further, a tax on personal property may be secured or cross-secured by real property. [A tax on personal property is a lien against real property if the personal property belongs to the owner of the real property on which it is located and the lien is noted on the secured roll.] If either of these conditions exists, the personal property so secured will be assessed on the secured roll. All other personal property is assessed on the unsecured roll.

Although it is commonly assumed that property on the unsecured roll consists almost exclusively of personal property, "possessory interests" in land generally are assessed on the unsecured rolls. [Possessory interests include leases, and as almost one-half of all the land in California is owned by the state or federal government, possessory interests are a significant portion of the unsecured tax dollar. Just a small listing of some of the possible possessory interests includes the possession of public property by commercial, residential, and industrial leases in such locations as harbors, airports, marinas, golf courses, parks, stadiums, government facilities, forest land, and recreational areas.]

In short, although the property tax system distinguishes between real and personal property and also between secured and unsecured property, the two classification systems overlap. As a result, the secured and unsecured rolls each contain both real and personal property. Taxes on property assessed on the secured roll are payable in two equal installments, due November 1 and February 1 of each year. The first installment becomes delinquent on December 10 and the second installment on April 10. Taxes on the unsecured roll, however, are due March 1 preceding the fiscal year for which the taxes are levied and, if included on the assessment roll as of July 31, become delinquent on August 31.

In addition to the differences in due dates and delinquency dates, one of the fundamental distinctions between secured and unsecured taxes lies in the fixing of the tax rate. The tax rate for the secured roll is established by the board of supervisors of each county on or before September 1 of each year. Taxes on unsecured property, however, are levied at the rate fixed for the secured roll in the prior tax year.

Two of Proposition 13's four critical elements are:

Section 1 imposes a limitation on the tax rate applicable to real property. The maximum amount of any ad valorem tax on real property shall not exceed 1 percent (1%) of the full cash value of such property.

Section 2 imposes a limitation on the assessed value of real property, commonly referred to as the valuation "rollback" provision. The full cash value means the county assessor's valuation of real property as shown on the 1975–1976 tax bill under "full cash value" or, thereafter, the appraised value of real property when purchased, newly constructed, or a change in ownership has occurred after the 1975 assessment.

The issue is whether these limitations apply to both real and personal property on the unsecured roll for the tax year 1978–1979. The controversy is rooted in the previously discussed and apparently conflicting requirements that the tax on personal property shall not be higher than that on real property and that the unsecured roll be taxed at the prior year's secured rate.

The judgment is reversed. [The 1 percent (1%) limitation of Proposition 13 does not apply to the unsecured rolls for 1978–1979. However, for the 1979 to 1980 year and every year thereafter, the 1 percent rule will apply. This is because a previous year would include a year with a 1 percent limitation.]

APPLY THE LAW

continued

STUDY QUESTIONS (TRUE–FALSE)

1. The first installment of real estate property taxes is due November 10.

2. If the second installment of taxes is not paid by April 10, 1979, the taxes become a lien as of March 1, 1978.

3. When the property is declared "tax delinquent" for nonpayment of taxes, the owner is no longer permitted to live on the property.

4. The property is deeded to the state only after the owner's five-year redemption period has expired.

5. Under the new law, taxes generally may not exceed 1 percent of the property's value carried on the assessor's rolls.

6. When a husband and wife transfer title by deed between themselves from joint tenancy to community property, reappraisal of the property is required.

7. The new law eliminated the concept of assessed value as 25 percent of property's fair market value.

8. The homeowner's exemption is $1,750 off the total taxes otherwise due on the property.

9. A tax lien created in 1978 takes priority over a mortgage executed in 1952.

10. The foreclosure of a tax lien extinguishes any deeds of trust on the property.

Chapter 18

NATURE AND AMOUNT

Nature

The homestead protects a portion of a debtor's family home from creditors. Its purpose is to preserve the family by protecting them from a forced sale of their home.

There are two types of homesteads. The first is the *declared homestead*, which is created by filing a document declaring the property homesteaded *C.C.P. 704.910 et seq*. The other homestead arises when a homeowner files after a creditor tries to sell the property to enforce a judgment. The creditor must give special notice and opportunity for a homeowner to file a special homestead, called a *dwelling house homestead*, which has the same effect as a declared homestead. *C.C.P. 704.710 et seq.*

Amount

There are three different homestead amounts. The first is the family homestead for $100,000. The debtor must live in the property with his or her spouse or with at least one other person who has no ownership interest in the residence. The second exemption is the age 65 or disabled homestead. The amount is $175,000. The debtor or spouse must either be age 65 or older, or be physically or mentally disabled such that he or she cannot engage in gainful employment. The homestead also covers people age 55 or older who earn less than $15,000 a year ($20,000 if married). Finally, there is the regular homestead. The regular homestead covers all other homestead situations and is worth $75,000. *C.C.P. 704.730.*

Homesteads

Equity Protection

The homestead exemption provides an equity protection over and above all liens, regardless of the value of the home. However, the dollar limitations do prevent a family from residing in total luxury to the exclusion of creditors.

Ninety Percent Limitation

A homeowner is further protected because the law requires that a creditor cannot even sell the home without obtaining a bid for the home that is equal to the greater of (1) 90 percent of the home's fair market value as determined by the court before the sale or (2) an amount over and above all liens and encumbrances on the property and the homestead amount. In other words, the court wants to be sure that the home will be sold at a fair value and that the sales proceeds will be sufficient to make at least partial payment to the creditor.

Selling Procedure

The procedure by which a home is sold is somewhat complicated, but in simplified terms it provides that at least 140 days must pass between the time the creditor first notifies the homeowner of an intent to sell (levy on) the home and the time of the actual sale. During this time, the homeowner must be served with a document containing specified statutory language that in plain English and Spanish tells the owner that he can still file a homestead and what the effects of not filing a homestead are. *C.C.P. 704.740–704.850.*

Effect of Increase

The amount of a homestead has increased many times since its inception in 1872. The latest increase was on January 1, 2010, when the current $175,000, $100,000, and $75,000 amounts became effective. With each statutory increase, the existing homestead is automatically increased to the larger amount; no action needs to be taken by the declarant. Figure 18.1 shows the effect of a homestead increase on a creditor.

Creditors Protected

The recent pattern has been to increase the amount of the homestead at least every other year. Although there is no guarantee that this pattern will continue, it is always prudent to check the *Code of Civil Procedure Section 704.730* for the current amounts. A thorough check should also include the legislative updates to see if any amendments have been passed that will take effect in the next calendar year. The homestead increases since 1987 are shown in Table 18.1.

FIGURE 18.1   Examples of homestead calculations.

Examples of Homestead Calculations

Facts: The following documents, in order of priority, are recorded against a home: $50,000 first deed of trust ("D/T"); $100,000 family homestead; and $10,000 judgment lien ("J/L")

Effect: The fair market value ("FMV") of the home rises during inflation. Assuming a forced sale and no change in the homestead amounts, the effect would be:

FMV Home	$150,000	$155,000	$170,000
– D/T	– 50,000	– 50,000	– 50,000
Equity	$ 100,000	$ 105,000	$ 120,000
– Homestead	– 100,000	– 100,000	– 100,000
Attachable Equity	$ 0	$ 5,000	$ 20,000
– to Judgment Lien	$ 0	– 5,000	– 10,000
Remainder to Debtor	$ 0	$ 0	$ 10,000

Note: When, as in the first example above, the value of the property is less than the value of the senior liens and homestead, the judgment creditor is prevented even from executing against the property to satisfy the judgment.

TABLE 18.1   Recent homestead increases.

Effective Date	Age 65 or Disabled	Family Homestead	Regular Homestead
1/1/10	$175,000	$100,000	$75,000
1/1/04	$150,000	$ 75,000	$50,000
1/1/98	$125,000	$ 75,000	$50,000
1/1/91	$100,000	$ 75,000	$50,000
1/1/89	$ 75,000	$ 45,000	$30,000
1/1/87	$ 60,000	$ 45,000	$30,000

Although any increase in the homestead exemption automatically applies to the homeowner and to any new creditors, such increases do not always affect preexisting creditors. Under the old law, the rules were complex and depended on when the debt was incurred. Current law simplifies the matter and looks to when the judgment lien was recorded or otherwise perfected. *C.C.P. 704.965.*

Homestead Recorded First

If the debtor recorded a homestead before a judgment lien, then the homestead obtains the benefit of any increases. For example, assume that a 67-year old debtor recorded a homestead followed by a creditor recording a judgment lien. Now assume that the legislature increased the over age 65 homestead amount from $175,000 to $200,000. The homeowner would be entitled to the $200,000 homestead amount.

Judgment Recorded First

If a creditor records a judgment or otherwise perfects a lien before a homestead is recorded, that lien has a special advantage. As to that one lien, the original homestead amount continues to apply regardless of any future increases. As an example, assume that a creditor recorded a lien, followed by the debtor recording a homestead. Then assume that the legislature increased the age 65 homestead amount from $175,000 to $200,000. As to that one judgment lien, the homestead amount for that senior will always remain at $175,000.

APPLY THE LAW

Thorsby v. Babcock
36 C.2d 202 (1950)

[Defendant, Babcock, realizing he was facing financial difficulties, filed a homestead on his property. He then sold his home; however, the proceeds of that sale were tied up in escrow pending the outcome of a lawsuit. On the

APPLY THE LAW

continued

judgment eight months after the sale of his home, the funds in escrow were released to Babcock. Plaintiff immediately filed this suit, claiming he was entitled to the proceeds because they had not been reinvested in a home within the statutory six-month protection period. Defendant appeals from a judgment awarding the funds to plaintiff.]

EDMONDS, JUSTICE. Babcock contends that the ruling was erroneous. He argues that a creditor should not be permitted, by delaying payment of proceeds to a homestead claimant through litigation for more than six months, to destroy the exemption of such proceeds. Relying upon the Civil Code which exempts the proceeds from sale of a homestead for the period of six months, he reasons that the time during which he cannot obtain the proceeds because they are under the control of a court looking into the validity of the exemption should be no part of such period.

Alternatively, a sale, voluntary transfer or involuntary conveyance where the deed or instrument is executed by all claimants having homestead rights will extinguish the homestead. other methods of termination are not permitted, mere abandonment is insufficient for termination. A person cannot have two homesteads simultaneously. Thus, if a person purchases a second home and declares a homestead on it, while still retaining his first homestead house, the second declaration will be ineffective, and the original property will be the one with the homestead.

By the Constitution, the Legislature is directed to protect from forced sale a certain portion of the homestead and other property of all heads of families. The object of all homestead legislation is to provide a place for the family and its surviving members where they may reside and enjoy the comforts of a home, freed from any anxiety that it may be taken from them against their will, whether by reason of their own necessity or improvidence, or from the importunity of their creditors. In addition to exempting the home, the Legislature has included protection of the proceeds arising from the sale of the homestead by the owner to the extent of the value allowed for a homestead exemption for a period of six months following such sale. The obvious purpose of that exemption is to allow the owner of the homestead to substitute one family home for another without losing his exemption.

Although, in granting an exemption to the proceeds of a voluntary sale of the homestead for a period of six months, the Legislature has imposed no requirement of reinvestment. Obviously, the true purpose of giving the owner that time is to permit him to move his family to another home with the retention of protection from forced sale. Clearly, the Legislature has not required a purchase of other property immediately. Rather it has given the seller the reasonable time of six months within which to complete the transaction. However, the legislative purpose is thwarted if the proceeds from the sale of the homestead cannot be obtained by the owner, through no fault of his own, during the six-month period.

continued

Under the circumstances shown by this record, his homestead rights have not been concluded by this lapse of time. The order is reversed. [Babcock has six months from the date he receives the funds in which to reinvest in another home, during which time the proceeds are exempt.]

PRIORITIES

Recording Priority

Once recorded, homesteads are generally senior to (and therefore protected against) all subsequently recorded judgments, liens, and encumbrances. There are three major exceptions.

1. Mechanic's liens, regardless of their date of creation, are always **senior liens** to homesteads.
2. Deeds of trust or mortgages signed by the husband and wife, or by an unmarried claimant, are always senior to homesteads, regardless of their date of creation and whether or not they are recorded.
3. Federal tax liens, regardless of their date of creation, are always senior to homesteads. (State tax liens are like any other lien and take their priority from the date of recording.) *C.C.P. 690.030.*

Dwelling House Exemption

Besides the regular declared homestead, which is recorded before a judgment is recorded, since 1976 there has been a second type of homestead. This homestead is called a dwelling house exemption. It offers almost exactly the same protection as a declared homestead, but it can be recorded after the judgment. A creditor who begins the process to foreclose and sell the debtor's house must first provide the debtor with a special notice, prescribed by statute, which states the debtor's right to homestead the house and the effect for failure to do so.

The reason for this homestead was well stated by one court.

When the dwelling house exemption was first enacted, the Legislature was quite obviously concerned with the large

> *number of homeowners who were not receiving the benefits of the homestead because of their ignorance of the law or their failure to satisfy the technical requirements for declaring a homestead. The new law gave the debtor–homeowner additional protection for his home against the claims of creditors. He could now either declare a homestead (the declared homestead) or obtain a "dwelling house exemption." The latter is in certain respects a superior and more effective method, for no longer would execution turn on the outcome of the race to the recorder's office with the resultant loss to the debtor if the abstract of judgment preceded the recordation of the homestead.* San Diego White Trust Corp. v. Swift (1979) 96 C.A.3d 89, 92.

Effect

A homestead protects a debtor's equity from creditors. Under the old law, it also prevented one spouse from transferring the homestead property and limited a person's ability to will that property. The new law abolishes these restraints. *C.C.P. 704.940.* A spouse can transfer, will, or encumber property with a homestead as freely as if there were no homestead. If the property is recorded as community property, it will take both spouses' signatures to transfer that property because of the laws affecting transfer of community property.

CREATION AND TERMINATION

Creation Requirements

A homestead is easily created. The declarant must only execute and record a formal declaration of homestead. To be valid, a homestead declaration must meet several requirements. *C.C.P. 704.930.* (See Figure 18.2.)

Identity of Declarant

The document must identify the declarant and his or her status. If both spouses are the declarants, they must jointly own the property. Furthermore, the declarant must state that the facts stated in the declaration are true and correct from personal knowledge. Although not required, if the declarant is age 65 or older, that fact should also be included in the document.

FIGURE 18.2 Declaration of homestead.

Homestead

(Jointly Declared by Husband and Wife)

We, JOHN HUSBAND and JANE WIFE, residents of the City of _____, County of _____, State of California, hereby certify and declare:

I.

We, JOHN HUSBAND and JANE WIFE, are married, and declare this homestead in both our names on our jointly owned property.

II.

The property we are homesteading is a single-family residence, commonly known as_____ Street, in the City of _____, County of _____, State of California, and is more fully described as ____[legal description]____.

III.

The property which we are hereby homesteading is our principal dwelling, and we actually reside in this property on the date this declaration of homestead is recorded.

IV.

This declaration of homestead is executed on this _____ day of _____, 20_____, in the City of _____, County of _____, State of California.

_____   _____
[Husband's Signature]   [Wife's Signature]

We, JOHN HUSBAND and JANE WIFE, certify and declare that we are the declarants herein, and that the above facts are true and correct and known to be so from our own personal knowledge. We declare under penalty of perjury the foregoing is true and correct, and therefore we execute this homestead on this _____ day of _____, 19_____, in the City of _____, County of _____, State of California.

_____   _____
[Husband's Signature]   [Wife's Signature]

(Notary)

Residency Stated

Second, the document must state that the declarant is residing on the premises. The law requires that the declarant live on the premises as a principal residence. (While residency is needed for a declared homestead, the automatic dwelling house homestead allows situations where a person does not live on the property because of dissolution of marriage or legal separation. *C.C.P. 704.720.*

Property Description

The document must also contain a sufficient description of the premises. Although not mandatory, legal descriptions are generally used.

Signed by the Declarant

Finally, the document must be signed by the declarant, acknowledged, and recorded in the county in which the property lies.

Termination of Homestead

Homesteads can be terminated only by prescribed methods. *C.C.P. 704.980, 704.990.* A formal declaration of abandonment, properly executed and recorded, will terminate the homestead. Alternatively, a homestead can be terminated by a homeowner recording a new homestead of a different property. No other methods of abandonment are recognized by statute. If at any time a homeowner ceases to meet the requirements of a homestead, the homestead will become invalid. Thus, if a homeowner moves to a new home without recording a new homestead or recording an abandonment of the old homestead, the homestead would be ineffective. The homeowner would fail to meet the requirement of living on the homesteaded property as a principal residence.

STUDY QUESTIONS (TRUE–FALSE)

1. The amount of a homestead for a retired man, age 70, living alone, is $175,000.

2. The homestead is limited to houses situated on less than 20 acres and costing not more than twice the cost of an average home in California.

3. If the fair market value of a home is $170,000 and the husband and wife file a homestead, against which there is only a $70,000 deed of trust, a creditor may not attach any of the homeowner's equity.

4. An unrecorded mortgage executed by the homeowner in 1995 is junior to a homestead recorded in 1990.

5. If a homeowner, who has homesteaded a house, goes on a two-year vacation, the homestead is abandoned.

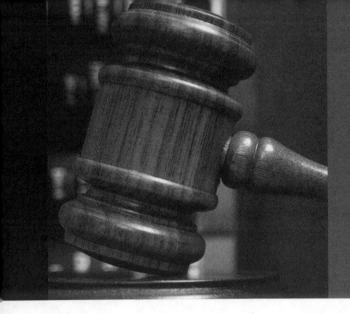

Chapter 19

NATURE OF PRIVATE RESTRICTION

Types of Restrictions

Frequently, private parties desire to control or limit the use of their land. Two individuals who dislike swimming pools may agree between themselves that neither they nor any future owner of their land may ever build a swimming pool. A subdivider who wants to keep all lots free from certain activities and types of buildings may bind each lot by a tract restriction. In each case, owners of land contract away certain rights affecting the potential use of their property. These restrictions on use are either covenants or conditions, cumulatively known as restrictions. Commonly, private limitations on land are called *covenants, conditions*, and *restrictions* (CC&Rs).

The term **restriction** is a generic word having no real significance today. Originally, it denoted a type of covenant or condition that *restricted* the use of property, as opposed to granting or enlarging a use of the land. For historical reasons, the term is retained and included in the declaration filed by subdividers.

Limitations

Owners are generally free to limit their land in any manner not against the law. Racial restrictions are in violation of the Constitution and invalid. The courts have further held that restrictions that create a monopoly are unenforceable. Although other legal limits exist, the parties basically have great flexibility in restricting the use of their property through contract.

Private Restrictions on Land

Effect of Restrictions

When one parcel is burdened by a restriction, another parcel generally benefits from that limitation. For example, if parcel A is restricted from housing a structure over two stories tall, adjoining parcel B would benefit because the view from that lot would be assured against blockage by a tall home on parcel A. The restricted land may be a single parcel or an entire subdivision, just as the benefited land may be one or more parcels. Occasionally, no specific lot is directly benefited; for example, a lot outside a subdivision might be restricted through a condition subsequent from being used for commercial purposes.

Creation of Restrictions

Covenants, conditions, and restrictions normally arise in one of three ways. Most often, they are created as part of a *general plan* of a subdivision. As such, they bind each lot in that tract of land. Occasionally, CC&Rs are created *by contract* between private landowners. Finally, and infrequently, restrictions are imposed *in the deed* to property as a condition of the grant.

CONDITIONS AND COVENANTS

Conditions in Contracts

In the context of CC&Rs, conditions are qualifications in a grant of an estate, not conditions in a contract. Nevertheless, understanding how conditions function in ordinary contracts best explains the nature and function of conditions in general.

Conditional Promises

A person who promises to do something is legally bound to do it, and failure to perform gives rise to damages or other legal remedies. To avoid the unconditional obligation wherein the promisor must perform regardless of future difficulties and burdens, the promisor may make his performance conditional on the occurrence of certain events or acts. Such conditions may be either *precedent* or *subsequent* to the duty of performance.

Conditions Precedent

A **condition precedent** requires an act, event, or fact to occur before the promisor has a duty to perform. For example, if a contract to purchase real estate contains a condition "subject to financing," the buyer is not obligated to purchase the property unless the stated financing has been obtained. If the financing is not secured, the buyer has no duty or liability to complete the sale.

Conditions Subsequent

A **condition subsequent** stipulates that when an act or event occurs the promisor no longer has any duty of performance. Such conditions are rarely encountered in contracts. (See Table 19.1.)

Conditions in Real Property Law

A **condition** is a fact or event the occurrence or nonoccurrence of which creates an estate or interest (and is called a condition precedent) or extinguishes an obligation or estate of the promisor (and is called a condition subsequent).

TABLE 19.1   Types of conditions.

	Conditions Precedent	Conditions Subsequent
Nature	Upon the occurrence of an act or event, an estate is created or enlarged.	Upon the occurrence of an act or event, an estate is destroyed or limited.
Example 1	I'll give you $1 if it rains today.	Here is $1; if it rains today you must give it back.
Example 2	Mother grants Blackacre to Mother until son reaches age 21, at which time it vests in (is transferred to) son.	Mother grants Blackacre to son, until son reaches age 21, at which time it reverts (is transferred back) to mother.

Covenant

A **covenant** is a mere promise to do something, contractual in nature and not tied to the creation or defeating of an estate. The person making the promise is called the *covenantor*, whereas the person to whom it is made is called the *covenantee*.

Comparison of Covenants and Conditions

The most important distinction between covenants and conditions is the remedies available on their violation. The violation of a condition subsequent results in the forfeiture of the estate, whereas the breach of a covenant permits only damages or equitable remedies. No loss of an estate is permitted for violation of a covenant. Other distinctions, although significant, are less important. (See Table 19.2.)

TABLE 19.2 Comparison of conditions and covenants.

	Condition	Covenant
Definition	A qualification added to a conveyance, specifying that upon the occurrence or nonoccurrence of some event, an estate shall be created or defeated.	A contractual agreement whereby one of the parties promises to perform or to refrain from certain acts.
Creation	Almost exclusively in the deed (or other instrument of conveyance).	Generally, by separate contract between parties, although rarely it may be part of the language in the deed.
Run with the land	Yes, it always runs with the land to bind successors in interest, since it is part of the estate (title).	No, unless it meets the special statutory requirements for running with the land. Otherwise, it remains a personal obligation that binds the covenantor and terminates upon his death.
Title	Creates a fee simple defeasible estate; a condition of title.	No effect on the title (ownership) of the estate.
Language	Since not favored by courts, found only if determined to be the clear and unmistakable intent of the grantor.	Construction favored by courts, so only reasonable intent to create a contractual obligation is needed.
Enforcement	The condition or title creates a defeasible fee, the breach of which is subject to termination of an estate.	A contractual promise, it is enforced by an injunction or lawsuit for damages. A breach does not involve forfeiture of the estate.

Construction of Ambiguous Language

The courts abhor forfeitures and penalties and strive, whenever possible, to construe any ambiguity toward the least offensive penalty. Because conditions involve the greater penalty—loss of an estate—the courts express extreme reluctance to find a condition. Only if the language is clear and unequivocal will conditions be found and upheld. Covenants imply lesser penalties—usually damages—so the courts tend to find covenants whenever possible. Finally, if possible, the courts will seek to find no covenant or condition at all, holding that only a fee simple absolute estate was created.

APPLY THE LAW

Boughton v. Socony Mobil Oil Co.
231 C.A.2d. 188 (1964)

LILLIE, JUSTICE. Plaintiffs, owners of a parcel of real property, sued to have the court declare a restriction prohibiting the dispensing of petroleum products thereon to be invalid and unenforceable. Judgment was entered for defendant adjudging the restriction to be valid and enforceable against plaintiffs; they appeal therefrom. On June 22, 1959, General Petroleum Corporation, by corporation grant deed, conveyed to Kelley and Clark as tenants in common a parcel of real property for the dispensing of petroleum products to November 1, 1979. Should the property be used for service station purposes prior to November 1, 1979, the title should be revested and revert to General Petroleum Corporation. Thereafter, General Petroleum was merged into Socony Mobil Oil Company, Inc., defendant herein. In March 1962, Kelley and Clark conveyed the property to plaintiffs subject to "covenants, conditions, reservations, restrictions, rights, rights of way, and easements of record."

It is settled law of California that a condition subsequent prohibiting the carrying on of a particular business upon property conveyed is valid and will be upheld where the question of monopoly is not involved or the purpose of the condition is not unlawful, and possibly other exceptions that do not exist here. The mere allegation that the purpose of the restriction is to prevent competition in that area, although uncontroverted, does not itself imply a monopoly. The courts have upheld similar use restrictions in conveyances in which the premises were reasonably limited on the theory that as the owner of property has the right to withhold it from sale, he can also, at the time of sale, impose conditions upon its use.

Moreover, while the cases are uniform in refusing to enforce a contract wherein one is restrained from pursuing an entire business, trade, or profession, where one is barred from pursuing only a small or limited part of a business, trade or profession, the contract has been upheld as valid. In the case at bar, plaintiffs are not prohibited from carrying on the lawful business of selling petroleum products or operating

APPLY THE LAW
continued

a service station but, as grantees of this particular piece of property, they are barred merely from doing so on those premises and then only for a limited time.

The restriction in the deed is neither a covenant running with the land nor a personal covenant, as urged by the appellants. The intention of the parties to provide a forfeiture and termination of the estate in the event the property is used for service station purposes prior to November 1, 1979, is readily apparent from the language employed in the restriction; it reflects a condition subsequent.

The nature of a restriction in a deed is determined by the language used. A condition subsequent is not favored in the law because a breach involves a forfeiture, and a clause in a deed imposing a restriction on a grant is subject to a strict construction wherein the language, if possible, will be interpreted as a mere declaration of purpose or a personal covenant. Conditions subsequent "can be created only by apt or appropriate language," but if the condition is so clearly stated as to leave no room for construction, or if the words used reflect a clear and unmistakable intention to create a condition subsequent, it will be enforced as such, even though it results in forfeiture. In light of the fact that language here employed clearly declares a condition and imports a forfeiture, the judgment is affirmed. [If the condition is violated, the property will pass to defendant Socony Mobil Oil Company.]

CONDITIONS RUNNING WITH THE LAND
Nature

When two people execute a contract, there is no problem in binding the two of them to its terms. However, if one of the parties sells, assigns, or otherwise transfers an interest in that contract, the question frequently arises whether that new party is bound by all the requirements of the contract. With land, if the covenant binds successors in interest, it is said to *run with the land*.

As to Covenants and Conditions

Conditions always run with the land because they are part of the estate contained in the grant. A grantor can convey no greater estate than he owns; hence, the condition passes with title. However, covenants affecting land are mere promises between two or more landowners, which will run to bind the heirs only if certain requirements are met.

Requirements

The once complex requirements for a covenant to run with the land have been eliminated. A covenant that meets only the following five statutory requirements will run with the land, binding all heirs and assigns. *C.C. 1468.*

1. The covenant must be in writing, as required by the statute of frauds.
2. The property affected by the covenant must be adequately described in the instrument so that there will be no question as to which property is burdened.
3. The document must state that it shall run with the land, thereby evidencing the parties' intent to bind their successors and assigns.
4. The document must be recorded in each county in which the property lies.
5. Finally, the document must *touch and concern* the land. That is, it must relate to the use of land (e.g., as to easements, covenants to pay taxes, options to purchase), as opposed to being a purely personal agreement between the parties.

Equitable Servitude

If the covenant cannot run because it does not meet the statutory requirements, it may still bind the successors under equitable circumstances. If the new owner had full knowledge of the covenant, it would be inequitable to enable him or her to escape its requirements and obligations simply because it failed to meet one of the five requirements. Equity binds the successor: Such a **quasi-covenant** is called an *equitable servitude;* that is, it is a burden on land binding successors through equitable principles.

GENERAL PLAN RESTRICTIONS (SUBDIVISIONS)

Nature and Purpose

Most developers impose covenants, conditions, and restrictions, known as **general plan restrictions**, on each lot in a subdivision. The builder hopes to ensure homogeneous development of the lots by each owner of a tract parcel. The restrictions are encumbrances on the land, appurtenant to the property. Each lot in the tract is burdened by the general plan restrictions in the same manner as the other lots; similarly, each lot shares the benefit of the CC&Rs with all other lots in the subdivision. Each property owner (including the subdivider, while he is still a lot owner) may enforce the restrictions against any other subdivision lot owner.

Scope of Restrictions

Most modern subdivisions are governed by general plan restrictions and such master deed restrictions can be almost as broad and all encompassing as bylaws in a condominium association. The author once lived in a large subdivision of thousands of single-family detached dwelling where each owner had to have a grass lawn and a palm tree in their front yard. One owner decided he wanted rock, and ripped out the lawn to cover the area with an attractive rock garden. The homeowners' association had the rock removed, reseeded new grass and planted another tree. It charged the owner for labor and materials in removing the rock, new grass, and tree. The moral of the story is not only the binding effect of the CC&Rs but also the need to review those documents before buying a house in a most subdivisions.

Equitable Servitude

Prior to 1969, general plan restrictions would not bind future owners and run with the land at law, because the owner could not meet the technical requirements that each lot be mutually bound by a direct benefit between common owners. The 1969 changes in the law minimize the differences between covenants running "in law" and "at equity." Equitable servitudes run under the equitable theory that a purchaser who has notice of the restriction should be bound by it, even if that restriction fails to meet the technical requirements to run at law. For all present and future owners of subdivision lots to be bound by general plan restrictions, the future owners need only have notice of the covenant. Notice is provided by meeting two requirements: notice of the restriction in the original deed and a full description of the benefited or burdened property.

Notice and Intent Stated in Subdivider's Original Deed

The notice of an intent to create a general plan restriction must be stated in the first deed to each parcel in the tract. Usually, this notice is accomplished by reference to another recorded document. After the subdivision map is recorded, but before the first deed is issued, the subdivider records a *Declaration of Covenants*, Conditions, and Restrictions. Thereafter, each deed contains language indicating that the recorded CC&Rs are incorporated in it by reference, with the same effect as if they were set out in full by the deed itself. Thereafter, all subsequent owners are bound by the general plan restrictions. Successors in interest are bound even if their deeds contain no direct reference to the restrictions, because all appurtenant encumbrances attach to the land and pass with each grant of that property. *Citizens for Covenant Compliance v. Anderson (1996) 39 C.A.4th 312.*

Description of Land Bound by General Plan

A notice of the intent to create a general plan restriction must describe the entire property bound by that general plan. A description of the entire subdivision creates a title chain providing constructive notice to all successors in interest.

Modification and Termination

General plan restrictions become unenforceable and terminate for the same reasons applicable to restrictions in general, including changed circumstances, public policy, waiver, expiration of term, and mutual agreement. If there is no stated requirement of the number of lot owners needed to effectuate a change, then all lot owners must consent before a modification becomes effective.

However, the real estate commissioner will not approve for filing any condominium project that does not provide the homeowners with the right to amend the CC&Rs. This document must be amendable by a written vote of (1) not less than 51 percent nor more than 75 percent of the total voting power of the Homeowner's Association and (2) at least 51 percent of the voting members of the association, excluding the developer. The 51 percent requirement was added to protect homeowners so that one large owner or the developer with many unsold lots would not individually control and amend the CC&Rs. Furthermore, any amendment that materially affects most rights of ownership or property use requires the prior approval of the real estate commissioner. *Regs. 2792.24.*

TERMINATION AND UNENFORCEABILITY

Enforcement

Covenants, conditions, and restrictions are enforced in an action seeking an injunction to prevent further violations, by a lawsuit seeking damages for the depreciation in value to the property caused by the violation, or through an action for declaratory relief seeking a court interpretation of the validity of the limitation.

Defenses to Enforcement

The courts maintain ultimate control over restrictions on the use of land. If the court finds that enforcement of a restriction would be inequitable or unreasonable, the court will refuse to enforce that condition. Additionally, the court may also quiet title to the property, eliminating the condition as a cloud on the title of the land. The most common defenses to enforcement are changed circumstances, violation of public policy, and waiver.

Changed Circumstances

When the condition has become obsolete and enforcement would be oppressive, enforcement will be denied. Typically, as in the principal case, the surrounding neighborhood has so changed that the original purpose is unachievable or impractical, and any enforcement would be inequitable under the new circumstances.

Public Policy

If enforcement would violate a public policy, there will be no court action. Commonly, the condition creates a monopoly or discriminates on the basis of race, religion, or national origin.

Waiver

If the plaintiff has expressly or impliedly waived rights to enforcement, has been guilty of laches (implied **waiver** resulting from unreasonable delay to the detriment of the defendant), or has personally materially violated the restriction, the courts will deny enforcement.

Natural Termination

Certain restrictions terminate automatically without court action. Some conditions state that they will expire after a set period of time (such as 20 years), in which case they automatically terminate at that expiration date. Other conditions terminate by merger. Whenever the benefited and burdened properties are acquired by the same person, the restrictions are automatically destroyed. Occasionally, restrictions provide the parties with the right to modify, add, or delete any conditions upon appropriate vote of affected landowners.

APPLY THE LAW

Bolotin v. Rindge
230 C.A.2d 741 (1964)

FILES, JUSTICE. This is an action for declaratory relief and to quiet title against tractwide deed restrictions that limit the use of plaintiff's property to single-family residential purposes. The trial court gave judgment declaring the restrictions to be unenforceable in part. Defendants have appealed.

Plaintiffs own an unimproved lot situated at the northeast corner of Wilshire Boulevard and Hudson Avenue in the City of Los Angeles. This lot is a part of a tract that was subdivided in 1923. Defendants are owners of other lots in the same tract. All the lots in the tract are subject to deed restrictions imposed by the original subdivider. These restrictions require, among other things, that each lot shall be used solely for single,

APPLY THE LAW

continued

private residences. There is no dispute that the Hancock Park area is one of the most desirable and expensive residential areas in the community. It is also undisputed that the character of Wilshire Boulevard has changed greatly since 1923. The changes in the uses of property abutting Wilshire Boulevard and the increase in vehicular traffic on said boulevard along said lot have resulted in said lot having no substantial value solely for single-family residential purposes, but said lot has a market value in excess of $200,000 for business purposes.

A court will declare deed restrictions to be unenforceable when, by reason of changed conditions, enforcement of the restrictions would be inequitable and oppressive, and would harass plaintiff without benefiting the adjoining owners. Also well recognized is the rule that a building restriction in the nature of a servitude will not be enforced where changed conditions in the neighborhood have rendered the purpose of the restrictions obsolete. But, if the original purpose of the covenant can still be realized, it will be enforced even though the unrestricted use of the property would be more profitable to its owner.

The difficulty in the present case is that there is no finding that the purposes of the restrictions have become obsolete, or that the enforcement of the restrictions on the plaintiffs' property will no longer benefit the defendants. The trial court's finding as to the effect upon defendants is limited to the statement that there will be no adverse effect upon market value. This is not the test.

The purpose of the deed restrictions was to preserve the tract as a fine residential area by excluding from the tract many of the activities that might be offensive to the residents or that would create noise, traffic, congestion, or other conditions that would lessen the comfort and enjoyment of the residents. Bringing the prohibited activities into the neighborhood might or might not depreciate the market value of the homes. If the restrictions should be broken, and a commercial building erected on the Wilshire frontage, speculators might be willing to pay more for the other parcels in anticipation of future expansion of the commercial development. Thus, the intrusion of an office building might increase market values even though it offended the senses of the residents and destroyed the physical conditions that had made their neighborhood a desirable one for them.

There is nothing in the record to support any inference that the trial court considered or decided whether the purpose of the deed restrictions had become obsolete, or whether the enforcement of the restrictions against plaintiffs' lot would benefit defendants in any respect other than market value. It is for the trial court to resolve this issue of fact. The judgment is reversed. [Plaintiff may not use his lot for commercial purposes based on the evidence presented.]

STUDY QUESTIONS (TRUE–FALSE)

1. The courts prefer to find conditions rather than covenants when the language permits.

2. Wording in a deposit receipt stating that "this offer is subject to financing" indicates a condition precedent.

3. The buyer in question 2, who could not, in good faith, obtain financing, would have absolutely no legal duty to purchase the property.

4. If A and B own adjoining parcels of property and create a covenant between them, and if A sells to X, and B sells to Y, then X can enforce the covenant against Y only if it runs with the land.

5. To run, a covenant must touch and concern the use of land.

6. An owner who breaches a covenant faces the possibility of losing the land, paying damages, or having an injunction issued against him or her.

7. Generally, whenever an agreement relating to the use of land is stated in the deed, it is a covenant included in and considered part of that deed.

8. If the court finds an intentional violation of a covenant, it must award damages or penalties against the violator.

9. An obsolete condition that causes hardship by its enforcement will generally not be enforced by the courts.

10. B covenants with A not to sell liquor on the premises, but A nevertheless does so openly. B usually purchases liquor from A. B has waived the right of enforcement by participating in the violation.

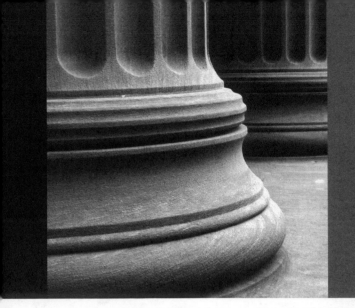

Chapter

20

NATURE OF ZONING

Definition and Use

Zoning is the division of property into sections, called *zones*, and the regulation of uses within each zone. Each different zone permits different uses, aiming toward an overall pattern of logical, systematic development, land use, and population regulation. One zone might permit only residential dwellings; another requires broad open space and environmental greenbelts; still another prohibits nonindustrial development. By comprehensive planning on a citywide and even regional basis, a community strives for an orderly, logical growth pattern, the prevention of slums, the regulation of traffic patterns, the control of population centers, the enhancement of fire safety, and the general protection of the public health, safety, and welfare.

Zoning History

Although rudimentary zoning existed centuries ago, the first modern attempt at comprehensive zoning was not made until 1916 in New York City. Most early zoning was simplistic in scheme, having only two or three categories. Generally, these few zones were *cumulative*. That is, if residential was the most protected use, residential zones excluded commercial and industrial use. Commercial was the next higher zone, permitting both residential and commercial use, whereas industrial zones permitted all three uses. Exceptions to the zoning **ordinances** existed, such as variances, although their use was rarely anticipated or encouraged. These simple zones are often labeled *Euclidean*, after the type of zoning involved in a case of that name. In fact, it was in this case, in 1926, that the U.S. Supreme Court

Zoning

finally upheld the constitutionality of comprehensive zoning. *Euclid v. Amber Realty Co. (1926) 272 U.S. 365.*

Modern Zoning

Current zoning differs dramatically from the early concepts and ordinances. Today zoning generally classifies land for 10 or more uses, sometimes as many as 30 to 40. The zones tend to be *noncumulative* (exclusive), permitting only the one designated use, or *partially exclusive*, permitting, for example, only different types of cumulative commercial uses in a commercial zone. Finally, modern zoning allows considerable flexibility through variances and conditional use permits as exceptions to the zoning plan.

Interim Zoning

If the zoning's purpose is to protect public health, safety, or welfare, as most zoning does, then the agency can adopt an interim zoning ordinance. Such temporary zoning bypasses the normal zoning process. Thus, counties have an expeditious method of providing interim protection while they work to adopt a final zoning ordinance. *Gov.C. 65858.*

Authority for Zoning

Zoning is an exercise of the *police power*, the right of a government to regulate the health, safety, and welfare of its citizens. The California Constitution (*Art. XI, Sec. 11*) specifically permits a city, county, town, or township to make and enforce its police, sanitary, and other regulations, provided they do not conflict with the general law. Furthermore, special statutes authorize local ordinances to regulate the use of buildings; the use of land for agricultural, industrial, business, residential, and other purposes; the location, height, size, bulk, and type of buildings; the yard space, ratio of home to lot size, setback requirements, and open space of buildings; the public parks, business districts, greenbelt areas, and other special districts; and the general city planning and land use controls. *Gov.C. 65800.* Additionally, many city charters authorize and regulate zoning.

Limits on Zoning

Zoning is regulated by the broad police power doctrine and circumscribed by the general limits of health, safety, and welfare. Some authorities have questioned whether these concepts are really limits or are so broad as to be almost meaningless. One recent U.S. Supreme Court case included the following statement:

> *Public safety, public health, morality, peace and quiet, law and order–these are some of the more conspicuous examples of the traditional applications of the police power to municipal affairs. Yet they merely illustrate the scope of the power and do not delimit it.* Berman v. Parker (1954) 348 U.S. 26.

Distinct from Eminent Domain

Zoning is a mere **regulation** of property, requiring no reimbursement to the owner. The regulation of property is one of the prices we pay for the privilege of living in the community. However, an owner is not required to give property to the state. Any actual taking of property by the power of eminent domain requires full compensation to the owner. Theoretically, the distinction between regulation and taking is clear, although in practice it is often difficult and imprecise. The procedures of and distinctions between police power and eminent domain are discussed in detail in Chapter 10.

EXPANDED USES OF ZONING AND PLANNING

New Orientations

Originally, zoning sought merely to regulate land uses within a city, often in a haphazard manner with little thought of the future. Modern zoning includes numerous applications never envisioned by early planners. Government agencies carefully delineate long-range *general plans* for a community's growth and proposed development. Then the community seeks to implement these plans by zoning. Furthermore, zoning authorities frequently coordinate their efforts with those of other communities to seek a comprehensive, overall regulation beneficial to the entire region. Additionally, there have been highly controversial attempts to do what some see as regulating citizens' morals through zoning.

General Plan

To coordinate a community's development, the planning authorities carefully outline its long-range goals and the most likely procedures for achieving them. These guidelines, known as general plans (formerly master plans), are required by every county and city having a planning department. Each plan must include a text and diagrams outlining the proposed future growth and development of the community, considering at least nine minimum elements: land use, circulation, housing, conservation, open space, seismic safety, noise pollution, scenic highway development, and protection from fires and geological hazards. *Gov.C. 65302*. Of course, the general plan may and often does include numerous other elements of concern.

Difference from Zoning

The general plan is a long-term outline of a community's objectives, whereas zoning is the most important method of implementing that general plan—the actual regulation of land to accomplish set objectives. Someone whose property is adversely affected by the zoning plan would lack standing to state a claim for a taking in an inverse condemnation suit. *Selby Realty Co. v. City of San Buenaventura (1973) 10 C.3d 110*. However, any adverse effect to property caused by zoning would create at least the right to litigate the issue of inverse condemnation. As a condition to bringing such lawsuit, the local government must first be notified within 90 days of the date that the government damaged the land's economic value. *Hensler v. City of Glendale (1994) 8 C.4th 1*. Finally, all zoning must be consistent with the general plan. *Gov.C. 65860*.

Regional Planning

When communities were isolated units, totally and physically independent of and separate from each other, zoning and planning were matters of purely local concern. However, today, because of the strong interdependence among communities, similarities in their goals, and common boundaries, communities have been forced to cooperate and coordinate certain types of planning. Cities and counties have together created common agencies to aid in planning and development: regional commissions, district associations, special study agencies, and joint community boards. Most of these intercity and intercounty entities were created through voluntary association, although some are of statutory creation. The voluntary associations range from having almost no authority except advisory fact-finding functions to having almost total planning control over certain programs.

San Francisco Bay Area as an Example

Because of the interdependence among communities in the San Francisco Bay Area, several regional agencies have been created. The eight counties of Alameda, Contra Costa, Marin, Napa, San Francisco, San Mateo, Santa Clara, and Sonoma, and the cities located within each respective county have formed a regional commission called the Association of Bay Area Governments. This association operates under a joint powers agreement among its members, investigating interregional needs, coordinating regional planning, and providing guidance to individual members. The state legislature created the Metropolitan Transportation Commission (MTC) to control regional transportation planning. The MTC approves all transbay bridges, intercounty transit systems, and most state highway routes. *Gov.C. 66500 et seq.* The legislature created the San Francisco Bay Conservation and Development Commission (BCDC) to regulate all developments affecting the San Francisco Bay. The BCDC approves all permits of any project dumping fill in, removing earth from, or affecting waterland around the bay. *Gov.C. 66650 et seq.*

LAFCO Planning

To further regulate urban sprawl, regional planning, and intercommunity competition, the state legislature created a special commission called the Local Agency Formation Commission. This commission must exist in each county and city having a planning department. It regulates the policies and procedures for incorporating new cities, merging two cities, and annexing land to existing cities or counties. The commission's review ensures that such incorporation or annexation is in conformity with that community's general plan. *Gov.C. 54774.1 et seq.*

APPLY THE LAW

Selby Realty Co. v. City of San Buenaventura
10 C.3d 110 (1973)

[Part of plaintiff–landowner's lawsuit concerned property he owned, which he claimed was adversely affected by a general plan adopted by Ventura County. The general plan indicated extension of existing streets into and across plaintiff's land, which plaintiff asserted was a taking of his property. Plaintiff in part requested a judicial determination (declaratory relief) that the general plan amounted to a taking of his property for which he should be compensated through an inverse condemnation action.]

APPLY THE LAW

continued

MOSK, JUSTICE. Under the Government Code, the legislative body of each city and county must establish a planning agency that shall adopt a comprehensive, long-term general plan for the physical development of the city or county. The plan may be changed after notice and hearing if the legislative body deems a change to be in the public interest. Cooperation between city and county planning agencies is encouraged, and a city and county may adopt the same general plan.

The code is less specific as to the implementation of a general plan. Prior to 1971, it provided only that the planning agency should make recommendations and reports to the legislative body and consult with others regarding implementation of the plan, and that legislative bodies are required to give consideration to conformity with the general plan in the acquisition or abandonment of property or the construction of public works. Recent legislation requires county and city zoning ordinances to be consistent with the general plan.

The county has taken no action with respect to plaintiff's land except to enact a general plan describing proposed streets, as required by state law. The fact that some of the proposed streets, if ultimately constructed, will cross plaintiff's property gives this plaintiff no greater right to secure a declaration as to the validity of the plan or its effect upon his land than that available to any other citizen whose property is included within the plan. The plan is by its very nature merely tentative and subject to change. Whether eventually any part of plaintiff's land will be taken for a street depends upon unpredictable future events. If the plan is implemented by the county in the future in such manner as actually to affect plaintiff's free use of his property, the validity of the county's action may be challenged at that time.

The adoption of a general plan is a legislative act. Because the wisdom of the plan is within the legislative and not the judicial sphere, a landowner may not maintain an action in declaratory relief to probe the merits of the plan absent allegation of a defect in the proceedings leading to its enactment.

Although plaintiff did not originally allege that the county's adoption of the general plan amounted to inverse condemnation of its property, it now asserts that the county's action in adopting the plan amounted to a "taking" of its property. No decision of which we are aware holds that the enactment of a general plan for the future development of an area, indicating potential public uses of privately owned land, amounts to inverse condemnation of that land.

The adoption of a general plan is several leagues short of a firm declaration of an intention to condemn property. It is too clearly established to require extensive citation of authority that under certain circumstances, a governmental body may require the dedication of property as a condition for its development, and it may not be necessary for the county to acquire the land by eminent domain even if it is

APPLY THE LAW
continued

ultimately used for a public purpose. In order to state a cause of action for inverse condemnation, there must be an invasion or an appropriation of some valuable property right that the landowner possesses and the invasion or appropriation must directly and specially affect the landowner to his injury.

The county has not placed any obstacles in the path of plaintiff in the use of its land. Plaintiff has not been refused permission by the county to build on or subdivide its county land, and its posture is no different from that of any other landowner along the streets identified in the plan. Furthermore, the plan is subject to alteration, modification, or ultimate abandonment, so that there is no assurance that any public use will eventually be made of plaintiff's property.

The deleterious consequences of haphazard community growth in this state and the need to prevent further random development are evident to even the most casual observer. The legislature has attempted to alleviate the problem by authorizing the adoption of long-range plans for orderly progress. Thus, it has provided not only for the adoption of general plans but also regional plans, specific plans, district plans, and a comprehensive plan for the conservation of San Francisco Bay. In addition, the voters recently passed an initiative measure providing the mechanism for adoption of plans to preserve and protect the state's coastline.

If a governmental entity and its responsible officials were held subject to a claim for inverse condemnation merely because a parcel of land was designated for potential public use on one of these several authorized plans, the process of community planning would either grind to a halt, or deteriorate to publication of vacuous generalizations regarding the future use of land. We indulge in no hyperbole to suggest that if every landowner whose property might be affected at some vague and distant future time by any of these legislatively permissible plans was entitled to bring an action in declaratory relief to obtain a judicial declaration as to the validity and potential effect of the plan upon his land, the courts of this state would be inundated with futile litigation.

It is clear, under all the circumstances, that plaintiff has not stated a cause of action against the county defendants for either declaratory relief or inverse condemnation. [The landowner has suffered no damages, may not recover any compensation, and has failed to state a valid complaint against the county for a lawsuit.]

Broadened Use of Zoning

Originally and traditionally, zoning sought to regulate land use, primarily to create areas conducive to residential living. All incompatible commercial and industrial uses were excluded from residential zones.

Although the residential purpose still remains the major purpose of zoning, it is now only one of the goals. Zoning has evolved from merely segregating residential, commercial, and industrial uses. Like many other functions of government, some of the uses and applications of zoning have become highly controversial. Some authorities think that zoning has been used to regulate indirectly the conduct and morals of society by means not available through direct legislation. Other experts hold that zoning has merely evolved to meet the needs of a complex society. Whatever one's opinion, it is clear that many areas of zoning are controversial, with ill-defined limits that can be determined only case by case. Zoning has clearly controlled open space, affected life patterns, and limited communities' growth patterns.

Open Space and Minimum Lot Size

Provided the regulation is reasonable, communities may zone in open-space areas and scenic vistas. Large areas can be zoned open greenbelt preserves, whereas small open areas can be required around cluster housing communities like planned unit developments. On the theory that small residential lots foster slums, overcrowding, traffic congestion, and unhealthy environments, communities have been allowed to zone minimum lot sizes. The courts have seemingly ignored arguments that minimize lot sizes discriminate against the poor and racial minorities. One case held that a zoning ordinance could prohibit the sale or subdivision of land less than 18 acres in size. *Gisler v. County of Madera (1974) 38 C.A.3d 303.*

Life Patterns

The most controversial use of zoning is the regulation of citizens' conduct through controlled land use. The rules are vague. For example, in the conservative village of Belle Torre, New York, the inhabitants sought to restrict college students and youths from living together. The planning department passed an ordinance prohibiting three or more unrelated individuals from living together in one dwelling. In upholding the ordinance the U.S. Supreme Court stated:

> *The police power is not confined to elimination of filth, stench, and unhealthy places. It is ample to lay out zones where family values, youth values, and the blessings of quiet seclusion and clear air make the area a sanctuary for people.* Village of Belle Torre v. Boraas (1974) 416 U.S. 797.

However, the Court later invalidated a Cleveland ordinance that regulated the number and type of related individuals who could live together, claiming that such restrictions exceed the boundaries of reasonable regulation and amount to an unconstitutional invasion of privacy. *Moore v. East Cleveland (1977) 431 U.S. 494.* Communities have been permitted to restrict the location of certain undesirable business establishments through zoning. A city may lawfully restrict adult movies from operating within 1,000 feet of each other or within 500 feet of a residential area. *Young v. American Mini Theatres, Inc. (1976) 427 U.S. 50.* Similarly, San Francisco has been permitted to restrict cocktail lounges from operating within 500 feet of a residential area without a conditional use permit. *Floresta, Inc. v. City Council (1961) 190 C.A.2d 599.*

Growth Limitations and Character

Recently, communities have been permitted to regulate their growth and development to preserve their rural character and life-style. For example, the California city of Petaluma adopted its Petaluma Plan, designed to limit and regulate future growth, preserve its small-town character, and provide for orderly expansion. The courts have held such purposes a valid exercise of zoning. *Construction Industry of Sonoma County v. City of Petaluma (1976) 522 F.2d 897.* Similarly, the community of Los Altos Hills, California, constitutionally limited single-family residences to 1-acre-minimum lots and totally excluded all future commercial uses. Such bans on commercial development by exclusionary zoning have been ruled valid if reasonable in scope and purpose. *Los Altos Hills v. Adobe Creek Properties (1973) 32 C.A.3d 488.*

RELIEF FROM ZONING

Sources of Relief

Disliking the application of specific zoning to property, an owner can seek relief from one of the three branches of government. The owner can seek a legislative change by asking the zoning authorities to amend or rescind the zoning ordinance or ask the courts to declare the statute or its application unconstitutional. The third and most popular and successful approach is to request administrative assistance in the form of a conditional use permit or a variance. (See Table 20.1.)

Legislative Relief

The property owner seeks legislative relief by asking the zoning authorities to amend the statute, either by changing the nature of the zone or by excluding his property from the zone. Generally, legislative relief is difficult to obtain because the owner must show a genuine

TABLE 20.1 Types of relief from zoning.

	Conditional Use Permit	Variance	Amendment
Action	Administrative	Administrative	Legislative
Purpose	For public good	To avoid hardship	For public good
Effect	Changes a zone	No effect on zone	Creates a new zone
Requirements	Must be a use authorized by zoning ordinance and not be detrimental to the public health	Must alleviate hardship and not adversely affect public as a whole or the neighboring properties	Must not be arbitrary and must have substantial relation to the public health, safety, or morals
Discretion	Restricted, usually limited to uses enumerated in the ordinance	Very broad (there had never been a case in California before 1966 that overruled a variance)	Very broad, with the same restrictions as zoning
Uses	Usually limited to public or quasi-public purposes (airports, cemeteries, dumps, etc.) whose needs are difficult to predict	Usually applies to private, individual properties that need relief and the creation of the zoning ordinance	To change the zoning plan to better satisfy new or existing needs of the community

public need before a zoning change will occur. Mere changes in circumstances or undue harshness to a particular parcel of property fail as reasons for rezoning. *Robinson v. Los Angeles (1956) 146 C.A.2d 810.*

Judicial Relief

The owner of property petitioning the court for judicial relief faces the extremely difficult task of convincing the court of an unconstitutional application of zoning. The courts generally refuse to substitute their opinions of good planning for those of the legislative bodies. As the U.S. Supreme Court stated in a landmark case:

> *A court should not set aside the determination of public officers in such a matter unless it is clear that their action has no foundation in reason and is a mere arbitrary or irrational exercise of power having no substantial relation to the public health, the public morals, the public safety, or the public welfare in its proper sense.* Nectow v. City of Cambridge (1927) 277 U.S. 783.

Attack against Ordinance's Application

Because it is so difficult to attack the constitutionality of the zoning ordinance as a whole, most court attacks are based on the application of zoning to a particular parcel of property. Probably the best judicial statement of the grounds for such an attack was made in *Wilkins v. San Bernardino (1946) 29 C.2d 332.* The court found four types of invalid applications of zoning.

> *(1) Where the zoning ordinance attempts to exclude or prohibit existing and established uses or businesses that are not nuisances; (2) where the restrictions create a monopoly; (3) where the use of adjacent property renders the land entirely unsuited to or unusable for the only purpose permitted by the ordinance; and (4) where a small parcel is restricted and given less rights than the surrounding property, as where a lot in the center of a business or commercial district is limited to use for residential purposes, thereby creating an "island" in the middle of a larger area devoted to other uses.*

Administrative Relief

The most successful form of relief from the application of zoning comes administratively. The property owner asks for a special exception from the application of the zoning ordinance, and any relief so granted has no effect on the validity of the zoning ordinance itself. The legislative body functioning in an administrative capacity rules on the landowner's request for a conditional use permit or a variance.

Variance

A variance is special relief granted from the effects of a zoning ordinance because of a unique hardship suffered by the property owner. An ordinance applies uniformly to numerous parcels within that zone, and when one of these lots is uniquely different from its neighboring parcels, it may suffer unduly from the zoning ordinance. The variance will be granted if (1) it will not adversely affect the public and the surrounding properties, and (2) the property is special because of its size, shape, topography, location, or surroundings. *Gov.C. 95906.*

Conditional Use Permit

A conditional use permit is another form of relief from the effects of zoning, granted by meeting certain conditions in the statute and demonstrating that relief from the statute is in the public interest. It is designed to cover situations for which it is difficult to establish adequate conditions in advance. Certain, often vague, conditions established in the zoning statute must be met, as well as conditions imposed by the zoning authorities, before the permit will be granted. *Gov.C. 65901.*

Tustin Heights Assn. v. Bd. of Supervisors
170 C.A.2d 619 (1959)

[The Roman Catholic Archbishop of Los Angeles petitioned the Orange County planning department for a conditional use permit to construct a church and parochial school in a predominantly residential zone. The planning department denied the application on the grounds of insufficient public parking and the detrimental effect on the neighborhood. In a closed hearing, under unusual circumstances, the board of supervisors nevertheless permitted oral amendment of the application and granted the amended permit without referral to the planning department. Petitioners, the neighborhood landowners, sought a writ of mandate from the courts ordering the board of supervisors to set aside their conditional use permit. Petitioners lost in the trial court and appealed.

Each county has its own zoning ordinances. The then existing Orange County ordinance permitted the board of supervisors to issue conditional use permits for "specified types of uses and buildings under conditions which will preserve the integrity and character of the district and the general welfare of the neighborhood on the condition that the plans be approved by the planning commission." However, the board of supervisors could grant variances without approval from the planning department "in cases where practical difficulty, unnecessary hardship, or results inconsistent with the general purpose and intent of the ordinance occur through strict application of such regulation."

Respondent, the board of supervisors, in its argument to the court, held that because it could grant variances without planning department approval, it should be able to grant conditional use permits without such authorization. In short, it wanted to read the two sections as one related grant of power.]

STONE, JUSTICE. Aside from disregarding the plain wording of the ordinance that treats conditional uses and variances separately, this argument ignores the basic distinction between conditional use permits and variance permits.

Classically, a master zoning ordinance establishes the basic uses permitted within the particular zoned area. Usually such permitted uses are not exclusive and the zoning act also enumerates certain other uses known as exceptions that do not comply with the ordinance but that may, nonetheless, be permitted upon application and hearing. Although various jurisdictions use different terminology when referring to such exceptions, they fall within three categories, and the attributes of each type are essentially the same in all jurisdictions.

The first is the nonconforming use. It is a use of property that was in effect prior to the enactment of the zoning ordinance. Although

APPLY THE LAW

continued

prohibited, it may be permitted if shown that it is not a menace to the health, welfare, and safety of the public.

The second type of exception is the conditional use, which is sometimes referred to by the general term exception. A conditional use may be permitted if it is shown that its use is essential or desirable to the public convenience or welfare and, at the same time, that it will not impair the integrity and character of the zoned district. It must also be shown that it is not detrimental to public health, public morals, or public welfare. Hardship is not a prerequisite to the issuance of a conditional use permit, and there is no burden on the applicant to show hardship in any nature.

The third type of use exception permitted under applicable circumstances is known as the variance. The essential requirement of the variance is a showing that strict enforcement of the zoning limitations would cause unnecessary hardship. Thus, a conditional use and variance are not one and the same and the provisions for each of them are not to be construed together as reciprocal parts of an integrated ordinance unless the particular act in question specifically and unequivocally so provides.

Respondent's next contention concerns the constitutionality of the ordinance in that this section fails to specify definite standards for the granting of a conditional use permit. Respondents argue this leaves the way open for arbitrary and discriminatory action by the planning commission.

There are standards provided by [the ordinance] but, admittedly, they are broad and permit the exercise of discretion by the planning commission. To devise standards to cover all possible situations that could be exceptions, that is, which would warrant the granting of a conditional use permit or a variance permit, would be a formidable task and one that would tax the imagination. If a legislative draftsman blessed with such omniscience were available and he could draft standards to govern the likely as well as the possible contingencies that a conditional use permit or variance is designed to relieve, there would be no need for a conditional use or a variance. There would be no discretion whatever, and anyone meeting the detailed and definite standards would be entitled to a permit without question, as his proposed use would be authorized by the ordinance.

All of which goes to point out that if the purposes of zoning are to be accomplished, the master zoning restrictions or standards must be definite while the provisions pertaining to a conditional use or a variance, designed to relieve against certain eventualities, must of necessity be broad and permit an exercise of discretion.

We conclude (based on the wording of the conditional use permit enacted in Orange County at the time of this case) that the board of supervisors violated the provisions of the zoning ordinance by granting a conditional use permit contrary to the recommendations of the planning commission. There is no provision for such overriding by the board in the ordinance.

Judgment reversed. [The board of supervisors is bound by the wording of its ordinance and, hence, must disallow the conditional use permit for the church.]

STUDY QUESTIONS (TRUE–FALSE)

1. Zoning is a taking of private property for which no compensation need be paid to the landowner.

2. Whenever an owner's property is regulated so severely as to reduce its value by over 50 percent, such regulation amounts to a taking, for which the owner may be compensated.

3. A community could zone houses to minimum 20-acre lots, a rule that, although it may tend to exclude minorities and poor people, would generally still be valid.

4. When the planning department refuses to grant relief from zoning, it is generally easy to obtain relief through court action. This is why the courts are so commonly involved in zoning.

5. Even if judges unequivocally feel that the planning department could have made a better decision, they will rarely overturn a zoning ordinance or decision.

6. Amendments to zoning ordinances are a legislative decision, designed to prevent hardship to a property owner.

7. A variance creates a new and special zone, exempt from the prior existing zone.

8. Before a variance will be granted, there must be a showing of individual hardship.

9. Traditionally, conditional use permits were used for airports, cemeteries, and other quasi-public purposes.

10. The property owner who can demonstrate a hardship because of the zoning ordinance has greatly improved the chances of obtaining a conditional use permit.

NEED FOR CONTROLS

Spaceship Earth

Faced with the inescapable conclusion that Earth is a closed ecological system with exhaustible resources, Congress acted to protect those resources, the ecological systems, and the quality of the environment. Many people contend that the extensive legislation in this field is unduly strict, overly oppressive, and harmful to natural growth, whereas others hold that the current controls are ineffective, overly narrow in their application, and biased toward exploitation of our environment.

Besides the normal environmental controls, local governments exercise significant controls on the environment through subdivision laws. The creation of a subdivision, from a large-scale residential development to a small condominium conversion, can come under the tight controls and supervision of the subdivision laws. Communities can regulate the amount and type of growth in a direct manner through these statutes. Any developer can relate the frustrations and patience needed to develop a subdivision.

Recent Power

Although certain common law remedies have always been available, only in the last 20 years or so have the statutory enactments provided environmentalists an effective tool for enforcing their rights.

Environmental Controls and Subdivision Laws

FEDERAL ENVIRONMENTAL LAWS

National Environmental Policy Act

At the federal level, the strongest legislation is the **National Environmental Policy Act of 1969 (NEPA)**. *42 USC 4321 et seq*. NEPA declares environmental protection to be a national policy in which all agencies of the federal government will, to the fullest extent possible, directly promote efforts to prevent or eliminate damage to the environment and biosphere. The most far-reaching and significant aspect of the NEPA is the requirement that all federal agencies must prepare, file, and consider an environmental impact statement before approving any major federal action that could have a significant effect on the environment.

Application of the NEPA

The terms *major federal action* and *significant effect* on the environment are undefined by statute. Courts have construed them to include any action in which the federal government has a proprietary or financial interest or in which government action will have a direct or indirect effect on the environment. A private apartment complex funded by the Department of Housing and Urban Development, a reduction of interstate freight rail rates, and the construction of a federal prison have all been held to be within the compass of the NEPA, thereby necessitating an environmental impact report before approval.

Other Legislation

Other federal environmental acts include the *Clean Air Amendments of 1970 (42 USC 1857d)*, which is very familiar to Detroit automakers and other large industries. The *Water Quality Control Act of 1965* and the *Clean Water Restoration Act of 1966* protect against pollution of federally controlled waters. Finally, solid waste disposal controls are regulated by the *Solid Waste Disposal Act of 1965* and the *Resource Recovery Act of 1970*. However, the most effective federal control is the *National Environmental Policy Act of 1969*.

CALIFORNIA ENVIRONMENTAL LAWS

Environmental Quality Act

California responded to the national concern about the environment by enacting the *Environmental Quality Act of 1970. Pub.Res.C. 21000 et seq*. The California act was closely modeled after and incorporated most of the concepts of the national act, the NEPA. One of the express intentions of the state legislature in enacting the statutes was "that all agencies of the state government which regulate activities of private individuals, corporations, and public agencies which are found to affect the quality of the environment, shall regulate such activities so that major consideration is given to preventing environmental damage." *Pub.Res.C. 21000*. The Environmental Quality Act (EQA) requires any agency or individual considering any project that may have a significant effect on the environment to prepare an **environmental impact report (EIR)**; the appropriate agencies must conduct hearings on the report.

Although the agency must consider the environmental impact report, it need not evaluate the feasibility of all the other alternatives or even select the best alternative. The agency need only choose an alternative that reduces the significant impact to an appropriate level.

Thus, in one case, the developer requested a building permit for a 95-unit single-family subdivision. Although the EIR found the project environmentally acceptable, it stated that a 63-unit condominium project would have a better environmental impact. The agency approved the builder's 95-unit plan, and the decision was upheld by the courts. *Laural Hills Home Assn. v. Los Angeles (1978) 83 C.A.3d 515*.

Government Projects

Although the act refers only to "projects" by government agencies, government action includes all of the following activities. *Pub.Res.C. 21065*.

By Agency

A project includes activities directly undertaken by an agency. For example, if the Department of Public Works undertook to construct a road or build a bridge, such activities would fall within the act. Furthermore, direct regulation brings any agency within the compass of the EQA. Thus, approval for an increase in bridge tolls and a decision to salt the roads at Lake Tahoe were included projects.

With Agency Support

Activities undertaken by a person that are supported in whole or in part by contracts, grants, subsidies, loans, or other forms of assistance from one or more public agencies fall within the scope of the act.

Through Agency Function

Finally, the act includes activities involving the issuance to a person of a lease, permit, license, certificate, or other entitlement for use by one or more public agencies. The act covers any builder, developer, or private citizen who builds, repairs, or alters any private project that requires the issuance of zoning variances, the issuance of conditional use permits, and the approval of tentative subdivision maps. *Pub.Res.C. 21080.*

Significant Effect

Even though all the activities described previously are within the scope of the EQA, only those activities that have or may have a significant effect on the environment require the preparation, submission, and consideration of an environmental impact report.

Preliminary Survey

If the agency is unable to determine whether the project will or may have a significant effect on the environment, then the agency must conduct a preliminary survey to ascertain whether a report is required. If an individual is involved, the agency may require the private citizen to investigate and discover whether the project has a potentially significant effect on the environment.

Broadly Defined

By code, projects that have a *significant effect* include those that may potentially degrade the environment and even those whose short-range goals will be achieved to the disadvantage of long-term environmental goals. Furthermore, any project that will have direct or indirect adverse effects on people is significant. *Pub.Res.C. 21068.* Also, the California supreme court has ruled that a serious public controversy over a project's effects is sufficient to require an environmental impact report. *Northern Oil Inc. v. L.A. (1974) 13 C.A.3d 68.*

Timing and Procedure

Once an EIR has been prepared, the appropriate government agency must make that report available to the public and other interested government agencies. The statutes do not designate what constitutes an "adequate" opportunity to respond to the report. Federally, the NEPA requires three months for the draft report and one month for the final report. Although large public projects in California sometimes adopt federal standards, it is the agency's responsibility to establish whatever period it deems adequate. *27 Code of Regs. 15160c.*

Formal Hearings Not Required

Formal public hearings on the report are not required. However, the public must have the opportunity to attend meetings at which the report is considered. Such opportunity includes a notice of the hearing that needs only be the type of notice usually adopted for other regularly scheduled hearings. *27 Code of Regs. 15085g.*

Effect of Violations

Failure to follow the appropriate procedure permits interested citizens to challenge the action in court. However, the statutes limit the period for such challenge. Suit must be filed within three months of the approval of an environmental impact report or of the incorrect determination of the need for the preparation of an EIR. If a project has been approved or commenced without consideration of whether it requires an EIR, the citizen has 180 days in which to file a lawsuit. *Pub.Res.C. 21167.*

APPLY THE LAW

Friends of Mammoth v. Board of Supervisors
9 C.3d 247 (1972)

[A private developer filed and obtained a conditional use permit from Mono County to construct a large condominium and specialty shop complex. The Friends of Mammoth, an association composed largely of local property owners in Mammoth Lakes, sought to block construction of the large project. They asserted that the newly passed EQA covered this private activity. Furthermore, the Friends of Mammoth argued that because an environmental impact report was not prepared the conditional use permit must be revoked.

Defendant–developer argued that the law covered only government agencies. The developer concluded that because he was a private individual, because the project was privately funded, and because the only possible link to a government agency was the issuance of a zoning permit, the project was exempt from the EQA. The trial court concurred, and plaintiff, Friends of Mammoth, appealed.]

MOSK, JUSTICE. California's Environmental Quality Act of 1970 requires various state and local governmental entities to submit environmental impact reports before undertaking specified activities. These reports compel state and local agencies to consider the possible adverse consequences to the environment of the proposed activity and to record such impact in writing.

APPLY THE LAW

continued

The environmental impact reports required by the act set forth the following information: "(a) The environmental impact of the proposed action. (b) Any adverse environmental effects which cannot be avoided if the proposal is implemented. (c) Mitigation measures proposed to minimize the impact. (d) Alternatives to the proposed action. (e) The relationship between local short-term uses of man's environment and the maintenance and enhancement of long-term productivity. (f) Any irreversible environmental changes that would be involved in the proposed action should it be implemented."

The specific provision involved in the case at hand states: "All other local governmental agencies shall make an environmental impact report on any project they intend to carry out which may have a significant effect on the environment and shall submit it to the appropriate local planning agency as part of the report." Only if the provision covers the issuance of a permit does the mandate of the act govern here. This determination necessarily turns on whether the term "project" includes private activity for which a government permit is necessary.

The National Environmental Policy Act (NEPA) was signed into law January 1, 1970. The EQA was passed and signed by the governor on September 18, 1970. Not only do the timing and the titles of the two acts tend to indicate that the EQA was patterned on the federal act, the key provisions of the two acts, the environmental impact report, is the same. Indeed, much of the phraseology of the EQA either is adopted verbatim from or is clearly patterned upon the federal act.

In view of the relationship between the two acts and the fact that both are subject to a broad judicial interpretation, it is manifest that the word "project" and other provisions of the EQA includes the issuance of permits, leases and other entitlements. Accordingly, we hold that in the case at bar defendants were required to consider whether the proposed condominium construction "may have a significant effect on the environment" and, if so, to prepare an environmental impact report prior to the decision to grant the conditional use and building permits.

We emphasize that by the terms of the act an environmental impact report is required only for a project "that may have a significant effect on the environment." Two general observations may be made at this time. On one hand, in view of the clearly expressed legislative intent to preserve and enhance the quality of the environment, we stress that the

continued

legislature has mandated an environmental impact report not only when a proposed project will have a significant effect, but also when it "may" or "could" have such an effect. On the other hand, common sense tells us that the majority of private projects for which a government permit or similar entitlement is necessary are minor in scope—e.g., relating only to the construction, improvement, or operation of an individual dwelling or small business—and hence, in the absence of unusual circumstances, have little or no effect on the public environment. Such projects, accordingly, may be approved exactly as before the enactment of the EQA.

The order is reversed. [Private projects requiring government permits are included within the EQA. Because this project may have a significant effect on the environment, an environmental impact report is required. Because an EIR was not prepared and considered by the government agency before the issuance of the permit, the conditional use permit is revoked.]

HAZARDOUS WASTE LAWS

Legislation

Almost everyone buying or selling property needs to be aware of hazardous waste laws and the potential liability and costs that these statutes impose. The federal law is known as the *Comprehensive Environmental Response, Compensation, and Liability Act* (known as *CERCLA* or *Superfund*). *42 USC 9601 et seq.* California's version is commonly called *California Superfund. H&S.C. §25300 et seq.* There are other statutes that regulate hazardous material, but *California Superfund* is the one that most commonly controls property purchases. The act is designed to aid the cleanup of hazardous wastes and to *shift* the financial burden of cleanup from the government to the property owners and potentially responsible parties.

Typical Hazardous Wastes

Any property containing hazardous wastes can require an expensive cleanup, sometimes exceeding even the cost of the property itself. The most common sources of contamination concern soil, building, groundwater, and storage tanks.

1. *Soil.* The soil can become contaminated from intentional, negligent, and even innocent dumping of toxic chemicals. Sometimes toxics leaked from aboveground activities occurring from uses on the property many years ago. Storage tanks and chemical drums

might leak into the soil or be buried underground. Even excessive use of certain agricultural pesticides can contaminate the soil.

2. *Building.* Most building contamination arises from asbestos and polychlorinated biphenyls (PCBs). Asbestos material was commonly used as a fire retardant, insulation for pipes, ceiling tiles, and in ceiling sprays. PCBs are normally restricted to electrical equipment.

3. *Groundwater.* Anything that seeps through the soil can contaminate groundwater located below the surface.

4. *Storage tanks.* Many businesses, especially before the 1980s, stored hazardous chemicals in tanks and barrels. Some containers were buried underground, whereas others remained aboveground or within buildings. Some of these storage facilities were only oil drums, whereas others were extensive storage tanks. Many of the structures may have been removed, but seepage and spill from the tanks remain in the soil.

People Liable

By purchasing property, the buyer normally becomes liable for the cost of cleaning up all toxic waste found on the property, even though he or she did not cause the contamination. The minute you are a part of the chain of title during a time when the property is contaminated, you become liable for the cost of cleanup. (There are two major exceptions, discussed later in this text. The first is for the purchasers using due diligence and the second is for purchasers buying the property for cleanup.) The laws that impose strict liability clearly attempt to hold people liable for the cleanup so that the government will not have to bear the cost. Strict liability means that you do not have to cause the contamination to be liable.

There are four ways a person becomes liable under *Superfund*, and it is important to realize just how easily someone can become responsible for the cost of cleanup. The following four classes of people might potentially be responsible for the cost of cleanup. *42 USC 9607a.*

1. *Current Owners or operators.* There is liability for anyone who currently owns polluted property or who currently operates a facility on this land. The person need contribute to or be the cause of the hazardous waste. The person need only be an owner of the property or operate a business on such land. The definition is so broad that in some cases active owners and operators of corporations have been held personally liable. *Levin Metals, Corp. v. Parr-Richmond Terminal Co. N.D. Cal. (1991) 781 F. Supp. 1454.*

In one case a trustee of a trust sold a parcel of real estate that was contaminated. Not only was the trust held liable for the cost, but also the trustee was held personally responsible and had to make payment from his own bank account. *City of Phonix v. Garbage Services Co. D. Ariz. (1993) 827 F.Supp. 600.*

2. *Owners or operators at time of contamination.* Anyone who owned the property or operated a facility on the land at a time when hazardous waste was contaminating the property is liable. Anyone who was in the chain of title during a period when the land was being contaminated or who contributed to already existing contamination is liable. Former owners and operators are only liable if toxics were released during their involvement. *Ecodyne Corp. v. Shah N.D. Cal. (1989) 718 F. Supp. 1454.*

3. *Arranger or transporter of toxic material.* Anyone who makes arrangement for the removal or transportation of toxic material or who actually transports such material for disposal or treatment bears legal responsibility. This holds a person liable for removing toxic material from land and moving it elsewhere, even if it is to another off-site location. In one extreme case a city hired a contractor to prepare the land for a housing project. The contractor prepared the site as instructed, by digging and moving the excavated dirt to the other side of the same lot. Nobody realized at the time that the dirt contained toxic waste. The contractor was held liable as a "transporter" of hazardous waste. *Kaiser Aluminum & Chem. Corp. v. Catellus Dev. Corp. (1993) 976 F.2d 1338.*

4. *Accepts toxic material.* Anyone who currently accepts or who in the past has accepted toxic material for transportation to disposal sites or to treatment centers can be held accountable.

Innocent Landowner Exception

The prime exception to *Superfund* liability is the innocent landowner defense. Anyone who bought contaminated property, without realizing it was contaminated, before purchase had no reason to know of the contamination, and who did not contribute to the contamination is not liable for the cleanup costs. To use the defense, the purchaser "must have undertaken, at the time of acquisition, *all appropriate inquiry* in the previous ownership and uses of the property consistent with good commercial or customary practice in an effort to minimize liability." *42 U.S.C. 9601(35)(B).*

The level of inquiry required is vague and undefined by statutes or regulations and varies on a case-by-case basis. It appears that merely asking the prior owner if he or she knows of any contamination without conducting a separate investigation does not meet the test of "all appropriate inquiry." In large commercial projects that are believed free of toxic material, a Phase One Environmental Report (also known as a Preliminary Site Assessment) is probably required. Such reports require a search of various governmental records for known or suspected toxic sites. It includes asking these governmental agencies if they have any reason to suspect contamination of this property. Usually, the report involves interviews with past owners and operators of the property and in some cases of surrounding properties. The investigation generally includes a visual inspection of the property for visible signs of toxicity.

If there are suspected toxins on the property, the buyer will have to do a Phase Two Environmental Report, which includes everything on a Phase One report plus actual analysis of soil (and possibly even water) samples.

Any property owner who is "aware" (defined term) of toxic problems has a duty to notify the government, the owners of the property, and all responsible parties. Since 1998, there is a special procedure for sellers who find toxic problems under the Environmental Responsibility Acceptance Act. *C.C. 850 et seq.* This act designates a resolution of the costs and expenses of cleanup with potential buyers. The purpose of the Act is to encourage cleanup and the settlement of costs between the parties without the need for litigation.

Prior, Innocent Owner

Even an innocent prior owner can escape liability for merely being in the chain of title, if that person did not cause some kind of leak, spill or otherwise actively contaminate the property. Thus, if a person bought contaminated property not knowing it was contaminated, and in no way contributed to the contamination during his or her ownership, that person would not be liable if the property was later sold to someone else. *Carson Harbor Village Ltd. v. Unocal Corp., 270 F.3d 863 (9th Cir. 2001).*

New Owner Restoring Property Exception

The second big exception to *Superfund* liability is for new owners who are purchasing contaminated property for cleanup. Congress felt many contaminated properties remained undeveloped, because new owners feared becoming liable for the entire cost of the cleanup. To rectify this situation, Congress passed the *Brownsfields Revitalization and Environmental Restoration Act of 2001.* This law encourages owners to purchase and restore contaminated property by shielding them from federal liability. The Act provides that a new owner of contaminated land will not be liable for the restoration costs provided the new owner does not contribute to the contamination and cleans up the property using the approved guidelines. Because Congress also allocated $200 million for cleanup, certain properties being restored may qualify for federal funds.

Lender and Fiduciary Exemption

Lenders have a partial exemption in that they hold title to protect their security interest and do not participate in the management of the facility. Unfortunately, lenders sometimes find it difficult not to participate in the management to protect their interests. Fiduciaries like trustees and executors were concerned that they could be personally liable if the cleanup costs exceeded the value of assets held in their capacity. Generally, with some exceptions, if a fiduciary will not be personally liable unless he or she negligently causes or contributes to the release of hazardous materials. *42 U.S.C. 9607(n)(3)*. Still, this is an area where lenders and fiduciaries should act cautiously and carefully.

Purchaser Protections

A purchaser should consider how much risk to take. If the cost of a Phase One report seems excessive, it is possible that the courts might consider a lesser investigation reasonable. The statutes do not state what kind of investigation is actually required. Certainly, some checking and investigation are almost always warranted, and a Phase One report is usually considered a "safe harbor."

A buyer should also consider a clause in the deposit receipt warranting that the property is uncontaminated. Sellers often refuse to sign a complete warranty, but will often guarantee that they and anyone else during their ownership have not contaminated the property. The seller should also warrant that to their knowledge no governmental agency has investigated, inquired, or begun proceeding about environmental problems on the property. The warranties could also be included in the grant deed so that they will survive close of escrow. The buyers might ask for an indemnification agreement. Although agreements allocating costs and responsibility are invalid as to the government, they are binding as between the parties. *42 U.S.C. 9607(e)(1)*. However, buyers should not be too surprised if sellers balk at providing a complete release.

The deposit receipt should also grant the buyer access to the seller's environmental records, the right to discuss environmental issues with people on or associated with the property, and the ability to conduct environmental tests.

CALIFORNIA SUBDIVISION LAWS

Two Separate Statutes

Before land can be subdivided or before already subdivided land can be offered for sale, certain statutory requirements must be satisfied. In California, subdivisions are regulated by the *Subdivided Lands Act* and by the *Subdivision Map Act*. Although the names of the two acts are similar, the purpose and scope of each statute is completely distinct and unrelated. The Subdivided Lands Act controls the sale to the public of land that is already subdivided, while the Subdivision Map Act regulates the physical design and development that a developer must adopt in subdividing his land (see Table 21.1).

Other statutes may control certain aspects of the subdivision process. If the property is from an out-of-state subdivision of more than 50 lots, it may come under jurisdiction of the federal *Interstate Land Sales Full Disclosure Act*. Many subdivisions under the Map Act come under and require compliance with state or federal environmental protection statutes.

SUBDIVIDED LANDS ACT

Nature of Statute

The Subdivided Lands Act governs the sale of existing subdivisions or subdivided land to the public by carefully regulating the type of advertising and marketing techniques that may be used. The act primarily operates as a full disclosure statute, trying to prevent fraudulent and deceptive marketing. The statute enacted a statewide control over subdivision sales under the jurisdiction of the California Real Estate Commissioner. Before anyone can sell subdivided land in California, the land must either be exempt from the statute or be covered by a *public report* issued by the Department of Real Estate. Until the report is obtained, it is unlawful to cash deposits or accept binding contracts of purchase.

Definition of Subdivision

A subdivision (also known as subdivided land) under the act is defined as any "improved or unimproved land or lands divided or proposed to be divided for the purpose of sale or lease or financing, whether immediate or future, into five or more lots or parcels." *B.&P.C. 11000.* A subdivision also includes a division of land into five or more undivided interests, such as tenants in common or joint tenancy. However, the commissioner specifically exempts divisions into undivided

TABLE 21.1   The subdivision acts.

	Subdivided Lands Act	Subdivision Map Act
	I. Nature Of Acts	
Basic purpose	To prevent fraud in marketing new subdivision lots	To ensure appropriate and orderly development of physical conditions of subdivision with surrounding community (e.g., proper sewage, water, utilities, streets, open spaces, schools, drainage, etc.)
Subdivision definition	Division or proposed division into five or more lots, condominiums, co-ops, or other undivided units	Division into two or more lots, condominiums, or community apartment projects
Major exceptions	Lots of 160 acres or larger	Subdivision of noncontiguous lots, lot line adjustments, and mere division into cotenancy (undivided) interests
Jurisdiction	Any California or out-of-state subdivisions marketed in California	Only applies to California subdivisions
Administrator	California Real Estate Commissioner	Generally county, otherwise city government
Code sections	B.&P.C. 11000-11030 and Comm. Regs 2790 et seq.	Gov.C. 66410 et seq. and local municipal ordinances
	II. Application Process	
Basic process	1. File Notice of Intention with questionnaire and application with Department of Real Estate	1. File tentative map (if required) with Planning Department or other appropriate government agency
	2. Preliminary report ("pink report") issued, if applicable. Authorizes receipt of reservations to purchase and deposits (which must be escrowed), and gives buyers the right to rescind anytime without penalty	2. After necessary hearings, usually with Planning Department, and input from other government agencies, a tentative map is approved
	3. Final public report ("white report") issued; authorizes sales	3. Final map approval (within 1 year of preliminary map, with possible 18-month extension, if requested)
		4. Final map recorded

interests if the division is between family members or if the division is among 10 or fewer sophisticated investors who waive their normal subdivision rights. *B.&P.C. 11000.1.* The creation of five or more condominiums, cooperatives, or other similar entities is a subdivision. (Before 1981, division into two or more condominiums was a subdivision.)

The statutory definition makes no distinction among (1) improved and unimproved land, (2) immediate division or merely common plans for distant future division, and (3) division for sale, or merely for lease, or solely for financing. Because of the broad scope, owners sometimes unintentionally and unknowingly create illegal divisions. For example, if an owner divides his land into four units, he is exempt from the act. However, if he later subdivides one of those parcels, he would cumulatively have exceeded five lots and would need to qualify as a subdivision. There is no time limit in the act as to when the divisions must occur. Another not uncommon violation concerns leases in community apartment projects. If an individual purchased five residential condominiums for speculation and leased them out on leases over one year in duration, that person would need to qualify that transaction as a subdivision.

Exemptions from Definition

Obviously, division into four or fewer units is exempt from the statutory definition of a subdivision (provided such division is not made with the intent of evading the statute by planning future divisions). The statute also exempts divisions into county-recognized parcels of 160 acres or larger.

Procedure for Compliance

Because no subdivision can be sold in California without first having the Final Public Report and as the processing time can be lengthy and complicated, developers usually file immediately upon beginning the subdivision process. The Subdivided Lands Act is totally separate from the Subdivision Map Act; however, the *Final Subdivision Report* cannot be issued until there has been a completed subdivision map under the Map Act. Consequently, most developers file under both acts simultaneously so that the final subdivision report can be processed and ready for issuance promptly upon receiving the final subdivision map under the Map Act. The actual process for obtaining a final report requires two or three formal steps.

Notice and Questionnaire

Application for a subdivision is made on the Real Estate Commissioner's form, called the *Notice of Intention and Subdivision Questionnaire*. It includes a lengthy questionnaire. Detailed information about the subdivision is required, including data about the financing and manner of sale to the public, the soil conditions, the projected costs of maintaining any common areas, the availability of common facilities, the location of nearby schools, and numerous other supporting reports and documents. If a condominium is involved, copies of the articles, bylaws, and CCRs must be submitted and reviewed to ensure that those documents meet the legal requirements on voting, membership rights, and other requirements set by the commissioner.

Preliminary Public Report

Until the final public report has been issued, the developer cannot accept any binding contracts of purchase or cash any deposits. However, the developer frequently desires to begin accepting bids and advertising his property. If it appears to the commissioner that the final report will be issued, then the developer can obtain a *Preliminary Subdivision Public Report*. This report is commonly known as the pink report, because it is issued on pink paper. It enables the developer to accept offers and deposits, although the deposits can only be placed in a special escrow or trust account. The offers are bids only, which are totally revocable by the purchaser at any time. If revoked, the purchaser must receive a full refund of his deposit.

Final Public Report

The commissioner issues the Final Subdivision Public Report when the subdivider has met all the subdivision law requirements. The requirements include proof of the following: that all blanket deeds of trust have been satisfied or bonded, that title to the property is marketable, that sufficient funds will be impounded or bonded to ensure that all common facilities will be completed, and that the subdivider will not engage in any deceptive marketing. Because the final report is issued on white paper, it is often called the white report. The final report must be given to each purchaser before a binding contract is signed. The report authorizes sales for a period of five years, at which time it must be renewed.

SUBDIVISION MAP ACT

Nature of the Statute

The Subdivision Map Act regulates the physical design, layout, and construction of subdivisions. The act is uninvolved with the marketing or salability of completed subdivisions. Rather, the Subdivision Map Act controls the creation and development of subdivisions by stipulating the following:

1. That the physical design (e.g., street alignment, road grading and widths, lot size and configuration, sewage and sanitary facilities, lot grading and drainage, location and size of easements, etc.) will be adequate for the subdivision;
2. That the subdivision will have adequate utilities (e.g., water, gas, electricity, sewer drainage, telephones, etc.), which will not unduly tax existing county utilities;

3. That the existing community amenities and facilities (e.g., transportation systems, traffic patterns on roads, schools, parks, hospitals, fire protection, etc.) can conscientiously support the subdivision; and

4. That the subdivision is compatible with the neighborhood and the county master plan and, further, that the subdivision will have no significant environmental impact on the community.

Unlike the Subdivided Lands Act, the Subdivision Map Act is controlled through the local communities. Each city or county sets local standards in conformity with the purposes and goals of the Map Act. The Map Act is regulated by local agencies whose community Map Act ordinances may vary significantly among local jurisdictions. No one may subdivide property without complying with the subdivision map requirements.

Definition of Subdivision

The Map Act defines a subdivision as "the division by any subdivider of any unit or units of improved or unimproved land, or any portion thereof, shown on the latest equalized county assessment roll as a unit or continuous unit, for the purpose of sale, lease or financing, whether immediate or future." *Gov.C. 66424.* This definition differs in part from that used in the Subdivided Map Act. A division of any parcel or lot into two or more units is a subdivision. Also, the land must be contiguous to be a subdivision, although streets and easements do not break the parcel's continuity. Mere division of land into undivided co-tenancy interest is excluded from the definition, as are mere lot line adjustments between adjacent parcels. Creation or division of condominiums and community apartment projects is a subdivision.

Obtaining the Final Map

For all divisions into five or more lots and in other situations directed by local ordinance, the developer must obtain a *final map* before he can legally divide the property. The first step in obtaining the map is to file an application with the city or county agency having jurisdiction over the land. Usually, this is the planning department. At the filing stage, most developers have an informal meeting with the planning staff to discuss the proposed subdivision, to explore solutions to potential problem areas, and to discuss that county's ordinance procedure.

The developer then submits a *tentative subdivision map*, which is usually prepared by an architect or surveyor. The map diagrams the proposed development, but is usually not drawn from a survey. The planning department forwards this map to all pertinent agencies for comment. These other agencies, such as the parks department, review the map and state the conditions and changes that they would want before their department would approve the map. Once the tentative map is approved, the subdivider has 12 months (plus any extensions that are granted) to obtain the *final map*. If the developer fails to satisfy all the conditions and requirements imposed by the tentative map within that time period, he must start the process anew and obtain a new tentative map.

The final subdivision map contains an accurate survey and layout of the subdivision. It is executed by all the owners and prepared by the engineer or surveyor. After the map is executed by the appropriate government officials, it is recorded. The final map signifies that the developer has met all of the requirements of the Map Act.

Dedication Requirements

Most planning departments require the developer to dedicate (give) sections of his or her land to the public for streets, utilities, parks, or other public uses as a condition to final map approval. As an alternative, some agencies permit the developer to pay certain fees equivalent in lieu of dedication. The California Supreme Court approved the practice of conditioning final map approval upon dedication, so most developers expect and budget dedication as a cost of the subdivision. *Assoc. Homebuilders, Inc., v. Walnut Creek (1971) 4 C.3d 633.*

Exceptions to Obtaining the Final Map

At one time, certain land divisions were exempt from the Map Act. However, since 1975, these former exceptions are included in the Map Act, although less stringent requirements are imposed. In the following four situations, plus any other situation where a *final map* is not required by statute, the developer need only obtain a *parcel map*:

1. Subdivision of a parcel of less than five acres, where each lot abuts on a public street.
2. Subdivision into parcels of 20 acres or more, where each parcel has access to a public street.
3. Subdivision into commercial or industrial lots, where each parcel has access to a public street.
4. Subdivision into 40-acre or larger lots. (No street access is required in such divisions.)

Additionally, in all situations where parcel maps are required, the local map act ordinance can direct that no map of any kind is required if the planning department finds that the requirements of the Map Act are satisfied. Often, counties requiring a parcel map or waiving parcel map requirement will require a tentative map.

Condominium Conversions

Conversion of existing rental units into condominiums or stock co-operatives is considered a subdivision, which may be subject to the Subdivided Lands Act, the Subdivision Map Act, and local conversion ordinances. If the conversion comes under the Subdivision Map Act and is a conversion of existing apartment or dwelling units, then before final approval, the developer must, among other provisions, meet the following requirements. *Gov.C. 66427.*

1. All tenants must be given four months' notice before termination of their tenancy.
2. All tenants must have the right to purchase their own unit on the same or better terms than the general public for a period of not less than 90 days after issuance by the state (under the Subdivided Lands Act) of the subdivision public report, the white report.

Additionally, most local jurisdictions have their own local ordinances, which are usually far more restrictive and demanding, especially for residential condominium conversions. For example, San Francisco requires, among its other provisions, that in any conversion of five or more units 10 percent of the units be made available for rental or purchase by low- or moderate-income people at a sale price of not more than two and one-half times the median income for low-income residences, or at a rental of not more than the low-income rental, adjusted by the consumer price index. As an alternative, the developer could either build an equivalent number of low-income units elsewhere or pay the city of San Francisco the equivalent cost of building such alternative units. Additionally, the price to existing tenants not purchasing their units must have their moving costs paid up to a $1,000 limit. Elderly tenants have the right to demand and receive lifetime leases, expiring on their death, if they do not wish to buy or move. Over and above these and other requirements, San Francisco only allows 1,000 units to be converted each year, with the balance of the application for conversions going on a waiting list (*S.F. Municipal Code*, Chapter 8).

Federal legislation entitled The Condominium and Co-operative Conversion Protection and Abuse Relief Act also affects the conversion of five or more residential units. *42 U.S.C. 3601 et seq.* The act leaves most of the control and supervision to the states, although residents through their homeowner's association may set aside any unconscionable leases made with a developer. The act also mandates the states to act in establishing condominium conversion legislation.

Vested Rights

Once a subdivider obtains a permit to build or subdivide, the issue often arises as to whether the developer can rely on that permit if there is a change in the law. Property can always be rezoned, and the owner has no way to immunize himself against future zoning. However, if the owner obtained a conditional use permit and in good faith detrimentally relied on the excepting permit, he acquires a **vested right** in the permit and can proceed under it despite the change in the law. The owner can only be denied the protection of his permit if he has not significantly and detrimentally relied on his permit, if the owner violates the terms of his permit, or if the current use amounts to a nuisance. *O'Hagen v. Board of Zoning Adjustment (1971) 19 C.A.3d 151.*

Similarly, once a subdivider obtains a *final* subdivision map or a *final* building permit (which means that no possible appeal or further governmental permissions are possible) and in good faith substantially and detrimentally relies on the permit, he acquires a vested interest in the grant. New laws cannot revoke the authority, unless there is a violation of the permit, insignificant reliance on the permit, or use that amounts to a nuisance. *Russian Hill Improvement Assn. v. Board of Permit Appeals (1967) 66 C.2d 34.*

STUDY QUESTIONS (TRUE–FALSE)

1. An environmental impact report must specifically consider both the long- and short-term effects of any project.

2. The NEPA requires every agency of the federal government to consider the environment as a top priority in its decision making.

3. The NEPA is federal; hence, private developers are not regulated by it.

4. If the Golden Gate Bridge District in San Francisco wanted to raise automobile tolls, it would first have to prepare an environmental impact report.

5. If a person sells real estate that is contaminated with toxic waste, which the seller did not know about or cause, the seller has no liability.

6. There are only two statutes in California affecting subdivisions.

7. The Subdivided Lands Act regulates the physical design and development of subdivisions.

8. The entire state of California is subject to the same laws under the Subdivided Lands Act.

9. The Subdivision Map Act is applicable to conversion of a two-unit apartment into condominiums, even if no physical work need be done on the building to make the division.

10. The entire state of California is subject to the same laws under the Subdivision Map Act.

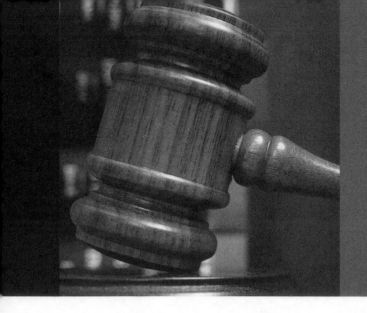

NATURE OF TITLE INSURANCE

Purpose

A title insurance policy insures that title to real estate is free from defects in title, undisclosed liens, and adverse claims. Under that policy, the title company agrees to pay any covered loss up to the face amount of the policy, in addition to reasonable costs incurred in defending that title through litigation.

Legally Optional

Although title insurance is not mandatory for the purchase of real estate, almost every California lender requires a policy before lending on real estate. Most buyers of real estate also demand insurable title, as evidenced by a title policy, as a condition of purchase. Consequently, title insurance has become essential and customary in most California real estate transactions.

Nature of Policy and Company

Title insurance is an insurance contract. However, the policy and the insuring title company differ materially from ordinary insurance policies and from typical insurance companies.

Unique Type of Insurance

Title insurance guarantees against risk of loss from defects existing at the date the policy was issued; ordinary insurance covers only losses arising from future events. Title insurance involves only one premium, payable at close of escrow; typical insurance policies require periodic payments to maintain the policy. Ordinary insurance policies

Title Insurance and Escrow

are issued for fixed periods of time and are often freely transferable; title insurance policies are issued for an indefinite period and remain effective for the entire duration of the insured's exposure to risk. Additionally, the title policy is nontransferable, except to the insured's estate or heirs.

Regulation of Title Companies

Title companies are regulated by the insurance commissioner. Such regulation is limited to requirements affecting the company's financial stability, provisions necessitating the publication of the company's charges and fees, and restrictions against rebates and reduced fees for special customers. *Ins.C. 12340 et seq.* Although title companies have no other state regulation, they are highly regulated by title industry requirements adopted by title associations. Fee schedules, title insurance coverage and policy provisions, and general title practices are standardized within the industry by its own regulatory agencies.

APPLY THE LAW

Hocking v. Title Ins. & Trust Co.
37 C.2d 644 (1951)

[Plaintiff purchased two adjacent parcels of vacant land in Palm Springs, insuring those lots by a standard policy of title insurance issued by defendant title company. The title policy insured the plaintiff against any loss she might sustain (1) by reason of not owning the property in fee simple absolute, (2) by reason of any unmarketability of title, and (3) by reason of any defect, lien, or encumbrance against the title. The policy also contained numerous exceptions to its coverage, including lack of coverage for any losses resulting from any government act or regulation restricting and/or regulating the use of land.

APPLY THE LAW

continued

The city of Palm Springs allegedly violated a city ordinance by approving a subdivision map without first obtaining agreements and bonds from the developers for grading and paving the streets. Because of the violation, the property remains unimproved and the city refuses to issue any building permits. Consequently, the plaintiff's property is almost valueless, and she sued the title company, claiming she was insured against such a loss. Plaintiff further asserts that because her land is currently worthless, she does not own title in fee simple absolute. The court, as a matter of law, held the loss was not covered and found for defendant. Plaintiff appealed.]

SAHAUER, JUSTICE. Plaintiff relies upon the rule of construction of title policies [that holds that] not only the provisions of the policy as a whole, but also the exceptions to the liability of the insurer, must be construed so as to give the insured the protection that he reasonably had a right to expect, and to that end doubts, ambiguities, and uncertainties arising out of the language used in the policy must be resolved in his favor.

The courts have also announced that when the language employed in an insurance contract is ambiguous, or when a doubt arises in respect to the application, exceptions to, or limitations of, liability thereunder, they should be interpreted most favorably to the insured. Such contracts are to be interpreted in the light of the fact that they are drawn by the insurer, and are rarely understood by the insured, to whom every rational indulgence should be given, and in whose favor the policy should be liberally construed. Where the language and terms of a policy are framed and formulated by the insurer, every ambiguity and uncertainty therein should be resolved in favor of the insured.

The words "good title" import that the owner has the title, legal and equitable, to all the land, and the words "defective title" means that the party claiming to own has not the whole title, but some other person has title to a part or portion of the land. A person who has contracted to purchase real estate is entitled to a perfect title; and if the estate or interest of the vendor is subject to defeasance upon the happening of a contingent event or the nonperformance of a condition, the title tendered is not perfect or "marketable." A seller frequently agrees to furnish a "good and perfect title." Such an agreement imports a title that must not only be good in point of fact, but it must also be apparently perfect when exhibited—that is, free from reasonable objection, such as litigation, palpable defects and grave doubts fairly deducible of record, and unencumbered.

Much learning has been expended in giving definitions as to good and marketable titles. The following appears to be one supported by the weight of authority: A marketable title, to which the vendee in a contract for the sale of land is entitled, means a title that a reasonable purchaser, well informed as to the facts and their legal bearings, willing and anxious to perform his contract, would, in the exercise of that prudence, which business men ordinarily bring to bear on such transactions, be willing and ought to accept.

APPLY THE LAW
continued

Because, says plaintiff, "the Palm Springs subdivision ordinance required these easements to be in a certain condition, namely, graded and paved" and "as such conditions did not exist in this matter," plaintiff's title is not perfect. Plaintiff also contends that the acceptance and recording of the subdivision map in violation of existing law "results in the entire subdivision being in a litigious state as the same is either wholly void or voidable," and she is deprived of a record title.

It is defendants' position that plaintiff confuses title with physical condition of the property she purchased and of the adjacent streets, and that "one can hold perfect title to land that is valueless; one can have marketable title to land while the land itself is unmarketable." The truth of this proposition would appear elementary.

It appears to be the condition of her land in respect to improvements related thereto (graded and paved streets), rather than the condition of her title to the land, which is different from what she expected to get.

Although it is unfortunate that plaintiff has been unable to use her lots for the building purposes she contemplated, it is our view that the facts that she pleads do not affect the marketability of her title to the land, but merely impair the market value of the property. She appears to possess fee simple title to the property for whatever it may be worth; if she has been damaged by false representations in respect to the condition and value of the land her remedy would seem to be against others than the insurers of the title she acquired. It follows that plaintiff has failed to state a cause of action under the title policy.

The judgment is affirmed. [Plaintiff cannot state a valid claim covered by the title policy. The defect ran to the value of the property rather than of its title.]

TYPES OF TITLE POLICIES

Types of Policies

There are two types of title policies: the homeowner's policy (CLTA) and the lender's policy (ALTA). The CLTA policy is the standard form approved by the California Land Title Association, although newer ALTA Residential policy is discussed below under *Other Types of Policies.* (See Figure 22.1 for a sample Homeowner's Policy.) This

FIGURE 22.1   Homeowner's title insurance policy.

 Chicago Title Insurance Company

POLICY NO.: SAMPLE

HOMEOWNER'S POLICY OF TITLE INSURANCE FOR A ONE-TO-FOUR FAMILY RESIDENCE

Issued by

Chicago Title Insurance Company

OWNER'S INFORMATION SHEET

Your Title Insurance Policy is a legal contract between You and Us.

It applies only to a one-to-four family residence and only if each insured named in Schedule A is a Natural Person. If the Land described in Schedule A of the Policy is not an improved residential lot on which there is located a one-to-four family residence, or if each insured named in Schedule A is not a Natural Person, contact Us immediately.

The Policy insures You against actual loss resulting from certain Covered Risks. These Covered Risks are listed beginning on page 2 of the Policy. The Policy is limited by:
- *Provisions of Schedule A*
- *Exceptions in Schedule B*
- *Our Duty To Defend Against Legal Actions on page 3*
- *Exclusions on page 6*
- *Conditions on pages 6 and 7.*

You should keep the Policy even if You transfer Your Title to the Land. It may protect against claims made against You by someone else after You transfer Your Title.

IF YOU WANT TO MAKE A CLAIM, SEE SECTION 3 UNDER CONDITIONS ON PAGE 6.

The premium for this Policy is paid once. No additional premium is owed for the Policy.

This sheet is not Your insurance Policy. It is only a brief outline of some of the important Policy features. The Policy explains in detail Your rights and obligations and Our rights and obligations. Since the Policy – and not this sheet – is the legal document,

YOU SHOULD READ THE POLICY VERY CAREFULLY.

If You have any questions about Your Policy, contact:
Chicago Title Insurance Company
P.O. Box 45023
Jacksonville, FL 32232-5023
Attn: Claims Department

HOMEOWNER'S POLICY OF TITLE INSURANCE FOR A ONE-TO-FOUR FAMILY RESIDENCE

TABLE OF CONTENTS

	Page		Page
OWNER'S COVERAGE STATEMENT	2	CONDITIONS	
COVERED RISKS	2	1. Definitions	6
OUR DUTY TO DEFEND AGAINST LEGAL ACTIONS	3	2. Continuation of Coverage	6
SCHEDULE A	4	3. How to Make a Claim	6
Policy Number, Premium, Date (and Time) and Amount		4. Our Choices When We Learn of a Claim	6
Deductible Amounts and Maximum Dollar Limits of Liability		5. Handling a Claim or Legal Action	6
Street Address of the Land		6. Limitation of Our Liability	6
1. Name of Insured		7. Transfer of Your Rights to Us	7
2. Interest in Land Covered		8. This Policy is the Entire Contract	7
3. Description of the Land		9. Increased Policy Amount	7
SCHEDULE B – EXCEPTIONS	5	10. Severability	7
EXCLUSIONS	6	11. Arbitration	7
		12. Choice of Law	7

ALTA Homeowner's Policy of Title Insurance (1/1/08)

FIGURE 22.1 *(Continued).*

HOMEOWNER'S POLICY OF TITLE INSURANCE FOR A ONE-TO-FOUR FAMILY RESIDENCE

As soon as You Know of anything that might be covered by this Policy, You must notify Us promptly in writing at the address shown in Section 3 of the Conditions.

OWNER'S COVERAGE STATEMENT

This Policy insures You against actual loss, including any costs, attorneys' fees and expenses provided under this Policy. The loss must result from one or more of the Covered Risks set forth below. This Policy covers only Land that is an improved residential lot on which there is located a one-to-four family residence and only when each insured named in Schedule A is a Natural Person.

Your insurance is effective on the Policy Date. This Policy covers Your actual loss from any risk described under Covered Risks if the event creating the risk exists on the Policy Date or, to the extent expressly stated in Covered Risks, after the Policy Date.

Your insurance is limited by all of the following:
- The Policy Amount
- For Covered Risk 16, 18, 19 and 21, Your Deductible Amount and Our Maximum Dollar Limit of Liability shown in Schedule A
- The Exceptions in Schedule B
- Our Duty To Defend Against Legal Actions
- The Exclusions on page 6
- The Conditions on pages 6 and 7.

COVERED RISKS

The Covered Risks are:
1. Someone else owns an interest in Your Title.
2. Someone else has rights affecting Your Title because of leases, contracts, or options.
3. Someone else claims to have rights affecting Your Title because of forgery or impersonation.
4. Someone else has an easement on the Land.
5. Someone else has a right to limit Your use of the Land.
6. Your Title is defective. Some of these defects are:
   a. Someone else's failure to have authorized a transfer or conveyance of your Title.
   b. Someone else's failure to create a valid document by electronic means.
   c. A document upon which Your Title is based is invalid because it was not property signed, sealed, acknowledged, delivered or recorded.
   d. A document upon which Your Title is based was signed using a falsified, expired, or otherwise invalid power of attorney.
   e. A document upon which Your Title is based was not properly filed, recorded, or indexed in the Public Records.
   f. A defective judicial or administrative proceeding.
7. Any of Covered Risks 1 through 6 occurring after the Policy Date.
8. Someone else has a lien on Your Title, including a:
   a. lien of real estate taxes or assessments imposed on Your Title by a governmental authority that are due or payable, but unpaid;
   b. Mortgage;
   c. judgment, state or federal tax lien;
   d. charge by a homeowner's or condominium association; or
   e. lien, occurring before or after the Policy Date, for labor and material furnished before the Policy Date.
9. Someone else has an encumbrance on Your Title.
10. Someone else claims to have rights affecting Your Title because of fraud, duress, incompetency or incapacity.
11. You do not have actual vehicular and pedestrian access to and from the Land, based upon a legal right.
12. You are forced to correct or remove an existing violation of any covenant, condition or restriction affecting the Land, even if the covenant, condition or restriction is excepted in Schedule B. However, You are not covered for any violation that relates to:
    a. any obligation to perform maintenance or repair on the Land; or
    b. environmental protection of any kind, including hazardous or toxic conditions or substances
    unless there is a notice recorded in the Public Records, describing any part of the Land, claiming a violation exists. Our liability for this Covered Risk is limited to the extent of the violation stated in that notice.
13. Your Title is lost or taken because of a violation of any covenant, condition or restriction, which occurred before You acquired Your Title, even if the covenant, condition or restriction is excepted in Schedule B.
14. The violation or enforcement of those portions of any law or government regulation concerning:
    a. building;
    b. zoning;
    c. land use;
    d. improvements on the Land;
    e. land division; or
    f. environmental protection,
    if there is a notice recorded in the Public Records, describing any part of the Land, claiming a violation exists or declaring the intention to enforce the law or regulation. Our liability for this Covered Risk is limited to the extent of the violation or enforcement stated in that notice.
15. An enforcement action based on the exercise of a governmental police power not covered by Covered Risk 14 if there is a notice recorded in the Public Records, describing any part of the Land, of the enforcement action or intention to bring an enforcement action. Our liability for this Covered Risk is limited to the extent of the enforcement action stated in that notice.
16. Because of an existing violation of a subdivision law or regulation affecting the Land:
    a. You are unable to obtain a building permit;
    b. You are required to correct or remove the violation; or
    c. someone else has a legal right to, and does, refuse to perform a contract to purchase the Land, lease it or make a Mortgage loan on it.
    The amount of Your insurance for this Covered Risk is subject to Your Deductible Amount and Our Maximum Dollar Limit of Liability shown in Schedule A.
17. You lose Your Title to any part of the Land because of the right to take the Land by condemning it, if:
    a. there is a notice of the exercise of the right recorded in the Public Records and the notice describes any part of the Land; or
    b. the taking happened before the Policy Date and is binding on You if You bought the Land without Knowing of the taking.
18. You are forced to remove or remedy Your existing structures, or any part of them – other than boundary walls or fences – because any portion was built without obtaining a building permit from the proper government office. The amount of Your insurance for this Covered Risk is subject to Your Deductible Amount and Our Maximum Dollar Limit of Liability shown in Schedule A.
19. You are forced to remove or remedy Your existing structures, or any part of them, because they violate an existing zoning law or zoning regulation. If You are required to remedy any portion of Your existing structures, the amount of Your insurance for this Covered Risk is subject to Your Deductible Amount and Our Maximum Dollar Limit of Liability shown in Schedule A.
20. You cannot use the Land because use as a single-family residence violates an existing zoning law or zoning regulation.
21. You are forced to remove Your existing structures because they encroach onto Your neighbor's land. If the encroaching structures are boundary walls or fences, the amount of Your insurance for this Covered Risk is subject to Your Deductible Amount and Our Maximum Dollar Limit of Liability shown in Schedule A.
22. Someone else has a legal right to, and does, refuse to perform a contract to purchase the Land, lease it or make a Mortgage loan on it because Your neighbor's existing structures encroach onto the Land.
23. You are forced to remove Your existing structures which encroach onto an easement or over a building set-back line, even if the easement or building set-back line is excepted in Schedule B.
24. Your existing structures are damaged because of the exercise of a right to maintain or use any easement affecting the Land, even if the easement is excepted in Schedule B.
25. Your existing improvements (or a replacement or modification made to them after the Policy Date), including lawns, shrubbery or trees, are damaged because of the future exercise of a right to use the surface of the Land for the extraction or development of minerals, water or any other substance, even if those rights are excepted or reserved from the description of the Land or excepted in Schedule B.

ALTA Homeowner's Policy of Title Insurance (1/1/08)

FIGURE 22.1   (Continued).

26.   Someone else tries to enforce a discriminatory covenant, condition or restriction that they claim affects Your Title which is based upon race, color, religion, sex, handicap, familial status, or national origin.
27.   A taxing authority assesses supplemental real estate taxes not previously assessed against the Land for any period before the Policy Date because of construction or a change of ownership or use that occurred before the Policy Date.
28.   Your neighbor builds any structures after the Policy Date – other than boundary walls or fences – which encroach onto the Land.
29.   Your Title is unmarketable, which allows someone else to refuse to perform a contract to purchase the Land, lease it or make a Mortgage loan on it.
30.   Someone else owns an interest in Your Title because a court order invalidates a prior transfer of the title under federal bankruptcy, state insolvency, or similar creditors' rights laws.
31.   The residence with the address shown in Schedule A is not located on the Land at the Policy Date.
32.   The map, if any, attached to this Policy does not show the correct location of the Land according to the Public Records.

OUR DUTY TO DEFEND AGAINST LEGAL ACTIONS

We will defend Your Title in any legal action only as to that part of the action which is based on a Covered Risk and which is not excepted or excluded from coverage in this Policy. We will pay the costs, attorneys' fees, and expenses We incur in that defense.

We will not pay for any part of the legal action which is not based on a Covered Risk or which is excepted or excluded from coverage in this Policy.

We can end Our duty to defend Your Title under Section 4 of the Conditions.

THIS POLICY IS NOT COMPLETE WITHOUT SCHEDULES A AND B.

IN WITNESS WHEREOF, CHICAGO TITLE INSURANCE COMPANY has caused this policy to be signed and sealed by its duly authorized officers.

Chicago Title Insurance Company

BY _____ President

ATTEST

_____ Secretary

ALTA Homeowner's Policy of Title Insurance (1/1/08)

FIGURE 22.1   (*Continued*).

SCHEDULE A

Our name and address is: Chicago Title Company, 555 Main Street, Anytown, USA

Policy No.: SAMPLE

Premium: $ 2,376.00   Policy Amount: $ 750,000.00

Policy Date: January 5, 2010 at 08:00 AM

Deductible Amounts and Maximum Dollar Limits of Liability
for Covered Risk 16, 18, 19 and 21:

	Your Deductible Amount	Our Maximum Dollar Limit of Liability
Covered Risk 16:	1.00% of Policy Amount Shown in Schedule A or $ 2,500.00 (whichever is less)	$ 10,000.00
Covered Risk 18:	1.00% of Policy Amount Shown in Schedule A or $ 5,000.00 (whichever is less)	$ 25,000.00
Covered Risk 19:	1.00% of Policy Amount Shown in Schedule A or $ 5,000.00 (whichever is less)	$ 25,000.00
Covered Risk 21:	1.00% of Policy Amount Shown in Schedule A or $ 2,500.00 (whichever is less)	$ 5,000.00

Street Address of the Land: 12345 Property Street, Santa Ana, California

1.   Name of Insured:

        Bryan B. Buyer and Belinda B. Buyer

2.   Your interest in the Land covered by this Policy is:

        A Fee

3.   The Land referred to in this Policy is described as:

        SEE EXHIBIT "A" ATTACHED HERETO AND MADE A PART HEREOF

THIS POLICY VALID ONLY IF SCHEDULE B IS ATTACHED

4

ALTA Homeowner's Policy of Title Insurance (1/1/08)

FIGURE 22.1   (*Continued*).

Policy No. CACTI7701-7701-5590-0000201006-CTIC-2010-20

LEGAL DESCRIPTION

EXHIBIT "A"

THE LAND REFERRED TO HEREIN BELOW IS SITUATED IN THE COUNTY OF ORANGE, STATE OF CALIFORNIA, AND IS DESCRIBED AS FOLLOWS:

Lot 222, Block 444, Tract 111, County of Orange, State of California, as per map recorded in Book 777, Page 888 of Maps, in the office of the County Recorder of said County.

APN: 123-45-678-9

4.1

ALTA Homeowner's Policy of Title Insurance (1/1/08)

FIGURE 22.1   (Continued).

Policy No. CACTI7701-7701-5590-0000201006-CTIC-2010-20

SCHEDULE B

EXCEPTIONS

In addition to the Exclusions, You are not insured against loss, costs, attorneys' fees, and expenses resulting from:

1. Covenants, conditions and restrictions but omitting any covenants or restrictions, if any, including but not limited to those based upon race, color, religion, sex, sexual orientation, familial status, marital status, disability, handicap, national origin, ancestry, or source of income, as set forth in applicable state or federal laws, except to the extent that said covenant or restriction is permitted by applicable law, as set forth in the document

    Recording Date: January 15, 2000
    Recording No: Instrument No. 2000-234567

2. A deed of trust to secure an indebtedness in the amount shown below,

    Amount: $600,000.00
    Dated: January 2, 2010
    Trustor/Grantor Brian B. Buyer and Belinda B. Buyer, husband and wife as joint tenants
    Trustee: XYZ Bank
    Beneficiary: XYZ Bank
    Loan No.:   55555555
    Recording Date: January 5, 2010
    Recording No: 2010-1234565

END OF SCHEDULE B

ALTA Homeowner's Policy of Title Insurance (1/1/08)

FIGURE 22.1 (Continued).

EXCLUSIONS

In addition to the Exceptions in Schedule B, You are not insured against loss, costs, attorneys' fees, and expenses resulting from:

1. Governmental police power, and the existence or violation of those portions of any law or government regulation concerning:
   a. building;
   b. zoning;
   c. land use;
   d. improvements on the Land;
   e. land division; and
   f. environmental protection.
   This Exclusion does not limit the coverage described in Covered Risk 8.a., 14, 15, 16, 18, 19, 20, 23 or 27.

2. The failure of Your existing structures, or any part of them, to be constructed in accordance with applicable building codes. This Exclusion does not limit the coverage described in Covered Risk 14 or 15.

3. The right to take the Land by condemning it. This Exclusion does not limit the coverage described in Covered Risk 17.

4. Risks:
   a. that are created, allowed, or agreed to by You, whether or not they are recorded in the Public Records;
   b. that are Known to You at the Policy Date, but not to Us, unless they are recorded in the Public Records at the Policy Date;
   c. that result in no loss to You; or
   d. that first occur after the Policy Date - this does not limit the coverage described in Covered Risk 7, 8.e., 25, 26, 27 or 28.

5. Failure to pay value for Your Title.

6. Lack of a right:
   a. to any land outside the area specifically described and referred to in paragraph 3 of Schedule A; and
   b. in streets, alleys, or waterways that touch the Land.
   This Exclusion does not limit the coverage described in Covered Risk 11 or 21.

CONDITIONS

1. DEFINITIONS

a. Easement – the right of someone else to use the Land for a special purpose.

b. Known – things about which You have actual knowledge. The words "Know" and "Knowing" have the same meaning as Known.

c. Land – the land or condominium unit described in paragraph 3 of Schedule A and any improvements on the Land which are real property.

d. Mortgage – a mortgage, deed of trust, trust deed or other security instrument.

e. Natural Person – a human being, not a commercial or legal organization or entity. Natural Person includes a trustee of a Trust even if the trustee is not a human being.

f. Policy Date – the date and time shown in Schedule A. If the insured named in Schedule A first acquires the interest shown in Schedule A by an instrument recorded in the Public Records later than the date and time shown in Schedule A, the Policy Date is the date and time the instrument is recorded.

g. Public Records – records that give constructive notice of matters affecting Your Title, according to the state statutes where the Land is located.

h. Title – the ownership of Your interest in the Land, as shown in Schedule A.

i. Trust – a living trust established by a human being for estate planning.

j. We/Our/Us – Chicago Title Insurance Company.

k. You/Your – the insured named in Schedule A and also those identified in Section 2.b. of these Conditions.

2. CONTINUATION OF COVERAGE

a. This Policy insures You forever, even after You no longer have Your Title. You cannot assign this Policy to anyone else.

b. This Policy also insures:
   (1) anyone who inherits Your Title because of Your death;
   (2) Your spouse who receives Your Title because of dissolution of Your marriage;
   (3) the trustee or successor trustee of a Trust to whom You transfer Your Title after the Policy Date; or
   (4) the beneficiaries of Your Trust upon Your death.

c. We may assert against the insureds identified in Section 2.b. any rights and defenses that We have against any previous insured under this Policy.

3. HOW TO MAKE A CLAIM

a. Prompt Notice Of Your Claim

(1) As soon as You Know of anything that might be covered by this Policy, You must notify Us promptly in writing.

(2) Send Your notice to **Chicago Title Insurance Company**, P.O. Box 45023, Jacksonville, FL 32232-5023, Attn: Claims Department. Please include the Policy number shown in Schedule A, and the county and state where the Land is located. Please enclose a copy of Your policy, if available.

(3) If You do not give Us prompt notice, Your coverage will be reduced or ended, but only to the extent Your Failure affects Our ability to resolve the claim or defend You.

b. Proof Of Your Loss

(1) We may require You to give Us a written statement signed by You describing Your loss which includes:
   (a) the basis of Your claim;
   (b) the Covered Risks which resulted in Your loss;
   (c) the dollar amount of Your loss; and
   (d) the method You used to compute the amount of Your loss.

(2) We may require You to make available to Us records, checks, letters, contracts, insurance policies and other papers which relate to Your claim. We may make copies of these papers.

(3) We may require You to answer questions about Your claim under oath.

(4) If You fail or refuse to give Us a statement of loss, answer Our questions under oath, or make available to Us the papers We request, Your coverage will be reduced or ended, but only to the extent Your failure or refusal affects Our ability to resolve the claim or defend You.

4. OUR CHOICES WHEN WE LEARN OF A CLAIM

a. After We receive Your notice, or otherwise learn, of a claim that is covered by this Policy, Our choices include one or more of the following:
   (1) Pay the claim;
   (2) Negotiate a settlement;
   (3) Bring or defend a legal action related to the claim;
   (4) Pay You the amount required by this Policy;
   (5) End the coverage of this Policy for the claim by paying You Your actual loss resulting from the Covered Risk, and those costs, attorneys' fees and expenses incurred up to that time which We are obligated to pay;
   (6) End the coverage described in Covered Risk 16, 18, 19 or 21 by paying You the amount of Your insurance then in force for the particular Covered Risk, and those costs, attorneys' fees and expenses incurred up to that time which We are obligated to pay;
   (7) End all coverage of this Policy by paying You the Policy Amount then in force, and those costs, attorneys' fees and expenses incurred up to that time which We are obligated to pay;
   (8) Take other appropriate action.

b. When We choose the options in Sections 4.a.(5), (6) or (7), all Our obligations for the claim end, including Our obligation to defend, or continue to defend, any legal action.

c. Even if We do not think that the Policy covers the claim, We may choose one or more of the options above. By doing so, We do not give up any rights.

5. HANDLING A CLAIM OR LEGAL ACTION

a. You must cooperate with Us in handling any claim or legal action and give Us all relevant information.

b. If You fail or refuse to cooperate with Us, Your coverage will be reduced or ended, but only to the extent Your failure or refusal affects Our ability to resolve the claim or defend You.

c. We are required to repay You only for those settlement costs, attorneys' fees and expenses that We approve in advance.

d. We have the right to choose the attorney when We bring or defend a legal action on Your behalf. We can appeal any decision to the highest level. We do not have to pay Your claim until the legal action is finally decided.

e. Whether or not We agree there is coverage, We can bring or defend a legal action, or take other appropriate action under this Policy. By doing so, We do not give up any rights.

6. LIMITATION OF OUR LIABILITY

a. After subtracting Your Deductible Amount if it applies, We will pay no more than the least of :
   (1) Your actual loss;
   (2) Our Maximum Dollar Limit of Liability then in force for the particular Covered Risk, for claims covered only under Covered Risk 16, 18, 19 or 21; or
   (3) the Policy Amount then in force.
   and any costs, attorneys' fees and expenses that We are obligated to pay under this Policy.

b. If We pursue Our rights under Sections 4.a.(3) and 5.e. of these Conditions and are unsuccessful in establishing the Title, as insured:
   (1) the Policy Amount then in force will be increased by 10% of the Policy Amount shown in Schedule A, and
   (2) You shall have the right to have the actual loss determined on either the date the claim was made by You or the date it is settled and paid.

c. (1) If We remove the cause of the claim with reasonable diligence after receiving notice of it, all Our obligations for the claim end, including any obligation for loss You had while We were removing the cause of the claim.

(2) Regardless of 6.c.(1) above, if You cannot use the Land because of a claim covered by this Policy:
   (a) You may rent a reasonably equivalent substitute residence and We will repay You for the actual rent You pay, until the earlier of:
      (i) the cause of the claim is removed; or
      (ii) We pay You the amount required by this Policy. If Your claim is covered only under Covered Risk 16, 18, 19 or 21, that payment is the amount of Your insurance then in force for the particular Covered Risk.
   (b) We will pay reasonable costs You pay to relocate any personal property You have the right to remove from the Land, including transportation of that personal property for up to twenty-five (25) miles from the Land, and repair of any damage to that personal property because of the

Page 6

ALTA Homeowner's Policy of Title Insurance (1/1/08)

FIGURE 22.1   (Continued).

relocation. The amount We will pay You under this paragraph is limited to the value of the personal property before You relocate it.

d.   All payments We make under this Policy reduce the Policy Amount then in force, except for costs, attorneys' fees and expenses. All payments We make for claims which are covered only under Covered Risk 16, 18, 19 or 21 also reduce Our Maximum Dollar Limit of Liability for the particular Covered Risk, except for costs, attorneys' fees and expenses.

e.   If We issue, or have issued, a Policy to the owner of a Mortgage that is on Your Title and We have not given You any coverage against the Mortgage, then:

(1)   We have the right to pay any amount due You under this Policy to the owner of the Mortgage, and any amount paid shall be treated as a payment to You under this Policy, including under Section 4.a. of these Conditions;

(2)   Any amount paid to the owner of the Mortgage shall be subtracted from the Policy Amount then in force; and

(3)   If Your claim is covered only under Covered Risk 16, 18, 19 or 21, any amount paid to the owner of the Mortgage shall also be subtracted from Our Maximum Dollar Limit of Liability for the particular Covered Risk.

f.   If You do anything to affect any right of recovery You may have against someone else, We can subtract from Our liability the amount by which You reduced the value of that right.

7.   TRANSFER OF YOUR RIGHTS TO US

a.   When We settle Your claim, We have all the rights and remedies You have against any person or property related to the claim. You must not do anything to affect these rights and remedies. When We ask, You must execute documents to evidence the transfer to Us of these rights and remedies. You must let Us use Your name in enforcing these rights and remedies.

b.   We will not be liable to You if We do not pursue these rights and remedies or if We do not recover any amount that might be recoverable.

c.   We will pay any money We collect from enforcing these rights and remedies in the following order:

(1)   to Us for the costs, attorneys' fees and expenses We paid to enforce these rights and remedies;

(2)   to You for Your loss that You have not already collected;

(3)   to Us for any money We paid out under this Policy on account of Your claim; and

(4)   to You whatever is left.

d.   If You have rights and remedies under contracts (such as indemnities, guaranties, bonds or other policies of insurance) to recover all or part of Your loss, then We have all of those rights and remedies, even if those contracts provide that those obligated have all of Your rights and remedies under this Policy.

8.   THIS POLICY IS THE ENTIRE CONTRACT

This Policy, with any endorsements, is the entire contract between You and Us. To determine the meaning of any part of this Policy, You must read the entire Policy and any endorsements. Any changes to this Policy must be agreed to in writing by Us. Any claim You make against Us must be made under this Policy and is subject to its terms.

9.   INCREASED POLICY AMOUNT

The Policy Amount then in force will increase by ten percent (10%) of the Policy Amount shown in Schedule A each year for the first five years following the Policy Date shown in Schedule A, up to one hundred fifty percent (150%) of the Policy Amount shown in Schedule A. The increase each year will happen on the anniversary of the Policy Date shown in Schedule A.

10.   SEVERABILITY

If any part of this Policy is held to be legally unenforceable, both You and We can still enforce the rest of this Policy.

11.   ARBITRATION

a.   If permitted in the state where the Land is located, You or We may demand arbitration.

b.   The law used in the arbitration is the law of the state where the Land is located.

c.   The arbitration shall be under the Title Insurance Arbitration Rules of the American Land Title Association ("Rules"). You can get a copy of the Rules from Us.

d.   Except as provided in the Rules, You cannot join or consolidate Your claim or controversy with claims or controversies of other persons.

e.   The arbitration shall be binding on both You and Us. The arbitration shall decide any matter in dispute between You and Us.

f.   The arbitration award may be entered as a judgment in the proper court.

12.   CHOICE OF LAW

The law of the state where the Land is located shall apply to this policy.

ALTA Homeowner's Policy of Title Insurance (1/1/08)

policy is issued to homeowners and noninstitutional lenders. The other policy, the ALTA, is the standard lender's form approved by the American Land Title Association, and is issued to banks, savings and loan associations, and other institutional lenders.

Two Policies Generally Issued

Most California real estate transactions involve both the CLTA issued to the buyer–owner, as well as the ALTA policy, issued to the lender. A seller taking back a purchase money deed of trust on the sale of property would receive a CLTA. Typically, the buyer pays for the cost of the lender's policy as part of the incidental fees for the loan, and the cost of the CLTA Policy is paid by one or both parties, depending on county custom.

Other Types of Policies

Title companies offer numerous other services besides the CLTA or Homeowner's Policy and ALTA policies, but such other policies are beyond the scope of this chapter. Briefly, the five most common other policies issued by title companies are the following:

1. *Preliminary title report.* This report is issued before and later replaced by a basic title policy. It contains some information as a basic title report, showing the status of the title and the legal description. It is primarily used to discover clouds on title and other title problems to resolve before close of escrow.

   The policy states that it is issued without liability by the title company. Since 1982, title companies will not be liable for negligence in failing to disclose conditions about title. Preliminary reports can no longer be relied on as "a representation of the condition of title to real property." Also since 1982, they are only an "offer" containing "the terms and conditions upon which the insurer is willing to issue its title policy." *Ins.C. 12340.11.*

2. *Foreclosure guarantee reports.* Whenever a deed of trust or other lien is foreclosed, all necessary parties must receive notice or they may not be bound by the foreclosure. This report guarantees to list all necessary parties. It also describes all liens against the property and provides a legal description. It is ordered in most lien foreclosure actions.

3. *Litigation guarantee reports.* When attorneys commence litigation against title to property, they must also name all necessary parties or those people may be unaffected by the outcome of the litigation. This report supplies all those names, the status and recorded address of those persons, and their purported interest in the property.

4. *Name run reports.* This report, also known as a real property guarantee report, provides a list of all property of record owned by a person. For example, if you have a judgment to enforce, this report will disclose recorded properties, which may be seized to satisfy the judgment.

5. *ALTA-Residential policy.* Some insurers are offering an ALTA-Residential policy. This policy is designed specifically for residential homeowners, and it would seem that it should have been offered by CLTA. However, because so many of its provisions parallel the lender's coverage and because it was developed for a national market, it was offered through ALTA. Because of increased competition between title companies, this policy is beginning to find its way into common usage.

The four biggest differences between a conventional CLTA policy and the ALTA-Residential policy is the plain language, coverage for easements, protection against mechanics' liens, and defense against encumbrances. First, the policy is written in *plain English*, so it is simple and easy to understand. The policy insures against a neighbor having an easement across the property, even if not of public record. The policy covers mechanics' liens that arise because of work performed or materials supplied before the policy is issued but becoming a lien later. Additionally, the title policy insures against any liens, assessments, or homeowner's association charges that are not yet of record. The policy is, indeed, far broader than the standard CLTA policy.

Elements of a Policy

Both ALTA and CLTA policies contain five sections. The first part, the Title page, describes the extent of the policy's coverage. Next is Schedule A, which includes such insurance information as the amount of the insurance policy, the estate or interest insured by the policy, and the vesting of that estate or interest. The third part is Schedule B, which lists the exclusions and exemptions from coverage. Part I of Schedule B details the standard preprinted exemptions from every policy and is found on the reverse side of the title page. Part II of Schedule B lists the specific exceptions for that property, including those items found of public record. The fourth part is Schedule C, which provides the legal description of the real estate covered by the policy. The final part, called Conditions and Stipulations, states certain other exceptions from coverage, and lists specific procedural requirements that must be followed to collect in the event of a loss. See Table 22.1 for detailed information on the parts and purposes of a title policy.

TABLE 22.1   Comparison of CLTA and ALTA policies.

	CLTA	ALTA
Unrecorded encumbrances: Covers facts not of public record, such as unrecorded liens, encumbrances, taxes, assessments, mining claims, and water rights	No	Yes
Physical inspection: Covers facts ascertainable by a physical inspection of the land, such as rights of an adverse possessor, building encroachments, potential mechanic's liens, and facts discoverable from a survey of the land	No	Yes
Competent deed and parties: Covers off-the-record defects such as forgery of deeds, fraudulently obtained deeds, improper delivery of deeds, legal capacity of the parties to the deed, and marital rights of the grantor's spouse	Yes	Yes
Police power, etc.: Covers violations of laws, ordinances, and other government regulations affecting the use of property, such as zoning laws, building codes, subdivision acts, unrecorded condemnation action, and police power regulation	No	No
Undisclosed facts: Covers facts known to the insured and not of public record, and which are not disclosed to the title company in writing	No	No

Difference between Policies

Both the CLTA and the ALTA policies cover competency of the deed and parties in the chain of title, and both exclude coverage for exercises of the police power and facts known to the insured and not disclosed to the title company. However, the CLTA policy is significantly less comprehensive than the ALTA policy, excluding also unrecorded encumbrances and facts disclosed by a physical inspection (see Table 22.2).

California Land Title Association Policy

The CLTA policy is designed to cover the risks commonly demanded by homeowners. It insures the homeowner or the noninstitutional lender that there are no unrecorded liens or ownership interests in the property except those stated in the policy. Thus, the policy does not insure against liens that are unrecorded. It also does not insure against interests that are discoverable by a physical inspection of the property. The most common unprotected interests are unrecorded mechanic's liens, adverse possessors, tenants under unrecorded leases, and boundary liens. Because zoning laws, setback lines, and

TABLE 22.2 How to read a title policy.

How to Read a Title Insurance Policy

The typical CLTA title insurance policy issued to homeowners is generally standardized and contains the identical wording whichever title insurance company is used. What varies is the typed attachments that limit the risks assumed and the exclusions. It is basically the reverse of the old adage, "what the large print giveth the small print takes away." In title insurance policies, it is the large print–the attachments–that reduce the amount of coverage. CLTA title policies have five sections as described below. (See Figure 23.1 for a sample policy.)

1. *Title page.* The title page or cover page describes the policy's coverage and limitations. The section starts with a generalized statement of coverage. It then lists several specifically covered items, such as vestings, liens, encumbrances, and marketability. The clause provides that such coverage is "subject to Schedule B" and other restrictions found in other parts of the policy.

2. *Schedule A.* Schedule A includes basic insurance information. It lists the face amount of the policy, the estate or interest insured by the policy, and the vesting of that estate or interest.

3. *Schedule B.* Schedule B lists two sets of exclusions and exemptions from coverage. Because the two parts are on different pages, understanding the limitations may at first seem confusing.

   A. *Schedule B, Part 1.* Part 1 of Schedule B details the standardized exclusions, such as current taxes, items not of public record but discoverable by a physical inspection, claims not of record, and the like. Part 1 is preprinted and located on the back of the title page. The page merely lists numerous items, without any introduction or statement as to why the items are listed.

   B. *Schedule B, Part 2.* Part 2 of Schedule B is a specially typed page stating that it does not insure against losses listed in Parts 1 and 2. One small, preprinted sentence states that Part 1 is located on the inside of the cover sheet. All the rest of Part 2 is specially typed and lists the specific exemptions for that property. These exemptions are those of public record that apply to the insured property such as tax liens, recorded easements, deeds of trust and other such recorded items.

4. *Schedule C.* Schedule C contains a legal description of the property. In California such descriptions of urban property are usually defined by lot and block or metes and bounds. The government survey method of township and range occurs mostly in remote, rural property.

5. *Conditions and stipulations.* The conditions and stipulations contain the legalese that is so hard to read. It defines terms, tells how to make a claim, explains the title company's obligations, and specifies what happens when the estate or interest is transferred. This section starts on the back side of the cover page and continues on the last page of the policy.

violations of police powers are also not of public record, they are excluded. Because it would be almost financially impossible to investigate each property to insure it meets plumbing codes, height restrictions, electrical codes, and zoning ordinances, police power regulations must, by necessity, be excluded. Finally, the policy does not cover anything known to the insured and not disclosed in writing to the title company.

NATURE OF ESCROW AND ESCROW COMPANIES

Use and Definition

Although an escrow is not mandatory in a real estate transaction, the complexity of the transaction and the significant sums of money involved usually require the parties to rely on an escrow. An escrow is simply a neutral third party (stakeholder) who holds deeds, documents, or something else of value according to stated instructions for its delivery on completion of certain documents or occurrence of certain events.

Typical Escrow

In the typical real estate purchase, the seller entrusts the deed and other documents to the escrow agent. Similarly, the buyer deposits all funds and instruments necessary for the purchase of the property. The escrow agent collects the data needed for transfer of the documents, prepares all necessary instruments for signature, makes the required prorations and monetary adjustments, and arranges for title insurance. When everything is completed, the escrow agent records all the documents, disburses the funds (including possible payment of existing encumbrances against the property), and dispenses the executed instruments to the appropriate parties.

Regulation of Escrow

Escrows must be licensed escrow corporations, having specified monetary reserves, and bound by strict regulations under the escrow law. *Fin.C. 17000–17654.* Banks, savings and loans, trust companies, insurance companies, certain attorneys, and specified real estate brokers in limited situations are exempt from the requirement of being a licensed escrow corporation. *Fin.C. 17006.* No other person may act as escrow agent or receive compensation for similar services under penalty of civil and criminal sanctions.

Exemptions

A real estate broker or attorney may act as an escrow only in the course of, or incident to, a transaction in normal business. Furthermore, the California Department of Real Estate requires that the broker, in addition to acting in the course of or incidental to the real estate business, must also be either the selling or listing broker. *California Department of Real Estate Bulletin, Summer 1977: 4.*

ESCROW IS A DOUBLE AGENT

Dual Agency

Most of the litigation and problems affecting escrow agents concern the nature and effect of their dual agency. The escrow holder is the holder for both parties until all conditions have been satisfied, at which time he becomes the individual agent for each party. Once the conditions have been performed, then the escrow agent becomes the individual agent of the seller to deliver the purchase money and the individual agent of the buyer to deliver the documents of title.

Limited Agency

The escrow is only a limited agent and is not bound by all the disclosure and fiduciary obligations of a general agent. The escrow's only obligations are those stated in the instructions. Thus, absent a specific instruction, the escrow is forbidden from disclosing certain facts concerning the subject transaction. Additionally, as a limited dual fiduciary, in the event of controversy or dispute between the parties on an issue or condition concerning the escrow, the escrow may, and usually does, refrain from making a determination. As a mere stakeholder, the escrow may petition the court (in a declaratory relief action or by impleading the other claimants) to decide the issues involved.

Risk if Agent Decides

Indeed, an escrow agent who resolves a controversy between the parties personally, without instructions from both parties or a ruling from the court, and the escrow's resolution is incorrect, is legally liable for all damages resulting from that error in judgment.

Elements of an Escrow

The essential elements of an escrow are (1) the irrevocable deposit of money or documents with a third person (2) under a valid and enforceable contract that (3) calls for the delivery of that money or those documents on the occurrence of some condition.

Valid Contract

Without a valid and enforceable contract between the parties, the deposit with the third person is revocable by the depositor. The third person would then be an agent only of the depositor and subject to the depositor's specific and unilateral instructions. Hence, a true escrow requires a valid underlying agreement between the parties. Only by such a contract is delivery to the third party made irrevocable at the will of the depositors.

Form of Contract

Generally, the underlying contract supporting the escrow is a deposit receipt, exchange agreement, or other standard real estate form. Once the matching buyer's and seller's escrow instructions are executed, those instructions become a separate and enforceable contract between the parties.

Escrow Instructions Prevail over Earlier Contract

If the escrow instructions differ from the underlying contract to the extent that the terms of the two agreements are not inconsistent, they are interpreted together to derive one entire agreement between the parties. *C.C. 1642.* However, to the extent that the escrow instructions are inconsistent with the earlier contract, the terms of the escrow instructions prevail (see Figure 22.2 for escrow instructions).

FIGURE 22.2   Escrow instructions.

Escrow Instructions

These escrow instructions are made on this 5th day of January, 20XX, by and between _____, "Seller," _____, "Buyer," and you, XYZ TITLE COMPANY, as escrow, and are based on the following definitions, terms and provisions:

1. **Definition - Subject Property.** The term, the "Subject Property," shall refer to the property commonly known 123 Jones Street, San Rafael, California, a single-family residence, described as:

   > Lot #1 of Block A, as shown on that certain map entitled "Tract 12345," and filed for record on January 15, 1990, as Book 123 in Page 567, in the Official Records of the County of Marin, State of California.

2. **Seller Deliver Deed.** The Seller will give you a deed conveying the Subject Property to the Buyer.

3. **Buyer Deliver Cash, Notes And Loan Proceeds.** The Buyer will give you and/or caused to be delivered to you, prior to close of escrow, a total of $250,000, as follows:

A.	**Deposit**. A deposit now held by broker:	$5,000
B.	**Down Payment**. Cash:	$45,000
C.	**New Loan**. The proceeds of a new loan secured by Buyer from ABC BANK, in the amount stated at the right, to be secured by a promissory note and deed of trust, in first priority position, fully executed by Buyer, in favor of ABC BANK.	$200,000

4. **Authority To Close Escrow.** You may close escrow, disburse all funds, deliver and/or record all documents, when you issue a current CLTA Owner's Title Insurance Policy (and any lender's ALTA policy as may be required by Buyer's lender, ABC BANK), in the face amount of $250,000, or such amount as may be required by Buyer's lender, whichever is greater.

5. **Exceptions On Title Policy.** Your title policies may contain the following exceptions:

   A. **Current Taxes**. A real property taxes and special taxes for the County of Marin for the current fiscal year, but not any bonds or special assessments.

   B. **CCR&E Of Record**. All covenants, conditions, restrictions, rights of way, easements and reservations of record.

FIGURE 22.2 (*Continued*).

ESCROW INSTRUCTIONS
CONTINUED, Page 2 of 2

C.   **New Deed Of Trust**. A first deed of trust in the amount of $200,000, which is to secure an installment promissory note, of the same amount, executed by Buyer, in favor of ABC BANK, both forms to be drawn on your standard form. The note will provide for installments of $2,057.26, or more per month, for 30 years, beginning 30 days from close of escrow, including interest, at the rate of 12% per annum from close of escrow. Note and deed of trust to contain your standard acceleration/due-on-sale clause, and your prepayment clause 3-A.

6. **Prorations**. All prorations are to be made as of close of escrow.

7. **Escrow And Title Costs**. At close of escrow, charge the following costs to the Buyer and Seller as provided below:

(To Seller)

1/2 of Document Preparation, Documentary Transfer Tax Stamps, and
1/2 of Escrow Fee

(To Buyer)

Owner's CLTA Title Insurance Premium, Lender's ALTA Title Insurance Premium,
1/2 of Document Preparation, 1/2 of Escrow Fee, Recording Fees, and Insurance Premium

8. **Fire And Hazard Insurance**. Buyer shall provide a new policy for at least $200,00, with a loss payable endorsement in favor of ABC BANK.

9. **Lender's Instructions.** Buyer will cause you to receive lender's instructions from ABC BANK, for the above $200,000 loan. You are authorized to comply with all instructions of the lender, and Buyer will pay all costs in connection with those instructions.

These instructions may only be amended by a document signed by all parties.

| *BUYER* | *SELLER* | *XYZ TITLE CO.* |

Delivery, Title, and Risk

Although the seller must deposit in escrow an executed deed, which cannot be revoked or withdrawn during that escrow, the mere deposit of the deed in the escrow is not a legal delivery of that deed. The grantor has no intent to cast off title immediately and unconditionally. Legal title remains with the seller, who may collect all the rents from the property and use it personally. If the property is destroyed or damaged during escrow, the loss is borne by the seller, who is still the legal owner. For the same reason, any unexplained loss or embezzlement of the buyer's funds in escrow is borne by the buyer. Once all the conditions are met, legal title to the property passes automatically to the buyer. From that moment on, any damage to the property is the problem of the buyer, and the seller bears any loss of purchase money from the escrow.

Kellogg v. Curry
101 C.A.2d 856 (1951)

[Defendants, Mr. and Mrs. Curry, executed a deposit receipt to purchase a home from plaintiffs. Defendants also gave the seller's broker, G. K. Wies, $100 on deposit for purchase of that property. Shortly thereafter, the escrow instructions were executed, and the buyer delivered to the escrow agent $1,200 cash, of which the $100 was part thereof, with the balance of the purchase price to follow before close of escrow. Before the time for close of escrow, defendants notified the sellers that they refused to complete the purchase of the property. After the escrow term had expired, plaintiff sold the property to other buyers for a higher sales price than the original contract. Plaintiff–sellers then sought to quiet title to the original buyers' $1,200 deposit in escrow, and the trial court awarded it to them. Defendants appealed.]

WOODS, JUSTICE. Defendants contend that plaintiffs cannot quiet title to the money in escrow because they had no title to it. They argue that a deposit in escrow is conditional and title remains in the depositor until the conditions under which it was deposited have been fulfilled; that plaintiffs were not entitled to the money in escrow for the reason there was no forfeiture clause in the escrow instructions; and that because the property was resold to a third person within six weeks after this escrow was opened, for more than the contract price herein, the plaintiffs were not damaged and should not have the aid of the court to enforce a forfeiture.

Under the standard form of escrow instructions that provide for the exchange of money and a deed upon stipulated conditions, the buyer retains ownership of the money and the seller retains ownership of his deed and title to his property. The escrow holder acts as agent of the buyer as to the money and as agent of the seller as to the deed until the stipulated conditions have been met. When performance has been rendered by each party the escrow holder then becomes the agent of the seller as to the money and the agent of the buyer as to the deed.

Failure of performance on the part of either party does not accomplish a transfer of title. If the buyer, having deposited money in escrow, fails to deposit the balance in accordance with the agreement, the money he has deposited does not ipso facto become the property of the seller.

[For example, in another case] the plaintiffs (sellers) sought unsuccessfully to quiet title to money deposited in escrow by the buyers of real property. The sellers therein extended the term of the escrow, and while the buyers were still endeavoring to raise the additional money required by the escrow, the sellers sold and conveyed the property to a

APPLY THE LAW

continued

third person. The payment of that deposit and the delivery of the deed were mutually dependent upon each other. The title to the money remained in appellants, and after July 22, 1944 [the original expiration date of the escrow], they were entitled to withdraw it even though they were liable in damages for failure to complete the transaction as provided by the terms of the escrow. The title to money deposited in escrow to be paid to the vendor of property does not pass until all conditions of the escrow have been fulfilled.

A buyer's agreement that his money shall be paid to the seller for a deed is not, of course, an agreement that it shall be paid to the seller in case of the buyer's default. Of course, an escrow agreement may incorporate additional provisions defining the rights of the parties with respect to the deposited money in the event of the buyer's default. The purposes of the widely used escrow arrangement would be largely defeated if the default of one party or the other would work a forfeiture of the property he has deposited into escrow, in the absence of an agreement that he should suffer that loss. To hold that the money in question here became the property of plaintiffs would amount to a rewriting of the agreement with respect to the sum of $1,100.

[The court then noted that the broker was acting as a trustee for the owners, that the escrow instructions required the plaintiff to deposit their deed in escrow, and that sellers had to provide marketable title as evidenced by a standard form title insurance policy.] The plaintiffs did not perform the conditions of the escrow instructions on their part to be performed. They did not deposit their deed or a policy of title insurance as required by the instructions or at all. In view of the fact that the title to the property stood of record in the name of Wise, and that Wise purportedly was acting in several different capacities in the transaction, it was especially important and material herein that plaintiffs perform the conditions on their part to be performed. Under such circumstances, in this proceeding in equity to quiet title, it cannot properly be said that it would have been a useless act for plaintiffs to perform the conditions required of them by the escrow agreement.

The deposit receipt provided for retention by the sellers of the money paid and also that one-half of the deposit should be applied on the real estate agent's commission but not to exceed the full amount of the commission, $312.50. The sum of $100, having been paid to the sellers on the contract, was not recoverable by defendants.

The escrow instructions contained no provision with relation to the deposit of $1,100 in the event of the buyers' default. That sum was not to be retained as liquidated damages or as security for any loss the seller might sustain, nor was there any agreement that it would be forfeited to

continued

the sellers. While such an agreement is not necessary to enable the sellers to retain the $100 they received on the contract in the event of the buyers' default, they cannot lay claim to money deposited in escrow except upon the terms stipulated in the buyers' instructions.

Judgment reversed. [To pay the same to the broker, the plaintiff is under these facts entitled to the $100 provided for default under the deposit receipt, but the balance, the $1,100 deposited in escrow, must be returned to defendants. Plaintiffs did not perform all of the conditions in escrow, nor could they establish damages enabling them to claim the right to any additional funds.]

REAL ESTATE SETTLEMENT PROCEDURES ACT

Nature of RESPA (Reg. X)

Most loans to purchase or refinance a residence for occupancy by consumers are bound by the Real Estate Settlement Procedures Act (commonly called "RESPA" or "Reg X"). *12 USC §2601 et seq.* RESPA is a broad act that among its provisions: (1) simplifies the wording of settlement cost statements, (2) requires borrowers to be given a good faith estimate of the costs they would incur if they chose that loan, and (3) prohibits kickbacks on others disallowed fees. RESPA forms and requirements are sometimes called *Regulation X* forms or requirements because it was section X of the law that Congress passed.

Good Faith Estimate Form

RESPA requires all lenders making loans covered by RESPA provide the borrower with a good faith estimate of the anticipated costs. The estimate also includes a booklet that explains the nature of the estimated charges. All the good faith estimate of charges must be reported on a standardized form so it will be easier for consumer to compare costs from different lenders. Before 2010, sample forms were found in *24 CFR 3500.7(a)* and if a lender still uses the old form, it does not count as compliance with the new law. Since 2010, lenders must use the standardized Good Faith Estimate HUD form. (See Figure 22.3). Borrowers sometimes confuse the Good Faith Estimate HUD with the final HUD Settlement Form. (See Figure 22.4).

FIGURE 22.3   HUD good faith estimate.

OMB Approval No. 2502-0265

Good Faith Estimate (GFE)

Name of Originator	Borrower
Originator Address	Property Address
Originator Phone Number	
Originator Email	Date of GFE

Purpose

This GFE gives you an estimate of your settlement charges and loan terms if you are approved for this loan. For more information, see HUD's *Special Information Booklet* on settlement charges, your *Truth-in-Lending Disclosures*, and other consumer information at www.hud.gov/respa. If you decide you would like to proceed with this loan, contact us.

Shopping for your loan

Only you can shop for the best loan for you. Compare this GFE with other loan offers, so you can find the best loan. Use the shopping chart on page 3 to compare all the offers you receive.

Important dates

1. The interest rate for this GFE is available through [   ]. After this time, the interest rate, some of your loan Origination Charges, and the monthly payment shown below can change until you lock your interest rate.

2. This estimate for all other settlement charges is available through [   ].

3. After you lock your interest rate, you must go to settlement within [ ] days (your rate lock period) to receive the locked interest rate.

4. You must lock the interest rate at least [ ] days before settlement.

Summary of your loan

Your initial loan amount is	$
Your loan term is	years
Your initial interest rate is	%
Your initial monthly amount owed for principal, interest, and any mortgage insurance is	$ per month
Can your interest rate rise?	☐ No ☐ Yes, it can rise to a maximum of %. The first change will be in .
Even if you make payments on time, can your loan balance rise?	☐ No ☐ Yes, it can rise to a maximum of $
Even if you make payments on time, can your monthly amount owed for principal, interest, and any mortgage insurance rise?	☐ No ☐ Yes, the first increase can be in and the monthly amount owed can rise to $. The maximum it can ever rise to is $.
Does your loan have a prepayment penalty?	☐ No ☐ Yes, your maximum prepayment penalty is $.
Does your loan have a balloon payment?	☐ No ☐ Yes, you have a balloon payment of $ due in years.

Escrow account information

Some lenders require an escrow account to hold funds for paying property taxes or other property-related charges in addition to your monthly amount owed of $[   ].

Do we require you to have an escrow account for your loan?

☐ No, you do not have an escrow account. You must pay these charges directly when due.

☐ Yes, you have an escrow account. It may or may not cover all of these charges. Ask us.

Summary of your settlement charges

A	Your Adjusted Origination Charges *(See page 2.)*	$
B	Your Charges for All Other Settlement Services *(See page 2.)*	$
A + B	Total Estimated Settlement Charges	$

FIGURE 22.3 *(Continued).*

Understanding
your estimated
settlement charges

Your Adjusted Origination Charges

1. **Our origination charge**
   This charge is for getting this loan for you.

2. **Your credit or charge (points) for the specific interest rate chosen**
   ☐ The credit or charge for the interest rate of ☐ % is included in "Our origination charge." (See item 1 above.)

   ☐ You receive a credit of $ ☐ for this interest rate of ☐ %. This credit **reduces** your settlement charges.

   ☐ You pay a charge of $ ☐ for this interest rate of ☐ %. This charge (points) **increases** your total settlement charges.

   The tradeoff table on page 3 shows that you can change your total settlement charges by choosing a different interest rate for this loan.

| **A** | Your Adjusted Origination Charges | $ |

Your Charges for All Other Settlement Services

Some of these charges can change at settlement. See the top of page 3 for more information.

3. **Required services that we select**
   These charges are for services we require to complete your settlement. We will choose the providers of these services.

   | Service | Charge |

4. **Title services and lender's title insurance**
   This charge includes the services of a title or settlement agent, for example, and title insurance to protect the lender, if required.

5. **Owner's title insurance**
   You may purchase an owner's title insurance policy to protect your interest in the property.

6. **Required services that you can shop for**
   These charges are for other services that are required to complete your settlement. We can identify providers of these services or you can shop for them yourself. Our estimates for providing these services are below.

   | Service | Charge |

7. **Government recording charges**
   These charges are for state and local fees to record your loan and title documents.

8. **Transfer taxes**
   These charges are for state and local fees on mortgages and home sales.

9. **Initial deposit for your escrow account**
   This charge is held in an escrow account to pay future recurring charges on your property and includes ☐ all property taxes, ☐ all insurance, and ☐ other ☐ .

10. **Daily interest charges**
    This charge is for the daily interest on your loan from the day of your settlement until the first day of the next month or the first day of your normal mortgage payment cycle. This amount is $ ☐ per day for ☐ days (if your settlement is ☐).

11. **Homeowner's insurance**
    This charge is for the insurance you must buy for the property to protect from a loss, such as fire.

    | Policy | Charge |

| **B** | Your Charges for All Other Settlement Services | $ |

| **A** + **B** | Total Estimated Settlement Charges | $ |

 Good Faith Estimate (HUD-GFE) 2

FIGURE 22.3 *(Continued).*

Instructions

Understanding which charges can change at settlement

This GFE estimates your settlement charges. At your settlement, you will receive a HUD-1, a form that lists your actual costs. Compare the charges on the HUD-1 with the charges on this GFE. Charges can change if you select your own provider and do not use the companies we identify. (See below for details.)

These charges **cannot increase** at settlement:	The total of these charges **can increase up to 10%** at settlement:	These charges **can change** at settlement:
■ Our origination charge ■ Your credit or charge (points) for the specific interest rate chosen *(after you lock in your interest rate)* ■ Your adjusted origination charges *(after you lock in your interest rate)* ■ Transfer taxes	■ Required services that we select ■ Title services and lender's title insurance *(if we select them or you use companies we identify)* ■ Owner's title insurance *(if you use companies we identify)* ■ Required services that you can shop for *(if you use companies we identify)* ■ Government recording charges	■ Required services that you can shop for *(if you do not use companies we identify)* ■ Title services and lender's title insurance *(if you do not use companies we identify)* ■ Owner's title insurance *(if you do not use companies we identify)* ■ Initial deposit for your escrow account ■ Daily interest charges ■ Homeowner's insurance

Using the tradeoff table

In this GFE, we offered you this loan with a particular interest rate and estimated settlement charges. However:

- If you want to choose this same loan with **lower settlement charges,** then you will have a **higher interest rate.**
- If you want to choose this same loan with a **lower interest rate,** then you will have **higher settlement charges.**

If you would like to choose an available option, you must ask us for a new GFE.

Loan originators have the option to complete this table. Please ask for additional information if the table is not completed.

	The loan in this GFE	The same loan with lower settlement charges	The same loan with a lower interest rate
Your initial loan amount	$	$	$
Your initial interest rate[1]	%	%	%
Your initial monthly amount owed	$	$	$
Change in the monthly amount owed from this GFE	No change	You will pay $ **more** every month	You will pay $ **less** every month
Change in the amount you will pay at settlement with this interest rate	No change	Your settlement charges will be **reduced** by $	Your settlement charges will **increase** by $
How much your total estimated settlement charges will be	$	$	$

[1] *For an adjustable rate loan, the comparisons above are for the initial interest rate before adjustments are made.*

Using the shopping chart

Use this chart to compare GFEs from different loan originators. Fill in the information by using a different column for each GFE you receive. By comparing loan offers, you can shop for the best loan.

	This loan	Loan 2	Loan 3	Loan 4
Loan originator name				
Initial loan amount				
Loan term				
Initial interest rate				
Initial monthly amount owed				
Rate lock period				
Can interest rate rise?				
Can loan balance rise?				
Can monthly amount owed rise?				
Prepayment penalty?				
Balloon payment?				
Total Estimated Settlement Charges				

If your loan is sold in the future

Some lenders may sell your loan after settlement. Any fees lenders receive in the future cannot change the loan you receive or the charges you paid at settlement.

 Good Faith Estimate (HUD-GFE) 3

FIGURE 22.4 HUD closing costs.

OMB Approval No. 2502-0265

A. Settlement Statement (HUD-1)

B. Type of Loan					
1. ☐ FHA 2. ☐ RHS 3. ☐ Conv. Unins. 4. ☐ VA 5. ☐ Conv. Ins.	6. File Number:	7. Loan Number:	8. Mortgage Insurance Case Number:		

C. Note: This form is furnished to give you a statement of actual settlement costs. Amounts paid to and by the settlement agent are shown. Items marked "(p.o.c.)" were paid outside the closing; they are shown here for informational purposes and are not included in the totals.

D. Name & Address of Borrower:	E. Name & Address of Seller:	F. Name & Address of Lender:
G. Property Location:	H. Settlement Agent:	I. Settlement Date:
	Place of Settlement:	

J. Summary of Borrower's Transaction		K. Summary of Seller's Transaction	
100. Gross Amount Due from Borrower		**400. Gross Amount Due to Seller**	
101. Contract sales price		401. Contract sales price	
102. Personal property		402. Personal property	
103. Settlement charges to borrower (line 1400)		403.	
104.		404.	
105.		405.	
Adjustment for items paid by seller in advance		**Adjustments for items paid by seller in advance**	
106. City/town taxes to		406. City/town taxes to	
107. County taxes to		407. County taxes to	
108. Assessments to		408. Assessments to	
109.		409.	
110.		410.	
111.		411.	
112.		412.	
120. Gross Amount Due from Borrower		**420. Gross Amount Due to Seller**	
200. Amounts Paid by or in Behalf of Borrower		**500. Reductions In Amount Due to Seller**	
201. Deposit or earnest money		501. Excess deposit (see instructions)	
202. Principal amount of new loan(s)		502. Settlement charges to seller (line 1400)	
203. Existing loan(s) taken subject to		503. Existing loan(s) taken subject to	
204.		504. Payoff of first mortgage loan	
205.		505. Payoff of second mortgage loan	
206.		506.	
207.		507.	
208.		508.	
209.		509.	
Adjustments for items unpaid by seller		**Adjustments for items unpaid by seller**	
210. City/town taxes to		510. City/town taxes to	
211. County taxes to		511. County taxes to	
212. Assessments to		512. Assessments to	
213.		513.	
214.		514.	
215.		515.	
216.		516.	
217.		517.	
218.		518.	
219.		519.	
220. Total Paid by/for Borrower		**520. Total Reduction Amount Due Seller**	
300. Cash at Settlement from/to Borrower		**600. Cash at Settlement to/from Seller**	
301. Gross amount due from borrower (line 120)		601. Gross amount due to seller (line 420)	
302. Less amounts paid by/for borrower (line 220)	( )	602. Less reductions in amount due seller (line 520)	( )
303. Cash ☐ **From** ☐ **To Borrower**		**603. Cash** ☐ **To** ☐ **From Seller**	

The Public Reporting Burden for this collection of information is estimated at 35 minutes per response for collecting, reviewing, and reporting the data. This agency may not collect this information, and you are not required to complete this form, unless it displays a currently valid OMB control number. No confidentiality is assured; this disclosure is mandatory. This is designed to provide the parties to a RESPA covered transaction with information during the settlement process.

FIGURE 22.4 *(Continued).*

L. Settlement Charges			
700. Total Real Estate Broker Fees		Paid From Borrower's Funds at Settlement	Paid From Seller's Funds at Settlement
Division of commission (line 700) as follows:			
701. $	to		
702. $	to		
703. Commission paid at settlement			
704.			
800. Items Payable in Connection with Loan			
801. Our origination charge	$	(from GFE #1)	
802. Your credit or charge (points) for the specific interest rate chosen $		(from GFE #2)	
803. Your adjusted origination charges		(from GFE A)	
804. Appraisal fee to		(from GFE #3)	
805. Credit report to		(from GFE #3)	
806. Tax service to		(from GFE #3)	
807. Flood certification		(from GFE #3)	
808.			
900. Items Required by Lender to Be Paid in Advance			
901. Daily interest charges from to @ $ /day		(from GFE #10)	
902. Mortgage insurance premium for months to		(from GFE #3)	
903. Homeowner's insurance for years to		(from GFE #11)	
904.			
1000. Reserves Deposited with Lender			
1001. Initial deposit for your escrow account		(from GFE #9)	
1002. Homeowner's insurance months @ $ per month $			
1003. Mortgage insurance months @ $ per month $			
1004. Property taxes months @ $ per month $			
1005. months @ $ per month $			
1006. months @ $ per month $			
1007. Aggregate Adjustment –$			
1100. Title Charges			
1101. Title services and lender's title insurance		(from GFE #4)	
1102. Settlement or closing fee	$		
1103. Owner's title insurance		(from GFE #5)	
1104. Lender's title insurance	$		
1105. Lender's title policy limit $			
1106. Owner's title policy limit $			
1107. Agent's portion of the total title insurance premium	$		
1108. Underwriter's portion of the total title insurance premium	$		
1200. Government Recording and Transfer Charges			
1201. Government recording charges		(from GFE #7)	
1202. Deed $ Mortgage $ Releases $			
1203. Transfer taxes		(from GFE #8)	
1204. City/County tax/stamps Deed $ Mortgage $			
1205. State tax/stamps Deed $ Mortgage $			
1206.			
1300. Additional Settlement Charges			
1301. Required services that you can shop for		(from GFE #6)	
1302.	$		
1303.	$		
1304.			
1305.			
1400. Total Settlement Charges (enter on lines 103, Section J and 502, Section K)			

FIGURE 22.4   (Continued).

Comparison of Good Faith Estimate (GFE) and HUD-1 Charges		Good Faith Estimate	HUD-1
Charges That Cannot Increase	**HUD-1 Line Number**		
Our origination charge	# 801		
Your credit or charge (points) for the specific interest rate chosen	# 802		
Your adjusted origination charges	# 803		
Transfer taxes	#1203		

Charges That in Total Cannot Increase More Than 10%		Good Faith Estimate	HUD-1
Government recording charges	# 1201		
	#		
	#		
	#		
	#		
	#		
	#		
	#		
Total			
Increase between GFE and HUD-1 Charges		$ or	%

Charges That Can Change		Good Faith Estimate	HUD-1
Initial deposit for your escrow account	#1001		
Daily interest charges	# 901 $ /day		
Homeowner's insurance	# 903		
	#		
	#		
	#		

Loan Terms

Your initial loan amount is	$
Your loan term is	▨ years
Your initial interest rate is	▨ %
Your initial monthly amount owed for principal, interest, and and any mortgage insurance is	$ ▨ includes ☐ Principal ☐ Interest ☐ Mortgage Insurance
Can your interest rate rise?	☐ No. ☐ Yes, it can rise to a maximum of ▨%. The first change will be on ▨ and can change again every ▨ after ▨ . Every change date, your interest rate can increase or decrease by ▨ %. Over the life of the loan, your interest rate is guaranteed to never be **lower** than ▨ % or **higher** than ▨ %.
Even if you make payments on time, can your loan balance rise?	☐ No. ☐ Yes, it can rise to a maximum of $ ▨ .
Even if you make payments on time, can your monthly amount owed for principal, interest, and mortgage insurance rise?	☐ No. ☐ Yes, the first increase can be on ▨ and the monthly amount owed can rise to $ ▨ . The maximum it can ever rise to is $ ▨ .
Does your loan have a prepayment penalty?	☐ No. ☐ Yes, your maximum prepayment penalty is $ ▨ .
Does your loan have a balloon payment?	☐ No. ☐ Yes, you have a balloon payment of $ ▨ due in ▨ years on ▨ .
Total monthly amount owed including escrow account payments	☐ You do not have a monthly escrow payment for items, such as property taxes and homeowner's insurance. You must pay these items directly yourself. ☐ You have an additional monthly escrow payment of $ ▨ that results in a total initial monthly amount owed of $ ▨ . This includes principal, interest, any mortgage insurance and any items checked below: ☐ Property taxes ☐ Homeowner's insurance ☐ Flood insurance ☐ ▨ ☐ ▨ ☐ ▨

Note: If you have any questions about the Settlement Charges and Loan Terms listed on this form, please contact your lender.

Limits On Good Faith Estimate Increase

Before 2010, lender only needed to make a good faith estimate, and if the final amount required at settlement varied, the lender had little responsibility. If the final loan closing ("settlement") figures differed from the good faith estimate ("GFE"), the borrower was suddenly required to come up with the additional funds on the day before or the day of the closing. The U.D. Department of Housing and Urban Development (HUD) felt lenders were abusing the good faith estimates requirement. One of the biggest changes HUD made in the 2010 regulations was the limit placed on which amounts in the GFE could change and by how much.

Three Categories of GFE Charges

Since 2010, there are three categories of good faith estimates ("GFE"). The first category represents settlement values that cannot change from the GFE, and includes items totally under a lender's control such as lender's origination fees, points, and transfer taxes. The second category limits any settlement values from exceeding 10% more than the GFE unless there are "changed circumstances." This category includes all other lender-required services, title insurance policy (if identified by name on the GFE or if lender selected), and government recording charges. The final category includes all other costs, and these can vary without limit provided the lender made a good faith estimate of their probable costs at time of the GFE statement. Typical examples include title insurance policy costs not identified by name on the GFE, services chosen by the borrower such as homeowners insurance, and daily interest costs.

The regulations specify what qualifies as "changed circumstances" that permit the settlement amount to increase by up to 10% over the GFE. The changed circumstances are limited to such emergencies as acts of war, disasters, and other causes of nature. It also allows information regarding the transaction or the borrower that arose after the GFE, and was either (1) inaccurate through no fault of the lender, (2) newly discovered and not relied upon in making the GFE, or (3) involved unique circumstances such as boundary line disputes, need for flood insurance, or environmental issues. Therefore, mere fluctuations in the market would not qualify as changed circumstances.

However, if the interest rate on the loan was locked in and that locked in rate expired, or if there was no lock on the interest rate, then the rate at time of settlement can change, as well any costs directly relevant to the rate charged on that loan.

Example of Allowed Changes to GFE

Because RESPA amounts were well-litigated areas of the law and was a frequent method of attack when challenging a lender, it is worth understanding exactly how the limits work. When the limits are exceeded and this error is brought to the lender's attention, the lender must reimburse all excess charges.

For example, assume the borrower is taking out a $500,000 loan. The lender quotes 1.5 points on the GFE statement, and the ALTA policy by a named title insurance company listed on the GFE is estimated to cost $850. At closing, the settlement statement lists 2 points and $1,000 for the title insurance policy. Under Regulation X, the points cannot exceed 1.5, and the lender must reimburse the borrower for the extra ½ point. Further, the title policy cost cannot exceed $935 ($850 + 10% maximum increase). Therefore, the borrower would be due a refund of $2,500 for points and $65 for title insurance.

STUDY QUESTIONS (TRUE–FALSE)

1. Title insurance policies ensure that title to real estate is free from all liens and encumbrances.

2. Title insurance is essential and mandatory in the purchase of real estate in California.

3. The homeowner's and the lender's policies of title insurance both insure against the risk of forgery.

4. Usually, either the lender orders an ALTA policy or the buyer orders a CLTA policy, but rarely do both parties obtain title policies on the same parcel of real estate.

5. The ALTA policy insures against unrecorded mechanic's lien.

6. Neither the ALTA nor the CLTA policy protects against violations of zoning ordinances.

7. Real estate brokers may, and often do, offer escrow services to other brokers and clients as a means of supplementing their normal income.

8. An escrow is a general agent and bound by the general rules of good faith, full disclosure, and loyalty to the principals.

9. If a seller deposits a termite report in escrow and later wants it returned, even if the buyer objects, the escrow agent may return it because it was and is the seller's report and the seller deposited it.

10. RESPA requires all lenders making loans covered by RESPA provide the borrower with a good faith estimate of the anticipated costs.

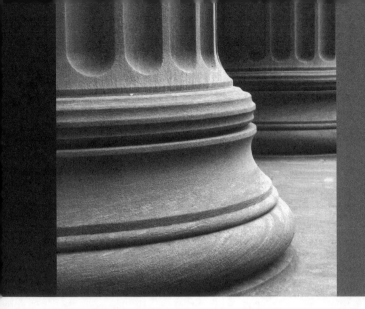

NATURE AND CREATION OF AGENCY RELATIONSHIPS

Nature of Agency

An agency relationship arises whenever one person, called the agent, represents another person, called the **principal**, in dealings with third parties. *C.C. 2295.* The creation of any agency relationship automatically imposes on the agent certain fiduciary duties of good faith and of high standards of trust.

Classification of Agencies

Agencies are categorized as *special* or *general* relationships. A special agent is employed for a particular act or transaction; all others are general agents. The mere fact that one person represents another in a series of transactions does not make that person a general agent. Because real estate brokers are employed to negotiate the transfer of special or limited parcels of property, they are special agents.

Comparison to Employee Relationship

An employee has no private trade or business. Rather, the employee works for and renders services in an employer's business and under the control and direction of that employer. An agent works for the employer, but also acts for and in the place of that principal for the express purpose of representation in creating legal relationships with third persons. The same person may be both an agent and an employee; as an agent, that person *represents* the principal. In practice, there is seldom a need to distinguish the services of an employee from those of an agent, because most of the rules relating to duties, authority, and liability apply equally to employees and to agents.

Agency and Broker's Relationship

Comparison to Independent Contractors

An independent contractor renders services for an employer while functioning independently in a private trade, business, or profession. Independent employment in a profession or occupation allows the option of determining the procedures, policies, and manner of work. The contractor is responsible to an employer only as to the results of that work, retaining the sole right to decide on procedures and means by which the work is to be accomplished. Distinguishing between an independent contractor and an employee is often difficult. The key distinction is the extent of control exercised or capable of being exercised by the employer.

Importance of Distinction

Classification as an employee or as an independent contractor may have significant legal ramifications. An employer sometimes escapes liability for the wrongful acts of an independent contractor, although the employer always retains full liability for the acts of an employee committed within the course and scope of employment. Also, an employer has no responsibility to pay Social Security or deduct it from the contractor's paycheck. Finally, the contractor is not covered by workmen's compensation or eligible for unemployment compensation based on work for the employer.

Creation of Express Agency

The typical agency relationship is created by an express contract or by authorization. The contract may be oral unless the statute of frauds or other regulations require it to be in writing. Under the equal dignities rule of the statute of frauds, almost all real estate contracts must be in writing; therefore, so, too, must the agency relationships dealing with those contract rights.

Creation of Implied Agency

An agency may be implied by the conduct of the parties, sometimes against the will of one of the parties. Because consideration is not a requirement for the formation of an agency relationship, a gratuitous offer of assistance may bind a broker to the fiduciary obligations of an agent and create a liability for failure to act. Furthermore, the acts of the parties may themselves create an agency relationship. For example, the acceptance of a deposit from a buyer for the purpose of depositing it in an escrow makes the broker the buyer's agent as to that deposit.

Ostensible Agents

An **ostensible agency** (an agency implied by law) may arise when the principal negligently or intentionally causes a third person reasonably to believe that another is the agent. In this situation, even though that other person is not actually employed by the principal, the law prevents (estops) the principal from denying the creation of an agency relationship. *C.C. 2300.* Thus, if a seller leads others to believe that a person is a broker acting on behalf of the seller, that seller will be bound by the person's act.

Termination of Agency Relationship

An agency relationship may be terminated through the acts of the parties or by operation of the law.

End of Employment

Typically, in real estate, the relationship ends at the expiration of the listing term or upon completion of the sales transaction. The courts are clear that a broker's duties end upon close of escrow and the broker has no further duties towards that client. *Robinson v. Grossman (1997) 57 C.A. 4th 634.* Even though most parties call their agent if a dispute arises after escrow, and most brokers do try to offer limited help, the agents have no legal obligation to do so.

Death or Incapacity

Generally, the death or incapacity of either the principal or the agent terminates the agency. Thus, under most powers of attorney, the death of an owner would automatically terminate any existing listing agreement. It is possible to execute a special power of attorney, called a *durable power of attorney*, that provides that the subsequent incapacity of the principal shall not revoke or inhibit the effect of the agency relationship. *C.C. 2400 et seq.*

Revocation

The principal may revoke the listing at any time. If the **revocation** occurs because of the broker's failure to use due diligence, the broker receives no commission. However, if the agency is revoked without legal justification, the principal will be liable to the broker for damage, which usually amounts to the full amount of the broker's commission. *Blank v. Borden (1974) 11 C.3d 963.*

Irrevocable if Coupled with an Interest

An agency, coupled with an interest, is irrevocable. However, such an agency arises only when it is created for the benefit of the agent (such as to protect some title or right of the agent), and mere use of words, such as "irrevocable" or "agency coupled with an interest," is insufficient. A real estate broker's listing does not qualify as irrevocable, because the broker's sole interest is "in the proceeds" as compensation for the agency and not "in the subject of the agency." *Jay v. Dollarhide (1970) 3 C.A.3d 1001.*

Real Estate Activities on Internet

The Internet has and is changing the way that some firms and individuals market real estate. Despite the erroneous belief that the World Wide Web ("Web") is like the unregulated "wild, wild west," users are still bound by the normal laws affecting transactions. Regulatory law tends to view the Internet merely as a vehicle for reaching a wide audience, but does not exempt it from the usual laws and regulations concerning real estate, contracts, and torts.

Most firms have Web sites that promote their company, explain their services, and offer various amount of consumer information. Firms often consider a Web site as a mandatory requirement of doing business. The question becomes more complicated, when companies may be "virtual offices," having no physical office except on the Web.

The California Department of Real Estate requires that any activities for which a real estate license is required must be by a licensee. The mere fact that the medium used is the Internet does not excuse any license violations. For example, out-of-state brokers may not solicit California residents unless they are licensed in this state. Thus, a Nevada broker might state on the Web that the property being sold is only available to Nevada inhabitants, or not to California residents.

The Web is evolving both in methods of use and in the number of laws specifically regulating its use. The federal government accounting office ("GAO") did a report in 2005 that identified the following four levels of Internet use in the real estate area:

Full-Service Discount Brokerages

These firms use the Internet as an adjunct to their normal functions of listing, selling, appraising, and closing real estate transactions, but they do so for a reduced fee. Such offices were not uncommon before the Web, but with the popularity of the Internet, their number has mushroomed. The laws governing such brokerages in California have not changed.

Limited-Service Discount Brokerages

These firms offer discounts but also perform fewer services than a full service discount broker performs. Frequently such firms offer less marketing, relying on pictures and virtual tours to sell the property, with less emphasis on physical tours of the available property. Frequently, property posted on these Internet sites is not listed with the Multiple Listing Service, thereby saving the MLS fees.

Information and Referral Companies

There is a wide variety of this type of company, some of whom merely act as a referral service. They find customers who want to buy or sell their property and steer them to real estate brokers enrolled the referral program and extracting a referral fee.

Alternative Listing Web Sites

The Web site provides an alternative way of displaying a large number of properties for sale. It is analogous in function to but separate from the Multiple Listing Service ("MLS"). Most commonly, such sites are used by individuals who want to sell their own property. They are the Web equivalents of the classified ads in the local newspapers, and include such traditional sites as Craig's list, eBay, and other such venues.

REAL ESTATE BROKERS

Definition of Broker

A real estate **broker** is someone who, for compensation or expectation of compensation, represents another in the sale or transfer of an interest in real estate. *B.&P.C. 10131.* Brokers include not only those who negotiate or solicit the sale, purchase, and exchange of property, but also those who negotiate loans and leases, manage property, service trust deeds, and are involved in most other transactions of real estate in which they act on behalf of others in expectation of a commission. *B.&P.C. 10131–10131.3.* Thus, even the operation of a rental data agency that merely supplies information about available rentals requires a real estate license. *Rees v. Dept. of Real Estate (1977) 76 C.A.3d 286.*

Exception for Own Property

Anyone dealing with personal property or operating under a power of attorney is exempt from licensure. Also exempt are attorneys working as such, trustees selling property under a deed of trust, and certain institutional lenders. Finally, resident managers of apartments (not condominiums) and their employees are exempt, as are ordinary office and clerical help functioning as such.

Exceptions for Finders

Finders (intermediaries) require no licenses. The finder who engages in any negotiation or does more than merely introduce the parties to a transaction ceases to become a finder. Any act other than mere introduction of the parties by the finder (such as solicitation or negotiation of terms) is illegal and in violation of the Real Estate Law unless the finder is a licensed broker or salesperson.

Salespersons

A **salesperson** is any licensed person employed by the broker in a professional capacity. *B.&P.C. 10132.* A salesperson must work for a broker and may not operate independent of the broker's supervision. For example, the employing broker must maintain reasonable supervision over the salespeople, including such rules, procedures, and systems as are necessary for such supervision. *Comm. Regs. 2725.* However, since 1997, brokers are no longer required by regulation to review and initial all deposit receipts and other important documents relating to real estate transactions within five working days of execution.

The distinction between a broker and a salesperson is significant. The broker, because of his education and experience, is able to work for the public. The broker is an agent of the parties to the transaction, usually the seller. The salesperson, on the other hand, is solely an agent of the broker. The salesperson cannot contract with the public or accept money from anyone other than the broker. All contracts and commissions must be paid to the broker. A broker can make a secured real estate loan at 25 percent interest, but if a salesperson makes the same loan, the salesperson will be guilty of usury. *People v. Asuncion (1984) 152 C.A.3d 422.* The salesperson may work for only one broker at a time, may not contract in his or her own name, and must receive any commissions through the employing broker. Furthermore, the employment agreement must be in writing and retained by the broker for at least three years after termination of employment.

See Figure 23.1 for a typical agreement that a salesperson or broker-association might sign when working with a real estate broker.

FIGURE 23.1   Independent contractor agreement.

CALIFORNIA
ASSOCIATION
OF REALTORS®

INDEPENDENT CONTRACTOR AGREEMENT
(Between Broker and Associate-Licensee)
(C.A.R. Form ICA, Revised 4/09)

This Agreement, dated _____, is made between _____
_____ ("Broker") and
_____ ("Associate-Licensee").
In consideration of the covenants and representations contained in this Agreement, Broker and Associate-Licensee agree as follows:

1. **BROKER:** Broker represents that Broker is duly licensed as a real estate broker by the State of California, ☐ doing business as _____ (firm name), ☐ a sole proprietorship, ☐ a partnership, or ☐ a corporation. Broker is a member of the _____ Association(s) of REALTORS®, and a subscriber to the _____ Multiple Listing Service(s). Broker shall keep Broker's license current during the term of this Agreement.

2. **ASSOCIATE-LICENSEE:** Associate-Licensee represents that: **(i)** he/she is duly licensed by the State of California as a ☐ real estate broker, ☐ real estate salesperson, and **(ii)** he/she has not used any other names within the past five years, except _____. Associate-Licensee shall keep his/her license current during the term of this Agreement, including satisfying all applicable continuing education and provisional license requirements.

3. **INDEPENDENT CONTRACTOR RELATIONSHIP:**
   A. Broker and Associate-Licensee intend that, to the maximum extent permissible by law: **(i)** This Agreement does not constitute an employment agreement by either party; **(ii)** Broker and Associate-Licensee are independent contracting parties with respect to all services rendered under this Agreement; and **(iii)** This Agreement shall not be construed as a partnership.
   B. Broker shall not: **(i)** restrict Associate-Licensee's activities to particular geographical areas, or **(ii)** dictate Associate-Licensee's activities with regard to hours, leads, open houses, opportunity or floor time, production, prospects, sales meetings, schedule, inventory, time off, vacation, or similar activities, except to the extent required by law.
   C. Associate-Licensee shall not be required to accept an assignment by Broker to service any particular current or prospective listing or parties.
   D. Except as required by law: **(i)** Associate-Licensee retains sole and absolute discretion and judgment in the methods, techniques, and procedures to be used in soliciting and obtaining listings, sales, exchanges, leases, rentals, or other transactions, and in carrying out Associate-Licensee's selling and soliciting activities; **(ii)** Associate-Licensee is under the control of Broker as to the results of Associate-Licensee's work only, and not as to the means by which those results are accomplished; **(iii)** Associate-Licensee has no authority to bind Broker by any promise or representation; and **(iv)** Broker shall not be liable for any obligation or liability incurred by Associate-Licensee.
   E. Associate-Licensee's only remuneration shall be the compensation specified in paragraph 8.
   F. Associate-Licensee who only performs as a real estate sales agent, shall not be treated as an employee for state and federal tax purposes. However, an Associate-Licencee who performs loan activity shall be treated as an employee for state and federal tax purposes unless the activity satisfies the legal requirements to establish an independent contractor relationship.
   G. The fact the Broker may carry workers' compensation insurance for Broker's own benefit and for the mutual benefit of Broker and licensees associated with Broker, including Associate-Licensees, shall not create an inference of employment.
   (Workers' Compensation Advisory: Even though Associate-Licensees may be treated as independent contractors for tax and other purposes, the California Labor and Workforce Development Agency considers them to be employees for workers' compensation purposes. According to that Agency: **(i)** Broker must obtain workers' compensation insurance for Associate-Licensees and **(ii)** Broker, not Associate-Licensees, must bear the cost of workers' compensation insurance. Penalties for failure to carry workers' compensation include, among others, the issuance of stop-work orders and fines of up to $1,000 per agent, not to exceed $100,000 per company.)

4. **LICENSED ACTIVITY:** All listings of property, and all agreements, acts or actions for performance of licensed acts, which are taken or performed in connection with this Agreement, shall be taken and performed in the name of Broker. Associate-Licensee agrees to and does hereby contribute all right and title to such listings to Broker for the benefit and use of Broker, Associate-Licensee, and other licensees associated with Broker. Broker shall make available to Associate-Licensee, equally with other licensees associated with Broker, all current listings in Broker's office, except any listing which Broker may choose to place in the exclusive servicing of Associate-Licensee or one or more other specific licensees associated with Broker. Associate-Licensee shall provide and pay for all professional licenses, supplies, services, and other items required in connection with Associate-Licensee's activities under this Agreement, or any listing or transaction, without reimbursement from Broker except as required by law. Associate-Licensee shall work diligently and with his/her best efforts to: **(i)** sell, exchange, lease, or rent properties listed with Broker or other cooperating Brokers; **(ii)** solicit additional listings, clients, and customers; and **(iii)** otherwise promote the business of serving the public in real estate transactions to the end that Broker and Associate-Licensee may derive the greatest benefit possible, in accordance with law. Associate-Licensee shall not commit any unlawful act under federal, state or local law or regulation while conducting licensed activity. Associate-Licensee shall at all times be familiar, and comply, with all applicable federal, state and local laws, including, but not limited to, anti-discrimination laws and restrictions against the giving or accepting of a fee, or other thing of value, for the referral of business to title companies, escrow companies, home inspection companies, pest control companies and other settlement service providers pursuant to the California Business and Professions Code and the Real Estate Settlement Procedures Acts (RESPA). Broker shall make available for Associate-Licensee's use, along with other licensees associated with Broker, the facilities of the real estate office operated by Broker at _____ and the facilities of any other office locations made available by Broker pursuant to this Agreement.

Broker's Initials   (_____)(_____)
Associate-Licensee's Initials (_____)(_____)

Reviewed by _____ Date _____

EQUAL HOUSING OPPORTUNITY

ICA REVISED 4/09 (PAGE 1 OF 3)

INDEPENDENT CONTRACTOR AGREEMENT (ICA PAGE 1 OF 3)

FIGURE 23.1 *(Continued)*.

5. **PROPRIETARY INFORMATION AND FILES: (A)** All files and documents pertaining to listings, leads and transactions are the property of Broker and shall be delivered to Broker by Associate-Licensee immediately upon request or termination of this Agreement. **(B)** Associate- Licensee acknowledges that Broker's method of conducting business is a protected trade secret. **(C)** Associate-Licensee shall not use to his/her own advantage, or the advantage of any other person, business, or entity, except as specifically agreed in writing, either during Associate-Licensee's association with Broker, or thereafter, any information gained for or from the business, or files of Broker.

6. **SUPERVISION:** Associate-Licensee, within 24 hours (or ☐ _____) after preparing, signing, or receiving same, shall submit to Broker, or Broker's designated licensee: **(i)** all documents which may have a material effect upon the rights and duties of principals in a transaction, **(ii)** any documents or other items connected with a transaction pursuant to this Agreement in the possession of or available to Associate-Licensee; and **(iii)** all documents associated with any real estate transaction in which Associate-Licensee is a principal.

7. **TRUST FUNDS:** All trust funds shall be handled in compliance with the Business and Professions Code, and other applicable laws.

8. **COMPENSATION:**

   A. **TO BROKER:** Compensation shall be charged to parties who enter into listing or other agreements for services requiring a real estate license:

   ☐ as shown in "Exhibit A" attached, which is incorporated as a part of this Agreement by reference, or

   ☐ as follows: _____

   _____

   Any deviation which is not approved in writing in advance by Broker, shall be: **(1)** deducted from Associate-Licensee's compensation, if lower than the amount or rate approved above; and, **(2)** subject to Broker approval, if higher than the amount approved above. Any permanent change in commission schedule shall be disseminated by Broker to Associate-Licensee.

   B. **TO ASSOCIATE-LICENSEE:** Associate-Licensee shall receive a share of compensation actually collected by Broker, on listings or other agreements for services requiring a real estate license, which are solicited and obtained by Associate-Licensee, and on transactions of which Associate-Licensee's activities are the procuring cause, as follows:

   ☐ as shown in "Exhibit B" attached, which is incorporated as a part of this Agreement by reference, or

   ☐ other: _____

   _____

   C. **PARTNERS, TEAMS, AND AGREEMENTS WITH OTHER ASSOCIATE-LICENSEES IN OFFICE:** If Associate-Licensee and one or more other Associate-Licensees affiliated with Broker participate on the same side (either listing or selling) of a transaction, the commission allocated to their combined activities shall be divided by Broker and paid to them according to their written agreement. Broker shall have the right to withhold total compensation if there is a dispute between associate-licensees, or if there is no written agreement, or if no written agreement has been provided to Broker.

   D. **EXPENSES AND OFFSETS:** If Broker elects to advance funds to pay expenses or liabilities of Associate-Licensee, or for an advance payment of, or draw upon, future compensation, Broker may deduct the full amount advanced from compensation payable to Associate-Licensee on any transaction without notice. If Associate-Licensee's compensation is subject to a lien, garnishment or other restriction on payment, Broker shall charge Associate-Licensee a fee for complying with such restriction.

   E. **PAYMENT: (i)** All compensation collected by Broker and due to Associate-Licensee shall be paid to Associate-Licensee, after deduction of expenses and offsets, immediately or as soon thereafter as practicable, except as otherwise provided in this Agreement, or a separate written agreement between Broker and Associate-Licensee. **(ii)** Compensation shall not be paid to Associate-Licensee until both the transaction and file are complete. **(iii)** Broker is under no obligation to pursue collection of compensation from any person or entity responsible for payment. Associate-Licensee does not have the independent right to pursue collection of compensation for activities which require a real estate license which were done in the name of Broker. **(iv)** Expenses which are incurred in the attempt to collect compensation shall be paid by Broker and Associate-Licensee in the same proportion as set forth for the division of compensation (paragraph 8(B)). **(v)** If there is a known or pending claim against Broker or Associate-Licensee on transactions for which Associate-Licensee has not yet been paid, Broker may withhold from compensation due Associate-Licensee on that transaction amounts for which Associate-Licensee could be responsible under paragraph 14, until such claim is resolved. **(vi)** Associate-Licensee shall not be entitled to any advance payment from Broker upon future compensation.

   F. **UPON OR AFTER TERMINATION:** If this Agreement is terminated while Associate-Licensee has listings or pending transactions that require further work normally rendered by Associate-Licensee, Broker shall make arrangements with another associate-licensee to perform the required work, or Broker shall perform the work him/herself. The licensee performing the work shall be reasonably compensated for completing work on those listings or transactions, and such reasonable compensation shall be deducted from Associate-Licensee's share of compensation. Except for such offset, Associate-Licensee shall receive the compensation due as specified above.

9. **TERMINATION OF RELATIONSHIP:** Broker or Associate-Licensee may terminate their relationship under this Agreement at any time, with or without cause. After termination, Associate-Licensee shall not solicit: **(i)** prospective or existing clients or customers based upon company- generated leads obtained during the time Associate-Licensee was affiliated with Broker; **(ii)** any principal with existing contractual obligations to Broker; or **(iii)** any principal with a contractual transactional obligation for which Broker is entitled to be compensated. Even after termination, this Agreement shall govern all disputes and claims between Broker and Associate-Licensee connected with their relationship under this Agreement, including obligations and liabilities arising from existing and completed listings, transactions, and services.

Broker's Initials (_____)(_____)
Associate-Licensee's Initials (_____)(_____)

ICA REVISED 4/09 (PAGE 2 OF 3)

Reviewed by _____ Date _____

EQUAL HOUSING OPPORTUNITY

INDEPENDENT CONTRACTOR AGREEMENT (ICA PAGE 2 OF 3)

FIGURE 23.1 (Continued).

10. **DISPUTE RESOLUTION:**
    A. Mediation: Mediation is recommended as a method of resolving disputes arising out of this Agreement between Broker and Associate-Licensee.
    B. Arbitration: All disputes or claims between Associate-Licensee and other licensee(s) associated with Broker, or between Associate-Licensee and Broker, arising from or connected in any way with this Agreement, which cannot be adjusted between the parties involved, shall be submitted to the Association of REALTORS® of which all such disputing parties are members for arbitration pursuant to the provisions of its Bylaws, as may be amended from time to time, which are incorporated as a part of this Agreement by reference. If the Bylaws of the Association do not cover arbitration of the dispute, or if the Association declines jurisdiction over the dispute, then arbitration shall be pursuant to the rules of California law. The Federal Arbitration Act, Title 9, U.S. Code, Section 1, et seq., shall govern this Agreement.
11. **AUTOMOBILE:** Associate-Licensee shall maintain automobile insurance coverage for liability and property damage in the following amounts $_____/$_____. Broker shall be named as an additional insured party on Associate-Licensee's policies. A copy of the endorsement showing Broker as an additional insured shall be provided to Broker.
12. **PERSONAL ASSISTANTS:** Associate-Licensee may make use of a personal assistant, provided the following requirements are satisfied. Associate-Licensee shall have a written agreement with the personal assistant which establishes the terms and responsibilities of the parties to the employment agreement, including, but not limited to, compensation, supervision and compliance with applicable law. The agreement shall be subject to Broker's review and approval. Unless otherwise agreed, if the personal assistant has a real estate license, that license must be provided to the Broker. Both Associate-Licensee and personal assistant must sign any agreement that Broker has established for such purposes.
13. **OFFICE POLICY MANUAL:** If Broker's office policy manual, now or as modified in the future, conflicts with or differs from the terms of this Agreement, the terms of the office policy manual shall govern the relationship between Broker and Associate-Licensee.
14. **INDEMNITY AND HOLD HARMLESS; NOTICE OF CLAIMS: A.** Regarding any action taken or omitted by Associate-Licensee, or others working through, or on behalf of Associate-Licensee in connection with services rendered or to be rendered pursuant to this Agreement: (i) Associate-Licensee agrees to indemnify, defend and hold Broker harmless from all claims, disputes, litigation, judgments, awards, costs and attorney's fees, arising therefrom and (ii) Associate-Licensee shall immediately notify Broker if Associate-Licensee is served with or becomes aware of a lawsuit or claim regarding any such action. **B.** Any such claims or costs payable pursuant to this Agreement, are due as follows:
    ☐ Paid in full by Associate-Licensee, who hereby agrees to indemnify and hold harmless Broker for all such sums, or
    ☐ In the same ratio as the compensation split as it existed at the time the compensation was earned by Associate-Licensee or
    ☐ Other: _____

    Payment from Associate-Licensee is due at the time Broker makes such payment and can be offset from any compensation due Associate-Licensee as above. Broker retains the authority to settle claims or disputes, whether or not Associate-Licensee consents to such settlement.
15. **ADDITIONAL PROVISIONS:** _____
16. **DEFINITIONS:** As used in this Agreement, the following terms have the meanings indicated:
    (A) "Listing" means an agreement with a property owner or other party to locate a buyer, exchange party, lessee, or other party to a transaction involving real property, a mobile home, or other property or transaction which may be brokered by a real estate licensee, or an agreement with a party to locate or negotiate for any such property or transaction.
    (B) "Compensation" means compensation for acts requiring a real estate license, regardless of whether calculated as a percentage of transaction price, flat fee, hourly rate, or in any other manner.
    (C) "Transaction" means a sale, exchange, lease, or rental of real property, a business opportunity, or a manufactured home, which may lawfully be brokered by a real estate licensee.
17. **ATTORNEY FEES:** In any action, proceeding, or arbitration between Broker and Associate-Licensee arising from or related to this Agreement, the prevailing Broker or Associate-Licensee shall be entitled to reasonable attorney fees and costs.
18. **ENTIRE AGREEMENT:** All prior agreements between the parties concerning their relationship as Broker and Associate-Licensee are incorporated in this Agreement, which constitutes the entire contract. Its terms are intended by the parties as a final and complete expression of their agreement with respect to its subject matter, and may not be contradicted by evidence of any prior agreement or contemporaneous oral agreement. This Agreement may not be amended, modified, altered, or changed except by a further agreement in writing executed by Broker and Associate-Licensee.

Broker:

_____
(Brokerage firm name)

By _____
Its Broker/Office manager (circle one)

_____
(Print name)

_____
(Address)

_____
(City, State, Zip)

_____
(Telephone)   (Fax)

Associate-Licensee:

_____
(Signature)

_____
(Print name)

_____
(Address)

_____
(City, State, Zip)

_____
(Telephone)   (Fax)

Published and Distributed by:
REAL ESTATE BUSINESS SERVICES, INC.
a subsidiary of the California Association of REALTORS®
525 South Virgil Avenue, Los Angeles, California 90020

ICA REVISED 4/09 (PAGE 3 OF 3)

Reviewed by _____ Date _____

EQUAL HOUSING OPPORTUNITY

INDEPENDENT CONTRACTOR AGREEMENT (ICA PAGE 3 OF 3)

Status of Real Estate Broker

The real estate broker is an independent contractor who also functions as an agent of the principal. However, the salespersons working for the broker are classified differently, depending on the purpose of the classification. The common practice of designating the salesperson as an independent contractor is not determinative or controlling.

Employee for General Purposes

Under general law, the salesperson is an employee. *Gipson v. Davis Realty Co. (1963) 215 C.A.2d 190*. The broker has a law-imposed duty to supervise and direct the activities of salespersons; hence, the salesperson lacks the freedom of action to qualify as an independent contractor. Consequently, the broker remains liable to any third parties for acts and damages caused by the salesperson in the course and scope of employment. Brokers should therefore carry and require public liability insurance on all salespersons and be named as a coinsured on each policy.

Employee Eligibility for Workman's Compensation

If a salesperson truly operates as an independent contractor, he or she is not covered by worker's compensation. *Payne v. White House Properties (1980) 112 C.A.3d 465*. However, in most cases the broker retains so much control that the person is really an employee, and the broker must provide worker's compensation insurance. *Lab. C. 3351, 3353*. Because the penalty is so severe for not having insurance, a broker would be wise to always carry insurance unless otherwise advised by an attorney.

Independent Contractor Eligibility for Unemployment Rights

For California state unemployment insurance, the salesperson paid entirely by commission qualifies as an independent contractor. *Un.I.C. 650*.

Employee Eligibility for Payment of Commission

The salesperson is held by law to be an employee for purposes of payment of, or disputes about, earned commissions. Therefore, if a broker fails to pay agents their share of a commission, the salesperson can use the services of the California Labor Commission. *Resnik v. Anderson & Miles Corp. (1980) 109 C.A.3d 569*.

Status Varies for IRS Purposes

Real estate salespersons may be independent contractors, where they pay their own Social Security and self-employment tax. Alternatively, the salesperson could be an employee for tax purposes. If so, the broker would need to contribute to the salesperson's Social Security and make withholdings from the salesperson's salary.

At one time, the distinction was difficult. Most California salespersons were considered employees because of the degree of supervision and responsibility that the law imposed on brokers. Finally, the Internal Revenue Code was amended to simplify and clarify the issue. *I.R.C. 3508.* For tax purposes, a licensed salesperson is considered an independent contractor if

1. Substantially all the remuneration received by the salesperson is related to sales or output, rather than the number of hours worked, and
2. The salesperson has a written contract that states that the relationship will be as an independent contractor and that the person will not be treated as an employee for federal tax purposes.

Whose Agent Is Broker?

Real estate brokers often unknowingly become the agents of different parties during a single transaction. Generally, the broker is the agent of the first employer, which is usually the seller. However, a broker who meets the buyer first and aids the buyer alone in purchasing the property from the seller is the buyer's agent. For purposes of imputing knowledge to a party or deciding who is to bear losses resulting from the broker's conduct, the broker may have a limited agency responsibility to the other party. Absent special facts to the contrary, the broker is the agent of the seller because the seller is the party paying the broker.

Subagents

The law of cooperating brokers, or *subagents*, remains unclear and conflicting in terms of the subagents' liability and right to sue for commissions. The relationship between the principal and the cooperating broker almost needs to be decided case by case.

REGULATION OF BROKERS

Basic Regulations

Besides having the ordinary duties and responsibilities of their agency relationship, brokers are further regulated by the Real Estate Law, *B.&P.C. 10000 et seq.*, and the real estate commissioner's regulations. These laws and regulations protect the public and ensure the competence of licensed individuals. Failure to observe the law or regulations may result in civil penalties, disciplinary action, and even loss of license. Most violations and disciplinary actions against brokers concern mishandling of trust funds and violations of *B.&P.C. 10176* or *10177*.

Handling of Deposits

Any funds received by the broker on behalf of a principal must be promptly given to the principal or deposited in a qualified escrow or trust account. With few exceptions, if the funds are not deposited by the next business day, the broker is guilty of *commingling* those funds. *Comm.Regs. 2832 et seq*. Detailed records must be maintained in the designated format for all trust funds handled by the broker. *B.&P.C. 10145; Comm.Regs. 2830*.

Unlawful Acts of Brokers

B.&P.C. 10176 lists the violations for which a licensee operating as a broker will be disciplined. The most important acts include making false statements or concealing material facts from a principal (misrepresentation); acting as an agent for more than one party without the full consent of all principals (divided agency); mixing the principal's fund with the broker's personal accounts (commingling); failing to disclose broker's full profit to his principal, including surreptitiously purchasing the property at a low price for resale (secret profit); and other forms of dishonest dealing. Other sections regulate false promises, continued misrepresentation, lack of termination dates on exclusive listings, exercising option listings without full disclosure, and forcing property listings from sale of a business opportunity.

Referral Fees

Brokers can pay referral fees only in limited circumstances. A referral fee can be cash, property, or other legal value, and the law varies depending on whom the referral fee is paid. Brokers are allowed to pay referral fees to other brokers and salespeople, provided there is full disclosure to the principals. *B.&P.C. 10176(g)*. Salespeople cannot pay or receive any kind of fee except through their own broker. *B.&P.C. 10137*. Neither brokers nor salespeople can receive a straight referral fee from an escrow company, title, pest control or lender. *B.&P.C. 10177.4* and under federal law, *24 C.F.R. 3500.14*. Finally, the broker can pay a **finder's fee** to an unlicensed person provided that person has not engaged in any activities or negotiations for which a license is required. *78 OPS Ca.l Atty. Gen. 71*.

Unlawful Acts as Individuals

B.&P.C. 10177 covers brokers and prospective licensees while they are not acting as agents in a professional capacity. Included in this section of the code are prohibitions against obtaining a license by fraud; being convicted of a criminal act involving moral turpitude; false or misleading advertising; misuse of the term realtor; violation of any restricted license provisions; misuse of government records; inducing panic selling on the basis of race, color, creed, or national origin; violating the franchise law; and failure to supervise salespersons adequately. A catchall provision covers any other violation of the Real Estate Law.

Other Regulations

Numerous provisions of the Real Estate Law regulate the activities of brokers, including hiring or compensating an unlicensed person who performs real estate acts, failure to inform the parties to a transaction of the selling price, neglecting to give a copy of any document signed by a party to that party, not maintaining one's license available for public inspection, and false or incomplete advertising.

For example, beginning in 2009 licensees must put their Department of Real Estate license number on all "solicitation materials intended to be the first point of contact with consumers." This broad description includes business cards, letterhead stationary, advertising flyers, "for sale" signs, and other solicitation materials.

Real Estate Recovery Fund

A plaintiff can obtain recovery for an uncollectable judgment against a licensee for fraud or misrepresentation from the Real Estate Education, Research, and Recovery Fund, maintained by the Department of Real Estate. The recovery is limited to the amount of the uncollectable judgment or $50,000 per transaction, whichever is less. (The limit is $20,000 for causes of action arising between 2008 and 1980.) This transaction limit applies regardless of the number of plaintiffs, the quantity of parcels involved, or the number of licensees engaged in the transaction. Finally, in no event may the recovery against any one licensee during his or her lifetime exceed $250,000 (however, the lifetime amount is $100,000 for causes of action arising between 2008 and 1980). *B.&P.C. 10474.* The court of appeals ruled that the term licensee only applies to brokers and not to salespeople. Thus, recovery against the Real Estate Recovery Fund only lies for actions committed by brokers.

Thus, if A and B were real estate brokers who defrauded L, M, N, O, P, and Q of $1,000,000 in the sale of a ranch, L, M, N, O, P, and Q could jointly collect only a maximum of $50,000 total from the fund. The number of licensees or parties involved is immaterial, because the one-transaction rule applies. *Fox v. Prime Ventures Ltd. (1978) 86 C.A.3d 333.* However, if L, M, N, O, P, and Q were each defrauded out of $100,000 on six separate transactions by X, a licensee, then the $250,000 per licensee limit would apply. Instead of receiving $50,000 each, they would probably each share proportionately in the $250,000 maximum recovery.

No Special Liability When Acting as Principal

It is not uncommon for a broker to act as a principal and to purchase property personally. In such situations, the broker is not an agent, because the definition of an agent is someone who acts for another person. As a principal the broker has no special obligations or duties toward the other principal. Still, the author feels it would be prudent to notify the other side that one is a licensee. The author had an interesting dialog with the Department of Real Estate on this very point. Although their response is nonbinding, it is set forth in Figure 23.2 because of the informative discussion of brokers' duties when acting as a principal. On April 13, 2004, the Department of Real Estate indicated that the letter in the author's book dated April 6, 1977 "still reflects the state of the law today."

On the flip side, a licensee acting as principal is not entitled to a commission, even if the contract specifies a fee. Because the licensee cannot act as an agent to himself or herself, by law there is no right to a real estate commission. *Horning v. Shilberg (2005) 130 C.A.4th 197.*

APPLY THE LAW

De St. Germain v. Watson
95 C.A.2d 862 (1950)

[A real estate broker, the respondent, accepted a nonnegotiable promissory note from a buyer as a deposit toward the purchase price. The broker made no mention to the seller, his client, about the nature of the deposit, and the deposit receipt (contract of purchase) merely acknowledged acceptance of a $1,000 deposit. The buyer later defaulted on the promissory note and refused to complete the sale.

The seller filed a complaint with the real estate commissioner, the appellant. The respondent broker personally made a partial payment on the promissory note to the seller, who thereafter sought to withdraw the complaint that he had filed with the department of real estate. However, the commissioner investigated the complaint on his own, found the broker guilty of violating the real estate law, and suspended the broker.

continued

The broker sued the commissioner to have the suspension set aside. The trial court vacated the suspension, finding that there was no intent to defraud or any dishonesty, and the commissioner appealed.]

BRAY, JUSTICE. Section 10176 of the Business and Professions Code (the Real Estate Law) provides that the commissioner on his own motion may, and if any person files a verified complaint, shall, investigate the actions of any person engaged in the business or acting in the capacity of a real estate licensee and may temporarily or permanently revoke a real estate license where [among other provisions] the licensee has been guilty of making any substantial misrepresentation or any other conduct, whether of the same or a different character than specified in this section, which constitutes fraud or dishonest dealing. The commissioner found that respondent's action in failing to disclose to his principal that the $1,000 mentioned in the deposit receipt as having been received from the buyer was not cash but a non-negotiable promissory note to respondent, violated the above law.

The trial court found that the petitioner did not intend to nor did mislead the sellers and it is true that the petitioner did not act in a fraudulent nor dishonest manner in his dealings with the said sellers. We agree with such finding insofar as intentional fraud or dishonesty is concerned. However, in spite of the fact that respondent acted in good faith in the matter, he still violated the spirit and letter of the Real Estate Law.

It is a well known fact that prior to the enactment of this law, there were a considerable number of persons engaged in the real estate business who were carrying on that business in an unethical manner, and that one of the purposes of the law was to raise the standards of that profession and to require its members to act fairly and ethically with their clients. Some of the things that brokers had done theretofore, and which were not necessarily illegal or unethical, were prohibited in the interests of protecting the public.

Thus, commingling the money or other property of his principal with his own is expressly prohibited. There were many brokers, prior to the enactment of the law, who placed moneys received for their clients in their personal accounts, and yet who scrupulously paid their clients every cent coming to them. It was not that commingling moneys meant necessarily that the client would be defrauded, but that such a practice might result in fraud or injury to the client. So it is with the undisclosed acceptance of a promissory note. In this case, the broker was well able to make good the full amount of the note had the seller insisted. But the possibilities of fraud, and of injury to a seller by the undisclosed acceptance of a promissory note are unlimited.

APPLY THE LAW

continued

In the first place, the seller is entitled to know before entering into a binding obligation to tie up his property by an agreement to sell, that for some reason the buyer either cannot or will not put up cash. He, rather than his broker, should determine whether the reason for the buyer's not paying cash is satisfactory. He, rather than his broker, should determine whether he is satisfied that a promissory note be accepted as a payment, even though the broker stands ready, as here, to guarantee its payment.

The seller has a right to believe that if the buyer for any reason refused to go on with this agreement, there was that much of the buyer's money to be forfeited and kept by the seller. But when a promissory note is accepted, the money is not there to be kept. The seller has a lawsuit on his hands to collect on the note. He, at least, is entitled to know from his own agent that that might be the situation before he signs the agreement of sale. When a person gives a check he represents that he has the money in the bank to cover it, and that the bank will pay the amount called for. Moreover, if he does not have the money in the bank it may constitute a crime. A note, even one payable on demand, makes no such representation, and the failure to pay when presented is not a crime. In modern business checks are universally accepted as money; promissory notes are not.

The law of California imposed on the real estate agent the same obligation of undivided service and loyalty that it imposes on a trustee in favor of his beneficiary. Violation of his trust is subject to the same punitory consequences that are provided for a disloyal or recreant trustee. Such an agent is charged with the duty of fullest disclosure of all material facts concerning the transaction that might affect the principal's decision.

A real estate broker, like a trustee, has an affirmative duty to disclose all material facts that might influence the decision of his principal; the fact that the prospective buyer cannot or does not make the down payment on the purchase of real property in money but by a promissory note is a material fact that the seller is entitled to know before agreeing to sell; here the agent failed to make such disclosure and hence violated the Real Estate Law as above set forth.

The judgment is reversed [and the broker's suspension is upheld].

FIGURE 23.2   Letter from department of real estate.

STATE OF CALIFORNIA   EDMUND G. BROWN JR., Governor

DEPARTMENT OF REAL ESTATE
714 P Street
Sacramento, CA   95814
(916) 445-6112

April 6, 1977

Ted H. Gordon, Esq.
4280 Redwood Highway, Suite 10
San Rafael, California   94903

Dear Mr. Gordon:

This letter is in answer to the question that you pose in
your letter of April 4, 1977. You ask whether a real
estate broker acting as a principal (buyer) in a real estate
transaction has any duties or obligations to the other
principal (seller) in the transaction beyond what would
be owed by a prospective lay purchaser.

I know of no statutory law, regulations nor decisional
law which imposes any special duty upon a real estate
licensee acting exclusively as a principal in a real estate
transaction. There are, of course, innumerable cases that
discuss the duty that a licensee has where he is an agent
in the transaction to disclose any interest that he will
acquire as a purchaser or through his relationship to the
purchaser. If the licensee does not purport to be acting
in the capacity of an agent in the transaction, I know of
no decisional law that even goes so far as to say that he
must disclose the fact that he is a real estate licensee.

There are cases in which the duty that a real estate
licensee owes to the purchaser of real property in a
transaction is distinguished from the fiduciary duty that
the licensee owes to the seller. This duty is referred to
as a duty of "fair and honest dealing" imposed upon all
real estate licensees ... in all of their dealings as such
licensees." Realty Projects, Inc. v. Smith, 32 CA 3d 204.
While this standard is somewhat less demanding than that
imposed upon a fiduciary, it nevertheless only applies in
those instances where a licensee is acting in an agency
capacity in a transaction.

Sincerely,

W. Jerome Thomas
Chief Legal Officer

WJT/pk

MEMBER: National Association of Real Estate License Law Officials

BROKER'S OBLIGATION TO CLIENTS

Nature of Duties

Several separate sets of standards regulate the real estate broker's conduct toward the client. First, under civil law, the fiduciary duties are due by all agents to their principal. The term *fiduciary* encompasses the broad legal duties of integrity and fidelity owed by all agents. It emphasizes honest dealings, loyalty, and utmost good faith, rather than mere legal obligation. Indeed, the agent's fiduciary duties correspond exactly to those imposed by law on a trustee acting on behalf of the beneficiaries of a trust. *C.C. 2322.* Second, as a professional agent claiming expertise within a specialized area, the broker is charged with operating under the standard of care expected of similar experts. Finally, the broker is bound to the special rules and standards imposed by the Real Estate Commission.

Violation of Duties

A broker who violates any fiduciary duties is deemed to have committed fraud on the principal. *C.C. 2234.* The principal may recover any secret profits made by the broker. Furthermore, the principal may recover any profits lost by the broker's breach of duty. *Jolton v. Mister Graf & Co. (1942) 53 C.A.2d 516.* Generally, the principal may recover any losses sustained because of the broker's ineptitude or misconduct. *C.C. 3333, 1709.* Furthermore, the broker is subject to disciplinary action by the real estate commissioner. *B.&P.C. 10176, 10177.*

Duty of Good Faith

The real estate broker "is bound to act in the highest of good faith" toward the principal and "may not obtain any advantage" over that client "by the slightest misrepresentation, concealment, threat, or adverse pressure of any kind." *C.C. 2228, 2322.* This duty of good faith includes total truthfulness, absolute integrity, and total fidelity to the client and the client's interest.

Example

In one case the broker, employed by the lessor, suggested that a prospective tenant hold out and obtain a longer lease than the landlord wanted to give. The court held that the broker had violated fiduciary duty, denied a commission, and held him liable for any damages suffered by the principal. The court also recognized that a similar situation arises if a seller's broker advises a buyer to try to obtain the seller's property at a lower price or on more favorable terms than those asked by the seller. *Mitchell v. Gould (1928) 90 C.A. 647.* Any such statements are made at the broker's risk, although they must be evaluated on the basis of reasonableness, distinguishing between honest negotiation and unpermitted disclosure.

Duty of Full Disclosure

The broker owes the principal a duty of full and complete disclosure of all material facts that may in any way influence the principal's decision, actions, or willingness to enter into a transaction. *C.C. 2020.* The broker must not only disclose all material facts known or discovered during an agency, but must also inform the principal of all relevant information acquired and known through general knowledge as a broker. Normally a broker's duty to disclose does not include an obligation to advise or warn about adverse tax consequences. *Carleton v. Tortosa (1993) 14 C.A.4th 745.*

Example

A broker receives two offers on a property, but fails to disclose either the higher or the lower offer. The broker has violated the duty of full disclosure by not communicating all offers on the property, even, apparently, unenforceable oral offers. *Duin v. Security First Natl. Bank (1955) 132 C.A.2d Supp. 904.*

Duty of Loyalty: No Adverse Interest

Closely tied to the duties of good faith and full disclosure is the broker's obligation to refrain from acquiring any interest adverse to that of the principal without a full and complete disclosure of all material facts. *C.C. 2231, 2230.* This duty prevents a broker from acting for two clients without the full consent of each principal. *B.&P.C. 10176d.* Furthermore, and frequently litigated, a broker may not obtain *secret profit* out of the agency without the principal's full and knowledgeable consent. *B.&P.C. 10176g.* Secret profits extend beyond mere sales to dummy corporations and to friends who hold the property for the broker. The duty also includes option listing and net listing sales, as well as any other situation in which the broker has a potential for an undisclosed profit, obtained either directly or indirectly.

Example

The broker presented to the seller an offer from a corporation of which, the broker disclosed, he was the president and in which he was financially involved. The court found the broker liable for failing to reveal that he and his wife were the only shareholders and that the corporation was not the ultimate purchaser. *Baston v. Strehlow (1968) 68 C.2d 662.*

Duty to Use Professional Standard of Care

The real estate broker, as a professional agent, must use a higher degree of skill and knowledge than the average layperson. The broker is charged with and responsible for operating in a manner consistent with that expected of the ordinary and reasonable professional in the field. Because the client can and usually does rely on the broker's advice, the broker is bound to investigate and discover that information and those facts necessary to advise the principal on the real estate transaction.

Example

A broker sold a house located on filled land that was not properly compacted. The seller had experienced problems, but concealed the fact from the broker and the buyer. The broker never had actual knowledge of the problem, but when he inspected the property, he noticed certain "red flags" indicative of soil problems and failed to investigate and discover the condition. The broker was held liable in negligence for failing to discover the problem. *Easton v. Strassburger (1984) 152 C.A.3d 90.*

Duty to Account

The real estate broker is responsible to the client for all monies received from or on behalf of that client. *C.C. 2229.* These funds belong exclusively to the principal, and they must be paid over on demand. Furthermore, the broker may not commingle the client's funds with personal money. *B.&P.C. 10176e.* Rather, all funds must be maintained in a separate trust account.

Example

A broker receives $1,000 cash deposit from the buyer toward the purchase price on the seller's property. The broker deposits the money in a business account and issues a $1,000 check to the seller promptly when the offer is accepted. The broker is guilty of commingling. *B.&P.C. 10176e.*

BROKER'S OBLIGATION TO THIRD PERSONS

General Duties

Both the Real Estate Law and the general laws of agency charge the broker with the responsibility of acting fairly and honestly with all parties. The broker is liable for a tort even if acting under the direction of the principal. *C.C. 2343.* However, if the broker commits a tort under the principal's instructions or within the course and scope of that agency, the principal will be jointly and severally liable with the broker. Generally, any tortious acts further provide grounds for discipline by the Real Estate Commission.

Fraud

Because a broker is a professional agent earning compensation through an agency relationship, the law imposes a personal liability for fraud similar to that of any other principal. *Fraud* is a generic term encompassing false representation, concealment, and misleading statements or acts intending to deceive another. Basically, this broad tort requires (1) an intentional misrepresentation, negligent representation, concealment, or false promise; (2) knowingly made or done with intent to deceive, or (which is regarded as the equivalent) without sufficient information to know whether the statement or act is true; (3) for the purpose of inducing the plaintiff to act or refrain from acting; (4) and upon which the plaintiff justifiably relies; and (5) to his detriment and damage.

Intentional Misrepresentation

An intentional misrepresentation is an affirmative suggestion or statement of a material fact that the broker knows is untrue. *C.C. 1710, 1572.* For example, the broker would commit fraud by saying that a house had 2,000 square feet when, in fact, it had only 1,500 square feet. The broker may not be obliged to disclose certain facts, but any volunteered statement must be the truth.

Puffing

Ordinarily, a broker's statements of opinion, describing property as the best buy in town or forecasting possible profits, are considered mere puffing on which the public is not entitled to rely. However, because the broker qualifies as an expert in the field, the public may rely on certain opinions if a reasonable person under similar circumstances would justifiably believe that such "dealer's talk" was actually statement of fact.

Negligent Misrepresentation

A negligent misrepresentation is a false statement by a broker who believes it to be true but has no reasonable grounds for his belief. *C.C. 1710, 1572.* The broker either knows or should realize a lack of sufficient information to make the statement. He or she makes a careless statement, as opposed to an intentional and knowing misstatement. If the broker tells a purchaser that hardwood floors are under the carpeting, something believed although never checked, the broker will be guilty of fraud.

Concealment

Concealment is the affirmative act of hiding defects in the property to prevent investigation and discovery by the other party. *C.C. 1710, 1572.* For example, the broker might plaster and paint over structural defects in a building. Partial concealment is true statements by the broker that nevertheless mislead because they reveal only part of the truth. For example, a broker might tell a purchaser that all the apartments in a building are rented, but fail to disclose that many tenants are given free rent.

Nondisclosure

The broker has an obligation to disclose any known material fact that a third person is ignorant of and unable to discover upon reasonable observation. *Lingsch v. Savage (1936) 213 C.A.2d 729.* For example, a broker is obligated to disclose that a building rests on filled land or that the property violates local zoning ordinances. Furthermore, a broker has a duty to disclose any fraudulent acts committed by the principal. *Willig v. Gold (1946) 75 C.A.2d 809.*

False Promise

A promise made by the broker with no intent to perform is a false promise of a fraudulent nature. *C.C. 1710, 1572.* A broker might promise to buy light fixtures for a living room or to paint a building but, in fact, have no intention of doing so. This type of fraud is difficult to prove and is generally established by eyewitness statements or circumstantial evidence.

Secret Profits

Clearly, brokers have always been liable to their principals (clients) for secret profits. However, because the code provides that brokers must be fair and honest with everyone, the courts hold brokers liable for any secret profits. Hence, a third party (who has no contractual relationship to the broker) may force the broker to return any secret profit. *Ward v. Taggart (1959) 52 C.2d 736.*

Negligence

Under the ordinary rules of **negligence**, a broker is liable to anyone injured as a result of his or her negligence or that of any of the salespeople. Although salespeople may be independent contractors for many purposes, they are agents–employees for purposes of imputing their negligence to their broker under the doctrine of **respondeat superior**. *Gipson v. Davis Realty Co. (1963) 215 C.A.2d 190.*

Principal's Contracts

Generally, a broker has no personal liability for any contracts signed on behalf of the principal. However, if when executing the contract the broker is acting in bad faith (i.e., knowing that he has no authority to sign the agreement), then the broker becomes personally liable as a principal. *C.C. 2343*. Furthermore, a broker acting without authority or in excess of authority also becomes personally liable for damages based on a breach of implied warranty of agency authority. *C.C. 2343, 3318*. Finally, a broker who signs a contract without indicating agent status will generally be held liable as a principal. *Otis Elevator Co. v. Berry (1938) 28 C.A.2d 430*. Consequently, a broker must always be sure to sign any contract as "Joe Buyer, by Ted Broker, agent."

Disclosure of Property's Condition

The famed case of *Easton v. Strassburger (1984) 152 C.A. 3d 90* held that a listing broker owed a duty to the buyer, even though the broker had no contractual obligation toward the buyer and even though the buyer had his own broker. The court held that in a residential sale, the broker had a duty to investigate and inspect the residential property and advise the buyer of any known or reasonably discoverable defects. This duty cannot be abrogated by the seller signing a statement to the broker that the property is in good shape.

To clarify and limit *Easton*, the California legislature added *C.C. 2079*, which provides that it "is the duty of a real estate broker—to a prospective purchaser of real property comprising one to four family units—to conduct a reasonably competent and diligent visual inspection of the property offered for sale and to disclose to that prospective purchaser all facts materially affecting the value or desirability of the property that such an investigation would reveal." The above requirements only apply if the broker has a written listing agreement with the seller, or the broker works in cooperation with a broker having a written listing.

APPLY THE LAW

Sands v. Eagle Oil & Refining Co.
83 C.A.2d 312 (1948)

[Respondent, Eagle Oil & Refining Company, hired real estate broker J. H. Tarman, one of the appellants, to find service stations for lease. Over the years, broker Tarman found several leases for respondent and, as was customary in real estate, the lessors always paid broker Tarman's commission.

APPLY THE LAW

continued

Through the advice and services of broker Tarman, respondent executed a lease for a service station from appellant Sands. The lease proved disadvantageous, and when respondent contacted Sands, the lessor, they discovered that he was the brother-in-law of broker Tarman and that Tarman was the real owner of the property. Respondent, who was sued for unpaid rent, defended by claiming that broker Tarman breached his fiduciary duty as an agent of loyalty and full disclosure. Respondent then sought to rescind the lease and recover damages.]

NOURSE, JUSTICE. Of appellants' contentions, the question of the existence or nonexistence of an agency relation between Tarman and respondent is of primary importance as the requirements of constructive fraud by breach of a confidential relation differ from those as to actual fraud.

Although not all professional contact between a real estate broker and a person desiring to buy or lease real estate need lead to a relation of agency between them, as the broker can act solely in behalf of the adverse party or sometimes only as a middleman whose duty is performed when he has brought the parties together, the facts above stated support the finding of an agency relation in the present case. The fact that Tarman was required to look to the lessors for compensation does not militate against him being the agent of respondent. The custom that commission for the conclusion of a lease is paid by the lessor cannot deprive the lessee of the possibility of having the confidential assistance of a broker.

If it be accepted that a relation of principal and agent existed between respondent and Tarman, then the evidence clearly supports the conclusion that Tarman violated his fiduciary duties as an agent. The law of California imposes on the real estate agent the same obligation of undivided service and loyalty that it imposes on a trustee in favor of his beneficiary. Violation of his trust is subject to the same punitory consequences that are provided for a disloyal or recreant trustee.

Such an agent is charged with the duty of fullest disclosure of all material facts concerning the transaction that might affect the principal's decision. The law prohibits an agent from concluding with himself directly or indirectly any transaction in which he is employed as an agent, without the fullest disclosure of the fact and all circumstances relating to it, and without permission or acquiescence of the principal with full knowledge of all these facts. Here Tarman himself testified that he was the lessor concealed behind the dummy Sands.

It is true that, in general, the knowledge of an agent, which he is under a duty to disclose to his principal or to another agent of the principal, is to be imputed to the principal. However, this rule is not without exceptions pertinent to this case. One is that if the agent and the third party act in

continued

the knowledge of the agent. Another excludes application of the general rule when the third party knows that the agent will not advise the principal.

The general rule that imputes an agent's knowledge to the principal is well established. The underlying reason for it is that an innocent third party may properly presume the agent will perform his duty and report all facts that affect the principal's interest. But, this general rule does not apply when the third party knows there is no foundation for the ordinary presumption—when he is acquainted with circumstances plainly indicating that the agent will not advise his principal. The rule is intended to protect those who exercise good faith, and not as a shield for unfair dealings.

When, as in this case, the agent concludes a real estate transaction with himself without the knowledge of his principal, such a transaction will always be set aside at the option of the principal. Absence of actual fraud in the transaction; of undue advantage for the agent; of injury to the principal or of other similar features is then immaterial. The rule is intended to prevent temptation and the possibility of wrong. Only ratification by the principal after full knowledge of all facts can defeat his right to avoid the transaction.

The only allegations required as to the cause of action of respondent were those relating to the existence of the agency, the violation by surreptitious transaction in the agent's own behalf, and the difference between the amounts paid under the lease and the fair value of the use of the premises, which respondent's allegations in these respects were sufficient to state a cause of action.

Although a transaction by which an agent deals with himself without the consent of the principal in a matter in which he is employed as an agent is not absolutely void, as it may be ratified by the principal upon full knowledge of all the facts; nevertheless, where there is no such ratification, it may be treated as void without a formal rescission as there is no meeting of the minds of two parties.

Judgment affirmed [and respondent may rescind the lease and recover damages from broker Tarman].

STUDY QUESTIONS (TRUE–FALSE)

1. A person acting as an agent is bound by fiduciary obligations toward the principal.

2. A person may not be both an agent and an employee.

3. A real estate salesperson who signs an independent contractor agreement with a broker under general law will still be considered an employee.

4. Until the broker contracts to act for a principal and the principal agrees to accept that employment, the broker has not become an agent.

5. A secretary who provides rental information about available property is violating the law unless he or she is a real estate licensee.

6. A broker who violates fiduciary duties is deemed to have committed fraud on the principal.

7. If a broker, through negligence, causes the seller to lose $30,000, the seller can sue and recover the $30,000 from the broker.

8. If a broker employed by the seller suggests that a prospective buyer can probably buy the property for less than the highly inflated listing price, the broker has violated the law.

9. A broker is charged with a responsibility to advise a prospective purchaser or seller of any adverse tax consequences of that real estate sale.

10. A broker for the seller owes no duty or obligation to the buyer if the buyer is represented by another broker.

Appendix A
Useful Web Sites

Note. These Web sites are a way to search for more information or to discover laws and cases relative to a particular topic. As will all Web sites, while the address ("URL") is current as of this date, it is not uncommon for Web sites to change their address. In such case, it would be easy to find the new address by using a search engine such as Google or Yahoo. These sites are the author's favorite selection of real estate and law Web sites, but represent only a miniscule listing of the enormous number of Web sites on the World Wide Web.

STATE LAW WEB SITES

California Statutes

http://www.leginfo.ca.gov/calaw.html

This page is part of the California legislative Web site. It allows the user to retrieve the full text of any statute found in any of the 29 California codes. The site allows searching by code section, by a set of codes, or by keywords. For people who need to check the wording of a statute, or ascertain if a certain statute exists, this is a very helpful Web site. The one negative about the site is that when you search for a statute, it often delivers both the desired code section and the other code numbers adjacent to that selected code. The site is free and there is no charge for searching.

Status of California Bills

http://www.leginfo.ca.gov/bilinfo.html

This page of the California legislative Web site allows searching for any existing or recently introduced bill. The search will reveal the full text of the bill, the text of any amendments, and the final resolution of that bill. It lists which bills have passed and become laws and which have died in committees. The site is free and there is no charge for searching.

Interesting Property Cases

http://www.calbar.ca.gov/state/calbar/

From the homepage, select the "real property section" of the California State Bar Association options. Then in the "section" page, choose the "new cases and opinions" from the list on the left side of the Web page. Here is a list of what attorneys consider the important property law cases decided by the California courts. The "new cases and opinions" portion lists a one-sentence description of each case, but provides a hyper-link to see more information. It is a quick way to keep apprised of what leading real estate cases are decided by the California Supreme Court and Court of Appeals. This page is free and available, but other pages on the Web site are limited to attorneys.

Full Text of Court Cases

http://www.courtinfo.ca.gov/opinions/continue.htm

The California Judicial Council is a quasi-governmental organization administering the courts. This site allows search for court cases, by court, by date, or by name. Further links provide a full and complete text of the court's decision, and in some cases, it even shows what libraries will carry the legal briefs filed by the attorneys in the case. Generally, in understanding the law, it is necessary to read the exact words of the case. It is one of the better ways to find a California case. The site is free, as is the unlimited searching.

Judicial Council Forms

http://www.courtinfo.ca.gov/forms/

Many pleadings and other forms have been standardized by the Judicial Council. When a form has been standardized, as a general rule (with some exceptions) any party wanting to file a document must use the standardized form. This site, part of the Judicial Council Web page, lists all the standardized documents. They can be downloaded for free and filed with the court or used as needed. Use of the site is free.

Code of Regulations

http://ccr.oal.ca.gov/

Many of the rules governing administrative bodies, like the Department of Motor Vehicles, Toxic Cleanup rules, and other departmental regulations are contained in California's Code of Regulations. (This used to be called the Administrative Code.) This site allows you to browse or search the regulations for any subject or department. It is free.

Find Law of Other States and California Laws

http://www.findlaw.com/

Find Law is a site that has links to all of the statutes in the United States. Thus, it is easy to find the law of any state. The use is free, because the site makes its money by advertising and listing attorneys. It is a helpful site for finding the law and for searching for cases (it contains reference to many recent judicial decisions). The site also sells many forms and contracts, although it offers links to some law firms that provide free legal information and documents.

Professional Web Search Site—Westlaw

http://west.thomson.com/store/default.asp

The best search engines are the professional search engines, and unfortunately, they charge for their use. Still, most attorneys do their law searches on this Web site or the one below (LexisNexis) because they are so thorough, and since they can search for any law or case. The search engines are spectacular, and you can search the thousands and thousands of cases for particular words in a case, or search by most other criteria.

Professional Web Search Site—LexisNexis

http://www.lexisnexis.com/

The competing site to Westlaw is LexisNexis. Attorneys doing online legal research generally use one of these two professional search sites. Besides covering and finding the law, this site also allows searches into tax records, company profiles and numerous other type investigations of public records. Like Westlaw, it is probably too expensive for a casual search by an occasional user.

FEDERAL LAW WEB SITES

U.S. Supreme Court Decisions

http://supct.law.cornell.edu/supct/index.html

This excellent site allows searching for a United State Supreme Court decision by a party's name, year, recent decisions, and sometimes by topic. For selected cases, it also provides references to sources that house a copy of the transcripts of oral arguments or copies of briefs that have been filed. The site provides a full and complete copy of the court's decision, including any dissenting options. Use of the site and searching is free.

United States Codes

http://www4.law.cornell.edu/uscode/

This site allows you to retrieve a full and complete copy of any law found in any volume of the United States Code ("USC"). Searching is done by statute name, by popular name, or just by browsing the various code sections. It also has a key word search engine. The site is free.

United State Code of Federal Regulations

http://www.gpoaccess.gov/cfr/index.html

Many times laws are enacted by Congress, but implementing regulations are issued by the appropriate agencies. These regulations interpret the law and define the rules and regulations operative under that statute. The regulations are housed in the Code of Federal Regulations ("CFR"). This site searches the CFR by name, regulation number or key words. The site is free.

Federal Register

http://www.findlaw.com/casecode/fed_register.html

The Federal Register contains all the rules, proposed rules, notices issued by federal agencies, plus documents and executive orders issued by the President. The Federal Register is a daily publication of the U.S. Government, and this site contains copies of the Federal Registers since 1995. Searches are by key words or by date. It is free.

U.S. Courts of Appeals

http://www.findlaw.com/casecode/

This site is part of "Find Law," and it provides a method of researching cases from the federal Courts of Appeals. California is in the 9th Judicial District. Searching is by case name, a party's name, key words, or by date. It is free.

Appendix B
Answers to Study Questions

Chapter 1

1.	True	Demonstrators in a shopping center.
2.	False	Also bound by federal Constitution and laws.
3.	False	Balance rights (e.g., no free speech in one's home).
4.	True	All rights in a democracy are relative.
5.	True	Holding of *In re Estate of Larkin*.
6.	False	United States uses creation of law doctrine.
7.	False	Former Soviet Union; no right to own land and other property.
8.	True	Under creation of law concept.
9.	False	Only pay for a taking, not a limitation.
10.	True	Property is a bundle of rights, not a thing.

Chapter 2

1.	False	Developed from common law.
2.	False	Higher courts not bound by lower court decisions.
3.	True	Advantages of small claims court.
4.	True	Total damages must be under $25,000.
5.	True	Appellate courts correct errors of law.
6.	True	Court must grant discretionary certiorari.
7.	False	Goes directly to U.S. Supreme Court.
8.	True	Of courts having jurisdiction, venue is proper place.
9.	False	Rule certain contracts must be in writing.
10.	False	Federal government owns 45 percent of total land.

Chapter 3

1.	False	Owns airspace he reasonably and beneficially uses.
2.	True	Minerals in place pass with deed.
3.	False	Owns right to drill only.
4.	False	If mortgaged, then constructively severed.

5. True   Similar to gas and oil and other liquid minerals.
6. False   Intent is the most important test.
7. False   Only if all others test equal, tenant prevails.
8. True   Parties bound, not others (without prior notice).
9. False   U.C.C.–1 is personal property security instrument.
10. True   Qualifies as a trade fixture.

Chapter 4

1. False   Unenforceable contract (executory contract).
2. False   Bilateral; both sides bound.
3. True   Contract by minor void.
4. False   Revocable before acceptance (unless consideration).
5. True   Rejection extinguishes offer permanently.
6. True   Is rejection and counteroffer.
7. False   If executed, but consideration generally required.
8. False   Statute of frauds requires writing.
9. True   For residential real estate.
10. True   Rising property values reduce damages.

Chapter 5

1. False   Also receipt for deposit, commission agreement.
2. False   There is no standard form.
3. True   Changes not incorporated until approved.
4. True   Contract may be illusory in some situations.
5. True   Offer generally revocable at will until accepted.
6. True   Risk generally passes with possession or title.
7. False   Enforceable and commonly used.
8. False   Revocable at will until accepted.
9. True   CAR requires signature plus delivery.
10. True   Statute of fraud requirements.

Chapter 6

1. False   Employment contract; no authority to sell.
2. True   Fiduciary duties not always dependent on contract.
3. False   Depends on listing wording; otherwise, true.
4. True   Sale by anyone except owner yields commission.

5. False   Writing mandatory, even if broker misled.
6. False   Not required (e.g., for exclusive right to sell).
7. True   If contract provides withdrawal clause.
8. False   Must have termination date.
9. False   Earned on sale.
10. True   If community property, generally both must sign to list.

Chapter 7

1. True   Only appurtenant easement has dominant estate.
2. True   See Table 7.1 on need and rationale.
3. True   Benefit of using statutory *C.C. 1008* signs.
4. False   General signs risky and not always conclusive.
5. False   Need only constructive, not actual notice.
6. False   Generally duty falls entirely to dominant estate.
7. False   Only for easements acquired by prescription.
8. True   Definition of license and not a contract.
9. True   Implied license arises by conduct.
10. True   Licenses are personal to owner.

Chapter 8

1. True   Definition of ownership in severalty.
2. True   Definition; key words so long as.
3. False   Only fee simple absolute has no future interests.
4. False   When X dies, B loses estate.
5. True   B's estate lasts as long as X lives.
6. True   Lease is possession, not use.
7. False   Tenancy for years, has fixed ending date.
8. True   Generally, month to month. Terminates on notice.
9. False   Now requires 30 days' notice to terminate.
10. False   Must be written only if over one year.

Chapter 9

1. False   Warranty against conveyance and encumbrance.
2. False   Quitclaim deeds contain no warranties.
3. True   Deed given by gift is valid.

4. True   Minors cannot sign deeds.

5. True   Not irrevocable transfer. A wants it back if he survives.

6. False   Just cannot sell; many own property by gift.

7. False   No witnesses in holographic will.

8. True   All community property passes to surviving spouse.

9. True   This is one reason for its unpopularity.

10. True   Contract usually passes possession immediately.

Chapter 10

1. False   Many cases involve improved property.

2. False   Only one of five elements for adverse possession, not notice.

3. True   Must be of public record to be marketable.

4. False   Constructive notice only; so visit your property.

5. False   Under color of title.

6. False   Continuous use is not constant use.

7. False   Usually, both owner and possessor pay taxes.

8. False   Eminent domain is the right, condemnation is exercise of that right.

9. True   Costs are not included; generally property only.

10. True   Why agencies prefer police power.

Chapter 11

1. False   Cannot will joint tenancy property.

2. True   Any transfer automatically dissolves joint tenancy.

3. False   B, C, and D are joint tenants; R is tenant in common.

4. False   Hold as tenants in common; joint tenancy never presumed.

5. True   Tenancy in common presumed.

6. True   Joint venture governed as general partnership.

7. False   Wife set aside within one year (three if fraud).

8. False   Table 11.4. Community property all to spouse.

9. False   Inheritances are separate property; no community property effort.

10. True   Purchases with community property remain community property.

Chapter 12

1.	False	Highest duty to invitee.
2.	False	Child trespasser higher duty than unknown trespasser.
3.	True	Opening to juries gives more protection.
4.	True	So owners often phone county; do not fix by self.
5.	False	Table 12.1. Noise or odor can be nuisance.
6.	False	Usually balance the equities, if not intentional.
7.	True	One of few times self-help remedy available.
8.	False	More than 10 feet is spite fence.
9.	True	Table 12.3. Definitions.
10.	False	Depends on depth of pool and notice.

Chapter 13

1.	False	Can only evict by court action.
2.	False	No notice to terminate estate for years.
3.	False	Must state quit or pay rent.
4.	True	Unlawful detainer cheapest and fastest.
5.	True	May assign at will.
6.	True	New. *C.C. 1942.4.* No charge if uninhabitable.
7.	False	Need notice and for certain purposes.
8.	True	Recover only if provided in contract.
9.	True	Code limits amount of deposits collected.
10.	True	Always refundable; code time limits.

Chapter 14

1.	False	Valid between parties. Not to BFP.
2.	True	First BFP to record win. Assumes A is BFP.
3.	True	Defects cured after one year.
4.	True	Once recorded, prevents others from being BFP.
5.	False	Actual notice prevents A from being BFP.
6.	True	A's occupancy gives constructive notice.
7.	False	All mechanic's liens equal.
8.	True	Lien on all real estate.
9.	False	Gives notice; prevents BFP; does not prohibit transfer.
10.	True	Lawsuits not constructive notice until recorded.

Chapter 15

1. False   Lender is beneficiary, borrower the trustor.
2. False   Allows unpaid installments declared immediately due.
3. False   Many statutory exemptions; also may be waiver, etc.
4. False   Covers multiple parcels, but all still bound by lien.
5. False   Disclosure statute only, no monetary limits.
6. True   First step toward trustee's sale.
7. True   Why junior liens are so risky.
8. True   Probably only major advantage of judicial foreclosure.
9. False   Hard money purchase money limited to one-to-four-family units.
10. True   Definition. No limit on type of property involved.

Chapter 16

1. False   Infrequent use because of new code limitations.
2. False   Also laborers and materialmen.
3. False   Required only if no direct contract with owner.
4. False   Is either 30 or 60 days.
5. True   Forces mechanic to act or lose lien.
6. False   Breach of contract, bond, etc.
7. True   Why need responsible management.
8. False   Must first be recorded.
9. True   Expires unless renewed in 10 years.
10. False   Equal except between themselves, keep old priorities.

Chapter 17

1. False   No Darn Fooling Around; November 1.
2. True   Lien March 1 preceding tax year.
3. False   Bookkeeping entry only.
4. True   Tax deeded to state at end of five years.
5. True   But assessor's value often has no relation to true fair market value.
6. False   Exempts interspousal transfers.
7. True   No longer use 25 percent of fair market value.
8. False   Old law $1,750. Now $70 less tax.
9. True   Tax liens superior to private liens.
10. True   Foreclosed senior lien cuts off junior.

Chapter 18

1. True $175,000 for age 65 or older.
2. False   No dollar or land size limitations.
3. True $70,000 + $100,000 = $170,000 protection.
4. False   One of three exceptions to normal priorities.
5. False   Temporary absence, not abandonment.

Chapter 19

1. False   Courts prefer covenants. No forfeiture.
2. True   Precedent means condition before duty occurs.
3. True   No obligation unless condition occurs.
4. False   Also enforce if found equitable servitude.
5. True   Must relate to use of land.
6. False   No forfeiture of property.
7. False   Table 19.2, creation. Usually condition.
8. False   May be defenses (e.g., waiver).
9. True   Changed circumstances are a defense.
10. True   B allowed, thereby waiving rights.

Chapter 20

1. False   Not a taking, but a regulation.
2. False   No compensation, mere regulation.
3. True   Provided not patently discriminatory.
4. False   Courts infrequently interfere.
5. True   Unless arbitrary and irrational decision.
6. False   For public good, not hardship.
7. False   No new zone. Exempt zone's effect.
8. True   Purpose is to avoid hardship.
9. True   Traditionally so used. Now broadened.
10. False   Hardship is variance.

Chapter 21

1. True   One of six items that must be included.
2. True   NEPA set as a national goal.
3. False   HUD funding, for example, makes federal.
4. True   Is governmental project.

5. False   Strict liability; need not know or cause.

6. False   Environmental laws, federal laws, zoning, etc.

7. False   Regulates marketing of existing divisions.

8. True   Administered by D.R.E. on statewide basis.

9. True   Any common division into two or more units.

10. False   Each county sets it own laws and requirements.

Chapter 22

1. False   Insures free undisclosed liens.

2. False   Optional, although many lenders require.

3. True   Part of competence of parties.

4. False   Usually, both ordered, for each party.

5. True   A major reason lenders get CLTA.

6. True   See Table 22.1, Police Power.

7. False   Only if incident to pending deal.

8. False   Limited, not general agent.

9. False   Stakeholder, not decide controversy.

10. True   RSPA (Reg X) requires lenders make the estimate.

Chapter 23

1. True   All general agents so bound.

2. False   Many agents employed by principal.

3. True   Contractor agreement for limited purposes.

4. False   May arise gratuitously or by implication.

5. True   Considered a licensee's activity.

6. True   Law considers breach as fraud.

7. True   Always liable for one's negligence.

8. True   Violation of duty of good faith.

9. False   Certified public accountant's duty, not broker's.

10. False   Must act fairly and honestly with all parties. Also see Easton ruling.

Appendix C
Sample Test #1

The answers to Appendix C can be found in Appendix E.

Chapter 1

1. The "creation of law" doctrine states that:
   a. Created by law, property becomes independent of future laws.
   b. Property does not exist without the protection of the law.
   c. Property existed before law, and is separate and unregulated.
   d. None of the above.

2. "Property" is:
   a. An intangible bundle of rights, created by laws.
   b. Commonly considered a physical element, such as land.
   c. Both (a) and (b).
   d. Neither (a) nor (b).

3. When the constitutional rights of "private property" and "free speech" conflict:
   a. The more important right, private property, prevails.
   b. The more important right, free speech, prevails.
   c. The more important right in that fact situation prevails.
   d. Local ordinances determine which right prevails.

4. The part of the U.S. Constitution that prohibits the federal government from taking a person's property without just compensation is:
   a. Third Amendment.
   b. Eighth Amendment.
   c. Fifth Amendment.
   d. Implied by the constitution.

5. Where could individuals most likely demonstrate in a nondisruptive manner without being evicted?
   a. Shopping centers
   b. In front of jails
   c. On your neighbor's front lawn
   d. All of the above

Chapter 2

6. Common law originated in:
   a. The United States.
   b. Ancient Rome.
   c. Ancient Greece.
   d. England.

7. Which of the following is true about small claims court?
   a. Plaintiff may not appeal if he loses
   b. It may never hear cases over $7,500 in damages
   c. Participants may not be represented by attorneys
   d. All of the above

8. Which of the following is or can act as an appellate court?
   a. Supreme Court
   b. Superior Court
   c. Both (a) and (b)
   d. Neither (a) nor (b)

9. According to the Statute of Frauds, which of the following contracts are unenforceable unless in writing?
   a. Leases over one year
   b. Contract for broker's commission on sale of real estate
   c. Options to purchase real estate
   d. All of the above

10. A seller has a written contract to sell his property for $200,000, but the parties have an oral agreement to increase the price to $210,000. In court:
    a. Only evidence on the $200,000 contract can be introduced.
    b. Only evidence on the $210,000 contract can be introduced.
    c. Neither contract can be introduced.
    d. Evidence on both contracts can be introduced.

Chapter 3

11. The most important test of whether or not an item is a fixture is:
    a. Method of attachment.
    b. Adaptability of an item.
    c. Relationship of the parties.
    d. Intent of the installer.

12. Which of the following is considered part of the real property?
    a. Fixtures
    b. Appurtenances
    c. Mineral rights
    d. All of the above

13. The "relationship of the parties test" for determining whether an item is a fixture favors which party:
    a. Buyer over seller
    b. Tenant over landlord
    c. Lender over borrower
    d. All of the above

14. With respect to airspace, one can:
    a. Sell his airspace totally separate from the land.
    b. Own all airspace under 1,000 feet.
    c. Both of the above.
    d. Neither (a) nor (b).

15. Which of the following is not a difference between real and personal property?
    a. Property included in a will
    b. Attachment of judgment liens
    c. Method of transfer of title
    d. Jurisdiction of laws relating to that property

Chapter 4

16. A contract that lacks an essential element and may be avoided by one party is called:
    a. Void contract.
    b. Voidable contract.
    c. Unenforceable contract.
    d. Executory contract.

17. Buyer A makes an offer to Buyer B on June 1, which states that it is irrevocable until June 3. A can revoke this offer:
    a. Never, as it is in writing
    b. At any time
    c. After June 3
    d. During June 1

18. B offers to cook a wild turkey if A will come to dinner. A agrees. This is:
    a. A binding contract.
    b. No contract.
    c. A voidable contract.
    d. A void contract.

19. On March 2, a contract is made for B to buy a house for $90,000. On May 1, the house is worth $90,000 and B breaches the contract. Seller resells the house on June 1 for $80,000. Seller's general damages are:
    a. $10,000.
    b. $80,000.
    c. $90,000.
    d. None ($0).

20. A buyer agrees to purchase A's house for $100,000. The contract provides for $5,000 liquidated damages, the amount of the deposit. The liquidated damage clause is:
    a. Absolutely and unconditionally valid.
    b. Valid, but seller recovers lesser of $5,000 or actual damages, and has burden of proving the amount of actual damages.
    c. Valid, but seller recovers less of $5,000 or actual damages, and buyer has burden to prove damages not $5,000.
    d. Voidable, as over three percent of selling price.

Chapter 5

21. A deposit receipt is a(an):
    a. Offer to purchase.
    b. Commission agreement.
    c. Acceptance of contract.
    d. All of the above.

22. If a person signs a deposit receipt, then later discovers he or she misunderstood certain facts, then that person:
    a. Is presumed to have read and understood what he signed, and is normally bound by the contact terms.
    b. Can claim the contract voidable, because there would be no "meeting of the minds" necessary to contract formation.
    c. Can claim the contract void, because there is no meeting of the minds.
    d. The contract is automatically void, because there is no meeting of the minds.

23. Which of the following is a person fully capable of executing a deposit receipt?
    a. Minors
    b. Corporation to be formed
    c. Incompetents
    d. None of the above

24. When a contract clause states that "time is of the essence," it means:
    a. Only reasonable time is permitted to perform all obligations.
    b. Normally all time limits are deemed material and binding.
    c. Has no meaning in California forms.
    d. That all months will be calculated as a 30-day month.

25. Title reports are paid for by:
    a. The seller.
    b. As provided by the contract.
    c. The buyer.
    d. By county custom.

Chapter 6

26. A listing agreement is governed by the laws of:
    a. Subcontract law.
    b. Agency law.
    c. Fiduciary code.
    d. Broker's law.

27. A listing that permits a broker to obtain a commission if the seller sells the property is:
    a. Exclusive agency.
    b. Exclusive right to sell.
    c. Net listing.
    d. All of the above.

28. Which listing gives a broker a commission if any broker sells the property?
    a. Open listing
    b. Option listing
    c. Net listing
    d. None of the above

29. Where property is sold, the commission is based on a percent of the:
    a. Property's fair market value.
    b. Listing price.
    c. Selling price.
    d. Deposit.

30. Brokers must complete a "residential disclosure statement":
    a. On all property.
    b. Only on qualified residential property.
    c. On any property not sold "as is."
    d. Only if the buyer asks for this inspection and will pay the inspection fee.

Chapter 7

31. An easement appurtenant requires:
    a. Dominant estate.
    b. Servient estate.
    c. Both (a) and (b).
    d. Neither (a) nor (b).

32. A profit á prendre is:
    a. A typical easement.
    b. A negative easement.
    c. An easement with power to consume.
    d. A lease for minerals.

33. To prevent adverse use, an owner may:
    a. Grant a license.
    b. Post a sign as permitted by the Civil Code.
    c. Record a notice of consent to use land.
    d. All of the above.

34. In the absence of an agreement, who pays for maintenance of an easement?
    a. Dominant estate
    b. Servient estate
    c. They split it
    d. The court decides

35. A normal license is:
    a. Revocable at any time upon reasonable notice.
    b. Revocable at any time upon 24 hours notice.
    c. Revocable at any time and without notice.
    d. Only revocable as allowed in the license.

Chapter 8

36. Which of the following is not a freehold estate?
    a. Reversion
    b. Life estate
    c. Estate for years
    d. None of the above

37. An estate owned by one person is called?
    a. A sole proprietorship.
    b. Ownership a prendre.
    c. Ownership in severalty.
    d. A fee simple absolute.

38. Fee simple defeasible:
    a. Terminates automatically on violation of the condition.
    b. Is any fee simple that is subject to a condition.
    c. Is a commonly granted fee in California.
    d. All of the above.

39. Which of the following can be created orally?
    a. A periodic tenancy
    b. Estate at sufferance
    c. Tenancy at will
    d. All of the above

40. An estate for years must be in writing to be enforceable if:
    a. It is to be used for residential purposes.
    b. The term is over one year.
    c. Minor children will be living in the property.
    d. All of the above.

Chapter 9

41. Which of the following is true about minors?
    a. They are competent grantees
    b. They are competent grantor
    c. Both of the above
    d. Neither of the above

42. Which deed contains no warranties?
    a. Grant deed
    b. Warranty deed
    c. Quitclaim deed
    d. All of the above

43. A "statutory will":
    a. Is a valid California will.
    b. Allows a testator to check boxes.
    c. Both of the above.
    d. None of the above.

44. An executor is:
    a. Appointed by the state.
    b. Appointed by the will.
    c. Appointed by the beneficiaries.
    d. Appointed by drawing ballots among qualified people.

45. Under an installment land sales contract:
    a. They have lost most of their popularity in California.
    b. The buyer gets a refund on part of his payments on default.
    c. Possession always passes to the buyer upon close of escrow.
    d. All of the above.

Chapter 10

46. Adverse possession can lie against:
    a. Unused streets.
    b. Commercial property.
    c. Both of the above.
    d. None of the above.

47. Adverse possession differs from an easement by prescription in that adverse possession:
    a. Requires use, not possession, of the property.
    b. Requires possession, not use, of the property.
    c. Both require occupation of the property.
    d. Both require use of the property.

48. Which of the following is true about acquiring title by adverse possession under a claim of right?
    a. A defective instrument is involved
    b. Entire property mentioned in document is acquired
    c. Entire property may be claimed although claimant occupies only a portion
    d. None of the above

49. A county decides it would be beneficial to add a park in the largely rural part of the county. The next day a homeowner requests a building permit to add a second story on his house situated. The county decides homeowner, who has 500 acres of land, has more than he needs, and will only grant permit if homeowner will dedicate ten acres to the public as a park. This condition requiring dedication before issuing a building permit:
    a. Is valid. The county can do anything it wants any time it wants under police power.
    b. Is valid as long as the county really needs the park.
    c. Both of the above.
    d. Is invalid. Need for park is not reasonably tied to burden of allowing second story.

50. Which of the following is a requirement for a state to take property by condemnation?
    a. The property must be taken for the public good
    b. The property must be necessary for the proposed public use
    c. The owner must be justly compensated for the property
    d. All of the above

Chapter 11

51. A and B own Blackacre as tenants in common. B dies leaving his interest to X. Which of the following is true?
    a. A owns all the property, free and clear of B's debts
    b. A owns all the property, subject to B's debts
    c. A and X each own half the property
    d. None of the above

52. Which of the following is a separate property?
    a. Property the spouses cannot remember how it was acquired
    b. Property acquired by the credit of one spouse
    c. Commingling of separate property and community property
    d. None of the above

53. Donna is given a gift of a summer home by her grandmother. Donna is married. The property is considered:
    a. Community property.
    b. Separate property.
    c. Community assets.
    d. b and c

54. On the death of a joint tenant, the surviving joint tenants:
    a. Automatically receive title. No formal action is needed.
    b. Receive title, but need to record documents for marketable title.
    c. Receive title if decedent's will so provides.
    d. Cannot receive title, only equitable interest.

55. Community property:
    a. Developed from English common law
    b. Developed from Spanish-Mexican law
    c. Developed from American common law
    d. Developed from statutory creation

Chapter 12

56. Under the old common law, which of the following persons would have been a licensee upon entering another's land with permission:
    a. Social guest
    b. Mail carriers
    c. Police officer
    d. All of the above

57. The owner of property is liable for injury occurring on the sidewalk in front of his property when:
    a. Anyone is injured.
    b. The owner creates a dangerous condition on the sidewalk.
    c. The property is within city limits.
    d. All of the above.

58. Which of the following cannot be an encroachment?
    a. A fence
    b. Corner of house hanging over property
    c. Trespasser
    d. Tree branch

59. An encroachment can be a:
    a. Tort.
    b. Tree branch overhanging on another's land.
    c. Either a trespass or a nuisance.
    d. All of the above.

60. An owner has a boundary-line fence between the land and that of the neighbor. The fence needs repair, and the neighbor doesn't want to spend any money to fix it. The owner can:
    a. By law force the neighbor to pay for half the cost of repair.
    b. Do nothing to force the neighbor to contribute.
    c. Pay for all work, and declare the fence entirely owned by the owner.
    d. Force the neighbor to pay for all the cost by refusing to voluntarily act.

Chapter 13

61. To terminate a lease for cause, the landlord uses a:
    a. 30-day notice (60-day notice if the tenant has been there for over one year).
    b. Three-day notice.
    c. Termination for cause notice.
    d. Eviction notice.

62. The steps in proper order to evict a tenant are:
    a. Unlawful detainer, terminate lease, and sheriff evict.
    b. Terminate lease, unlawful detainer, and sheriff evict.
    c. Writ of immediate possession, unlawful detainer, and sheriff evict.
    d. Forcible entry, unlawful detainer, and sheriff evict.

63. For the sheriff to evict, the sheriff must first:
    a. Serve a five-day advance notice.
    b. Make sure tenant is nonviolent.
    c. Call a locksmith.
    d. Collect back rent due.

64. A tenant can rent an unfurnished apartment for $400 per month. The maximum deposits that can be collected, in addition to the first month's rent is:
    a. $400.
    b. $800.
    c. $1200.
    d. Whatever the market will allow.

65. If a tenant finds the apartment being rented lacks hot water, the tenant can by statute pay for the repairs and deduct that sum from future rent if:
    a. The amount does not exceed two months' rent.
    b. The tenant has not used this remedy during the lease term.
    c. The sole cause of no hot water is the landlord's negligence.
    d. All of the above.

Chapter 14

66. Recording does not:
    a. Impart constructive notice.
    b. Guarantee priority as of date of recording.
    c. Create a presumption of delivery.
    d. Make a copy of the document available at recorder's office.

67. An unrecorded document:
    a. May not bind the parties.
    b. Is invalid and unrecognized.
    c. Is binding between parties.
    d. Suggests fraudulent intent.

68. Which of the following imparts constructive notice?
    a. Seeing a copy of a deed
    b. Seeing people living on property
    c. Seeing the actual deed
    d. All of the above

69. In February, "X" sells his vacant land to "A" who does not record. In March, "X" sells that same land to "B" who records. Neither "A" nor "B" has actual notice of the other's claim. Who owns the property:
    a. A
    b. B
    c. X
    d. It's up to the courts to decide as you can't tell from the facts

70. In February, "X" begins digging a foundation. In March, "Y" loans and records a deed of trust on the property. In April, "Z" builds the building and records a mechanic's lien. As to "Y" and "Z," who wins:
    a. Y
    b. Z
    c. Neither, X wins
    d. Up to the courts

Chapter 15

71. Which of the following is not required for a promissory note to be negotiable:
    a. Payment on demand or set date
    b. Conditional promise to pay
    c. Signed by lender
    d. None of the above

72. Under our usury laws, in which of the following loans can a lender charge any interest the market will bear:
    a. Loans made by a bank
    b. Secured loans made through real estate brokers
    c. Both of the above
    d. Neither (a) nor (b)

73. In a deed of trust, the person who borrows the money and puts his or her property up for security, the person who makes the loan, and the person holding bare legal title in trust are respectively called:
    a. Trustor, trustee, and beneficiary.
    b. Trustor, beneficiary, and trustee.
    c. Beneficiary, trustor, and trustee.
    d. Trustee, trustor, and beneficiary.

74. If a senior lien forecloses, which of the following is not a remedy available to the holder of a junior deed of trust?
    a. Reinstate the senior lien
    b. Immediately sue the borrower personally rather than wait for foreclosure
    c. Do nothing and hope there would be excess proceeds from the sale
    d. Foreclosure simultaneously with the senior lien

75. If a seller takes back a deed of trust executed by the buyer and secured by the property being purchased, on which of the following properties is it a purchase money loan:
    a. 100-unit apartment
    b. Owner-occupied home
    c. Office building
    d. All of the above

Chapter 16

76. _____ lien arises out of a lawsuit.
    a. Mortgage
    b. Execution
    c. Mechanic's
    d. Creditor's

77. Which of the following is true about attachment liens?
    a. Can be used in any type of lawsuit
    b. Can only arise against business persons, in contract cases, over $500, where property to be attached is not for home or family use
    c. Can only be used in criminal or tort actions over $500
    d. Can no longer be used in California

78. A judgment was entered in 1975 and recorded in 1990. The judgment lien would be good until:
    a. 2000.
    b. 1995.
    c. 1990.
    d. No lien created.

79. A judgment lien is:
    a. A voluntary lien.
    b. An involuntary lien.
    c. Either voluntary or involuntary, depending on circumstances.
    d. None of the above.

80. If "A" dug a foundation in January, and "B" bank-loaned money secured by a deed of trust in February, and "C" painted in June and recorded a mechanic's lien, "C" lien would have priority as of:
    a. January.
    b. February.
    c. June.
    d. When project was finished.

Chapter 17

81. The amount of the Veteran's exemption for real property taxes is:
    a. $40 off tax bill.
    b. $70 off tax bill.
    c. $1000 off assessed value.
    d. 10% of tax bill.

82. Which of the following pays no real property tax of any amount?
    a. Church building
    b. Public High School
    c. City hospital
    d. All of the above

83. Real property taxes are due:
    a. Once a year, on April 15th.
    b. Once a year, on December 31st.
    c. Twice a year.
    d. In monthly installments.

84. Which of the following results in a reassessment of all or part of the real property?
    a. Adding a new room to a house
    b. Death of wife, holding as joint tenants with husband
    c. Transfer of husband's separate property to wife
    d. All of the above

85. In 1994, assume you bought a home for $350,000. Assume you qualify for a homeowner's exemption. Your first year's real property taxes would be:
    a. $3,500.
    b. $8,000.
    c. $3,430.
    d. $7,930.

Chapter 18

86. The amount of a family homestead, where husband and wife reside is:
    a. $50,000.
    b. $75,000.
    c. $100,000.
    d. $175,000.

87. If you are single, aged 21, and purchasing your first house using the proceeds of an inheritance, for $2,000,000, all cash, your homestead amount would be:
    a. $75,000
    b. $100,000
    c. No homestead when purchasing home over $1,000,000
    d. No homestead, since too much equity

88. The amount of a homestead for a person aged 77 is:
    a. $75,000.
    b. $100,000.
    c. $175,000.
    d. $150,000 (amount of two homestead amounts combined).

89. Which of the following will terminate a homestead?
    a. Taking a four-year vacation
    b. Moving and living in an apartment, while renting out the house
    c. Marrying and living in a home with a single person homestead
    d. All of the above

90. Assume a homeowner has no outstanding debts. Assume that homeowner filed a homestead in 1985, when the amount was $45,000, and never refiled each time the homestead amounts were increased. If this same person were to record a homestead now, the amount would be $75,000. What is the amount of the person's original homestead worth now:
    a. $75,000
    b. $45,000
    c. $45,000 plus 2% per year increase from 1985
    d. Invalid as homestead must be renewed to remain effective

Chapter 19

91. If an offer to purchase property is subject to a favorable zoning report, the offer is subject to:
    a. Invalid condition, as zoning is legal.
    b. Condition subsequent.
    c. Condition precedent.
    d. Covenant.

92. Which of the following is not a remedy for breach of a covenant?
    a. Injunction
    b. Damages
    c. Forfeiture of the estate
    d. None. All of above are remedies

93. For a covenant to run with the land, it must:
    a. Touch and concern the land.
    b. State it runs with the land.
    c. Describe the property.
    d. All of the above.

94. Which of the following suggests a covenant rather than a condition?
    a. Created by contractual agreement
    b. Only remedy allowed by instrument is damages
    c. Does not affect title to property
    d. All of above

95. An equitable servitude involves CC&Rs and usually applies:
    a. To subdivision land
    b. To commercial property
    c. In contract and criminal actions
    d. In actions by RE Commissioner

Chapter 20

96. The authority for zoning is predominantly based on:
    a. Eminent domain
    b. Civil code
    c. Police power
    d. Res ipsa loquitur

97. Police power is separate and distinct from:
    a. Eminent domain.
    b. Taking of property.
    c. Compensation to property owners.
    d. None of the above.

98. General plans are:
    a. Required by statute for all counties.
    b. Not actually zone property.
    c. Long-range plans.
    d. All of the above.

99. Which of the following remedies is based on hardships?
    a. Amendment to zoning ordinance
    b. Variance
    c. Conditional use permit
    d. None of the above

100. Which of the following is type of administrative relief from zoning?
    a. Amendment to zoning ordinance
    b. Declare statute unconstitutional
    c. Conditional use permit
    d. All of the above

Chapter 21

101. What is the major environmental legislation at the federal level?
    a. EQA
    b. EIS
    c. NEPA
    d. EIR

102. California's major environmental legislation requires an environmental impact document whenever there is a government project that:
    a. Has a significant impact on the environment.
    b. Has or may have a significant impact on the environment.
    c. Has a significant—adverse—impact on the environment.
    d. Has or may have a significant—adverse—impact on the environment.

103. A person could become liable under superfund for the cost of toxic cleanup to land if he or she is:
    a. Current operator of a facility on toxic land, but who did not cause the problem.
    b. Prior owner of property 25 years ago who, when they owned the land, contaminated it.
    c. The person who arranges for toxic material to be dumped on someone else's land.
    d. All of the above.

104. Which of the following regulates the orderly development and physical conditions of subdivisions built within the State of California:
    a. Subdivision Act
    b. Subdivided Lands Act
    c. Subdivision Map Act
    d. Interstate Subdivision Sales Qualification Act

105. The most important report to a developer under the Subdivided Lands Act is the:
    a. Pink Report.
    b. White Report.
    c. Unrestricted Sales Clearance Report.
    d. None of the above. Reports concern the Subdivision Map Act.

Chapter 22

106. An ALTA title insurance policy insures against violations of:
    a. Incorrect zoning
    b. Height restrictions
    c. Building code
    d. None of the above

107. Which of the following is not covered by a CLTA title policy?
    a. Recorded mechanic's liens
    b. Building encroachments
    c. Recorded tax liens
    d. None of above covered

108. The noninstitutional lender obtains which type of title policy?
    a. ATLA
    b. CTLA
    c. CLTA
    d. ALTA

109. Which of the following is not an essential and mandatory element of an escrow?
    a. Irrevocable deposit of money
    b. Valid contract
    c. Title insurance policy
    d. All above are required

110. Which of the following need not be licensed as an escrow agent to so act?
    a. Title insurance companies
    b. Attorneys
    c. Real estate brokers
    d. All above need licenses

Chapter 23

111. In an agency relationship, if "A" asks "B" to represent him, then "A" would be called the:
    a. Agent.
    b. Attorney-in-fact.
    c. Principal.
    d. None of the above.

112. A real estate broker can never be an agent unless:
    a. The agency was created by written agreement.
    b. The broker is an express agent of the seller.
    c. The broker is not representing himself.
    d. All of the above.

113. A salesperson:
    a. Can only work under a broker.
    b. Must have all real estate contracts reviewed by the broker.
    c. Must have a written contract relationship with a broker.
    d. All of the above.

114. A broker represents a seller. In direct response to a question by a prospective buyer, the broker truthfully replies the seller would probably accept a lower price than the listing price. The broker has violated:
    a. No law.
    b. Duty of good faith.
    c. The duty of full disclosure.
    d. Duty of loyalty—no adverse interest.

115. A broker represents a seller, and presents a full price, very fair, all cash offer from the broker's brother-in-law. If the broker forgets to mention the buyer's family relationship, the broker has violated:
    a. No law.
    b. Duty of good faith.
    c. The duty of full disclosure.
    d. Duty of loyalty—no adverse interest.

Appendix D
Sample Test #2

The answers to Appendix D can be found in Appendix E.

Chapter I

1. The "natural law" doctrine states that:
   a. Created by law, property becomes independent of future laws.
   b. Property does not exist without the protection of the law.
   c. Property existed before law, and is separate and unregulated.
   d. None of the above.

2. Under ancient property law:
   a. Trespassers could be shot.
   b. Land could be used anyway the owner wanted.
   c. Land was "owned" until someone stronger took it away.
   d. All of the above.

3. Demonstrators going onto a shopping center that has no policy regarding demonstrators, do so against the owner's permission. They will:
   a. Win, because property becomes public for free speech.
   b. Win, because free speech takes priority over private property.
   c. Lose, because they are trespassing.
   d. Lose, because property is open to the public only to shop.

4. The state governments are prohibited from taking a private citizen's property without just compensation, because of:
   a. Equal protection.
   b. In Re Estate of Larkin.
   c. 14th Amendment—due process.
   d. State sovereignty.

5. Which statement is true about state restrictions on the use of property?
   a. Restrictions can vary between neighboring parcels of property.
   b. Restrictions on same property can vary from year to year.
   c. Both of the above statements.
   d. Neither of the above statements.

Chapter 2

6. The principal of Stare Decisis:
   a. Forces all inferior courts to follow rulings of higher courts.
   b. Strongly influences courts to follow rulings of equal courts.
   c. Both (a) and (b).
   d. Neither (a) nor (b).

7. If a tenant fails to pay his $600 monthly rent on the home he is renting, the landlord can sue in:
   a. Small claims court
   b. Superior Court
   c. Supreme Court
   d. Either small claims or superior court

8. The California Supreme Court:
   a. Must hear all cases that come to it through the appellate process.
   b. May and does hear only those cases it deems worthy of review.
   c. Must hear a fixed percentage of cases that come to it.
   d. None of the above.

9. The Statute of Limitations states that if you are going to sue for breach of a written lease, you must do so within:
   a. Four years.
   b. Three years.
   c. Two years.
   d. One year.

10. Approximately what percent of the land in the State of California is owned by private citizens and not by any government:
    a. About 25%
    b. About 50%
    c. About 75%
    d. About 90%

Chapter 3

11. Ted has homes in San Francisco (his residence) and Chicago. If he dies intestate (without a will), the art works in each home would be subject to the laws of:
    a. California.
    b. Chicago.
    c. The state where located.
    d. Federal laws on probate.

12. Which of the following is true about crops on leased land?
    a. It is always personal property.
    b. It is always real property.
    c. It depends on the circumstances and the lease terms.
    d. It always belongs to the tenant.

13. _____ is not an appurtenance.
    a. Land
    b. Water rights
    c. Easements
    d. Mineral rights

14. Trade fixtures:
    a. Only occur in certain lease situations.
    b. Are exceptions to the rule about removing fixtures.
    c. Cannot be removed if they cause irreparable injury.
    d. All of the above.

15. A good faith improver erroneously installs a small building on his neighbor's land. Which of the following is true?
    a. He is trespassing; the neighbor owns the building.
    b. He can probably remove the building if he can do so without injury to the neighbor's land.
    c. He owns the building and must pay rent to the neighbor.
    d. The neighbor has option to keep the building or force its removal.

Chapter 4

16. A contract that is not fully performed is called:
    a. Executory contract.
    b. Unperformed contract.
    c. Executed contract.
    d. Implied contract.

17. A offers to buy B's house for $90,000. B says he will sell it for $95,000. A then says no. B then says he will accept the $90,000 offer. There is:
    a. A contract for $90,000.
    b. No contract, as B's rejection destroyed the offer.
    c. No contract. Now B's counter offer to sell for $90,000.
    d. Both (b) and (c).

18. On March 2, a contract is made for B to buy a house for $90,000. On May 1, the house is worth $70,000 and B breaches the contract. Seller resells the house on June 1 for $60,000. Seller's general damages are:
    a. $20,000.
    b. $30,000.
    c. $70,000.
    d. $60,000.

19. A written contract is silent on the provisions for modification. It may be modified by:
    a. An executed oral agreement.
    b. Cannot be modified.
    c. A new written contract.
    d. Both (a) and (c).

20. Which of the following is a remedy for default of a real estate purchase contract?
    a. Commercial frustration
    b. Novation
    c. Both of the above
    d. Neither (a) nor (b)

Chapter 5

21. Real estate brokers must use a deposit receipt that:
    a. Conforms to the State Real Estate Board standard form.
    b. Conforms to the local real estate board standard form.
    c. Covers all necessary details, regardless of form.
    d. Contains no legal words that are undefined.

22. When a deposit receipt requires the "place of execution" at the top of the form, it is referring to the city where:
    a. Property is located.
    b. Buyer signs the contract.
    c. Seller is located.
    d. The buyer's residence lies.

23. If a contract provides for attorney's fees to the seller and the contract is breached, then:
    a. The seller recovers attorney's fees.
    b. The buyer recovers attorney's fees.
    c. Whichever party wins recovers attorney's fees.
    d. Both parties recover their attorney's fees.

24. Which of the following is a description of property that can be used in a deposit receipt?
    a. Street address
    b. County assessor's parcel number
    c. A descriptive name (e.g., "Gordon Ranch") if it is commonly known what that name means
    d. All of the above

25. In the C.A.R. deposit receipt form, acceptance occurs upon:
    a. "Acceptance" of the offer by the seller and signing the offer.
    b. Giving a signed copy of the "accepted" contract to the buyer.
    c. Failure to make a counteroffer.
    d. Opening the escrow.

Chapter 6

26. A multiple listing can only be which type of listing:
    a. Exclusive agency
    b. Exclusive right to sell
    c. Net listing
    d. All of the above

27. Which listing gives a broker a commission if any broker sells the property?
    a. Exclusive agency
    b. Exclusive right to sell
    c. Net listing
    d. Both (a) and (b)

28. _____ clause gives a broker a commission even after the listing expires.
    a. Exculpatory
    b. Safety
    c. Ready, willing, and able
    d. Procuring

29. An exclusive agency and exclusive right to sell listings are voidable by the seller unless the form includes:
    a. Termination date.
    b. Beginning date.
    c. Both of the above.
    d. Neither (a) nor (b).

30. Which of the following relates to an agency?
    a. Fiduciary
    b. Attorney-in-fact
    c. Principal
    d. All of the above

Chapter 7

31. An easement in gross requires:
    a. Dominant estate.
    b. Servient estate.
    c. Both (a) and (b).
    d. Neither (a) nor (b).

32. Which of the following methods will create an easement?
    a. Hostile use
    b. Notorious use
    c. Open use
    d. None of the above

33. An easement by necessity requires before the lot split:
    a. Discussions implying an easement
    b. Implied intent to reserve an easement
    c. Language in the deed reserving an easement
    d. None of the above

34. An easement recorded by deed cannot be terminated by which of the following methods:
    a. Non-use for five years
    b. Merger—dominant and servient estate under an owner
    c. Contract and grant releasing easement
    d. All of the above

35. Dedication:
    a. Is a gift of private property to the public.
    b. Can be expressed (i.e., by grant) or implied (by use).
    c. Can be of fee ownership to land or just an easement.
    d. All of the above.

Chapter 8

36. If a grant contains ambiguous language as to the type of estate granted, a court will:
    a. Attempt to construe it as a covenant, and if that fails will attempt to construe it as a condition on the estate.
    b. Attempt to construe it as a condition of the estate first, and as a covenant if that fails.
    c. Interpret the language as it believes to be equitable and fair.
    d. Void the grant as vague.

37. A fee simple absolute is:
    a. Presumed by every grant by an owner of full title.
    b. Not subject to any conditions or future interests.
    c. The largest estate permitted by law.
    d. All of the above.

38. The future interest associated with a life estate is a:
    a. Reversion.
    b. Reverting nonfreehold.
    c. Possibility of reverter.
    d. Contingent reverter.

39. Notice to terminate a month-to-month tenancy, without cause, when the tenant has only lived in the property six months, must be given how many days in advance?
    a. Exactly 30 days for California leases
    b. Length of rental pay period, but not less than seven days, and presumed to be 30 days (60 days if the tenant lived on the property over one year)
    c. By county ordinance
    d. Seven days

40. Notice to terminate a periodic tenancy:
    a. Must be given at the beginning of the period.
    b. Can be given anytime as long as the termination date coincides with the last day of that period.
    c. Must be given at the end of a period so that a tenant is out by the end of the next period.
    d. Can be given anytime during the month so long as the length of the notice equals the length of one period.

Chapter 9

41. Which of the following is not a valid California will?
    a. Oral will in fear of death
    b. Nuncupative will
    c. Quitclaim will
    d. None of the above

42. A grant deed warrants as to the conveyed property:
    a. That the grantor owns title
    b. That there are no liens or encumbrances
    c. Both of the above
    d. None of the above

43. Which of the following can be a valid legal description on a deed?
    a. Meets and bounds description
    b. The "Gordon Ranch" in San Rafael, California
    c. Home at 123 Jones Street, San Rafael, California
    d. All of the above

44. Escheat is:
    a. The money portion of a decedent's personal property.
    b. The property passing to the state for nonpayment of taxes.
    c. What happens to your property when you die intestate.
    d. None of the above.

45. If Ted was using a power of attorney to sign for "Joe Seller," grantor, he should:
    a. Have the form approved by the title company.
    b. Have the form recorded.
    c. Sign "Joe Seller by Ted Gordon under Power of Attorney."
    d. All of the above.

Chapter 10

46. Which of the following will stop a person from acquiring property by adverse possession?
    a. File an eviction or trespass suit within five years
    b. Give written consent to use the property within five years
    c. Have the sheriff remove the person within the five-year period
    d. All of the above will prevent adverse possession.

47. The rationale for the doctrine of adverse possession is:
    a. To penalize a property owner who "sleeps on his rights."
    b. To reward a delinquent trespasser who utilizes the land.
    c. To prevent property from standing unused.
    d. All of the above.

48. Which of the following is not a proper method for a state to acquire private property?
    a. Eminent domain
    b. Police power
    c. Condemnation
    d. All of the above

49. Generally, when the state condemns property it includes not only the cost of the property, but also:
    a. Appraisal fees and other costs of experts to the owner
    b. Owner's attorney's fees (to the extent they are reasonable)
    c. None of the above
    d. All of the above

50. Ted has a forged deed to Blackacre, a 100-acre farm. Ted only occupies the west 40 acres. If he meets and claims title by adverse possession, how much land could he claim:

    a. 40 acres

    b. 60 acres

    c. 100 acres

    d. None. Because the deed is invalid.

Chapter 11

51. The four unities needed for a joint tenancy are:

    a. Interest, possession, deed, and title.

    b. Interest, unity, time, and deed.

    c. Possession, time, interest, and title.

    d. Time, deed, interest, and possession.

52. In a limited partnership, limited partners are:

    a. Only liable for the amount of their investment.

    b. Only liable for their proportionate share of the liability.

    c. Only liable to the amount not covered by the general partner.

    d. Only liable for an equal share of the liabilities.

53. A syndication:

    a. Is not a legal entity.

    b. Is a limited partnership.

    c. May be a corporation, trust, or general partnership.

    d. All of the above.

54. Ted gives friend, Husband and Wife property, the deed reading "Husband and Wife." Ted intends to grant title as tenants in common. Husband and wife hold title:

    a. As tenants in common.

    b. As joint tenants.

    c. As community property.

    d. In trust until court determines.

55. Which of the following will sever a joint tenancy?

    a. Naming the real estate in a will to a nontenant

    b. Orally agreeing title is to be held as tenants in common

    c. Creditor of one joint tenant foreclosing against property

    d. All of the above

Chapter 12

56. A landowner now owes a duty of care:
    a. To anyone who comes on the land.
    b. Only to people who are invited on the land.
    c. To invited people and police and fire people.
    d. To guests and business invitees.

57. If water runs down an uphill owner's land, injuring the downhill neighbor's property, the uphill owner is liable if that owner:
    a. Improved the uphill property and created the dangerous runoff situation.
    b. Left property in its natural condition, made no changes to the land, but the land had dangerous run-off conditions.
    c. Both (a) and (b).
    d. Neither (a) nor (b).

58. An owner built an expensive garage, which unintentionally extended three inches onto the neighbor's land. If the neighbor sued for an injunction to force its removal, the court would:
    a. Allow it, and force the neighbor to sell owner 3 inches of land.
    b. Order its removal—the owner does not own the land it is on.
    c. Take a poll of all neighbors and decide accordingly.
    d. Refer to planning department for a variance.

59. A factory that emits dangerous sulfur dioxide that pollutes a lake:
    a. Is a public nuisance.
    b. Is a nuisance per incident.
    c. Can be stopped by injunction.
    d. All of the above.

60. An owner plans to build a 30-story building, plus two basement floors (below street level). If the adjacent neighbor's land or house is damaged by the excavation, the owner is:
    a. Liable under the doctrine of subjacent support, because excavation is over 9 feet deep.
    b. Liable under the doctrine of lateral support, because excavation is over 9 feet deep.
    c. Liable only if no notice is given to neighbor, with time for neighbor to protect neighbor's land.
    d. Not liable. The owner has right to use the land as needed, as long as there is no violation of zoning ordinance or building permit requirements.

Chapter 13

61. To terminate a periodic tenant without cause, the landlord uses a:

    a. 30-day notice (60-day notice if tenant been there over one year)

    b. Three-day notice

    c. Termination-for-cause notice

    d. Eviction notice

62. Which of the following is an advantage of an unlawful detainer action?

    a. Five days to answer a complaint

    b. Judgment can be tripled

    c. No cross complaints

    d. All of the above

63. Which of the following is proper wording for a three-day notice?

    a. Get off the premises within three days

    b. Cure the defect within three days

    c. Cure the defect or leave within three days

    d. Cure the defect and leave within three days

64. A tenant can rent a small, furnished office for $400 per month. The maximum deposits that can be collected, in addition to the first month's rent, is:

    a. $400.

    b. $800.

    c. $1200.

    d. Whatever the market will allow.

65. If a tenant complains to the health department about problems in living conditions of the tenant's apartment, the landlord can serve a 30-day notice (60-day notice for tenants over one year) to terminate the tenancy because of the tenant's complaint:

    a. At any time

    b. Never

    c. After 180 days

    d. After 60 days

Chapter 14

66. Recording provides constructive notice:

    a. To anyone for any and all purposes.

    b. Only to subsequent purchasers and encumbrancers.

    c. Only to bona fide purchasers without notice.

    d. And actual notice to anyone with a potential interest.

67. To be a "bona fide purchaser" ("BFP") a person must:

    a. Be a purchaser or encumbrancer.

    b. Have no notice of prior interests.

    c. Pay value.

    d. All of the above.

68. In February, "X" sells his vacant land to "A" who does not record. In March, "X" sells that same land to "B" who does not record. Neither "A" nor "B" has actual notice of the other's claim. Who owns the property:
    a. A owns the property.
    b. B owns the property.
    c. X owns the property.
    d. Up to the courts.

69. Ted owns only one piece of property, Blackacre. In February, "A" records a judgment against Ted, and in March "B" also records a judgment against Ted. In September, Ted purchases Whiteacre. Both properties are in Marin County, the county where the judgments were recorded. Which of the following is true:
    a. A's lien has priority over B's lien on both Blackacre and Whiteacre.
    b. A's lien has priority over B's lien on Blackacre, both liens are equal on Whiteacre.
    c. A's lien and B's lien have equal priority on both Blackacre and Whiteacre.
    d. A's lien has priority over B's lien on Blackacre; neither lien attaches to Whiteacre.

70. In January, "A" sues "B" in court claiming title, and records a lis pendens. In February, "X" buys the property. In March, "A" wins the lawsuit, and records the judgment. Between "A" and "X," who wins:
    a. A wins.
    b. X wins.
    c. Neither. B wins.
    d. Up to the courts.

Chapter 15

71. Even if a loan contains a due-on-sale provision, this clause cannot be enforced in which of the following transfers involving residential property occupied by the borrower:
    a. Homes passing to a relative because of the death of the borrower
    b. Death of a joint tenant borrower, where transfer is to another joint tenant
    c. Transfers to a revocable trust, where the borrower is the primary beneficiary and there is no change in the right to occupy the property
    d. All of the above are exempt.

72. A clause in a promissory note that reads "should default be made in payment of any installment when due, the whole sum of principal and interest shall become immediately due and payable at the option of the lender" is called:
    a. Due-on-sale clause.
    b. Alienation clause.
    c. Acceleration clause.
    d. All of the above.

73. What is the order to foreclose a deed of trust nonjudicially?
    a. File lis pendens, notice of default, reinstatement period, notice of sale, sale
    b. Notice of default, reinstatement period, notice of sale, sale
    c. Reinstatement period, notice of default, notice of sale, sale
    d. Notice of default, reinstatement period, court judgment, notice, sale

74. Which of the following relieves a borrower of any primary or contingent liability for payment of a loan secured by a deed of trust?
    a. Novation
    b. Assumption
    c. Subject to
    d. Release agreement

75. Which of the following is a purchase money loan?
    a. Loan to refinance an owner-occupied home
    b. Loan to remodel an owner-occupied home
    c. Both of the above
    d. Neither (a) nor (b)

Chapter 16

76. What is the natural order in which the following liens arise?
    a. Mechanic's lien, judgment lien, attachment lien
    b. Garnishment lien, attachment lien, mechanic's lien
    c. Attachment lien, judgment lien, execution lien
    d. Execution lien, judgment lien, attachment lien

77. Which of the following can never be a mechanic?
    a. Laborer
    b. Person selling nails and lumber
    c. General contractor
    d. None; all could be.

78. A judgment is recorded in Marin County and creates a lien on all nonexempt real property owned by the judgment debtor in:
    a. Marin County.
    b. Debtor's City of Residence.
    c. United States.
    d. California.

79. If an owner filed a notice of completion, a subcontractor would have how long to file a mechanic's lien:
    a. 30 days
    b. Never. Notice stops any liens.
    c. 90 days
    d. 60 days

80. If an owner wanted to protect himself from work ordered by a tenant, the owner would use:
    a. Notice of nonliability.
    b. Notice of nonresponsibility.
    c. Notice of completion.
    d. Notice of nonrecourse.

Chapter 17

81. The amount of the Homeowner's exemption for real property taxes is:
    a. $40 off tax bill.
    b. $70 off tax bill.
    c. $1,750 off assessed value.
    d. 10% of tax bill.

82. The first installment of real property taxes is delinquent on:
    a. March 10.
    b. April 10.
    c. November 10.
    d. December 10.

83. After property is marked "tax delinquent property" for unpaid taxes:
    a. A homeowner loses possession of the property.
    b. Property must be auctioned to the highest bidder within one year.
    c. Deed must be promptly executed to the State.
    d. None of the above.

84. Which of the following would not result in a reassessment of all or part of the real property involved in the following transfer?
    a. Brothers holding as joint tenants changing to tenants in common
    b. Father transferring from self to self and son as joint tenants
    c. Transfer from self to revocable trust with you as sole beneficiary
    d. None of the above causes a reassessment

85. Assume you bought a house in 1991 for $200,000, and made no improvements or changes in ownership since then. In 1994, your real property taxes (without any homeowner's exemption) would be:
    a. $206,000.
    b. $208,000.
    c. $212,000.
    d. $212,242.

Chapter 18

86. If you are single, aged 21, and purchasing your first house, a low-income home, the amount of your homestead would be:
   a. $75,000.
   b. $50,000.
   c. $100,000.
   d. $175,000.

87. If you are wheelchair bound, totally unable to work, and decide to homestead your home that has a mortgage of $200,000 on a house that has a fair market value of $210,000, the amount of your homestead would be:
   a. $75,000.
   b. $100,000.
   c. $175,000.
   d. No homestead as your property is not worth enough.

88. To be valid, a homestead must:
   a. Be recorded.
   b. Describe the property.
   c. Both of the above.
   d. Neither (a) nor (b).

89. Which of the following is true about claiming a homestead on a house?
   a. Can be claimed by a child if the parents do not claim
   b. One can be claimed by child, and another one claimed by parents
   c. Cannot be claimed by a child, only by parents
   d. Can be claimed by anyone, but only on behalf of the parents

90. Once a homestead is recorded, it generally protects against any future recorded liens, except which of the following liens are always superior to and have priority over even a recorded homestead:
   a. Mechanic's liens
   b. Deeds of trust
   c. Federal tax liens
   d. All of the above are always superior to homesteads.

Chapter 19

91. If an offer to purchase property only arises if the offeror receives a $1,000,000 inheritance by January 1986, the offer is subject to:
   a. Invalid condition, as illusory.
   b. Condition subsequent.
   c. Condition precedent.
   d. Covenant.

92. Which of the following does the court most favor in interpreting ambiguous language?
   a. Covenant
   b. Fee simple absolute
   c. Condition precedent
   d. Condition subsequent

93. Which of the following restrictions is valid?
    a. No minorities live on this land
    b. Permits houses of prostitution
    c. Creates a monopoly
    d. None of the above

94. Which of the following will render CC&Rs unenforceable?
    a. Totally circumstances, but before end date of CC&Rs
    b. Where CC&Rs are found to violate public policy
    c. Where plaintiff in lawsuit has waived the right to enforcement
    d. All of the above

95. _____ is the most important element in finding an equitable servitude.
    a. Contract between parties
    b. Successive equitable principles
    c. Notice of the restriction
    d. Constructive evidence

Chapter 20

96. Which of the following is not a proper purpose of zoning?
    a. Health
    b. Welfare
    c. Peace and quiet
    d. None; all proper

97. If a zoning ordinance acting for a proper public purpose renders $1,000,000 property worth less than $1,000, the owner can receive:
    a. No compensation.
    b. $999,000 cash compensation.
    c. $999,000 tax write-off only.
    d. $999,000 over 10 years.

98. The most successful attack on exempting property from the effects of zoning is:
    a. Administrative.
    b. Legislative.
    c. Judicial.
    d. Inverse condemnation.

99. If an R-3 zone automatically allows all R-2 and R-1 uses, then it is:
    a. Retrogressive zoning.
    b. Illegal.
    c. Cumulative zoning.
    d. General plan zoning.

100. ABAG, the Association of Bay Area Governments, located in the San Francisco Bay Area, is an example of:
    a. General plan zoning.
    b. Regional agencies to coordinate local zoning and development.
    c. Selecting delegates to electoral college and regional mayors.
    d. A strong, viable political group lobbying against zoning.

Chapter 21

101. The major California environmental act requires a report describing and evaluating the impact on the environment. This report is called:
    a. Environmental impact statement (EIS).
    b. Environmental impact document (EID).
    c. Environmental impact report (EIR).
    d. Environmental impact sheet (EIS).

102. Which of the following projects would not fall under the control of the Environmental Quality Act (EQA) by a landowner working on building a private shopping center?
    a. Seeking a variance
    b. Seeking a government funding
    c. Landowner is agency of the government.
    d. None of the above. All are under EQA.

103. Which of the following regulates the sale of existing subdivisions within the State of California?
    a. Subdivision Act
    b. Subdivided Lands Act
    c. Subdivision Map Act
    d. Interstate Subdivision Sales Qualification Act

104. Which of the following is regulated by the California Commissioner of Real Estate at the state level, and not by planning departments and other local agencies?
    a. Subdivision Map Act
    b. Interstate Subdivision Sales Qualification Act
    c. Subdivision Act
    d. Subdivided Lands Act

105. Which of the following would be defined as a subdivision under the Subdivision Map Act and subject to its provisions?
    a. Dividing a parcel of property into two separate parcels
    b. Dividing a parcel of property into five or more separate parcels
    c. Dividing a parcel of property into four or fewer separate parcels
    d. Dividing a parcel of property into three lots, each 160 acres or larger

Chapter 22

106. The title insurance premium is paid:
    a. Once, at close of escrow.
    b. Monthly, during the life of the policy.
    c. Annually, during the life of the policy.
    d. All of the above, as the borrower desires.

107. The institutional lender obtains which type of title policy:
    a. ATLA
    b. CTLA
    c. CLTA
    d. ALTA

108. An escrow officer is the agent of:
    a. The seller.
    b. The buyer.
    c. Both buyer and seller.
    d. One who pays agent's fee.

109. Escrow is to close in February. In January, the seller deposits the deed into escrow. The "transfer" in January of the instrument:
    a. Is legal delivery of the deed.
    b. Creates a presumption of delivery.
    c. Is never delivery.
    d. Delivery is not an element of transfer

110. If the express provisions of the deposit receipt conflict with the provisions of the escrow instructions, which prevail:
    a. Deposit receipt, as major document and purpose for escrow
    b. Deposit receipt, as first in time
    c. Escrow instructions, as later in time
    d. Neither prevails, and courts must decide conflict.

Chapter 23

111. A real estate broker is:
    a. Special agent.
    b. Ostensible agent.
    c. Statutory agent.
    d. All of the above.

112. Which of the following individuals are required by law to hold a real estate broker's license?
    a. Apartment manager
    b. Finders and "middlemen"
    c. Selling own property
    d. None of the above

113. A broker is always the agent of:
    a. The seller.
    b. The person who pays the commission.
    c. The buyer.
    d. None of the above.

114. A broker simultaneously receives two all-cash offers on the seller's property, one for $200,000 and the other for $210,000. The broker only presents the higher offer. The broker has violated:

    a. No law.

    b. Duty of good faith.

    c. The duty of full disclosure.

    d. Duty of loyalty—No adverse interest.

115. In establishing a selling price, a broker advises the seller to reduce the value by $15,000 because of an easement on the property. The seller accepts the advice and sells the property $15,000 below market value. The broker's error was unintentional and based on the broker's honest belief. The broker has:

    a. Violated no law.

    b. Committed Malpractice.

    c. Violated duty of full disclosure.

    d. Committed fraud.

Appendix E

Answers to Sample Tests #1 and #2

TEST #1

1. (b) The creation of law doctrine holds that laws created property. Therefore laws can and do regulate the nature, definition, and rights of property owners. (See page 5.)

2. (c) Strictly and legally speaking, property is only a creation of the law. However, most people speak of the tangible item as property. (See page 5.)

3. (c) The courts "balance the rights" and decide depending on the fact pattern involved. It is the constitution, not local ordinances that prevail. The Fifth Amendment and 14th Amendment are the two most important property clauses in the U.S. Constitution. (See page 2.)

4. (d) The Fifth Amendment to the U.S. Constitution prohibits the federal government from taking private property for public good without just compensation. The 14th Amendment contains a similar restriction against the States taking property without just compensation. (See page 2.)

5. (a) Shopping centers, in most cases, are analogous to public streets because they are open to the public. In many situations you can demonstrate absent specific restrictions by the shopping centers. Conversely, jails are designed for security purposes and not open to the public, and homes are private property also restricted to the public. (See page 5.)

6. (d) Common law originated in England, as opposed to civil law that originated in ancient Rome. (See page 12.)

7. (d) All are true. (See page 15.)

8. (c) Superior courts hear appeals from small claims; the Supreme Court hears appeals from courts of appeals. (See pages 20 and 23.)

9. (d) All contracts for the sale or transfer of real estate and leases over one year must be in writing to be enforceable. (See page 68.)

10. (a) The parol evidence rule does not allow oral testimony to be introduced that contradicts the terms of a written contract. (See page 28.)

11. (d) All other tests are really subjective tests used to determine the intent of the owner. (See page 147.)

12. (c) Fixtures are personal property so affixed to the reality as to become real property. Appurtenances (such as easements, water rights, and minerals) are part of the land. Minerals are just a type of appurtenance. (See page 34.)

13. (d) All of the above parties, all other facts being equal, will be favored in determining if an item is a fixture. (See page 39.)

14. (a) A landowner only owns that airspace that he can reasonably and beneficially used. (See page 39.)

15. (a) There is no difference as to which property can be included in a will. However, the method of transfer, attachment of liens, and jurisdiction are different between real and personal property. (See pages 34 and 35.)

16. (b) This is the definition of a voidable contract. (See page 54.)

17. (b) An offer can be revoked at any time, until it is accepted, or unless made irrevocable by separate consideration. (See page 76.)

18. (b) It is a social obligation, not a contract. The offer was not made with "contractual intent," and there is no consideration. (See pages 54 and 55.)

19. (d) The general damages are the contract price less the fair market value at time of breach. (See page 64 and the Royer case on page 73.)

20. (b) In home purchase contracts, contracts over 3 percent of the selling price are valid, but the burden of proof is on the seller to prove his damages, and he may not collect more than his actual damages. (See page 65.)

21. (d) The deposit receipt serves all of the above functions. (See page 76.)

22. (a) Absent fraud, a person is ordinarily bound by what he signs, assuming he is mentally capable of understanding what is written. This doctrine is the principle of the *Meyer v. Benko* case in this chapter. (See page 78.)

23. (d) Minors and incompetents lack legal capacity to sign such legal documents. A corporation to be formed is not yet a legal entity in existence, and hence cannot sign. Promoters sometimes sign in the name of a corporation to be formed, but they run the very real risk that the contract could be voidable. (See page 63.)

24. (b) "Time is of the essence" means that all time periods stated in the contract are deemed material, and the obligations must be performed within the stated time periods. Normally, such time periods will not be waived. (See page 176.)

25. (b) The person who pays is decided by the contract between the parties. Most often such fees are paid according to county custom, but the decision to do so comes from an agreement to that effect found in the contract. (See page 117.)

26. (b) The other answers are fictitious laws or names. (See page 142.)

27. (b) Only the exclusive right to sell gives the broker a commission on a sale by the owner. (See pages 145 and 146.)

28. (d) Option and net listings can attach to any type of listing, and open listings only give the selling broker a commission. (See pages 145 and 146.)

29. (c) The percentage is based on selling price. In homes, the typical commission is six or seven percent of the selling price. (See page 146.)

30. (b) The famed Easton case, now codified, requires the broker to complete this form in all residential transactions—with certain minor exceptions. (See page 169.)

31. (c) An easement appurtenant requires two separately owned parcels, the one that is burdened (encumbered) by the easement, called the servient estate, and the one that is benefited by the easement, called the dominant estate. (See page 180.)

32. (c) A profit á prendre is a special easement, granting another access (and right-of-way) and the right to remove (power to consume) natural resources on the land. Traditionally, it is granted for timber, coal, or oil. Often, leases, not profit á prendres are used. (See page 182.)

33. (d) All of the above indicate permission to use land, which prevents use from being "hostile" and thereby being one of the elements needed for an easement by prescription. (See page 185.)

34. (a) Because the dominant estate enjoys the benefits of the easement, he also has the burdens. Of course, the parties are free to contractually provide any arrangement they want. Frequently, there is no prior agreement, so the statute controls. (See page 186.)

35. (c) A license can be revoked at any time, even indirectly by conduct. For example, a license to use a road is revoked if a locked fence blocks the road. No notice need be given, other than the fact the license's purpose is prevented. (See page 192.)

36. (c) The terminology arose in ancient England, where a freehold estate was one that could be owned by a free man. All others (e.g., serfs) could only own nonfreehold estates, commonly known as leases. An estate for years is a leasehold estate (See page 198.)

37. (c) The definition of ownership in severalty is ownership by one person. (See page 200.)

38. (b) It does not terminate automatically, but takes a court action and proof that no waiver of the condition occurred. It is rarely encountered. (See page 202.)

39. (d) Probably most periodic tenancies are month-to-month and created orally. Tenancies at will are rarely written. Estates at sufferance arise orally and by law. (See page 210.)

40. (b) Under the Statute of Frauds, leases over one year (or where the expiration date is more than one year away) must be in writing to be enforceable. This applies to all leases, regardless of the type of property or whether or not minors live there. (See Table 8.2 on page 211.)

41. (a) Minors can and often do hold title to real estate. However, they lack capacity to transfer title. A guardian is needed to execute and convey title on behalf of the minor. (See pages 222 and 223.)

42. (c) The quitclaim contains no warranties, not even a warranty that the grantor owns any interest in the property described in the deed. For this reason, it is often used to clear land of potential or actual clouds on title. (See Table 9.1 on page 215.)

43. (c) Since 1983, California recognized a new will, the statutory will. It is a form that allows only limited flexibility. For people whose estate plan coincides with the forms, it can be an inexpensive, enforceable, professionally prepared will. The only problem is to know if your tax planning and estate plan fully match the testator's needs. (See page 224.)

44. (b) The testator in drafting his will nominates his executor, and usually names alternate executors in case the first named executor cannot serve. (See page 225.)

45. (a) Because the Garn-St. Germain Act holds transfers by land sales contract allows acceleration of the due-on-sale clause in a mortgage, these documents are not commonly used in California. Option (c) is incorrect. Possession does not pass on C.O.E. without wording in the document. The refund on default is not automatic, so (b) is false. A refund requires payments in excess of the seller's damages. (See page 226.)

46. (b) While it may be difficult to imagine a situation where you could occupy commercial property for five years without the owner taking action, adverse possession can be had against all privately owned real estate. Adverse possession cannot be used against publicly owned property, whether occupied or unused. (See page 232.)

47. (b) You only need to use the property to acquire an easement to it, but you need to occupy (possess) the property to acquire it by adverse possession. Adverse possession also requires payment of taxes. (See pages 233 and 234.)

48. (d) All of the above refer to acquisition of title by "color of title." Claim of right occurs when the occupant knows he has no rights to title or mistakenly believes he has a right to occupancy, but no written document is involved. Further, he can only acquire that which is actually occupied. (See page 235.)

49. (d) Adding second story is not reasonably related ("essential nexus") to the county's need for park. Adding second story will not impact need for the park. The county must prove the

specific problem (the need for a park) somehow arises from or significantly increases by allowing a second story to the house. Further, the county must prove that the land or funds demanded are roughly proportional to the cost of correcting or reducing the problem arising from allowing a second story. It can do neither here. (See page 239.)

50. (d) The property must be for the public good and further the taking agency must adopt a resolution that the condemnation action is for public necessity. Finally, the owner must be paid a just compensation. (See page 238.)

51. (c) Property held as tenants in common passes by will or intestacy. There is no right of survivorship. (See page 249.)

52. (d) All property is presumed to be community property. Credit is considered like property, and because it is based on earnings, it is community property. (See page 258.)

53. (b) Anything acquired by gift, even during marriage is a separate property. (See page 258.)

54. (b) You must record an affidavit of death of joint tenant and a death certificate. (See page 250.)

55. (b) Community property came from Spanish law and only eight states in the nation have it. (See page 257.)

56. (d) Social guests and government employees whose job takes them on another's land are all licensees. (See pages 279 and 280.)

57. (b) Generally, the owner is not liable for injuries arising on the sidewalk in front of his or her property unless the owner modified the sidewalk, or created a dangerous condition. (See page 282.)

58. (c) An encroachment is a relatively permanent object that extends onto or over the land of another. A person is neither an object nor a relatively permanent obstruction. (See page 292.)

59. (d) An encroachment is the tort of either a nuisance or a trespass, where an object extends onto or over another's land. (See Table 12.3 on page 292.)

60. (a) Adjacent landowners have an obligation to pay for half the cost of repairs for boundary line fences, under C.C. 841. (See pages 291 and 292.)

61. (b) A three-day notice is used to terminate a lease for cause. (See pages 298 and 299.)

62. (b) First terminate the lease, usually by 3-day or 30-day notice (60-day notice if tenant has been there over one year), then obtain unlawful detainer judgment, and then have sheriff enforce the judgment and evict the tenant. (See page 301.)

63. (a) Before the sheriff can physically evict, he must first serve a five-day notice of eviction, either on the tenant personally, or by mailing a copy and positing one on the door. (See pages 307 and 308.)

64. (b) The total deposits cannot exceed two months' rent for unfurnished residential property. (See page 320.)

65. (a) The tenant cannot use this remedy more than twice in a 12-month period. The cause is immaterial, as long as the tenant did not substantially create the condition. (See page 321.)

66. (b) Recording establishes priorities, but does not guarantee priority as of date of recording. Mechanic's liens, for example, usually have a different priority date. (See page 344.)

67. (c) It is binding between the parties, but is subject to challenge by a BFP. (See page 350.)

68. (b) People living on the property suggest they have some sort of interest, which is a type of constructive notice. Seeing the actual or copy of a deed is "actual" notice. (See page 347.)

69. (b) The first bona fide purchaser ("BFP") to record without notice wins. This is the advantage of the recording statutes. (See page 347.)

70. (b) The mechanic's lien gets its priority as of the date work commenced, which is February. This is why lenders require ALTA title policies to protect against mechanic's liens that can have priority over earlier recorded documents. (See page 350.)

71. (c) It is signed by the maker, not the lender. The lender is not promising to pay; the borrower is obligating himself or herself. (See page 363.)

72. (c) Banks loans and loans made or arranged by real estate brokers that are secured by deeds of trust are currently unregulated. (See page 377.)

73. (d) The definition of the party's names. (See page 367.)

74. (b) To sue the borrower personally, the loan must first be a non-purchase money loan, which is nonjudicially foreclosed, that produces a deficiency at the sale, and the lender had sought a deficiency judgment from the court. You cannot just sue the borrower immediately and before any foreclosure. (See page 384.)

75. (d) "Soft money" deeds of trust taken back by the seller have no type of property limitations. (See page 385.)

76. (b) Once a judgment has been obtained, it is enforced by obtaining a writ of execution, which creates an execution lien. A mortgage is a voluntary lien, and a mechanic's lien is available only to certain people who work on or supply material to property. A creditor's lien has no application to lien enforcement. (See page 415.)

77. (b) The law severely restricts the use of these attachments because of the potential for violation of the Fifth Amendment (taking of property without due process of law). (See pages 406 and 407.)

78. (d) Any lien would expire ten years from date of the judgment (1985). The 1990 recording has no validity. (See page 409.)

79. (b) It is called involuntary because it arises without any action by the owner, and indeed, is often against the owner's wishes. (See page 416.)

80. (a) A mechanic's lien relates back to the date when work first commences on the property. For this reason, lenders require ALTA title insurance policies for protection from as yet unrecorded liens. (See pages 416 and 419.)

81. (a) If the veteran qualifies, the tax bill is reduced by $40. (See page 432.)

82. (d) Government properties and properties of churches, schools, hospitals, charities, and other welfare institutions are exempt, under normal nonprofit operations. (See page 431.)

83. (c) The mnemonic phrase "no darn fooling around" is helpful. (See page 432.)

84. (a) A new room causes reassessment of that room. All transfers between spouses are exempt from reassessments. (See page 438.)

85. (c) One percent of $350,000 is $3,500, your first year's gross tax, less $70 homeowner's exemption, for a tax due of $3,430. (See pages 431 and 432.)

86. (c) The amount is $100,000. (See page 448.)

87. (a) The amount is $75,000, a single person's homestead. It is immaterial if your home is your first or your last, or the amount of the purchase price. (See page 448.)

88. (c) The amount for a person over age 65 is $175,000, the same as for a person who is disabled and unable to work. (See page 448.)

89. (b) One of the requirements of a homestead is to live on the homestead property. A vacation is not an abandonment. Two or more people living in homestead property is not grounds for termination. (See page 456.)

90. (a) Once the homestead is filed, it continues to automatically increase each time the legislature increases the amount. No action need be taken by the homeowner. There were no outstanding debts. (If there are outstanding debts, as to those outstanding obligations, and only as to those limited outstanding debts, the amount sometimes remains static if there is insufficient equity in the home). (See page 453.)

91. (b) A condition subsequent holds that a party has a duty that terminates on the happening of the condition. Here the obligation to purchase property would be excused by the condition subsequent. (See page 460.)

92. (c) Damages and injunction are proper remedies, but forfeiture only applies to conditions. (See page 461.)

93. (d) A covenant must be written, recorded, and meet all of the above requirements to run with the land. (See page 461.)

94. (d) Covenants are generally contractual in nature, not affecting title, and thereby not allowing a forfeiture of the estate as a remedy. (See page 461.)

95. (a) Such actions rarely arise outside the subdivision general plans. Equitable servitude arises by notation on deeds that do not meet the formal requirements to "run with the land." (See pages 464 and 465.)

96. (c) The source of zoning is the police power, the right of a government to regulate property for the health, safety, and welfare of its citizens. (See pages 471 and 472.)

97. (d) Zoning is a mere "regulation" of property, while (a), (b), and (c) concern a "taking" of property. (See pages 471 and 472.)

98. (d) Master plans are required for long range planning for all zoning communities. Zoning must follow the general plan, but the plan itself does not zone. (See the Selby Realty Co. case in the chapter). (See page 473.)

99. (b) The variance is obtained by showing a unique hardship suffered by the property owner because of the effect of zoning. (See page 480.)

100. (b) The administrative (executive) branch of government, usually represented by the planning commission or the board of supervisors, can grant conditional use permits, if permitted by ordinance. (See page 480.)

101. (c) The National Environmental Protection Act ("NEPA") is the major environmental act. (See page 485.)

102. (b) If the project has or may have a significant impact, such a report is needed. It must ascertain the short-term and long-range impact, adverse environmental effects, alternative options, and other issues, besides just any adverse effects. (See page 486.)

103. (d) All of the above are liable. Anyone who currently owns polluted property or currently operates a facility on such land is liable. Anyone who owned the land or operated a facility at the time of contamination is liable, even if that ownership/operation was several generations of owners back. Finally, anyone who arranges for transportation or who transports toxic material may be held liable. (See pages 490 and 491.)

104. (c) The Subdivision Map Act is administered by local agencies and regulates the physical development and design that is required for the creation of subdivisions. (See page 495.)

105. (b) The White Report is the final report by the Commission and evidences that the subdivider has met all the requirements of the Subdivided Lands Act. The Pink report is only a preliminary

report, not allowing the developer at this state to accept any binding contracts or cash any deposits. (See page 498.)

106. (d) Neither CLTA nor ALTA policies insure against violations of police power regulations. (See Table 22.1 on page 515 and see page 513.)

107. (b) Both (a) and (c) are covered because they are recorded, although they would have been uncovered if they were unrecorded. (See Table 22.1 on page 515 and see page 513.)

108. (c) The California Land Title Association policy (CLTA) is obtained by noninstitutional lenders and buyers. (See page 515.)

109. (c) There is no requirement that title insurance be obtained, although it is rare that such insurance is not obtained in purchase-sale escrows and institutional-lender involved escrows. (See page 530.)

110. (a) Both attorneys and real estate brokers may act as escrows, although unlicensed as such, if incident to a transaction in which they are involved in their professional capacity. (See pages 504 and 505.)

111. (c) An agent represents a principal. (See page 532.)

112. (c) An agent must represent someone other than himself. An agency can arise by implication of law. The agent can represent a buyer, seller, lender, or any other party to a transaction. (See page 536.)

113. (d) A salesperson must work for a broker, who must review and initial all contracts written by the salesperson. The "employment" agreement between the broker and salesperson must be in writing. (See page 537.)

114. (b) A broker must act in utmost good faith and total fidelity to the principal. Suggesting negotiating strategy adverse to the client is violation of that duty, and is grounds to deny the broker a commission and hold the broker liable for any damages sustained by seller. (See pages 541 and 542.)

115. (d) A broker must disclose relationships that can or may influence a seller, regardless of the fairness of the offer. Here the broker could be charged with "secret profits" or "adverse interest." (See page 550.)

TEST #2

1. (c) The natural law doctrine, which is now not followed in any country, holds property exists outside and not because of the law. (See page 7.)

2. (d) At one time land was held by force. Might made right. Now laws replace force and define an owner's rights. (See page 2.)

3. (a) As long as the demonstrators are reasonably nondisruptive, free speech prevails on the private property treated as if it were public property. (See page 5.)

4. (c) The 14th Amendment prohibits states from taking its citizens property without due process of law (just compensation). (See page 3.)

5. (c) Zoning, building codes, etc. do not infrequently treat neighboring properties differently. As laws and ordinances change or are amended, so do property restrictions change. (See page 4.)

6. (c) Only lower courts are "bound" by stare decisis. (See page 13.)

7. (d) The landlord has a choice, although if he sues in small claims court and loses, he has no right of appeal. (See page 20.)

8. (b) The Supreme Court hears only a small percentage of the cases appealed, accepting those cases it desires to hear by issuing a "writ of certiorari." (See page 23.)

9. (a) Suit must be brought on written contracts within four years, or become unenforceable if the defendant raises the defense of the Statute of Limitations. (See page 27.)

10. (b) About 50 percent of all land in the State of California is owned by federal, state, or local government, with the federal government owning about 45 percent of all California property. (See page 32.)

11. (a) Personal property is subject to the laws of the decedent's residence. Real estate is subject to the laws where the property is located. (See page 37.)

12. (c) The parties can agree between themselves that crops shall be real or personal property. Absent agreement, on agricultural leases, it remains the property of the tenant; if not harvested by the end of the lease, it passes to the landlord (absent constructive severance). (See page 43.)

13. (a) Appurtenances are those rights and things incidental to (but not part of) the surface land. (See page 39.)

14. (d) Trade fixtures only occur if the fixture was installed by the tenant for trade or domestic use and can be removed without irreparable injury to the premises. (See page 48.)

15. (b) A good faith improver can remove fixtures, upon paying expenses thereto, if it will cause no injury to the property and the removal will not be inequitable under the circumstances. (See page 49.)

16. (a) This is the definition of an executory contract. (See page 54.)

17. (d) A rejection destroys the offer. B has created an offer to sell, which A can accept or reject. (See page 60.)

18. (a) The general damages are the contract price less the fair market value at time of breach. (See page 72.)

19. (d) If the oral agreement is fully executed by both parties it can modify a written agreement. This is an exception to the "equal dignities" rule. While the original contract may need to be in writing, a fully executed agreement can be oral. Naturally, a new contract can modify an old one. (See page 64.)

20. (d) Novation and commercial frustration concern excuses for discharge of contract. They are not remedies for a breach of contract. (See pages 65 and 66.)

21. (c) There is no required form that must be followed. Many local boards urge adoption of their forms, but such use is not mandatory under law or by Real Estate Commissioners' regulations. (See page 78.)

22. (b) The place where the buyer physically signs the contract is the place of purchase. (See page 89.)

23. (c) Attorney's fee clauses are double-edged provisions. If it authorizes one party, then whichever party prevails recovers its fees. (See page 125.)

24. (d) Any description by which a person could identify that particular property as the parcel described is adequate. *C.C. 1092.* However, it is preferable to use meets and bounds, government survey, or reference to a recorded map as the description. (See page 90.)

25. (b) Unlike most deposit receipt forms that provide that acceptance occurs upon execution of the contract by the seller, the C.A.R. form requires an additional step. The executed form must be delivered to the buyer before a contract is formed. (See page 76.)

26. (d) New laws now require MLS to list any type of listing, not just exclusive right to sell listings. (See page 146.)

27. (d) Both the exclusive right to sell and the exclusive agency yield a commission on a sale by any other broker. (See page 145.)

28. (b) A sale during the "safety" time period to a prior prospective buyer, registered with the seller, yields a commission. (See page 148.)

29. (a) A contract does not need a beginning date, although the Commissioner's Regulations make it voidable without an ending date. (See page 143.)

30. (d) An agency creates a fiduciary obligation by the agent, sometimes called an attorney-in-fact. (See page 142.)

31. (b) An easement in gross has no dominant estate, because it belongs to a person rather than an estate. It only has a servient (encumbered) estate. (See page 181.)

32. (d) All of the above are part of the elements needed to establish an easement by prescription. However, none of the above will, by themselves, creates an easement. (See page 185.)

33. (d) An easement by necessity requires strict necessity. It rests on the public policy (not contract, agreement, or implication) and holds that land should not be landlocked and rendered unusable. (See Table 7.1 on page 184.)

34. (a) Nonuse will not terminate easements (except one acquired by prescription). An easement is an interest in property. Just as nonuse of your land for five years does not lose the parcel, neither does five years' nonuse of the easement forfeit that interest in the property. (See page 189.)

35. (d) Subdividers often dedicate land in fee for schools or parks and easements for roads. Landowners can lose an easement by dedication by five years' use by the public under specified conditions. In either case, it is considered a gift to the public, for which no compensation need be paid. (See page 195.)

36. (a) Because the "courts hate forfeitures," the courts will attempt to construe any defeasible language in the way that allows the least forfeiture. A covenant is first, because it dies with the original parties. Next is a condition, which "runs with the land." (c) is incorrect because the court is bound by the law and the language in the deed. (See page 199.)

37. (d) All are true. It is presumed, not defeasible and the largest estate at law. (See page 200.)

38. (a) A reverter (possibility and contingent follow a fee simple subject to a condition subsequent estate). A nonfreehold estate would be a leasehold estate. (See page 203.)

39. (b) In a month-to-month tenancy this would be 30 days, unless the tenant lived on the property over one year, in which case 60 days notice is required. Absent the 60-day rule for long-term tenancies, in a week-to-week tenancy, the notice need only be given 7 days in advance. County ordinances (e.g., rent control) may control the right to give notices, but have not affected the Civil Code time periods involved in giving notices. (See page 209.)

40. (d) Notice can be given at any time. If the notice is given in the middle of a month-to-month lease (e.g., on January 15th) effective 30 days later, then on the February 1st, the tenant would only pay half a month's rent. (See page 209.)

41. (d) The nuncupative will, also called the oral will, was a valid will in California until 1983. This will is still valid in some other states, but not in California. (See page 224.)

42. (d) The warranties of (a) and (b) are "full" warranties, and grant deeds have only limited warranties. A grant deed only warrants that the grantor has not previously conveyed the designated interest (not that he owns it) and he has not encumbered the property (not that it is free and clear). (See page 214.)

43. (d) Any description that describes only one specific piece of property is valid. The informal description like (b) and (c) are seldom used in professionally prepared deeds, but they are valid. (See page 223.)

44. (d) Escheat is property passing to the State of California, because the decedent has no heirs who can claim his estate. (See page 226.)

45. (d) Only (a) is not absolutely mandatory. However, unless the title company approves the form, it may not issue a title policy. Without the title policy there probably would be no sale. Still, title company approval is not a legal requirement, only a business necessity. (See page 222.)

46. (c) All of the named methods will prevent adverse possession, as they stop the "open, notorious, and continues possession." (See page 232.)

47. (d) Adverse possession is designed to reward the diligent and punish the lazy, while keeping as much property as possible in the commerce and use of the people within the state. (See page 232.)

48. (b) Police power is a regulation of property, while eminent domain, through the method of condemnation, results in an actual taking of the property. (See pages 238 and 239.)

49. (c) One of the difficulties is the state almost never seems to pay what the owner feels the property is worth. In addition, the owner, if he decides to challenge the amount paid by the state, often spends considerable sums in attorney's fees, appraisal fees, and to other experts, for which he is not reimbursed. (See page 245.)

50. (c) Under a color of title, an adverse possessor is entitled to all of the land described in the deed, even though only 40 acres were actually occupied. It is presumed that he constructively occupied the entire property. (See Table 10.2 on page 236.)

51. (c) Time, title, interest, and possession are required at common law. In California, only possession and part of interest is needed. (See page 252.)

52. (a) The advantage of limited partnerships is the limited risk. (See page 267.)

53. (d) The syndication is a means of jointly pooling resources to acquire property, but it is not a legal entity. (See page 272.)

54. (c) All property acquired by spouse is presumed to be community property unless the deed states otherwise. (See page 257.)

55. (c) Foreclosure causes actual title transfer. Wills and oral agreements have no effect on joint tenancy property. (See page 250.)

56. (a) An owner owes a duty to everyone, even if it is only a duty to refrain from intentionally injuring them. (See page 278.)

57. (c) The uphill owner is liable in negligence for having property in a condition that creates dangerous risk of runoff. (See page 293.)

58. (a) For unintentional trespasses, the court would "balance the equities" and find three inches of land were unnecessary to the owner. The trespasser would have to pay the owner for the reasonable cost of three inches of property. (See page 292.)

59. (d) The nuisance is public, arises because of the nature of the factory's operation (per incident), for which an injunction will be issued. (See page 288.)

60. (b) By excavating over 9 feet deep, the owner is strictly liable for all damages, unless the neighbor refused to allow the owner (at owner's expense) onto neighbor's land to protect it from potential damage. (See page 294.)

61. (a) A 30-day notice is used to terminate a periodic tenancy without cause. If the tenant has lived in the apartment for one year, then the landlord must use a 60-day notice. The three-day notice is to terminate "for cause." (See page 303.)

62. (d) Cross complaints cannot be used, a judgment can be tripled for willful retention of the premises by the tenant, and a five-day response time are all advantages of unlawful detainer actions. (See page 306.)

63. (c) The notice must be stated in the alternative ("or") to pay rent or quit the premises. (See page 305.)

64. (d) The restrictions on the size of deposits only apply to residential property. (See page 320.)

65. (c) It is not illegal to retaliate and evict after six months from the date of a complaint for habitability. (See pages 326 and 327.)

66. (b) It is not "notice to the world"; rather, notice is limited to people without notice who are either purchasers or encumbrancers. (See page 344.)

67. (d) A bona fide purchaser must be a purchaser or encumbrancer who pays value for the interest and have no notice of prior interests. (See page 348.)

68. (a) The first document in time wins when nothing is recorded. (See page 350.)

69. (a) A judgment lien attaches to all after acquired property in the county, so both liens attach to Whiteacre. While both liens attach at the time of purchase to the newly acquired Whiteacre, between themselves, they retain their original priorities. Because A's lien was recorded first, it has priority on both parcels. (See page 355.)

70. (b) A judgment relates back and obtains the priority of the date of recording a lis pendens. This is why it is so hard to sell property once a lis pendens is recorded against property. (See page 356.)

71. (d) All of the above are special exemptions in which the lender cannot enforce a due-on-sale clause, despite its presence in a promissory note. (See Table 15.2 on page 372.)

72. (c) There is nothing concerning transfer of the property as the default "trigger" so (a) and (b) are inapplicable, as is (d). This clause is a standard acceleration clause. (See page 371.)

73. (b) The notice of default is recorded, wait the reinstatement period, public notice of sale, hold sale. (See pages 391 and 392.)

74. (a) Only a novation releases contingent liability. (See page 404.)

75. (d) The home is already owned, so the proceeds are not used to purchase the home. (See page 386.)

76. (c) The attachment lien arises before judgment, the judgment is recorded to create a lien, and the execution arises on enforcement of the judgment. (See pages 406 and 409.)

77. (d) All could be mechanics. Options (a) and (c) are part of the definitions of mechanics, and (b) would be a materialman. (See page 416.)

78. (a) It would have to be recorded in every county in California to be a lien throughout the state. (See page 410.)

79. (a) The short delay is one of the key reasons for filing a notice of completion. (The general contractor would have 60 days.) (See page 419.)

80. (c) It must be posted and recorded within 10 days after the owner has actual or constructive notice of the commencement of the work. (See page 426.)

81. (b) If the homeowner occupies the property as of March 1, under the old law, pre-Proposition 13, the exemption was answer (c). (See page 432.)

82. (d) The mnemonic phrase "no darn fooling around" is helpful. (See page 432.)

83. (d) Marking property "tax-defaulted property" is only a bookkeeping entry, having no effect on possession. It starts the five-year period for redemption running. Until a few years ago, such notation was called "sale to the state," but so much confusion resulted, that the name was changed. (See page 433.)

84. (d) *R.&T.C. 61–65* exempts all of the above transfers. Options (a) and (c) have no tax because there is no change in "real" ownership interests. Option (b) has no tax because creation of the joint tenancy has the grantor remaining as a joint tenant. (See pages 438 and 439.)

85. (d) 1991 value of house is $200,000. At 2 percent per year increase, it would be $204,000 in 1992; and $208,080 in 1993; and $212,242 in 1994. (See page 443.)

86. (a) The amount is $75,000, a single person's homestead. It is immaterial if your home is your first or your last, or the amount of the purchase price. (See page 448.)

87. (c) The amount is $175,000 for a disabled person. Obviously, with only $10,000 equity, $165,000 of the homestead amount would be unused. The unused amount remains to shelter future appreciation in the home. (See page 448.)

88. (c) A homestead must be recorded to be valid. Further, it must contain a description of the homestead property so that creditors will know which parcel is exempted. (See page 454.)

89. (c) The homestead can only be claimed by either a husband or a wife, and then only for their benefit. Children and others have no rights to file on their behalf. (See page 454.)

90. (d) All three are senior to homesteads, even when recorded years after the homestead. (See page 453.)

91. (c) A condition precedent holds that a party has no duty to perform unless and until the happening of the condition. Here the obligation to purchase property arises on receipt of the inheritance. (See page 460.)

92. (b) The courts favor that solution that involves the least threat of forfeiture. Because (b) has absolutely no restrictions on title, it is the most favored. (See page 462.)

93. (d) None are lawful; (a) violates the constitution, and (b) and (c) violate state statutes. (See page 460.)

94. (d) Changed circumstances is the most common attack, although occasionally an attack on the legality of the restriction (e.g., creates a monopoly) succeeds, and sometimes the plaintiff waives the right to sue by inequitable conduct. (See page 467.)

95. (d) The critical element is that the future owner takes the property with full notice of the restriction, so that it would be inequitable not to bind the new owner. This is an equitable action, not one based on contract. (See page 465.)

96. (d) As the U.S. Supreme Court stated: "Public safety, public health, morality, peace and quiet, law and order ... merely illustrate the scope of the power and do not delimit it." (See page 472.)

97. (a) The proper exercise of zoning never results in compensation to an owner, even if property is rendered almost valueless. (See page 438.)

98. (a) The administrative remedies of variances and conditional use permits are the most effective and frequently used remedy. (See page 480.)

99. (c) Cumulative zoning allows all lesser included zoning within the current zone. (See page 480.)

100. (b) ABAG helps the eight San Francisco Bay area counties on regional zoning and development, because of the close interdependence of the counties on each other. Thus, zoning can and is being done on both the county and the regional level. (See page 474.)

101. (c) The environmental impact statement (EIS) is the federal document; and (c), the environmental impact report (EIR), is the California report. (See page 486.)

102. (d) Any action by the government, itself (c) or through its funding or involvement (b) or by the issuance of permits or other entitlements (a) qualifies as "state" action. (See page 486.)

103. (b) The Subdivided Lands Act is administered by the California Real Estate Commission, and concerns the sale of existing subdivisions. (See page 495.)

104. (d) The Subdivided Lands Act is administered by the California Real Estate Commission, and concerns the sale of existing subdivisions. (See page 495.)

105. (a) Division into two or more contiguous lots is a subdivision under the Subdivision Map Act. The "five or more" lots and the "160-acre exemption" concern the Subdivided Lands Act. (See page 499.)

106. (a) The premium is only paid once, at close of escrow. (See page 504.)

107. (d) The American Land Title Association policy (ALTA) is obtained by institutional lenders. (See page 513.)

108. (c) The escrow is a dual agent, representing both the buyer and the seller in the capacity of a limited agent. (See page 518.)

109. (c) Delivery occurs at close of escrow, or as otherwise specified in the escrow instructions, which allow for legal delivery of the deed upon satisfaction of certain conditions (e.g., payment of all sums by buyer). (See page 517.)

110. (c) The latest contract on a subject is deemed controlling, which in this case would be the escrow instructions. (See page 519.)

111. (a) An "ostensible agency" arises by operation of law as an imputed agency. There is no such term as a statutory agent. (See page 534.)

112. (d) Answer (c) is not an agency, and (a) and (b) are statutory exceptions to the real estate licensing law. (See page 537.)

113. (d) The broker can be the agent of the buyer, seller, lender, tenant, or other party. While the broker is usually an agent of the person who pays the commission, such statements are only rules of thumb that are generally true. (See page 536.)

114. (c) A broker must disclose all material facts about the property, including all offers. Perhaps one "buyer" has better financial ability, requires a shorter escrow, or any other fact that the seller may consider. (See page 550.)

115. (b) A broker is required to possess the degree of skill and knowledge about property and its value consistent with that of other professionals in the area. (See page 551.)

Glossary of Real Estate and Legal Terms

A

Abstract of judgment: A summary of a money judgment. The summary is usually prepared so that it may be recorded, thereby creating a (judgment) lien on real estate owned by the judgment debtor.

Acceleration clause: A clause in a promissory note, deed of trust, or mortgage that provides that upon default of a payment or some other stated event, the entire unpaid balance becomes immediately due and payable.

Acceptance: An essential element of every contract, it is the consent to be bound by the offer. In deeds, it is the consent to accept a grant of real property.

Accord and satisfaction: The discharge of an existing contract by accepting the performance under a substitute contract. Generally, consideration under the new contract is different from and of lesser value than under the original contract. Accord is the substitution of a new contract, and satisfaction is the performance of that contract; the combination discharges the original contract.

Acknowledgment: A formal statement (usually before a notary public) by the person signing a deed or document that the instrument was actually and freely signed.

Actual notice: Information of which a person has actual or physical knowledge.

Adjacent: Located next to or near an object or parcel of property.

Adjoining: Located so as to touch an object or share a common property line.

Adverse possession: A method of acquiring property through continuous use of that property while paying taxes on it.

Affidavit: A written statement of facts sworn to be true under penalty of perjury or other affirmation and taken before a notary public or other public official.

Agency: A special relationship of trust by which one person (agent) is authorized to conduct business, sign papers, or otherwise act on behalf of another person (principal).

Agent: Someone authorized to act for another (called the principal) in business matters.

Agreement: A mutual understanding or compact between parties. Although often used as synonymous with contract, technically it denotes mutual promises that fail as a contract for lack of consideration.

Alienation: Conveyance or transfer of title to real estate from one person to another person.

Alienation clause: In a deed of trust or mortgage, a provision that, if the secured property is sold or transferred, the lender has the option of accelerating the loan and declaring the entire unpaid balance immediately due and payable. Also called a due-on-sale clause.

ALTA policy: The title insurance policy issued to institutional lenders. The initials stand for the American Land Title Association, an organization that regulates and standardizes the provisions within title policies.

Alter ego: A doctrine that holds that a corporation is really owned by shareholders as their own property and, therefore, should not be considered as a separate entity. Usually used to try to hold shareholders liable for corporate debts.

Alternate Dispute Resolution: A method of settling disputes outside of court, most commonly through mediation or arbitration.

Ambulatory: Capable of being changed or revoked. In wills, it refers to the concept that a will may be revoked or modified at any time up to the testator's death.

Ameliorating waste: Improvements to property that, although not damaging the value of the property, technically qualify as waste. For example, an apartment building constructed on property designated only for single-family structures is considered ameliorating waste.

Amortization: The method or plan for the payment of a debt, bond, deed of trust, and so forth, by installments or sinking fund.

Anticipatory breach: Advance notice of intention to violate the terms of a contract.

Appeal: The review or rehearing by a higher court of a lower (inferior) court's decision.

Appellant: The party appealing a court decision. Either party may appeal; hence, the appellant could have been either the plaintiff or the defendant in the trial court.

Appraisal: An opinion or estimate of the fair market value of a property.

Appurtenant: Attached to or considered part of land, because of being considered necessary and incidental to the use of that land. Commonly applied to easements that are considered part of a property.

Arbitration: The equivalent of an informal, abbreviated trial held outside the judicial system under the guidance of an arbitrator. The arbitrator seeks to hear the evidence and arrive at an appropriate award.

Assessed value: A value used by the tax assessor before July 1978. It represented 25 percent of the assessor's fair market value. After deducting any exemptions from assessed value, one applied the tax rate to the net figure to determine annual property taxes.

Assignment: The transfer of one's entire interest in property. Generally, the term is limited to intangible personal property (i.e., stocks, bonds, promissory notes) and to leasehold estates.

Assignment of rents clause: A clause in a deed of trust or mortgage providing that, in the event of default, all rents and income from the secured property will be paid to the lender to help reduce the outstanding loan balance.

Assumption: Acceptance of personal liability for another's debt or obligation. In the case of the sale of real estate, the buyer personally accepts and promises to pay off the existing deed of trust.

Attachment: The actual or constructive seizure of property by court order during a lawsuit.

The usual purpose is to hold the assets as security for the satisfaction of a judgment.

Attachment lien: A lien on property arising because of an attachment of that property.

B

Balloon payment: An installment promissory note providing for the last payment to be much larger than any previous payment. By statute, any payment more than twice the smallest payment is a balloon payment, although in practice generally the term refers only to the last payment.

Beneficiary: The creditor (lender) under a deed of trust.

Bequest: A gift of personal property by will.

Bilateral contract: A contract in which the consideration given by each party is a promise: that is, a promise for a promise.

Blanket deed of trust: A deed of trust binding more than one parcel of property as security. It is frequently encountered in subdivisions, where every lot in the subdivision is bound by the same deed of trust. As the lots are sold, they are released from the deed of trust by a partial release provision.

Bona fide purchaser (BFP): A purchaser who pays fair value for property in good faith and without notice of adverse claims.

Bond: A certificate representing a contract for the payment of money, often used to repay certain loans or held as security to ensure the performance of a stated act.

Breach: The violation of or failure to perform an obligation.

Broker: An agent who earns income by arranging sales and other contracts. A real estate broker is an individual licensed by the state of California to arrange the sale or transfer of interests in real property for compensation.

Business and Professions Code: One of the 25 California codes containing the laws passed by the state legislature. It contains the statutes regulating the conduct of real estate brokers and establishes the Department of Real Estate.

C

CAR: Abbreviation for the California Association of Realtors.

Cause of action: A legal right; facts giving rise to an enforceable claim.

CCR: Abbreviation for covenants, conditions, and restrictions. Often used synonymously with general plan restrictions on a subdivision.

Certiorari: The Supreme Court order indicating that the court has decided to exercise its discretion and accept a case offered on appeal. The court reviews only those select cases that it deems worthy of review.

Chain of title: A history of the recorded ownership of real estate and claims against title to real estate.

Chattel: The old name for personal property.

Civil Code: One of the 25 California codes containing the statutes passed by the state legislature. The most important code relating to contracts and real estate, the Civil Code defines the nature and requirements for contracts and real estate transactions, among its many other provisions.

Civil law: A system of jurisprudence, sometimes called Roman law, wherein all the laws are set forth in advance to regulate conduct (as opposed to common law, wherein the principles of law develop on a case-by-case basis). In California, the term also refers to the law relating to and between individuals, as opposed to criminal law.

Cloud on title: A claim or document that affects title to real estate. The actual cloud may ultimately prove invalid, but its existence mars the title.

Code of Civil Procedure: One of the 25 California codes that contain the statutes passed by the state legislature. It contains most of the procedural requirements for enforcing rights granted by other codes, including the procedures for evictions, foreclosures, and lawsuits.

Codicil: An amendment to a will.

Color of title: A document that appears to convey title, but, in fact, is ineffective, conveying no title at all. It is one of the requirements for adverse possession and easement by prescription.

Commingling: The mixing of different funds so that they can no longer be distinguished. In domestic law, it refers to the combination of separate property and community property so that the separate and community funds can no longer be distinguished; in such cases all property is considered community property. For brokers, it refers to the mixing of clients' money with the broker's separate bank accounts.

Common law: A body of unwritten law that developed in England from the general customs and usage. It was adopted in the United States and exercised by court decisions following the ancient English principles and the precodified law of a state.

Community property: Property owned in common by a husband and wife as a kind of marital partnership.

Conclusive presumption: A legal assumption that cannot be rebutted and is, therefore, accepted as true and binding on the courts.

Condemnation: The taking of private property for public use through the exercise of the power of eminent domain.

Condition: (1) A restriction added to a conveyance that, on the occurrence or nonoccurrence of some act or event, causes the estate to be defeated. (2) A contractual provision that, on the occurrence or nonoccurrence of a stated act or event, causes an obligation to be created, destroyed, or defeated.

Condition precedent: A condition that must occur before an estate is created or enlarged or before some other right or obligation occurs.

Condition subsequent: A condition that, on its failure or nonperformance, causes the defeat or extinguishment of an estate, right, or obligation.

Conditional sales contract: A contract for the sale of property by which possession is delivered to the buyer, but title remains with the seller until full payment or the satisfaction of other stated conditions.

Conditional use permit: An exception to or relief from the application of a zoning ordinance, because of special authorization granted by the zoning authorities. The issuance rests on public policy benefits and prior authorization in the zoning ordinance.

Condominium: The ownership of an individual unit in a multiunit structure, combined with joint ownership of common walkways, land, and other portions of the property.

Consideration: The inducement for entering into a contract; usually money, services, or a promise, although it may consist of a legal benefit to the promisor or any legal detriment to the promisee.

Construction: The interpretation of an ambiguous term or provision in a statute or agreement.

Constructive: A fiction imputed by law.

Constructive eviction: A breach of the landlord's warranty of quiet enjoyment. Any acts by the landlord that substantially interfere with the tenant's use and enjoyment of the premises.

Constructive notice: (1) Notice given by a recorded document. (2) Notice imputed by law because a person could have discovered certain facts on reasonable investigation, and a "reasonable man" in the same situation would have conducted such an investigation.

Contingent: Conditional, uncertain, conditioned on the occurrence or nonoccurrence of some uncertain future event.

Contract: A legally binding agreement between parties. An agreement to do or not to do a certain thing, supported by consideration.

Conversion: (1) In tort, an unauthorized claim of ownership over another's personal property. (2) In property, the change of character of property from real to personal or vice versa.

Conveyance: The transfer of title to real estate from one person to another.

Corporation: An artificial entity given authority to conduct business and possess many of the rights of natural persons. One of the key characteristics is that of perpetual existence.

Co-tenancy: Any form of joint ownership.

Counteroffer: The rejection of an offer by the submission of another offer that is different in terms from the original offer. Any purported acceptance of an offer that introduces new terms is a rejection of that offer and amounts to a counteroffer.

Covenant: A contractual agreement whereby one of the parties promises to perform or to refrain from doing certain acts.

D

Damages: Compensation ordered by the courts for the injury to one's person or the loss of one's property.

Declaratory relief: A court's decision on the rights of the parties in a question of law, without ordering anything to be done.

Dedication: A gift of privately owned land to the public or for public use. It may be voluntary or involuntary.

Deed: A written instrument used to transfer ownership in property.

Deed of trust: A security instrument transferring title to property to a third person (trustee) as security for a debt or other obligation.

Default: Failure to perform a legal duty or to discharge a promise.

Default judgment: A judgment obtained because the defendant failed to appear and defend his case.

Defeasible: Capable of being defeated. A defeasible estate is one that has a condition attached to the title, which, if broken, causes the termination of that estate.

Defendant: The party being sued in a lawsuit; the party against whom an action is filed.

Deficiency judgment: A court decree holding a debtor personally liable for the shortage or insufficiency realized on the sale of secured property. The debtor owes the difference between the sale price of the property and the amount of the secured debt.

Delivery (of a deed): The unconditional, irrevocable intent of a grantor immediately to divest (give up) an interest in real estate by a deed or other instrument.

Deposit: Money given to another as security to ensure the performance of a contract. The money is usually intended to be applied toward the purchase price of property or forfeited on failure to complete the contract.

Deposit receipt: The name given to most real estate contracts containing the terms of the sale of real estate and a receipt for earnest money (deposited).

Devise: A gift of real property by deed.

Dictum: A written observation, remark, or opinion by a judge to illustrate or suggest an argument or rule of law not incidental to the case at hand, and which, therefore, although persuasive, is not binding on the judge.

Dissolution of marriage: A divorce.

District court: The main trial court in the federal court system and the lowest federal court. It has jurisdiction in civil cases in which the plaintiffs and defendants are from different states (diversity of citizenship) and the amount in controversy is over $50,000 and in cases involving a federal question.

Divestment: The elimination or removal of a right or title, usually applied to the cancellation of an estate in land.

Domicile: A person's permanent residence.

Dominant tenement: That parcel of land that benefits from an easement across another parcel of property (servient tenement).

Donee: A person who receives a gift.

Donor: A person who makes a gift.

Double escrow: An escrow that will close only on the condition that a prior escrow is consummated. The second escrow is contingent on and tied to the first escrow. Although double escrow is not illegal, unless there is full and fair disclosure of the second escrow, there may be a possibility of fraud or other actionable conduct by the parties.

Due-on-encumbrance clause: A clause in a deed of trust or mortgage that provides that, on the execution of additional deeds of trust or other encumbrances against a secured parcel of property, the lender may declare the entire unpaid balance of principal and interest due and owing.

Due-on-sale clause: A clause in a deed of trust or mortgage that provides that if the secured property is sold or transferred the lender may declare the entire unpaid balance immediately due and payable. Its use has been severely limited by recent court decisions. Also called an *alienation clause.*

Due process of law: A constitutional guarantee that the government will not interfere with a person's private property rights without following procedural safeguards prescribed by law.

E

Easement: A legal right to use another's land for one's benefit or the benefit of one's property (right-of-way).

Easement appurtenant: An easement created for the benefit of a particular parcel of property. There is both a dominant and a servient estate. The easement is annexed to and part of the dominant property.

Easement in gross: An easement that benefits a particular individual, not a parcel of property. Involves only a servient estate. A public utility easement is an example.

Egress: Exit; the act or avenue of leaving property.

Eminent domain: The constitutional or inherent right of a government to take private property for public good on the payment of just compensation.

Encroachment: A structure or natural object that unlawfully extends into another's property.

Encumbrance: A claim, lien, or charge on property.

Environmental Impact Report (EIR): A report that must be prepared whenever any agency or individual considers a project that may have a significant impact on the environment, as directed by the California Environmental Quality Act.

Equal protection: The Fourteenth Amendment to the U.S. Constitution and similar provisions in the California Constitution require each citizen to receive equal protection of the laws. There are no minimum standards of protection; all equally situated individuals must simply be treated equally. (The due process clause of the Constitution imposes certain minimum standards of protection.)

Equity: (1) Law based on fairness under the circumstances, rather than on fixed legal principles or statutes. (2) Ownership in property, determined by calculating the fair market value less the amount of liens and encumbrances.

Escalator clause: A clause in a promissory note, lease, or other document that, provides that on the passage of a specified time or the happening of a stated event, the interest rate shall increase.

Escheat: Reversion of property to the state on the death of an owner who has no heirs able to inherit.

Escrow: The neutral third party (stakeholder) who holds deeds or other documents pursuant to instructions for delivery on completion or occurrence of certain conditions.

Estate: (1) Ownership interest in real estate. (2) The quality and quantity of rights in property.

Estate at will: A leasehold tenancy, which at common law could be terminated by either party at any time without advance notice. Thirty days of notice are now required to terminate this type of estate in California.

Estate for life: A freehold estate whose duration is measured by and limited to the life or lives of one or more persons.

Estate for period to period: A leasehold tenancy that continues indefinitely for successive periods until terminated by proper notice. When the periods are one month in duration, it is often called a month-to-month tenancy.

Estate for years: A leasehold tenancy of a fixed duration, being a definite and ascertainable period of a year or any fraction or multiple thereof. It has a definite beginning and ending date, and, hence, a known and definite duration.

Estop: To ban, stop, or impede.

Estoppel: The doctrine that prevents a person from exercising a legal right, because that person previously acted in an inconsistent manner so that a third person detrimentally relied on the earlier acts.

Et al.: Abbreviation meaning "and others" (other persons).

Et ux.: Abbreviation meaning "and wife."

Eviction: Dispossession by legal process, as in the termination of a tenant's right to possession through re-entry or other legal proceedings.

Evidence: All relevant information, facts, and exhibits admissible in a trial.

Exclusive agency: A contract hiring the broker as the exclusive agent for the seller. If anyone, except the seller, finds a buyer, the broker has earned the commission.

Exclusive right to sell agency: A contract hiring the broker as the only person authorized to sell property. If anyone, including the seller, finds a buyer, the broker earns the commission.

Exculpatory clause: A provision in leases and other instruments seeking to relieve one party of liability for his negligence and other acts. In residential leases, such clauses are invalid, and in other leases the courts have limited the landlord's ability to escape liability for intentional acts and for acts of affirmative negligence.

Execute: To sign a document, intending to make it a binding instrument. The term is also used to indicate the performance of a contract.

Execution lien: A lien arising because of an execution on property. A judgment is not self-executing; however, when a writ of execution has been obtained, the sheriff will levy (seize) property, which creates a lien on the property.

Executor: A personal representative appointed in a will to administer a decedent's estate.

Ex parte: By only one party or side. For example, an injunction obtained by evidence presented by only one side, without notice to the other parties.

F

Fee: An estate of inheritance or for life.

Fee simple absolute: The highest estate known at law. A freehold estate of indefinite duration, incapable of being defeated by conditions or limitations. Sometimes simply called fee or fee estate.

Fee simple defeasible: A fee simple estate to which certain conditions or limitations attach, such that the estate may be defeated or terminated on the happening of an act or event. Also called a fee-simple subject to a condition subsequent estate.

Fee simple subject to a condition subsequent: A fee simple defeasible estate that requires the holder of the future interest to act promptly to terminate the present interest for that interest to be terminated.

Financing statement: The security interest in personal property. It is analogous to a mortgage on real property, except that it secures personal property. Under the U.C.C., it may be filed in Sacramento with the secretary of state.

Finder's fee: Money paid to a person for finding someone interested in selling or buying property. To conduct any negotiations of sale terms, the finder must be a licensed broker or he violates the law.

First Amendment: The constitutional amendment guaranteeing freedom of speech, press, assembly, and religion.

Fixture: An item of personal property that has been so attached to real property as to be considered part of that real property.

Forcible detainer: Wrongful retention of property by actual or constructive force.

Forcible entry: Entry into property without the consent of the owner by acts that constitute more than mere trespass.

Foreclosure: The process by which secured property is seized and sold to satisfy a debt. A mortgage or involuntary lien must be sold by a court-ordered sale; a sale under a deed of trust may be either by court action or through a private trustee's sale.

Forfeiture: Loss of a legal right, interest, or title by default.

Formal will: A will signed by the testator in the presence of two or more witnesses, who must themselves sign the will.

Fourteenth Amendment: The constitutional amendment that directs that no state can deprive a person of life, liberty, or property without due process or equal protection of the law.

Fraud: False representation or concealment of material facts that induces another justifiably to rely on it to his detriment.

Freehold: An estate of fee.

Fructus: Fruits, crops, and other plants. If the vegetation is produced by human labor, such as crops, it is called fructus industriales; vegetation growing naturally is called fructus naturales.

Future advances: Future (additional) loans made by a lender and secured under the original deed of trust. The advances may be either optional or obligatory, but the deed of trust or mortgage must provide in the security instrument that it will cover any such future advances.

Future interest: An estate that does not or may not entitle one to possession or enjoyment until a future time.

G

Garnishment: A legal process to seize a debtor's property or money in the possession of a third party.

General plan restrictions: Covenants, conditions, and restrictions placed on a subdivision or other large tract of land, designed to benefit and burden each lot in that tract.

Gift: A voluntary transfer of property without consideration.

Grant: A transfer or conveyance of real estate.

Grant deed: A deed used to transfer property in California. By statute, it impliedly contains only two limited warranties.

Grantee: The buyer or person to whom a grant is made.

Grantor: The seller or person who executes a grant.

H

Heirs: Persons who succeed to the estate of someone who dies intestate (without a will). It sometimes indicates anyone who is entitled to inherit a decedent's property.

Holder in due course: Someone who acquires a negotiable instrument in good faith and without any actual or constructive notice of defect. The acquisition must occur before the note's maturity. Such a holder takes the note free from any personal defenses (such as failure of consideration, fraud in the inducement) that may be available against the maker.

Holographic will: A will that is entirely written, dated, and signed by the testator in the testator's handwriting. No witnesses are needed.

Homeowner's exemption: An exemption or reduction in real property taxes available to those who reside on their property as of March 1. The current amount is $70 off the normal tax bill otherwise due.

Homeowner's title insurance policy: The title insurance policy issued to homeowners and noninstitutional lenders. The initials stand for the California Land Title Association, an organization that regulates and standardizes the provisions within title policies.

Homestead: A special, limited exemption against certain judgments available to qualified homeowners.

Hypothecate: To pledge property; to pledge a security interest in property without the transfer of possession.

I

Illusory contract: An agreement that gives the appearance of a contract, but, in fact, is not a contract because it lacks one of the essential elements.

Implied: Not expressed by words, but presumed from facts, acts, or circumstances.

Indebtedness: A debt or obligation.

Indemnification: Compensation to a person who has already sustained a loss. For example, insurance payment for a loss under a policy.

Ingress: The act of or avenue for entering property.

Inherit: To take property through a deceased's estate.

Injunction: A court order prohibiting certain acts or ordering specific acts.

Installment: A partial payment of a debt due in a series of payments.

Interest: The charge or cost for the use of money.

Intestate: A person who dies without a will.

Invitee: A person who enters another's land because of an express or implied social invitation, such as a social guest. The term also covers certain government workers who enter someone's land, such as police officers and firefighters. Classification of such status was revoked by a recent court case.

Irrevocable: Unrecallable; incapable of being repealed or changed.

J

Joint tenancy: Property held by two or more people with right of survivorship.

Joint venture: In legal effect, it is a partnership for a limited, specific business project.

Judgment: The final decision by a court in a lawsuit, motion, or other matter.

Judgment affirmed: A decision by an appellate court reaffirming, approving, and agreeing with an inferior court's decision.

Judgment debtor: A person who has an unsatisfied money judgment levied against him or her.

Judgment lien: A money judgment that, because it has been recorded, has become a lien against the judgment debtor's real property.

Judgment reversed: A decision by an appellate court disagreeing with an inferior court's decision and modifying that decision to conform with its findings.

Junior lien: A lien lower in priority or rank than another or other liens.

Jurisdiction: The power of a court to hear and decide a case or issue.

L

Landlocked: Property totally surrounded by other property with no means of ingress or egress.

Landlord: The person who leases property; the owner of the property.

Land sales contract: A contract for the sale of property, by which possession is delivered to the buyer, but title remains with the seller until full payment or the satisfaction of other stated conditions.

Lateral support: The support that soil receives from adjacent property.

Lease: A contract for possession of land, in consideration for rent.

Legacy: A gift of money by will.

Lessee: A tenant; the person who is entitled to possession of property under a lease.

Lessor: A landlord; the property owner who executes a lease.

Levy: To execute on; to seize and sell property to obtain money to satisfy a judgment.

License: Personal, nonassignable authorization to enter and perform certain acts on another's land.

Licensee: Under the law before 1968, which classified persons who entered on others' land, a licensee was someone who entered on land with the owner's express or implied permission for a business purpose.

Lien: A charge or claim against property as security for payment of a debt or obligation.

Life estate: An estate in property whose duration is limited to and measured by the life of a natural person or persons.

Limited partnership: A special partnership composed of limited and general partners. The general partners have unlimited liability and total management, whereas the limited partners have no voice in the management and their only financial exposure is to the extent of their investment. In some ways, the limited partners' interest is similar to that of stockholders in a corporation.

Liquidated damages clause: An agreement between the parties that in the event of a breach, the amount of damages shall be liquidated (set or fixed). The amount is set before the breach, usually at the time of making the contract, on the assumption that the exact amount of damages is difficult to determine because of the nature of the contract.

Lis pendens: A recorded notice that a lawsuit is pending, the outcome of which may affect title to property.

Listing agreement: An employment contract authorizing a broker to sell, lease, or exchange an owner's property.

Litigation: A civil lawsuit; a judicial controversy.

M

Mandamus: A court decree ordering a lower court judge, public official, or corporate officer to perform an act required of that office.

Mechanic's lien: Whenever a contractor, laborer, or materialman provides labor or materials to improve real property and is not paid, that person is entitled to a lien against the property as a means of securing payment. Certain statutory steps must be taken to file, record, and foreclose the lien.

Mediation: A process outside the judicial system where a neutral third party, called a mediator, tries to help the parties reach a compromise and resolution. Most commonly, the mediator acts as a facilitator, seeking to help the parties reach an agreement without imposing his or her own views into the process.

Memo to set: A document filed in a lawsuit that asks to be placed on the waiting list (docket) for the next available court date.

Merger of title: The combination of two estates. Also refers to the joining of one estate burdened by an encumbrance and another estate benefited by the encumbrance. Whenever a benefit and a burden are merged, the encumbrance is extinguished.

Minor: Someone under age 18.

Misrepresentation: An intentional or negligent suggestion or statement of a material fact in a false manner with the intent of deceiving someone into taking a course of action that he would not otherwise normally pursue.

Mitigation: Facts or circumstances that tend to justify or excuse an act or course of conduct.

Month-to-month tenancy: A lease of property for a month at a time, under a periodic tenancy that continues for successive months until terminated by proper notice, usually 30 days.

Mortgage: A contract by which property is hypothecated (pledged without delivery) for the repayment of a loan.

Mortgagee: A creditor (lender) under a mortgage.

Mortgagor: A borrower (property owner) of money under a mortgage.

Multiple listing: A listing taken by a broker and shared with other brokers through a specialized distribution service, usually provided by the local real estate board. Generally, such listings are exclusive right to sell listings.

Municipal court: An inferior trial court having jurisdiction in cases involving up to $25,000 in money damages. Since 1998, most counties have elected to abolish their municipal court in favor of a combined superior court that hears all the cases.

Mutual assent: An agreement between the parties in a contract. The offer and acceptance of a contract.

N

Negative amortization: Occurs when normal payments on a loan are insufficient to cover all interest then due so that unpaid interest is added to principal. Thus, even though payments are timely made, the principal grows with each payment.

Negligence: Either the failure to act as a reasonable, prudent person or the performance of an act that would not be done by a reasonable, prudent person.

Negotiable instrument: A check or promissory note that meets specified statutory requirements and is therefore easily transferable in somewhat the same manner as money. The negotiable instrument can be passed by endorsement and delivery (or in some cases by mere delivery), and the transferee takes title free of certain real defenses (such as failure of consideration or fraud in the inducement) that might exist against the original maker of the negotiable instrument.

NEPA: Abbreviation for the National Environmental Protection Act, a federal statute requiring all federal agencies to prepare an Environmental Impact Statement and meet other requirements whenever a major federal action is anticipated that could significantly affect the environment.

Net listing: An employment agreement that entitles the broker to a commission only in the amount, if any, that the sales price of the property exceeds the listing price.

Nonfreehold estate: A lease tenancy. A rental. There are four types of nonfreehold estates: estates for years, estates for period to period, estates at sufferance, and estates at will.

Nonjudicial foreclosure: Foreclosure and sale of property without resort to court action, by private sale. For deeds of trust the foreclosure provisions are outlined by the statutes and the requirements in the security instrument, which include a notice of default, right to reinstate, publication of sale, and trustee's sale.

Notary public: An individual licensed by the state to charge a fee for acknowledging signatures on instruments.

Note: Shortened name for a promissory note.

Notice of completion: A notice recorded after termination of work on improvements, limiting the time in which mechanic's liens can be filed against the property.

Notice of default: Recorded notice that a trustor has defaulted on his secured debt.

Notice of nonresponsibility: Notice relieving an owner from mechanic's liens for work on property not ordered by that owner.

Notice to quit: Also called a three-day notice. Notice given to a tenant in default of his lease terms or on his rent, which directs him either to cure the default or to vacate the premises.

Novation: The acceptance of a new contract in substitution for the old contract, with the intent that the new contract will extinguish the original contract. Sometimes encountered in transfers of deeds of trust, where the new owner assumes the debt and the lender, through novation, releases the former owner from any liability under the original promissory note and deed of trust.

Nuisance: A legal wrong arising from acts or use of one's property in a way that unreasonably interferes with another's use of his property.

O

Offer: A proposal to create a contract, which signifies present intent of the offeror to be legally bound by his proposal.

Open listing: An employment contract made to numerous brokers, promising a commission only to that broker, if any, who produces a qualified buyer.

Option: The right of a person to buy or lease property at a set price at any time during the life of a contract.

Option listing: A listing that also includes an option, permitting the broker to buy the property at the stated price at any time during the listing period.

Ordinance: A law passed by a political subdivision of the state (such as a town, city, or county).

Or-more clause: A simple prepayment clause that permits the borrower to make normal payment or any larger amount, up to and including the entire outstanding balance, without a prepayment penalty.

Ostensible agency: An agency implied by law because the principal intentionally or inadvertently caused a third person to believe someone to be his agent, and that third person acted as if that other person was, in fact, the principal's agent.

Ownership: The right of a person to use and possess property to the exclusion of others.

P

Parol: Oral, verbal.

Parol evidence rule: A rule of courtroom evidence that, once the parties make a written contract, they may not then introduce oral agreements or statements to modify the terms of that written agreement. An exception exists for fraud or mistake, which will permit the parties to offer evidence to vary the terms of the writing.

Partial reconveyance: In a deed of trust or mortgage, a clause that permits release of a parcel or part of a parcel from the effects and lien of that security instrument. The release usually occurs on the payment of a specified sum of money.

Partition action: The physical division of property between co-owners, usually through court action.

Partnership: An agreement of two or more individuals jointly to undertake a business enterprise. If it is a general partnership, all partners have unlimited liability and, absent other agreements, share equally in the management and profits of the business.

Periodic tenancy: A leasehold estate that continues indefinitely for successive periods until terminated by proper notice. When the periods are one month in duration, it is often called a month-to-month lease.

Personal injury: A term commonly used in tort (e.g., negligence cases) indicating an injury to one's being or body (e.g., cuts or broken bones) as opposed to injury to his property.

Personal property: Property that is movable, as opposed to real property, which is immovable; also includes intangible property and leasehold estates.

Petitioner: A person who petitions the court on a special proceeding or a motion.

Plaintiff: The party who initiates a lawsuit; the person who sues another.

Police power: The power of the state to prohibit acts that adversely affect the public health, welfare, safety, or morals. (Zoning and building codes are examples of exercise of the police power.)

Power of attorney: A document authorizing a person (an attorney-in-fact) to act as an agent.

Power of termination: The future interest created whenever there is a grant of a fee simple subject to a condition subsequent estate. The future interest matures into a present interest estate only if the holder timely and properly exercises his rights on a breach by the current holder of the fee estate.

Prejudgment attachment: An attachment of property made before the trial, with the intent of holding that property as security to have an asset to sell if the court judgment is favorable to the attaching party.

Prepayment clause: A provision in a promissory note, deed of trust, or mortgage permitting the debtor to pay off the obligation before maturity.

Prepayment penalty: A fee or charge imposed on a debtor who desires to pay off his loan before its maturity. Not all prepayment clauses provide for a penalty, and in many real estate transactions, the law regulates the amount of penalty that may be charged.

Prescription: A method of obtaining an easement by adverse use over a prescribed period.

Present interest: An estate in land that gives the owner the right to occupy his property immediately; as opposed to a future interest, which grants only the right to occupy the premises at some future date.

Presumption: A conclusion or assumption that is binding in the absence of sufficient proof to the contrary.

Prima facie: Facts, evidence, or documents that are taken at face value and presumed to be as they appear (unless proved otherwise).

Principal: Someone who hires an agent to act on his behalf. The term also refers to the amount of an outstanding loan (exclusive of interest).

Priority: Superior, higher, or preferred rank or position.

Probate: Court supervision of the collection and distribution of a deceased person's estate.

Procedural law: The law of how to present and proceed with legal rights (e.g., laws of evidence or enforcement of judgments). It is the opposite of substantive law.

Procuring cause: Proximate cause. A broker is the procuring cause of a sale if his or her efforts set in motion an unbroken chain of events that resulted in the sale.

Profit á prendre: An easement coupled with a power to consume resources on the burdened property.

Promissory note: A written promise to pay a designated sum of money at a future date.

Property: Anything of value in which the law permits ownership.

Punitive damages: Money awarded by the court for the sole purpose of punishing the wrongdoer and not designed to compensate the injured party for his damages.

Purchase money instrument: A mortgage or deed of trust that does not permit a deficiency judgment in the event of foreclosure and sale of the secured property for less than the amount due on the promissory note. It is called purchase money because the deed of trust or mortgage was used to buy all or part of the property.

Q

Quasi: Almost as if it were.

Quasi-contract: A contract implied by law; that is, the law will imply and consider certain relationships as if they were a contract.

Quiet title action: A lawsuit designed to remove any clouds on title to property. It forces the claimant of an adverse interest in property to prove his right to title; otherwise, he will be forever barred from asserting it.

Quitclaim deed: A deed that transfers only whatever right, title, or interest, if any, the grantor owns, without implying any warranties.

R

Ratification: Approval and confirmation of a prior act performed on one's behalf by another person without previous authority.

Ready, willing, and able buyer: A purchaser of property, who is willing to buy on terms acceptable to the seller and who further possesses the financial ability to consummate the sale. Producing such a buyer sometimes earns the broker a commission, even though a sale is not forthcoming.

Real estate investment trust (REIT): A specialized form of holding title to property that enables investors to pool their resources and purchase property, while still receiving considerable tax advantages, without being taxed as a corporation.

Real property: Land, buildings, and other immovable property permanently attached thereto.

Realtor: A broker who is a member of a real estate board affiliated with the National Association of Realtors.

Rebuttable presumption: A presumption that applies unless proved inapplicable by the introduction of contradictory evidence.

Receiver: A neutral third party appointed by the court to collect the rents and profits from property and distribute them as ordered by the court. Often used as a remedy when mere damages are inadequate.

Reconveyance: The transfer of property back from a lender who holds an interest as security for the payment of a debt. In a deed of trust, the beneficiary reconveys property on satisfaction of the promissory note.

Recordation: The act of having a document filed for record in the county recorder's office. Once recorded, the instrument gives constructive notice to the world.

Redemption: The repurchasing of one's property after a judicial sale.

Regulations: The rules and formal requirements issued by a government agency. Among the most common are the regulations issued by the Internal Revenue Service interpreting the Internal Revenue Code.

Reinstatement: A right available to anyone under an accelerated promissory note secured by a deed of trust or mortgage on property. If a deed of trust is foreclosed by trustee's sale, the debtor may have up to three months from the recording of the notice of default to pay the amount in arrears plus interest and costs, thereby completely curing the default (reinstating) without penalty.

Rejection: Refusal to accept an offer. Repudiation of an offer automatically terminates the offer.

Release: To give up or abandon a right. The release of rights may be voluntary, as when one voluntarily discharges an obligation under a contract. The release may be involuntary, by operation of the law; for example, one's wrongful conduct may bar him from asserting his rights. In deeds of trust a partial release clause frees certain property from the security of the deed of trust on the payment of specified sums of money.

Remainder: Most commonly, an estate (future interest) that arises in favor of a third person after a life estate.

Remand: To send back to a lower court for further action.

Remedy: The means by which a right is enforced, preserved, or compensated. Some of the more common remedies are damages, injunctions, rescission, and specific performance.

Rent: The consideration paid by a tenant for possession of property under a lease.

Rescission: The unmaking of a contract and the restoring of each party to the same position each held before the contract arose.

Respondeat superior: This Latin phrase, "let the master answer," means that an employer is liable for the tortious acts of an employee, and a principal is liable for the acts of an agent. To be liable, the acts must be within the "course and scope" of the agency or employment. For example, an employer would not be liable for the acts of an employee while at home and not doing work for the employer.

Respondent: The person against whom an appeal is taken; the opposite of an appellant.

Restriction: An encumbrance on property that limits the use of it; usually a covenant or condition.

Retaliatory eviction: A landlord's attempt to evict a tenant from a lease because the tenant has used the remedies available under the warranty of habitability.

Reversion: Any future interest (estate) left in the grantor. The residue of an estate left in the grantor after the termination of a lesser estate.

Revocation: Withdrawal of an offer or other right, thereby voiding and destroying that offer or right. It is a recall with intent to rescind.

Right-of-way: An easement granting a person the right to pass across another's property.

Rule against perpetuities: A complex set of laws designed to prevent excessive restrictions on the transferability of property. The rule holds that "no interest is good unless it must vest, if at all, not later than 21 years after some life in being at the creation of the interest."

S

Safety clause: In a listing agreement, a provision that, if anyone found by the broker during his listing period purchases the property within a specified time after the expiration of the listing, the broker receives his full commission.

Salesperson: An individual licensed to sell property, but who must at all times be under the supervision and direction of a broker.

Satisfaction: Discharge of an obligation or indebtedness by paying what is due.

Secured debt: An obligation that includes property held as security for the payment of that debt; on default, the property may be sold to satisfy the debt.

Security deposit: A sum of cash given as collateral to ensure faithful performance of specified obligations.

Senior lien: A lien that is superior to or has priority over another lien. Also, the first deed of trust or lien on a property.

Separate property: Property held by a married person that is not community property; it includes property owned before marriage and property acquired after marriage by gift or inheritance.

Servient estate: That parcel of property that is burdened by and encumbered with an easement.

Severalty: Sole ownership of property. Ownership by one person.

Small claims court: A branch of the municipal court. The rules of this court forbid parties to be assisted by attorneys, dispense with most formal rules of evidence, and have all trials heard by judges. The monetary limit of cases before the court is $5,000.

Sold to the state: A bookkeeping entry on the county tax rolls indicating that the property taxes are delinquent. The entry begins the five-year redemption period, after which the property may be physically sold to the public for back taxes.

Specific performance: A contract remedy by which one party is ordered by the court to comply with the terms of the agreement.

Spouse: A person's husband or wife.

Stare decisis: A fundamental principle of law, which holds that courts should follow prior decisions on a point of law. A proper decision is a binding precedent on courts having the same facts in controversy.

Statute: A written law.

Statute of frauds: A law that requires certain contracts (including most real estate contracts) to be in writing to be enforceable.

Statute of limitations: A statute that requires lawsuits to be brought within a certain time to be enforceable. The basic periods are one year for personal injury, two years for oral contracts, three years for damages to real or personal property, four years for written contracts, and three years from date of discovery for fraud.

Stepped-up basis: A higher, increased tax value of property given as the result of most sales or taxable transfers. The tax basis is used in computing capital gains and losses on the transfer of property.

Stop notice: A notice served on the owner of property or custodian of funds. It requests, with certain penalties for noncompliance, that any funds due to a general contractor be paid to the claimant, laborer, or materialman.

Straight note: A promissory note that is unamortized. The principal is paid at the end of the term of the note.

Subchapter-S corporation: A corporation that, for federal tax purposes only, is taxed similarly to a partnership. The corporate entity is disregarded for most federal tax purposes, and the shareholders are generally taxed as individual partners.

Subjacent support: The support that soil receives from land beneath it.

Subject to: (1) Burdened by and liable for an obligation. (2) A method of taking over a loan without becoming personally liable for its payment.

Subordination agreement: In a mortgage or deed of trust, a provision that a later lien shall have a priority interest over the existing lien. It makes the existing lien inferior to a later lien, in effect exchanging priorities with that later lien.

Subrogate: To substitute one person for another's legal rights to a claim or debt.

Substantive law: The laws describing rights and duties. Differs from procedural law, which only describes how to enforce and protect rights.

Succession: The inheritance of property.

Successor in interest: The next succeeding owner of an interest in property. The transferee or recipient of a property interest.

Superior court: The principal trial court of the state; a court of unlimited monetary and subject matter jurisdiction and an appeal court for decisions of municipal courts (in counties where such courts exist) and of small claims courts.

Supreme Court: The highest court in the California and the federal court structure. This court is almost exclusively an appeals court, accepting (by certiorari) only those cases that, in the court's discretion, involve issues of significant magnitude and social importance.

Syndication: A group of individuals pooling their resources to purchase property through the holding vehicle of a partnership, corporation, or other association. Each individual owns shares in the legal entity formed to acquire and hold title to the property.

T

Tax: A compulsory charge on property or individuals, the payment of which supports a government.

Tax basis: The tax value of property to the taxpayer. It is a figure used to compute capital gains and losses.

Tenancy: A leasehold estate. (For specific types of leases, see Chapter 8.)

Tenancy in common: Ownership of property by two or more persons who hold an undivided interest without the right of survivorship.

Tenant: A lessee; one who leases property.

Testamentary disposition: A gift passing by will.

Testate: Describes a person who dies leaving a will.

Testator: A person who makes a will. Technically, a testator is a male and a testatrix is a female, although in common use testator refers to anyone who makes a will.

Thirty-day notice: A notice terminating a periodic tenancy without cause, by ending a tenancy thirty days from date of service.

Three-day notice: A notice giving a tenant three days in which to cure a default or quit the premises. It is the first step in an unlawful detainer action, as the means of terminating a lease for cause. When rent is delinquent, it is sometimes called a notice to quit or pay rent.

Title: (1) The right of ownership. (2) The evidence of a person's ownership or interest in property.

Title insurance: A special policy of insurance issued by a title company, insuring the owner against loss of or defect in title to the insured property. The policy may be either a CLTA policy, issued to the property owner and to noninstitutional lenders, or an ALTA policy, issued to institutional lenders.

Tort: A civil wrong not arising from a breach of contract. Most torts lie in negligence, although they could also be intentional torts (such as assault and battery or trespass) or strict liability torts.

Tortfeasor: A person who commits a tort.

Tortious: Conduct that amounts to a tort.

Trade fixtures: Fixtures installed to further one's trade, business, or profession. They are an exception to the general rule that fixtures are part of a building. Such fixtures installed by a tenant may be removed before the expiration of the tenancy.

Transfer: Conveyance; passage of title.

Transferee: The person to whom a transfer is made.

Transferor: The person who makes a transfer.

Trespass: (1) Unauthorized entry onto another's land. (2) Invasion of another's rights or property.

Trespasser: One who trespasses. The importance of this classification of individuals on property is created by the methods for removal and the liability of the property owner if the trespasser is injured on his property.

Trust: Arrangement whereby one person holds property for the benefit of another under fiduciary (special confidential) relationship.

Trust deed: A deed of trust.

Trustee: The person who holds property in trust for another. In a deed of trust, the person who holds bare legal title in trust.

Trustee's deed: The deed issued by the beneficiary after the foreclosure and sale under a deed of trust.

Trustee's sale: The private sale of property held by a trustee under a deed of trust as part of the foreclosure proceedings.

Trustor: (1) The person who places property in trust. (2) The owner of property who executes a deed of trust.

Truth in lending law: A complex set of federal statutes designed to provide a borrower with a means of discovering and comparing the true costs of credit. Under Regulation Z of the act, certain borrowers of property have three days after accepting a loan to rescind without cost or liability.

U

Undue influence: Using a position of trust and confidence improperly to persuade a person to take a course of action. By relying on the trusted confidant, the decision maker fails to exercise his free will and independent judgment.

Unenforceable: Incapable of being enforced at law. An example of an unenforceable contract is an oral listing agreement to pay a broker a commission.

Uniform Commercial Code: Statutes regulating commercial transactions, which have been drafted by national committees and adopted by most states (including California) as their laws. The code covers sales, commercial paper, bank deposits, letters of credit, bulk transfers, warehouse receipts and documents of title, investment securities, and secured transactions.

Unilateral: One-sided, ex parte.

Unjust enrichment: A legal doctrine that prevents a person from inequitable benefiting from another's mistake, poor judgment, or loss. In a land sales contract the vendor may no longer keep both the property and the buyer's excess payments (over his damages) in the event of breach, because to do so would unjustly enrich him at the buyer's expense.

Unlawful: Illegal.

Unlawful detainer: A lawsuit designed to evict a defaulting tenant or anyone unlawfully in possession of property from premises. It is summary in nature, entitled to a priority court trial, and litigates only the right to possession of property (and damages resulting therefrom).

Unsecured debt: A debt not backed by specific property to satisfy the indebtedness in case of default.

Usury: Charging a greater rate of interest on loans than the rate allowed by law (10 percent in many cases).

V

Valid: Fully effective at law; legally sufficient.

Variable interest rate (VIR): An interest rate that fluctuates in a set proportion to changes in an economic index, such as the cost of money. Extensive regulations cover use of VIRs in loans on residential property.

Variance: An exception granted to a property owner, relieving him from obeying certain aspects of a zoning ordinance. Its granting is discretionary with the zoning authorities and is based on undue hardship suffered by the property owner because of unique circumstances affecting his property.

Vendee: Purchaser or buyer of real property.

Vendor: Seller of real property.

Venue: The location in which a cause of action occurs; it determines the court having jurisdiction to hear and decide the case. For real estate, the court having proper venue is one in the county in which the property is located.

Verification: Written certification under oath and penalty of perjury, confirming the truth of the facts in a document.

Versus: Against (abbreviated v.). Used in case names, with the plaintiff's name given first.

Vested: Absolute, not contingent or subject to being defeated.

Veteran's exemption: A deduction from the annual property tax allowed to a qualified veteran residing on residential property. Since July 1978, it has amounted to $40 off the normal tax bill.

Void: Unenforceable, null, having no legal effect.

Voidable: May be declared void, but is valid unless and until declared void.

W

Waiver: Giving up of certain rights or privileges. The relinquishment may be voluntary and knowing, or it may occur involuntarily through action of the parties. The action resulting in the waiver is unilateral, and requires no action or reliance by the other party.

Warranty: An absolute undertaking or promise that certain facts are as represented. Occasionally used interchangeably with guarantee.

Warranty deed: Used predominantly in states that do not have title insurance companies. This deed contains six full warranties of protection to the buyer, including warranties that the seller owns the property, that it is unencumbered, and that the seller will defend title against any defects.

Warranty of habitability: Implied warranty in residential leases. The landlord covenants by implication that the premises are suitable for human occupancy. The implied warranties are found in the statutes and implied by common law.

Waste: The destruction, injury, material alteration, or abusive use of property by a person rightfully in possession, but who does not own the fee or entire estate (e.g., by a lessee or life tenant).

Will: A document that directs the disposition of one's property after death.

Witnessed will: A formal will, signed by the testator in the presence of two or more witnesses, each of whom must also sign the will.

Wraparound deed of trust: A sophisticated financing package that permits the seller to sell his property without paying off the outstanding deed of trust. The buyer's larger loan, which is used to purchase the property, includes provisions for paying off the seller's existing loan.

Writ: An order from the court to the sheriff or other law-enforcement officer directing and authorizing a specific act.

Writ of attachment: A writ authorizing and directing the physical attachment (seizure) of property.

Writ of execution: An order directing the sheriff to seize property to satisfy a judgment.

Writ of immediate possession: An order authorizing a landlord to obtain immediate possession of a tenant's premises, pending the outcome of an unlawful detainer action or other court proceeding.

Z

Zoning: A government's division of a city or other geographic area into districts, and the regulation of property uses within each district.

Index of Cases

Note: Cases in bold include extensive analysis

Ablett v. Clauson, 56
Adderly v. Florida, 4
Alamo School District v. Jones, 205–207
Alexander v. McKnight, 134
Allen v. Enomoto, 73
Allstate S.&L. Assn. v. Murphy, 386
Anderson v. Superior Court, 20
Andrade Development Co. v. Martin, 263–265
Angell v. Rowlands, 168
Annenberg v. So. Cal. Dist. Council, 3
Assoc. Homebuilders, Inc. v. Walnut Creek, 500
Augustine v. Trucco, 147

Bargioni v. Hill, 389–390
Baston v. Strehlow, 550
Bd. Ssupervisors v. Lenergan, 445–447
Beauchamp v. Los Gatos Golf Course, 281
Beazel v. Kane, 144
Beebe v. Richards, 49
Berman v. Parker, 472
Blank v. Borden, 149, 159, 161, 535
Bolotin v. Rindge, 467–468
Booska v. Patel, 291
Born v. Koop, 60
Bouchard v. Orange, 73
Boughton v. Socony Mobil Oil Co., 462–463
Braun v. Vallade, 280
Bread v. Alexandria, 3
Brown v. Board of Education, 13
Buckaloo v. Johnson, 147, 153–154

Cable Connection v. Direct TV, 26

C.B. Webster Real Estate v. Richard, 159
California Auto Court Assn. v. Cohn, 148
Calkins v. Steinbach, 255
Carleton v. Tortosa, 550
Carlsen v. Zane, 159
Carpenter v. Brenham, 398
Carpenter v. Lewis, 236
Carson Harbor Village Ltd. v. Unocal Corp., 493
Chang v. Tsang, 132
Chapman v. Gilmore, 149
Cisco v. Van Lew, 89
Citizens for Covenant Compliance v. Anderson, 465
City of Phoenix v. Garbage Services Co. D. Ariz, 492
Coleman v. Mora, 159
Complaint forms, 17–19
Construction Industry of Sonoma County v. City of Petaluma, 478
Coon v. Shry, 362
Covina Manor, Inc. v. Hatch, 211–212
Cowell v. Snyder, 211
Crimmins v. Gould, 189–192

De St. Germain v. Watson, 545–547
Debble v. Stearns, 77
Delano v. Jacoby, 222
Dolan v. City of Tigard, 239
Droeger v. Friedman, Sloan & Ross, 131, 168
Duin v. Security First Natl. Bank, 550

Easton v. Strasburger, 135, 169, 551, 554
Ecodyne Corp. v. Shah N.D. Cal., 492
Ellis v. Klaff, 29–31

Euclid v. Amber Realty Co., 471
Evans v. Faught, 219–221

Field v. Century 21 Klowden-Forest Realty, 134
First Lutheran Etc. Church v. County of Los Angeles, 239
Fleischer v. Cosgrove, 72
Floresta, Inc. v. City Council, 478
Fox v. Prime Ventures Ltd., 545
Freedman v. Rector, 72
Friedman v. Isenbruck, 318
Friends of Mammoth v. Board of Supervisors, 488–490
Froelich Motor Co. v. Kohler Estate, 253

Gans v. Smull, 129
Garcia v. Wetzel, 377
Gelfand v. O'Haver, 289–290
Geotheral Kinetics v. Union Oil Co. of California, 39–41
Gibbs v. American Savings & Loan Assn., 61–62
Gilardi v. Hallam, 233
Gilligan v. Jamco Dev. Corp., 342
Gion v. Santa Cruz, 196
Gipson v. Davis Realty Co., 541, 553
Giraud v. Milvich, 328
Gisler v. County of Madera, 477
Glenn R. Sewell Sheet Metal, Inc. v. Loverde, 324
Golden Gateway Center v. Golden Gateway Tenants Assn., 310

Granberry v. Islay Investments, 322

Green v. Superior Court, 325

Greenbach Bros. Inc. v. Burns, 69

Grubb & Ellis Co. v. Bello, 167

Gustafson v. Dunman, Inc., 216

Hall Street Associates LLC v. Mattel Inc., 26

Harri's v. Capital Growth Investors XIV, 342

Hart v. Burnett, 14–15

Havley v. Bank of America, 414–415

Hawaii Housing Authority v. Midkiff, 241

Hedges v. Carrigan, 124

Henrioville v. Marin Ventures, Inc., 340

Herz v. Clark's Market, 159

Hess v. Fair Employment and Housing Commission, 342

Higgins v. Ova, 255

Hignell v. Gebala, 337

Hinman v. Wagon, 305

Hocking v. Title Ins. & Trust Co., 505–507

Holtz v. Sup. Ct., 296

Honey v. Henry's Franchise Leasing Corp., 229–230

Horning v. Shilberg, 545

Howard Jarvis Taxpayer's Assn. v. Whittier Union H.S. Dist., 7, 437

Howden-Goetzl v. Superior Court, 358

Huijers v. DeMarrais, 174

IGA Aluminum Products v. Manufacturer's Bank, 417

Ilkhchooyi v. Best, 331

In re Duncombe, 352–354

In re Estate of Larkin, 8–10

In re Estate of Porter, 214

In re Garner, 354

In re Hoffman, 3

In re Jones, 410

In re Lane, 6

In re Sanders, 354

Jamison v. Texas, 3

Jay v. Dollarhide, 535

Jolton v. Mister Graf & Co., 549

Jones v. Alfred Mayer Co., 341

Jones v. Deeter, 282

Jones v. Tierney-Sinclair, 185

Jordan v. Talbot, 299–301, 305, 329

Kaiser Aluminum & Chem. Co. v. Catelus Dev. Corp., 492

Karbelning v. Brothwell, 337

Katemis v. Westerlund, 130

Kellogg v. Curry, 521–523

Keys v. Romley, 293

Kirk v. Source One Mortgage Services Corp., 382

Kneiser v. Balasco-Blackwood Co., 280

Knight v. Hallsthammer, 325

Kraemer v. Smith, 153

Kritt v. Athens Hills Dev. Co., 132, 149

Kroger v. Baur, 64

Kucera v. Lizza, 182

Kwock v. Bergren, 305

Lathrop v. Gauger, 77

Laural Hills Home Assn. v. Los Angeles, 486

Leamon v. Krfajkiewcz, 24

Lehman v. Richfield Oil Corp., 280

Levin Metals Corp. v. Parr-Richmond Terminal Co., 491

Lewis & Queen v. Ball & Sons, 158

Lewis v. Superior Court, 349

Lingsch v. Savage, 553

Livingston v. Rice, 355

Los Altos Hills v. Adobe Creek Properties, 478

M.P. Moller, Inc. v. Wilson, 49–50

Madhani v. Cooper, 286

Manhattan Loft, LLC v. Mercury Liquors, Inc., 27

Marin Co. Bd. of Realtors, Inc. v. Palsson, 146

Marin Mun. Water Dist. v. N.W. Pac. R.R. Co., 296

McDonald v. Morly, 252

Mendiondo v. Greitman, 144

Meyer v. Benko, 78–80

Mitchell v. Gould, 549

Moncharish v. Heily & Blasé et al, 26

Moore v. East Cleveland, 478

Mt. States Tel. & Tel. Co. v. Kelton, 345

Nakasone v. Randall, 408

Nakatsukasa v. Wade, 78

Nectow v. City of Cambridge, 479

Nelson v. Mayer, 147

Nollan v. Calif. Coastal Commission, 239, 241–244

Nork v. Pac. Coast Medical Ent. Inc., 307

Northern Oil Inc. v. L.A., 487

O'Hagen v. Board of Zoning Adjustment, 502

Oroville-Wyandotte Irr.Dist. v. Ford, 48

Otis Elevator Co. v. Berry, 554

Ott Hardware Co. v. Yost, 427

Pacific Trust Co. v. Fidelity Federal Savings, 402

Patten-Blinn Lumber Co. v. Francis, 358–360

Payne v. White House Properties, 541

Pease v. Brown, 129

Peiser v. Mettler, 330

People v. Asuncion, 377, 537

Pereira v. Pereira, 259

Pollard v. Saxe & Yolles Dev. Co., 216, 219
Potts v. Grover, 419
Pratt v. Hodgson, 185

Randone v. Appellate Department, 408
Rees v. Dept. of Real Estate, 537
Resnik v. Anderson & Miles Corp., 541
Riddle v. Harmon, 253–254
Rivadell, Inc. v. Raso, 89
Robins v. Pruneyard Shopping Center, 4
Robinson v. Grossman, 534
Robinson v. Los Angeles, 479
Roven v. Miller, 53
Rowland v. Christian, 278, 281–284
Royer v. Carter, 73–74
Russian Hill Improvement Assn. v. Board of Permit Appeals, 502

Salton Comm. Services Dist. v. Southard, 337
San Diego White Trust Corp. v. Swift, 454
Sands v. Eagle Oil & Refining Co., 554–556
Sarten v. Pomatto, 92
Secretary of Housing and Urban Dev. v. Layfield, 325

Selby Realty Co. v. City of San Buenaventura, 473, 474–476
Shapiro v. Hu, 136
Sierra Club v. City of Hayward, 431
Silacci v. Abramson, 292
Smith v. Fair Employment and Housing Com'n, 342
Smith v. Richard, 135
Southern Land Co. v. McKenna, 236
Southland Corp. v. Superior Court, 282
Specialty Restaurants Corp. v. Los Angeles, 36
States Shingle Co. v. Kaufman, 427–428
Steiner v. Thexton, 124
Stoltenberg v. Harveston, 340
Stratton v. Tejani, 129
Strout Western Realty Agency, Inc. v. Lewis, 147
Summers v. Freeman, 168

Thompson v. Thompson, 256
Thorsby v. Babcock, 451–453
Tustin Heights Assn. v. Bd. of Supervisors, 481–483

U.S. v. 3814 N.W. Thurman St., 381
U.S. v. Estate of Romani, 445

Valencia v. Michaud, 286
Van Camp v. Van Camp, 259
Village of Belle Torre v. Boraas, 477

Ward v. Taggart, 553
Warsaw v. Chicago Metallic Ceiling, Inc., 188
Wellencamp decision, 227–228
West v. Evans, 237–238
Weston Inv. Co. v. State of California, 434–436
Wharam v. Investment Underwriters, Inc., 295
Wheeler v. Bainbridge, 304
Wilkins v. San Bernardino, 480
Williams v. Fassler, 374
Willig v. Gold, 553
Wilson v. Lewis, 92
Wood Court II Ltd. v. McDonald, 358
Wyatt v. Union Mortgage Co., 268

Young v. American Mini Theatres, Inc., 478

Zeibak v. Nasser, 267
Zellers v. State of California, 194
Ziegler v. Bonnel, 250

Index of Codes

Business & Professions Code (B&PC)

7031(b), ...425
7071.6 et seq, ...420
7159, ...425
10000 et seq, ...542
10131, ...536
10131.6, ...178
10131-10131.3, ...536
10132, ...537
10137, ...543
10142, ... 143, 168
10145, ...543
10147.5, ... 146, 160
10176, ... 168, 543
10176d, ...550
10176e, ... 144, 551
10176f, ... 143, 158
10176g, ...550
10176(g), ...543
10176h, ...146
10177, ... 168, 543, 544
10177.4, ...543
10232.4, ...382
10240, ... 367, 379
10240 et seq, .379
10244, ...366
10245, ...379
10250 et seq, .269
10474, ...544
11000, ...495
11003.2, ...270
11004, ...269
11423, ...381

California Constitution

Art. XI, Sec. 11, ...471
Art. XIII, Sec 1-1/4, ...432
Art. XIIIA, ...436

California Real Estate Commission Regulations (Comm.Regs.)(Regs.)

2725, ...537
2792.24, ...466
2830, ...543
2832, ... 93, 144, 543
2900, ...78
2901, ...78

Civil Code (C.C.)

18, ...349
25, ...222
33, ...54
34-36, ...54
51-2, ...341
54.1, ...341
328, ...236
654, ...34
657, ...34
659, ...39
660, ...39
662, ...39
682.1(a), ...266
783, ...269
789, ...211
789.3, ...329
791, ...303
798.70, ...178
798.75, ...178
798 et seq, ...308
811.4, ...189
813, ...196
818, ...204
819, ...43
827, ... 304, 338
827(b), ...305
832, ...295
841, ...291
841.4, ...292
846, ...281
850 et seq, ...493
864, ...403
865, ...403
871.1-871.7, ...49
882.020 et seq, ...360
885.020, ...202
885.030, ...203
896, ...422
897, ...423
1007, ...232
1008, ...196

1009, ... 196
1019, ... 48
1058.5, ... 354
1091, ... 211
1092, ... 90
1096, ... 222
1102, ... 135
1102.2, ... 136
1102.4, ... 137
1102.6b, ... 139
1102.6(c), ... 136
1105, ... 214
1113, ... 214
1161.1(c), ... 337
1161.5, ... 305
1173, ... 219
1174.2, ... 326
1189, ... 345
1207, ... 351
1213, ... 344
1214, ... 344, 350
1350 et seq, ... 269
1351, ... 270
1354, ... 270
1366, ... 270
1368, ... 178
1468, ... 464
1541, ... 66
1572, ... 552–553
1583, ... 62
1585, ... 57
1587, ... 60
1624, ... 63, 64, 131, 147, 168, 211, 341
1632, ... 310
1642, ... 27, 519
1668, ... 165, 340
1671, ... 71, 72
1671b, ... 69
1671c,d, ... 69, 71
1671 et seq, ... 127
1675, ... 70
1675a, ... 70
1675c,d, ... 70
1675e, ... 70
1676, ... 72
1677, ... 70, 71, 72
1677a, ... 70
1678, ... 70
1689, ... 65, 159
1695.13-1695.14, ... 400

1695-1695.12, ... 400
1697, ... 340
1698, ... 340
1699, ... 66
1710, ... 552–553
1710.2, ... 139
1717, ... 126, 339
1785.20a, ... 338
1786.10 et seq, ... 338
1846.7, ... 309
1914, ... 376
1916-1, ... 376, 377
1916-3, ... 378
1916.5, ... 366
1922.1, ... 144
1927, ... 328
1940.9, ... 323
1941.1, ... 324
1942.3, ... 326
1942.4, ... 326
1945, ... 211
1946, ... 303, 337, 338
1946.1(b), ... 304
1947, ... 318
1950.5, ... 326
1950.5b, ... 333
1950.5c, ... 320, 321
1950.5d, ... 322
1950.5e, ... 320, 321
1950.5f, ... 332
1950.5(g)(4), ... 321
1950.5k, ... 322
1950.6, ... 321
1950.7, ... 321
1950.7c, ... 320
1950.8, ... 331
1951, ... 334
1951.2, ... 332, 333
1951.3, ... 334
1951.4, ... 334
1952.3, ... 308
1953a5, ... 340
1954, ... 328
1954.27, ... 319
1954.50 et seq, ... 319
1980-1991, ... 335
1981, ... 335
1984-1985, ... 335
1985.20.3, ... 321
1988, ... 335

1993, ... 335
1995.010-1995.340, ... 330
2020, ... 550
2079, ... 169, 554
2079.7, ... 139
2228, ... 549
2229, ... 551
2230, ... 550
2231, ... 550
2234, ... 549
2295, ... 532
2300, ... 534
2322, ... 549
2343, ... 551, 554
2373, ... 173
2400 et seq, ... 535
2876, ... 402
2904, ... 416
2923.5, ... 392, 394
2923.52, ... 395
2924, ... 36, 392
2924b, ... 392
2924c, ... 394
2924c(b)(1), ... 393
2924e, ... 401
2924f, ... 394, 397
2924g, h, ... 397
2924i, ... 367
2937, ... 381
2954, ... 382
2954.5, ... 373
2954.7, ... 382
2954.9, ... 374
2954(b), ... 374
2966, ... 367
2985.1, ... 227
2985.2, ... 227
2985.3, ... 227
2985.4, ... 227
2985.6, ... 227
3085, ... 420
3090, ... 417
3095, ... 416
3096, ... 420
3097, ... 418
3104, ... 416
3109-3153, ... 416, 419
3114, ... 418
3115, ... 419
3116, ... 419

3128, ... 426
3129, ... 426
3143, ... 421
3144, ... 419
3147, ... 419
3148, ... 419
3152, ... 419
3156-3175, ... 420
3235, ... 420
3236, ... 420
3260.1, ... 420
3294, ...72
3300, ...66
3307, ... 72, 73–74
3318, ... 554
3333, ... 549
3345, ... 211
3384-3387, .68
3479, ... 286
4800, ... 260
5107, ... 258
5108, ... 258
5110, ... 258
5118, ... 258
5125, ... 258
5127, ... 258, 260, 265

Code of Civil Procedure (C.C.P.)

7, ... 129
10, ... 302
12, ... 302
12a, ... 129, 302
12b, ... 302
85, ...16
98, ...16
116.220, ...16
116.221, ...16
318, ... 260
328, ... 236
337, ...27
338.4, ... 260
340, ...27
409, ... 356
409.2, ... 358
481.010-492.090, ... 408
483.010, ... 408
484.010-484.110, ... 408
485.010-485.540, ... 408
486.010, ... 409

487.010, ... 409
488.010 et seq, ... 409
488.310, ... 307
580b, ... 385, 389
638, ...26
685.010, ... 409
690.030, ... 453
697.310, ... 410, 413
697.340, ... 410
697.350, ... 409
697.380(g), ... 355, 413
701.510, ... 415
701.540-701.545, ... 399
701.590(c), ... 399
704.710 et seq, ... 448
704.720, ... 456
704.730, ... 448, 450
704.740-704.850, ... 449
704.910 et seq, ... 448
704.930, ... 454
704.940, ... 454
704.965, ... 451
704.980, ... 456
704.990, ... 456
726, ... 389
729.010, ... 400
1021, ... 339
1021-1035, ... 339
1033, ...16
1049, ... 409
1159-1179a, ... 306
1161, ... 337
1161.1, ... 211, 303
1162, ... 337
1166a, ... 308
1167, ... 306
1174, ... 307
1175b, ... 334
1177, ... 307
1179a, ... 306
1180.1, ...20
1230.010-1273.060, ... 244
1240.010, ... 244
1240.030, ... 244
1245.244, ... 245
1245.270, ... 245
1263.330, ... 245
1263.510, ... 245
1856, ...28

Code of Federal Regulations (CFR)

12 CFR 226.2(a)17, ... 378
12 CFR 226.15, ... 379
12 CFR 226.34, ... 384
12 CFR 555.15, ... 374
12 CFR 591.2(b), ... 372
12 CFR 591.5(b)(I)(i), ... 373
12 CFR 3445, ... 374
24 CFR 3500.7(a), ... 523
24 CFR 3500.14, ... 543
29 CFR 1630, ... 341

Code of Regulations

10 Code of Regs 2844, ... 379
10 Code of Regs 2944, ... 379
27 Code of Regs 15085g, ... 488
27 Code of Regs 15160c, ... 488
Comm. Regs. *See* California Real Estate
   Commission Regulations

Commercial Code (Comm.C.)

1459, ... 363
3305, ... 364
3306, ... 363
9102, ...43
9105f, ...43
9313, ...48

Corporations Code (Corp. C.)

15006, ... 266
15501 et seq, ... 267
17000 et seq, ... 268

Evidence Code

1152.5, ...26

Family. C.

297, ... 257
297.5, ... 257

Financial Code

1236, ... 270
4970-4978.8, ... 382
4970-4979.8, ... 383
4973(c), ... 383
4973(f), ... 383
7153.4, ... 270
17000-17654, ... 517
17006, ... 517

Government Code

38780, ... 137
51200 et seq, ... 431
54774.1 et seq, ... 474
65302, ... 473
65800, ... 472
65858, ... 471
65901, ... 480
66410 et seq, ... 195
66424, ... 499
66427, ... 501
66650 et seq, ... 474
72055, ...16
95906, ... 480

Health & Safety Code

17980.7, ... 326
25300 et seq, ... 490
26100-26156, ... 140
35720 et seq, ... 341

Insurance Code

12340.11, ... 513
12340 et seq, ... 505

Internal Revenue Code (I.R.C.)

856-858, ... 269
1031, ... 269
1445, ... 169
2036, ... 203
3508, ... 542
I.R.C. *See* Internal Revenue Code

Labor Code

2810, ... 425
3351, ... 541
3353, ... 541

Probate Code (Prob.C.)

56.3, ... 224
201, ... 225
10160.5, ... 150
10161-10168, ... 150
10510 et seq, ... 150

Public Resources Code (Pub.Res.C.)

21000 et seq, ... 486
21068, ... 487
21080, ... 487
21167, ... 488
21403, ...42

Public Utilities Code

10009.6, ... 323

Pub.Res.C. *See* Public Resources Code

Regs. *See* California Real Estate Commission
   Regulations

Revenue & Tax Code (R&TC)

61, ... 442
61-65, ... 438
69.5, ... 442
110.1, ... 437
205.5, ... 432
218, ... 432
480.4, ... 439
1463, ... 169
2192.1, ... 444
3520, ... 434
3712, ... 444
3900, ... 445
11911, ... 348
11912, ... 348
17980.7, ... 326
18662, ... 173
18805, ... 169
20501, ... 442
20601, ... 442
24436.5, ... 326

San Francisco Municipal Code

Chapter 8, ... 501

Streets and Highways Code

5610, ... 282

Unemployment Insurance Code

650, ... 541

Uniform Commerical Code (U.C.C.)

9601, ...36

United States Code

12 USC 2601 et seq, ... 523
12 USC 2605, ... 381
15 USC 1601 et seq, ... 378
15 USC 1615, ... 366
15 USC 1691(d)(1), ... 381

42 USC 901 et seq, ...490

42 USC 1437f, ...309

42 USC 1857d, ...485

42 USC 3601 et seq, ... 341, 501

42 USC 4321 et seq, ...485

42 USC 4852d(a)(3), ...137

42 USC 9601(35)(B), ...492

42 USC 9607a, ...491

42 USC 9607(e)(1), ...494

42 USC 9607(n)(3), ...494

42 USC 12101-12213, ...341

Water Code

100, ...45

101, ...45

106, ...44, 46

1225, ...44

1250, ...44

Subject Index

AAA (American Arbitration Association), 24, 128

Abandonment, lease agreements, 334–335

Abstract of judgment, 410–412

Acceleration clauses, 370–373

Acceptance, 57, 60, 131–133, 224

Accord and satisfaction, 65

Acknowledgment, 345–346

ADA (Americans with Disabilities Act), 341–342

Adjoining property, 282, 294–296

Adjustable rate loans, 366

ADR (alternative dispute resolution), 23–27, 270–271

Advance deposits, 319–322

Adverse possession
   additions and subtractions by water, 245–246
   condemnation (eminent domain), 238–245
   defined, 232
   vs. easement by prescription, 233
   requirements of, 233–238
   use of, 232–233

Affidavit of death of joint tenant, 251

Affirmative easements, 181

Agency Disclosure Addendum, 174–175

Agency relationships
   creation of, 533–534
   deposit receipt form, 90–91
   escrow, 518
   Internet activities, 535–536
   lease agreements, 340
   listing agreements, 165, 173–174

nature of, 532–533
   termination of, 534–535

AIREA. *See* American Industrial Real Estate Association

Airspace, 41–42

Alienation provision, 371–373

Allocation of costs, deposit receipt form, 98

Alluvium, 246

ALTA (American Land Title Association), 112, 120, 507–516

Alterations, lease agreements, 328

Alternative dispute resolution (ADR), 23–27, 270–271

Ambulatory, defined, 226

American Arbitration Association (AAA), 24, 128

American Industrial Real Estate Association (AIREA), 317

American Land Title Association (ALTA), 112, 120, 507–516

Americans with Disabilities Act (ADA), 341–342

Antiwaiver, lease agreements, 336–337

Appellate courts, 20, 23

Appraisals, 97–98, 144–145, 381

Appurtenances, 39, 180

Arbitration, 24–25, 128, 167

"As is," deposit receipt form, 99, 116–117, 136

Assignees, 89

Assignment and sublease, 329–330

Assignment of rents clause, 373

Association of Bay Area Governments, 474

Assumption, 403–404

Attachment liens, 406–409

Attachments, 408

Attorney fees, 126, 166, 339

Avulsion, 246

Balance the equities, 288–289

Balloon payments, 366–367

Bankruptcy, 66

Bay Area Rapid Transit, 296

BCDC (San Francisco Bay Conservation and Development Commission), 474

Bequests, 226

Bilateral contracts, 52, 76

Bill of Sale, 37

Blanket deed of trust, 375

Bona fide purchaser (BFP), 348–349

Bonds, 420

Breach of contract
   damages, 66, 334
   defined, 66
   general damages, 72–73
   lease agreements, 332–334
   liquidated damages, 68–72
   rescission actions, 65, 68
   specific performance, 68

Brokers
   commissions, 64, 76–77, 132, 146–150, 153
   defined, 536–537
   deposit receipt form, 131–133
   disclaimers, lease agreements, 341
   listing agreement form, 158, 164–165, 168
   obligation to clients, 549–551
   obligation to third persons, 551–556

regulation of, 542–548
vs. salespersons,
  537–538, 541–542
Brownsfields Revitalization
  and Environmental
  Restoration Act (2001),
  493–494
Buyers
  defaults, 149, 161
  deposit receipt form,
    89, 117, 120, 131
  land sales contracts and,
    227–229
  ready, willing and
    able, 148

California Association of
  REALTORS®
  arbitration, 24
  commission agreements, 77
  Confirmation of Real
    Estate Agency Relation-
    ships form, 174, 177
  contingency for sale or
    purchase of other
    property form, 123
  deposit receipt forms,
    81–101, 112–122,
    124–133
  Disclosure Regarding
    Real Estate Agency
    Relationship form,
    174–176
  dispute resolution, 23–24
  Independent Contractor
    Agreement, 538–540
  lease form and analysis,
    311–342
  listing agreement form,
    154–161, 163–168
  natural hazard disclosure
    statement form, 138
  Notice of Prospective
    Buyers/Transferees
    form, 162
  Real Estate Transfer
    Disclosure Statement,
    170–172
  receipt for increased deposit
    form, 94

statewide buyer and seller
  advisory, 102–111
California Land Title
  Association (CLTA),
  112, 120, 507–516
Cancellation of contract,
  65–67
C.C.&R.s (covenants, condi-
  tions, and restrictions),
  269, 458–468
CERCLA (Comprehensive
  Environmental
  Response, Compensation,
  and Liability Act),
  490–493
Certiorari, 23
Chain of title, 351
City transfer fees, 113
Civil law, 12
Civil Rights Act (1968), 341
Claim of right, 235–236
Clean Air Amendments
  (1970), 485
Cleaning deposit, 320
Clean Water Restoration Act
  (1966), 486
Closings, deposit receipt
  form, 113–114
CLTA (California Land Title
  Association), 112, 120,
  507–516
Codicils, 226
Color of title, 235–236
Commencement date, listing
  agreement form, 158
Commercial leases, 317, 324,
  327, 335
Commercial loans, 377
Commingling deposits, 144,
  543
Commissions
  deposit receipts and,
    132, 146–150
  listing agreements and,
    64, 76–77, 153,
    160–161, 163–164
Common areas, 285
Common interest develop-
  ments, 270–271
Common law, 12–13

Community property, 32,
  168, 225, 257–260
Community property with
  right of survivorship,
  266
Competent parties, 63
Comprehensive Environmen-
  tal Response, Compen-
  sation, and Liability Act
  (CERCLA), 490–493
Concealment, 553
Condemnation
  dedication as, 239
  guidelines for, 244–245
  inverse, 238–239
  vs. police power, 240–241
Conditional estates, 199
Conditional releases, 422
Conditional use permits,
  479, 480
Condition of premises, lease
  agreement, 323–324
Condition of property,
  deposit receipt form,
  116–117
Condition precedents/
  subsequents, 460
Conditions, defined,
  460–461
Conditions running with the
  land, 463–464
Condominium and Co-
  operative Conversion
  Protection and Abuse
  Relief Act, 501
Condominium/planned unit
  development disclosures
  deposit receipt form, 115
  leases, 327
Condominiums, 178,
  269, 501
Confirmation of acceptance,
  deposit receipt
  form, 132
Consideration, 62–63
Constant reduction notes,
  366
Constitutional rights, 2–3, 9
Constructive notice, 426
Consumer loans, 376–377

Contingency for sale or purchase of other property form, 123
Contingent life estates, 204
Contracts. *See also* Breach of contract; Deposit receipts
  alternative dispute resolution, 23–27
  cancellation of, 65–67
  classifications of, 52–56
  defined, 52
  discharge and unenforceability, 64–66
  elements of, 56–64
  general damages, 72–74
  liquidated damages, 68–72
Conveyance, 317
Cooperatives, 270
Co-ownership. *See also* Ownership
  common interest developments, 270–271
  community property, 32, 168, 225, 257–260
  community property with right of survivorship, 266
  condominiums, 269
  cooperatives, 270
  corporations, 267–268
  joint tenancy, 168, 249–254, 438–439
  joint ventures, 267
  limited liability companies, 268–269
  limited partnerships, 267
  partnerships, 266
  real estate investment trusts, 269
  syndications, 269
  tenancy in common, 168, 254–257
  types of, 248, 261–263
Corporate Securities Law, 267
Corporations, 267–268
Correlative rights doctrine, 45–46
Costa-Hawkins Rental Housing Act, 319

Cotenancy agreements, 256–257
Counter offers, 58–59
County transfer fees, 113
Courts
  appellate, 20, 23
  Federal, 23
  small claims, 16, 20, 21–22
  superior, 15–16, 20
Covenant of quiet enjoyment, 328
Covenants, conditions, and restrictions (C.C.&R.s), 269, 458–468
Covenants, defined, 461
Creation of law doctrine, 7–8
Credit check, lease agreements, 338
Crisis Period Loans, 391–392
Crops/vegetation, 43

Damages
  for breach of contract, 66, 334
  general, 72–73
  liquidated, 68–72
  to premises, 336
  special, 73
Data base disclosure, deposit receipt form, 113
Death on the premises disclosures, 139
Declaration of Covenants, Conditions and Restrictions, 465
Declared homesteads, 448
Dedication of property, 195–196, 239, 500
Deeds
  defined, 214
  land sales contracts, 226–230
  requirements for, 221–224
  types of, 214–221
  wills and intestacy, 224–226
Deeds of trust
  deficiency judgments and, 384
  foreclosure and, 400–403
  future advances, 356

vs. mortgages, 367–370
  promissory notes and, 370–376
  time periods, 360
  transfer of property and, 403–404
Default of payment clause, 371
Defaults, 149, 161
Defeasible estates, 201
Deficiency judgments, 384–390, 399–400, 404
Delivery of deeds, 223–224
Department of Housing and Community Development (HCD), 178, 309
Department of Housing and Urban Development (HUD), 112, 341, 524–529
Department of Motor Vehicles, 178
Deposit receipts
  California Association of REALTORS® forms, 80–140
  characteristics of, 52, 76–78
  deeds and, 219
  drafting requirements, 78
  mediation clauses in, 25–26
  rescission of, 65
  termination of offer and, 57
Deposits (earnest money), 143–144, 165, 543
Deposits, advance, 319–322
Description of property
  deposit receipt form, 89–90
  listing agreement, 159
Devise, defined, 226
Dicta, 28–29
Disclosure of Information on Lead-Based Paint and/ or Lead-Based Paint Hazards, 331

Disclosures
  agency disclosure statement, 173–174
  condominium/planned unit development disclosures, deposit receipt form, 115
  data base disclosure, deposit receipt form, 114
  death on the premises, 139
  environmental hazards, 139
  full, of brokers, 550
  general duty, 133–134
  lead-based paint warning, 137, 139, 331
  lease agreements, 331
  listing agreements, 173–177
  Mello-Roos assessments, 114, 139
  natural hazard disclosure statement form, 138
  Real Estate Transfer Disclosure Statement, 117
  residential disclosure statements, 114, 134–136, 169
  statutory disclosures and cancellation rights, deposit receipt form, 114–115, 116–117
  subdivisions, 139
  toxic mold, 139
  transfer disclosure statements, 114
Discrimination, lease agreements, 341–342
Dispute resolution, listing agreement, 167
District Court, 23
District Court of Appeal, 20
Doctrine of correlative rights, 45–46
Doctrine of reasonableness, 28
Documentary Transfer Tax, 346
Domestic partnerships, 257
Domestic violence, 309
Domicile, 35
Dominant tenement, 180

Dual agency, 518
Due-on-encumbrance clause, 373
Due-on-sale clause, 227, 371–373
Due process, 9
Durable power of attorney, 222, 534
Dwelling house homesteads, 448, 453–454

Earnest money, 143–144, 165, 543
Easements
  creation of, 182–187
  dedication of property, 195–196, 239, 500
  defined, 180
  in gross, 180–181
  licenses, 192–194
  by prescription, 233
  purpose of, 181–182
  termination of, 188–189
  types of, 180–181
  use, maintenance, and repair, 187–188
Easton disclosure statements. *See* Residential disclosure statements
Economic Stabilization Act (1970), 318
Effectiveness, 60–62
EIR (environmental impact report), 486
Eminent domain, 238, 240, 296, 472
Encroachments, 292–293
Entry, lease agreements, 328–329
Environmental hazards disclosures, 139
Environmental impact report (EIR), 486–488
Environmental laws
  California, 486–490
  federal, 485–486
  hazardous waste laws, 490–494
Environmental Quality Act (1970), 486, 488–490

Environmental Responsibility Acceptance Act., 493
Equal dignities rule, 64
Equal housing opportunity
  deposit receipt form, 126
  listing agreement, 166
Equal protection laws, 2–3, 9
Equitable servitude, 464, 465
Escheat, 226
Escrow
  defined, 517
  delivery, title and risk, 520–523
  deposit receipt form, 101–102, 133
  dual agency, 518
  elements of, 518–520
  good faith estimates, 523–531
  instructions, 519–520
  regulation of, 517
  RESPA, 523, 531
Estate for years, 208
Estates
  classification of, 198–200
  freehold, 198, 200–207
  nonfreehold, 207–212
Estoppel, 189, 338
Euclidean zones, 470
Eviction. *See also* Leases
  limitations on, 298–299
  nonfreehold estates and, 208, 210–211
  process, 301–309
  retaliatory, 326–327
Exclusive agency listings, 145
Exclusive right to sell agency, 145, 158
Exculpatory clause, lease agreements, 339–340
Executed oral agreements, 64
Executed *vs.* executory contracts, 54, 66
Execution liens, 415–416
Executors, 226
Ex parte order, 408
Express agency, 533
Express *vs.* implied contracts, 54

Fair Debt Collection Practices Act, 305

Fair Employment Practices Commission, 341

False promise, 553

Fanny Mae, 381

Federal Arbitration Act., 26, 128

Federal Consumer Credit Protection Act, 381

Federal Consumer Protection Act, 378

Federal courts, 23

Federal Deposit Insurance Corporation (FDIC), 381

Federal Home Loan Bank Board (FHLBB), 374

Federal Reserve, 384

Federal Truth in Lending Act, 378

Fee simple absolute estates, 199–203

Fee simple defeasible estates, 201

Fee simple subject to condition subsequent estates, 200–202

Fences, 291–292

FHA, 112, 160, 381–382

Fifth Amendment, 2–3

Final Subdivision Public Report, 498

Final walk through, 125

Finance charges, 376–384

Finance section, deposit receipt form
  additional financing terms, 93
  all cash offer, 98
  appraisal contingency and removal, 97
  balance and total purchase price, 95
  first loan, 93
  increased deposit, 93
  initial deposit, 91–92
  loan applications, 95
  loan contingency removal, 96–97
  no loan contingency, 97
  terms, 91
  verification of down payment and closing costs, 95

Financing statement, 38, 48

Finders, 537

FIRPTA (Foreign Investment in Real property Tax Act), 169

First Amendment, 3

Fixtures, 39, 46–50, 115

Forcible detainer, 298

Foreclosure. *See also* Involuntary liens
  effects on other deeds of trust, 400–403
  guarantee reports, 513
  judicial, 398–400
  judicial *vs.* nonjudicial, 391
  sale of residential property, 400
  trustee's foreclosure (nonjudicial) process, 391–398

Foreign Investment in Real property Tax Act (1980), 169

Formal wills, 224

Forms
  abstract of judgment, 411–412
  acknowledgment, 346
  affidavit of death of joint tenant, 251
  Confirmation of Real Estate Agency Relationships form, 174, 177
  contingency for sale or purchase of other property, 123
  deed of trust, 368–369
  deposit receipt, 81–101, 112–122, 124–133
  Disclosure Regarding Real Estate Agency Relationship form, 174–176
  escrow instructions, 519–520

good faith estimates, 524–526

grant deed, 217

grant of easement, 183–184

homeowner's title insurance policy, 507–512

homestead declaration, 455

Independent Contractor Agreement, 538–540

lease, 311–317

license agreement, 193

lis pendens, 357

listing agreement, 154–161, 163–168

mechanic's lien, 417

natural hazard disclosure statement, 138

Notice of Consent to Use Land, 186

notice of default, 393–394

Notice of Prospective Buyers/Transferees form, 162

Notice of Trustee's Sale of Property, 396–397

preliminary 20-day notice, 418

Preliminary Change of Ownership Report, 440–441

promissory note, 365

quitclaim deeds, 218

Real Estate Transfer Disclosure Statement, 170–172

receipt for increased deposit, 94

release for final payment, conditional, 425

release for final payment, unconditional, 426

release for progress payment, conditional, 423

release for progress payment, unconditional, 424

Report of Sale and Order Confirming Sale of Real Property form, 151–152

Request for Notice of Default and Sale, 395
settlement statement (HUD), 527–529
statewide buyer and seller advisory, 102–111
thirty-day notice, 303, 304
three-day notice, 306
Transfer Tax Affidavit, 347–348
waiver of mechanic's lien by general contractor, 421
For sale signs, 166
Fourteenth Amendment, 2–3, 9
Fraud, 307, 388–389, 549, 552. *See also* Statute of frauds
Freddy Mac, 381
Freehold estates, 198, 200–207
Free speech, 2–3
Fructus, 43
Full disclosure, 550
Future advances clauses, 375–376
Future interest, 200

Garnishment, 407
Garn-St. Germain Act, 371, 373, 374–375, 401, 403
General duty disclosures, 133–134
General plan restrictions, 464–466
General plans, 472–476
Good faith estimates, 523–531
Good faith improver, 49
Good-faith trespasser, 49
Government property, 430
Government requirements and retrofits, deposit receipt form, 101
Grant deeds, 37, 214, 217
Grant of easement, 182–184
Gross leases, 55
Guarantee, lease agreements, 342

Habitability, 324–326
Hazardous waste laws, 490–494
HCD (Department of Housing and Community Development), 178
Historical overview, 31–32
HOA (homeowners' associations), 113, 270
Holder in due course, 363
Holographic wills, 224
Homeowners' associations (HOA), 113, 270
Homeowner's exemption, 432
Homeowner's title insurance policy, 507–512
Homestead Act, 32
Homesteads, 344, 448–456
Home warranty, 113
Hostile use, 185, 234
HUD (Department of Housing and Urban Development), 112, 309, 341, 524–529

IAEA (Independent Administration of Estates Act), 149–150
Illusory contracts, 55–56, 63
Implied agency, 534
Implied easements, 182, 184, 196
Implied *vs.* express contracts, 54
Impound accounts, 382
Independent Administration of Estates Act (IAEA), 149–150
Independent Contractor Agreement, 538–540
Independent contractors, 538–541
Industrial leases, 317
Initial deposits, 91–92
Inspections, 99–101, 117, 332–334
Installment notes, 364
Installment sales contracts, 72

Insurance, 336. *See also* Private mortgage insurance; Title insurance
Intentional misrepresentations, 552
Interim occupancy agreement, 120
Internal Revenue Service, 169
Internet activities, 535–536
Interpreter/translator, lease agreements, 340–341
Intestacy, 225
Intestate, 35
Investigative Consumer Reporting Agencies Act, 338
Invitees, 280
Involuntary liens
attachment liens, 406–409
creation of, 406
execution liens, 415–416
judgment liens, 409–415
mechanic's lien, 416–428
Involuntary sales, 36, 39
Irrevocable contracts, 57, 159, 193–194
Items included
deposit receipt form, 115
listing agreement, 159

JAMS (Judicial Arbitration and Mediation Services, Inc.), 24, 128
Jarvis-Gann Initiative, 436
Joint and individual obligations, lease agreements, 331
Joint escrow instructions, deposit receipt form, 127
Joint tenancy, 168, 249–254, 438–439
Joint ventures, 267
Judgment liens, 36, 39, 228, 344, 355, 409–415
Judicial Arbitration and Mediation Services, Inc. (JAMS), 24, 128
Judicial system
alternative dispute resolution, 23–27

Judicial system (*continued*)
appellate courts, 20, 23
civil *vs.* common law, 12–13
Federal courts, 23
legal terms and concepts,
27–29
state trial courts, 15–20
Jurisdiction, 27, 35
Just compensation, 245

Keys and locks, lease
agreements, 328

Laborer, defined, 416
Land
additions and subtractions
by water, 245–246
C.C.&R.s, 269, 458–468
defined, 39, 41
eminent domain,
238, 240, 296
lateral support, 294–295
sales contracts, 226–230
subjacent support, 296
Landlords
liability of, 284–286
relationship with tenant,
309–317
Landowner's liability,
278–284, 491–494
Last month's rent, 320
Late charges clause
lease agreement, 322
promissory note, 373
Lateral support, 294–295
Lead-based paint warning,
137, 139, 331
Leasehold estates, 198
Leases. *See also* Eviction;
Tenancy
American Industrial Real
Estate Association form,
317
California Association of
REALTORS® form and
analysis, 310–342
deposit receipt form, 120
gross, 55
landlord-tenant
relationships, 309–310

liability and, 284–286
net-net-net, 55, 317
triple net, 55, 317
violation of, 298–299
Legacy, defined, 226
Legal object, 63
Legal terms and concepts,
27–29
Lender/Purchaser Disclosure
Statement, 382
Level payment notes,
364–365
Liability
of landlords, 284–286
of landowners,
278–284, 491–494
under Superfund, 491–494
Licensees, 279–280
Licenses, 192–194
Life estates, 200, 203–204
Limited liability companies,
268–269
Limited partnerships, 267
Liquidated damages
breach of contract and,
68–72
deposit receipt form, 127
receipt for increased
deposit/liquidated
damages form, 94
Lis pendens, 27, 356–358
Listing agreements
agency and contract, 143
agency disclosure
statement, 173–174
California Association of
REALTORS® form,
154–161, 163–168
commission and,
64, 76–77, 146–150,
153, 160–161, 163–164
condominiums, 178
Confirmation of Real
Estate Agency Relation-
ships form, 174, 177
deposits, 143–144
Disclosure Regarding Real
Estate Agency Relation-
ship form, 174–176
employment contract, 142

mediation and, 26
mobile homes, 174, 178
Real Estate Transfer
Disclosure Statement
form, 170–173
Report of Sale and Order
Confirming Sale of
Real Property form,
151–152
requirements, 143–144
residential disclosure
statement and, 169
types of, 145–146
withholding statements
and, 169, 173
List price, 159–160
Litigation guarantee
reports, 513
Loans
adjustable rate, 366
applications, 379–382
approval types, 96t
commercial, 377
consumer, 376–377
Crisis Period, 391–392
fraudulent, 388–389
Predatory Lending Law,
382–383
subprime, 383–384
truth in lending and,
378–379
Local Agency Formation
Commission, 474
Lockbox, 166

Maintenance and fitness
(habitability), 324–326
Management approval, 166
Manner of service, lease
agreements, 337
Map Act. *See* Subdivision
Map Act
Materialman, defined, 417
Mechanic's liens, 354–355,
416–428, 453
Mediation, 24–25, 128, 167,
338–339
Megan's Law, 331
Mello-Roos assessments, 114,
139, 436–437

Metropolitan Transportation Commission (MTC), 474
Mineral rights, 42–43
MLS. *See* Multiple listing service
Mobilehome Residency Law, 308
Mobile homes, 174, 178, 308–309
Modification, lease agreements, 340
Mortgages
  vs. deeds of trust, 367–370, 384
  as obligation, 362
MTC (Metropolitan Transportation Commission), 474
Multiple listing service (MLS)
  deposit receipt form, 126
  Internet listings, 536
  listing agreements and, 146, 164
  shared commissions and, 163
Municipal courts, 15
Mutual assent, 56

Name run reports, 514
National Environmental Policy Act of 1969 (NEPA), 485, 486, 489
Natural hazard disclosure statement form, 114, 138
Natural rights doctrine, 7
Negative amortization, 367
Negative easements, 181
Negligence, 553
Negligent misrepresentations, 552
Negotiable instruments, 363
Neighborhood conditions, lease agreements, 327
NEPA (National Environmental Policy Act of 1969), 485, 486, 489
Net listings, 145–146
Net, net, net leases, 55, 317
Newly constructed property, 442

Nixon, Richard, 318
Nominees, 89
Nondisclosure, 553
Nonfreehold estates, 198, 207–212
Nonresidential property, 72
Notices
  bona fide purchaser, 349
  conflicting claims to property, 351
  of Consent to Use Land, 186
  of default, 393–394
  of Intention and Subdivision Questionnaire, 497
  lease agreements, 337–338
  of nonresponsibility, 426
  of Prospective Buyers/ Transferees form, 162
  of recission, 394
  of Trustee's Sale of Property, 396–397
Notorious use, 185, 234
Novations, 65, 404
Nuisances, 286–290, 293

Occupants, 317–318
Offers
  acceptance, 57, 60, 131–132
  characteristics of, 56–57
  counter offers, 58–59
  deposit receipt form, 76, 131
  effectiveness of, 60, 63
  termination of, 57
Open listings, 145
Open-space exemption, 431
Open space zoning, 477
Option listings, 146
Options, 53
Oral agreements, 64–65, 130
Ordinances, 470
Original contractor, defined, 416
Or-more clause, 374
Ostensible agency, 534
Ownership, 34, 42, 200, 248. *See also* Co-ownership

Parking, lease agreement, 323
Parole evidence rule, 28
Partial release clauses, 376
Partnerships, 266
Patents, 32
Performance bonds, 420
Periodic tenancy, 208–210
Personal property, 34–39, 115, 335
Pets, lease agreements, 327
PITI (principle, interest, taxes and insurance), 55
Place of execution, deposit receipt form, 89
Planned unit development (PUD), 115
Police power, 240–241, 471
Possession, lease agreements, 331–332
Power of termination, 202
Powers of attorney, 222, 534
Preapproval, 96t
Predatory Lending Law, 382–383
Preemption, 32
Prejudgment attachments, 408
Preliminary 20-day notice, 418
Preliminary Change of Ownership Report, 346, 348, 440–441
Preliminary Subdivision Public Report, 498
Preliminary title report, 513
Pre-move out inspections, 332
Prepayment clause, 373–375
Prequalification, 96t
Principle, interest, taxes and insurance (PITI), 55
Prior Appropriation Rights, 44
Priorities
  homesteads, 453–454
  property tax liens, 444–447
  recording, 349, 350–356
Private mortgage insurance (PMI), 381–382

Private *vs.* public property, 2–3. *See also* Property
Probate sales, 149–150
Procuring cause, 147–148
Profit á prendre, 182
Progress payments, 422
Promissory notes, 363–367, 370–376
Property. *See also* Zoning
    adjoining, 282
    community, 32, 168, 225, 257–260
    condition of, deposit receipt form, 116–117
    dedication of, 195–196, 239, 500
    descriptions, 89–90
    exempt from taxes, 430–432
    newly constructed, 442
    ownership, 34
    private *vs.* public, 2–3
    real *vs.* personal, 34–39
    regulation of, 472
    restrictions on use, 4–7
    separate, 225, 258
    theories of, 7–9
    transfer of secured, 403–404
Proposition 2, 377–378
Proposition 13, 436–437, 445–447
Proposition 39, 437
Proposition XIII, 346, 348
Prorations, deposit receipt form, 126
Public good, 244–245
Public *vs.* private property, 2–3
PUD (planned unit development), 115
Puffing, 552–553
Purchase money instruments, 385–386

Quasi-covenants, 464
Quitclaim deeds, 215, 218

Race-notice recording statute, 350
Ready, willing and able buyers, 148

Real Estate Education, Research, and Recovery Fund, 544
Real estate investment trusts (REIT), 269
Real Estate Settlement Procedures Act of 1974 (RESPA), 112, 121, 379, 382, 523, 531
Real Estate Transfer Disclosure Statement
    California Association of REALTORS® Form, 170–172
    known defects and, 117
    toxic mold and, 139
Real property
    elements of, 39
    fixtures, 39, 46–50
    land, 39–46
    vs. personal, 34–39
Real Property Loan Act, 379
Reasonableness, 28
Receipt for increased deposit form, 94
Recission rights, 379
Recording
    bona fide purchaser, 348–349
    limits, 360–361
    lis pendens, 356–360
    nature and effect of, 344–350
    priorities, 349, 350–356
    title insurance, 349–350
Referral fees, 543
Regional planning, 473–476
Regulation of property, 472
Regulation X. *See* RESPA
Regulation Z, 384
Releases, 422–425
Reliction, 246
Remedies, 292–293
Rent, 318–319
Rent controls, 318–319
Repairs, 125
Repairs, deposit receipt form, 118
Request for Notice of Default and Sale, 395
Rescissions, 65, 68, 159

Reservation of easement, 182
Residential disclosure statements, 114, 134–136, 169
Residential property
    liquidated damages and, 70–71
    prepayment fees, 374–375
Resource Recovery Act (1970), 486
RESPA (Real Estate Settlement Procedures Act of 1974), 112, 121, 379, 382, 523, 531
Respondeat superior, 553
Restrictions, 458
Retaliatory eviction, 326–327
Right of reentry, 202, 329
Right-of-way, 180
Riparian Rights, 44
Rule against perpetuities, 204–205
Rules and regulations, lease agreements, 327
Rumford Fair Housing Act, 341

Safety clause, 148–149, 161
Sale of buyer's property, deposit receipt form, 121–122
Salespersons, 537–538, 541–542
San Francisco Bay Conservation and Development Commission (BCDC), 474
Screening fees, 321
Secret profits, 553
Section 8 housing, 309
Security deposits, 320
Security transactions. *See also* Deeds of trust; Mortgages
    listing agreements, 165
    obligation and, 362
    promissory notes, 363–367
    transfer of secured property, 403–404

Selection of service providers, deposit receipt form, 126
Seller
  deposit receipt form, 131
  land sales contracts and, 226–228
  listing agreement form, 154, 158, 164, 168
Semi-public leases, 285
Senior liens, 453
Separate property, 225, 258
Servient tenement, 180
Settlement statement (HUD), 527–529
Shopping centers, 4–7
Sidewalks, 282
Signs, lease agreements, 329
Small claims courts, 16, 20, 21–22
Solid Waste Disposal Act (1965), 486
Specific performance, 68
Stanford, Leland, 201
Stare decisis, 13–14
State Water Resources Control Board, 44
Statewide buyer and seller advisory form, 102–111
Statute of frauds, 27–31, 63–64, 66, 153–154
Statute of limitations, 27, 66, 260
Statutory disclosures and cancellation rights, deposit receipt form, 114–115
Statutory wills, 224
Stepped-up tax basis, 8
Storage, lease agreement, 323
Storm damage, 293–294
Straight notes, 364
Structural pest control, 99–100
Subagents, 542
Subchapter-S corporations, 267
Subcontractor, defined, 416
Subdivided Lands Act, 139, 495–498
Subdivision Map Act, 139, 195, 496, 498–502

Subdivisions
  disclosures, 139
  general plan restrictions, 464–466
  laws, 495–502
Subjacent support, 296
Subleases, 329–330
Subordination agreements, 376
Subprime loans, 383–384
Superfund. *See* CERCLA
Superior courts, 15–16, 20
Supreme Court, 20, 23
Surface water, 43
Survivorship, 249
Syndications, 269

Taxes
  calculation of, 443–444
  due dates, 432–436
  exempt property, 430–432
  nonpayment effects, 430
  priority of liens, 444–447
  real *vs.* personal property, 35–36
  taxing procedure, 436–442
Tax free exchanges, 173
Tax liens, 444–447
TDS (transfer disclosure statements), 114
Temporary relocation, lease agreements, 335–336
Tenancy, 207–212. *See also* Leases
Tenancy at sufferance, 210–211
Tenancy at will, 210
Tenancy in common, 168, 254–257
Tenant's obligations upon vacating premises, 332
Termination
  of agency relationships, 534–535
  of C.C.&R, 466–468
  of contract, 65–66
  of easement, 188–189
  of homestead, 456
  of lease, 332
  listing agreement form, 158

  of offer, 57
  powers of, 361
  of tenancy, 303–306
Termite inspections, 99–100
Term of lease, 318
Terms and conditions of offer, deposit receipt form, 129
Terms of sale, 160
Testate/testator, 225–226
Thirty-day notice form, 303, 304
Three-day notice, 305–306
Time of essence, deposit receipt form, 129–130
Time periods and contingencies, on deposit receipt form, 119–122
Title
  color of, 235–236
  deposit receipt form, 120–121
  listing agreement, 164
Title insurance
  conflicting claims and, 349–350
  nature of, 504–507
  types of, 507–516
Tort interference, 147
Toxic mold, 139
Toxic Mold Protection Act, 140
Trade fixtures, 48–49
Transfer disclosure statements (TDS), 114
Transferee, 363
Transfer Tax Affidavit, 346–348
Treaty of Guadalupe Hidalgo, 31
Trees, 290–291
Tresspass, 278–279, 287, 293
Triple net leases, 55, 317
Trustee, 367–369
Trustee's sale, 385

UCC-1 Statements, 48
Unconditional releases, 422
Underground waters, 44

Unenforceable contracts, 55, 64–66
Unilateral contracts, 53
Unities, 252
Unlawful detainer, 299, 306–307, 325
Unlisted encumbrances, 120
Unregulated loans, 377
Unruh Civil Rights Act, 341
U.S. Supreme Court, 23
Usury, 376–378
Utilities, lease agreement, 323

VA (Veterans Administration), 112, 160, 382
Valid contracts, 54
Variances, 480
Vendor/vendee, 226
Venue, 27
Vested rights, 502
Vesting of title, deposit receipt form, 120–121

Veteran's exemption, 432
View easements, 181–182
Voidable contracts, 54
Void contracts, 54

Waiver of mechanic's lien by general contractor, 421
Warranty deeds, 215
Water, additions and subtractions by, 245–246
Waterbeds, 336
Water Quality Control Act (1965), 486
Water rights, 43–46
Welfare institutions, 431
Williamson Act, 431
Wills and intestacy, 224–226
Withholding taxes
deposit receipt form, 115
listing agreements, 169, 173

Witnessed wills, 224
Wood destroying pest inspection, deposit receipt form, 99–100
Wraparound deeds of trust, 375
Writ of attachment, 407
Writ of execution, 415–416
Writ of immediate possession, 308
Writ of mandamus, 241
Writ of possession, 307–308

Zoning
authority for, 471–472
defined, 470
eminent domain and, 472
expanded use of, 472–478
history, 470–471
relief from, 478–483